Computing for Numerical Methods Using Visual C++ / Shaharuddin Salleh, Albert Y. Zomaya, and Sakhinah A. Bakar

Architecture-Independent Programming for Wireless Sensor Networks / Amol B. Bakshi and Viktor K. Prasanna

High-Performance Parallel Database Processing and Grid Databases / David Taniar, Clement Leung, Wenny Rahayu, and Sushant Goel

Algorithms and Protocols for Wireless and Mobile Ad Hoc Networks / Azzedine Boukerche (*Editor*)

Algorithms and Protocols for Wireless Sensor Networks / Azzedine Boukerche (*Editor*)

Optimization Techniques for Solving Complex Problems / Enrique Alba, Christian Blum, Pedro Isasi, Coromoto León, and Juan Antonio Gómez (*Editors*)

Emerging Wireless LANs, Wireless PANs, and Wireless MANs: IEEE 802.11, IEEE 802.15, IEEE 802.16 Wireless Standard Family / Yang Xiao and Yi Pan (*Editors*)

High-Performance Heterogeneous Computing / Alexey L. Lastovetsky and Jack Dongarra

Research in Mobile Intelligence / Laurence T. Yang (*Editor*)

Advanced Computational Infrastructures for Parallel and Distributed Adaptive Applicatons / Manish Parashar and Xiaolin Li (*Editors*)

Market-Oriented Grid and Utility Computing / Rajkumar Buyya and Kris Bubendorfer (*Editors*)

Advanced Computational Infrastructures for Parallel and Distributed Adaptive Applications

Advanced Computational Infrastructures for Parallel and Distributed Adaptive Applications

Edited by

Manish Parashar
Xiaolin Li

WILEY

A JOHN WILEY & SONS, INC., PUBLICATION

Published by John Wiley & Sons, Inc., Hoboken, New Jersey
Published simultaneously in Canada.

Library of Congress Cataloging-in-Publication Data:

Advanced computational infrastructures for parallel and distributed adaptive applications / Manish Parashar, Xiaolin Li.
p. cm.
Includes bibliographical references and index.
ISBN 978-0-470-07294-3 (cloth)
1. Parallel processing (Electronic computers) 2. Electronic data processing–Distributed processing. 3. Adaptive computing systems. I. Parashar, Manish, 1967- II. Li, Xiaolin, 1973-
QA76.58.A375 2010
004'.35–dc22

2009031419

Printed in the United States of America

10 9 8 7 6 5 4 3 2 1

To our parents....

Shyam and Shashi – Manish Parashar
Guangdong and Meixian – Xiaolin Li

Contents

Preface

INTRODUCTION

The last decade has witnessed a dramatic increase in computing, networking, and storage technologies. In the meantime, the emerging large-scale adaptive scientific and engineering applications are requiring an increasing amount of computing and storage resources to provide new insights into complex systems. Furthermore, dynamically adaptive techniques are being widely used to address the intrinsic heterogeneity and high dynamism of the phenomena modeled by these applications. Adaptive techniques have been applied to real-world applications in a variety of scientific and engineering disciplines, including computational fluid dynamics, subsurface and oil-reservoir simulations, astronomy, relativity, and weather modeling. The increasing complexity, dynamism, and heterogeneity of these applications coupled with similarly complex and heterogeneous parallel and distributed computing systems have led to the development and deployment of advanced computational infrastructures that provide programming, execution, and runtime management support for such large-scale adaptive implementations. The objective of this book is to investigate the state of the art in the design, architectures, and implementations of such advanced computational infrastructures and the applications they support.

This book presents the state of the art in advanced computational infrastructures for parallel and distributed adaptive applications and provides insights into recent research efforts and projects. The objective of this book is to provide a comprehensive discussion of the requirements, design challenges, underlying design philosophies, architectures, and implementation and deployment details of the advanced computational infrastructures. It presents a comprehensive study of the design, architecture, and implementation of advanced computational infrastructures as well as the adaptive applications developed and deployed using these infrastructures from different perspectives, including system architects, software engineers, computational scientists, and application scientists. Furthermore, the book includes descriptions and experiences pertaining to the realistic modeling of adaptive applications on parallel and distributed systems. By combining a "bird's eye view" with the "nitty-gritty" of advanced computational infrastructures, this book will serve as a comprehensive cross-disciplinary reference and a unique and valuable resource for students, researchers, and professionals alike.

We believe that this book can be used as a textbook for advanced courses in computational science and software/systems engineering for senior undergraduate and graduate students. It can also serve as a valuable reference for computational scientists, computer scientists, industry professionals, software developers, and other researchers in the areas of computational science, numerical methods, computer science, high-performance computing, parallel/distributed computing, and software engineering.

OVERVIEW OF THE BOOK

The book is organized in three separate parts. Part I titled "Adaptive Applications in Science and Engineering" focuses on high-performance adaptive scientific applications and includes chapters that describe high-impact, real-world application scenarios. The goal of this part of the book is to emphasize the need for advanced computational engines as well as outline their requirements. Part II titled "Adaptive Computational Infrastructures" includes chapters describing popular and widely used adaptive computational infrastructures. Part III is titled "Dynamic Partitioning and Adaptive Runtime Management Frameworks" focuses on the more specific partitioning and runtime management schemes underlying these computational toolkits. The three parts are described in more detail below.

Part I consists of seven chapters. Chapter 2 presents the use of adaptive mesh refinement techniques in large-scale fusion simulations modeled using megnetohydrodynamics (MHD). The emphasis of this work is on understanding the large-scale macroscopic processes involved in the redistribution of mass inside a tokamak during pellet injection and to support experimentation using ITER. Chapter 3 introduces adaptive models and parallel computing engines for subsurface imaging such as hydraulic tomography. Chapter 4 proposes a new parallel imaging algorithm and its implementation in oil reservoir simulations. The algorithm is based on decomposing the observed seismic data into plane wave components that correlate to angles of incidence in the subsurface and the degree of lateral variability. Chapter 5 focuses on assessments of uncertainty in climate models and climate prediction. Chapter 6 focuses on high-fidelity computational fluid dynamics (CFD) models for hazardous airborne materials in urban environments. The rapid embedded boundary gridding method in AMR is proposed to support efficient adaptive operations for this application. Chapter 7 presents the parallel adaptive simulation of cardiac fluid dynamics using the immersed boundary method and an unstructured adaptive mesh refinement technique. Chapter 8 introduces quantum chromodynamics and presents a scalable implementation on the IBM BlueGene/L supercomputer. The work presented in this chapter was awarded the 2006 Gordon Bell Special Achievement Award.

Part II consists of six chapters. Chapter 9 presents the SCIJump problem solving environment (PSE), which builds on its successful predecessor SCIRun and is based on the DOE common component architecture (CCA) scientific component model.

SCIJump supports multiple component models under a metacomponent model. Chapter 10 describes the Uintah computational framework, which provides a set of parallel software components and libraries that facilitate the solution of partial differential equations (PDEs) on structured AMR (SAMR) grids. This framework uses an explicit representation of parallel computation and communication to enable integration of parallelism across multiple simulation methods. Chapter 11 focussing on the complexity of parallel adaptive finite element applications describes the Sierra Framework, which supports a diverse set of finite element and finite volume engineering analysis codes. Chapter 12 presents the grid adaptive computational engine (GrACE), an object-oriented framework supporting the large-scale SAMR application, and providing support dynamic partitioning, scheduling, and automatic data migration. Over the years, GrACE has evolved into a widely used tool for supporting autonomic partitioning and runtime management of large-scale adaptive applications. Chapter 13 introduces the adaptive MPI model and presents an implementation using the Charm++ framework. An intelligent adaptive runtime system using migratable objects and various adaptive strategies is presented in this chapter. Chapter 14 presents the Seine framework for data/code coupling for large-scale coupled parallel scientific simulations. Seine provides the high-level abstraction as well as efficient runtime mechanisms to support MXN data redistributions required by such coupled applications.

Part III consists of eight chapters. Chapter 15 presents a hypergraph approach for dynamic partitioning and load balancing in scientific applications. Chapter 16 presents the PART framework and its mesh partitioning algorithms that can support scientific applications across geographically distributed systems. Chapter 17 presents a meshing partitioning framework, called variable partition inertia (VPI), for repartitioning adaptive unstructured meshes considering resource and application heterogeneity. Chapter 18 presents the Nature + Fable framework, a hybrid and flexible partitioning tool dedicated to structured grid hierarchies. Nature + Fable is shown to effectively cope with demanding, complex, and realistic SAMR applications. Chapter 19 proposes and implements a flexible mesh database based on a hierarchical domain decomposition to partition and manage evolving adaptive unstructured meshes. Chapter 20 presents a hybrid runtime management framework (HRMS) that provides a suite of partitioning and managing strategies. HRMS decomposes computational domain and selects an appropriate partitioner for each partition based on the partition's local characteristics and requirements. Chapter 21 presents an autonomic programming framework PARM, which can dynamically self-configure the application execution environment to exploit the heterogeneity and the dynamism of the application execution states. Chapter 22 presents the DistDLB framework, which is equipped with hierarchical load balancing algorithms to support global balancing and local balancing phases. DistDLB is specifically targeted to SAMR simulations in cosmology.

Once again, the objective of this book is to investigate the state of the art in the design, architectures, and implementations of such advanced computational infrastructures and the applications they support. We do hope that it will lead to new insights into the underlying concepts and issues, current approaches and research efforts, and outstanding challenges of the field and will inspire further research in this promising area.

ACKNOWLEDGMENTS

This book has been made possible due to the efforts and contributions of many individuals. First and foremost, we would like to acknowledge all the contributors for their tremendous efforts in putting together excellent chapters that are comprehensive, informative, and timely. We would like to thank the reviewers for their excellent comments and suggestions. We would also like to thank Professor Albert Zomaya for the opportunity to edit this book as part of the Wiley Book Series on Parallel and Distributed Computing and to Michael Christian and the rest of the team at John Wiley & Sons, Inc. for patiently helping us put this book together. Finally, we would like to acknowledge the support of our families and would like to dedicate this book to them.

MANISH PARASHAR
Department of Electrical and Computer Engineering, Rutgers
The State University of New Jersey
Piscataway, NJ, USA

XIAOLIN LI
Department of Computer Science
Oklahoma State University
Stillwater, OK, USA

Contributors

Marsha Berger, Courant Institute, New York University, New York, NY, USA

Gyan Bhanot, Department of Molecular Biology and Biochemistry & Physics, Rutgers, The State University of New Jersey, Piscataway, NJ, USA

Erik G. Boman, Discrete Algorithms and Mathematics Department, Sandia National Laboratories, Albuquerque, NM, USA

Doruk Bozdağ, Department of Biomedical Informatics, The Ohio State University, Columbus, OH, USA

Xing Cai, Simula Research Laboratory, Lysaker, Norway; Department of Informatics, University of Oslo, Oslo, Norway

Umit V. Catalyurek, Department of Biomedical Informatics, The Ohio State University, Columbus, OH, USA

Kyle Chand, Lawrence Livermore National Laboratory, Livermore, CA, USA

Jian Chen, Department of Computer Science, Brown University, Providence, RI, USA

Fotini K. Chow, Civil and Environmental Engineering, University of California, Berkeley, CA, USA

Kostadin Damevski, Scientific Computing and Imaging Institute, University of Utah, Salt Lake City, UT, USA

Karen D. Devine, Discrete Algorithms and Mathematics Department, Sandia National Laboratories, Albuquerque, NM, USA

Ciprian Docan, Department of Electrical and Computer Engineering, Rutgers, The State University of New Jersey, Piscataway, NJ, USA

Harold C. Edwards, Sandia National Laboratories, Livermore, CA, USA

Boyce E. Griffith, Courant Institute of Mathematical Sciences, New York University, New York, NY, USA

James Guilkey, Department of Mechanical Engineering, University of Utah, Salt Lake City, UT, USA

Salim Hariri, Department of Electrical and Computer Engineering, The University of Arizona, Tucson, AZ, USA

Todd Harman, Department of Mechanical Engineering, University of Utah, Salt Lake City, UT, USA

Robert Heaphy, Discrete Algorithms and Mathematics Department, Sandia National Laboratories, Albuquerque, NM, USA

Richard D. Hornung, Center for Applied Scientific Computing, Lawrence Livermore National Laboratory, Livermore, CA, USA

Gabriel Huerta, Department of Mathematics and Statistics, University of New Mexico, Albuquerque, NM, USA

Charles S. Jackson, Institute for Geophysics, The University of Texas at Austin, Austin, TX, USA

Christopher R. Johnson, Scientific Computing and Imaging Institute, University of Utah, Salt Lake City, UT, USA

Laxmikant V. Kale, University of Illinois at Urbana-Champaign, Urbana, IL, USA

Ayla Khan, Scientific Computing and Imaging Institute, University of Utah, Salt Lake City, UT, USA

Branko Kosovic, Lawrence Livermore National Laboratory, Livermore, CA, USA

Zhiling Lan, Department of Computer Science, Illinois Institute of Technology, Chicago, IL, USA

Hans P. Langtangen, Simula Research Laboratory, Lysaker, Norway; Department of Informatics, University of Oslo, Oslo, Norway

Xiaolin Li, Department of Computer Science, Oklahoma State University, Stillwater, OK, USA

Yawei Li, Illinois Institute of Technology, Chicago, IL, USA

Justin Luitjens, Department of Mechanical Engineering, University of Utah, Salt Lake City, UT, USA

David M. McQueen, Courant Institute of Mathematical Sciences, New York University, New York, NY, USA

Chuen-Fa Ni, Department of Hydrology and Water Resources, The University of Arizona, Tucson, AZ, USA

Manish Parashar, Department of Electrical and Computer Engineering, Rutgers, The State University of New Jersey, Piscataway, NJ, USA

Steven G. Parker, Department of Mechanical Engineering, University of Utah, Salt Lake City, UT, USA

Charles S. Peskin, Courant Institute of Mathematical Sciences, New York University, New York, NY, USA

Reynam C. Pestana, Instituto de Geociências, Universidade Federal da Bahia, Campus Universitário da Federação, Salvador, Bahia, Brazil

Lee A. Riesen, Discrete Algorithms and Mathematics Department, Sandia National Laboratories, Albuquerque, NM, USA

Ravi Samtaney, Princeton Plasma Physics Laboratory, Princeton University, Princeton, NJ, USA

Roustam K. Seif, Institute for Geophysics, The University of Texas at Austin, Austin, TX, USA

Mrinal K. Sen, Institute for Geophysics, The University of Texas at Austin, Austin, TX, USA

Seegyoung Seol, Scientific Computation Research Center, Rensselaer Polytechnic Institute, Troy, NY, USA

Mark S. Shephard, Department of Civil Engineering, Rensselaer Polytechnic Institute, Troy, NY, USA

Johan Steensland, Advanced Software Research and Development, Sandia National Laboratories, Livermore, CA, USA

Paul L. Stoffa, Institute for Geophysics, University of Texas at Austin, Austin, TX, USA

Ashwin Swaminathan, Scientific Computing and Imaging Institute, University of Utah, Salt Lake City, UT, USA

Valerie E. Taylor, Department of Computer Science and Engineering, Texas A&M University, College Station, TX, USA

Pavlos M. Vranas, Lawrence Livermore National Laboratory, Livermore, CA, USA

Chris Walshaw, Computing & Mathematical Sciences, University of Greenwich, London, UK

Andrew Wissink, ELORET Corporation, NASA Ames Research Center, Moffett Field, CA, USA

Bryan Worthen, Department of Mechanical Engineering, University of Utah, Salt Lake City, UT, USA

Tian-Chyi J. Yeh, Department of Hydrology and Water Resources, The University of Arizona, Tucson, AZ, USA; Department of Resources Engineering, National ChengKung University, Tainan, Taiwan

Li Zhang, Department of Electrical and Computer Engineering, Rutgers, The State University of New Jersey, Piscataway, NJ, USA

Yeliang Zhang, Department of Electrical and Computer Engineering, The University of Arizona, Tucson, AZ, USA

Gengbin Zheng, University of Illinois at Urbana-Champaign, Urbana, IL, USA

Junfeng Zhu, Department of Hydrology and Water Resources, The University of Arizona, Tucson, AZ, USA

Biographies

Manish Parashar is Professor of Electrical and Computer Engineering at Rutgers University and codirector of the NSF Center for Autonomic Computing. He is also the Associate Director of the Rutgers Center for Information Assurance (RUCIA), is affiliated with CAIP, WINLAB, CBIM, and IMCS at Rutgers, holds a joint research appointment with the Center for Subsurface Modeling, The University of Texas at Austin, and a visiting position at the e-Science Institute at Edinburgh, United Kingdom. He has been a visiting fellow at the Department of Computer Science and DOE ASCI/ASAP Center, California Institute of Technology, at the DOE ASCI/ASAP FLASH Center, University of Chicago, and at the Max-Planck Institute in Potsdam, Germany. His research is in the broad area of applied parallel and distributed computing and computational science. A key focus of his current research is on solving scientific and engineering problems on very large systems and the integration of physical and computational systems.

Manish received the IBM Faculty Award (2008), the Rutgers Board of Trustees Award for Excellence in Research (The Award) (2004–2005), the NSF CAREER Award (1999), TICAM (University of Texas at Austin) Distinguished Fellowship (1999–2001), Enrico Fermi Scholarship, Argonne National Laboratory (1996), is a senior member of IEEE/IEEE Computer Society, and a senior member of ACM. He is also the Vice Chair of the IEEE Computer Society Technical Committee on Scalable Computing (TCSC) and a member of the executive committee of the IEEE Computer Society Technical Committee on Parallel Processing (TCPP) and part of the IEEE Computer Society Distinguished Visitor Program (2004–2007). He is the cofounder of the IEEE International Conference on Autonomic Computing (ICAC), has served as general or program chair for over 30 international conferences/workshops, and is actively involved in the organization of several conferences and workshops. He also serves on various steering committees and journal editorial boards.

Manish has coauthored over 250 technical papers in international journals and conferences, has coauthored/edited over 20 books and proceedings, and has contributed to several others, all in the broad area of computational science and applied parallel and distributed computing.

Manish received a BE degree in Electronics and Telecommunications from Bombay University, India, and MS and PhD degrees in Computer Engineering from Syracuse University. For more information, please visit http://www.ece.rutgers.edu/~parashar/.

Xiaolin Li is an Assistant Professor and the director of the Scalable Software Systems Laboratory in the Computer Science Department at Oklahoma State University. His research has been sponsored by the National Science Foundation, the Department of Homeland Security, the Oklahoma Center for the Advancement of Science and Technology, AirSprite Technologies Inc., and OSU. He was a visiting scholar at UT Austin, a research staff at the Institute for Infocomm Research, and a research scholar at the National University of Singapore (NUS). His research interests include parallel and distributed systems, sensor networks, and network security. More information about his research can be found at http://s3lab.cs.okstate.edu/. He is on the executive committee of IEEE Technical Committee of Scalable Computing (TCSC) and is also the coordinator of Sensor Networks. He has been a TPC chair for several conferences and workshops and an associate editor for several journals. He has coauthored over 40 technical papers in international journals and conferences and has contributed to several books in parallel and distributed systems, networks, and security. He received the PhD in Computer Engineering from Rutgers University. He is a member of IEEE and ACM.

Chapter 1

Introduction: Enabling Large-Scale Computational Science—Motivations, Requirements, and Challenges

Manish Parashar and Xiaolin Li

1.1 MOTIVATION

The exponential growth in computing, networking, and storage technologies has ushered in unprecedented opportunities for parallel and distributed computing research and applications. In the meantime, emerging large-scale adaptive scientific and engineering applications are requiring an increasing amount of computing and storage resources to provide new insights into complex systems. Furthermore, dynamically adaptive techniques are being widely used to address the intrinsic heterogeneity and high dynamism of the phenomena modeled by these applications. Adaptive techniques have been applied to real-world applications in a variety of scientific and engineering disciplines, including computational fluid dynamics, subsurface and oil reservoir simulations, astronomy, relativity, and weather modeling. The increasing complexity, dynamism, and heterogeneity of these applications, coupled with similarly complex and heterogeneous parallel and distributed computing systems, have led to the development and deployment of advanced computational infrastructures that provide programming, execution, and runtime management support for such large-scale adaptive implementations. The objective of this book is to investigate the

Advanced Computational Infrastructures For Parallel and Distributed Adaptive Applications. Edited by Manish Parashar and Xiaolin Li

state of the art in the design, architectures, and implementations of such advanced computational infrastructures and the applications they support.

1.2 REQUIREMENTS AND CHALLENGES

Compared to numerical techniques based on static uniform discretization, adaptive techniques, for example, structured adaptive mesh refinement (SAMR), can yield highly advantageous ratios for cost/accuracy by adaptively concentrating computational effort and resources on appropriate regions of the domain at runtime. Large-scale parallel implementations of such adaptive applications have the potential for accurately modeling complex physical phenomena and providing dramatic insights. However, due to the dynamism and space–time heterogeneity, the scalable parallel implementation remains a significant challenge. Specifically, these adaptive applications are inherently dynamic because the physical phenomena being modeled and the corresponding adaptive computational domain change as the simulation evolves. Further, adaptation naturally leads to a computational domain that is spatially heterogeneous, that is, different regions in the computational domain and different levels of refinements have different computational and communication requirements. Finally, the adaptive algorithms require periodically regridding the computational domain, which causes regions of refinement to be created/deleted/moved to match the physics being modeled, that is, it exhibits temporal heterogeneity.

For example, parallel implementations of SAMR applications typically partition the adaptive grid hierarchy across available processors, and each processor operates on its local portions of this domain in parallel. The overall performance of parallel SAMR applications is thus limited by the ability to partition the underlying grid hierarchies at runtime to expose all inherent parallelism, minimize communication and synchronization overheads, and balance load.

Furthermore, communication overheads of parallel SAMR applications primarily consist of four components: (1) *interlevel communications*, defined between component grids at different levels of the grid hierarchy and consist of prolongations (coarse to fine transfer and interpolation) and restrictions (fine to coarse transfer and interpolation); (2) *intralevel communications*, required to update the grid elements along the boundaries of local portions of a distributed component grid, consisting of near-neighbor exchanges; (3) *synchronization cost*, which occurs when the load is not balanced among processors; and (4) *data migration cost*, which occurs between two successive regridding and remapping steps.

1.3 A TAXONOMY FOR ADAPTIVE APPLICATIONS AND MANAGEMENT STRATEGIES

To provide an overview of the applications and management strategies presented in this book, we develop a simple taxonomy that is based on the characteristics of the applications and application-level partitioners. This taxonomy, shown in Tables 1.1 and 1.2, decouples the classification of applications and their partitioners. This not

Table 1.1 Classification of Application Characteristics

Application characteristics	Categories
Execution	Computation intensive, communication intensive, IO intensive
Activity	Dynamic (localized adaptivity, scattered adaptivity), static
Granularity	Fine grained, coarse grained, indivisible
Dependency	Independent, workflow, hybrid

only provides a better understanding of both aspects but also implicitly indicates that different partitioners can be potentially applied to address different application characteristics. The SAMR application is used to illustrate the taxonomy in the discussion below.

In Table 1.1, applications are characterized based on their execution behavior, activity, granularity, and dependency. The execution behavior can be computation intensive, communication intensive, or IO intensive [1, 2]. For example, most SAMR applications are computation intensive, belonging to high-performance scientific computing category. Due to deep levels of adaptive refinements, SAMR applications can also be communication intensive. In some cases, when dealing with large amounts of data, SAMR applications can fall into IO-intensive category. Experiments show that during the entire course of execution, SAMR applications may run in different execution modes as the simulated physical phenomena evolve [1, 2]. Application activities are classified as dynamic or static. Many embarrassingly parallel applications belong to the static application category, for example, parallel geometrical transformations of images and Monte Carlo simulations [3]. SAMR applications, on the other hand, are dynamic in nature because of their dynamic adaptivity. The dynamic behavior of SAMR applications may demonstrate localized adaptivity pattern or scattered adaptivity pattern in different execution phases. From the perspective of divisibility, some applications are fine grained [4], some are coarse grained [5], while others are not divisible at all [6, 7]. Workloads in the divisible load scheduling class are assumed to be homogeneous and arbitrarily divisible in the sense that each portion of the load can be independently processed on any processor on the network. Coarse-grained divisible applications typically involve dependencies among subtasks. Indivisible tasks are atomic and cannot be further divided into smaller subtasks and have to be completely processed on a single processor. SAMR applications can fall into the fine-grained or coarse-grained divisible categories. When the underlying physical domain being modeled exhibits more homogeneity, the load associated with this domain belongs to the fine-grained divisible category. However, when the physical domain exhibits scattered heterogeneity with deep refinements, the load may be classified as coarse-grained divisible. Note that SAMR applications involve iterative operations and frequent communications and obviously cannot be considered as embarrassingly parallel. The last criterion in the table is dependency. Independent applications are common in the divisible load scheduling category, such as parallel low-level image processing and distributed database query processing [4]. Workflow

Table 1.2 Classification of Application Partitioners

Partitioner characteristics	Categories
Organization	Static single partitioner, adaptive single partitioner (meta-partitioner), adaptive hierarchical multiple partitioner
Decomposition	Data decomposition (domain based, patch based, hybrid), functional decomposition
Partitioning method	Binary dissection, multilevel, SFC based, and others
Operations	Dynamic Repartitioning policy (periodic, event driven), system sensitive
	Static

applications are composed of several modules or subtasks that must run in order, for example, data-driven parallel applications, scientific simulations, and visualization applications. In the case of SAMR applications, although load partitions can be processed independently, they need communications iteratively. If dynamic load balancing strategies are adopted, repartitioning may result in load movement or process migration, thus exhibiting a hybrid dependency.

As shown in Table 1.2, application-level partitioners/schedulers are classified with respect to their organization, decomposition method, and operations. The organization of partitioners falls into three categories: static single partitioner, adaptive single partitioner, and adaptive multiple partitioner. In the case of static single partitioning approaches, one predefined partitioning and repartitioning strategy is adopted throughout the entire life cycle of the applications. However, in the case of adaptive single partitioner approaches, also termed meta-partitioner in the literature [2], the most appropriate partitioning routine is selected based on the runtime behavior of the applications. Adaptive multiple partitioner approaches not only select appropriate partitioning strategies based on the runtime state of the application but also apply multiple partitioners simultaneously to local relatively homogeneous regions of the domain based on the local requirements.

Decomposition methods can be classified as data decomposition and functional decomposition. Functional decomposition exploits functional parallelism by dividing problems into a series of subtasks. Pipelining techniques can often be used to speed up applications with limited functional parallelism. Data decomposition is commonly applied to achieve data parallelism for applications that require the same operations to be performed on different data elements, for example, SPMD (single program multiple data) applications.

In the case of SAMR applications, data decomposition methods can be further classified as patch based and domain based. Patch-based decomposition methods make partitioning decisions for each patch at different refinement levels independently [8–10]. Patch-based techniques result in well-balanced load distribution as long as each patch is sufficiently large. Since the workload is balanced for each patch, an implicit feature of this scheme is that it does not need redistribution when a patch is deleted at runtime. However, the scheme does not preserve locality and can result in considerable communication overheads. Moreover, these communications may lead to serializing of the computation and severe performance bottleneck. Interlevel communications occur during restriction and prolongation data transfer operations between parent–children (coarser–finer) patches.

In contrast, domain-based approaches partition the physical domain rather than the individual patches at each refinement level [9, 10]. A subdomain includes all patches on all refinement levels in that region. Domain-based schemes maintain the parent–child locality while striving to balance overall workload distribution. As a result, these techniques substantially eliminate interlevel communication overheads and the associated communication bottleneck. However, strict domain-based partitioning may result in a considerable load imbalance when the application has deep refinements on very narrow regions with strongly localized features. In these cases, hybrid schemes that combine patch-based and domain-based techniques are required.

1.4 A CONCEPTUAL ARCHITECTURE FOR COMPUTATIONAL INFRASTRUCTURES

The functionality of a computational infrastructure includes partitioning applications at runtime and distributing each partition to available resources to efficiently utilize resources and minimize the execution time of applications. Figure 1.1 presents an illustrative conceptual architecture for such an infrastructure as a middleware system

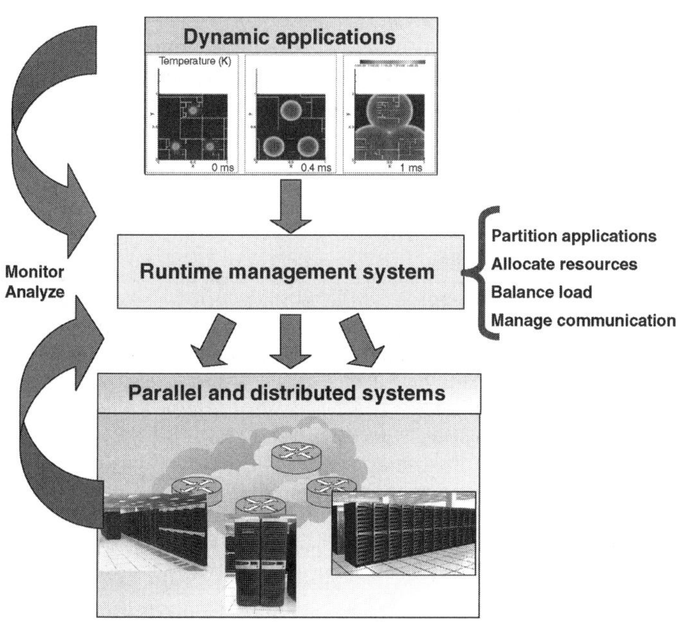

Figure 1.1 An illustrative conceptual architecture for computational infrastructures.

that bridges the gap between applications and operating systems and provides efficient runtime support, including monitoring, dynamic partitioning, resource allocation, coordination, load balancing, and runtime adaptation. In the figure, the illustrative input application is a combustion simulation of hydrogen–air mixture with three initial ignition spots. The infrastructure monitors the runtime states of applications and resources, analyzes requirements, and delivers a plan for partitioning, scheduling, and executing the application on parallel and distributed systems to maximize their performance, efficiency, and utilization. In case of such dynamically adaptive applications, the system should also address the dynamism and space–time heterogeneity in applications.

1.5 OVERVIEW OF THE BOOK

The objective of this book is to investigate the state of the art in the design, architectures, and implementations of such advanced computational infrastructures and the applications they support. The book is organized in three separate parts. Part I, Adaptive Applications in Science and Engineering, focuses on high-performance adaptive scientific applications and includes chapters that describe high-impact, real-world application scenarios. The goal of this part of the book is to motivate the need for advanced computational engines as well as outline their requirements. Part II, Adaptive Computational Infrastructures, includes chapters describing popular and widely used adaptive computational infrastructures. Part III, Dynamic Partitioning and Adaptive Runtime Management Frameworks, focuses on the more specific partitioning and runtime management schemes underlying these computational toolkits.

We do hope that it will lead to new insights into the underlying concepts and issues, current approaches and research efforts, and outstanding challenges of the field and will inspire further research in this promising area.

REFERENCES

1. S. Chandra, J. Steensland, M. Parashar, and J. Cummings. An experimental study of adaptive application sensitive partitioning strategies for SAMR applications. In *2nd Los Alamos Computer Science Institute Symposium* (also *Best Research Poster at Supercomputing Conference 2001*), 2001.
2. J. Steensland, M. Thune, S. Chandra, and M. Parashar. Towards an adaptive meta-partitioner for parallel SAMR applications. In *IASTED PDCS 2000*, 2000.
3. B. Wilkinson and M. Allen. *Parallel Programming: Techniques and Applications Using Networked Workstations and Parallel Computers*, 1st edition. Pearson Education, 1999.
4. B. Veeravalli, D. Ghose, V. Mani, and T.G. Robertazzi. *Scheduling Divisible Loads in Parallel and Distributed Systems*. IEEE Computer Society Press, Los Alamitos, CA, 1996.
5. G. Allen, T. Dramlitsch, I. Foster, N.T. Karonis, M. Ripeanu, E. Seidel, and B. Toonen. Supporting efficient execution in heterogeneous distributed computing environments with cactus and globus. In *Proceedings of the 2001 ACM/IEEE Conference on Supercomputing (CDROM)*, Denver, CO, 2001, p. 52.
6. S. Bokhari. *Assignment Problems in Parallel and Distributed Computing*. Kluwer Academic Publishers, Boston, MA, 1987.

7. B.A. Shirazi, A.R. Hurson, and K.M. Kavi. *Scheduling and Load Balancing in Parallel and Distributed Systems*. IEEE Computer Society Press, Los Alamitos, CA, 1995.
8. S. Kohn. SAMRAI: structured adaptive mesh refinement applications infrastructure. Technical report, Lawrence Livermore National Laboratory, 1999.
9. M. Parashar and J. Browne. On partitioning dynamic adaptive grid hierarchies. In *29th Annual Hawaii International Conference on System Sciences*, 1996, pp. 604–613.
10. J. Steensland. *Efficient partitioning of structured dynamic grid hierarchies*. PhD thesis, Uppsala University, 2002.

Part I

Adaptive Applications in Science and Engineering

Chapter 2

Adaptive Mesh Refinement MHD Simulations of Tokamak Refueling

Ravi Samtaney

2.1 INTRODUCTION

2.1.1 Background

Einstein's famous formula $E = mc^2$ implies that a change in a tiny amount of mass leads to a large change in energy by a factor equal to the square of the speed of light. It is precisely this formula that scientists rely upon in the quest of extracting energy from atoms. In fusion energy, a tiny amount of mass is lost when hydrogen (or rather heavier isotopes of hydrogen: deuterium and tritium) atoms combine to form helium. This process is the source of energy of our sun, and it is this source of energy that the community of controlled fusion scientists seek to harness. Furthermore, fusion as a source of essentially unlimited energy has several advantages: no pollution, no high-level nuclear waste, no risk of nuclear accidents, and virtually unlimited amount of fuel.

To recreate conditions on the sun, fusion scientists heat up the hydrogen gas to enormously high temperatures (these can easily surpass 500 million degrees, which exceeds the core temperature of the sun by a factor of more than 20!) until a gas

Advanced Computational Infrastructures For Parallel and Distributed Adaptive Applications. Edited by Manish Parashar and Xiaolin Li

undergoes a transition to another state of matter called *plasma*.[1] This plasma is too hot to be held in material containers, and *magnetic confinement* is one technique to suspend the plasma in a vacuum chamber using a magnetic field. In the 1960s, a magnetic confinement device called the *tokamak*[2] (toroidalnaya kamera and magnitnaya katushka, meaning "toroidal[3] chamber" and "magnetic coil") was first developed. We note that there are other confinement devices such as stellarators, which are not the focus of the present work. As we fast forward to the twenty-first century, we are at the beginning of the construction of the world's largest tokamak called ITER ("The Way" in Latin—formerly, ITER stood for International Thermonuclear Experimental Reactor, although this usage is now obsolete). ITER is a joint international research and development project that aims to demonstrate the scientific and technical feasibility of fusion power. The partners in the project are the European Union, Japan, China, India, South Korea, Russia, and the United States. ITER will be constructed in Europe, at Cadarache in the south of France. ITER is based on the tokamak concept and is the culmination of decades of research in tokamaks. When completed, ITER may well be the world's most expensive scientific experiment ever undertaken. The aim of ITER is to demonstrate that fusion could be used to generate electrical power and to gain the necessary data to design and operate the first electricity-producing plant.

Refueling of ITER is a practical necessity due to the burning plasma nature of the experiment and significantly longer pulse durations ($\mathcal{O}(100)$–$\mathcal{O}(1000)$ s). An experimentally proven method of refueling tokamaks is by *pellet*[4] *injection* [1, 2]. Pellet injection is currently seen as the most likely refueling technique for ITER. Furthermore, the use of "killer" pellets has been suggested as a method for fast shutdown of large tokamaks [11]. Thus, it is imperative that pellet injection phenomena be understood via simulations before very expensive experiments are undertaken in ITER. The emphasis of the present work is to understand the large-scale macroscopic processes involved in the redistribution of mass inside a tokamak during pellet injection. Such large-scale processes are best understood using magnetohydrodynamics (MHD)[5] as the mathematical model. Before proceeding further we will first briefly describe magnetohydrodynamics.

[1]The fourth state of matter. A collection of electrically charged electrons and ions that is approximately "charge neutral" macroscopically.

[2]A device for containing a plasma inside a torus chamber by using a combination of two magnetic fields—one created by electric coils around the torus, while the other created by intense electric current in the plasma itself.

[3]In a ring doughnut, the direction parallel to the large circumference.

[4]Small slug of frozen deuterium/tritium fuel of a few mm diameter range fired frequently (between 50 and 7 Hz) into the plasma to maintain sufficient fuel density in the plasma core.

[5]The study of the motions of an electrically conducting fluid in the presence of a magnetic field. The motion of the fluid gives rise to induced electric currents that interact with the magnetic field, which in turn modifies the motion.

2.1.2 Magnetohydrodynamics

A true description of plasma motion must rely on kinetic equations for each plasma species. As this approach is too costly for simulation of full magnetic fusion devices, a fluid description of the plasma is often used, which is obtained from taking velocity moments of the kinetic equations describing a plasma under certain closure assumptions (see Ref. [9] for details). The often used term "resistive MHD" is a single-fluid model of a plasma in which a single velocity and pressure describe both the electrons and ions. Mathematically, single-fluid resistive MHD is a system of nonlinear partial differential equations describing conservation of mass, momentum, and energy for an ionized gas coupled with Faraday's induction law describing the evolution of the magnetic field and Ohm's law. The resistive MHD model of a magnetized plasma does not include finite Larmor radius (FLR) effects and is based on the simplifying limit in which the particle collision length is smaller than the macroscopic length scales. A more sophisticated set of models, hereafter referred to as *extended MHD*, can be derived from more realistic closure approximations. In the present work, we loosely employ the phrase "extended MHD" to mean resistive MHD that includes additional models relevant to pellet injection.

2.1.3 Pellet Injection

One can loosely classify the launch trajectories of pellet injection into two categories: HFS (or high-field side) launch in which the pellet is injected from the inside of the tokamak and LFS (or low-field side) launch in which the pellet is injected from the outside of the tokamak. It was experimentally observed that the HFS launches of the pellet lead to a significantly better fueling efficiency of the core of the tokamak than the LFS launches. Identifying and quantifying the causal MHD mechanisms in HFS versus LFS pellet launches are the goals of this research.

As a frozen pellet of hydrogen or deuterium is injected into the hot plasma tokamak fusion reactor, it is rapidly heated by long mean-free-path electrons streaming along magnetic field lines, leading to ablation at the frozen pellet surface, with a shield of neutral gas and an ionized high-density plasma cloud around it. This forms a local high-β[6] plasmoid, which implies a localized region of high pressure. This can trigger MHD instabilities [26]. Furthermore, the high-β plasmoid expands along the magnetic field lines, and the plasma cloud drifts in the direction of the major radius. This drift was observed in experiments on ASDEX[7] Upgrade tokamak, as well as DIII-D[8] and JET [16]. Thus, pellets injected on the high-field side showed a much better penetration and fueling efficiency than pellets injected on the low-field side.

[6]The ratio of gas pressure and magnetic pressure, that is, $2p/B^2$.

[7]A fusion facility tokamak in Germany.

[8]A national fusion facility tokamak located at General Atomics.

Pellet injection has been associated with transitions from L-mode[9] to H-mode[10] [8] and formation of cloud striations [18], as well as the occurrence of neoclassical tearing modes [16]. It is interesting to note that none of these phenomena has been simulated *a posteriori* or predicted *a priori*.

The literature on computational investigations of pellet injection can be broadly classified into two categories: global investigations versus local investigations. We briefly examine each type below.

Global Simulations: These are simulations of pellet injection in the full tokamak geometry. Strauss and Park [26] can be credited with the first global simulations of pellet injection. Their 3D resistive MHD simulations qualitatively captured the drift of the pellet mass toward low-field-side though they lacked the details of pellet ablation and realistic pellet parameters. An improvement of such large-scale simulations was obtained by Samtaney et al. [25] using an MHD code based on the Chombo[11] AMR (adaptive mesh refinement) package [6]. The HFS/LFS differences were also observed in this work that employed an analytical pellet ablation model as a moving density source.

Local Simulations: The emphasis here is to capture the details of pellet ablation by simulating the phenomenon in a small neighborhood surrounding the pellet. Most works in this area tend to be two dimensional. In their work, Parks et al. [20] theoretically explained the motion across flux surfaces invoking curvature and $\mathbf{E} \times \mathbf{B}$ drifts. The ablation process involves complex interactions between the partially conducting ablation cloud, the background plasma and magnetic field, and the motion of the pellet itself. The ablation of tokamak pellets and its influence on the tokamak plasma have been studied using several approaches. Among the pellet ablation models, a semianalytical neutral gas shielding (NGS) model by Parks and Turnbull [22] has achieved a significant success in explaining experimental data. This 1D steady-state hydrodynamics model provides the scaling of the ablation rate with respect to the pellet radius, plasma temperature, and plasma density. However, it neglects MHD, geometric effects, and atomic effects such as dissociation and ionization. Theoretical studies of the magnetic field distortion [17], equilibrium pellet shape under high ablation pressures [21], radial displacement of the pellet ablation material [19, 20], and cloud oscillation [18] have also been performed. A detailed investigation of the ablation process, including the dissociation, ionization, and the nonlocal electron heating of the pellet cloud, was simulated with two-dimensional hydrodynamics, that is, the background plasma and magnetic field were stationary [14, 15]. More recently, two-dimensional hydrodynamic simulations have been performed that include solid-to-gas phase transition treatment, dissociation, ionization, and a kinetic

[9]A confinement regime in a tokamak in which the confinement time is low, named after discovery of the H-mode (high mode) of operation.

[10]High mode, a regime of operation attained during auxiliary heating of divertor tokamak plasmas when the injected power is sufficiently high. A sudden improvement in particle confinement time leads to increased density and temperature.

[11]Infrastructure for adaptive mesh refinement developed at Lawrence Berkeley National Laboratory.

Table 2.1 Resolution Requirements for Pellet Injection for Three Tokamaks

Tokamak	Major radius (m)	N	N_{steps}	Space–time points
CDXU[a] (small)	0.3	2×10^7	2×10^5	4×10^{12}
DIII-D (medium)	1.75	3.3×10^9	7×10^6	2.3×10^{17}
ITER (large)	6.2	1.5×10^{11}	9×10^7	1.4×10^{19}

N is the number of spatial points and N_{steps} is the number of timesteps required.
[a]A modest sized tokamak located at PPPL.

heat flux model. These simulations showed the presence of shocks in the pellet cloud as well as the flattening of the pellet due to fluidization, which can shorten the pellet lifetime by as much as a factor of 3 if the pellet is assumed to be rigid and stationary [10].

The emphasis of the present work is on global simulations of pellet injection but using as much of the detailed local physics as possible in the vicinity of the pellet.

2.1.4 Numerical Challenges

The physical dimensions of the pellet typically range from a submillimeter to a few millimeters in radius. This is three orders of magnitude smaller than the device size (for ITER, the minor radius is 2 m). We can estimate the resolution requirements if the high-density cloud around a pellet is to be resolved. Assuming uniform meshing, we estimate the computational resources required to simulate pellet injection in tokamak ranging from small (CDXU), to medium (DIII-D), to large (ITER) in Table 2.1. It is clear that some form of adaptive meshing is necessary to overcome the large resolution requirements arising from the fact that the region around the pellet has to be well resolved.

The large range of spatial scales is somewhat mitigated by the use of adaptive mesh refinement. Our approach is that of block-structured hierarchical meshes, as championed by the seminal work of Berger and Oliger [3] and Berger and Colella [4]. We employ the Chombo library for AMR and further details on this can be found in the Chombo documentation [6]. The effectiveness of local mesh adaptiveness has been demonstrated in the context of pellet injection by Samtaney et al. [25].

Apart from the wide range of spatial scales, the physical phenomena have several timescales: the fastest timescale is the heat exchange time between electrons and singly charged ions ($\tau_e \approx \mathcal{O}(10^{-8}\text{ s})$), followed by the fast magnetosonic timescales of expansion ($\tau_f \approx \mathcal{O}(10^{-7}\text{ s})$). The timescales of interest are those at which the pellet cloud drifts toward the low-field side on Alfvén wave[12] transit timescales

[12]A type of oscillation of plasma particles, consisting of transverse waves propagating along the magnetic field lines in a plasma. Also called magnetohydrodynamic wave.

($\tau_a \approx \mathcal{O}(10^{-6}\,\text{s})$) and the motion along magnetic field lines on acoustic timescales ($\tau_s \approx \mathcal{O}(10^{-4}\,\text{s})$). Finally, the entire process last until the pellet has been completely ablated $\mathcal{O}(10^{-3}\,\text{s})$. At present, the fast electron heating is handled by a semianalytical model described later, which leads to evaluating integrals of density along field lines. This poses technical challenges on hierarchical adaptive meshes.

The other numerical challenges stem from the large gradients in density and pressure at the edge of the pellet cloud. Traditional nondissipative finite difference schemes have large dispersive errors. These large spatial gradients are effectively treated with high-resolution upwind methods, which have been effectively used in shock capturing in computational fluid dynamics.

2.2 MATHEMATICAL MODELS, EQUATIONS, AND NUMERICAL METHOD

We begin by writing the equations of compressible resistive MHD in near-conservation form in cylindrical coordinates. These equations describe the conservation of mass, momentum, and energy, coupled with Maxwell's equations for the evolution of the magnetic field.

$$\frac{\partial U}{\partial t} + \underbrace{\frac{1}{R}\frac{\partial RF}{\partial R} + \frac{\partial H}{\partial z} + \frac{1}{R}\frac{\partial G}{\partial \phi} + S}_{\text{hyperbolic or ideal MHD terms}} = \underbrace{\frac{1}{R}\frac{\partial RF_{\text{D}}}{\partial R} + \frac{\partial H_{\text{D}}}{\partial z} + \frac{1}{R}\frac{\partial G_{\text{D}}}{\partial \phi}}_{\text{diffusion terms}} + S_{\text{D}} + S_{\text{pellet}}, \tag{2.1}$$

where $U \equiv U(R, \phi, Z, t)$ is $U = \{\rho, \rho u_R, \rho u_\phi, \rho u_Z, B_R, B_\phi, B_Z, e\}^T$. Here ρ is the density; u_R, u_Z, and u_ϕ are the radial, axial, and azimuthal components of velocity; B_R, B_Z, and B_ϕ are the radial, axial, and azimuthal components of the magnetic field; and e is the total energy per unit volume. The hyperbolic fluxes and source terms are given by

$$F \equiv F(U) = \left\{ \begin{array}{c} \rho u_R \\ \rho u_R^2 + p_{\text{t}} - B_R^2 \\ \rho u_R u_\phi - B_R B_\phi \\ \rho u_R u_Z - B_R B_Z \\ 0 \\ u_R B_\phi - u_\phi B_R \\ u_R B_Z - u_Z B_R \\ (e + p_{\text{t}})u_R - (B_k u_k) B_R \end{array} \right\},$$

$$H \equiv H(U) = \left\{ \begin{array}{c} \rho u_Z \\ \rho u_R u_Z - B_R B_Z \\ \rho u_Z u_\phi - B_Z B_\phi \\ \rho u_Z^2 + p_\mathrm{t} - B_Z^2 \\ u_Z B_R - u_R B_Z \\ u_Z B_\phi - u_\phi B_Z \\ 0 \\ (e + p_\mathrm{t}) u_Z - (B_k u_k) B_Z \end{array} \right\},$$

$$G \equiv G(U) = \left\{ \begin{array}{c} \rho u_\phi \\ \rho u_R u_\phi - B_R B_\phi \\ \rho u_\phi^2 + p_\mathrm{t} - B_\phi^2 \\ \rho u_Z u_\phi - B_Z B_\phi \\ u_\phi B_R - u_R B_\phi \\ 0 \\ u_\phi B_Z - u_Z B_\phi \\ (e + p_\mathrm{t}) u_\phi - (B_k u_k) B_\phi \end{array} \right\}, \quad S(U) = \frac{1}{R} \left\{ \begin{array}{c} 0 \\ B_\phi^2 - \rho u_\phi^2 - p_\mathrm{t} \\ \rho u_R u_\phi - B_R B_\phi \\ 0 \\ 0 \\ u_\phi B_R - u_R B_\phi \\ 0 \\ 0 \end{array} \right\}.$$

The diffusive fluxes and source terms are given by the following:

$$F_\mathrm{D}(U) = \left\{ \begin{array}{c} 0 \\ T_{RR} \\ T_{R\phi} \\ T_{RZ} \\ 0 \\ \eta J_Z \\ -\eta J_\phi \\ T_{RR} u_R + T_{R\phi} u_\phi + T_{RZ} u_Z + \kappa \frac{\partial T}{\partial R} - A_R \end{array} \right\},$$

$$H_\mathrm{D}(U) = \left\{ \begin{array}{c} 0 \\ T_{ZR} \\ T_{Z\phi} \\ T_{ZZ} \\ \eta J_\phi \\ -\eta J_R \\ 0 \\ T_{RZ} u_R + T_{Z\phi} u_\phi + T_{ZZ} u_Z + \kappa \frac{\partial T}{\partial Z} - A_Z \end{array} \right\},$$

$$G_{\mathrm{D}}(U) = \left\{ \begin{array}{c} 0 \\ T_{\phi R} \\ T_{\phi\phi} \\ T_{\phi Z} \\ -\eta J_Z \\ 0 \\ \eta J_R \\ T_{R\phi} u_R + T_{\phi\phi} u_\phi + T_{\phi Z} u_Z + \frac{\kappa}{R}\frac{\partial T}{\partial \phi} - A_\phi \end{array} \right\}, \quad S_{\mathrm{D}}(U) = \frac{1}{R} \left\{ \begin{array}{c} 0 \\ -T_{\phi\phi} \\ T_{\phi R} \\ 0 \\ 0 \\ -\eta J_Z \\ 0 \\ 0 \end{array} \right\}.$$

In the above equations, p_{t} includes the magnetic energy ($p_{\mathrm{t}} = p + 1/2 B_k B_k$), and the term in the energy equation corresponding to the diffusive portion of the Poynting flux is denoted as $(A_R, A_\phi, A_Z) = \eta \boldsymbol{J} \times \boldsymbol{B}$. The equation of state gives $e = p/(\gamma - 1) + 1/2 B_k B_k + 1/2 \rho u_k u_k$, where $\gamma = 5/3$ is the ratio of specific heats. In the above equations, we have implicitly made use of resistive MHD form of Ohm's law: $\boldsymbol{E} = -\boldsymbol{v} \times \boldsymbol{B} + \eta \boldsymbol{J}$. The stress tensor $\mathbf{T}$ is related to the strain as $\mathbf{T} = \mu(\nabla \mathbf{u} + (\nabla \mathbf{u})^T) - 2/3 \mu \nabla \cdot \mathbf{u}$, where μ is the viscosity. Other plasma properties are the resistivity denoted by η and heat conductivity denoted by κ. The source terms denoted as S_{pellet}, due to pellet-specific ablation and heating physics are described later. In addition to the above, we have the constraint of no magnetic monopoles expressed as $\nabla \cdot \mathbf{B} = 0$.

A toroidal cross section (i.e., constant ϕ slice) of a tokamak is generally shaped by current-carrying coils leading to an elongated plasma with some triangularity. For such a shaped plasma, we employ a mapped grid in the (R, Z) plane: $(\xi, \zeta) \leftrightarrow (R, Z)$ (this mapping is a diffeomorphism), where $\xi \equiv \xi(R, Z)$ and $\zeta \equiv \zeta(R, Z)$. Conversely, $R \equiv R(\xi, \zeta)$ and $Z \equiv Z(\xi, \zeta)$. The Jacobian J and its inverse J^{-1} of the mapping are

$$J = \left| \frac{\partial(R, Z)}{\partial(\xi, \zeta)} \right| = R_\xi Z_\zeta - R_\zeta Z_\xi, \tag{2.2}$$

$$J^{-1} = \left| \frac{\partial(\xi, \zeta)}{\partial(R, Z)} \right|. \tag{2.3}$$

Note that R, Z, ξ, and ζ written with subscripts denote derivatives.

Equation (2.1) is then transformed to

$$\frac{\partial UJ}{\partial t} + \frac{1}{R}\frac{\partial R\tilde{F}}{\partial \xi} + \frac{1}{R}\frac{\partial R\tilde{H}}{\partial \zeta} + \frac{1}{R}\frac{\partial \tilde{G}}{\partial \phi} + \tilde{S} = \frac{1}{R}\frac{\partial R\tilde{F}_{\mathrm{D}}}{\partial \xi} + \frac{1}{R}\frac{\partial R\tilde{H}_{\mathrm{D}}}{\partial \zeta} + \frac{1}{R}\frac{\partial \tilde{G}_{\mathrm{D}}}{\partial \phi} + \tilde{S}_{\mathrm{D}}. \tag{2.4}$$

Here $\tilde{F} = J(\xi_R F + \xi_Z H) = Z_\zeta F - R_\zeta H$, $\tilde{H} = J(\zeta_R F + \zeta_Z H) = -Z_\xi F + R_\xi H$, $\tilde{G} = JG$, $\tilde{S} = JS$, $\tilde{F}_{\mathrm{D}} = J(\xi_R F_{\mathrm{D}} + \xi_Z H_{\mathrm{D}}) = Z_\zeta F_{\mathrm{D}} - R_\zeta H_{\mathrm{D}}$, $\tilde{H}_{\mathrm{D}} = J(\zeta_R F_{\mathrm{D}} + \zeta_Z H_{\mathrm{D}}) = -Z_\xi F_{\mathrm{D}} + R_\xi H_{\mathrm{D}}$, $\tilde{G}_{\mathrm{D}} = JG_{\mathrm{D}}$, and $\tilde{S}_{\mathrm{D}} = JS_{\mathrm{D}}$.

2.2.1 Pellet Physics Models

The source terms due to the pellet, S_{pellet}, are nonzero in the continuity and the energy equations. The continuity equation contains the density source term arising from the pellet ablation, while the energy equation contains the source and sink terms corresponding to the heating due to electrons streaming along field lines. Both these models are described below.

Pellet Ablation Model In the present model, the pellet is described by a sphere of frozen molecular hydrogen of radius r_{p}. The trajectory $x_{\text{p}}(x_i, t)$ of the pellet is prescribed with a given initial location $x_{\text{p}0} \equiv x_{\text{p}}(x_i, 0)$ and constant velocity u_{p}. The density source term arises from the ablation of the pellet and is written in terms of number density (i.e., atoms per unit volume per unit time) as

$$S_n = \dot{N}\delta(x - x_{\text{p}}), \tag{2.5}$$

where the delta function is approximated as a Gaussian distribution centered over the pellet with a characteristic size equal to $10r_{\text{p}}$. The ablation rate of the pellet, originally derived by Parks and Turnbull [22] and modified for hydrogen pellets by Kuteev [13] is given below (in atoms/s):

$$\dot{N} = -4\pi r_{\text{p}}^2 \frac{\mathrm{d}r_{\text{p}}}{\mathrm{d}t} 2n_{\text{m}} = 1.12 \times 10^{16} n_{\text{e}}^{0.333} T_{\text{e}}^{1.64} r_{\text{p}}^{1.33} M_i^{-0.333}, \tag{2.6}$$

where n_{e} is the background plasma density in cm^{-3}, T_{e} is the background plasma electron temperature in eV, M_i is the atomic mass number in atomic units, and $n_{\text{m}} = 2.63 \times 10^{22}/\text{cm}^3$ is the molecular density of frozen hydrogen. The source term S_n due to ablation is appropriately nondimensionalized and included in S_{pellet}.

Electron Heat Flux Model A heat source $-\nabla \cdot \bar{q}$ is included in the energy equation. This arises from the energy deposition by hot long-mean-free-path plasma electrons streaming into the ablation cloud along the magnetic field lines. It can be analytically approximated [10] as

$$-\nabla \cdot \bar{q} = \frac{q_\infty n_t(r, \phi, z)}{\tau_\infty} \left[g(u_+) + g(u_-) \right], \tag{2.7}$$

where $g(u) = u^{1/2} K_1 \left(u^{1/2} \right) / 4$ and K_1 is the Bessel function of the second kind. $u_\pm = \tau_\pm / \tau_\infty$ is the dimensionless opacity, where

$$\tau_+(R, \phi, Z) = \int_{-\infty}^{(R,\phi,Z)} n_t(r, \hat{\phi}, z) \mathrm{d}s,$$

$$\tau_-(R, \phi, Z) = \int_{(R,\phi,Z)}^{\infty} n_t(r, \hat{\phi}, z) \mathrm{d}s,$$

are the respective line-integrated densities penetrated by right-going (left-going) electrons arriving at the point (R, ϕ, Z) from infinity, and

$$\tau_\infty = \frac{T_{e\infty}^2}{8\pi e^4 \ln \Lambda},$$

where Λ is the Coulomb logarithm. The above model is derived by assuming half-Maxwellian distribution for electrons and neglecting pitch angle scattering.

To ensure energy conservation, we employ the following ansatz:

$$-\nabla \cdot q_e = \frac{1}{V_\psi - V_{\text{cloud},\psi}} \int_{\text{cloud},\psi} \nabla \cdot q_e. \tag{2.8}$$

This means that on the portion of each flux surface not covered by the pellet ablation cloud we have an average sink term. This ansatz allows cooling on the flux surface that is outside the ablation cloud. Clearly, this effect is physical. However, one should be aware that this model is not entirely appropriate when there are no longer any coherent flux surfaces present—a situation that arises in later stages of our simulations.

2.2.2 Initial and Boundary Conditions

The initial conditions correspond to a flow-free ideal MHD equilibrium obtained by solving $\nabla p = \boldsymbol{J} \times \boldsymbol{B}$. The magnetic field is expressed as $\boldsymbol{B} = \nabla\phi \times \nabla\psi + g(\psi)\nabla\phi$, where ψ is the poloidal[13] magnetic flux and $g(\psi)/R$ is the toroidal component of the magnetic field. The pressure $p \equiv p(\psi)$ is expressed as a function of the poloidal flux. This leads to a nonlinear elliptic equation called the Grad–Shafranov equation. There are a number of methods and codes that implement the Grad–Shafranov equation. We obtain the equilibrium from J-SOLVER (fixed-boundary, toroidal MHD equilibrium code, which solves the Grad–Shafranov equation for the poloidal flux using a finite difference scheme). The flux surfaces ψ are closed and nested, and in our implementation, these coincide with the ξ coordinate with $\xi = 0$ coincident on the magnetic axis and the $\xi = \xi_0$ forming the outermost flux surface. The boundary conditions at $\xi = 0$ are that of zero flux, while the $\xi = \xi_0$ surface is a perfect conductor. The boundaries in ζ and ϕ are periodic.

2.2.3 Numerical Method

We use a finite volume technique wherein each variable is stored at the cell center. At present, we employ a method-of-lines approach and evolve the equations in time using a second-order TVD Runge–Kutta method. In the future, we will replace this with a multidimensional unsplit method originally developed by Colella [5] and extended to MHD by Crockett et al. [7].

[13]Movement in the vertical plane intersecting the plasma torus along projections in that plane of any of the tokamak's nested toroidal flux surfaces.

Hyperbolic Fluxes At each stage of the Runge–Kutta time integration, the numerical fluxes of conserved quantities are obtained at the cell faces using upwinding methods. We first compute a vector of "primitive" variables $W = \{\rho, u_R, u_\phi, u_Z, B_R, B_\phi, B_Z, p_t\}^T$, where p_t is the total pressure including the magnetic pressure, in each cell and use these to fit a linear profile in each cell subject to standard slope-limiting techniques. Given the left and right states (W_L and W_R, respectively) at each cell interface, we use a seven-wave linearized Riemann problem to compute the solution at the cell interface as follows:

$$W_{rp} = W_L + \sum_{k,\lambda_k<0} \alpha_k r_k, \tag{2.9}$$

where $\alpha_k = l_k \cdot (W_R - W_L)$, and λ_k, l_k, and r_k are the eigenvalues and left and right eigenvectors, respectively, of the Jacobian, of the ideal MHD flux vector with respect to W. Note that in computing the above-mentioned Jacobian, the row and column corresponding to the normal component of the magnetic field are dropped. The solution to the Riemann problem is then used to compute the fluxes through the cell face. This method, as described above, can lead to numerical problems, that is, positivity is not guaranteed and negative pressures or densities may develop. If this occurs, we use the more robust and generally positivity preserving HLL flux as given below.

$$\begin{aligned}
F &= \frac{\lambda_{max} F(W_L) - \lambda_{min} F(W_R) + \lambda_{max}\lambda_{min}(U_R - U_L)}{\lambda_{max} - \lambda_{min}}, \quad \text{if } \lambda_{min} < 0 < \lambda_{max},\\
F &= F(W_L), \quad \text{if } \lambda_{min} > 0,\\
F &= F(W_R), \quad \text{if } \lambda_{max} < 0,
\end{aligned} \tag{2.10}$$

where F is notationally a generic flux through a cell face, U_L and U_R are the conserved quantities on the left/right side of the cell face, and λ_{min} and λ_{max} are, respectively, the minimum and maximum eigenvalues evaluated at the arithmetic average of the left and right states.

Diffusive Fluxes The diffusive fluxes in the resistive MHD equations are evaluated using second-order central differences. These are evaluated explicitly in the present implementation that can have an adverse effect on the timestep because the timestep restriction based on diffusion is quadratic in the mesh spacing. In the future, we plan to treat these terms implicitly in a fashion similar to Samtaney et al. [24].

Electron Heat Flux The electron heat flux term in the energy equation involves the computations of opacities by integrating the density along magnetic field lines. For example, consider $\tau_+(R, \phi, Z) = \int_{-\infty}^{(R,\phi,Z)} n_t(r, \hat{\phi}, z) ds$. It is clear that a brute-force approach to actually integrating along the field lines can be computationally expensive and, furthermore, lead to a complicated implementation in parallel especially on structured hierarchical adaptive meshes. Instead, we rewrite the integral equation as an advection–reaction equation as follows:

$$\frac{\mathrm{d}\tau}{\mathrm{d}s} = n(\boldsymbol{x}), \tag{2.11}$$

$$\hat{\boldsymbol{b}} \cdot \nabla\tau = n(\boldsymbol{x}), \tag{2.12}$$

$$\frac{\mathrm{d}\tau}{\mathrm{d}\vartheta} + \hat{\boldsymbol{b}} \cdot \nabla\tau = n(\boldsymbol{x}), \tag{2.13}$$

where $\hat{\boldsymbol{b}}$ is the unit vector along the magnetic field and ϑ is a "pseudotime" variable. Upon integrating the above to steady state (i.e., $\vartheta \to \infty$), we obtain the opacity τ at every point in our domain. Spatial derivatives in the above equation are evaluated in a standard upwind fashion by examining the sign of the "velocity" vector $\boldsymbol{b}$.

Preserving the Solenoidal Property of B The zero divergence condition on $\boldsymbol{B}$ is maintained numerically by using the central difference version of the constrained transport algorithm proposed by Toth [27]. We update the magnetic field using the method of lines described above. Then, the time average of the electric field is calculated as

$$\mathbf{E} = -\frac{1}{2}((\mathbf{v} \times \mathbf{B})^n - \eta J^n + (\mathbf{v} \times \mathbf{B})^{n+1} - \eta J^{n+1}). \tag{2.14}$$

The contravariant component of the magnetic field is then obtained at every mesh point. The following equation details the ξ-contravariant component of $\boldsymbol{B}$:

$$\begin{aligned}(B^{\xi})^{n+1}_{ijk} = (B^{\xi})^{n}_{ijk} &+ \frac{1}{RJ}\frac{(RE_{\phi})_{i,j+1,k} - (RJE_{\phi})_{i,j-1,k}}{2\Delta\zeta} \\ &- \frac{1}{RJ}\frac{E_{\zeta i,j,k+1} - E_{\zeta i,j,k-1}}{2\Delta\phi},\end{aligned} \tag{2.15}$$

where E_{ζ} and E_{ϕ} are covariant components of the electric field. The numerical approximation to $\nabla \cdot \boldsymbol{B}$ is zero in the following discrete sense:

$$\begin{aligned}(RJ\nabla \cdot \mathbf{B})_{ijk} = &\frac{(JRB^{\xi})_{i+1,j,k} - (JRB^{\xi})_{i-1,j,k}}{2\Delta\xi} \\ &+ \frac{(JRB^{\zeta})_{i,j+1,k} - (JRB^{\zeta})_{i,j-1,k}}{2\Delta\zeta} \\ &+ \frac{(JB^{\phi})_{i,j,k+1} - (JRB^{\phi})_{i,j,k+1}}{2\Delta\phi} = 0.\end{aligned} \tag{2.16}$$

2.2.4 AMR Implementation

We now briefly describe the main issues in implementing the above algorithm using block-structured adaptive meshes using the Chombo framework [6]. Each of the blocks is surrounded by a layer of guard cells that are filled either by exchanging data from sibling meshes at the same level or by interlevel interpolation from coarse to fine meshes. In the calculation of the second-order accurate hyperbolic fluxes, linear interpolation is sufficient, while the diffusive fluxes require a quadratic interpolation. We employ the Berger–Oliger timestepping technique in which the timesteps are determined by the CFL condition imposed by the ideal MHD wave speeds and are computed at the finest level and then appropriately coarsened by the refinement ratio to determine the larger stable timestep for coarser levels. We maintain flux registers that are used during synchronization when disparate levels reach the same physical time. During the refluxing procedure, the coarse-level fluxes at coarse–fine boundaries are replaced by the sum of the fine-level fluxes. At the end of the timestep on a coarser level, the portion of the mesh covered by a finer level mesh is replaced by averaging down the finer level solution. So far what we have described is fairly standard practice for structured hierarchical AMR meshes. We will now state a few of the difficulties stemming from AMR on generalized curvilinear meshes. Generally, one has to be careful when refining or coarsening on curvilinear meshes because the volume and surface areas are not conserved upon coarsening or refinement [12] and special care is required to maintain conservation. We have circumvented this issue by using the following method. We have the curvilinear representation only in the poloidal section. We precompute the equilibrium on the mesh at the finest level. Recall that the equilibrium determines the flux surfaces and the corresponding mesh. For all the coarser levels, we coarsen the flux surfaces in a manner that preserves the volume and the areas of the cell faces. The metric terms and the Jacobian used in the equations are thus predetermined at all the levels and stored. While this may be deemed excessive, we remind the reader that this is only required for the two-dimensional poloidal cross section.

2.3 SIMULATION RESULTS

In this section, we present results of pellet injection simulations using the methods described in the previous sections. The parameters of the simulation studies are as follows: the toroidal field at the magnetic axis is $B_{\mathrm{T}} = 0.375$ T, the number density of the ambient plasma is $n_{\infty} = 1.5 \times 10^{19}/\mathrm{m}^3$, the ambient plasma temperature is $T_{\infty} = 1.3$ keV, the major radius of the tokamak is $R_0 = 1$ m, and the minor radius is $a = 0.3$ m. The initial pellet radius is $r_{\mathrm{p}} = 1$ mm and the injection speed is $v_{\mathrm{p}} = 1000$ m/s. The pellet is instantaneously initialized on the same flux surface for both the LFS and HFS launches.

The mesh parameters for this run are the following. The coarsest mesh is 32^3 in size, which is refined by five levels, each with a refinement factor of 2 resulting in an effective mesh resolution of 1024^3. The mesh refinement criterion was a simple one: we refined the mesh where the density exceeded a certain threshold. This results in a mesh that can effectively resolve the pellet ablation cloud. We note that unless the pellet ablation cloud is resolved properly, the heating due to the electrons, which is directly proportional to the local density, drops precipitously and results

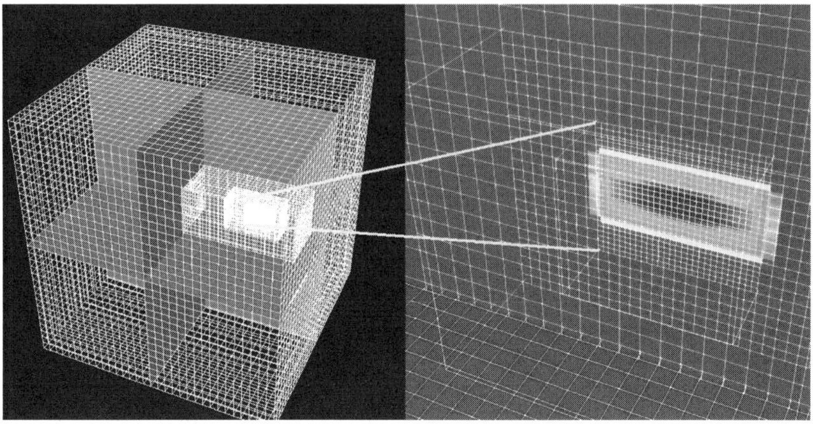

Figure 2.1 Mesh structure in pellet injection. The right image is a magnification of the pellet cloud region showing that this cloud has been adequately resolved.

in an inaccurate transport of the ablated mass. A snapshot of the mesh structure in computational coordinates is shown in Figure 2.1, which includes a magnification of the pellet region showing the pellet cloud in the finest mesh.

A time history of the density field for both LFS and HFS is shown in Figure 2.2. In both cases, we observe that pellet ablated mass has a dominant motion along field lines (mostly along the toroidal direction) accompanied by the so-called anomalous transport across flux surfaces in the direction of increasing major radius. This cross-field transport is further quantified and flux-averaged density profiles are plotted in Figure 2.3, wherein we observe a significant penetration toward the core of the pellet mass in the HFS case and a pileup of the mass on the outer flux surface in the LFS case. This observed motion of the pellet mass toward the low-field side in these adaptive mesh three-dimensional simulations of pellet injection is in qualitative agreement with experimental observations.

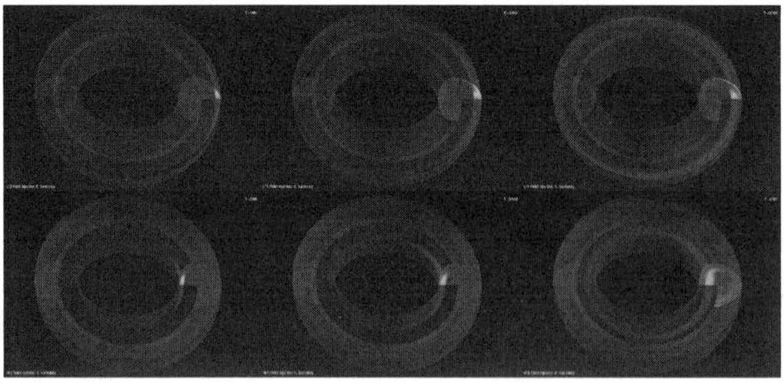

Figure 2.2 Density field images in pellet injection in a tokamak. The top row shows a time sequence for a LFS launch, while the bottom row is a time sequence for a HFS launch.

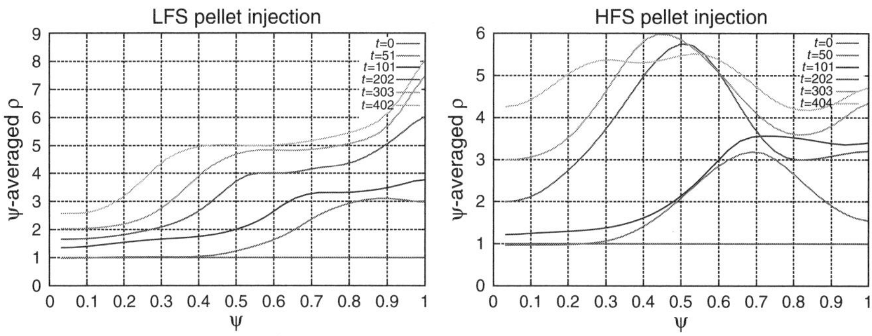

(**a**) Flux-averaged density profiles in LFS pellet injection.

(**b**) Flux-averaged density profiles in HFS pellet injection.

Figure 2.3 Flux-averaged density profiles of pellet injection into a tokamak indicate HFS launches have better core penetration than LFS.

2.4 SUMMARY AND FUTURE WORK

Pellet injection is a viable method to refuel a tokamak and will most likely be the fueling mechanism for ITER. We presented an adaptive mesh extended MHD method, including the electron heat flux models, to simulate pellet injection into a tokamak. We employed mapped curvilinear grids to handle shaped plasma in the toroidal cross section. Without AMR, resolved simulations of pellet injection become prohibitively expensive. Simulations using this code were used to investigate the differences and similarities between HFS and LFS pellet injection. It was found that, in qualitative agreement with experiments, HFS leads to better core fueling than LFS launches.

On the algorithmic side, in the future, we expect to use a multidimensional upwind method for the hyperbolic fluxes and implicit treatment of the diffusion terms. Finally, we hope to adopt the Jacobian-free Newton–Krylov approach to overcome the temporal stiffness. Such a method has been recently applied to resistive MHD by Reynolds et al. [23] albeit in a slab geometry. We expect to extend it to a tokamak geometry and combine it with adaptive mesh refinement. On the physics side, we expect to conduct more numerical experiments, validate our results against existing experiments, and make prediction for ITER-like parameters.

ACKNOWLEDGMENTS

We thank the SciDAC program of the Department of Energy for funding this work that was performed at the Princeton Plasma Physics Laboratory, Princeton University, under USDOE Contract No. DE-AC020-76-CH03073. This research used resources of the National Energy Research Scientific Computing Center, which is supported by the Office of Science of the U.S. Department of Energy under Contract No. DE-AC03-76SF00098. We acknowledge the contributions of the Applied Numerical Algorithms Group at the Lawrence Berkeley National Laboratory, especially Dr. Phillip Colella and Brian Van Straalen, in the development of the adaptive mesh refinement MHD code used for this research. We also acknowledge useful discussions with Dr. Stephen C. Jardin of PPPL and Dr. Paul Parks of General Atomics.

REFERENCES

1. L. Baylor, et al. Improved core fueling with high field pellet injection in the DIII-D tokamak. *Phys. Plasmas*, 7:1878–1885, 2000.
2. L. Baylor, et al. Comparison of fueling efficiency from different fueling locations on DIII-D. *J. Nucl. Mater.*, 313:530–533, 2003.
3. M. Berger and J. Oliger. Adaptive mesh refinement for hyperbolic partial differential equations. *J. Comput. Phys.*, 53:484–512, 1984.
4. M.J. Berger and P. Colella. Local adaptive mesh refinement for shock hydrodynamics. *J. Comput. Phys.*, 82(1):64–84, 1989.
5. P. Colella. Multidimensional upwind methods for hyperbolic conservation laws. *J. Comput. Phys.*, 87:171–200, 1990.
6. P. Colella, et al. Chombo software package for AMR applications design document.
7. R.K. Crockett, P. Colella, R. Fisher, R.I. Klein, and C.F. McKee. An unsplit, cell-centered Godunov method for ideal MHD. *J. Comput. Phys.*, 203:422–448, 2005.
8. P. Gohill, et al. Investigations of H-mode plasmas triggered directly by pellet injection in the DIII-D tokamak. *Phys. Rev. Lett.*, 86:644–647, 2001.
9. R.J. Goldston and P.H. Rutherford. *Introduction to Plasma Physics*. Institute of Physics Publishing, Bristol, 1997.
10. R. Ishizaki, et al. Two-dimensional simulation of pellet ablation with atomic processes. *Phys. Plasmas*, 11:4064–4080, 2004.
11. S.C. Jardin, et al. A fast shutdown technique for large tokamaks. *Nucl. Fusion*, 40:923–933, 2000.
12. J.B. Bell, P. Colella, J.A. Trangenstein, and M. Welcome. Adaptive mesh refinement on moving quadrilateral grids. In *Proceedings of the 9th AIAA Computational Fluid Dynamics Conference*, Buffalo, NY, June 1989.
13. B.V. Kuteev. Hydrogen pellet ablation and acceleration by current in high temperature plasmas. *Nucl. Fusion*, 35:431–453, 1995.
14. A.K. MacAulay. Two dimensional time dependent simulation of ablation of hydrogen pellets in hot magnetized fusion plasmas. PhD thesis, Princeton University, 1993.
15. A. K. MacAulay. Geometrical, kinetic and atomic physics effects in a two dimensional time dependent simulation of ablating fuel pellets. *Nucl. Fusion*, 34:43–62, 1994.
16. H.W. Müller, et al. High β plasmoid formation, drift, and striations during pellet ablation in ASDEX upgrade. *Nucl. Fusion*, 42:301–309, 2002.
17. P. Parks. Magnetic-field distortion near an ablating hydrogen pellet. *Nucl. Fusion*, 20:311–320, 1980.
18. P. Parks. Theory of pellet cloud oscillation striations. *Plasma Phys. Control. Fusion*, 38:571–591, 1996.
19. P. Parks, L.R. Baylor. Effects of parallel flows and toroidicity on cross field transport of pellet ablation matter in tokamak plasmas. *Phys. Rev. Lett.*, 94:125002, 2005.
20. P. Parks, et al. Radial displacement of pellet ablation material in tokamaks due to the grad-B effect. *Phys. Plasmas*, 7:1968–1975, 2000.
21. P. Parks and M. Rosenbluth. Equilibrium pellet and liquid jet shape under high ablation pressures. *Phys. Plasmas*, 5:1380–1386, 1998.
22. P. Parks and R.J. Turnbull. Effect of transonic flow in ablation cloud on lifetime of a solid hydrogen pellet in a plasma. *Phys. Fluids*, 21:1735–1741, 1978.
23. D.R. Reynolds, R. Samtaney, and C.S. Woodward. A fully implicit numerical method for single-fluid resistive magnetohydrodynamics. *J. Comput. Phys.*, 219:144–162, 2006.

24. R. Samtaney, P. Colella, T.J. Ligocki, D.F. Martin, and S.C. Jardin. An adaptive mesh semi-implicit conservative unsplit method for resistive MHD. In A. Mezzacappa, et al., editors, *SciDAC 2005*. San Francsico, June 26–30, 2005.
25. R. Samtaney, S.C. Jardin, P. Colella, and D.F. Martin. 3D adaptive mesh refinement simulations of pellet injection in tokamaks. *Comput. Phys. Commun.*, 164:220–228, 2004.
26. H.R. Strauss and W. Park. Pellet driven disruptions in tokamaks. *Phys. Plasmas*, 7:250–257, 2000.
27. G. Toth. The $\nabla \cdot B = 0$ constraint in shock-capturing magnetohydrodynamics codes. *J. Comput. Phys.*, 161:605–652, 2000.

Chapter 3

Parallel Computing Engines for Subsurface Imaging Technologies

Tian-Chyi J. Yeh, Xing Cai, Hans P. Langtangen, Junfeng Zhu, and Chuen-Fa Ni

3.1 INTRODUCTION

Multiscale heterogeneity of geologic media is a rule rather than an exception. The knowledge of detailed spatial distributions of hydraulic properties is imperative to predict water and solute movement in the subsurface at high resolution (see Refs. [22, 23]). Traditional aquifer tests (e.g., pumping and slug tests) have been widely employed for estimating hydraulic properties of the subsurface for the last few decades. Besides their costly installation and invasive natures, Beckie and Harvey reported in Ref. [2] that slug tests can yield dubious estimates of the storage coefficient of aquifers. Validity of classical analysis for aquifer tests was also questioned by Wu et al. [21]. They reported that the storage coefficient S, obtained from the traditional Theis analysis, primarily represents a weighted average of S values over the region between the pumping and observation wells. In contrast to the S estimate, the transmissivity T estimate is a weighted average of all T values in the entire domain with relatively high weights near the pumping well and the observation well. In concordance with the finding by Oliver [17], Wu et al. [21] concluded that the T estimate can be influenced by any large-sized or strong anomaly within the cone of depression. Thus, interpretation of the T estimates can be highly uncertain. As a result, previous assessments of transmissivity distributions of aquifers may be subject to serious doubt.

Advanced Computational Infrastructures For Parallel and Distributed Adaptive Applications. Edited by Manish Parashar and Xiaolin Li

Recently, viable alternatives to the direct characterization and traditional inverse modeling approaches have emerged in which data from the direct characterization and monitoring methods are supplemented with coverage of greater density from the indirect, minimally invasive hydrologic and geophysical tomographic surveys. These tomographic surveys are analogous to CAT (computerized axial tomography) scan technology that yields a 3D picture of an object that is more detailed than a standard X-ray and has been widely used in medical sciences to "see" into human bodies noninvasively. Unlike traditional hydrologic inverse modeling and geophysical surveys, the tomographic approaches excite the subsurface using artificial stimuli and then intelligently collect the same types of information to provide more independent information to constrain the inverse modeling in a cost-effective manner.

In hydrology, noticeably, hydraulic, pneumatic, as well as tracer tomography surveys have been developed recently; seismic, acoustic, electromagnetic (EM), and other tomography surveys have emerged in geophysics. Our discussion, however, will concentrate on hydraulic and tracer tomography and electrical resistivity tomography only.

Hydraulic tomography [3, 10, 14, 25, 29], in a simple term, is a series of cross-well interference tests. More precisely, hydraulic tomography involves stressing an aquifer by pumping water from or injecting water into a well and monitoring the aquifer's response at other wells (well hydrograph). A set of stress and response data yields an independent set of equations. Sequentially switching the pumping or injection location, without installing additional wells, results in a large number of aquifer responses induced by the stresses at different locations and, thus, a large number of independent sets of equations. This large number of sets of equations makes the inverse problem (i.e., using aquifer stress and response relation to estimate the spatial distribution of hydraulic parameters) better posed, and the subsequent estimates approach reality. Principles of tracer tomography [28] and electrical resistivity tomography [13, 26] are identical to that of hydraulic tomography, with the exception that tracer tomography uses tracers and electrical resistivity tomography uses electric currents as sources of excitation.

The large number of data sets generated during tomographic surveys often leads to information overload, substantial computational burdens, and numerical instabilities (see Ref. [11]). To overcome these difficulties, Yeh and Liu [25] developed a sequential successive linear estimator (SSLE) approach for hydraulic tomography. This approach eases the computational burdens by sequentially including information obtained from different pumping tests; it resolves the nonuniqueness issue by providing an unbiased mean of an abstracted stochastic parameter rather than the actual parameter. That is, it conceptualizes hydraulic parameter fields as spatial stochastic processes and seeks their conditional effective parameter distributions. The conditional effective parameters are conditioned on the measured data and governing physical principles of hydraulic tomography, as well as our prior knowledge of the geologic structure and directly measured parameter values (such as from slug tests or core samples). The SSLE approach in essence is the Bayesian formalism (see Ref. [12]). Sand box experiments by Liu et al. [14, 15] proved that the combination of hydraulic tomography and SSLE is a viable, cost-effective technique for delineating heterogeneity using a limited number of invasive observations. The work by Yeh and Liu [25], nonetheless, is limited to steady-state flow conditions, which may occur only under special field conditions. Because of this restriction, their method ignores transient head data before flow reaches steady-state conditions.

Several researchers have investigated transient hydraulic tomography (THT). Bohling et al. [3] exploited the steady-shape flow regime of transient flow data to interpret tomographic surveys. Similar to Vasco et al. [19], Brauchler et al. [4] developed a method that uses the traveltime of a pneumatic pressure pulse to estimate air diffusivity of fractured rocks. As in X-ray tomography, their approach relies on the assumption that the pressure pulse travels along a straight line or a curved path. Thus, an analytical solution can be derived for the propagation of the pressure pulse between a source and a pressure sensor. Many pairs of sources and sensors yield a system of one-dimensional analytical equations. A least-squares-based inverse procedure developed for seismic tomography can then be applied to the system of equations to estimate the diffusivity distribution. The ray approach avoids complications involved in numerical formulation of the three-dimensional forward and inverse problems, but it ignores interaction between adjacent ray paths and possible boundary effects. Consequently, their method requires an extensive number of iterations and pairs of source/sensor data to achieve a comparable resolution to that achieved from inverting a three-dimensional model. Vesselinov et al. [20] applied an optimization technique and geostatistics to interpret pneumatic cross-borehole tests in fractured rocks.

Recently, Zhu and Yeh [29] extended the SSLE approach to THT to estimate both spatially varying hydraulic conductivity and specific storage fields in three-dimensional random media. They demonstrated that it is possible to obtain detailed hydraulic conductivity and specific storage fields of aquifers using few wells with THT surveys. But as the size of the field site to be characterized and the demand of resolution increase, the computational burden increases significantly. A computationally efficient algorithm, therefore, must be developed for speedy analysis of the THT surveys. For basin-scale naturally recurrent tomographic surveys (such as river-stage tomography, Yeh et al. [24]), development of such a technology is imperative.

Speedy analysis of high-resolution THT as well as other types of hydrologic and geophysical tomographic surveys clearly calls for parallel computing. Therefore, both the numerical algorithms and software must be adapted to the parallel computing hardware. It is thus the purpose of this chapter to shed some light on this topic by presenting the design of parallel computing engines applicable to the above-mentioned problems. Section 3.2 will summarize the main types of partial differential equations and their related computations in the context of subsurface imaging. Thereafter, Section 3.3 will discuss a strategy of creating the numerical algorithms and resulting software with both parallelism and adaptivity. Afterward, numerical experiments will be shown in Section 3.4, before we give some concluding remarks in Section 3.5.

3.2 MATHEMATICAL MODELS AND NUMERICAL APPROACHES

Mathematically, subsurface imaging such as hydraulic tomography is equivalent to solving inverse problems defined through partial differential equations. The solutions need to be restricted with respect to scattered measurements, typically by a geostatistical approach in an iterative style. We will show in this section the most frequently encountered partial differential equations and their associated geostatistical computations, thus paving the way for Section 3.3 where parallel computing engines with adaptive capability will be devised.

3.2.1 Hydraulic Tomography

Hydraulic tomography is a high-resolution technique for characterizing the heterogeneous distribution of hydraulic properties in aquifers (see Refs. [3, 4, 10, 16, 18, 19, 25]). The setup of hydraulic tomography for a three-dimensional aquifer domain Ω is that at least two wells are bored, in which water pumping/injection and hydraulic measurement can be done alternately. A series of pumping tests ($P = 1, 2, \ldots, n_q$) is then carried out, during each test water is pumped or injected in one well at location $\mathbf{x}_p$, while inside all the other wells the response in the form of total hydraulic head H is measured. The aim is to portray subsurface hydraulic properties, such as the hydraulic conductivity $K(\mathbf{x})$, as heterogeneous fields in the entire three-dimensional domain Ω.

Steady-State Hydraulic Tomography: In the simplest steady-state form of hydraulic tomography, the hydraulic conductivity field $K(\mathbf{x})$ is the target of solution and is assumed to fit with the following elliptic partial differential equation:

$$\nabla \cdot [K(\mathbf{x})\nabla H(\mathbf{x})] + Q(\mathbf{x}) = 0, \tag{3.1}$$

where $Q(\mathbf{x})$ denotes the pumping rate of a specific pumping test. That is, for pumping test p, $Q(\mathbf{x})$ is zero for all positions $\mathbf{x}$ except for a very small region around $\mathbf{x}_p$. Equation (3.1) is to be restricted with respect to the H measurements obtained from all the pumping tests ($1 \leq p \leq n_q$) such that a suitable heterogeneous field $K(\mathbf{x})$ can be found.

As boundary conditions for (3.1), it is common to divide the boundary of Ω into two disjoint parts: $\Gamma = \Gamma_1 \cup \Gamma_2$, where on the Dirichlet boundary Γ_1, the value of H is prescribed:

$$H|_{\Gamma_1} = H^*,$$

whereas on the Neumann boundary Γ_2, the outflow flux is prescribed:

$$[K\nabla H] \cdot \mathbf{n}|_{\Gamma_2} = q,$$

where $\mathbf{n}$ denotes the outward unit normal on Γ_2.

Transient Hydraulic Tomography: When the time-dependent feature of the total hydraulic head H is of importance, as is in most real-life applications, *transient hydraulic tomography* (see Ref. [29]) should be used. In the transient case, the aim is to find both the hydraulic conductivity $K(\mathbf{x})$ and specific storage $S_s(\mathbf{x})$ that fit with the following parabolic partial differential equation:

$$\nabla \cdot [K(\mathbf{x})\nabla H(\mathbf{x}, t)] + Q(\mathbf{x}) = S_s(\mathbf{x})\frac{\partial H(\mathbf{x}, t)}{\partial t}. \tag{3.2}$$

Similar to steady-state hydraulic tomography, the above equation is to be restricted with respect to the $H(\mathbf{x}, t)$ measurements obtained from a series of pumping tests ($1 \leq p \leq n_q$), with suitable boundary and initial conditions. In each pumping test, the total hydraulic head H is measured at a set of locations $\mathbf{x}_j$ ($1 \leq j \leq n_h$) and for a set of time levels t_l ($1 \leq l \leq n_t$). THT is in effect an inverse problem with respect to K and S_s.

3.2.2 Electrical Resistivity Tomography

Electrical resistivity tomography is a geophysical survey technique, in the same style as steady-state hydraulic tomography. Instead of pumping or injecting water, DC currents are emitted at one location and the resulting electrical potential is measured at a set of other locations (see Refs. [26, 27]). The aim is to find the electrical conductivity field $\sigma(\mathbf{x})$ that fits with the following governing equation:

$$\nabla \cdot (\sigma(\mathbf{x})\nabla\phi(\mathbf{x})) + I(\mathbf{x}) = 0, \tag{3.3}$$

where ϕ denotes the electrical potential and I denotes the electrical current source. A detailed characterization of $\sigma(\mathbf{x})$ is important information needed for hydrological inverse modeling.

3.2.3 Tracer Tomography

To monitor the hazardous nonaqueous phase liquids (NAPLs), *partitioning tracer tomography* is an important subsurface imaging technique. The starting assumption is that there exists a steady flow field in form of a Darcy flux,

$$\mathbf{q}(\mathbf{x}) = -K(\mathbf{x})\nabla H(\mathbf{x}).$$

Each pumping test injects an impulse solution of *partitioning tracers* from a specific location $\mathbf{x}_p$ into Ω. The tracer concentration $c(\mathbf{x}, t)$ is then measured at a set of observation locations and for a set of time levels. The governing equation for the tracer flow in Ω is as follows:

$$\frac{\partial}{\partial t}(\theta_w c + K_n\theta_n c) = -\nabla \cdot (\mathbf{q}c) + \nabla \cdot (\theta_w \mathbf{D}\nabla c), \tag{3.4}$$

where θ_w and θ_n denote the saturation fields of water and NAPL, respectively. The NAPL saturation θ_n is the main target of solution, whereas the water saturation θ_w

is also unknown in most practical cases. In (3.4), K_n denotes the so-called partitioning coefficient and $\mathbf{D}$ denotes a known dispersion tensor field. Normally, the convection term $\nabla \cdot (\mathbf{q}c)$ is dominant in (3.4), in comparison with the dispersion term $\nabla \cdot (\theta_{\mathrm{w}}\mathbf{D}\nabla c)$. It should also be noted that tracer tomography is often carried out together with hydraulic tomography, because a detailed characterization of the hydraulic conductivity field $K(\mathbf{x})$ is vital for the accuracy of the computed θ_{n} field, that is, the NAPL distribution.

3.2.4 Geostatistically Based Inversion

In the preceding text, four subsurface inverse problems (3.1)–(3.4) have been presented. All of them are defined through partial differential equations, which need to be restricted with respect to scattered measurements of the total hydraulic head H, or electrical potential ϕ, or tracer concentration c obtained from a series of tests. Here, we will briefly describe a generic solution approach applicable to all the four inverse problems on the basis of geostatistics. More details can be found in Ref. [25].

Let χ be a generic symbol representing a primary variable to be estimated, based on *a priori* knowledge of χ_i^* at $1 \le i \le n_\chi$ locations and measurements of a secondary variable v_j^* at $1 \le j \le n_v$ locations. The initial estimate of χ is constructed as

$$\hat{\chi}^{(1)}(\mathbf{x}) = \sum_{i=1}^{n_\chi} \lambda_i(\mathbf{x})\chi_i^* + \sum_{j=1}^{n_v} \mu_j(\mathbf{x})v_j^*, \tag{3.5}$$

where the cokriging weights $[\lambda_i(\mathbf{x})]_{i=1}^{n_\chi}$ and $\left[\mu_j(\mathbf{x})\right]_{j=1}^{n_v}$ are derived from solving the following system of linear equations:

$$\begin{aligned}
\sum_{i=1}^{n_\chi} \lambda_i(\mathbf{x})R_{\chi\chi}(\mathbf{x}_\ell, \mathbf{x}_i) + \sum_{j=1}^{n_v} \mu_j(\mathbf{x})R_{\chi v}(\mathbf{x}_\ell, \mathbf{x}_j) &= R_{\chi\chi}(\mathbf{x}, \mathbf{x}_\ell) \quad 1 \le \ell \le n_\chi, \\
\sum_{i=1}^{n_\chi} \lambda_i(\mathbf{x})R_{v\chi}(\mathbf{x}_\ell, \mathbf{x}_i) + \sum_{j=1}^{n_v} \mu_j(\mathbf{x})R_{vv}(\mathbf{x}_\ell, \mathbf{x}_j) &= R_{v\chi}(\mathbf{x}, \mathbf{x}_\ell) \quad 1 \le \ell \le n_v.
\end{aligned} \tag{3.6}$$

In (3.6), $R_{\chi\chi}$ and R_{vv} denote the spatial covariance function of χ and v, respectively. The cross-covariance between χ and v is denoted by $R_{\chi v}$. The covariance function $R_{\chi\chi}$ of the primary variable is prescribed *a priori*, whereas R_{vv} and $R_{\chi v}$ are calculated using a first-order analysis based on $R_{\chi\chi}$ (see Ref. [25]). It should be noted that the above linear system is of dimension $(n_\chi + n_v) \times (n_\chi + n_v)$ and the system matrix is full due to nonzero (cross-)covariance function values. It should also be noted that $\chi(\mathbf{x})$ in (3.5) is numerically sought at a number of discrete locations of $\mathbf{x}$, such as the center of elements in a setting of finite element discretization. Therefore, the linear system (3.6) is to be solved repeatedly to find $[\lambda_i(\mathbf{x})]_{i=1}^{n_\chi}$ and $\left[\mu_j(\mathbf{x})\right]_{j=1}^{n_v}$ for each of the discrete locations.

Since the relation between χ and v is in general nonlinear, a successive linear estimator approach using iterations can be used. More specifically, suppose $\hat{\chi}^{(r)}(\mathbf{x})$

denotes the estimate of χ after iteration r, then $\hat{\chi}^{(r)}(\mathbf{x})$ is used to compute its corresponding $v^{(r)}(\mathbf{x})$, which is likely to be different from measured values v_j^* at the n_v measurement locations. The difference $v_j^* - v^{(r)}(\mathbf{x}_j)$ is thus used to improve the current estimate $\hat{\chi}^{(r)}(\mathbf{x})$ by

$$\hat{\chi}^{(r+1)}(\mathbf{x}) = \hat{\chi}^{(r)}(\mathbf{x}) + \sum_{j=1}^{n_v} \omega_j^{(r)}(\mathbf{x}) \left[v_j^* - v^{(r)}(\mathbf{x}_j) \right], \tag{3.7}$$

where the weights $\omega_j^{(r)}$ are found by solving a similar linear system as (3.6), which makes use of updated (cross-)covariance functions $R_{v\chi}^{(r)}$ and $R_{vv}^{(r)}$ (see Ref. [25]). The above iterations will continue until satisfactory convergence has been achieved for all the measurements obtained from one test. Once this test has been handled successfully, measurements from another test are added and the estimate $\hat{\chi}(\mathbf{x})$ is further improved by a new series of iterations of form (3.7). This one-by-one incorporation of the remaining tests is repeated until all the tests are processed. Such a geostatistical approach is termed *sequential successive linear estimator* (see Figure 3.1 for an illustration).

SSLE Applied to THT: The basic assumption is that the natural logarithm of both the hydraulic conductivity and specific storage is a mean value plus perturbation, that is, $\ln K = \bar{K} + f$ and $\ln S_s = \bar{S} + s$. Similarly, the hydraulic head H is assumed to be $H = \bar{H} + h$. These statistical assumptions give rise to the same parabolic equation as (3.2), but with K, S_s, and H being replaced by $\bar{K}_{\text{con}}$, $\bar{S}_{\text{con}}$, and $\bar{H}_{\text{con}}$, which represent *conditional effective* hydraulic conductivity, specific storage, and hydraulic head, respectively. The details can be found in Ref. [29] and the references therein.

When applying the SSLE approach to THT, the perturbations $f(\mathbf{x})$ and $s(\mathbf{x})$ are considered as the primary variables, whereas the perturbation $h(\mathbf{x}, t)$ is treated as the secondary variable. That is, $f(\mathbf{x})$ and $s(\mathbf{x})$ collectively replace χ in (3.5)–(3.7), whereas $h(\mathbf{x}, t)$ replaces v. It should be noted that a double summation $\sum_{l=1}^{n_t} \sum_{j=1}^{n_h}$ replaces all occurrences of the single summation $\sum_{j=1}^{n_v}$ in (3.5)–(3.7), because the measurements of $H(\mathbf{x}, t)$ exist at n_h spatial locations and n_t time levels.

The transient hydraulic head is assumed to be

$$H(\mathbf{x}, t) = \bar{H}(\mathbf{x}, t) + f(\mathbf{x}) \left. \frac{\partial H(\mathbf{x}, t)}{\partial \ln K(\mathbf{x})} \right|_{\bar{K},\bar{S}} + s(\mathbf{x}) \left. \frac{\partial H(\mathbf{x}, t)}{\partial \ln S_s(\mathbf{x})} \right|_{\bar{K},\bar{S}}, \tag{3.8}$$

where second and higher order terms have been neglected (see Ref. [29]). To compute the sensitivity terms $\partial H(\mathbf{x}, t)/\partial \ln K(\mathbf{x})$ and $\partial H(\mathbf{x}, t)/\partial \ln S_s(\mathbf{x})$ needed in (3.8), the following adjoint-state equation, which is in fact a backward transient problem, must be solved for each pair of measurement location $\mathbf{x}_j$ and measurement time level t_l:

$$S_s \frac{\partial \phi^*}{\partial t} + \nabla \cdot \left(K \nabla \phi^* \right) = \delta(\mathbf{x} - \mathbf{x}_j)(t - t_l), \tag{3.9}$$

with suitable boundary and final conditions. That is, (3.9) is solved backward in time from $t = t_l$ to $t = 0$. It should be noted that both (3.2) and (3.9) need to be solved during each iteration, when new estimates of $K(\mathbf{x})$ and $S_s(\mathbf{x})$ are updated.

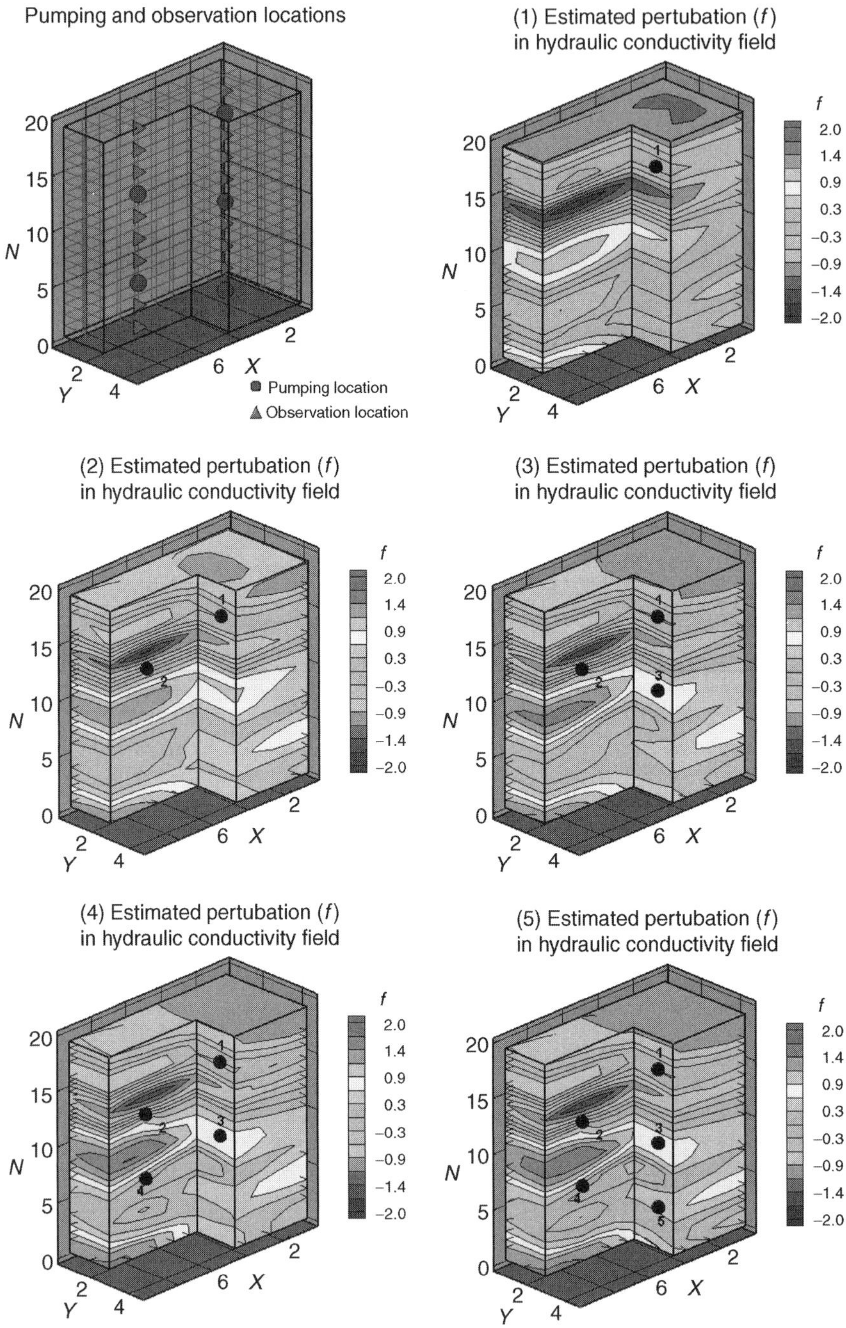

Figure 3.1 An example of hydraulic tomography using the SSLE approach, based on measurements obtained from five pumping tests.

Of course, the computational effort associated with solving (3.9) is much larger than solving (3.2), because there are altogether $n_t \times n_h$ occurrences of (3.9) inside each iteration.

The sensitivity terms that are required by (3.8) can be calculated for each computational location $\mathbf{x}_i$ in the aquifer domain Ω as follows:

$$\frac{\partial H(\mathbf{x}_j, t_l)}{\partial \ln K(\mathbf{x}_i)} = \int_T \int_\Omega \left\{ \frac{\partial K(\mathbf{x})}{\partial \ln K(\mathbf{x}_i)} \nabla \phi^* \cdot \nabla H \right\} \mathrm{d}\mathbf{x}\, \mathrm{d}t, \tag{3.10}$$

$$\frac{\partial H(\mathbf{x}_j, t_l)}{\partial \ln S_s(\mathbf{x}_i)} = \int_T \int_\Omega \left\{ \frac{\partial S_s(\mathbf{x})}{\partial \ln S_s(\mathbf{x}_i)} \phi^* \frac{\partial H}{\partial t} \right\} \mathrm{d}\mathbf{x}\, \mathrm{d}t. \tag{3.11}$$

Also, the covariance of h, the cross-covariance between h and f, and the cross-covariance between h and s all need to be updated by simple algebraic computations. We refer to Ref. [29] for more computational details.

3.2.5 Summary of Typical Computations

The most frequently encountered computations within the geostatistically based inversion approach are summarized below, they can be considered the computing engines of subsurface imaging.

- Solution of a stationary elliptic equation of form (3.1) or (3.3).
- Solution of a transient parabolic equation of form (3.2) or (3.9).
- Solution of a transient equation of form (3.4) with dominant convection.
- Calculation of sensitivity terms as expressed by (3.10) and (3.11).
- Solution of a linear system of form (3.6) with a full system matrix.

3.3 PARALLEL SUBSURFACE IMAGING WITH ADAPTIVITY

There are two main motivations for the use of parallel and adaptive computing in subsurface imaging. First, future hydrological and geophysical research need to address basin-scale investigations, which inevitably require computations involving millions of (or more) degrees of freedom. Second, the distribution of subsurface hydraulic properties is highly heterogeneous, with spatially (and possibly also temporarily) varying magnitude and direction. The computational resources should thus be utilized efficiently when doing very large-scale subsurface imaging computations. This ideally means that the finest mesh resolution should be applied to small and local areas with rapidly changing features, whereas the remaining areas of the solution domain use a relatively coarser mesh resolution. Consequently, the computational mesh for the entire solution domain becomes unstructured. The unstructured computational mesh may also need to be adaptively adjusted when solving transient equations. These heterogeneous and adaptive features will clearly complicate the parallelization of subsurface imaging computations. This section will thus provide some guidelines on how to parallelize the related numerical algorithms, such that we become well posed to solve the mathematical model problems discussed in Section 3.2.

3.3.1 An Example of Adaptive Mesh Refinement

Let us give a simple but motivating example of adaptive computing. In connection with tracer tomography (see Section 3.2.3), the following stationary convection-dominated equation often needs to be solved:

$$\mathbf{q} \cdot \nabla m_0 - \nabla \cdot (\theta_{\mathrm{w}} \mathbf{D} \nabla m_0) - Q = 0, \tag{3.12}$$

where the target of solution is the zeroth tracer moment $m_0(\mathbf{x})$, $\mathbf{q}(\mathbf{x})$ is a prescribed velocity field, $Q(\mathbf{x})$ is a given source function, and the definition of $\theta_{\mathrm{w}}(\mathbf{x})$ and $\mathbf{D}(\mathbf{x})$ is the same as in (3.4). Due to the dominant convection, some form of upwind discretization must be adopted to avoid nonphysical oscillations in the resulting m_0 solution. In terms of finite element discretization, a standard technique is the so-called *streamline upwind Petrov–Galerkin* (SUPG) finite element formulation (see Ref. [5]). However, using SUPG alone is often not enough for obtaining a satisfactory solution, as depicted in Figure 3.2. This figure has a rectangular domain where a source term is located close to the bottom right corner of Ω. By comparing two different m_0 solutions, which are respectively obtained on a uniform mesh and an unstructured mesh, we can see that adaptive mesh refinement helps to considerably improve the quality of the m_0 solution. The unstructured mesh has arisen from adaptively refining the uniform mesh in areas where the gradient of uniform mesh m_0 solution is large. We refer the reader to Ref. [1] for more mathematical and numerical details with respect to adaptive finite element computations.

Similar adaptive mesh refinement is also desirable in hydraulic tomography when the hydraulic conductivity $K(\mathbf{x})$ and/or the specific storage $S_s(\mathbf{x})$ are locally rapid varying functions of $\mathbf{x}$. Moreover, higher resolution around the location of the source term Q is often necessary and can be achieved by adaptive mesh refinement. However, unstructured computational meshes, which arise from adaptive mesh refinement,

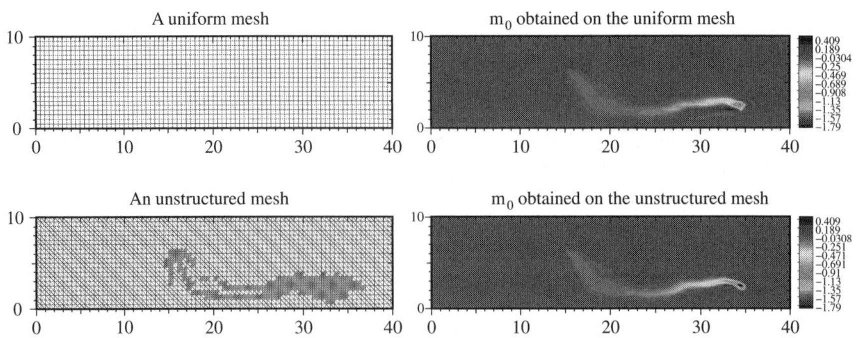

Figure 3.2 An example showing the necessity of using adaptively refined finite element meshes in connection with tracer tomography.

make domain decomposition a nontrivial task in connection with parallel computing. This is because straight planes or lines cannot be used to partition an unstructured global mesh, and load balancing becomes more complicated. The issue will be further discussed in Section 3.3.3.

3.3.2 Different Levels of Parallelism

It is now high time for analyzing why parallel computing is necessary and how it can be applied to the most frequently encountered computations of subsurface imaging, as mentioned in Section 3.2.5. For simplicity, we will only consider using finite elements in spatial discretizations, the reader is reminded that other common discretization strategies (such as finite difference and finite volume) can be parallelized using the same principles.

The transient partial differential equations (3.2), (3.4), and (3.9) are clearly the most computationally demanding, especially when high resolution is desired. Let N denote the number of elements in a spatial solution domain Ω. The associated computational cost for (3.2), (3.4), and (3.9) is of order $\mathcal{O}(N^{\alpha})$, where $\alpha > 1$. This is because first an increase in N will normally require more timesteps in the temporal integration when solving (3.2), (3.4), and (3.9) numerically. Second, during each time step of the temporal integration, a linear system that arises from the finite element discretization requires a computational effort of order $\mathcal{O}(N^{\beta})$, where $\beta \geq 1$. (The optimal case of $\beta = 1$ is obtained only when an optimal linear solver, such as multigrid [6], is used.)

Consequently, a large value of N, for example, of order $\mathcal{O}(10^6)$, will give rise to a huge amount of computation in SSLE. We recall that the computational work also grows with respect to the number of measurement locations n_h, the number of measurement time levels n_t, and the number of pumping tests n_q. All these factors call for the application of parallel computers to SSLE.

Parallelism arises from the following observations:

1. As mentioned in Section 3.2.4, the adjoint-state equation (3.9) needs to be solved for each pair of measurement location $\mathbf{x}_j$ and measurement time level t_l. These different solutions of (3.9) are totally independent of each other. This observation immediately calls for a *task parallel* approach to the parallelization, because a processor can be assigned to a number of solutions of (3.9). Note that the cost of each solution of (3.9) depends on the value of t_l, as (3.9) needs to be solved backward in time from $t = t_l$ to $t = 0$. This will clearly cause some nontriviality with respect to load balancing, but the real inconvenience is the fact that such a task parallel approach implies that every processor computes over the entire domain Ω. This parallelization approach may be impractical when N is too large for a single processor on a distributed memory machine, thus requiring a rethinking to be discussed later.
2. Equations (3.10) and (3.11) are used to compute the sensitivity terms associated with all the elements in Ω. The computation for one element is

independent of any other elements. Therefore, the computations associated with (3.10) and (3.11) can be parallelized using a *data parallel* approach, in the sense that one processor is assigned to a subset of the elements that constitute Ω. Likewise, the repeated solutions of the linear system (3.6), that is, one solution of (3.6) per element, can be divided among the processors.

3. When the values of n_h and n_t are relatively small, such that $n_h \times n_t$ is smaller than (or of the same size as) the number of available processors, we need to further consider parallelizing the linear system solver during each time step when (3.9) is integrated backward in time. Such a rethinking of parallelization for (3.9) is also necessary when N is too large for a single processor on a distributed memory machine. In general, parallelizing a linear system solver is more difficult than in the above two observations, because the degrees of freedom in a linear system are coupled with each other. A viable parallelization should be based on the so-called *subdomain-based* approach. This means that the degrees of freedom are divided following a domain decomposition of Ω. Each processor then becomes responsible for a piece of Ω and those degrees of freedom that are within the subdomain. In this way, iterative linear system solvers can be parallelized by letting each processor mostly carry out sequential computations, which are interleaved with interprocessor communication. We refer to Refs. [7, 8] for more in-depth discussions. The other partial differential equations (3.1)–(3.4) should always be parallelized using this subdomain-based approach. We note that not only the iterative linear system solvers are parallelizable in this way but also the finite element discretizations are straightforward for parallelization where each processor works only on its assigned subdomain.

We conclude from the above observations that a subdomain-based approach should lay the foundation for parallelizing the typical subsurface imaging computations. It should be noted that domain decomposition naturally gives rise to the data decomposition required by the parallelization of (3.6) and (3.10) and (3.11). In addition, when the values of n_h and n_t are large, the repeated solutions of (3.9) can be supplementarily parallelized using the task parallel approach.

3.3.3 Combining Adaptivity with Parallel Computing

From the preceding text, we know that adaptivity is necessary for an effective use of the computational resources (fine mesh resolution only where necessary), while parallelism is needed to handle large-scale computations. However, these two factors do not easily complement each other. This is because adaptivity often requires nontrivial mesh partitioning and dynamic load balancing. While partitioning unstructured finite element meshes is a well-studied topic with several good quality algorithms and software packages (see Ref. [9] and the references therein), dynamic load balancing is doable but normally incurs too much overhead (see Ref. [6]). To limit the cost of mesh partitioning and dynamic load balancing, we suggest the following strategy for creating unstructured subdomain finite element meshes:

1. Start with a coarse global uniform mesh for Ω. For a transient problem, this global uniform mesh should be the starting mesh for all the time steps.
2. The global uniform coarse mesh is refined adaptively a few times, possibly making use of the solution of the target equation obtained on the uniform coarse mesh. The result is a medium resolution unstructured mesh covering the entire spatial domain.
3. The unstructured global mesh is partitioned in P subdomains.
4. All the subdomains thereafter refine their own local subdomain mesh independently, each creating a hierarchy of subdomain unstructured meshes. The finest level of mesh resolution depends on both the accuracy requirement of the target solution and the available memory on each processor.
5. The final solution of the target equation is sought in parallel following the subdomain-based approach, at the finest level of mesh resolution.
6. If needed, each subdomain can use local multigrid as its subdomain solver in the parallelization of an iterative linear system solver.

The advantage of the above strategy is that adaptivity is injected into parallel computing, where load balance is also ensured (as long as each subdomain approximately refines the same amount of its elements). Moreover, the cost of partitioning an unstructured global mesh is limited, because the partitioning does not happen on the finest resolution level.

3.4 NUMERICAL EXPERIMENTS

Since (3.2) is the basic building block of any transient subsurface imaging problem, we test here the parallel efficiency of a three-dimensional code for solving (3.2). We mention that the original serial code was developed by the University of Arizona, and the parallelization has been done following the subdomain-based approach (see Section 3.3.2). Table 3.1 shows the associated speedup results, for

Table 3.1 Speedup Results Associated with Solving (3.2) in Parallel, Using the Subdomain-Based Parallelization Approach

Processors	CPU (min)	Speedup
1	29.55	N/A
2	15.45	1.91
4	7.89	3.75
8	4.07	7.26
16	1.81	16.33
24	1.27	23.27

which a three-dimensional finite element $45 \times 45 \times 45$ mesh has been used and the parallel computer is a Linux cluster consisting of 1.3 GHz Itanium II processors interconnected through a Gbit ethernet. It can be observed that satisfactory parallel performance has been achieved.

3.5 SUMMARY

Efficient numerical algorithms and parallel computers must be combined to handle basin-scale subsurface imaging problems in future. Based on summarizing the main types of involved partial differential equations and their associated computations, the present chapter has suggested a strategy for creating parallel numerical algorithms with adaptivity. The essence is to divide the spatial solution domain (such as a basin) into subdomains and assign each subdomain to a processor. The computations on each subdomain closely resemble the original serial computations on the entire spatial domain plus some additional intersubdomain communication. Therefore, an existing serial code has a good chance of reuse in the parallelized computations. This subdomain-based approach can often be mixed with task parallel and/or data parallel approaches to achieve satisfactory performance.

ACKNOWLEDGMENTS

The research is supported by NSF grant EAR-0229717, a SERDP grant, NSF IIS-0431079, and NSF EAR-0450388. In addition, partial support is provided by the Norwegian Research Council through Project 175128/D15.

REFERENCES

1. T.J. Barth and H. Deconinck, editors. *Error Estimation and Adaptive Discretization Methods in Computational Fluid Dynamics*, Vol. 25, Lecture Notes in Computational Science and Engineering. Springer-Verlag, 2003.
2. R. Beckie and C.F. Harvey. What does a slug test measure: an investigation of instrument response and the effects of heterogeneity. *Water Resour. Res.*, 38(12):1290, 2002.
3. G.C. Bohling, X. Zhan, J.J. Butler Jr., and L. Zheng. Steady shape analysis of tomographic pumping tests for characterization of aquifer heterogeneities. *Water Resour. Res.*, 38(12):1324, 2002.
4. R. Brauchler, R. Liedl, and P. Dietrich. A travel time based hydraulic tomographic approach. *Water Resour. Res.*, 39(12):1370, 2003.
5. A.N. Brooks and T.J.R. Hughes. Streamline upwind/Petrov–Galerkin formulations for convection dominated flows with particular emphasis on the incompressible Navier–Stokes equations. *Comput. Methods Appl. Mech. Eng.*, 32:199–259, 1982.
6. A.M. Bruaset and A. Tveito, editors. *Numerical Solution of Partial Differential Equations on Parallel Computers*, Vol. 51, Lecture Notes in Computational Science and Engineering. Springer-Verlag, 2006.
7. X. Cai. Overlapping domain decomposition methods. In H.P. Langtangen and A. Tveito, editors, *Advanced Topics in Computational Partial Differential Equations: Numerical Methods and Diffpack Programming*, Vol. 33, Lecture Notes in Computational Science and Engineering. Springer-Verlag, 2003, pp. 57–95.

8. X. Cai, E. Acklam, H.P. Langtangen, and A. Tveito. Parallel computing. In H.P. Langtangen and A. Tveito, editors, *Advanced Topics in Computational Partial Differential Equations: Numerical Methods and Diffpack Programming*, Vol. 33, Lecture Notes in Computational Science and Engineering. Springer-Verlag, 2003, pp. 1–55.
9. X. Cai and N. Bouhmala. A unified framework of multi-objective cost functions for partitioning unstructured finite element meshes. *Applied Mathematical Modelling*, 31:1711–1728, 2007.
10. J. Gottlieb and P. Dietrich. Identification of the permeability distribution in soil by hydraulic tomography. *Inverse Probl.*, 11:353–360, 1995.
11. D.L. Hughson and T.-C.J. Yeh. An inverse model for three-dimensional flow in variably saturated porous media. *Water Resour. Res.*, 36(4):829–839, 2000.
12. P.K. Kitanidis. Comment on "A reassessment of the groundwater inverse problem" by D. McLaughlin and L.R. Townley. *Water Resour. Res.*, 33(9):2199–2202, 1997.
13. S. Liu and T.-C.J. Yeh. An integrative approach for monitoring water movement in the vadose zone. *Vadose Zone J.*, 3(2):681–692, 2004.
14. S. Liu, T.-C.J. Yeh, and R. Gardiner. Effectiveness of hydraulic tomography: sandbox experiments. *Water Resour. Res.*, 38(4):1034, 2002.
15. W.A. Illman, X. Liu, and A. Craig. Steady-state hydraulic tomography in a laboratory aquifer with deterministic heterogeneity: Multi-method and multiscale validation of hydraulic conductivity tomograms. *Journal of Hydrology*, 341:222–234, 2007.
16. C.I. McDermott, M. Sauter, and R. Liedl. New experimental techniques for pneumatic tomographical determination of the flow and transport parameters of highly fractured porous rock samples. *J. Hydrol.*, 278(1):51–63, 2003.
17. D.S. Oliver. The influence of nonuniform transmissivity and storativity on drawdown. *Water Resour. Res.*, 29(1):169–178, 1993.
18. C.E. Renshaw. Estimation of fracture zone geometry from steady-state hydraulic head data using iterative sequential cokriging. *Geophys. Res. Lett.*, 23(19):2685–2688, 1996.
19. D.W. Vasco, H. Keers, and K. Karasaki. Estimation of reservoir properties using transient pressure data: an asymptotic approach. *Water Resour. Res.*, 36(12):3447–3466, 2000.
20. V.V. Vesselinov, W.I. Illman, Y. Hyun, S.P. Neuman, V. Di Federico, and D.M. Tartakovsky. Pronounced permeability and porosity scale-effect in unsaturated fractured tuffs. In *Proceedings of the Conference "Fractured Rock 2001"*, Toronto, Canada, March 26–28, 2001.
21. C.-M. Wu, T.-C.J. Yeh, J. Zhu, T.H. Lee, N.-S. Hsu, C.-H. Chen, and A.F. Sancho. Traditional analysis of aquifer tests: comparing apples to oranges? *Water Resour. Res.*, 41:W09402, 2005.
22. T.-C.J. Yeh. Stochastic modeling of groundwater flow and solute transport in aquifers. *J. Hydrol. Processes*, 6:369–395, 1992.
23. T.-C.J. Yeh. Scale issues of heterogeneity in vadose-zone hydrology and practical solutions. In G. Sposito, editor, *Dependence and Scale Invariance in Hydrology*. Cambridge University Press, 1998.
24. T.-C.J. Yeh, K. Hsu, C. Lee, J. Wen, and C. Ting. On the possibility of using river stage tomography to characterize the aquifer properties of the Choshuishi Alluvial Fan, Taiwan. Presentation at AGU 2004 Fall Meeting.
25. T.-C.J. Yeh and S. Liu. Hydraulic tomography: development of a new aquifer test method. *Water Resour. Res.*, 36(8):2095–2105, 2000.
26. T.-C.J. Yeh, S. Liu, R.J. Glass, K. Baker, J.R. Brainard, D.L. Alumbaugh, and D. LaBrecque. A geostatistically based inverse model for electrical resistivity surveys and its applications to vadose zone hydrology. *Water Resour. Res.*, 38(12):1278, 2002.
27. T.-C.J. Yeh and J. Šimůnek. Stochastic fusion of information for characterizing and monitoring the vadose zone. *Vadose Zone J.*, 1:207–221, 2002.
28. J. Zhu and T.-C.J. Yeh. A cost-effective method for characterizing NAPL source zones: hydraulic/tracer tomography. Poster at AGU 2005 Fall Meeting.
29. J. Zhu and T.-C.J. Yeh. Characterization of aquifer heterogeneity using transient hydraulic tomography. *Water Resour. Res.*, 41:W07028, 2005.

Chapter 4

Plane Wave Seismic Data: Parallel and Adaptive Strategies for Velocity Analysis and Imaging

Paul L. Stoffa, Mrinal K. Sen, Roustam K. Seif, and Reynam C. Pestana

4.1 INTRODUCTION

Seismic data from multiple sources and receivers need to be combined based on the traveltimes of the sound waves into the subsurface to form subsurface images. This process is known as Kirchhoff migration [13] and is routinely implemented in the data domain of the observations (space and time) using parallel computer architectures, particularly PC clusters [17]. However, the same data can first be transformed into a new spectral domain (plane wave component and vertical delay time) using a parallel algorithm as the field data are read, which regularizes the data to be processed. Once transformed, the imaging can again proceed in parallel since each plane wave component can be imaged independently. Computational resources can be dynamically adjusted as the data are transformed based on the number of plane wave components that will contribute to the final image. Efficiencies over conventional Kirchhoff migration algorithms range from 10–100 based on the reduced input data volume since the number of plane wave components employed will be less than the recorded data volume.

Advanced Computational Infrastructures For Parallel and Distributed Adaptive Applications. Edited by Manish Parashar and Xiaolin Li

A new double plane wave migration method is based on slant stacking [3, 5, 18, 19] over both shot positions and receiver positions (or offsets, which are the distances between the sources and receivers) for all the recorded data for either an entire survey or a subset of a survey. For seismic data recorded in a 3D mode of acquisition, the source may be positioned at the beginning, and/or end, and/or to the sides of the recording array. Further, the recording array will have more than one line of receivers. If an areal-receiving array is used and/or the sources are positioned to the sides of the receiving array, both in-line and cross-line data can be incorporated into the plane wave transform resulting in a vector or multidimensional phase space representation for the data. Also, seismic data are often not recorded on regular grids due to obstacles in the survey area. Since the true geometry is used in the plane wave transforms, this process results in a regularization of the data. In addition, because the number of plane wave components needed to represent the data is fewer than the original data volume, the transformation often results in a reduced data volume. By noting the maximum time changes versus distance for the recorded arrivals that are present in the data, the number of plane waves required can be estimated, and this, again, may result in a further data reduction.

We require vertical delay time computations (time taken by a wave to travel a vertical distance) for each particular plane wave component being used to image the plane wave transformed data. By combining these times for the source and receiver (or offset) plane waves, we can select the time samples to be used in the image. However, since we are in phase space, we do not need traveltimes for each source and receiver point in the survey; the plane wave vertical delay times can be registered to any surface (source or receiver) position by the addition of a simple time shift [20]. This considerably reduces the computational burden. Even so, each source and receiver plane wave component must be combined with all other receiver and source components for a complete diffraction summation. Many available traveltime techniques can be used to calculate the required imaging times, and because we are interested in just plane wave vertical delay times, problems with multipathing and first arrivals that are usually encountered in conventional traveltime computations for Kirchhoff imaging are minimal or absent.

We also investigate the applicability of this new technique to determine the velocity structure. The vertical delay times we need for imaging are derived from knowledge of the 3D subsurface velocity. This can be derived from the data using an optimization algorithm that searches the velocity model space until coherent images result for different viewing angles of the same subsurface target. Because the plane wave data can be selected to restrict the angles of incidence at each subsurface point or to emphasize subsurface targets with specific spatial variability or "dips," we can prune the imaging integrals to concentrate on selected targets. This leads naturally to an adaptive velocity estimation scheme.

The primary objective of this chapter is to demonstrate with examples parallel and adaptive strategies of our plane wave imaging and velocity analysis algorithms using a distributed architecture, like a PC cluster, to compute various plane wave sections, since they are independent of each other. By careful organization of the distribution of plane wave components for a given architecture, it is possible, in many cases, to achieve an in-memory solution even for a 3D survey or significant parts thereof. For adaptive velocity analysis, the number of compute nodes employed may be the same, but by restricting the number of plane wave components based on a staging strategy, the imaging time can be reduced and a non-linear optimization scheme, such as simulated annealing [15], becomes a viable solution.

4.2 THEORY

A plane wave or τ–$\mathbf{p}$ transform is computed for a recorded seismic trace relative to its source and receiver's absolute positions or the receiver's "offset" or distance from the source position [3, 5, 18, 19]. For today's dense source and receiver spacings with sources positioned every 50 m or less and receivers every 10 m or less, we can transform the data over source positions, receiver (or offset) positions, or both. Let the recorded data at the surface be $P(\mathbf{s}, \mathbf{r}, t)$, where $\mathbf{s}$ is the source location, $\mathbf{r}$ is the receiver location, and t is the time (Figure 4.1). Our first objective is to decompose these data into plane wave components.

In the frequency domain, the recorded data $P(\mathbf{s}, \mathbf{r}, t)$ can be decomposed into source and receiver plane wave components using a variant of slant stacking that applies a linear phase delay of each trace with respect to its shot or receiver position. For receiver plane waves, described by their horizontal slowness or ray parameter, $\mathbf{p_r}$, we have the following forward and inverse stacking formulas:

$$P(\mathbf{s}, \mathbf{p_r}, \omega) = \int P(\mathbf{s}, \mathbf{r}, \omega) \exp(+i\omega \mathbf{p_r} \cdot \mathbf{r}) d\mathbf{r},$$

$$P(\mathbf{s}, \mathbf{r}, \omega) = \omega^2 \int P(\mathbf{s}, \mathbf{p_r}, \omega) \exp(-i\omega \mathbf{p_r} \cdot \mathbf{r}) d\mathbf{p_r},$$

where ω is angular frequency and $P(\mathbf{s}, \mathbf{p_r}, \omega)$ represents the plane wave data with ray parameter $\mathbf{p_r}$ with respect to the absolute source and receiver positions.

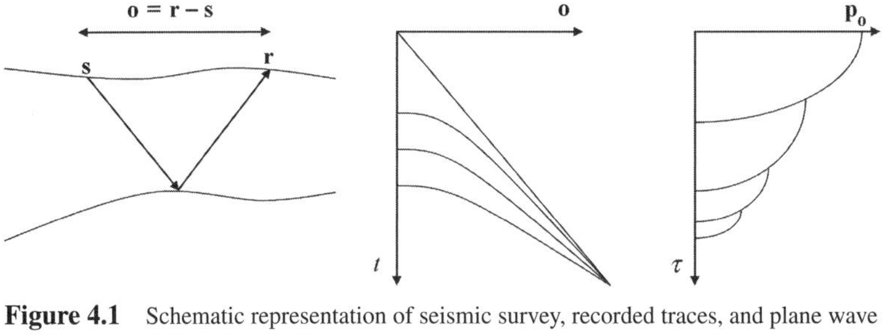

Figure 4.1 Schematic representation of seismic survey, recorded traces, and plane wave decomposition.

We can use the above transformation to decompose all recorded source and receiver data simultaneously:

$$P(\mathbf{p_s}, \mathbf{p_r}, \omega) = \iint P(\mathbf{s}, \mathbf{r}, \omega) \exp(+i\omega[\mathbf{p_r} \cdot \mathbf{r} + \mathbf{p_s} \cdot \mathbf{s}]) d\mathbf{s} d\mathbf{r}, \tag{4.1}$$

with the inverse slant stack given by

$$P(\mathbf{s}, \mathbf{r}, \omega) = \omega^4 \iint P(\mathbf{p_s}, \mathbf{p_r}, \omega) \exp(-i\omega[\mathbf{p_r} \cdot \mathbf{r} + \mathbf{p_s} \cdot \mathbf{s}]) d\mathbf{p_s} d\mathbf{p_r}. \tag{4.2}$$

To combine seismic data to form images of the subsurface, we start with the double downward continuation integral based on scattering theory [6, 8, 21]. The integral for wavefield continuation of sources and receivers to depth is

$$P(\mathbf{x}, \omega) = \int \partial_n G(\mathbf{x}, \mathbf{s}, \omega) d\mathbf{s} \int \partial_n G(\mathbf{x}, \mathbf{r}, \omega) P(\mathbf{s}, \mathbf{r}, \omega) d\mathbf{r}, \tag{4.3}$$

where $P(\mathbf{s}, \mathbf{r}, \omega)$ is the seismic wavefield measured at the surface, $\mathbf{s}$ is the source location, $\mathbf{r}$ is the receiver location, G is the Green's function, $\partial_n G$ is the surface normal derivative of the Green's function, $\mathbf{x}$ is the subsurface location, and $P(\mathbf{x}, \omega)$ is the predicted wavefield at depth. For heterogeneous media, the Green's function is approximated using asymptotic ray theory (ART)[4]:

$$G(\mathbf{x}, \mathbf{s}, \omega) = A(\mathbf{x}, \mathbf{s}) \exp(i\omega t(\mathbf{x}, \mathbf{s})),$$

where $A(\mathbf{x}, \mathbf{s})$ is an amplitude term and $t(\mathbf{x}, \mathbf{s})$ is the ray traveltime from the source position $\mathbf{s}$ to the image point $\mathbf{x}$.

Assuming that the amplitude is a slowly varying function of space [8], equation (4.3) becomes

$$P(\mathbf{x}, \omega) = -\omega^2 \iint W(\mathbf{x}, \mathbf{s}, \mathbf{r}) \exp(i\omega[t(\mathbf{x}, \mathbf{s}) + t(\mathbf{x}, \mathbf{r})]) P(\mathbf{s}, \mathbf{r}, \omega) d\mathbf{s} d\mathbf{r}, \tag{4.4}$$

where $t(\mathbf{x}, \mathbf{s})$ and $t(\mathbf{x}, \mathbf{r})$ are the traveltimes from the source and receiver locations, respectively, to the subsurface point $\mathbf{x}$, $\exp(i\omega[t(\mathbf{x}, \mathbf{s}) + t(\mathbf{x}, \mathbf{r})])$ corresponds to the time-delay operator and $W(\mathbf{x}, \mathbf{s}, \mathbf{r}) \approx \partial_n t(\mathbf{x}, \mathbf{s}) A(\mathbf{x}, \mathbf{s}) \partial_n t(\mathbf{x}, \mathbf{r}) A(\mathbf{x}, \mathbf{r})$.

Transforming simultaneously all shot and receiver gathers to plane waves according to equation (4.2) and defining the receiver and source vertical delay times [20], respectively, as

$$\tau(\mathbf{x}, \mathbf{s}, \mathbf{p_s}) = t(\mathbf{x}, \mathbf{s}) - \mathbf{p_s} \cdot \mathbf{s},$$

$$\tau(\mathbf{x}, \mathbf{r}, \mathbf{p_r}) = t(\mathbf{x}, \mathbf{r}) - \mathbf{p_r} \cdot \mathbf{r},$$

we get for the plane wave $(\mathbf{p_s}, \mathbf{p_r})$

$$P(\mathbf{x}, \mathbf{p_s}, \mathbf{p_r}, \omega) = -\omega^6 P(\mathbf{p_s}, \mathbf{p_r}, \omega) \iint W(\mathbf{x}, \mathbf{s}, \mathbf{r}) \exp(i\omega(\tau(\mathbf{x}, \mathbf{s}, \mathbf{p_s}) + \tau(\mathbf{x}, \mathbf{r}, \mathbf{p_r}))) d\mathbf{s} d\mathbf{r}. \tag{4.5}$$

Summing over all frequencies and all plane wave combinations forms the final image:

$$P(\mathbf{x}) = -\iiint \omega^6 P(\mathbf{p_s}, \mathbf{p_r}, \omega)\mathrm{d}\omega\mathrm{d}\mathbf{p_s}\mathrm{d}\mathbf{p_r}$$
$$\iint W(\mathbf{x}, \mathbf{s}, \mathbf{r}) \exp(i\omega(\tau(\mathbf{x}, \mathbf{s}, \mathbf{p_s}) + \tau(\mathbf{x}, \mathbf{r}, \mathbf{p_r}))\mathrm{d}\mathbf{s}\mathrm{d}\mathbf{r}. \quad (4.6)$$

Denoting by $\boldsymbol{\xi}$ the projection of $\mathbf{x}$ onto the measurement surface, we note that [20]

$$\tau(\mathbf{x}, \mathbf{s}, \mathbf{p_s}) = \tau(\mathbf{x}, \mathbf{p_s}) - \mathbf{p_s} \cdot \boldsymbol{\xi},$$
$$\tau(\mathbf{x}, \mathbf{r}, \mathbf{p_r}) = \tau(\mathbf{x}, \mathbf{p_r}) - \mathbf{p_r} \cdot \boldsymbol{\xi}, \quad (4.7)$$

where τ $(\mathbf{x}, \mathbf{p_s})$ and $\tau(\mathbf{x}, \mathbf{p_r})$ are the source and receiver vertical delay times computed from the origin to the isochron of $\mathbf{x}$. This result is critical to understanding the computational advantage of the method. Instead of requiring traveltimes for each source and receiver position, as in the conventional approach to Kirchhoff imaging, we now only require vertical delay times for the plane wave components actually in use. These are then registered to the reference point $\boldsymbol{\xi}$ by a simple time delay. Substituting (4.7) into (4.6) and after some simplification (which includes ignoring the filter ω^6) we obtain

$$P(\mathbf{x}) = L(\mathbf{x}) \iiint P(\mathbf{p_s}, \mathbf{p_r}, \omega)$$
$$\exp(i\omega(\tau(\mathbf{x}, \mathbf{p_s}) + \tau(\mathbf{x}, \mathbf{p_r}) - (\mathbf{p_s} + \mathbf{p_r}) \cdot \boldsymbol{\xi}))\mathrm{d}\omega\mathrm{d}\mathbf{p_s}\mathrm{d}\mathbf{p_r}, \quad (4.8)$$

where $L(\mathbf{x}) = -\iint W(\mathbf{x}, \mathbf{s}, \mathbf{r})\mathrm{d}\mathbf{s}\mathrm{d}\mathbf{r}$.

Noting that integral over frequencies represents a δ function, we finally arrive at the double plane wave imaging formula:

$$P(\mathbf{x}) = L(\mathbf{x}) \iint P(\mathbf{p_s}, \mathbf{p_r}, \tau(\mathbf{x}, \mathbf{p_s}) + \tau(\mathbf{x}, \mathbf{p_r}) - (\mathbf{p_s} + \mathbf{p_r}) \cdot \boldsymbol{\xi})\mathrm{d}\mathbf{p_s}\mathrm{d}\mathbf{p_r}, \quad (4.9)$$

Equation (4.9) can be rewritten in the more conventional source–offset coordinates. If we change variables $\mathbf{o} = \mathbf{r} - \mathbf{s}$, $\mathbf{s}' = \mathbf{s}$, then according to the chain rule $\mathbf{p_r} = \mathbf{p_o}$, $\mathbf{p_s} = \mathbf{p}'_\mathbf{s} - \mathbf{p_o}$. Assuming field invariance under the change of variables and dropping the primes, equation (4.9) becomes [20]

$$P(\mathbf{x}) = L(\mathbf{x}) \iint P(\mathbf{p_s}, \mathbf{p_o}, \tau(\mathbf{x}, \mathbf{p_s} - \mathbf{p_o}) + \tau(\mathbf{x}, \mathbf{p_o}) - \mathbf{p_s} \cdot \boldsymbol{\xi})\mathrm{d}\mathbf{p_s}\mathrm{d}\mathbf{p_o}, \quad (4.10)$$

and the equation used to transform the data is similar to Eq. (4.1):

$$P(\mathbf{p_s}, \mathbf{p_o}, \omega) = \iint P(\mathbf{s}, \mathbf{o}, \omega) \exp(+i\omega[\mathbf{p_o} \cdot \mathbf{o} + \mathbf{p_s} \cdot \mathbf{s}])\mathrm{d}\mathbf{s}\mathrm{d}\mathbf{r}. \quad (4.11)$$

Note that the plane wave migration method described above can be used to regularize the recorded data. As the data are read, the transform is computed in a distributed fashion by various compute nodes resulting in a regularly sampled plane wave data volume for imaging purposes. Depending on the data and the application (final imaging or velocity analysis), sparse subsets of the plane wave data may be used to improve performance or adapt the computational burden to the level of image resolution desired. Of particular importance is the fact that the same plane wave vertical delay times can be reused for source or receiver or offset plane waves, and, thus, we need to calculate these only once for a given subsurface velocity model. The independence of the plane wave components from each other and the ability to use subsets based on desired image resolution make this method ideal for parallel and adaptive computing.

Finally, since the plane wave domain is the equivalent of a phase velocity representation, anisotropy can be taken into account exactly, using, for example, the delay time computation methods described in [7, 12, 16].

4.3 PARALLEL IMPLEMENTATION

There are two parts to the algorithm that need to be considered. The first is the transformation of the original data into the plane wave domain. The second is the imaging algorithm. We can assume for all practical purposes that the input data are typically organized as they are recorded in the field. These shot "gathers" are a collection of all the time samples for each receiver (called a seismic trace). Typically, hundreds to thousands of receivers will record several thousand time samples for each source of seismic energy, resulting in as many traces per source. For each shot gather, we will know the position of the source and each receiver as we read the data from the field media. Essentially, we assume no order in these positions, and, indeed, prior trace editing based on difficulties in recording at some receiver positions make missing or edited traces a likely occurrence.

The integral we need to compute is equation (4.11). Each compute node of the system can be assigned a subset of plane waves to be computed based on the range of $\mathbf{p_s}$ and $\mathbf{p_o}$ plane wave components requested by the user and the number of compute nodes available. As a data trace is read, it may be subjected to conditioning algorithms, and then the Fourier transformed from time to frequency. The subset of frequencies of interest are broadcast to all the compute nodes along with the position information of this data trace, that is, its (x, y) source and receiver locations in the survey. Each compute node computes equation (4.11) for its plane wave components, using the position information and its knowledge of the frequency values it has received. Once all the data are included in the integrals, the frequency domain data are inverse Fourier transformed back to time.

As part of the integration process, weights may be applied to the input data, which act as spatial tapers to improve the transformation. Before the final inverse frequency to time Fourier transform, the data need to be reregistered to the correct frequency grid, and in some applications, zero samples will be appended to generate "sinc" interpolated data values in the time domain.

Figure 4.2 shows the details of the plane wave transform algorithm. The compute nodes are assigned their respective plane waves or $\mathbf{p}$ values and the data are read trace-by-trace, preprocessed, Fourier transformed, and then the subset of frequencies in use are broadcast to the compute nodes. Each compute node computes the integral

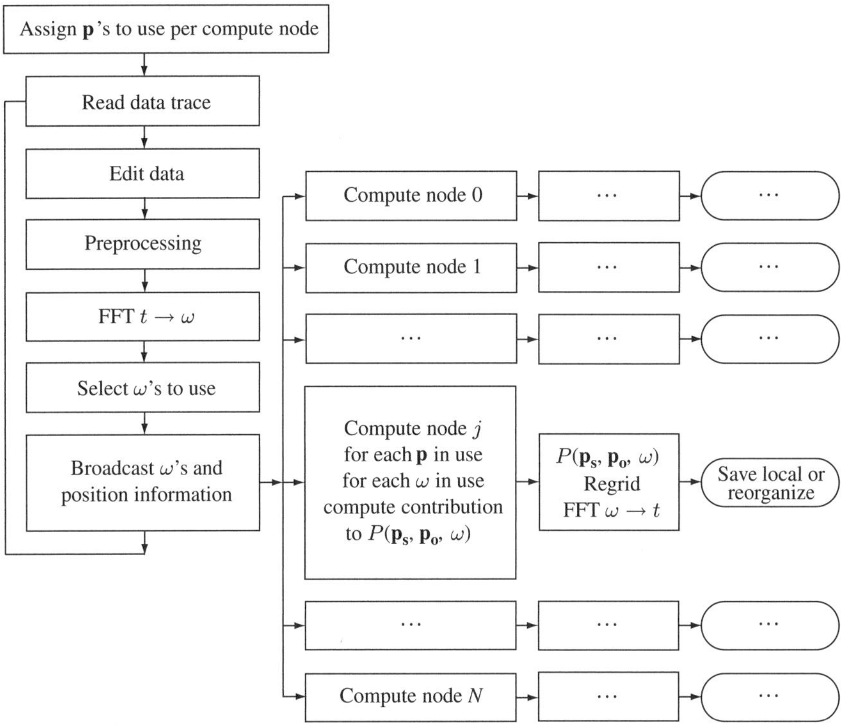

Figure 4.2 A flow diagram for the parallel realization of the $\tau - \mathbf{p_s} - \mathbf{p_o}$ transform on N compute nodes. Each compute node is assigned a set of **p** values, data are read, preprocessed, Fourier transformed from time to frequency, and the selected range of frequencies is broadcast to all compute nodes for independent computation of their contribution to $P(\mathbf{p_s}, \mathbf{p_o}, \omega)$. Results are postprocessed and stored locally.

according to equation (4.11) until all the data are included. The resulting sums for each plane wave are then moved to the correct frequency grid and inverse Fourier transformed back to time and then stored on local disk for the next processing stage. Anticipating the imaging algorithm requirements we will discuss below, some care must be taken in the distribution plan for the plane waves in the compute nodes. The above calculation is performed as the data are read. Typical numbers for a 2D survey would be 1000 shot gathers, each with 500 receivers that record 4000 time samples, for example, 8 GB of data. The plane wave domain for this survey would likely span -0.66 to $+0.66$ s/km for both the offset and source plane waves with sampling intervals of 0.0025 s/km for a total of 528×528, or 278,784 plane wave traces (instead of the original 500,000 data traces) or 4.46 GB, that is, 56% of the original data volume. For a similar sized but 3D survey, the number of shots would increase by the number of acquisition lines, for example, 250, and the number of cross-line receivers per shot, for example, 16. For marine seismic data, the cross-line receiver aperture is small compared to the in-line aperture, so we will need only eight cross-line receiver plane wave components. Similarly, for the shot positions, we will only require 125 cross-line plane wave components. The data volume increases by a factor of 250 × 16 or 4000, resulting in 32 TB to be read. But, the plane wave volume increases by only a factor of 125 × 8 or 1000. The final data volume to be imaged is 4.4 TB, which is a factor of 8 reduction. Additional savings could accrue based on inspections of the data. For example, in marine surveying, only positive offsets are recorded and the number of in-line receiver plane wave components can likely be reduced by another factor of 2.

For the 2D problem, we need to distribute 278,784 plane wave components of 16 KB each into the parallel system. Assuming 2 GB of memory per compute node and 100 compute nodes requires only 44.6 MB for the data per compute node. In the 3D case, we have a factor of 1000 more plane wave components that can be distributed among most likely a factor of 10 more compute nodes for a total of 1000. But now each compute node requires 4.46 GB of data memory per compute node. For the plane wave transformation algorithm, this increase in data memory does not necessarily present an obstacle, as the number of complex frequency samples typically in use is half or less the number of time samples and no other large memory requirements are necessary. For the imaging algorithm, other memory requirements include the image space and the vertical delay time tables that are of the same size as the image space. So, while the 2D imaging problem presents no obstacles to the above naive approach, for the 3D problem, only the plane wave transform might be able to be implemented, as described. However, the 3D imaging might require a more complex solution and one that can be extended as data volumes increase.

The algorithm we implemented organizes the plane wave components as all the $\mathbf{p_o}$ components per $\mathbf{p_s}$, or all the $\mathbf{p_s}$ components per $\mathbf{p_o}$. This decision is made based on the number of $\mathbf{p_s}$ or $\mathbf{p_o}$ components and the memory available per compute node. For example, in the case under consideration, the $\mathbf{p_o}$ cross-line aperture is small and results in a correspondingly small number, 16, of plane wave components. The total $\mathbf{p_o}$ components in use are then 528 × 16 or 8448 traces, while the number of 2D $\mathbf{p_s}$ components is 528 × 250 or 132,000. We will distribute the work based on the number of $\mathbf{p_s}$ components, each of which now requires only 135.2 MB of memory for the $\mathbf{p_o}$ data. The 3D image space, two traveltime tables, and velocity grid can be made to fit in the remaining memory by encoding the times and velocities using 1 or 2 byte arrays.

We target a system of about 1000 identical compute nodes (typically available) and organize the algorithm to work using multiple passes based on the number of $\mathbf{p_s}$ data volumes distributed into the system. For example, to image 132,000 $\mathbf{p_s}$ components using 1000 compute nodes would take 132 iterations of the algorithm (load balance is determined by keeping the $\mathbf{p_s}$ data volume as evenly distributed as possible). During each iteration, all the $\mathbf{p_o}$ components would be imaged. A global sum is then used to construct the partial images at each iteration with the last global sum producing the final image. The elapsed time is then the time per iteration (which includes the global sum) times the number of iterations.

Since the plane waves are in effect interchangeable, the above algorithm can be generalized further based on the memory per compute node, the number of compute nodes, the number of plane wave components, and the size of the image space. Once the total memory requirements are known for a given problem, the plane waves can be accordingly distributed. The above approach may be suboptimum in terms of overall memory efficiency, but optimum in that the delay times required for imaging have two components, one for the source and one for the offset wave. By organizing the plane waves so that there is one $\mathbf{p_s}$ per compute node each iteration, the $\mathbf{p_s}$ times are computed only once at the start of each iteration and reused for all the $\mathbf{p_o}$ times. Since the $\mathbf{p_o}$ times are the same for each iteration, they can either be stored after the first iteration and retrieved in subsequent iterations or recomputed, as needed, depending which is faster on a particular system. This is not just system dependent, but algorithm dependent, as more accurate delay time calculations can require more computational effort and storage and retrieval by each compute node can be more efficient when overlapped with the computations.

Figure 4.3 shows how the decision is made for data distribution based on the memory available, number of compute nodes, image space size, and others. This decision could be made before the plane wave transformation so that the plane wave components end up in the compute nodes that will do the imaging. Often the data volumes are such that this decision is postponed until imaging and then the

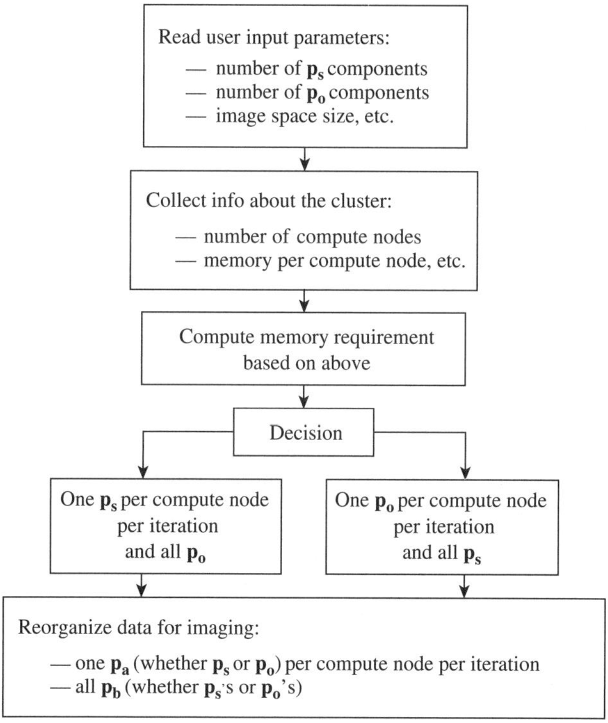

Figure 4.3 A flow diagram for job distribution decision: based on the user-requested plane wave components, image space size, and so on, available cluster architecture, and resulting memory requirements, the plane wave components to be imaged are distributed either as one $\mathbf{p_s}$ per compute node per iteration and all $\mathbf{p_o}$, or as one $\mathbf{p_o}$ per compute node per iteration and all $\mathbf{p_s}$.

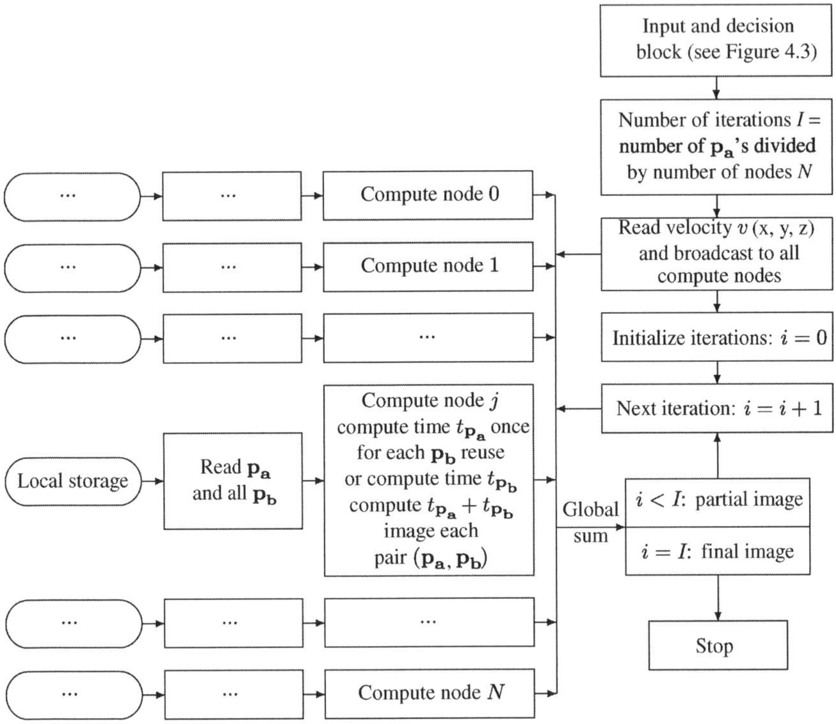

Figure 4.4 A flowchart for the imaging algorithm: all compute nodes are broadcast the velocity model and then locally stored plane wave data are read by each compute node, each compute node computes vertical delay traveltimes to be used in imaging. Once all compute nodes have computed their plane wave components' contributions to the image, the global sum is performed to combine individual contributions into final image.

transformed data, which are locally stored, must be reorganized between the compute nodes for imaging purposes. This will be the case mainly for very large problems where local storage will be used because an out-of-memory solution is required.

In Figure 4.4, we show the three-dimensional velocity being broadcast to all the compute nodes for their use at the start of the imaging algorithm. Figure 4.4 also shows the local plane wave data initially being read by each compute node and then each compute node independently computing the plane wave times it needs for imaging and then constructing its contribution to the image. At the end of the imaging, a global sum (whose size is the same as the image space being constructed) is performed over all the plane wave components to produce the final image. This is the primary communication challenge in this algorithm as it occurs once per plane wave being imaged.

One of the outstanding challenges in seismic imaging is to derive this velocity information from the observed data. These velocities are used to derive the imaging times $\tau - \mathbf{p}$ in equations (4.6), (4.9), and (4.10). Since the subsurface is heterogeneous and the data are band limited, typical iterative linear inverse methods fail [10]. The imaging method described here can be used for a nonlinear approach to the velocity analysis problem. But first we will describe how this is accomplished after showing an example of seismic imaging using this method.

4.4 IMAGING EXAMPLE

We used a 2D staggered grid elastic finite difference simulation [11] of the standard SEG/EAGE 3D salt model [2] to construct seismograms for a 2D slice from this model. The synthetic data were generated for 675 sources every 0.02 km along the top of the model (z = 0.0 km). We simulated an offshore survey where the receiving array has detectors every 0.02 km and is towed behind the shooting ship. Two hundred and forty channels were collected but the first gather with a full 240 channels recorded was when the source was at the grid position 240 ($X = 4.78$ km). We only recorded pressure since the source and receivers were located in the water layer of the model. Absorbing boundaries were added before and after the actual model to reduce artificial reflections from the edges and bottom of the model and to eliminate reverberations from the sea surface that is a perfect reflector. The recorded data were transformed into both source and offset plane waves using equation (4.11) for the range of −0.6 to +0.6 s/km every 0.01 s/km for both the source and offset plane waves. This process completely transformed the recorded data into its plane wave components.

The $\mathbf{p_s} - \mathbf{p_o}$ volume was migrated using equation (4.10) and an eikonal solver, see [14], to calculate the vertical delay times. The offset plane wave data were migrated independently and in parallel. The resulting partial images were then summed to create the subsurface image. Figure 4.5 shows the result of a parallel run on a PC cluster.

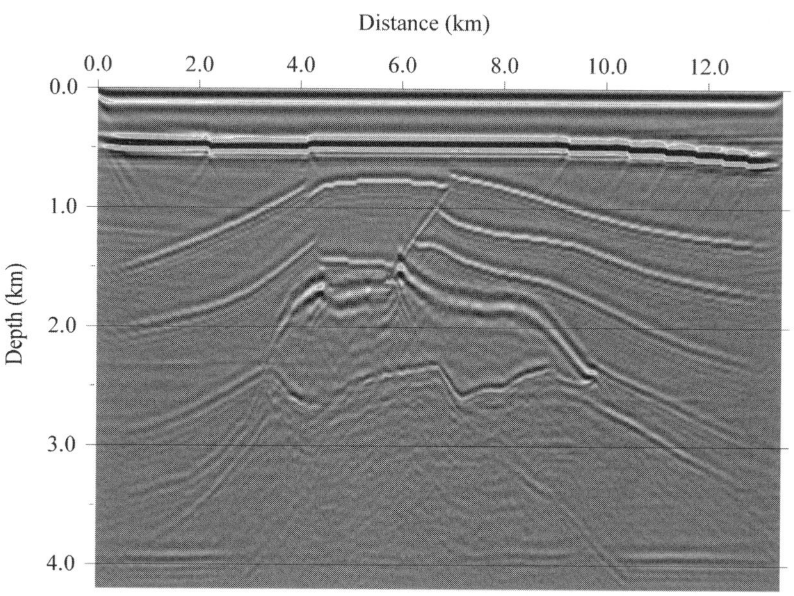

Figure 4.5 Final image for the synthetic data for the SEG/EAGE salt model. The challenge is to image beneath the high-velocity irregular-shaped salt body in the center of the model. This image was obtained by using our parallel double plane wave transform migration algorithm using 30 compute nodes.

4.5 VELOCITY ANALYSIS

The subsurface velocities used for imaging must be derived from the recorded data. Because of the considerable redundancy designed into seismic surveys, each subsurface point is illuminated from many angles (Figure 4.6). Images from varying angles of illumination are examined (these are called common image gathers CIGs)) to estimate velocities. The principal idea behind CIG velocity analysis is that the gathers become flat for true velocities. For incorrect velocities, these CIGs are nonflat. An optimization method can be used to find an optimal velocity model that flattens the CIGs. Conventional velocity analysis involves a repeated trial and error analysis that is based on forming coherent images from the data, which are transformed to depth. Either skilled interpreters assisted by computer-generated partial images, or semiautomated schemes based on interpreted arrival times in the data and tomographic inverse methods are used.

Our plane wave method makes it possible to automate this analysis by employing staging over velocity accuracy and structural complexity. This staging of the velocity analysis (which during implementation becomes a simple staging over data plane waves) makes it possible to employ a nonlinear optimization method. Very fast simulated annealing (VFSA), as described in [1, 9, 15, 22], is used to judge whether coherent images are being formed for trial velocity functions and to propose updates. Figure 4.7 shows in general how VFSA works and compares it to the classical Metropolis algorithm. The main difference between the two approaches is that VFSA draws new trials from a biased distribution based on a Cauchy distribution centered around the current model, which becomes narrower as the temperature decreases; whereas the classical Metropolis algorithm always uses a flat distribution. This speeds up convergence to a good solution at the risk of not adequately sampling the velocity model space.

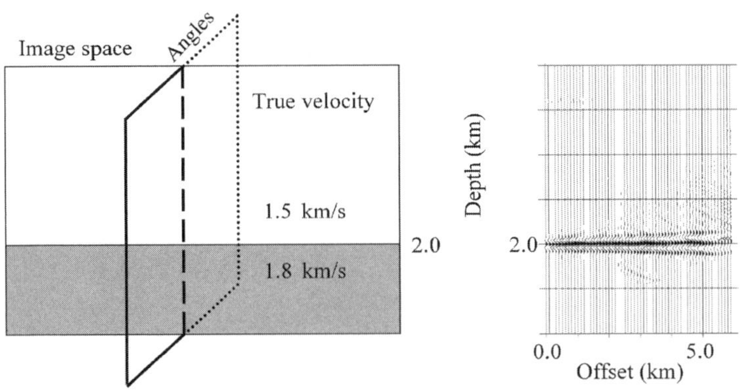

Figure 4.6 Reflections from a common subsurface point illuminated by waves occurring at different angles are examined for velocity analysis. Such panels are called common image gathers (left panel). For correct velocities, CIGs are flat (right panel).

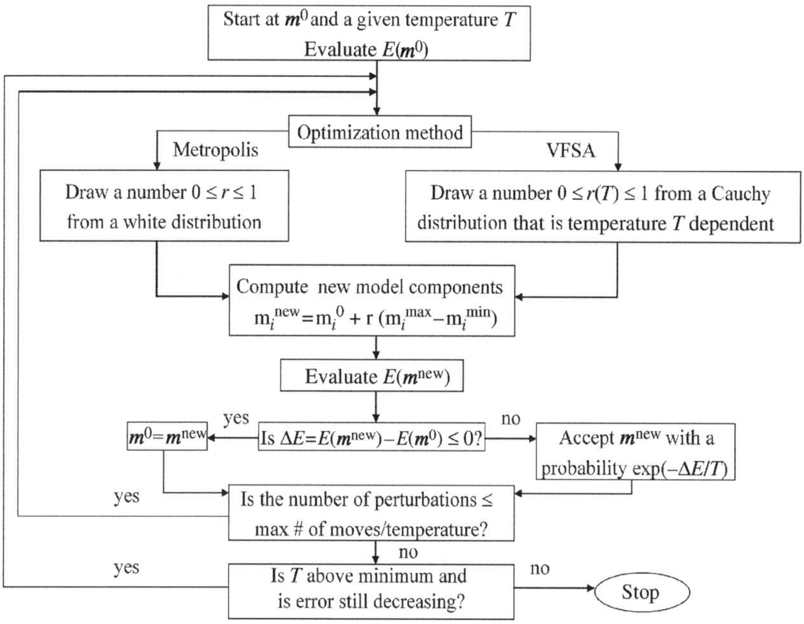

Figure 4.7 Simulated annealing flowchart with the Metropolis algorithm shown on the left and VFSA algorithm shown on the right.

The key to any velocity analysis method is the description of the subsurface. Here we use vertical "wells" defined by, for example, splines positioned throughout the image space. The values of the spline nodes are the parameters to be optimized by the VFSA algorithm. The splines are used to grid the velocity model to the scale necessary for imaging purposes.

Even VFSA requires many trials (on the order of hundreds), and this provided one of the motivations to develop the fast imaging method presented here. In addition, the decomposition of the original data into two types of plane wave components, each of which represents different aspects of the data, makes it possible to tune the imaging for purposes of velocity analysis, thereby, increasing the computational burden only as knowledge of the subsurface velocity and structure improves.

For example, the $\tau - \mathbf{p_o}$ data (Figure 4.8) correspond to a fixed received angle at the surface for each $\mathbf{p_o}$. By downward continuing these data and with knowledge of the velocity being employed, these data correspond to different scattering angles in the subsurface (Figure 4.9). The velocity is correct when the recorded events on all the different $\mathbf{p_o}$ data traces, when imaged to depth, register at the same depth. If the images for specific events for the different $\mathbf{p_o}$ plane waves are deeper or shallower, the velocity is wrong and must be updated.

For the image point $\mathbf{x} = (x, y, z)$ with surface location $(x, y, 0)$ and depth z, the common image gathers can be described by separating the integration with respect to

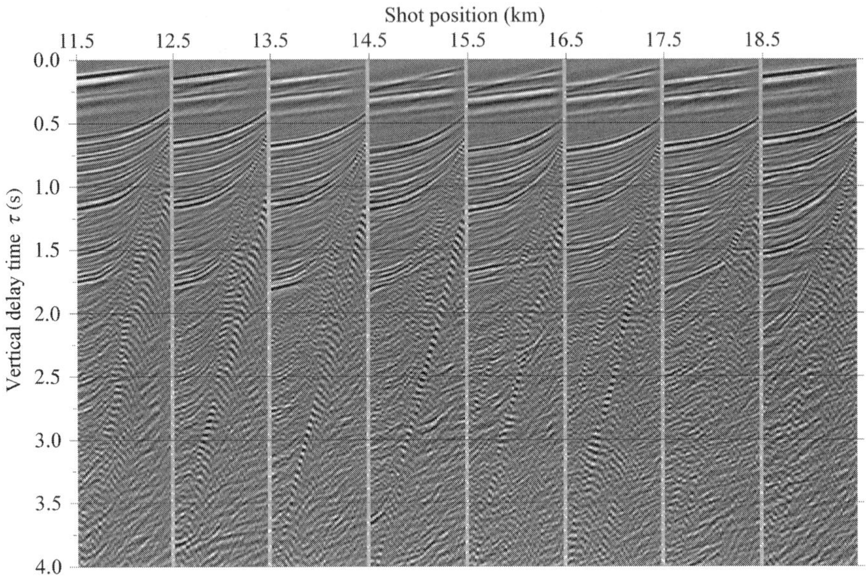

Figure 4.8 Seismic data transformed to the $\tau - \mathbf{p_o}$ domain but before the transform to $\mathbf{p_s}$. The $\mathbf{p_o}$ range in each panel shown is from 0.0 to +0.5 km every 0.01 km. The upward elliptic trajectories correspond to reflection events from subsurface structures.

$\mathbf{p_s}$ from equation (4.10), namely,

$$P(x, y, z, \mathbf{p_o}) = L(\mathbf{x}) \int P(\mathbf{p_s}, \mathbf{p_o}, \tau(\mathbf{x}, \mathbf{p_s} - \mathbf{p_o}) + \tau(\mathbf{x}, \mathbf{P_o}) - \mathbf{p_s} \cdot \boldsymbol{\xi}) d\mathbf{p_s}. \quad (4.12)$$

For the image points $\mathbf{x}_m = (x_0, y_0, z_m), m = 1, \ldots, N_z$, with fixed surface location $(x_0, y_0, 0)$, multiple depth levels $\{z_m\}, m = 1, \ldots, N_z$ and many $\mathbf{p_o}$ and $\mathbf{p_s}$ values, that is, $\{\mathbf{p_o}_j\}, j = 1, \ldots, N_{\mathbf{p_o}}$ and $\{\mathbf{p_s}_k\}, k = 1, \ldots, N_{\mathbf{Ps}}$, the discrete data set

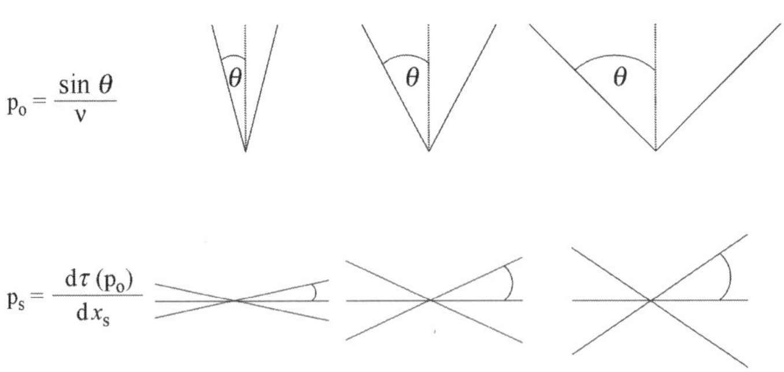

Figure 4.9 Upper row shows how $\mathbf{p_o}$ plane waves correspond to incidence angles through knowledge of the local velocity. Lower row $\mathbf{p_s}$ plane waves correspond to vertical delay time dips, which correspond to depth dips again through knowledge of the local velocity.

for CIGs can be described as

$$P(x_0, y_0, z_m, \mathbf{p_o}_j) = \frac{L(\mathbf{x}_m)}{N_{\mathbf{p_s}}} \sum_{k=1}^{N_{\mathbf{p_s}}} P(\mathbf{p_s}_k, \mathbf{p_o}_j, \tau(\mathbf{x}_m, \mathbf{p_s}_k - \mathbf{p_o}_j) + \tau(\mathbf{x}_m, \mathbf{p_o}_j) - \mathbf{p_s}_k \cdot \boldsymbol{\xi}). \quad (4.13)$$

where $\boldsymbol{\xi} = (x_0, y_0, 0)$. The corresponding error can be defined as

$$\text{err}(x_0, y_0) = \frac{1}{N_z} \sum_{m=1}^{N_z} \frac{L(\mathbf{x}_m)}{N_{\mathbf{p_o}}} \sum_{j=1}^{N_{\mathbf{p_o}}} (P(x_0, y_0, z_m, \mathbf{p_o}_j) - \tilde{P}(x_0, y_0, z_m))^2, \quad (4.14)$$

where

$$\tilde{P}(x_0, y_0, z_m) = \frac{1}{N_{\mathbf{p_o}}} \sum_{j=1}^{N_{\mathbf{p_o}}} P(x_0, y_0, z_m, \mathbf{p_o}_j) \quad (4.15)$$

is the average, or, as we call it, the "stacked" trace at position $(x_0, y_0, 0)$.

Figure 4.10 shows the data for many $\mathbf{p_o}$'s versus depth at one surface location. On the leftmost part of the figure, the data were imaged with a velocity that is too slow; on the right, the velocity is too fast, but in the center the velocity is nearly correct and in this case nearly all the depth-imaged events become horizontally aligned. The $\mathbf{p_o}$ aperture employed for this analysis can be selectively increased as knowledge of the velocity improves. For example, small values of $\mathbf{p_o}$, for example, <0.1 s/km correspond to small angles of incidence with respect to the vertical (Figure 4.9) and are a good measure of image event strength but not velocity as the differential times of arrival within such a small aperture are insufficient to discriminate between different velocity models. Thus, the VFSA algorithm can employ a small $\mathbf{p_o}$ aperture and then increase it to develop a more accurate velocity model. As more $\mathbf{p_o}$ plane waves are used, the compute nodes must work longer to form the trial image. Figure 4.10 can be used to illustrate the concept of staging over incidence angle by using more $\mathbf{p_o}$ traces in the velocity analysis. As we continue to add more traces, we are in effect increasing the local angles of incidence and the sensitivity of the data to the velocity increases. If you look at the data for the fast and slow velocity trials (left and right panels) for just the first one-third or so of the $\mathbf{p_o}$ traces, you see very little difference in the horizontal alignment of the arrivals. Most of the changes that indicate whether the velocity is correct or not come from the higher $\mathbf{p_o}$ traces.

In a similar way, the $\mathbf{p_s}$ aperture is related to the structural complexity of the subsurface in that it can be used to select different types of arrival for use in the analysis. For example, small values of $\mathbf{p_s}$, for example, <0.1 s/km correspond primarily to reflection events having little horizontal dip ($\mathbf{p_s}$ is a measure of the time dip in a constant $\mathbf{p_o}$ section and as such is related to the true dip in depth through the

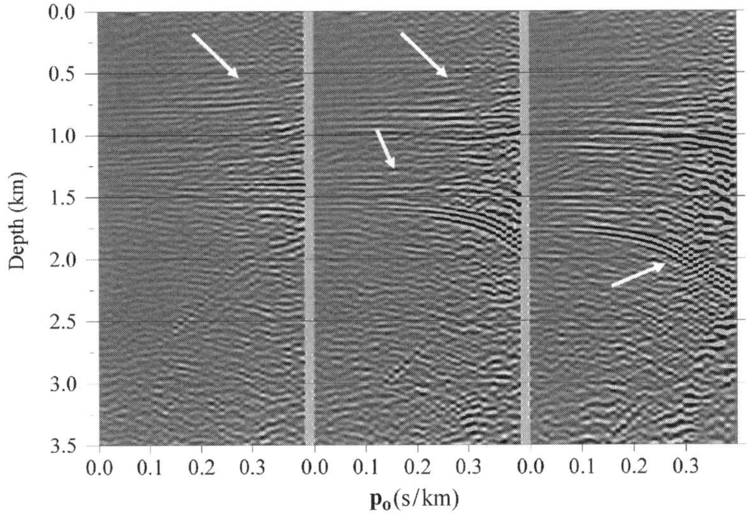

Figure 4.10 Common image gathers for a slow velocity (left) and fast velocity (right); the center panel is the best trial velocity since most events are horizontally aligned, see arrows. Arrow on the left panel shows an event that is overmigrated and the arrow on the right panel shows an event that is undermigrated.

velocity function). As the $\mathbf{p_s}$ aperture increases, more lateral variability is included (Figure 4.10). By staging over $\mathbf{p_s}$ aperture, the velocity analysis starts with the simpler structural components and then adds complexity (and more computation time) as more $\mathbf{p_s}$ plane waves are used in forming the trial images (Figure 4.11c and d).

Being able to control the angles of incidence and the structural complexity by simply limiting the velocity analysis to select groups of plane waves, depending upon the intent of the optimization, makes an adaptable algorithm that stages over resolution and complexity possible. Nonlinear methods, such as VFSA, which require many trial solutions before converging on the "best" velocity model, become viable to use as the low-resolution iterations require only a few tens of plane waves and the computational cost per iteration is quite small. As higher resolution is desired, the velocity model can be constrained using the prior lower resolution results, and only the details need to be found. This limits the number of iterations that require a large number of plane wave contributions.

Figure 4.11 shows two snapshots of the evolution of an image as more $\mathbf{p_s}$ plane waves are included in the velocity analysis. On the left are image data for multiple positions along the line (every 0.5 km), and at each position multiple viewing angles are represented by the $\mathbf{p_o}$ traces displayed. For these common image gathers only when the data at depth are completely horizontal for all the $\mathbf{p_o}$ traces is the velocity correct. The sum over all the $\mathbf{p_o}$ traces is shown on the right and represents the final image for this trial velocity model. In Figure 4.11 (a and b) the $\mathbf{p_s}$ aperture was only from -0.2 to $+0.2$ s/km or only 21 plane wave components. This is the reason for the low spatial frequency appearance in the image on the right. We then continued the VFSA velocity analysis, but included more $\mathbf{p_s}$ aperture, -0.6 to $+0.6$ s/km

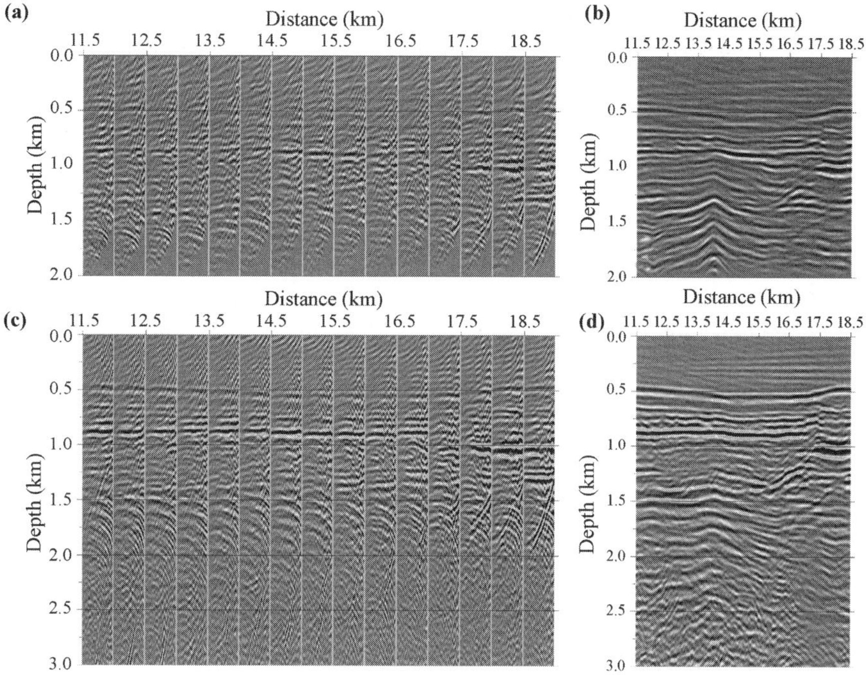

Figure 4.11 CIGs and trial image for a small $\mathbf{p_s}$ aperture -0.2 to $+0.2$ s/km (a and b) and for a $\mathbf{p_s}$ aperture, -0.6 to $+0.6$ s/km (c and d). For the larger $\mathbf{p_s}$ aperture, the spatial resolution is increased, but the imaging time is increased by a factor of 3.

(Figure 4.11c and d). We now see that not only are the events in the $\mathbf{p_o}$ gathers on the left better aligned but also the resulting image on the right has better spatial resolution. Also note that the general appearance of the two images on the right are very similar except for the horizontal spatial resolution. Closer inspection, however, shows that the depths of the reflectors being imaged are different, indicating that the velocity model is indeed different and better resolved in both dimensions.

This type of analysis can be carried out simultaneously at multiple analysis points throughout the study area and the velocity between evaluation points interpolated as part of the gridding and the image evaluation process. In the staging strategy presented here, we would distribute the computational load in the manner described above for the complete imaging. What may change is the distribution of plane wave components, depending on the size of the image volume being analyzed, the number of compute nodes, and the memory available for compute node. If more compute nodes are available, we can add them to the problems as the analysis progresses.

4.6 CONCLUSIONS

We have described an efficient method for seismic imaging that can be easily implemented in parallel. The key to the method is to decompose the observed seismic data into plane wave components that correlate to angles of incidence in the subsurface and the degree of lateral variability. By recognizing these relationships, we can develop an adaptive strategy for imaging, which gradually introduces larger angles of incidence and more structural complexity. Computational resources can be increased correspondingly, as more plane waves are included in the imaging.

One of the outstanding problems in seismic imaging is to determine the three-dimensional subsurface velocity function required for imaging. This function can be based on *a priori* information, but usually must be either defined or refined from the seismic survey data. We present an automated approach for velocity analysis based on the coherency of trial images, as observed from different viewing angles. As the optimization tool, we employ very fast simulated annealing to draw trial sparse velocity models based on, for example, spline coefficients, which are then gridded for the imaging algorithm. Repeated trials (on the order of hundreds) lead to coherent images with minimal need for manual intervention in the process. We stage the optimization process over model complexity and viewing angle to improve the rate of convergence. This adaptive strategy improves the velocity model by finding the slowly varying lateral components first, and then adding complexity and resolution, as more plane wave components are included.

The implementation strategy we describe is best on a distributed but relatively large memory parallel configuration, such as the clusters currently in use. Based on the size of the imaging task, the number of plane waves involved, and the availability of compute nodes and the memory of each, we present a strategy that tries to keep all data in memory and only requires an out-of-memory solution for very large problems. The careful distribution of plane wave data is key to this goal. Further, we organize the plane waves and the computational flow based on the plane wave distribution and the requirement that the only internode communication should be at the end of each cycle, where a global sum is required to actually form the image from the plane wave subimages.

The combination of effective plane wave distribution, minimal internode communications, and staging over plane waves makes a nonlinear optimization tool, like VFSA, a viable approach for both 2D and 3D seismic surveys.

ACKNOWLEDGMENT

The authors would like to thank Svein Vaage for many useful discussions on this approach to seismic imaging and velocity analysis.

REFERENCES

1. F.E. Akbar. Three-dimensional prestack planewave Kirchhoff depth migration in laterally varying media. PhD thesis, University of Texas at Austin, 1997.
2. R Aminzadeh, J. Brac, and T. Kunz. 3-D salt and overthrust models. *SEG/EAGE 3-D Modeling Series No.* 1, SEG, 1997.

3. H. Brysk and D.W. McCowan. A slantstack-procedure for point-source data. *Geophysics*, 51:1370–1386, 1986.
4. V. Cerveny. Seismic Ray Theory. Cambridge University Press, 2001.
5. J.F Claerbout. *Fundamentals of Geophysical Data Processing*. McGraw-Hill, 1976.
6. R.W. Clayton and R.H. Stolt. A Born-WKBJ inversion method for acoustic reflection data. *Geophysics,* 46:1559–1567, 1981.
7. E.L. Faria and P.L. Stoffa. Traveltime computation in transversely isotropic media. *Geophysics,* 59:272–281, 1994.
8. S.T. Hildebrand and R.J. Carrol. Radon depth migration. *Geophys. Prospect.,* 41:229–240, 1993.
9. L. Ingber. Very fast simulated re-annealing. *Math. Comput. Model,* 12:967–973, 1989.
10. M. Jervis, M.K. Sen, and P.L. Stoffa. Prestack velocity estimation by nonlinear optimization. *Geophysics,* 61:138–150, 1996.
11. A.R. Levander. Fourth-order finite-difference $P-SV$ seismograms. *Geophysics,* 53:1425–1436, 1988.
12. A. Mukherjee, M.K. Sen, and P.L. Stoffa. Traveltime computation and pre-stack time migration in transversely isotropic media. *J. Seism. Explor.,* 13:201–225, 2005.
13. W.A. Schneider. Integral formulation for migration in two and three dimensions. *Geophysics,* 43:49–76, 1978.
14. W.A. Schneider Jr., K.A. Ranzinger, A.H. Balch, and C. Kruse. A dynamic programming approach to first arrival traveltime computation in media with arbitrarily distributed velocities. *Geophysics,* 57:39–50, 1992.
15. M.K. Sen and P.L. Stoffa. *Global Optimization Methods in Geophysical Inversion.* Elsevier Science Publishers, 1995.
16. M.K. Sen and A. Mukherjee. $\tau-p$ analysis in transversely isotropic media. *Geophys. J. Int.,* 154:647–658, 2003.
17. V Sen, M.K. Sen, and P.L. Stoffa. PVM based 3-D Kirchhoff migration using dynamically computed traveltimes: an application in seismic data processing. *Parallel Comput.,* 25:231–248, 1999.
18. P.L. Stoffa, editor. Tau-p: a plane wave approach to the analysis of seismic data. Kluwer Academic Publishers, 1989.
19. P.L. Stoffa, P. Buhl, J.B. Diebold, and F. Wenzel. Direct mapping of seismic data to the domain of intercept time and ray parameter: a plane wave decomposition. *Geophysics,* 46:255–267, 1981.
20. P.L. Stoffa, M.K. Sen, R.K. Seifoullaev, R.C. Pestana, and J.T. Fokkema. Plane wave depth migration. *Geophysics,* 71:261–272, 2006.
21. R.H. Stolt and A.B. Weglein. Migration and inversion of seismic data. *Geophysics,* 50:2458–2472, 1985.
22. C.L. Varela, P.L. Stoffa, and M.K. Sen. Background velocity estimation using nonlinear optimization for reflection tomography and migration misfit. *Geophys. Prospect.,* 46:51–78, 1998.

Chapter 5

Data-Directed Importance Sampling for Climate Model Parameter Uncertainty Estimation

Charles S. Jackson, Mrinal K. Sen, Paul L. Stoffa, and Gabriel Huerta

5.1 INTRODUCTION

The 2001 Working Group I report from the Intergovernmental Panel on Climate Change documents a wide disparity among existing models of the climate system in their response to projected increases in atmospheric CO_2 concentrations. Predictions of global mean surface air temperature sensitivity to a doubling of atmospheric CO_2 concentration (in ~100 years) range from ~2 to 6°C [1, 2]. There are a number of possible reasons why these differences exist. Although each climate model has been tuned to reproduce observational means, each model contains slightly different choices of model parameter values as well as different parameterizations of underresolved physics (e.g., clouds, radiation, convection). Climate model uncertainties are primarily estimated from model intercomparison projects [3, 4, 5] (also see www.clivar.org/organization/aamp/publications/mips.htm for a list of 40 ongoing projects). It is often assumed that the range of behaviors exhibited by models that participate in the intercomparison projects is representative of a realistic range of probable outcomes [5]. Although there may be some recognition of which models perform better than others, the qualitative approach to evaluating model performance

Advanced Computational Infrastructures For Parallel and Distributed Adaptive Applications. Edited by Manish Parashar and Xiaolin Li

does not lend itself to assigning quantitative likelihoods to model predictions. The 2001 IPCC report, in its assessment of current research needs, calls for "...a much more comprehensive and systematic system of model analysis and diagnosis, and a Monte Carlo approach to model uncertainties associated with parameterizations..." (Section 8.10 [6]). The computational expense of typical atmosphere–ocean general circulation models (AOGCMs) is a major barrier to reaching this goal. Two approaches have been taken to address uncertainties arising from climate model parameters. One is based on a reduced complexity climate model [7, 8, 9,] and the other one distributes the computational burden among thousands of underutilized personal computers (see www.climateprediction.net [10, 11]). Data-directed importance sampling for climate model parameter uncertainty estimation involves an improved framework for taking advantage of distributed computing resources toward the goal of identifying multiple, nonlinearly related parameter values of a single climate model, which reflect observational constraints on climate model uncertainty. This goal is not trivial insofar as a single climate model experiment typically uses a 30-year simulation or 1500 cpu h to characterize a climate state, and one may need to complete millions of experiments to randomly sample all the potentially relevant combinations of 10 or more parameter values.

Predictive uncertainty up to this point has been mainly associated with uncertainty in CO_2 emissions and/or natural variability, factors that may be treated in a fairly straightforward manner. A far greater challenge is to represent the uncertainty that arises from arbitrary differences in climate model parameter values when the parameters themselves are nonlinearly related [12]. This fact presents unique challenges to those working to improve climate model predictions. One example of this challenge became apparent within a presentation at the 2001 NCAR Community Climate System Model (CCSM) Workshop in Breckenridge, Colorado. In an effort to improve simulations of arctic climate, changes were made within the infrared radiation scheme to make it more physical. This had the effect of improving the simulation of arctic climate but at the expense of drying out the tropics. This was remedied in part by increasing the amount of water that is allowed to evaporate from hydrometeors (rain drops) within unsaturated downdrafts of convective clouds. In another particularly dramatic example, Williams et al. [13] document the effect of specific changes made in the process of creating the next version of HadCM2 (Hadley Center Climate Model 2, United Kingdom). The authors noticed that the response of precipitation over the tropical Pacific to a doubling of atmospheric CO_2 concentration within HadCM3 was entirely different from the distribution found within HadCM2. The cause of these differences was found to originate from the combined influence of small changes within two parameters affecting mixing within the boundary layer and the critical humidity for cloud formation. Many of these nonlinear behaviors within models go unpublished, as the root causes are often hard to identify and there often is not a strong link to any particular science question. However, even these few examples underscore the need for a systematic approach for evaluating climate model performance and a way to navigate through the seemingly endless cycle of "educated guessing" that now takes place each time a new version of a climate model is released.

There are two useful objectives of an uncertainty analysis that considers how nonideal parameter value choices affect model predictions of climate. The first is to identify sets of model parameter values that define members of an ensemble that is assured to be representative of the combined uncertainty in the observations and model physics. The second is the ability to identify an optimal set of parameter values that maximizes climate model performance. As yet, there has been little progress on meeting these objectives outside of what can be gleaned from individual sensitivity experiments and model intercomparison projects. The principal reason for this lack of progress is that most traditional methods for meeting the first objective (e.g., Monte Carlo or Metropolis/Gibbs' "importance sampling") require 10^4–10^6 model evaluations (experiments) for problems involving fewer than 10 parameters.

Over the past decade, there has been significant progress within the mathematical geophysics community for solving nonlinear problems in geophysical inversion using statistical methods to account for the possibility of multiple solutions (interpretations) of geophysical data (for a review, see Ref. [14]). Like climate models, geophysical models are complex, computationally expensive, and involve many potential degrees of freedom. Within the geophysics community, particular emphasis has been on efficiency, although with some measured compromises. Similarly, dramatic advances have taken place within the statistics community over the past decade on a class of methods of statistical inference known as Markov Chain Monte Carlo (MCMC). In particular, greater awareness now exists for how different challenges in robust statistical inference can be addressed with Bayesian inference and sampling rules that obey the properties of a Markov chain. In what follows, we document progress being made on both these fronts to advance the feasibility of quantifying climate model uncertainties that stem from multiple, nonlinearly related parameters.

Other, potentially useful approaches exist to estimating parameters and uncertainties for complex systems. Examples include Latin-hypercube sampling and kriging interpolation techniques to reduce the number of experiments that may be needed to estimate the multidimensional dependencies [15, 16, 17, 18, 19]. Within the climate community, there has been some interest to apply the Ensemble Kalman Filter that uses time trajectories of the climate system in much the same way traditional data assimilation works in numerical weather prediction [20, 21, 22]. This may provide another computationally feasible approach to the tuning problem, but this approach still needs to prove its viability for the longer term climate problem. One concern is that many of the effects and feedbacks of model parameter changes take time to express themselves. The parameter choices constrained by short-term weather would not be the same or ideally suited for a model meant for predicting climate change [23]. The point that will be developed below is that estimates of the posterior distribution and optimization of model skill can be performed through direct sampling, in parallel, with relatively few iterations and without surface approximations.

5.2 COMPUTING CLIMATE MODEL PARAMETER UNCERTAINTIES IN PARALLEL

The computation of parametric uncertainties in a climate model will take advantage of two levels of parallelism: the parallelism of the climate model code and the parallelism permitted by the stochastic sampler. To appreciate the advantages of the choice

Table 5.1 Performance of CAM3.1 Over a Cluster of Dell PowerEdge 1955 Blade Servers

No. of processors	1	2	4	8	16	32	64
Simulated years/wall clock day	0.92	1.70	2.91	5.56	10.26	17.91	27.38
Simulated years/wall clock day per processor	0.92	0.883	0.729	0.696	0.641	0.560	0.429

of stochastic sampler, it will be helpful to first document the computational characteristics of the Community Atmosphere Model version 3.1 (CAM3.1) for which we are currently testing the effects of six model parameters important to clouds and convection. CAM3.1 resolves the physics and fluid motions of the atmosphere on a 64×128 spectral grid with 26 vertical levels. For parallelism, the code exploits domain decomposition by the 64 latitude bands, which place an effective upper limit on number of processors for which the model can be run efficiently. The performance of CAM3.1 may be expressed by the number of simulated years per wall clock day for a given number of processors. This number may be normalized by the number of processors (years per day per processor) to give a measure of the scaling efficiency of the code. Table 5.1 shows the performance of CAM3.1 on a distributed computing platform available at the Texas Advanced Computing Center. This platform consists of a distribution of Dell PowerEdge 1955 Blade servers, each with dual socket/dual core 2.66 GHz Intel 64 bit Xeon (Woodcrest) processors and a 1333 MHz Front Side Bus and dual channel 533 MHz fully buffered DIMMS. Each server is interconnected by an InfiniBand switch with a nominal bandwidth of 1 GB/s with 6 μs latency, the overhead time for sending a packet of information between any two processors. Climate models do not scale particularly well within distributed computing environments because of the frequency at which information needs to be shared among processors. This makes scaling performance numbers more sensitive to latency numbers.

The performance numbers of Table 5.1 provide a reality check on the enormity of the problem to systematically evaluate all possible combinations of parameter values. Without model parallelism, a single 10 year long experiment would take over a week. To take advantage of the data-directed importance sampling described below, one needs at least 150 of these experiments to be run sequentially. We, therefore, depend on the model parallelism in addition to the stochastic sampling algorithm parallelism to obtain scientifically relevant results within a reasonable time frame.

5.3 STOCHASTIC INVERSION

Bayesian statistics uses rules of conditional probabilities to infer how a set of parameters may be constrained by available observations given the knowledge of a system's physics. The desired result is known as *a posteriori* probability density function (PPD). The PPD is a powerful summary of information about how observational data can inform us about key relationships of a physical system. The key to making this work efficiently is to allow data to be involved in selecting candidate parameter values through a meaningful metric of the distance between observations and model predictions. That is, the improved efficiencies come from the process by which the choices of candidate parameter values depend on past values. This dependency is not great news for application in distributed computing environments as one wants to be completing as many experiments at once as possible. Moreover, most algorithms for choosing candidate parameter values are not terribly efficient, even when directed by data, and whatever efficiency they do achieve is sensitive to characteristics of the shape of the likelihood function, the metric of model-data discrepancies as a function of model parameters.

The optimal approach to stochastic inversion of data and/or computational demanding problems is a subject of current research [24]. One strategy that provides an adequate blend of efficiency and accuracy is multiple very fast simulated annealing (MVFSA) [25, 26]. It may be characterized as a sophisticated heuristic approach to approximating MCMC sampling. The rules for selecting samples is similar to a Metropolis/Gibbs sampler insofar as candidate parameter set values are either accepted or rejected (for stepping through parameter space) in proportion to a probability

$$P = \exp\left(\frac{-\Delta E}{T}\right), \tag{5.1}$$

where $\Delta E = E(\mathbf{m}_{k+1}) - E(\mathbf{m}_k)$ is the change in the metric of model-data discrepancies, also called the "cost function," for going from a model with parameter set values $\mathbf{m}_k$ to model with parameter set values $\mathbf{m}_{k+1}$. The mathematical form of $E(\mathbf{m})$ is defined below. The Metropolis/Gibbs sampler is sensitive to the algorithm "temperature" parameter T that controls how freely the stochastic sampler will jump around parameter space. If too high a temperature is selected, then the benefits of data-directed sampling are lost. If too low a temperature is selected, then sampling will not be representative of the range of possible solutions. Multiple very fast simulated annealing avoids the ambiguity of knowing in advance what the ideal temperature is by starting at a relatively high temperature and allowing the stochastic sampler to experience a range of temperatures according to the schedule in which iteration (k) has temperature

$$T_k = T_0 \exp\left(-0.9(k-1)^{1/2}\right). \tag{5.2}$$

The size of the steps that are taken through parameter space within MVFSA is connected to temperature with larger steps at higher temperatures and smaller steps as T approaches 0. After a relatively few number of iterations, depending primarily on the dimensionality of $\mathbf{m}$, the MVFSA algorithm will converge on a solution that tends to favor the global minimum of the cost function. The convergence process should be repeated 10–100 times to accumulate sufficient statistics to estimate the PPD. The advantage of MVFSA for distributed computing is that the convergence attempt chains can be run in parallel with the final estimate of the PPD coming from an accumulation of statistics across chains. Because of its data-directed sampling, MVFSA can be several orders of magnitude more efficient than the Metropolis/Gibbs

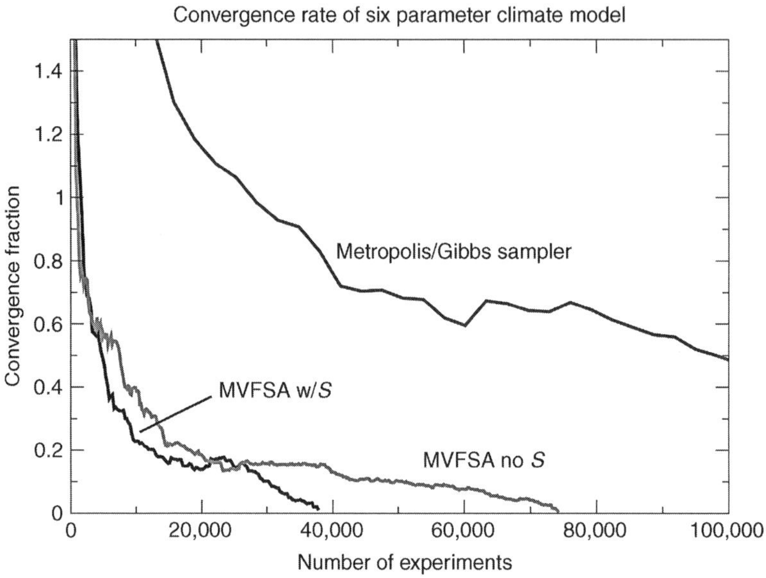

Figure 5.1 Convergence fraction as a function of experiment number for MVFSA not incorporating S into the stochastic sampling (gray line), MVFSA with incorporating S into the stochastic sampling (lower black line), and the Metropolis/Gibbs sampler (upper black line). Convergence fraction is given by the rms difference among the distributions for 6 climate model parameters as a function of experiment number and the final distribution. The climate model is described in Ref. [26].

sampler (Figure 5.1). So the combination of the sampling efficiency and the fact that one can separate the problem into multiple pieces bring a new class of problems within reach of Bayesian stochastic inversion.

5.4 APPLICATION TO CLIMATE PREDICTION

Within the Bayesian formulation of probability, the likelihood of a given choice in parameters is measured by an exponential of the effects of those parameters on model performance (i.e., the cost function) relative to all other parameter choices tested. The use of exponential implies Gaussian errors in both the data and observations. Many potential applications of Bayesian stochastic inversion may not know or may not depend heavily on quantifying these errors. For instance, in some cases it may be sufficient to simply identify the locations of the peaks in the PPD and exhibit the uncertainty as a qualitative reweighting of the PPD given the slightly different scaling factors S for the uncertainty in size in the error normalization (data covariance) part of the metric of model performance,

$$PPD(\mathbf{m}) = \frac{\exp(-S \cdot E(\mathbf{m}))}{\int \exp(-S \cdot E(\mathbf{m}))d\mathbf{m}}. \tag{5.3}$$

For the climate prediction problem, where there is more interest in quantifying the likelihood of extremes, it is necessary to develop a more formal way to incorporate information about sources of uncertainty. In the following two sections, we discuss why there exists a need for incorporating prior information acknowledging uncertainties in selecting S into the definition of the metric of model performance and its role in improving the efficiency and accuracy of estimating the PPD.

5.4.1 Definition of the Metric of Model Performance

The cost function $E(\mathbf{m})$ contains an inverse of the data covariance matrix $\mathbf{C}^{-1}$ that provides a means to normalize the significance of model-data mismatch among N different fields $\mathbf{d}_{\text{obs}}$ (e.g., surface air temperature, precipitation, and so on) and model predictions $g(\mathbf{m})$ at M points (note that each field may contain a different number of points M),

$$E(\mathbf{m}) = \sum_{i=1}^{N} \frac{1}{2N} \left[(\mathbf{d}_{\text{obs}} - g(\mathbf{m}))^T \mathbf{C}^{-1} (\mathbf{d}_{\text{obs}} - g(\mathbf{m})) \right]_i . \tag{5.4}$$

Equation (5.4) includes vector $\mathbf{m}$ of model parameter values and T for the matrix transpose. The data covariance matrix includes information about sources of observational or model uncertainty, including information about uncertainty originating from natural (internal) variability, measurement errors, or theory. This form of the mean square error E is the appropriate form for assessing more rigorously the statistical significance of modeled–observational differences when it is known that distributions of model and observational uncertainty are Gaussian. Our focus here will be entirely on sources of uncertainty that arise from natural variability.

If one assumes uncertainties are spatially uncorrelated, the data covariance matrix will contain nonzero elements only along the diagonal. When considering uncertainty originating from spatially uncorrelated natural variability, each of these elements is equal to the variance of the natural variability within the corresponding grid point where model predictions are compared to observations. However, data points are correlated in space, season, and among fields. Some points and/or fields have very little associated variance, such as rain over a desert. The cost function can be very sensitive to the choices one makes in accounting for these correlations and/or singularities within the data covariance matrix [27]. Estimating normalizing factors for complex systems is an area of active research ([28], p. 345). Although not satisfactory to a statistician, some have treated this unknown through a reweighting of the posterior distribution (i.e., S within equation (5.3)). The problem is that such a reweighting does not give the statistical sampling algorithm the opportunity to only sample from the posterior, which can lead to inefficiencies and biases in the results. A more statistically correct procedure would be to introduce a renormalizing factor before sampling. One empirical Bayesian approach is to estimate S in advance through an ensemble of experiment in which one imposes uncertainties. For instance, in the climate problem, where the uncertainty is from natural variability, one may consider how the cost function would be affected if the climate model (or data) was taken from different segments of a long integration. One may estimate a fixed renormalizing factor to be $S = 2/\Delta E$, where $\Delta E = E_{95} - E_0$ represents the 2σ range in cost function values that arise from internal variability. One may then apply the logic that parameter sets that are ΔE away from the optimal parameter set will be given a likelihood measure of exp(−2), which is equivalent to the 95% probability measure for a normalized Gaussian distribution.

5.4.2 Incorporating Uncertainties in Error Normalization in the Prior

The reweighting of samples according to equation (5.3) gives a skewed perspective of the PPD as it tends to have more narrow peaks and fat tails relative to a cost function that had been correctly normalized. This is because correlations among constraints in the data tend to increase the significance of changes in the cost function. Thus, stochastic sampling uninformed about the effects of these correlations will tend to sample more frequently the regions that end up being weighted down in equation (5.3). This represents a sampling inefficiency.

Along the lines suggested by Gelman et al. [28], it is possible to treat *S* as one of the uncertain parameters within MVFSA and use principles of Bayesian inference to select candidate choices of *S* from a prior Gamma distribution whose mean and variance are determined by a process similar to the choice of *S* in Section 5.4.1. The choice of a Gamma distribution was mostly for mathematical convenience and given that a Gamma prior is "conditionally conjugate" to our definition of the cost function. It is a mathematical way to express uncertainties in the denominator (i.e., the variance). The Gamma distribution looks alike a skewed Gaussian distribution with no probability for a value of 0, a mean value that corresponds to the choice of *S* from the previous section, and a tail that conveys uncertainties in defining an appropriate *S*. In a fully Bayesian approach, one can construct candidate choices of *S* to depend on a corresponding evaluation of $E(\mathbf{m})$ to incorporate uncertainties in the data covariance matrix into the stochastic sampling algorithm [29].

Although this revised method adds a randomly generated number *S* to the acceptance/rejection criterion (equation 5.1), there can be significant improvements in the accuracy and efficiency (Figure 5.1) to estimating the PPD. In fact, samples selected in the case where *S* is included through a prior no longer require weighting for estimating the PPD as these samples are now assumed to be drawn directly from a distribution that is proportional to the actual PPD. The effect of this choice can be dramatic, as illustrated in Figure 5.2 where the PPD derived from including *S* as a prior is a much better match to the target distribution of an idealized example than without it.

5.5 RESULTS

The MVFSA stochastic sampler has been applied to estimating the PPD of six parameters (Table 5.2) of the Community Atmosphere Model version 3.1 important

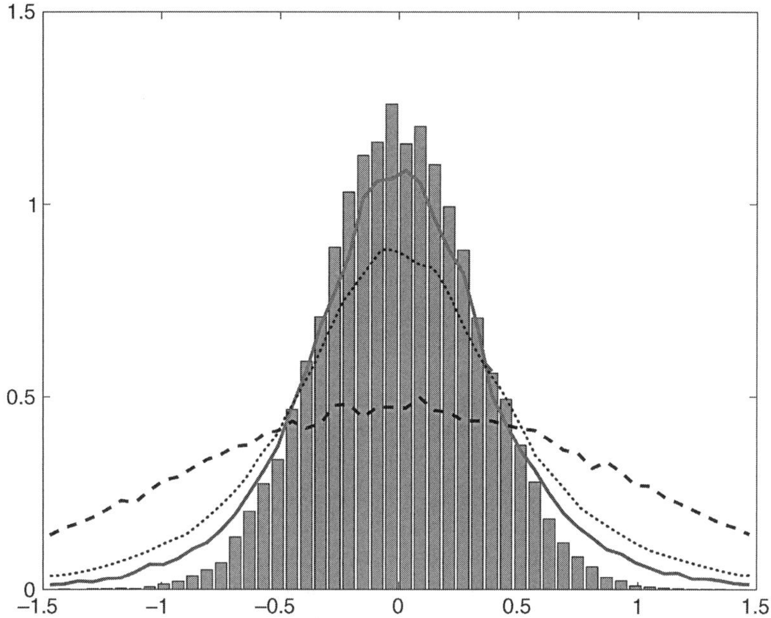

Figure 5.2 Idealized example using different sampling schemes. Sampling efficiency is improved when information about *S* is included within the prior. Target distribution (gray bars) was generated using Gibbs' sampling using a prior for *S*. Gibbs' sampling without a prior for *S* is given by the dashed line. MVFSA sampling using a prior for *S* is given by the solid black line and without using a prior for *S* is given by the dotted line.

to clouds and convection as constrained by observations or reanalysis of 15 fields separated into 4 seasons and 6 regions covering the globe [27]. In addition, MVFSA incorporates a prior distribution estimate for *S*, the parameter controlling inadequacies in properly defining the data covariance matrix [29].

Each experiment testing the sensitivity of CAM3.1 to combined changes in select parameters follows an experimental design in which the model is forced by observed

Table 5.2 Names and Descriptions of Parameters Important to Clouds and Convection in CAM3.1

Parameter	Description
RHMINL	Critical relative humidity for low cloud formation
RHMINH	Critical relative humidity for high cloud formation
ALFA	Initial cloud downdraft mass flux
TAU	Rate at which convective clouds consume available potential energy
ke	Environmental air to cloud entrainment rate coefficient
c0	Deep convection precipitation production efficiency parameter

sea surface temperatures (SST) and sea ice for an 11-year period (March 1990 through February 2001). The model includes 26 vertical levels and uses an approximately 2.8° latitude by 2.8° longitude (T42) resolution.

Up to this point, 518 experiments have been completed over 6 independent VFSA convergence attempt "lines." Each line starts at a randomly chosen point in the multidimensional parameter space. Each model experiment runs in parallel over 64 processors, bringing the total number of processors being occupied at any point in time to 384. The average number of experiments that we anticipate will be required to reach convergence for each line is 150 [26]. However, more lines may be necessary to have confidence that we are converging on a stationary estimate of the PPD.

Of the 518 completed experiments, 332 configurations have cost values the same or better relative to the default model configuration with the optimal experiments in each line averaging a respectable 10% improvement in their cost values. The size of the cost function gives a normalized perspective of the distance between observations and model predictions with the units relating to the size of the effect of internal variability on each component. Large cost values tend to be associated with fields that have very little variability. In this case, the field with the largest associated cost value in the default model configuration is the annual mean global mean radiative balance at the top of the atmosphere with a value of 202 cost units. The field with the lowest cost value is precipitation with a value of 24.2 cost units.

We have separately analyzed the six top performing experiments, one for each of the independent lines considered. The fields that improved the most across these six experiments were shortwave radiation reaching the surface (averaging 14% improvement), net radiative balance at the top of the atmosphere (33% improvement), and precipitation (12% improvement). However, the performance gains or losses for the other fields were not consistent. The similar cost values achieved for all six optimal model configurations are achieved through different compromises in model skill for predicting particular fields.

The marginal PPD for each of the six model parameters along with the position of the default model and the optimal values chosen by the six lines is shown in Figure 5.3. The PPD is generated only from the 332 configurations that have the same or better cost than the default configuration. The range of parameter values that improved model performance is quite broad for all parameters except for the critical relative humidity for low cloud formation. Also of interest is the desired result that the six optimal parameter sets are representative of the uncertainty as quantified by the PPD. Capturing climate model parametric uncertainties within a limited number of candidate model configurations is the key step in quantifying observational constraints on these important degrees of freedom for model development. For instance, one may use these different parameter sets to test the impacts of these uncertainties on the model's sensitivity to CO_2 forcing. Although we are still completing the number of necessary experiments to draw a firm conclusion, the implication of the wide ranges apparent in Figure 5.3 is that it may be very difficult to use available observations to constrain sufficiently some of the choices that need to be made in assigning values to parameters that are involved in clouds and convection, which are processes thought to be key sources of climate prediction uncertainty.

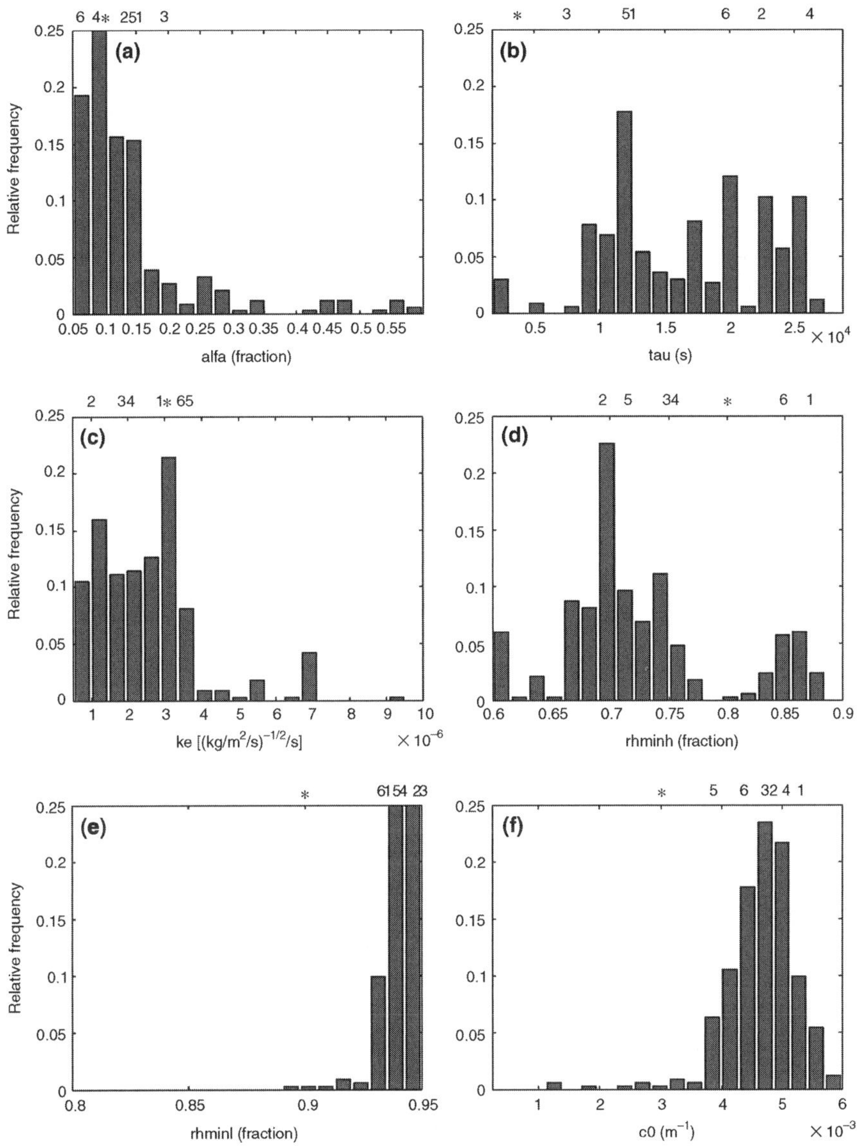

Figure 5.3 PPD for six parameters of CAM3.1 important to clouds and convection (see Table 5.2). The histograms are derived from the 332 experiments whose cost values were the same or showed an improvement over the default model configuration. The parameter values of the default model are given by an asterisk (*). The values of the top performing six parameter sets are labeled by the particular line number that produced them. Reproduced from [29] © Copyright 2008 AMS.

5.6 SUMMARY

The increase in availability in distributed computing provides an opportunity for the climate sciences to address more quantitatively the sources and impacts of uncertainties in climate model development on climate predictions. This is achieved through a selection of alternate climate model configurations that reflect the scientific values for how these models are constrained by observations (i.e., the definition of the cost function). One of the barriers to achieving this goal is the substantial computational expense of climate models where the ideal choice of multiple parameter values is interdependent. For these cases, one needs to draw inferences about the relative likelihood of different possible choices from a random sampling of candidate parameter combinations that do not bias the end result. Data-directed importance sampling achieves improved efficiency from sampling more often, and in proportion to the final PPD, those regions of parameter space that contribute effectively to the PPD. There exist many types of stochastic samplers that make use of data direction. However, many of these approaches depend on the sequential integration of experiments, which make it difficult to fully exploit available computational resources. Moreover, the efficiency of most methods depends on knowledge about the characteristics of the problem that may be difficult to gage without significant experimentation. We present multiple very fast simulated annealing as an alternative that is less sensitive to problem characteristics and produces helpful estimates of the PPD.

We also show that additional improvements in accuracy and efficiency of the MVFSA algorithm can be incorporated into data-directed importance samplers when prior information is incorporated about the size of the effects of sources of uncertainty on the cost function through a parameter S that is conceptually correcting for errors in defining a data covariance matrix that appropriately accounts for correlations that may exist among the many data constraints.

The results of estimating a PPD for six parameters of the CAM3.1 climate model reinforce the notion that there exist many possible model configurations that can do an equally adequate job in reproducing a multifield average skill score. More sampling will be required to establish with greater confidence the relative likelihood of the solutions that have been identified so far. The main point of this exercise is to illustrate the practicality of data-directed importance sampling and uncertainty characterization of parameters within a nonidealized climate model.

REFERENCES

1. H. LeTreut, and B.J. McAvaney. A model intercomparison of equilibrium climate change in response to CO_2 doubling. Note du Pole de Modelisation de l'IPSL, Number 18, Institut Pierre Simon LaPlace, Paris, France, 2000.
2. U. Cubasch, G.A. Meehl, G.J. Boer, R.J. Stouffer, M. Dix, A. Noda, C.A. Senior, S. Raper, K.S. Yap. Projections of future climate change. In Houghton, J.T., Y. Ding, D.J. Griggs, M. Noguer, P.J. van der Linden, X. Dai, K. Maskell, and C.A. Johnson, editors, *Climate Change 2001: The Scientific Basis. Contribution of Working Group I to the Third Assessment Report of the Intergovernmental*

Panel on Climate Change. Cambridge University Press, Cambridge, UK and New York, NY, USA, 2001, p. 881.

3. W.L. Gates, J.S. Boyle, C. Covey, C.G. Dease, C.M. Doutriaux, R.S. Drach, M. Fiorino, P.J. Gleckler, J.J. Hnilo, S.M. Marlais, T.J. Phillips, G.L. Potter, B.D. Santer, K.R. Sperber, K.E. Taylor, and D.N. Williams. An overview of the results of the Atmospheric Model Intercomparison Project (AMIP I). *B. Am. Meteorol. Soc.*, 80(1):29–56, 1999.
4. S. Joussaume, and K.E. Taylor. The paleoclimate modeling intercomparison project. In P. Braconnot, editor, *Paleoclimate Modeling Intercomparison Project (PMIP)*. Proceedings of the Third PMIP Workshop, Canada, 4–8 October 1999, WCRP-111, WMO/TD-1007, 2000, pp. 271.
5. G.A. Meehl, G.J. Boer, C. Covey, M. Latif, R.J. Stouffer. The Coupled Model Intercomparison Project (CMIP). *B. Am. Meteorol. Soc.*, 81(2):313–318, 2000.
6. B.J. McAvaney, C. Covey, S. Joussaume, V. Kattsov, A. Kitoh, W. Ogana, A.J. Pitman, A.J. Weaver, R.A. Wood, and Z.-C. Zhao. Model evaluation. In J.T. Houghton, Y. Ding, D.J. Griggs, M. Noguer, P.J. van der Linden, X. Dai, K. Maskell, and C.A. Johnson, editors, *Climate Change 2001: The Scientific Basis. Contribution of Working Group I to the Third Assessment Report of the Intergovernmental Panel on Climate Change*. Cambridge University Press, Cambridge, UK and New York, NY, USA, 2001, p. 881.
7. C. Forest, M.R. Allen, P.H. Stone, and A.P. Sokolov. Constraining uncertainties in climate models using climate change detection techniques. *Geophys. Res. Lett.*, 27(4):569–572, 2000.
8. C. Forest, M.R. Allen, A.P. Sokolov, and P.H. Stone. Constraining climate model properties using optimal fingerprint detection methods. *Climate Dyn.*, 18:277–295, 2001.
9. C. Forest, P.H. Stone, A.P. Sokolov, M.R. Allen, and M.D. Webster. Quantifying uncertainties in climate system properties with the use of recent climate observations. *Science*, 295:113–117, 2002.
10. M. Allen. Do-it-yourself climate prediction. *Nature*, 401:642, 1999.
11. D.A. Stainforth, T. Aina, C. Christensen, M. Collins, N. Faull, D.J. Frame, J.A. Kettleborough, S. Knight, A. Martin, J.M. Murphy, C. Piani, D. Sexton, L.A. Smith, R.A. Spicer, A.J. Thorpe, and M.R. Allen. Uncertainty in predictions of the climate response to rising levels of greenhouse gases. *Nature*, 433:403–406, 2005.
12. H. Kheshgi and B.S. White. Testing distributed parameter hypotheses for the detection of climate change. *J. Climate*, 14:3464–3481, 2001.
13. K.D. Williams, C.A. Senior, and J.F.B. Mitchell. Transient climate change in the Hadley Centre models: the role of physical processes. *J. Climate*, 14(12):2659–2674, 2001.
14. J. Barhen, J.G. Berryman, L. Borcea, J. Dennis, C. de Groot-Hedlin, F. Gilbert, P. Gill, M. Heinkenschloss, L. Johnson, T. McEvilly, J. More, G. Newman, D. Oldenburg, P. Parker, B. Porto, M. Sen, V. Torczon, D. Vasco, and N.B. Woodward. Optimization and geophysical inverse problems. Report of a workshop at San Jose, California, February 5–6, 1999. Lawrence Berkeley National Laboratory Report No. 46959, p. 33.
15. J. Sacks, S.B. Schiller, and W.J. Welch Designs for computer experiments. *Technometrics*, 31:41–47, 1989.
16. W.J. Welch, R.J. Buck, J. Sacks, H.P. Wynn, T.J. Mitchell, and M.D. Morris. Screening, predicting, and computer experiments. *Technometrics*, 34:15–25, 1992.
17. K.P. Bowman, J. Sacks, and Y.-F. Chang. On the design and analysis of numerical experiments. *J. Atmos. Sci.*, 50:1267–1278, 1993.
18. W.L. Chapman, W.J. Welch, K.P. Bowman, J. Sacks, and J.E. Walsh. Arctic sea ice variability: model sensitivities and a multidecadal simulation. *J. Geophys. Res.*, 99(C1):919–935, 1994.
19. T.J. Santner, B.J. Williams, and W.I. Notz. *The Design and Analysis of Computer Experiments*. Springer-Verlag, Inc, 2003.
20. G.A. Grell and D. Dévényi. A generalized approach to parameterizing convection combining ensemble and data assimilation techniques. *Geophys. Res. Lett.*, 29(14):1693, 2002. doi:10.1029/2002GL015311.
21. G. Evensen. The ensemble Kalman filter: theoretical formulation and practical implementation. *Ocean Dyn.*, 53:343–367, 2003.

22. J.D. Annan, and J.C. Hargreaves. Efficient estimation and ensemble generation in climate modeling. *Philos. Trans. R. Soc., A*, 365: 2077–2088, 2007. doi:10.1098/rsta.2007.2067.
23. D.J. Lea, M.R. Allen, and T.W.N. Haine. Sensitivity analysis of the climate of a chaotic system. *Tellus,* 52A:523–532, 2000.
24. A. Villagran, G. Huerta, C.S. Jackson, and M.K. Sen. Parameter uncertainty estimation in climate models. *Bayesian Analysis*, 3(4):823–850, 2008. doi:10.1214/08-BA331.
25. M.K. Sen and P.L. Stoffa. Bayesian inference, Gibbs' sampler and uncertainty estimation in geophysical inversion. *Geophys. Prospect.*, 44:313–350, 1996.
26. C. Jackson, M. Sen, and P. Stoffa. An efficient stochastic Bayesian approach to optimal parameter and uncertainty estimation for climate model predictions. *J. Climate*, 17(14):2828–2841, 2004.
27. Q. Mu, C.S. Jackson, and P.L. Stoffa. A multivariate empirical-orthogonal-function-based measure of climate model performance. *J. Geophys. Res.*, 109:D15101, 2004. doi:10.1029/2004JD004584.
28. A. Gelman, J.B. Carlin, H.S. Stern, and D.B. Rubin. *Bayesian Data Analysis, 2nd edition.* Chapman & Hall/CRC, 2004, p. 668.
29. C.S. Jackson, M.K. Sen, G. Huerta, Y. Deng, and K.P. Bowman. Error reduction and convergence in climate prediction. *Journal of Climate*, 21(24):6698-6709, 2008. doi: 10.1175/2008JCLI2112.1.

Chapter 6

Adaptive Cartesian Methods for Modeling Airborne Dispersion

Andrew Wissink, Branko Kosovic, Marsha Berger, Kyle Chand, and Fotini K. Chow

6.1 INTRODUCTION

The release of hazardous airborne materials is a dangerous, potentially life-threatening occurrence. Sources of such releases include industrial chemical releases, accidents incurred during transport of hazardous materials by truck or rail, or through a premeditated terrorist attack. Dangerous hazardous releases occur weekly in the United States. Fortunately, most of these events are minor, with major events requiring federal assistance occurring rarely. Still, it is important to have good computational tools available for planning, responding to, and assessing the consequences when they do happen. Numerical simulations provide an important predictive capability by giving a detailed understanding of the flow patterns and associated concentration distributions that may be used to guide emergency responders and the public in the event of a release. The NARAC/IMAAC center at Lawrence Livermore National Laboratory maintains a suite of operational computer models to predict atmospheric dispersion that have been used to respond to hundreds of major incidents involving federal assistance since its inception in 1979 (Figure 6.1).

High-fidelity computational fluid dynamics (CFD) models that solve the Navier–Stokes equations with turbulence models and accurately represent building boundaries are often needed to capture the important physics that affects dispersion in urban

Advanced Computational Infrastructures For Parallel and Distributed Adaptive Applications. Edited by Manish Parashar and Xiaolin Li

Figure 6.1 Simulation of an atmospheric release over a regional urban area performed by NARAC/IMAAC (courtesy Lawrence Livermore National Lab [33]).

environments. At the city or regional scale, flow is affected by buildings and other structures that impose an effective drag force that slows and mixes the flow in the urban boundary layer. Thermodynamics also plays an important role at this scale because the concrete structures can significantly impact heating and cooling characteristics, which affects lofting and mixing behavior. At increased fidelity is the neighborhood scale, where different building heights affect the turbulent characteristics and vertical mixing. At the finest fidelity is the street scale, where detailed flow channeling and lofting become apparent and flow is impacted by street-level obstructions such as traffic, trees, and building entrances.

Most operational atmospheric release advisory tools in use today use Gaussian puff-based models, which derive the dispersion patterns from wind fields produced by meso-scale atmospheric models. These models are used to predict atmospheric dispersion of contaminants and resulting concentration fields and determine appropriate plans of action, such as evacuation of residents or shelter-in-place recommendations. Gaussian puff models are fast and inexpensive and can be run on a PC. However, they do not resolve building boundaries or the complex flow patterns around them and hence are of limited utility in predicting concentrations in densely populated urban areas. While puff models can be parameterized to account for some urban effects, they do not fully incorporate the physical processes required to represent the complex fluid dynamics and thermodynamics that occur at many scales in urban environments [6]. High-resolution computational fluid dynamics models are often needed to capture the important physics that affect dispersion, such as channeling in street canyons, lofting, vertical mixing, and turbulence. Comparisons of Gaussian puff versus CFD models for urban environments reveal the need for resolving the microscale flow effects in urban settings for accurate concentration predictions [7, 30]. Evacuations based on miscalculated dispersion patterns from low-accuracy puff-based models could be disastrous.

High computational requirements generally preclude most CFD models from operational use today. Such models are, however, useful for planning and analysis and, together with experiments, may be used to define urban surface parameterization that may be used to improve the accuracy of puff-based models. Also, as computers become faster and cheaper and the use of parallel processing systems becomes more prevalent, models that are considered too computationally intensive today may become operationally usable in 5–10 years. With sufficient automation and efficiency improvements, CFD tools will soon become a viable option for operational use.

A variety of high-fidelity urban CFD models are in use today [5, 24, 28, 31]. Although they differ in their grid type (structured versus unstructured), discretization, and turbulence modeling approach (Reynolds-averaged Navier–Stokes (RANS), or large-eddy simulation (LES), they all solve the Navier–Stokes equations with turbulence models on building-resolved grids. The work described here uses the FEM3MP urban CFD model [8, 9, 32], an incompressible finite element Navier–Stokes code. The model has been tested against various urban field experiments, including Urban 2000 in Salt Lake City [11], Urban 2003 in Oklahoma City [10, 12], and the Urban Dispersion Program in New York City [26]. We discuss in this chapter how we utilized adaptive mesh refinement (AMR) and rapid grid generation infrastructures and applied them to FEM3MP to enhance the automation and efficiency of high-fidelity urban CFD modeling.

AMR allows dynamic control of the grid resolution so that the different scales of the urban flow field can each be resolved as needed, at significantly less computational cost than a comparably accurate uniform grid calculation. Parallel AMR capability was provided through the SAMRAI [22, 23] structured AMR package. The structured AMR approach lends itself well to incorporating legacy codes like FEM3MP. One needs to develop only a version of the code that operates on a single Cartesian block; it then forms the basis for the numerical kernel that is applied on each patch in the grid hierarchy. The rest of the AMR capabilities, dynamic grid generation, multilevel solvers, parallel load balancing, and so on are provided through the SAMRAI library's data structures and procedures.

To support the complex geometry requirements of the urban boundary, we utilize fast embedded boundary mesh generation. Unlike traditional gridding techniques that place grid points directly on the building boundaries, embedded boundary meshing simply cuts boundaries through the cells of the Cartesian grid Figure 6.2a. Advantages of this approach are that it is very fast and able to handle complex geometries in an automated way. Geometric information defining the urban terrain comes in two main forms: 2D polygonal definitions with an associated height and 3D surface triangulations. The polygonal definition usually comes from ESRI shapefiles [16], while surface triangulations come from more general representations of surface topography, such as terrain or light detection and ranging (LIDAR) data. Two software infrastructures were utilized to provide the rapid embedded boundary mesh generation capabilities using these geometric data definitions. *PatchCubes* is based

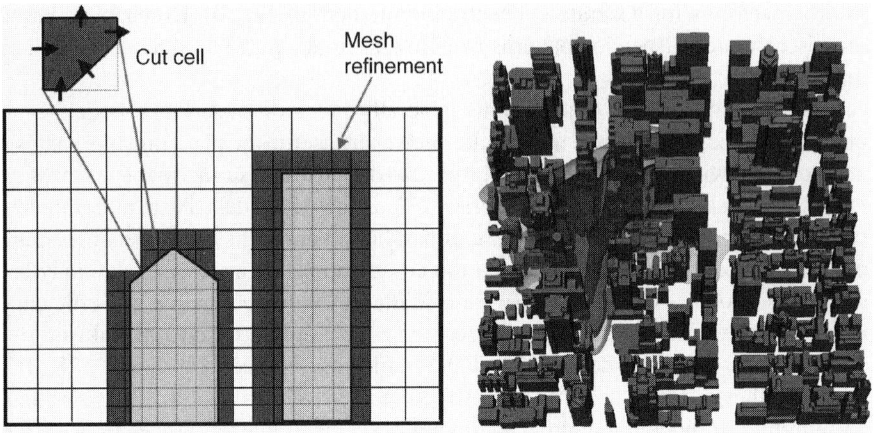

(a) Adaptive embedded boundary grid

(b) Times square calculation with FEM3MP using immersed boundary grid

Figure 6.2 Embedded boundary treatment imposes the presence of buildings by modifying the solution on cells of the Cartesian grid that are cut by the boundary, rather than conforming the grid to the building boundaries (courtesy Lawrence Livermore National Lab [37]).

on the mesh generator *cubes* that operates on surface triangulations and is part of the Cart3D [3] package. *Eleven* is a general complex geometry library that operates on ESRI shapefiles and is included as part of the Overture [21] package. Both packages are integrated with SAMRAI in a way that provides a fully parallel embedded boundary mesh generation capability.

The particular approach used in FEM3MP to enforce the boundary is an algorithm based on the immersed boundary formulation (see Ref. [27]), which is slightly different from traditional embedded boundary approaches (see, e.g., Ref. [15]); however, it uses the geometric information provided by the embedded boundary packages. In what follows, we use the term "embedded boundary" to refer to any of the Cartesian grid approaches where the boundary is not body fitted. SAMRAI can support either embedded or immersed boundary representations.

Although the discussion in this chapter will focus on the urban modeling application using FEM3MP, the framework we have put together is general purpose and can be applied to many other problems that require AMR, complex geometries, and parallel computing. Section 6.2 gives some background on the numerics in the FEM3MP model and the particular algorithmic changes that were made to operate on an adaptive Cartesian mesh with an embedded boundary representation of the building surfaces. Section 1.3 discusses the computational infrastructures that provide the adaptive grid capability on large-scale parallel computer systems with complex geometry. Section 1.4 discusses details of the parallel implementation. Finally, Section 6.5 deals with about future improvements that could be achieved through continued use of innovative computational infrastructures.

6.2 FINITE ELEMENT NUMERICAL SOLUTION

This section discusses the FEM3MP numerical model. The first section describes the finite element discretization used in FEM3MP. Next is a discussion of the adaptive implementation. Finally, we discuss how building boundary conditions are applied using an immersed boundary-type algorithm.

6.2.1 Model Equations

The FEM3MP model solves the filtered 3D Navier–Stokes momentum and scalar advection equations

$$\frac{\partial u_i}{\partial t} + u_j \frac{\partial u_i}{\partial x_j} = -\frac{1}{\rho}\frac{\partial p}{\partial x_i} + \nu \frac{\partial^2 u_i}{\partial x_j \partial x_j} - \frac{\partial \overline{u_i' u_j'}}{\partial x_j}, \tag{6.1}$$

$$\frac{\partial c}{\partial t} + u_j \frac{\partial c}{\partial x_j} = \nu_c \frac{\partial^2 c}{\partial x_j \partial x_j} - \frac{\partial \overline{c' u_j'}}{\partial x_j} \tag{6.2}$$

subject to the incompressibility constraint

$$\frac{\partial u_i}{\partial x_i} = \nabla \cdot \vec{u} = 0, \tag{6.3}$$

where $\vec{u}$, or u_i, is the velocity, ρ is the density, p is the pressure, c is a passive scalar, and ν and ν_c are the molecular viscosity and scalar diffusivity constants, respectively. Primed quantities denote fluctuations of the filtered (or averaged) quantities. The density ρ is defined as a field variable in the initial conditions and is subject to the Bousinesq approximation (it is unchanged by the momentum equation). Likewise, the temperature T is defined initially and is treated as a passive scalar in the solution. The overbar indicates either time or space averaging for RANS and LES, respectively. A turbulence closure model is applied to model the correlations of fluctuating quantities. Boundary conditions are defined in a variety of ways for different circumstances, but generally are Dirichlet for $\vec{u}$ and Neumann for p.

The velocity is defined at node centers and linear finite element discretizations are used for the advection and diffusion operators

$$N\left(u_j\right) u_i \equiv u_j \frac{\partial u_i}{\partial x_j}, \tag{6.4}$$

$$K u_i \equiv -\left(\nu \frac{\partial^2 u_i}{\partial x_j \partial x_j} - \frac{\partial \overline{u_i' u_j'}}{\partial x_j}\right). \tag{6.5}$$

Further details on these operators can be found in Ref. [19]. Pressure is defined at element centers and is constant over each element. The node-centered gradient operator for p in equation (6.1) is computed by averaging cell-centered values to element faces and computing the gradient at the nodes (Figure 6.3).

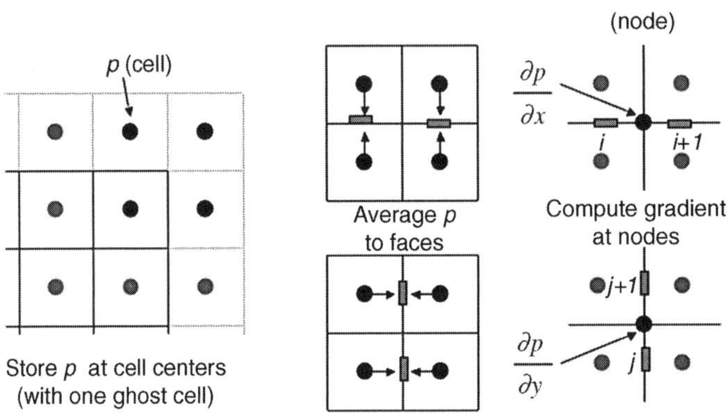

Figure 6.3 The pressure gradient is computed at nodes from pressures stored at element centers.

A mixed discretization, which enforces the divergence-free condition on velocity (equation (6.3)) through a finite volume discretization, has some advantages over the standard Q1Q0 discretization. The Q1Q0 discretization, described in Ref. [19], uses a linear representation for velocity (i.e., Q1) and a constant representation for pressure (i.e., Q0) over an element. With this type of discretization, application of the divergence operator can lead to "checkerboard" patterns due to instabilities in the operator. The mixed discretization, Q1FV, which is similar to Q1Q0 but uses a finite volume operator for the divergence, avoids these instabilities. It is also easier to implement in an adaptive context, where grids of different spacings align. The finite volume divergence operator is computed by first averaging the node-centered velocities to faces, and then computing with the integral form of the divergence operator (Figure 6.4).

The solution approach uses a dual projection scheme in which the momentum equation is first solved to get an initial velocity u_i^* (which does not satisfy the divergence-free constraint). Then, the divergence-free condition is enforced by doing

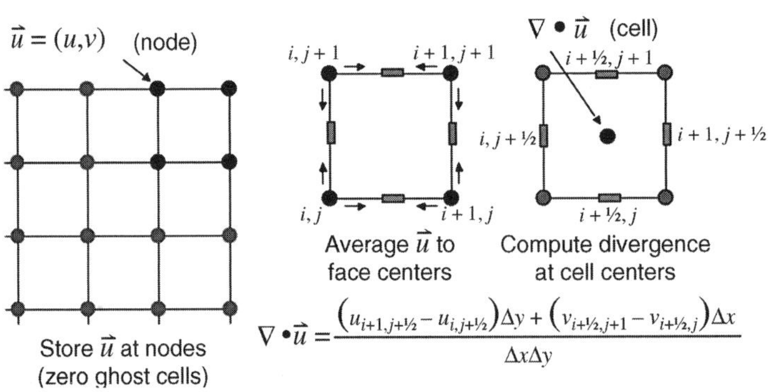

Figure 6.4 The divergence of velocity is computed by first averaging node-centered quantities to faces, and then applying the finite volume integral form of the divergence operator.

a projection solve based on the scheme by Chorin [13]. The projection solve obtains a scalar field ϕ and its gradient is used to correct the velocity such that it satisfies the divergence-free constraint. Finally, the pressure is updated through a second projection solve. The derivation behind the equation for pressure in the second projection solve arises from application of the divergence operator to the momentum equation (equation (6.1)). Once the new velocity and pressure fields are defined, scalar quantities are advected. Applying the finite element matrices given in equations (6.4) and (6.5), this five-step solution update process can be written as

$$\frac{u_i^* - u_i^n}{\Delta t} = -\left(N\left(u_j^n\right) + K\right)u_i^n - \frac{1}{\rho}\frac{\partial p^n}{\partial x_i}, \tag{6.6}$$

$$\nabla^2\phi = \nabla \cdot u_i^*, \tag{6.7}$$

$$u_i^{n+1} = u_i^n + \nabla\phi, \tag{6.8}$$

$$\nabla^2 p^{n+1} = -\nabla \cdot \left[\left(N\left(u_j^{n+1}\right) + K\right)u_i^{n+1}\right], \tag{6.9}$$

$$\frac{c^{n+1} - c^n}{\Delta t} = -\left(N\left(u_j^{n+1}\right) + K\right)c^n. \tag{6.10}$$

Equation (6.6) solves the momentum equations to get a prediction for velocity, equation (6.7) performs the first projection solve, and equation (6.8) corrects the velocity. After these three steps, the velocity field satisfies the divergence-free constraint. Equation (6.9) performs the second projection solve to get the pressure field, and equation (6.10) advects the scalar quantities according to the computed velocity and pressure field.

For purposes of clarity, the above process is presented in the context of a first-order forward Euler scheme. In practice, we use a third-order Runge–Kutta time stepping scheme (RK3), with the five-step solution algorithm shown above employed in each RK3 subiteration.

6.2.2 Adaptive Formulation

The standard FEM algorithm used in the FEM3MP CFD code had to be modified to operate on a Cartesian structured AMR (SAMR) grid system. Converting an algorithm from a single level to multiple levels is simple in concept. First, solve each level separately, as if it were a single-level calculation, using interpolated values from the coarser level as boundary conditions at level boundaries. Once the computation has finished on the finer level, restrict (coarsen) the more accurate solution to the coarser level and then repeat the process to the next coarser level.

The Q1FV algorithm requires consideration of two discretizations at the coarse–fine boundary: linear finite element discretization for node-centered quantities and finite volume discretization for element-centered quantities.

A finite element discretization accumulates contributions at each node from the element matrices of its surrounding elements. A multilevel discretization must account for contributions of elements on both levels. For example, suppose we apply the

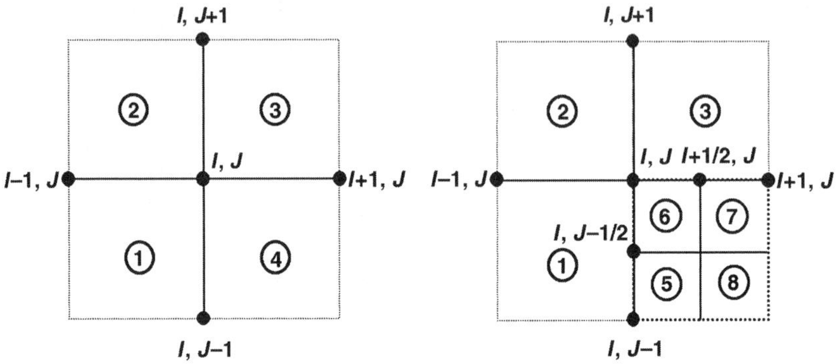

(**a**) Single-level discretization (**b**) Multilevel discretization

Figure 6.5 Finite element discretization at node (I, J) includes contributions from surrounding elements. If the node lies on the boundary between coarse and fine levels, the discretization must account for elements on both levels.

diffusion operator K (equation (6.5)) to compute diffusion r of one of the scalar velocity components $r = Ku$. On a single level, node (I, J) is surrounded by four elements, labeled 1–4 (Figure 6.5a) and the value of $r_{I,J}$ is determined by summing the K element matrix contributions from the surrounding elements:

$$\begin{aligned} r_{I,J} = r_{I,J} &+ \left(K_{01}^{(1)} + K_{00}^{(2)}\right) u_{I-1,J}, \\ &+ \left(K_{10}^{(3)} + K_{11}^{(4)}\right) u_{I+1,J}, \\ &+ \left(K_{10}^{(1)} + K_{00}^{(4)}\right) u_{I,J-1}, \\ &+ \left(K_{11}^{(2)} + K_{01}^{(3)}\right) u_{I,J+1}, \end{aligned} \tag{6.11}$$

where $K_{ij}^{(n)}$ denotes local contributions by element n at local node (x, y) on the element (0 = lower node and 1 = higher).

If we now apply this discretization to the multilevel mesh shown in Figure 6.5b, element 4 is replaced by elements 5–8 on the finer level and the discretization formula for node (I, J) becomes

$$\begin{aligned} r_{I,J} = r_{I,J} &+ \left(K_{01}^{(1)} + K_{00}^{(2)}\right) u_{I-1,J}, \\ &+ \left(K_{10}^{(3)} + K_{11}^{(7)}\right) u_{I+1,J}, \\ &+ \left(K_{10}^{(1)} + K_{00}^{(5)}\right) u_{I,J-1}, \\ &+ \left(K_{11}^{(2)} + K_{01}^{(3)}\right) u_{I,J+1}, \end{aligned}$$

$$+ \left(K^{(1)}_{1\frac{1}{2}} + K^{(5)}_{01} + K^{(6)}_{00} \right) u_{I,J-\frac{1}{2}},$$

$$+ \left(K^{(3)}_{\frac{1}{2}0} + K^{(6)}_{11} + K^{(7)}_{01} \right) u_{I+\frac{1}{2},J}. \tag{6.12}$$

Nodes at the coarse–fine boundary that do not overlap coarser level nodes (e.g., those at $(I, J - \frac{1}{2})$ and $(I + \frac{1}{2}, J)$ in Figure 6.5b) are designated "hanging" nodes. Quantities on the hanging nodes are not computed through discretization. Rather, their value is set to be an average of the nodal quantities of the surrounding nonhanging nodes. This is mathematically consistent with the linear representation of the quantity on the element. But since the solution on the hanging nodes is determined directly from the coarser level nodes, the accuracy at the coarse–fine boundary will be based on the coarser level spacing, not the finer. Although this causes a reduction in discretization accuracy across the coarse–fine boundary, the overall accuracy of the solution will remain intact as long as the boundary exists only in regions of the flow field where the flow is smooth and unchanging. This is accomplished by monitoring solution quantities, refining where the solution is changing frequently, and maintaining coarser grids where solution quantities are changing infrequently.

The gradient operator is treated in a similar fashion at the coarse–fine boundary. Recall that the gradient of element-centered quantities is computed at nodes by averaging the quantities to face centers and computing the gradient as the difference between faces on either side of the node (Figure 6.3). Once it has been computed on a coarser level, the gradient is copied to overlapping nodes on the finer level. Hanging nodes on the fine level are set to be an average of the nodal quantities on the coarser. This assures that the gradient will remain consistent between levels at the coarse–fine boundary. It will maintain the lower accuracy of the coarser level at the boundary, but the accuracy is consistent with the finite element discretization.

Solution of the Poisson equation in the two projection steps is done with a fast adaptive composite (FAC) algorithm, a multigrid-type scheme applied to nested refined grids that is particularly well suited to SAMR grid types. A red–black Gauss–Seidel smoother is used in each multigrid cycle and the discretization scheme proposed by Ewing et al. [17] is used at the coarse–fine boundaries. At the coarsest level, the multigrid solve is done through interfaces with the high-performance preconditioners (HYPRE) library [14].

6.2.3 Immersed Boundary Formulation

Implementing an immersed boundary representation into an existing Cartesian grid solver involves modifying the forcing on elements that contain the boundary, whether that is from modifying the actual equations solved or prescribing the boundary condition. In this work, we extend the finite difference-based immersed boundary method (IBM) of Tseng and Ferziger [34] to enforce boundary conditions for velocity and pressure in our finite element formulation.

In the IBM, the effect of a solid surface is included by modifying the values at ghost points so that the flow in the domain interior "feels" the presence of the wall. This allows inclusion of mountains, buildings, and other complex shapes without wrapping or stretching the grid. The ghost cell IBM of Ref. [34] is similar to other immersed boundary methods, for example, the method of Fadlun et. al [18] and the shaved cell approach of Adcroft et. al [1]. We chose the ghost cell method because, for our purposes, it offered the most flexibility and was straightforward to implement. The immersed boundary method is usually described as the addition of a force to the RHS of the momentum equations. The effect of the force is to prescribe the equivalent of a Dirichlet boundary condition on the solid immersed boundary. The desired velocity and pressure gradient boundary conditions can be applied directly without the need to solve the momentum equation at the boundary points. If the solid boundary happens to directly intersect Cartesian grid nodes, the scheme is equivalent to applying directly Dirichlet conditions at the grid node that intersects the boundary. With an arbitrary geometry, it is rare that grid points directly lie on the immersed boundary, so most boundary points are updated through interpolation (the details of which are in Ref. [34]).

Figure 6.6a gives an example of how the interior and exterior points are designated for an arbitrary boundary shape. A linear or quadratic interpolation procedure is used to represent (approximately) the prescribed conditions on the true immersed boundary using nearby points. The method uses points on the inside and outside of the immersed boundary. *Ghost points* are defined on the inside of the boundary and values at these points are assigned based on the *nearest neighbor* points just outside the boundary. Determination of ghost and nearest neighbor points is done automatically using the data computed through calls to geometry libraries (see Sections 6.3.2 and 6.3.3). As discussed in Ref. [34], instabilities can arise if the ghost point lies too close to the boundary. We circumvent this problem by simply assigning the point to the boundary (meaning the Dirichlet conditions are applied directly, with no interpolation) whenever the ghost point lies very close to the immersed boundary.

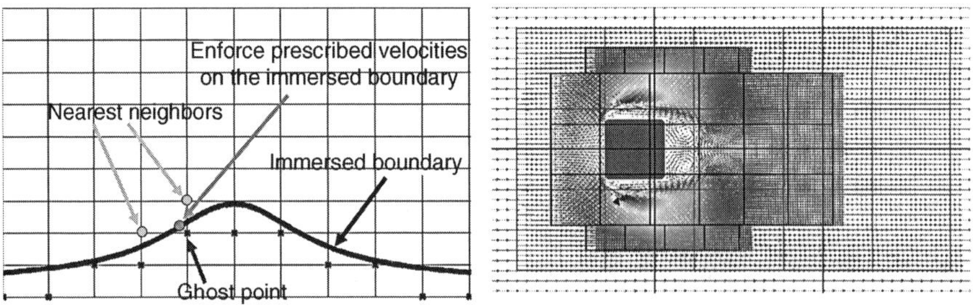

(a) Immersed boundary method

(b) Adaptive flow solution using FEM3MP and IBM

Figure 6.6 Immersed boundary treatment. Values are imposed on ghost points based on interpolated values from neighbor points in order to enforce the desired boundary condition.

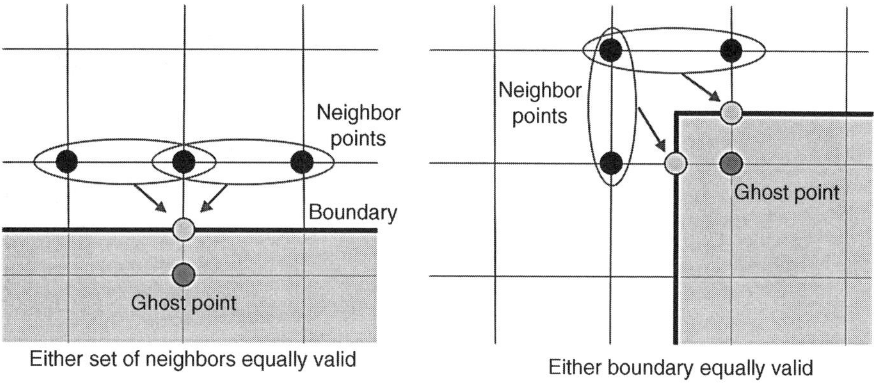

(a) Arbitrary choice of nearest neighbors

(b) Multiply-defined boundary for ghost point correction

Figure 6.7 Modeling polygonal shapes with an immersed boundary can introduce poorly defined correction scenarios, but these can be minimized through further grid adaptivity.

Some issues arise in modeling square and rectangular building boundaries with this IBM representation. Surfaces aligned with the Cartesian grid will have a degree of asymmetry in the choice of available nearest neighbor points (see Figure 6.7a). Also, in this scenario, the selection of which two of the three potential nearest neighbors can be arbitrary, with each particular choice potentially giving slightly different results. At corners, the ghost point could have a choice of multiple boundary locations from which it derives its corrected value (see Figure 6.7b). In practice, we found that these issues introduced some minor asymmetries in otherwise symmetric flow fields but the effects were generally minimal, particularly when summed over many components. More generous grid refinement in the affected regions further minimizes these effects.

Computing the identity and location of ghost points, boundary points, and nearest neighbors is nontrivial for geometrically complex boundaries. These quantities are computed by complex geometry infrastructures and provided for adaptive computations through SAMRAI. This interaction between these infrastructures is discussed in the next section.

6.3 INFRASTRUCTURES

Computational infrastructures played a critical role in the development of the adaptive embedded boundary formulation in FEM3MP. Building from scratch the core capabilities to perform parallel AMR calculations around thousands of buildings would have taken years of development. By leveraging existing infrastructures, we were effectively able to take advantage of significant amounts of code and algorithm development and testing that were originally directed at other applications.

Traditionally, urban simulations with FEM3MP have modeled buildings on grids that use contour mapping, an example of which is shown in Figure 6.8a. Grid lines are

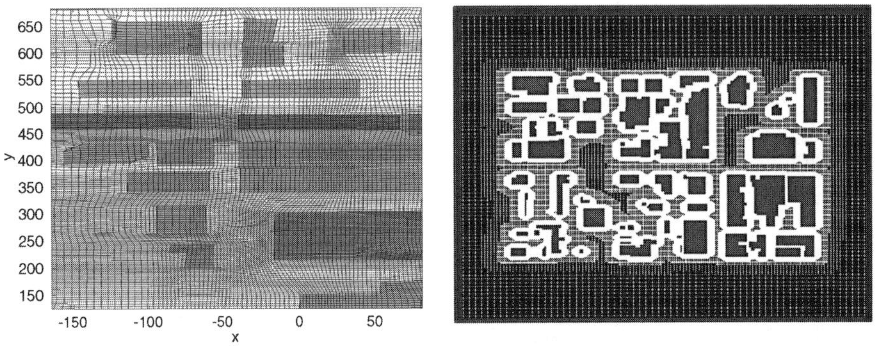

(a) Boundary conforming mesh (b) Adaptive embedded boundary grid

Figure 6.8 Boundary conforming meshes require tedious manual generation, while adaptive Cartesian embedded boundary meshes are fast and automatic. The five-level 1.7M grid point embedded boundary mesh shown above was generated in less than 2 min on a single processor workstation.

wrapped around buildings and points inside the building are blanked out. Although this approach yields accurate results in the flow calculations, the problem setup is not automated, and is time-consuming for large-scale cityscapes. This prompted our adoption of embedded boundary treatment, where solid geometry simply cuts through the cells of the Cartesian grid. Most of the domain is a uniform Cartesian grid, and only those cells or nodes next to the geometry need to be modified. This approach greatly alleviates the grid generation burden. For example, the grid in Figure 6.8a for buildings in Oklahoma City took almost a week of manipulation to generate. By contrast, the grid shown in Figure 6.8b for buildings in Salt lake City, with comparable complexity to the Oklahoma City case, was generated in less than 2 min using an embedded boundary approach.

To support different forms of urban geometry data, we adopted two complex infrastructures to handle complex geometry embedded boundary grid generation. *PatchCubes* operates on general surface triangulations representing surface topography coming from various terrain definitions or, in the case of complex buildings, through CAD-type engineering descriptions. *Eleven* manages grid generation from the polygonal descriptions in large-scale urban shapefiles. The ability to handle these different geometry types provides flexibility to operate on different geometric representations under different circumstances. For instance, shapefiles often contain geometric degeneracies that make it difficult to generate robust surface triangulations, requiring the polygonal capabilities in *Eleven*. At the same time, there are many shapes important to the urban flow field that cannot be defined through polygonal shapefiles (e.g., geometrically complex buildings, and hilly or mountainous terrain) that require triangulated surface representations and *patchCubes*. There are also circumstances where both infrastructures could be used simultaneously, an example of which would be embedding cityscape shapefiles together with topographic terrain information.

A good computational infrastructure should be flexible and extensible enough to work with different types of applications. Although in this work we implemented a particular numerical approach that operated on adaptive finite elements with an immersed boundary representation, our code framework provides a range of capabilities that can support cell- or node-based data and embedded or immersed boundary formulations. In this way, our adaptive complex geometry infrastructure could apply to other urban CFD codes as well.

The following sections provide further details of the *SAMRAI* framework that manages AMR operations, the *patchCubes* library that manages embedded boundary grid generation from triangulated surfaces, and the *Eleven* library that manages embedded or immersed boundary construction from shapefile definitions.

6.3.1 Structured AMR with *SAMRAI*

SAMRAI is an object-oriented framework developed at Lawrence Livermore National Lab that was designed from the outset to be a general purpose, extensible, and scalable infrastructure for a wide variety of parallel SAMR applications [22, 23]. It supports a variety of data representations (e.g., cell-, node-, and face-centered data) as well as data defined irregularly on the Cartesian mesh, examples of which are particles and the cut cell data structure used in this work. These features were designed to be fully extensible, so that users can configure their own data representations. SAMRAI manages the adaptive grid generation operations and parallel communication so that the application scientist using SAMRAI can focus on the numerical and algorithmic issues. Considerable work has gone into ensuring efficient scalable performance in SAMRAI for adaptive applications [20, 36].

SAMRAI uses a standard SAMR grid structure, consisting of a hierarchy of nested refinement levels with each level formed as a union of logically rectangular grid regions (Figure 6.9). All grid cells on a particular level have the same spacing, and the ratio of spacing between levels is generally a factor of 2 or 4, although it is possible in SAMRAI to use other refinement ratios as well. Simulation data are stored on patches in a structured fashion, using contiguous arrays that map directly to the grid cells without indirection, providing very efficient numerical operations.

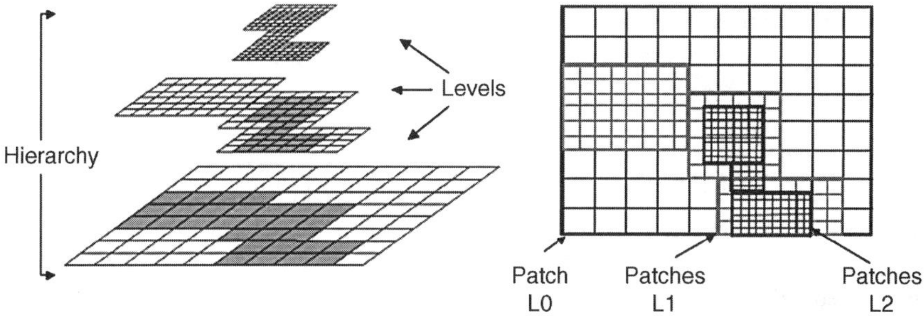

Figure 6.9 Block structured AMR implementation. The grid is composed of a hierarchy of nested levels of refinement, with each level consisting of logically rectangular regions referred to as "patches".

Levels are generated from coarsest to finest during initial construction of the grid hierarchy. The coarsest level defines the physical extent of the computational domain and each finer level is constructed by selecting cells on the next coarser level that require refinement. The criteria used to select cells for refinement is problem dependent. In our case, cells with close proximity to the solid geometry (i.e., those that were near to, or contained, a building boundary) were marked for refinement, as were those that exhibited flow conditions deemed important (e.g., regions of high shear stress, high contaminant concentration levels). Once marked, cells are then clustered to form the patches that will constitute the finer level. A consequence of this approach is that finer level patch boundaries always align with coarser cell boundaries. This facilitates data communication between levels and also the implementation of numerical methods on the hierarchy.

SAMRAI adaptively regenerates the patches to follow time-dependent features or track moving surfaces. Each "regrid" cycle involves constructing new levels and distributing them to processors. The initial grid generation steps are done in parallel by the CPU owning the old patch; once the patch layout for the new level is known, they are redistributed to processors in a load balanced way, and data are transferred from the old to the new set of patches. Specifically, the regrid algorithm proceeds using a four-step process: first, choose cells on the next coarser level that require refinement (i.e., *cell tagging*); second, construct new patch regions on the finer level from tagged cells on the coarser; third, move data from the old finer level to the newly generated one; and finaly, generate the new data dependency information required to exchange data at patch boundaries.

Between adaptive gridding steps, the governing equations are numerically integrated on the patches. Serial numerical operations are applied on each patch simultaneously by each processor. At specified synchronization points data are exchanged between processors using MPI communication operations to update the solution at patch boundaries. The patch boundary updates automatically apply the finite element discretization operations outlined in equations (6.11) and (6.12) at boundaries of patches on the same level, and at coarse–fine boundaries, respectively. The parallel communication for all these operations is entirely managed by SAMRAI.

To exploit the efficiency of structured Cartesian meshes, the same numerical integration algorithm is applied on all elements of the mesh, as if a boundary were not present. Then the solution is corrected on those elements containing the boundary to enforce the appropriate boundary conditions, using the algorithm outlined in Section 6.2.3.

6.3.2 Surface Triangulation Representation with *patchCubes*

The embedded boundary mesh generator *cubes* is part of the Cart3D [2] CFD package from NASA Ames. The package was developed in the 1990s and is currently used extensively for rapid analysis of geometrically complex aerospace vehicles. In this section, we describe the unstructured cell-based refinement used in *cubes* and

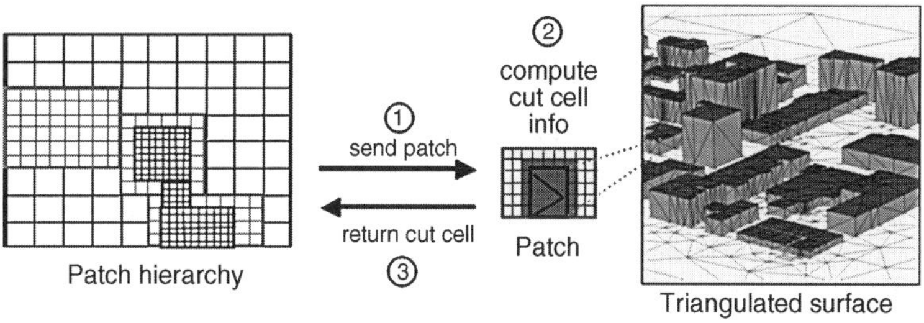

Figure 6.10 Interface between SAMRAI and *patchCubes*. SAMRAI dynamically constructs patches that make up the adaptive mesh hierarchy. PatchCubes is called by each patch to construct only the embedded boundary representation.

how it was converted to work on structured grid patches in a new library called *patchCubes*.

Cubes is a fast, unstructured, cell-based embedded boundary mesh generator that operates serially for steady-state flow computations. SAMRAI, at its core, can be viewed as a parallel, time-dependent memory and data structure manager, controlling patch placement and manipulating data in parallel. The *patchCubes* library provides a way to compute the cut cell embedded boundary information on each patch simultaneously using the serial, cell-based algorithms on each processor (Figure 6.10). Thus, SAMRAI's embedded boundary mesh is constructed completely in parallel. We first describe *cubes*, and then the simple modifications that allowed us to build this parallel version.

Cubes is a multilevel mesh generator originally developed for aerodynamic applications. It takes as input a watertight surface triangulation of the geometry and works in two phases. The first phase tags cells in an initially uniform coarse mesh until it reaches the desired level of mesh refinement. The refinement decision in this phase is purely based on geometry, using only the variation of triangle normals within cells. For efficiency, triangles are stored in an alternating digital tree [4] to easily determine the triangle–cell intersections. If a mesh cell is determined to need refinement, a buffer layer of cells around it is also refined, so that the resulting mesh is smooth. Interfaces between cells that have been refined are restricted such that adjacent cells are no more than one level apart. The second phase generates the detailed cut cell information for the embedded cells in this final multilevel mesh. The output consists of a list of all cells and faces in the Cartesian mesh, with the cells categorized as either full (i.e., uncut) or cut. Cells that lie within a solid surface are omitted. If a cell is cut, *cubes* computes the information needed by a second-order finite volume scheme: cell volume, face areas, cell and face centroids, as well as area and centroids of the triangles that intersect the cut cells.

Input parameters required for *cubes* include the surface triangulation, domain bounding box, initial coarse mesh size, and maximum number of refinement levels. This minimal set of information is the only parameter one needs to specify. *Cubes* uses a lightweight unstructured face-based data structure that consists of an array of cells and an array of faces where each face points to the left and right cells on either side.

The unstructured representation means that, although the mesh is Cartesian, there is no multidimensional IJK organization of cells as would be the case in a structured grid representation, so neighboring cells cannot be directly accessed.

When joined with SAMRAI, cubes no longer needs to decide where to refine. This, along with managing the construction of the mesh hierarchy and all of the AMR operations, is completely determined by SAMRAI. Since SAMRAI and *cubes* both use a Cartesian mesh description of the underlying domain along with a hierarchical description of each level, they already "speak the same language."

The decision of when and where to apply refinement is made by SAMRAI, so the algorithms in *cubes* that decide where to refine are no longer necessary, which led to a number of simplifications. There are two main conceptual differences between the unstructured mesh generator *cubes* and the cut cell engine needed for structured AMR patches. First, *patchCubes* is needed to separate the notion of the domain bounding box from the region of cut cell generation. In the original *cubes*, these were one and the same, but for patch-based treatment the region of cut cell generation is typically a small subset of the domain bounding box. The second more computationally important difference is that mesh faces between uncut cells do not need to be explicitly computed. SAMR does not need an explicit representation of an uncut face; it is implicitly available on a structured mesh, and all information about it is easily computed when needed. Only the cut face information needs to be supplied. This allows us to simplify *cubes* by refining only the cut cells, not the uncut cells, to the level of refinement of the requested patch. Large uncut cells could remain at the coarsest level in the intermediate mesh used by *cubes*, since the face information associated with the refinements was not needed.

These two simplifications made the interface rather straightforward. SAMRAI passes individual patches at a given level, and starting from the coarsest level, *patchCubes* "tags" all the cut cells in the patch bounding box until they reach the requested level. Only cut cells need to be tagged because if a large coarse cell is uncut, all its children are also uncut. For patches that lie on finer levels, *cubes* begins by using the underlying coarse representation. This is more efficient because it is faster to compute triangle intersection information on coarse cells and pass it on to the refined children rather than computing it from scratch on the finest level requested. However, one consequence is that the coarse cells often extend outside the requested boundaries of the patch because building a coarser representation of a requested fine cell region usually results in coarse cells extending outside the original patch boundaries (Figure 6.11). This is a relatively small inefficiency compared to the efficiency gained by using the coarse cell information to guide construction of the boundary on fine cells. In the final transfer of information from the internal data structure to the patch data structure, a coarse cell can simply mark its embedded fine cells as uncut, and no other information is needed. There is also no need to apply any mesh smoothing rules, so this part of the process that is typically done by *cubes* was turned off.

When cut cell information for a new patch is requested, SAMRAI already knows the type of cells (flow, cut, solid) on a coarser level. This allows SAMRAI to approximately load balance the cut cell generation along with the other computational estimates. This old information could be used for additional efficiency

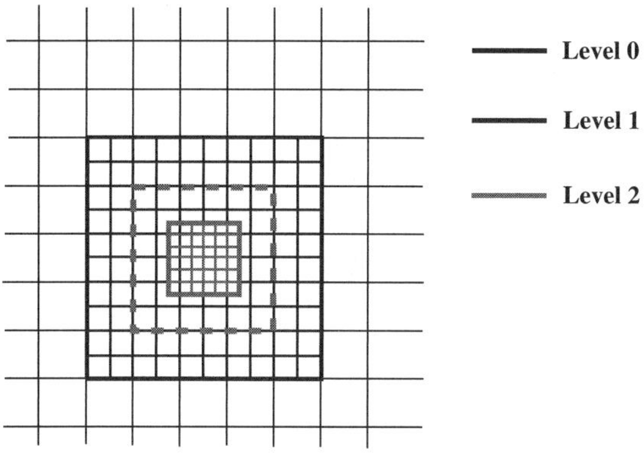

Figure 6.11 Example of finer level computations in *patchCubes*. The solid pink line shows a fine level 2 patch requested from SAMRAI. The patch is automatically enlarged to fit the grid on level 1, shown by the dotted pink line, and the level 1 region is enlarged to fit within the coarse level 0 grid. The enlargement operations all happen within *patchCubes*, only the requested patch data are actually returned to SAMRAI.

enhancements, such as shrinking the patch to include only the cut cells, or transferring cut cell information from overlapping old patches. In practice, we have found those steps to be slower than simply regenerating the information from scratch, but further investigation may be warranted in the future.

This patch-based approach suggests a natural domain decomposition approach for parallelization, which is further discussed in Section 6.4.

6.3.3 Polygonal and Curved Representation with *Eleven*

Eleven is a library that is part of the Overture [21] package from Lawrence Livermore National Lab. It supports cut cell grid generation for large-scale polygonal city representations through interfaces to ESRI shapefiles [16]. The ESRI shapefile data file is a standard method for representing large urban geometries. Shapefiles representing cities essentially consist of a collection of polygons; an accompanying database provides an elevation for each polygon. A single building is represented by one or more polygons extruded from a plane to the provided elevation. For example, Figure 6.12a depicts the collection of polygons used to represent the Chrysler building in New York City. The accompanying 3D depiction of the building in Figure 6.12b illustrates the geometry after extrusion by the provided elevations for each polygon. In this case, 186 polygons are used to represent a single building. In a city as large as New York, the number of polygons grows quickly as more of the city is included. Figure 6.13a shows a large section of lower Manhattan, consisting of more than 22,000 polygons. This large data set was read into *Eleven's* representation and rendered in less than 3 s.

Since shapefiles are limited to extrusions of polygons, complex buildings with overhangs and curved surfaces are not well represented. Furthermore, shapefiles often

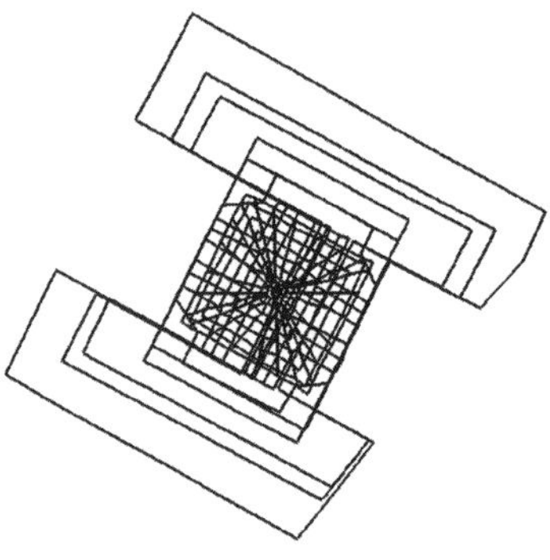

(a) Polygons representing the Chrysler building

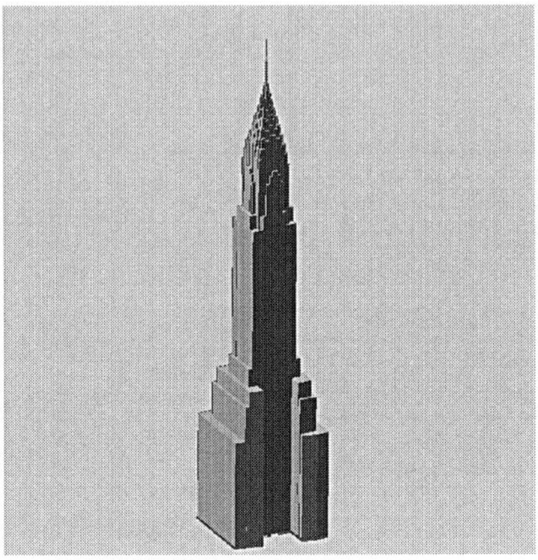

(b) The polygons extruded into a 3D representation

Figure 6.12 Shapefiles represent complicated buildings as the union of extruded polygons.

suffer from geometric degeneracies that, together with the sheer size of some data sets (more than 64,000 polygons), make the generation of watertight triangulations impractical. *Eleven* provides an interface for querying the polygonal geometry directly, thereby eliminating the need for a robust triangulation. The shapefile data are read into *Eleven*'s representation using an open source utility called *shapelib* [35]. This direct access to the geometry allows simulation tools to read in large data sets and generate grids in a matter of minutes. For example, 13 million cell grid of the Madison Square Garden region from a surface consisting of several thousand polygons shown in Figure 6.13b was generated in less than 10 min using SAMRAI's interface to *Eleven*.

(a) Polygonal representation of a section of lower Manhattan (22,000 polygons)

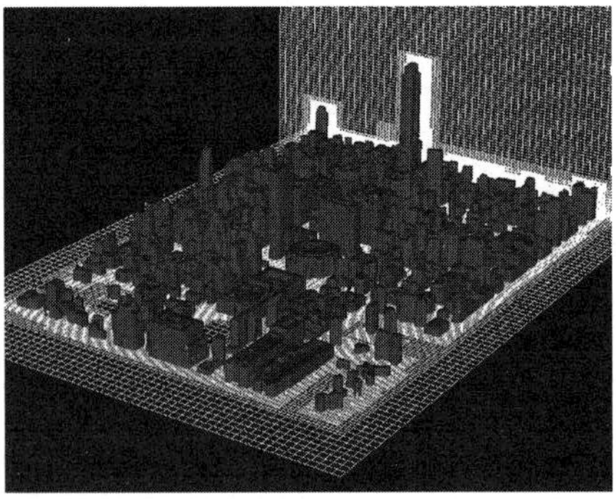

(b) Adaptive grid around the Madison Square Garden area

Figure 6.13 *Eleven* can efficiently represent large numbers of buildings and construct a boundary representation on the adaptive grid through queries on the large data set.

In urban applications, *Eleven* primarily operates on polygonal definitions, but its underlying representation for all curves and surfaces is the nonuniform rational B-Spline (NURBS) [29]. More complicated boundary representations can be represented as a collection of NURBS. Since shapefiles provide only piecewise linear curves, there are only as many control points as there are corners in the polygon. While higher order NURBS, that is, quadratic and higher curves, can be represented, only linear curves are currently utilized by the immersed boundary method described in Section 6.2.3. Collections of curves (2D) or surfaces (3D) may be used in the future to describe more complicated shapes. For data from shapefiles, NURBS curves are used to represent the polygon, while the elevation is stored as auxiliary data. Like the approach used in *patchCubes*, boundary generation queries are posed to a mesh patch, with the computations on each patch proceeding independently.

For the New York City dispersion calculation depicted earlier in Figure 6.2b, a first-order boundary approximation was used that requires the classification of nodes as either inside or outside a building. To determine the inside/outside classification for each node, *Eleven* uses a ray-tracing predicate combined with the mark-and-sweep algorithm depicted in Figure 6.14. The process begins by building a geometric search tree containing the bounding boxes of all the polygons provided by the shapefile. This search tree, based on the alternating digital tree described in Ref. [4], allows the fast determination of intersection candidates for the ray-tracing algorithm. Each

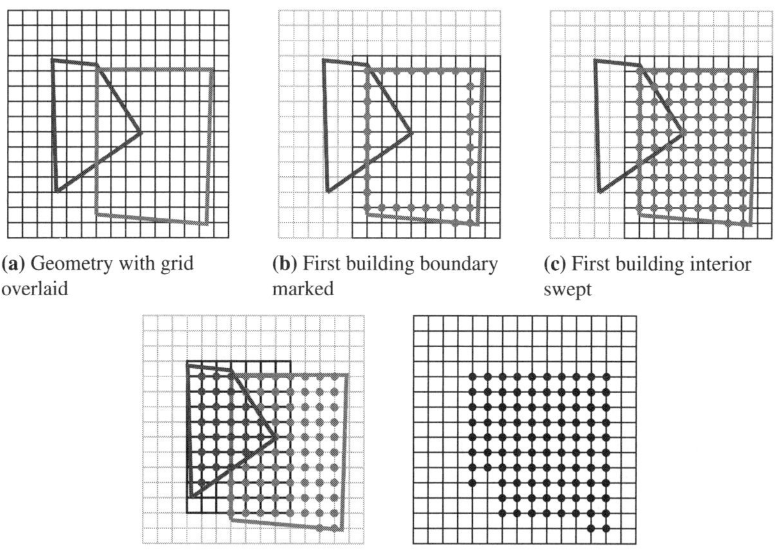

(a) Geometry with grid overlaid

(b) First building boundary marked

(c) First building interior swept

(d) Second building classification

(e) Complete classification

Figure 6.14 Vertices in a grid patch are classified as either inside or outside; dots mark inside points in this figure. Classification is performed only on the subpatch that covers a particular building. Expensive inside/outside computations are performed only on the points immediately near the boundary of the polygon line segments; the rest of the interior is swept from the boundary data.

x-y plane in the 3D is processed in 2D independently since the buildings are simple extrusions. Elevation from the shapefile database is incorporated by performing the 2D classification for each grid plane in the z direction. An additional condition is introduced that skips polygons whose elevation is below that of the current plane. This approach generates a 3D grid using essentially only 2D queries. Each polygon that overlaps the grid plane is used to classify points on the boundaries of the buildings, as shown in Figure 6.14a. This marking proceeds by looping through the line segments comprising each polygon; first, using the geometry of each line segment, determine nearby grid points, and then use the ray tracing algorithm to classify the nodes near the curve. The ray tracing is only performed for nodes that have not already been classified as inside. Given the classifications of the points along the boundaries of the buildings, the remainder of the grid can be filled by sweeping through each grid line.

Higher order accurate boundary conditions require more information about the boundary than the simple inside–outside classification. The immersed boundary method presented in Section 6.2.3 requires only the identification of the nodes immediately adjacent to the boundary and the closest points on the geometry to each of these nodes. The points immediately adjacent to the curve, but outside the geometry, that is, the ghost nodes, are found using a two-step process. A piecewise linear approximation (i.e., polygonal) to the curve is used to compute a provisional classification of the nodes as either inside or outside the geometry (as above). Once this provisional classification has been made, it is trivial to identify candidate ghost points. These points are only candidates, however, since using only the piecewise linear approximation often produces erroneous classifications when a higher order curve represents the geometry.

For each ghost point, P_g, the closest point on the curve is computed by minimizing

$$F(u_g) = \left|C(u_g) - P_g\right|^2. \tag{6.13}$$

where u_g is the parameter value of the closest point on the curve C. *Eleven* uses Newton's method, modified to accommodate composite curves, to solve this minimization problem. A by-product of this projection process is an approximation to the normal of the curve, $\mathbf{n}_g = P_g - C(u_g)$, at u_g. For many higher order boundary conditions, this information is sufficient [25, 34].

Once provisional ghost points have been identified using the piecewise linear approximation, $\mathbf{n}_g$ is compared to the normal, and $\mathbf{n}_c$ computed directly from the derivative of the curve at u_g. This normal is adjusted so that it always points outside the domain. With this orientation, points are misclassified if $\mathbf{n}_g \cdot \mathbf{n}_c < 0$; such nodes have their classifications switched. Three-dimensional extensions of this method are being developed that can query composite trimmed-NURBS boundary representations for immersed and embedded boundary applications.

6.4 PARALLEL IMPLEMENTATION

Urban CFD calculations are computationally intensive enough such that the efficiency improvements provided through mesh refinement and embedded boundary gridding alone are insufficient if they are limited to serial computer systems. To take advantage of the computing power available from parallel computer systems, all operations must be implemented with a scalable approach.

SAMRAI uses an MPI-based domain decomposition approach to parallelize the computational work. As discussed in Section 6.3.1, a simulation can be decomposed into numerical operations that advance the governing equations in time on a fixed set of patches, followed by adaptive gridding operations to construct new patches and transfer data from the old to new grid system. During the time advancement phase, serial numerical routines operate on data residing on separate patches, which have been assigned to different processors, and data are communicated between patches to copy or interpolate data at patch boundaries. This phase is highly scalable and exhibits good parallel performance if the patches are distributed to processors in a load balanced way. Indeed, many useful calculations can be run on a fixed set of refined grids. However, we are interested in using this tool to automatically adapt to changing plume conditions using a time-varying adaptive grid. Achieving scalable performance in the adaptive gridding operations is much more challenging. See Refs[20, 36] for further discussion of the issues of parallel adaptive gridding in SAMRAI. In the rest of this section, we focus specifically on new considerations for parallel embedded boundary grid generation. In particular, how to deal with the nonuniformity of the computational work on patches during parallel embedded boundary grid generation, and how this affects the performance of the overall adaptive gridding operations.

The total computational work on a patch is a sum of both the time advancement and the embedded boundary grid generation phases. The time advancement cost is affected by the total number of cells (or nodes) on the patch, while the grid generation cost is affected by the number of cut cells on the patch. If the number of cut cells is known, the total computational cost can be reliably estimated as

$$t_{\text{patch}} = t_{\text{n}} \times \#\text{Cells} + t_{\text{b}} \times \#CutCells + t_{\text{o}}. \tag{6.14}$$

where t_{n} is the per-cell time to compute the numerics (i.e., governing equations), t_{b} is the per-cell time to compute the embedded boundary, and t_{o} is a small overhead incurred by each patch. For example, a patch that does not intersect the boundary, and hence has no cut cells, will incur the cost of the numerics (t_{n} times the total number of cells on the patch) plus a small overhead t_{o} for calling *patchCubes* to determine that no cut cells were found on the patch. Patches that do intersect the boundary and have cut cells incur the additional cost of computing the information on those cells (t_{b} times the number of cut cells). The sum of these gives an estimate of the computational cost on a patch. Of course, the values of t_{n}, t_{b}, and t_{o} will depend on the characteristics of the machine and the algorithms used for the numerics and the embedded boundary construction but will be largely problem independent. We determined values of t_{n}, t_{b}, and t_{o} using a least squares fit from statistics gathered from a computation of a plume evolution around buildings in Salt Lake City. For this calculation, we recorded the total number of cells on the patch, the number of cut cells on the patch, and the computation time on that patch. From these data, we computed t_{n} and t_{o} by considering patches that contained no cut cells, and t_{b} by additionally considering those patches that did.

The estimate of the workload is used for load balancing the patches across parallel processors. Although the total number of cells on each patch is known before load balancing, the number of cut cells is not known exactly until after the patches have been distributed and the embedded or immersed boundary is computed. Hence, we have to rely on an estimate. Using information from the underlying coarse grid, as well as from old fine patches that overlap the new patch regions, we can get a relatively reliable estimate of the number of cut cells expected on the new patch. As the results will show, this approach works sufficiently well on clusters up to several hundred processors. For larger problems run on more processors, a more detailed investigation of the costs and overheads is likely needed.

Once the workload estimate is complete, patches are assigned to processors and each makes its own calls to the geometry libraries to compute the embedded/immersed boundary information. This can be done independently by each patch, without communication, making the procedure embarrassingly parallel. Each processor does have to know the surface representation, whether it be a surface triangulation or a shapefile description. This requires a small overhead at startup to broadcast the geometry. From a memory standpoint, the coarse surface representation is generally quite small and does not require significant storage. In practice, we have found that even a large surface geometry composed of several hundred thousand triangles, or tens or thousands of polygons, does not pose a problem on modern day machines.

Parallel performance for only the grid generation phase was measured on the MCR LINUX cluster at LLNL for a problem that tracked a plume moving over a set of arbitrary buildings in Salt Lake City (Figure 6.15a). A total of five levels were used, with horizontal grid spacing of 32 to 1m from the coarsest to finest levels, respectively. The grids automatically adapted to follow the plume as it moved around the buildings. The urban terrain was defined through a triangulated surface and the

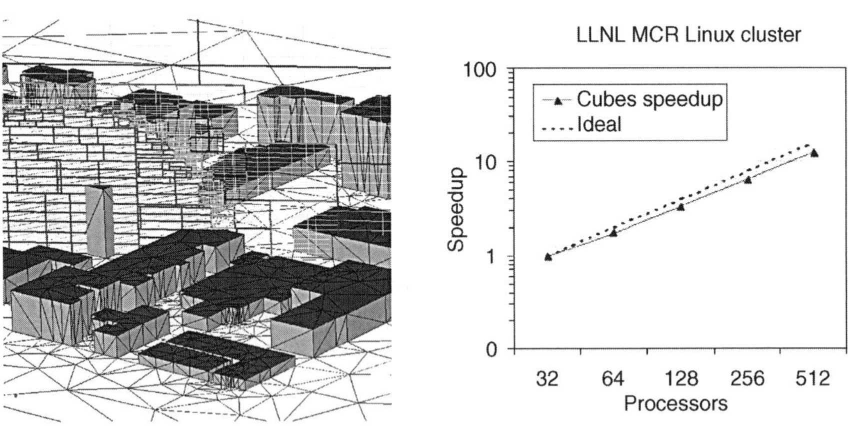

(a) Plume-tracking adaptive grid (b) Parallel performance

Figure 6.15 Parallel performance for adaptive grid generation. Adaptivity tracks an expanding plume over set of buildings defined by a triangulated surface. Shaded boxes show patch outlines at different levels.

boundary was computed using *patchCubes*. Figure 6.15b shows the parallel speedup of the grid generation only, measured on 32–512 processors. A load imbalance of 20–30% is observed on each processor partition, due to the extra cost of computing the embedded boundary on those patches that contain it. However, although the imbalance introduces some inefficiency, the level of imbalance remains roughly uniform across the different processor partitions tested, so the observed degree of scaling is quite good. Because the problem was not scaled, that is, the workload per processor decreases as the number of processors increase, some drop in scaling efficiency on the largest processor partitions is expected, independent of the embedded boundary calculation.

6.5 FUTURE WORK

Developing accurate predictive capabilities for flow in urban environments is an important but extremely complicated problem. The multiscale nature of urban environments, with turbulent physics and thermodynamic effects ranging from regional to the street-level scales, makes it a natural candidate for adaptive mesh refinement. This work demonstrated the potential advantages of AMR, showing that adaptive meshes could resolve flows at the building level with an order of magnitude fewer grid points than a comparably accurate uniform grid calculation. Our prototypes, however, only scratch the surface of a much more complicated problem. More work is needed in both algorithm development and validation in order to answer important unresolved questions, such as where to optimally place refinement to achieve the best results. Through the use of coarse mesh spacing to extend the far field boundaries, AMR offers the potential to extend the urban boundaries much farther than what is possible with a uniform grid code. This makes coupling with coarse resolution meso- or regional-scale models an attractive way to provide more accurate input conditions. This coupling of mesh *and* model refinement could extend the modeling framework to apply across many more scales in the urban atmospheric environment.

The use of rapid embedded boundary gridding technology for the complex urban topography demonstrated huge automation and efficiency improvements. For example, regions that formerly took a week to generate grids around could be gridded automatically in less than 2 min. Regions of downtown Manhattan that contained thousands of geometrically complex buildings, which would have taken weeks to months with manual tools, were gridded in less than 10 min with these tools. If a shapefile surface description is used, however, construction of the shapefile itself introduces a significant bottleneck. Shapefiles are difficult and time-consuming to generate and are consequently available only for a selected number of cities. This effectively limits the CFD tools to those cities where shapefiles exist. Aircraft-acquired high-resolution LIDAR terrain data provide a possible alternative to this limitation. LIDAR data exist for most regions of the United States and can be acquired in a couple of days for regions where it does not. The ability to use LIDAR data directly would significantly broaden the applicability of urban CFD models to a much wider variety of cityscapes. Because our gridding tools have the ability to handle general surface triangulations, they can operate directly on a terrain surface generated from

LIDAR. Automated tools are still needed to filter the data to remove "noisy" effects, and further study is needed on the accuracy ramifications.

Turbulence modeling in atmospheric applications is critical to achieving proper effects across the different scales of the problem. Although RANS models are appropriate for steady-state or slowly evolving continuous release flows, LES is more appropriate for time-dependent and rapidly evolving flows. AMR techniques hold the potential to dramatically improve LES simulations by automatically increasing resolution in regions of high velocity gradients where the turbulent eddies are formed. We did not investigate the use of AMR with LES, nor the effects from embedded boundary representations on the LES predictions. These important effects require further investigation.

Finally, it is important to point out the benefits that infrastructures provided to this work. Developing from scratch a code that is able to perform large-scale parallel AMR computations on urban geometries consisting of thousands of buildings would have taken years of code development. By adopting the computational infrastructure SAMRAI, and the gridding libraries *patchCubes* and *Eleven*, we were able to leverage numerous capabilities that were originally developed and tested for other applications. The overall code framework developed through linking these infrastructures was applied to urban dispersion applications with FEM3MP, but only the serial numerical kernels are specific to this application. The framework that manages parallel adaptive grid generation over complex urban topographies is general purpose and could be applied to any number of computational engineering applications.

ACKNOWLEDGMENTS

Brian Gunney and Craig Kapfer made numerous significant contributions to the codes and algorithms described. Stevens Chan and David Stevens were instrumental in assisting us with the FEM3MP code. The authors gratefully acknowledge the many useful discussions with the SAMRAI development team. The lead author resided at Lawrence Livermore National Laboratory during the development of the work described.

LLNL authors performed this work under the auspices of the U.S. Department of Energy by the University of California Lawrence Livermore National Laboratory under Contract No. W-7405-Eng-48 and Report No. UCRL-MI-223156.

The work of Marsha Berger was supported in part by AFOSR grant F49620-00-0099 and DOE grants DE-FG02-00ER25053 and DE-FC02-01ER25472.

REFERENCES

1. A. Adcroft, C. Hill, and J. Marshall. Representation of topography by shaved cells in a height coordinate ocean model. *Mon. Weather Rev.*, 125(9):2293–315, 1997.
2. M. Aftosmis, M. Berger, and J. Melton. Robust and efficient cartesian mesh generation for component-based geometry. *AIAA J.*, 36(6):952–960, 1998.

3. M. Aftosmis, M. Berger, and J. Melton. Adaptive Cartesian mesh generation. In J. F. Thompson, B. K. Soni, and N. P. Weatherill, editors, *Handbook of Grid Generation.* CRC Press, Boca Raton, FL, 1999, pp. 22-1–22-26.
4. J. Bonet and J. Peraire. An alternating digital tree (ADT) algorithm for 3D geometric searching and intersection problems. *Int. J. Numer. Methods Eng.*, 31:1–17, 1991.
5. J. P. Boris. The threat of chemical and biological terrorism: preparing a response. *Comput. Sci. Eng.*, 4(2):22–32, 2002.
6. R.E. Britter and S. R. Hanna. Flow and dispersion in urban areas. *Ann. Rev. Fluid Mech.*, 35:469–496, 2003.
7. M. J. Brown. Urban dispersion—challenges for fast response modeling. *5th Symposium on the Urban Environment, American Meteorological Society*, 2004. Paper 5.1.
8. S. Chan and D. Stevens. Evaluation of two advanced turbulence models for simulating the flow and dispersion around buildings. *The Millennium NATO/CCMS International Technical Meeting on Air Pollution Modeling and its Application*, Boulder, CO, May 2000, pp. 355–362.
9. S. Chan, D. Stevens, and W. Smith. Validation of two CFD urban dispersion models using high resolution wind tunnel data. *3rd International Symposium on Environmental Hydraulics*, 2001, p. 107.
10. S. Chan and M. Leach. A validation of FEM3MP with Joint Urban 2003 data. *J. Appl. Meteorol. Clim.*, 46(12):2127–2146, 2007.
11. S. T. Chan and M. J. Leach. Simulation of an urban 2000 experiment with various time-dependent forcing. *5th Symposium on the Urban Environment, American Meteorological Society*, 2004.
12. S. T. Chan and J. Lundquist. A verification of FEM3MP predictions against field data from two releases of the joint urban 2003 experiment. *9th GMU Conference on Atmospheric Transport and Dispersion Modeling*, Fairfax, VA, July 18–20, 2005.
13. A. J. Chorin. Numerical solution of the Navier–Stokes equations. *Math. Comput.*, 22:745–762, 1968.
14. E. Chow, A. J. Cleary, and R. D. Falgout. Design of the hypre preconditioner library. Technical Report UCRL-JC-132025, Lawrence Livermore National Laboratory, Livermore, CA, 1998.
15. P. Colella, D. T. Graves, B. J. Keen, and D. Modiano. A Cartesian grid embedded boundary method for hyperbolic conservation laws. *J. Comput. Phys.*, 211:346–366, 2006.
16. ESRI Shapefile Technical Description. Technical report, Environmental Systems Research Institute Inc. www.esri.com/library/whitepapers/pdfs/shapefile.pdf, 1997.
17. R. Ewing, R. Lazarov, and P. Vassilevski. Local refinement techniques for elliptic problems on cell-centered grids. *Numer. Math.*, 59(1):431–452, 1991.
18. E. A. Fadlun, R. Verzicco, P. Orlandi, and J. Mohd-Yusof. Combined immersed-boundary finite-difference methods for three-dimensional complex flow simulations. *J. Comput. Phys.*, 161(1):35–60, 2000.
19. P. M. Gresho and R. L. Sani. *Incompressible Flow and the Finite Element Method.* John Wiley & Sons, Ltd., New York, 1998.
20. B. T. N. Gunney, A. M. Wissink, and D. A. Hysom. Parallel clustering algorithms for structured AMR. *J. Parallel Distrib. Comput.*, 66:1419–1430, 2006.
21. W. D. Henshaw. Overture: an object-oriented framework for overlapping grid applications. In *Proceedings of the 32nd American Institute for Aeronautics Fluid Dynamics*, St. Louis, MO, June 24–27, 2002. See `http://www.llnl.gov/CASC/Overture`.
22. R. D. Hornung and S. R. Kohn. Managing application complexity in the SAMRAI object-oriented framework. *Concurrency Comput. Pract. Exper.*, 14:347–368, 2002.
23. R. D. Hornung, A. M. Wissink, and S. R. Kohn. Managing complex data and geometry in parallel structured AMR applications. *Eng. Comput.*, 22(3):181–195, 2006.
24. A. Huber, P. Georrgopoulos, R. Gilliam, G. Stenchikov, S. W. Wang, B. Kelly, and H. Feingersh. Modeling air pollution from the collapse of the World Trade center and assessing the potential impacts on human exposures. *Environ. Manager.*, 35–40, 2004.
25. H. O. Kreiss and N. A. Petersson. A second order accurate embedded boundary method for the wave equation with dirichlet data. *SIAM J. Sci. Comput.*, 27(4):1141–1167, 2006.

26. M. J. Leach, S. T. Chan, and J. K. Lundquist. High-resolution CFD simulation of airflow and tracer dispersion in New York City. *6th Symposium on the Urban Environment, 86th Annual Meeting of the American Meteorological Society*, 2006.
27. R. Mittal and G. Iaccarino. Immersed boundary methods. *Ann. Rev. Fluid Mech.*, 37:239–261, 2005.
28. G. Patnaik, J. P. Boris, F. F. Grinstein, and J. P. Iselin. Large scale urban simulation with the miles approach. *AIAA CFD Conference*. AIAA Paper 2003-4101, 2003.
29. L. Piegl and W. Tiller. *The NURBS Book 2nd edition*. Springer, 1997.
30. J. Pullen, J. P. Boris, T. Young, G. Patnaik, and J. Iselin. A comparison of contaminant plume statistics from a Gaussian puff and urban CFD model for two large cities. *Atmos. Environ.*, 39:1049–1068, 2005.
31. W. S. Smith, M. J. Brown, and D. S. DeCroix. Evaluation of CFD simulations using laboratory data and urban field experiments. Paper 1.6. *4th Symposium on the Urban Environment, American Meteorological Society*, 2002, p. 2.
32. D. E. Stevens, S. T. Chan, and P. Gresho. An approximate projection method for incompressible flow. *International J. Numer. Methods Fluids*, 40:1303–1325, 2002.
33. G. Sugiyama and J. S. Nasstrom. Overview of LLNL services and tools for the National Atmospheric Release Advisory Center (NARAC) and Interagency Modeling and Atmospheric Assessment Center (IMAAC). Technical Report UCRL-PRES-223394, Lawrence Livermore National Laboratory, Livermore, CA, 2006.
34. Y. H. Tseng and J. H. Ferziger. A ghost-cell immersed boundary method for flow in complex geometry. *J. Comput. Phys.*, 192(2):593–623, 2003.
35. F. Warmerdam. Shapefile C library v1.2. http://shapelib.maptools.org/, 1998.
36. A. M. Wissink, D. Hysom, and R. D. Hornung. Enhancing scalability of parallel structured AMR calculations. In *Proceedings of the 17th ACM International Conference on Supercomputing (ICS03)*, San Francisco, CA, June 2003, pp. 336–347.
37. A. M. Wissink, B. Kosovic, K. Chand, M. Berger, B. Gunney, C. Kapfer, and F. K. Chow. Adaptive urban dispersion integrated model. Paper J4.7. *6th Symposium on the Urban Environment, 86th Annual Meeting of the American Meteorological Society*, 2006.

Chapter 7

Parallel and Adaptive Simulation of Cardiac Fluid Dynamics

Boyce E. Griffith, Richard D. Hornung, David M. McQueen, and Charles S. Peskin

7.1 INTRODUCTION

Like many problems in biofluid mechanics, cardiac mechanics can be modeled as the dynamic interaction of a viscous incompressible fluid (the blood) and an incompressible viscoelastic structure (the muscular walls and the valves of the heart and the walls of the great vessels). The immersed boundary method [1] is both a mathematical formulation and a numerical approach to such problems of *fluid–structure interaction*. The immersed boundary method describes the configuration of the elastic structure with Lagrangian variables (i.e., variables indexed by a coordinate system attached to the elastic structure), and describes the momentum, velocity, and incompressibility of the coupled fluid–structure system with Eulerian variables (i.e., in reference to fixed physical coordinates). In the continuous equations of motion, these two descriptions are connected by making use of the Dirac delta function, whereas a regularized version of the delta function is used to link the Lagrangian and Eulerian quantities in the discretized equations of motion. This framework for fluid–structure interaction problems was introduced by Peskin to study the fluid dynamics of heart valves [2, 3] and has subsequently been used with three-dimensional models of the left ventricle [4, 5] and the whole heart and nearby great

Advanced Computational Infrastructures For Parallel and Distributed Adaptive Applications. Edited by Manish Parashar and Xiaolin Li

vessels [6, 7], as well as for a variety of other biofluid dynamic problems. Just in relation to cardiovascular physiology, it has also been used to simulate platelet aggregation [8–10], the deformation of red blood cells in shear flow [11, 12], and flow in blood vessels [13–16].

Simulating blood flow in the heart by the immersed boundary method requires the use of high spatial resolution, but this requirement is somewhat localized to the flow in the neighborhood of the immersed elastic structures, that is the heart valve leaflets, the muscular heart walls, and the walls of the great vessels. For the flow within the chambers of the heart but away from the immersed elastic structures, the need for high resolution is lessened somewhat, although it may be required in regions of high vorticity in the interior of the flow, for example near vortices that are shed from the free edges of the heart valve leaflets. For problems that possess localized fine-scale features, computational resources are more efficiently utilized by employing adaptive techniques, whereby high spatial resolution is deployed locally where it is most needed and comparatively coarse resolution is employed where it suffices.

Over the last several years, we have developed a new adaptive and distributed-memory parallel version of the immersed boundary method [17, 18]. This scheme is formally second-order accurate in the sense that second-order convergence rates are obtained for sufficiently smooth problems [19]. We take the same hierarchical structured grid approach as the two-dimensional adaptive immersed boundary method of Roma et al. [20, 21], but we use a somewhat different numerical scheme. Briefly, we employ a strong stability-preserving Runge–Kutta method [22] for the time integration of the Lagrangian equations of motion and a projection method [23–25] for the time integration of the Eulerian equations of motion that employs an implicit L-stable discretization of the viscous terms [26] and an explicit second-order Godunov method for the nonlinear advection terms [27–29]. As in most recent projection methods for locally refined grids [28–30], the present scheme does not produce a velocity field that "exactly" satisfies the discrete divergence-free condition. Instead, we employ a projection that is "approximate," so that the discrete divergence of the velocity only *converges* to zero at a second-order rate as the computational grid is refined. When such approximate projection methods are employed in the context of the immersed boundary method, we have demonstrated [17, 19] that it is beneficial to employ a *hybrid* approximate projection method similar to the inviscid scheme of Ref. [31], in which the updated velocity and pressure are determined by solving two different approximate projection equations. Such a scheme is described in the present work.

In the remainder of this chapter, we describe the immersed boundary formulation of problems of fluid–structure interaction and provide an overview of the particular numerical scheme we employ to solve the equations of motion. We then describe the parallel and adaptive implementation of this scheme and discuss the application of this parallel and adaptive version of the immersed boundary method to the simulation of cardiac fluid dynamics. Finally, we briefly describe future extensions to this parallel and adaptive framework for simulating heart function.

7.2 THE IMMERSED BOUNDARY METHOD

7.2.1 The Continuous Equations of Motion

Consider a system comprised of an incompressible viscoelastic structure immersed in a viscous incompressible fluid. Let the fluid possess uniform mass density ρ and uniform dynamic viscosity μ, and suppose that the incompressible viscoelastic structure is neutrally buoyant in the fluid and, moreover, that the viscous properties of the structure are identical to the fluid in which it is immersed. The momentum, velocity, and incompressibility of such a coupled fluid–structure system are described by the uniform density incompressible Navier–Stokes equations, augmented by an appropriately defined elastic body force.[1] Although the neutrally buoyant case is the simplest setting in which to present the immersed boundary approach to problems of fluid–structure interaction, it is important to note that this setting is in fact appropriate for simulating cardiac fluid dynamics since heart muscle is neutrally buoyant in blood.

In the immersed boundary formulation of this problem, the velocity of the coupled fluid–structure system is described by the incompressible Navier–Stokes equations in Eulerian form, whereas the elasticity of the structure is described in Lagrangian form. In particular, the velocity of the coupled fluid–structure system is described in terms of an Eulerian velocity field $\mathbf{u}(\mathbf{x}, t)$, where $\mathbf{x} = (x, y, z)$ are fixed physical (Cartesian) coordinates restricted to a region $U \subset \mathbb{R}^3$, which we take to be a cube with periodic boundary conditions. It is important to keep in mind that $\mathbf{u}(\mathbf{x}, t)$ is the velocity of *whichever* material is located at position $\mathbf{x}$ at time t. The Lagrangian description of the elasticity of the structure makes use of a curvilinear coordinate system attached to the elastic structure. Letting $\Omega \subset \mathbb{R}^3$ denote the curvilinear coordinate space, and letting $(q, r, s) \in \Omega$ denote curvilinear coordinates attached to the elastic structure, we denote the physical position of material point (q, r, s) at time t by $\mathbf{X}(q, r, s, t)$, and the configuration of the entire structure by $\mathbf{X}(\cdot, \cdot, \cdot, t)$. The curvilinear elastic force density (i.e., the elastic force density with respect to (q, r, s)) generated by the elasticity of the structure is denoted by $\mathbf{F}(\cdot, \cdot, \cdot, t)$ and is given by a time-dependent mapping of the structure configuration. The equations of motion for the coupled fluid–structure system can be written as

$$\rho\left(\frac{\partial \mathbf{u}}{\partial t} + (\mathbf{u} \cdot \nabla)\mathbf{u}\right) + \nabla p = \mu \nabla^2 \mathbf{u} + \mathbf{f}, \tag{7.1}$$

$$\nabla \cdot \mathbf{u} = 0, \tag{7.2}$$

[1] Even in the more complicated case in which the mass density of the structure differs from that of the fluid, the momentum, velocity, and incompressibility of the coupled fluid–structure system can still be described by the incompressible Navier–Stokes equations [1, 32, 33]. The case in which the viscosity of the structure differs from that of the fluid can also presumably be handled by a generalization of the methods we describe, but this has not yet been attempted in the context of the immersed boundary method.

$$\mathbf{f}(\mathbf{x}, t) = \int_{\Omega} \mathbf{F}(q, r, s, t)\, \delta(\mathbf{x} - \mathbf{X}(q, r, s, t))\, \mathrm{d}q\, \mathrm{d}r\, \mathrm{d}s, \tag{7.3}$$

$$\frac{\partial \mathbf{X}}{\partial t}(q, r, s, t) = \int_{U} \mathbf{u}(\mathbf{x}, t)\, \delta(\mathbf{x} - \mathbf{X}(q, r, s, t))\, \mathrm{d}\mathbf{x}, \tag{7.4}$$

$$\mathbf{F}(\cdot, \cdot, \cdot, t) = \mathcal{F}[\mathbf{X}(\cdot, \cdot, \cdot, t), t]. \tag{7.5}$$

Here, equations (7.1) and (7.2) are the incompressible Navier–Stokes equations written in Eulerian form, in which $p(\mathbf{x}, t)$ is the pressure and $\mathbf{f}(\mathbf{x}, t)$ is the (Cartesian) elastic force density. Equation (7.5) is the Lagrangian description of the elasticity of the structure, and the precise formulation of $\mathcal{F}$ will depend on the properties of the elastic structure that is being modeled.

In the immersed boundary formulation of the equations of motion, the Eulerian Navier–Stokes equations are connected to the Lagrangian description of the elasticity of the structure via two Lagrangian–Eulerian interaction equations, equations (7.3) and (7.4). Each of these equations makes use of the three-dimensional Dirac delta function, $\delta(\mathbf{x}) = \delta(x)\delta(y)\delta(z)$, as the kernel of an integral transformation. The first interaction equation, equation (7.3), converts the Lagrangian elastic force density $\mathbf{F}(q, r, s, t)$ into the equivalent Eulerian elastic force density $\mathbf{f}(\mathbf{x}, t)$. The second interaction equation, equation (7.4), uses the Dirac delta function to compute the value of the Eulerian velocity field at the location of material point (q, r, s), that is, to evaluate $\mathbf{u}(\mathbf{X}(q, r, s, t), t)$. Note that equation (7.4) is only valid if the Eulerian velocity field is continuous. In the present setting, the continuity of $\mathbf{u}(\mathbf{x}, t)$ follows from the presence of viscosity in both the fluid and the structure.

All that remains is to describe the elastic force density mapping. Although there are many possible choices for this mapping, we employ a formulation that is well suited for describing the highly anisotropic elastic properties of cardiac muscle tissue as well as heart valve leaflets. Suppose that the immersed elastic structure consists of a continuous collection of elastic fibers, where the material coordinates (q, r, s) have been chosen so that a fixed value of the pair (q, r) labels a particular fiber for all time. Let $\boldsymbol{\tau}$ denote the unit tangent vector in the fiber direction, so that for this choice of curvilinear coordinates,

$$\boldsymbol{\tau} = \frac{\partial \mathbf{X}/\partial s}{|\partial \mathbf{X}/\partial s|}. \tag{7.6}$$

Since the fibers are elastic, the fiber tension T (such that $T\boldsymbol{\tau}\, \mathrm{d}q\, \mathrm{d}r\, \mathrm{d}s$ is the force transmitted by the bundle of fibers $\mathrm{d}q\, \mathrm{d}r$) is related to the fiber strain, which is determined by $|\partial \mathbf{X}/\partial s|$. The fiber tension can be expressed by a generalized, time-dependent Hooke's law of the form

$$T = \sigma\,(|\partial \mathbf{X}/\partial s|\,; q, r, s, t)\,. \tag{7.7}$$

The explicit time dependence in equation (7.7) is important in the context of the heart, since cardiac muscle has drastically different mechanical properties in the different phases of the cardiac cycle. Indeed, it is this explicit time dependence that makes the heart beat. Note in particular that we do *not* prescribe the motion of the heart wall, nor do we prescribe the tension in the heart wall, but we do prescribe a position- and time-dependent relationship between strain and stress in the form of equation (7.7). It can be shown [1, 34] that the corresponding curvilinear elastic force density can be put in the form

$$\mathcal{F}[\mathbf{X}(\cdot,\cdot,\cdot,t),t] = \frac{\partial}{\partial s}(T\boldsymbol{\tau}). \tag{7.8}$$

Since T and $\boldsymbol{\tau}$ are both defined in terms of $\partial\mathbf{X}/\partial s$, $\mathcal{F}$ is a mapping from the structure configuration $\mathbf{X}(\cdot,\cdot,\cdot,t)$ to the curvilinear force density $\mathbf{F}(\cdot,\cdot,\cdot,t)$.

Before concluding this section, we briefly mention another way of viewing the formulation that is particularly useful for implementing a discretization of the foregoing continuous equations. It is important to note again that in the present formulation, many of the properties of the incompressible viscoelastic material, including its density and viscosity, are identical to those of the surrounding fluid. Thus, the viscoelastic material can be viewed as an idealized *composite* material with a viscous incompressible fluid component (the properties of which are described in Eulerian form) and an elastic fiber component (the properties of which are described in Lagrangian form). From this point of view, the sole purpose of the fibers is to provide a Lagrangian description of the additional elastic stresses that are present only in the viscoelastic material, stresses that are absent in the surrounding fluid. These additional fiber stresses are characterized by the elastic force density $\mathbf{F}(\cdot,\cdot,\cdot,t)$ as a function of the material configuration $\mathbf{X}(\cdot,\cdot,\cdot,t)$. As derived in Ref. [34], the Eulerian form of the stress tensor of such a composite material is

$$\sigma'_{ij} = -p\,\delta_{ij} + \mu\left(\frac{\partial u_i}{\partial x_j} + \frac{\partial u_j}{\partial x_i}\right) + T'\tau_i\tau_j, \tag{7.9}$$

where p is the pressure, δ_{ij} is the Kronecker delta, μ is the viscosity, $\mathbf{u} = (u_1, u_2, u_3)$ is the velocity, $\mathbf{x} = (x_1, x_2, x_3)$ are (Cartesian) physical coordinates, T' is the (Eulerian) fiber tension (so that $T'\boldsymbol{\tau}$ is the force per unit cross-sectional area transmitted by the fibers), and $\boldsymbol{\tau} = (\tau_1, \tau_2, \tau_3)$ is the unit tangent to the fibers. It can be shown [34] that the Eulerian fiber tension T' is related to the Lagrangian fiber tension T via

$$T'(\mathbf{X}(q,r,s,t),t) = \frac{|\partial\mathbf{X}/\partial s|}{J(q,r,s)}\,T(q,r,s,t), \tag{7.10}$$

where $J(q,r,s)$ denotes the Jacobian determinant of the coordinate transformation $(q,r,s) \mapsto \mathbf{X}(q,r,s,t)$. Note that the incompressibility of the viscoelastic structure implies that J is time independent.

7.2.2 The Numerical Scheme

In our adaptive version of the immersed boundary method, we discretize the Eulerian incompressible Navier–Stokes equations on a structured locally refined Cartesian grid, and we discretize the Lagrangian description of the elasticity of the model heart on a uniform lattice in the curvilinear coordinate space. As is typical in the immersed boundary context, we use a regularized version of the Dirac delta function in the discretizations of the Lagrangian–Eulerian interaction equations.

Spatial Discretizations In the uniform grid version of the scheme, the physical domain U is discretized on a Cartesian grid with uniform grid spacings $h = \Delta x = \Delta y = \Delta z$, whereas in the adaptive case, U is discretized on a locally refined Cartesian grid described in Section 7.3.1. For Eulerian quantities such as $\mathbf{u}(\mathbf{x}, t)$ that are defined on the Cartesian grid, we denote by $\mathbf{u}^n_{i,j,k}$ the value of $\mathbf{u}$ at the center of Cartesian grid cell (i, j, k) at time $t = t_n$. In both the uniform and the adaptive scheme, the curvilinear coordinate domain Ω is discretized on a fixed lattice in (q, r, s)-space with uniform meshwidths $(\Delta q, \Delta r, \Delta s)$. For Lagrangian quantities such as $\mathbf{X}(q, r, s, t)$ that are defined on the curvilinear mesh, we denote by $\mathbf{X}^n_{q,r,s}$ the value of $\mathbf{X}$ at curvilinear mesh node (q, r, s) at time t_n. From now on, note that the curvilinear coordinate indices (q, r, s) always refer to the nodes of the curvilinear computational lattice.

Although the discretization of the curvilinear coordinate space is fixed throughout a particular simulation, it is important to note that the physical locations of the nodes of the curvilinear mesh are free to move throughout the physical domain. In particular, the physical positions of the curvilinear mesh nodes are in no way required to conform to the Cartesian grid. As we describe in Section 7.3, however, in the adaptive scheme, the locally refined Cartesian grid *does* adapt to the evolving configuration of the curvilinear mesh to ensure that high spatial resolution is present in the vicinity of the immersed elastic structure.

Cartesian Grid Finite Difference and Projection Operators To approximate the incompressible Navier–Stokes equations in the uniform grid version of the method, we employ standard second-order accurate, cell-centered approximations to the gradient, divergence, and Laplace operators, as well as a cell-centered approximate projection operator defined below. For a scalar function ψ, we denote by $(\mathbf{G}\psi)_{i,j,k}$ the second-order accurate centered difference approximation to $\nabla\psi$ evaluated at cell (i, j, k). Similarly, for a vector field $\mathbf{u}$, the centered difference approximation to $\nabla \cdot \mathbf{u}$ evaluated at cell (i, j, k) is denoted by $(\mathbf{D} \cdot \mathbf{u})_{i,j,k}$. The evaluation of the standard 7-point approximation to $\nabla^2\psi$ at cell (i, j, k) is denoted by $(L\psi)_{i,j,k}$. In the adaptive case, it is necessary to develop approximations to the gradient, divergence, and Laplace operators for locally refined Cartesian grids. We employ an approach similar to that described in Ref. [29], except that, at coarse–fine interfaces, we employ a three-dimensional generalization of the discretization approach introduced in Ref. [35]. For a complete specification of these locally–refined finite difference approximations, see Refs. [17, 18]. In the remainder of this chapter, note that $\mathbf{G}$, $\mathbf{D}\cdot$, and L denote either the uniform grid or the locally refined versions of the finite difference operators, as appropriate.

Before we define the approximate projection operator we use to enforce the constraint of incompressibility to $\mathcal{O}(h^2)$, we first recall the discrete analogue of the Hodge decomposition, namely, that an arbitrary cell-centered vector field $\mathbf{w}_{i,j,k}$ can be uniquely decomposed as

$$\mathbf{w} = \mathbf{v} + \mathbf{G}\varphi, \tag{7.11}$$

where $(\mathbf{D}\cdot\mathbf{v})_{i,j,k} = 0$ and $(\mathbf{D}\cdot\mathbf{G}\varphi)_{i,j,k} = (\mathbf{D}\cdot\mathbf{w})_{i,j,k}$. The discretely divergence-free vector field $\mathbf{v}_{i,j,k}$ can be explicitly defined in terms of an *exact* projection operator P given by

$$\mathbf{v} = P\mathbf{w} = \mathbf{w} - \mathbf{G}\varphi = \left(I - \mathbf{G}\left(\mathbf{D}\cdot\mathbf{G}\right)^{-1}\mathbf{D}\cdot\right)\mathbf{w}. \tag{7.12}$$

Since $(\mathbf{D}\cdot\mathbf{v})_{i,j,k} = 0$, for any vector field $\mathbf{w}$, $P^2\mathbf{w} = P\mathbf{w}$, so P is indeed a projection operator.

In practice, the application of the exact projection operator defined by equation (7.12) requires the solution of a system of linear equations of the form $\mathbf{D}\cdot\mathbf{G}\varphi = \mathbf{D}\cdot\mathbf{w}$. On a uniform, periodic, three-dimensional Cartesian grid with an even number of grid cells in each coordinate direction, $\mathbf{D}\cdot\mathbf{G}$ has a eight-dimensional nullspace. This complicates the solution process when iterative methods (such as multigrid) are employed to solve for φ. Moreover, when P is used in the solution of the incompressible Navier–Stokes equations, this nontrivial nullspace results in the decoupling of pressure field on eight subgrids, leading to the so-called "checkerboard" instability. The difficulties posed by exact cell-centered projections are only compounded in the presence of local mesh refinement.

To avoid these difficulties, we employ an approximate projection operator defined by

$$\tilde{P}\mathbf{w} = \left(I - \mathbf{G}\left(L\right)^{-1}\mathbf{D}\cdot\right)\mathbf{w}. \tag{7.13}$$

It is important to note that $\tilde{P}$ is *not* a projection operator, since $L \neq \mathbf{D}\cdot\mathbf{G}$. For smooth $\mathbf{u}$, however, $\|\mathbf{D}\cdot\tilde{P}\mathbf{u}\| \to 0$ as the Cartesian grid is refined, and in the uniform grid case, $|\mathbf{D}\cdot\tilde{P}\mathbf{u}| = \mathcal{O}(h^2)$ pointwise. The use of approximate projection operators in place of exact projections was first proposed in Ref. [36]. In the uniform grid case, the approximate projection operator that we employ is the one first introduced in Ref. [37], and in the locally refined case, $\tilde{P}$ is similar to the one described in Ref. [29].

A Regularized Version of the Dirac Delta Function In its treatment of the Lagrangian–Eulerian interaction equations, the immersed boundary method makes use of a regularized version the Dirac delta function that is generally of the tensor product form

$$\delta_h(\mathbf{x}) = \frac{1}{h^3}\,\phi\left(\frac{x}{h}\right)\phi\left(\frac{y}{h}\right)\phi\left(\frac{z}{h}\right). \tag{7.14}$$

In this chapter, we use the *4-point delta function*, which is so named because it has a support of four meshwidths in each coordinate direction, yielding a total support of 64 grid cells in three spatial dimensions. It is defined in terms of the function

$$\phi(r) = \begin{cases} \frac{1}{8}\left(3 - 2|r| + \sqrt{1 + 4|r| - 4r^2}\right), & 0 \le |r| < 1, \\ \frac{1}{8}\left(5 - 2|r| - \sqrt{-7 + 12|r| - 4r^2}\right), & 1 \le |r| < 2, \\ 0, & 2 \le |r|. \end{cases} \tag{7.15}$$

The 4-point delta function satisfies two discrete moment conditions along with a quadratic condition that helps the immersed boundary method achieve approximate translation invariance with respect to the position of the immersed elastic structure relative to the Eulerian computational mesh. The moment conditions guarantee that the 4-point delta function conserves total force and total torque when it is used to spread force from the curvilinear mesh to the Cartesian grid, for example, in a discretization of equation (7.3). These moment conditions also imply that a discretization of the interpolation formula, equation (7.4), that employs the 4-point delta function is second-order accurate for a sufficiently smooth Eulerian velocity field $\mathbf{u}$. A detailed description of the construction of this regularized delta function is provided in Ref. [1]. In addition, see Ref. [19] for a comparison of the performance of the present version of the immersed boundary method for several different choices of δ_h, including the 4-point delta function.

Timestepping Let $\Delta t_n = t_{n+1} - t_n$ denote the size of the nth timestep. Even though the timestep duration is not uniform throughout the simulation of a cardiac cycle, we drop the subscript, so that $\Delta t = \Delta t_n$. All levels of the locally refined Cartesian grid hierarchy are advanced synchronously in time, that is, by the same time increment Δt. In particular, we do not employ *subcycled* timestepping, whereby the timestep size is refined locally along with the spatial meshwidth [29, 30].

At the beginning of each timestep $n \geq 0$, we possess approximations to the values of the state variables at time t_n, namely, $\mathbf{u}^n$ and $\mathbf{X}^n$. The pressure (which is in principle not a state variable) must be defined at half-timesteps to obtain a consistent second-order accurate method. Thus, at the beginning of each timestep $n > 0$, we also possess $p^{n-1/2}$, an approximation to a lagged pressure defined at the midpoint of the previous time interval.[2] Since the model heart is initially in a tension-free configuration, the initial value of the lagged pressure is taken to be $p^{-1/2} = 0$.

To advance the solution forward in time by the increment Δt, we first compute $\mathbf{X}^{(n+1)}$, where the parentheses around $n+1$ indicate that this is only a *preliminary* approximation to the locations of the nodes of the curvilinear mesh at time t_{n+1}. This initial approximation to the updated structure configuration is obtained by approximating equation (7.4) by

$$\mathbf{X}^{(n+1)}_{q,r,s} = \mathbf{X}^n_{q,r,s} + \Delta t \sum_{i,j,k} \mathbf{u}^n_{i,j,k}\, \delta_h(\mathbf{x}_{i,j,k} - \mathbf{X}^n_{q,r,s})\, h^3. \tag{7.16}$$

A discrete approximation to $\mathcal{F}[\mathbf{X}(\cdot,\cdot,\cdot), t]$ provides the curvilinear elastic force densities corresponding to structure configurations $\mathbf{X}^n$ and $\mathbf{X}^{(n+1)}$, which are denoted by $\mathbf{F}^n$ and $\mathbf{F}^{(n+1)}$, respectively. The equivalent Cartesian elastic force densities are

[2] In addition to $\mathbf{u}$, $\mathbf{X}$, and p, we also maintain an additional MAC [38] velocity field whose normal components are defined at the faces of the Cartesian grid cells. This additional velocity field is used in the second-order Godunov treatment of the nonlinear advection terms that appear in the momentum equation, but we omit the details of this advection scheme from the present discussion; see Refs [17, 19].

obtained by discretizing equation (7.3) and are given by

$$\mathbf{f}^n_{i,j,k} = \sum_{q,r,s} \mathbf{F}^n_{q,r,s}\, \delta_h(\mathbf{x}_{i,j,k} - \mathbf{X}^n_{q,r,s})\, \Delta q\, \Delta r\, \Delta s, \tag{7.17}$$

$$\mathbf{f}^{(n+1)}_{i,j,k} = \sum_{q,r,s} \mathbf{F}^{(n+1)}_{q,r,s}\, \delta_h(\mathbf{x}_{i,j,k} - \mathbf{X}^{(n+1)}_{q,r,s})\, \Delta q\, \Delta r\, \Delta s. \tag{7.18}$$

A timestep-centered approximation to the Cartesian elastic force density is then defined by $\mathbf{f}^{n+1/2} = \frac{1}{2}\left(\mathbf{f}^n + \mathbf{f}^{(n+1)}\right)$.

We next determine the updated velocity field by integrating the incompressible Navier–Stokes equations in time via a second-order projection method. We first obtain an intermediate velocity field $\mathbf{u}^*$ by solving an approximation to the momentum equation, equation (7.1), without imposing the constraint of incompressibility. Instead, the time-lagged pressure gradient $\mathbf{G}p^{n-1/2}$ is used to approximate the timestep-centered pressure gradient, so that

$$\begin{aligned}(I - \eta_2 \nu L)(I - \eta_1 \nu L)\mathbf{u}^* \\ = (I + \eta_3 \nu L)\mathbf{u}^n + \Delta t (I + \eta_4 \nu L)\left(-\mathbf{N}^{n+1/2} + \frac{1}{\rho}\left(\mathbf{f}^{n+1/2} - \mathbf{G}p^{n-1/2}\right)\right).\end{aligned} \tag{7.19}$$

Here, $\nu = \mu/\rho$ and $\mathbf{N}^{n+1/2}$ is the explicit second-order Godunov approximation to $[(\mathbf{u}\cdot\nabla)\mathbf{u}]^{n+1/2}$ detailed in Refs [17, 19]. In addition, we have that

$$\eta_1 = \frac{a - \sqrt{a^2 - 4a + 2}}{2}\Delta t, \quad \eta_2 = \frac{a + \sqrt{a^2 - 4a + 2}}{2}\Delta t,$$
$$\eta_3 = (1 - a)\,\Delta t, \qquad \eta_4 = (1/2 - a)\,\Delta t,$$

with $a = 2 - \sqrt{2} - \epsilon$, where ϵ is machine precision; see Ref. [26] for further details on this L-stable implicit treatment of the viscous terms. Next, we impose the constraint of incompressibility to $\mathcal{O}(h^2)$ by approximately projecting $\mathbf{u}^*$, obtaining

$$\mathbf{u}^{n+1} = \tilde{P}\mathbf{u}^*. \tag{7.20}$$

Here, $\tilde{P}$ is the approximate projection operator defined by equation (7.13).

We now describe the computation of the updated pressure. Although it is possible to determine this value in terms of the approximate projection of $\mathbf{u}^*$, we have demonstrated in the immersed boundary context [17, 19] that it is beneficial to determine $p^{n+1/2}$ by approximately projecting a *different* intermediate velocity field $\tilde{\mathbf{u}}^*$, which is obtained from an alternate treatment of the momentum equation, namely,

$$\begin{aligned}(I - \eta_2 \nu L)(I - \eta_1 \nu L)\tilde{\mathbf{u}}^* \\ = (I + \eta_3 \nu L)\mathbf{u}^n + \Delta t (I + \eta_4 \nu L)\left(-\mathbf{N}^{n+1/2} + \frac{1}{\rho}\mathbf{f}^{n+1/2}\right).\end{aligned} \tag{7.21}$$

Note that the only difference between equations (7.19) and (7.21) is that equation (7.19) includes an approximation to the timestep-centered pressure gradient, whereas equation (7.21) *does not*. To obtain $p^{n+1/2}$, we first compute $\tilde{\varphi}$, the solution to a discrete Poisson problem,

$$L\tilde{\varphi} = \mathbf{D} \cdot \tilde{\mathbf{u}}^*, \tag{7.22}$$

and then obtain $p^{n+1/2}$ by solving

$$p^{n+1/2} = \frac{\rho}{\Delta t}(I + \eta_4 \nu L)^{-1}(I - \eta_2 \nu L)(I - \eta_1 \nu L)\tilde{\varphi}. \tag{7.23}$$

Since we employ an approximate projection instead of an exact one, the values of $\tilde{P}\mathbf{u}^*$ and $\tilde{P}\tilde{\mathbf{u}}^*$ will generally be different. Moreover, the pressures obtained from the approximate projections of $\mathbf{u}^*$ and $\tilde{\mathbf{u}}^*$ are generally different. Note that $p^{n+1/2}$ has no influence on the value obtained for $\mathbf{u}^{n+1}$, but that it is used in the next timestep, when computing $\mathbf{u}^{n+2}$.

Having obtained the values $\mathbf{u}^{n+1}$ and $p^{n+1/2}$, we complete the timestep by computing $\mathbf{X}^{n+1}$ by means of

$$\mathbf{X}^{n+1}_{q,r,s} = \mathbf{X}^{n}_{q,r,s} + \frac{\Delta t}{2}\left(\sum_{i,j,k} \mathbf{u}^{n}_{i,j,k}\, \delta_h(\mathbf{x}_{i,j,k} - \mathbf{X}^{n}_{q,r,s})\, h^3 \right.$$
$$\left. + \sum_{i,j,k} \mathbf{u}^{n+1}_{i,j,k}\, \delta_h(\mathbf{x}_{i,j,k} - \mathbf{X}^{(n+1)}_{q,r,s})\, h^3 \right), \tag{7.24}$$

which is an explicit formula for $\mathbf{X}^{n+1}$, since $\mathbf{X}^{(n+1)}$ is already defined (see equation (7.16). Note that the evolution of the structure configuration via equations (7.16) and (7.24) takes the form of a second-order accurate strong stability-preserving Runge–Kutta method [22].

7.3 PARALLEL AND ADAPTIVE IMPLEMENTATION

7.3.1 Adaptive Mesh Refinement

In our adaptive version of the immersed boundary method, the incompressible Navier–Stokes equations are solved on a locally refined hierarchical Cartesian grid. Each level in the grid hierarchy is composed of the union of rectangular grid *patches*. The levels are numbered $\ell = 0, \ldots, \ell_{\max}$, where $\ell = 0$ indicates the coarsest level in the hierarchy and $\ell = \ell_{\max}$ indicates the finest level. All patches in a given level ℓ share the same grid spacings $(\Delta x_\ell, \Delta y_\ell, \Delta z_\ell)$, and in the present discussion we assume that $h_\ell = \Delta x_\ell = \Delta y_\ell = \Delta z_\ell$. The grid spacing on a particular level is not arbitrary; instead, we require that the grid spacing on level $\ell + 1$ is an integer factor $\mathfrak{r} > 1$ finer than the grid spacing on level ℓ, so that $h_{\ell+1} = h_\ell/\mathfrak{r}$. Typical choices for this *refinement ratio* are $\mathfrak{r} = 2$ or 4.

To simplify the numerical scheme as well as interlevel data communication, the patch levels are properly nested, that is, the union of the grid patches on level $\ell + 1$ is strictly contained in the union of the patches on level ℓ. In particular, we require that there is a buffer of at least one level ℓ cell between the boundary of the union of

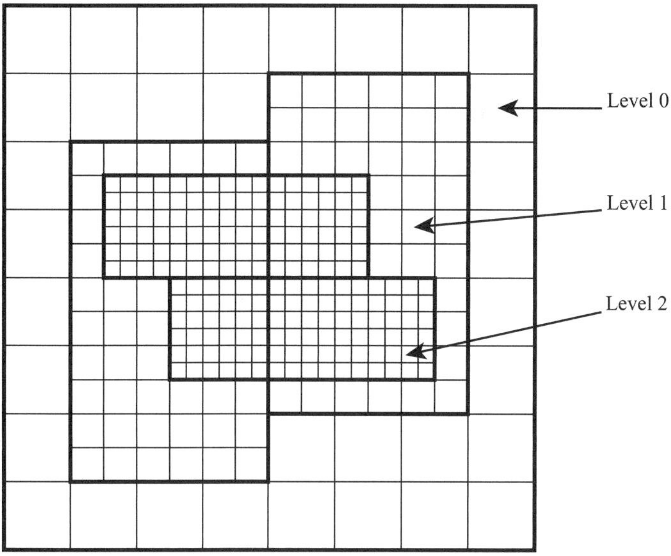

Figure 7.1 A two-dimensional structured locally refined Cartesian grid. Patch boundaries are indicated by bold lines. Each level in the hierarchy consists of one or more rectangular grid patches, and the levels satisfy the proper nesting condition. Here, the refinement ratio is given by $\mathfrak{r} = 2$.

the level $\ell + 1$ patches and the boundary of the union of the level ℓ patches. Note that this *is not* equivalent to requiring that each level $\ell + 1$ patch be contained (strictly or otherwise) within a single level ℓ patch. (Figure 7.1).

The levels in the patch hierarchy are constructed, either initially or at later times during the computation when adaptive regridding is needed, by a simple recursive procedure as follows. First, the coarsest level of the grid hierarchy is constructed as the collection of one or more grid patches whose union completely covers U, the physical domain.[3] Next, having constructed levels $0, \ldots, \ell < \ell_{\max}$, grid cells on level ℓ that require higher spatial resolution are tagged for further refinement. Tagged cells are clustered to form disjoint rectangular boxes of grid cells using a parallel implementation [39] of the Berger–Rigoutsos clustering algorithm [40]. The boxes generated on level ℓ by the clustering algorithm are further modified to enforce load balancing and proper nesting criteria. The resulting boxes are then refined by the refinement ratio $\mathfrak{r}$ to form the new level $\ell + 1$ patches. A consequence of this construction is that level $\ell + 1$ grid *patch* boundaries align with coarse level ℓ grid *cell* boundaries. This property further simplifies the interlevel data communication routines as well as the development of numerical methods for the locally refined grid structure. The level construction process is repeated until the specified maximum number of levels has been generated.

[3]Although the coarsest level of the hierarchy is always a uniform discretization of U, it may be comprised of multiple grid patches when the code is run in a parallel environment, since the load balancing of each hierarchy level is performed independently (see Section 7.3.2).

Multiple criteria are applied to select and tag grid cells for refinement. Primarily, cells are tagged for refinement whenever they contain any curvilinear mesh nodes. More precisely, cell (i, j, k) on level $\ell < \ell_{\max}$ is tagged if there exists a curvilinear mesh node (q, r, s) such that $\mathbf{X}^n_{q,r,s} \in \mathfrak{c}_\ell(i, j, k)$, where

$$\mathfrak{c}_\ell(i, j, k) = [ih_\ell, (i+1)h_\ell) \times [jh_\ell, (j+1)h_\ell) \times [kh_\ell, (k+1)h_\ell). \quad (7.25)$$

Here, $\mathfrak{c}_\ell(i, j, k)$ indicates the region in physical space occupied by Cartesian grid cell (i, j, k) on level ℓ. This tagging criterion ensures that the elastic structure is embedded in the finest level of the patch hierarchy.[4] Additional cells on level $\ell_{\max} - 1$ are tagged for refinement to form a buffer of level $\ell_{\max}$ grid cells between the immersed structure and the coarse–fine interface between levels $\ell_{\max} - 1$ and $\ell_{\max}$. In particular, when velocity interpolation and force spreading are performed via a regularized delta function with a support of d meshwidths in each coordinate direction, we ensure that the physical position of each node of the curvilinear mesh is at least $\lceil d/2 \rceil + 1$ grid cells away from the nearest coarse–fine interface on level $\ell_{\max}$. This buffer serves a dual purpose: It ensures that the structure is sufficiently far from the coarse–fine interface to avoid complicating the discretization of the Lagrangian–Eulerian interaction equations, and it prevents the structure from moving off the finest patch level prior to the subsequent regridding operation. It is important to emphasize that the positions of the curvilinear mesh nodes are *not* constrained to conform *in any way* to the locally refined Cartesian grid. Instead, the patch hierarchy is adaptively updated to conform to the evolving structure configuration.

Cartesian grid cells may also be tagged for refinement according to feature detection criteria or other error estimators. For instance, in an attempt to ensure that any vortices shed from the free edges of the valve leaflets remain within the finest level of the adaptively refined grid, cells are also tagged for refinement when the local magnitude of the vorticity exceeds a specified tolerance. In particular, cell (i, j, k) is tagged for refinement whenever $\left(\sqrt{\boldsymbol{\omega} \cdot \boldsymbol{\omega}}\right)_{i,j,k} \geq 0.25 \|\sqrt{\boldsymbol{\omega} \cdot \boldsymbol{\omega}}\|_\infty$, where $\boldsymbol{\omega} = \nabla \times \mathbf{u}$ is the vorticity. Although we do not presently do so, additional application-specific tagging criteria could be employed if desired.

Even though the curvilinear mesh nodes are constantly in motion during the course of an immersed boundary computation, it is not necessary to continuously update the configuration of the patch hierarchy. To determine the frequency at which the locally refined Cartesian grid must be updated, we first note that the explicit treatment of the nonlinear advection terms that appear in the momentum equation requires that the duration of the nth timestep satisfies a stability condition of the form

$$\Delta t = \Delta t_n \leq C \min_{\ell \in \{0 \ldots \ell_{\max}\}} h_\ell / \max_{\substack{(i,j,k) \in \\ \text{level } \ell}} \left(|u^n_{i,j,k}|, |v^n_{i,j,k}|, |w^n_{i,j,k}| \right), \quad (7.26)$$

[4]A generalization that we do not consider here is to assign portions of the elastic structure to levels other than the finest one.

where C is the CFL number. The Godunov scheme is stable so long as Δt satisfies equation (7.26) with $C < 1$. This CFL condition is not the only stability constraint that Δt must satisfy, however. In particular, a consequence of our explicit treatment of the Lagrangian equations of motion is that Δt must satisfy an additional constraint of the form $\Delta t = \mathcal{O}(h_{\ell_{\max}}^2)$ or even $\Delta t = \mathcal{O}(h_{\ell_{\max}}^4)$, depending on the definition of $\mathcal{F}$.[5] Consequently, Δt typically satisfies equation (7.26) for $C \ll 1$, so that in a single timestep, each curvilinear mesh node may move at most $C \ll 1$ fractional meshwidths per timestep in any coordinate direction. Over the course of $\lfloor 1/C \rfloor$ timesteps, each curvilinear mesh node will move less than one Cartesian meshwidth in any coordinate direction. By constructing the locally refined Cartesian grid according to the foregoing tagging criteria, it suffices to rebuild the patch hierarchy every $\lfloor 1/C \rfloor$ timesteps. For instance, by ensuring that Δt satisfies equation (7.26) for $C \leq 0.1$, it suffices to reconstruct the locally refined Cartesian grid every 10 timesteps.

7.3.2 Basic Approaches to the Distributed-Parallel Implementation of the Immersed Boundary Method

Developing a distributed-memory parallel implementation the immersed boundary method requires a number of design decisions, but perhaps the most important of these concerns the manner in which the Lagrangian and Eulerian data are partitioned across the available processors. Among the possible choices are:

1. Independently subdivide and distribute the Cartesian grid and the curvilinear mesh; or
2. First subdivide and distribute the Cartesian grid, and then subdivide and distribute the curvilinear mesh so that each curvilinear mesh node is assigned to the processor that "owns" the portion of the Cartesian grid in which that node is "embedded."

When considering these two possibilities, a third alternative may come to mind: First partition the curvilinear mesh and then partition the Cartesian grid accordingly; however, it is difficult to conceive of a reasonable way to implement such an approach without placing restrictions on the configuration of the curvilinear mesh.

A distributed-memory parallel implementation of a nonadaptive version of the immersed boundary method that follows the first of the aforementioned approaches to data partitioning has been developed as part of the Titanium project [42]. Since the curvilinear mesh and Cartesian grid are independently distributed among the processors, it is relatively straightforward to subdivide both in a manner that results in a nearly uniform distribution of the work associated with computations involving only Lagrangian or only Eulerian data. One drawback to this approach is that it potentially requires a large amount of interprocessor communication to evaluate the

[5] This severe constraint could presumably be avoided by making use of an implicit version of the immersed boundary method [41], but this has not yet been done in the adaptive context.

discrete interaction formulae, which involve both Lagrangian and Eulerian data. In particular, when the 4-point delta function is employed in three spatial dimensions, each curvilinear mesh node is coupled to 64 Cartesian grid cells, and a particular curvilinear mesh node will not necessarily be assigned to the same processor as the one that has been assigned the data corresponding to the nearby Cartesian grid cells. Moreover, the degree of coupling rapidly increases as the support of the delta function is broadened. For instance, the *6-point delta function*, which is similar to the 4-point delta function except that it satisfies two additional discrete moment conditions, can yield substantial improvements in the quality of the computed solutions [19]. Since the 6-point delta function results in each curvilinear mesh node being coupled to 216 Cartesian grid cells in three spatial dimensions, however, its use with a parallelization strategy that independently distributes the Cartesian grid and curvilinear mesh could result in a substantial amount of unstructured parallel communication when evaluating the interaction formulae.

In our parallel implementation, we use the second of the approaches listed above to distribute the Eulerian and Lagrangian data. We now describe this approach more precisely.

Each time a level in the locally refined Cartesian grid hierarchy is constructed, its patches are required to be *nonoverlapping*. The patches are distributed among processors according to a load balancing criterion that accounts for the present configuration of the curvilinear mesh (see below). After patch distribution, each processor has been assigned a subset of rectangular grid patches on each level. Note that each patch defines a region of the grid over which data are contiguous and local to a processor. Patches, once defined, are not further partitioned across processors to account for the curvilinear mesh data. Rather, the patches are used to *determine* the distribution of the curvilinear mesh. If the data distribution occurs at time t_n, each curvilinear mesh node (q, r, s) is assigned to whichever processor owns the level $\ell_{\max}$ patch that contains the Cartesian grid cell (i, j, k) that satisfies $\mathbf{X}^n_{q,r,s} \in \mathfrak{c}_{\ell_{\max}}(i, j, k)$. Since the grid patches on each level are nonoverlapping, this defines a unique decomposition and distribution of the curvilinear mesh to distributed processors. Note that $\mathfrak{c}_{\ell_{\max}}(i, j, k)$ is defined in equation (7.25) so that there is no ambiguity should a curvilinear mesh node fall on a patch boundary, either exactly or to machine precision.

Defining the distribution of the Lagrangian data in terms of the distribution of the Eulerian data in the foregoing manner ensures that relatively little interprocessor communication is required to evaluate the discrete interaction formulae. Unfortunately, this particular data distribution makes load balancing somewhat more challenging. To obtain good parallel performance, we must distribute the patches in a manner that yields a nearly uniform division of the computational work required to advance the numerical solution forward in time. In the present implementation, load balancing is performed independently for each level of the patch hierarchy. That is, the parallel distribution of the grid patches on a particular level does not depend on the parallel distributions of the patches that comprise the other levels of the hierarchy.

In the present adaptive scheme, recall that the immersed elastic structure is embedded within the finest level of the Cartesian patch hierarchy, that is, level $\ell_{\max}$. Consequently, we can associate computations involving Lagrangian data, including evaluations of the Lagrangian–Eulerian interaction formulae, with the finest level of the hierarchy. Moreover, the work associated with each level $\ell < \ell_{\max}$ can be considered to consist exclusively of Cartesian grid computations. Thus, for each level $\ell < \ell_{\max}$, we distribute the level ℓ patches so that each processor is assigned roughly the same number of level ℓ Cartesian grid cells.

Since we consider all computations involving Lagrangian data to be associated with the finest level of the locally refined Cartesian grid, we use a different load balancing strategy when distributing the level $\ell_{\max}$ patches. First, a workload estimate is computed in each cell on level $\ell_{\max}$ via

$$\text{work}^n_{i,j,k} = \alpha + \beta \left| \left\{ (q, r, s) : \mathbf{X}^n_{q,r,s} \in \mathfrak{c}_{\ell_{\max}}(i, j, k) \right\} \right|, \tag{7.27}$$

that is, the workload estimate in cell (i, j, k) is taken to be α plus β times the number of curvilinear mesh nodes embedded in cell (i, j, k), so that α determines the relative importance of the Eulerian workload and β determines the relative importance of the Lagrangian workload.[6] With the workload estimate so defined, the patches that comprise the finest level of the hierarchy are distributed to the available processors in a manner that attempts to ensure that the total estimated workload is roughly equal on each processor. Note that a benefit of this load balancing strategy is that the Lagrangian and Eulerian data distributions are able to adapt to the configuration of the elastic structure as it evolves during the course of a simulation.

7.3.3 Software Infrastructure

The implementation of our adaptive immersed boundary code derives much of its capability from two software libraries, SAMRAI [43, 44] and PETSc [45, 46]. SAMRAI is a general object-oriented software infrastructure for implementing parallel scientific applications that employ structured adaptive mesh refinement. SAMRAI provides the backbone of our implementation, managing the locally refined Cartesian grid patch hierarchy as well as the Eulerian data defined on the hierarchy. It also provides facilities for performing adaptive gridding, load balancing, and parallel data communication. PETSc is also an object-oriented toolkit for constructing parallel scientific applications, and its design makes it especially well suited for performing unstructured or nonadaptive structured grid computations. We employ PETSc vector objects to store quantities defined on the distributed curvilinear mesh, as well as PETSc sparse matrix objects to perform computations on the curvilinear mesh.

During each timestep, our numerical scheme requires the solution of several systems of linear equations on the locally refined Cartesian grid. These systems of equations are solved by preconditioned Krylov methods provided by PETSc. A modified version of the PETSc–SAMRAI interface provided by the SAMRAI library [47] allows this to be done without requiring data copying between SAMRAI and PETSc. Preconditioning is performed by an FAC solver described in Ref. [17].

[6]Presently, we simply set $\alpha = \beta = 1$. The optimal values are likely application and platform dependent and are almost certainly different from those that we are presently using.

7.3.4 Managing the Distributed Curvilinear Mesh with SAMRAI and PETSc

In our implementation, each of the Lagrangian quantities defined on the curvilinear mesh (for example, the curvilinear force density **F** or the configuration of the incompressible viscoelastic structure **X**) is stored as a separate PETSc `VecMPI` distributed-parallel vector object. Consequently, linear operations that are defined on the curvilinear mesh can be expressed in terms of one of the parallel sparse matrix objects provided by PETSc, for example, `MatMPIAIJ` or `MatMPIBAIJ`. In fiber-based descriptions of the material elasticity, such as the one used in the model heart, the discrete curvilinear force density is determined by evaluating finite difference approximations to $\partial/\partial s\mathbf{X}$ and to $\partial/\partial s\,(T\boldsymbol{\tau})$ at the nodes of the curvilinear mesh. A finite difference approximation to $\partial/\partial s$ can easily be described by a PETSc matrix, and once such a matrix object is initialized, it is straightforward to evaluate the curvilinear force density on the curvilinear mesh. Note that since we express these finite difference operations as distributed matrix–vector products, the application-specific force evaluation routines that must be implemented by the programmer can be made essentially independent of the details of the parallel distribution of the curvilinear mesh.

In addition to evaluating the curvilinear elastic force density, which is a computation that involves only Lagrangian data, we must also be able to *interpolate* the velocity from the Cartesian grid to the curvilinear mesh and *spread* the force density from the curvilinear mesh to the Cartesian grid. This is done by evaluating the discrete Lagrangian–Eulerian interaction formulae, that is, equations (7.16–7.18) and (7.24), on each level $\ell_{\max}$ grid patch. Performing these operations within a particular patch requires not only data in the patch interior but also data values in a ghost cell region outside the patch boundary. In particular, in the case of velocity interpolation, the Eulerian velocity **u** must be provided in a ghost cell region about each patch, whereas in the case of force spreading, the curvilinear force density **F** must be locally accessible both for the nodes that are located within the patch interior and also for those nodes that are embedded within the same ghost cell region.

To determine the size of this ghost cell region, suppose that force spreading is performed by the 4-point delta function, which has a support of four meshwidths in each coordinate direction. If a curvilinear mesh node (q, r, s) is more than 1.5 Cartesian meshwidths away from the interior of a particular Cartesian grid patch, the force associated with node (q, r, s) cannot be spread to any of the Cartesian grid cell centers in the interior of that patch. Since the curvilinear mesh nodes are in motion, however, it is useful to keep track of the curvilinear mesh nodes in a somewhat larger ghost cell region. Assuming that the nodes may move at most a single Cartesian meshwidth in any coordinate direction during a single timestep, it suffices to provide curvilinear mesh data within a 2.5-cell ghost cell region, although in practice we round this number up to 3. Similarly, interpolating the Eulerian velocity **u** from the Cartesian grid to an arbitrary location in the interior of a grid patch requires that values of **u** be provided in a 2-cell-wide ghost cell region about that patch. Again, since the curvilinear mesh nodes are free to move off of the patch interior and into

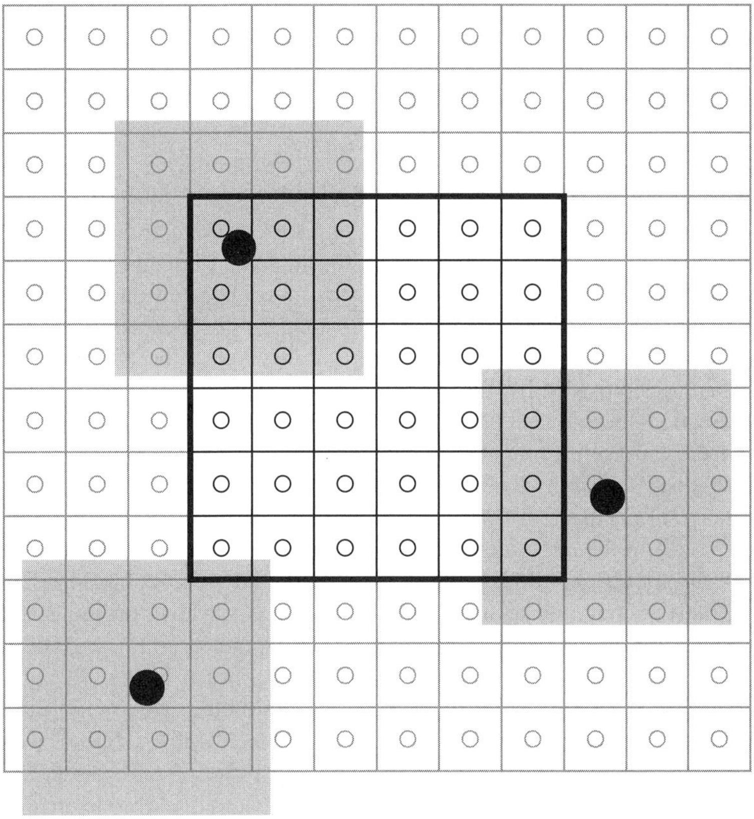

Figure 7.2 A two-dimensional Cartesian grid patch along with a 3-cell-wide ghost cell region. Cells interior to the patch appear in black, whereas the ghost cells appear in gray. Cartesian cell centers are indicated by open circles. Three isolated curvilinear mesh nodes appear as filled circles. The support of the 4-point delta function centered about each of these nodes is indicated in light gray. Note that in a typical immersed boundary simulation, the density of curvilinear mesh nodes would be substantially higher than that indicated in this figure.

the ghost cell region, we actually ensure that ghost cell values of **u** are provided in a 3-cell-wide ghost cell region. (See Figure 7.2. More generally, when interpolation and spreading are performed by a d-point regularized delta function, then we provide data within a $(\lfloor d/2 \rfloor + 1)$-cell-wide ghost cell region about each patch.

Since we use SAMRAI for all Cartesian grid data management, it is straightforward to ensure that the necessary Eulerian data are accessible on a particular patch, for example, by setting the size of the ghost cell region associated with **u** appropriately. Since the curvilinear mesh nodes are free to move throughout the Cartesian grid, however, efficiently determining which of the curvilinear mesh nodes must be accessible to a particular patch is more complicated. To do so, we introduce additional Cartesian grid data that are stored only on the finest level of the patch hierarchy. In particular, for each Cartesian grid cell (i, j, k) on level $\ell_{\max}$, we explicitly store the set of curvilinear mesh nodes embedded in that cell, namely,

$$\mathcal{Q}^n_{i,j,k} = \{(q, r, s) : \mathbf{X}^n_{q,r,s} \in \mathfrak{c}_{\ell_{\max}}(i, j, k)\}. \tag{7.28}$$

To store these data on the locally refined Cartesian grid, we introduce a version of the standard SAMRAI `IndexData` patch data type that has been specialized through the C++ template mechanism and class inheritance. For each Cartesian grid cell (i, j, k) that contains one or more curvilinear mesh nodes, this new patch data type maintains data corresponding to the set $\mathcal{Q}_{i,j,k}$, whereas no storage is allocated for those cells that do not contain any curvilinear mesh nodes.[7] Although this application-specific data type is not a part of the SAMRAI library, the parallel communication and data management facilities provided by SAMRAI are designed so that they can be used with such application-specific data types without modification. In particular, we use SAMRAI to fill the ghost cell values of $\mathcal{Q}$ on each patch on level $\ell_{\max}$, thereby allowing us to determine the identities of all of the curvilinear mesh nodes that are required to spread $\mathbf{F}$ to the interior cells of any particular patch in the level.

Since each node of the curvilinear mesh is constantly in motion, it may appear that the set of curvilinear coordinate indices associated with a particular Cartesian grid cell $\mathcal{Q}_{i,j,k}$ must be continuously updated. This is not the case, however, as a result of stability restrictions on the timestep duration Δt; see equation (7.26), and recall that for the present scheme, we generally have that Δt satisfies equation (7.26) for $C \ll 1$. As long as $\mathcal{Q}$ is updated every $\lfloor 1/C \rfloor$ timesteps, the value of $\mathcal{Q}_{i,j,k}$ indicates which curvilinear mesh nodes are within one Cartesian meshwidth of cell (i, j, k). Since we also must adaptively regrid the patch hierarchy every $\lfloor 1/C \rfloor$ timesteps to avoid complicating the discretizations of the interaction equations and to ensure that the curvilinear mesh does not escape the finest level of the locally refined Cartesian grid, it suffices to update the value of $\mathcal{Q}$ as part of the regridding process, as described below.

In our implementation, $\mathcal{Q}$ also plays an important role in simplifying the *redistribution* of the curvilinear mesh when the hierarchy configuration changes. In particular, each time that the patch hierarchy is regridded, $\mathcal{Q}$ is used to indicate which nodes of the curvilinear mesh are to be assigned to a particular processor. Since $\mathcal{Q}$ is defined on the locally refined Cartesian grid, its parallel redistribution is automatically handled by SAMRAI. Once the patch hierarchy has been reconfigured, the portion of the distributed curvilinear mesh that is assigned to a particular processor is determined from the values of $\mathcal{Q}$ defined on each of the *local* Cartesian grid patches on level $\ell_{\max}$. Using this information, we can then use PETSc to perform a parallel scatter of all the Lagrangian quantities from the old configuration of the distributed curvilinear mesh to the newly defined data distribution.

[7] Although we do not discuss this issue further in this chapter, this patch data type also maintains information regarding the connectivity of the curvilinear mesh; that is, it provides a local portion of a distributed *link table* that indicates which nodes in the curvilinear mesh are connected by elastic links, as well as the stiffnesses and resting lengths of those connections.

In summary, so long as the locally refined Cartesian grid is regenerated at least every $\lfloor 1/C \rfloor$ timesteps, it suffices to update the value of $\mathcal{Q}$ only during the regridding process. Thus, if we adaptively regrid the patch hierarchy at time t_n, we

1. Loop over all of the level $\ell_{\max}$ patches and set $\mathcal{Q}^n_{i,j,k} = \{(q, r, s) : \mathbf{X}^n_{q,r,s} \in \mathfrak{c}_{\ell_{\max}}(i, j, k)\}$ for each Cartesian grid cell (i, j, k) on level $\ell_{\max}$;
2. Regenerate and redistribute the locally refined Cartesian grid hierarchy, using the tagging and load-balancing criteria described in Sections 7.3.1 and 7.3.2;
3. Loop over all of the level $\ell_{\max}$ patches and use $\mathcal{Q}^n$ to determine the set of curvilinear mesh nodes that are located in each local level $\ell_{\max}$ patch interior, and the set of curvilinear mesh nodes that are located in the ghost cell region associated with each local level $\ell_{\max}$ patch;
4. Scatter the curvilinear mesh from the old data distribution to the new data distribution; and
5. Regenerate the matrices required to compute $\mathbf{F}$.

Note that in our implementation, step 2 is performed by SAMRAI, and step 4 is performed by PETSc. The implementation of the remaining operations is comparatively straightforward.

7.4 SIMULATING CARDIAC FLUID DYNAMICS

The model of the heart that is used in this study may be described overall as a system of elastic fibers that interacts with a viscous incompressible fluid in which the fibers are immersed. Some of these fibers have active, contractile properties, as described below. The fibers of the model represent the muscular heart walls, the flexible heart valve leaflets, and the walls of the great vessels that connect to the heart. The fluid (which is everywhere in an immersed boundary computation) represents the blood in the cardiac chambers, the intracellular and extracellular fluid within the thick heart walls, and the tissue that is external to the heart (for which a fluid model is admittedly oversimplified but at least accounts for the fact that when the heart moves, it has to push something out of the way).

The muscle fibers of the model have time-dependent elastic parameters. In particular, the stiffnesses and resting lengths of these fibers vary with time during the cardiac cycle, so that the muscle fibers of the model are stiffer and have shorter rest lengths during systole than during diastole. It is these time-dependent changes in elastic parameters that cause the beating of the model heart. In the present form of the model, the time-dependent changes in elastic parameters are synchronous within the atria, and then after a brief delay, similar time-dependent changes occur synchronously within the ventricles. In future work, we plan to simulate the wave of electrical activity that actually coordinates and controls the heartbeat, and to use the time-dependent intracellular Ca^{2+} concentration associated with this wave to drive a more realistic model of cardiac muscle mechanics, for example, Ref. [48].

The model heart includes representations of the left and right ventricles; the left and right atria; the aortic, pulmonic, tricuspid, and mitral valves; the ascending aorta and main pulmonary artery; and the superior and inferior vena cavae and the four pulmonary veins. Sources and sinks in the veins and arteries connect the model heart to pressure reservoirs through hydraulic impedances, so that the model heart operates under appropriate preload and afterload conditions. A source/sink external to the heart allows the total volume of the heart model to change during the cardiac cycle and also provides a convenient reference pressure with respect to which other pressures may be defined in a meaningful manner. Another option, not yet implemented, is to connect the venous sources and arterial sinks by differential equations that model the pulmonary and systemic circulations, so as to provide an even more natural setting for the model heart and to enable the study of the influence of the circulation on the function of the heart.

For further details concerning the construction of the model heart, see Ref. [7], and for the mathematics underlying the construction of the aortic and pulmonic valves of the model, see Refs [49, 50]. Although the anatomy of the model heart is realistic in many respects, there is considerable room for improvement, and indeed we have recently completed the construction of a next-generation version of the model in which cardiac computed tomography data are used during the construction process. We expect that the computational methods described in this chapter will produce even more realistic results when applied in the context of this more anatomically realistic next-generation heart model.

In Figures 7.3 and 7.4, we provide illustrative results obtained from the application of the parallel and adaptive version of the immersed boundary method described in this chapter to the simulation of a complete cardiac cycle. In this computation, the physical domain is described as a periodic box that has a length of 26.118 cm on each side. (For comparison, note that the circumference of the human mitral valve ring is approximately 10 cm and its diameter is approximately 3.2 cm.) The locally refined Cartesian grid consists of two levels, a global coarse level with 32 grid cells in each coordinate direction and a locally refined fine level with a refinement ratio of 4. The timestep size is specified to ensure that the CFL number never exceeds $C = 0.1$, so that it suffices to regrid the patch hierarchy every 10 timesteps.

To demonstrate the potential of our adaptive scheme to reduce the computational resources required to simulate cardiac fluid dynamics, we also performed the first 100 timesteps of this simulation with both uniform and locally refined Cartesian grids. In particular, we compare the performance of the adaptive immersed boundary method in three cases: (1) a uniform 128^3 Cartesian grid, (2) a two-level locally refined Cartesian grid with a coarse grid resolution of 64^3 and a refinement ratio of 2, and (3) a two-level locally refined Cartesian grid with a coarse grid resolution of 32^3 and a refinement ratio of 4. Note that in all the cases, the grid spacing on the finest level of the hierarchy corresponds to that of a uniform grid with 128 grid cells in each coordinate direction. These computations were performed on the Multiprogrammatic and Institutional Computing Capability Resource (MCR) at Lawrence Livermore National Laboratory, which is equipped with 1152 compute nodes, each consisting of two Intel 2.4 GHz Pentium 4 Xeon processors and 4 GB of memory.

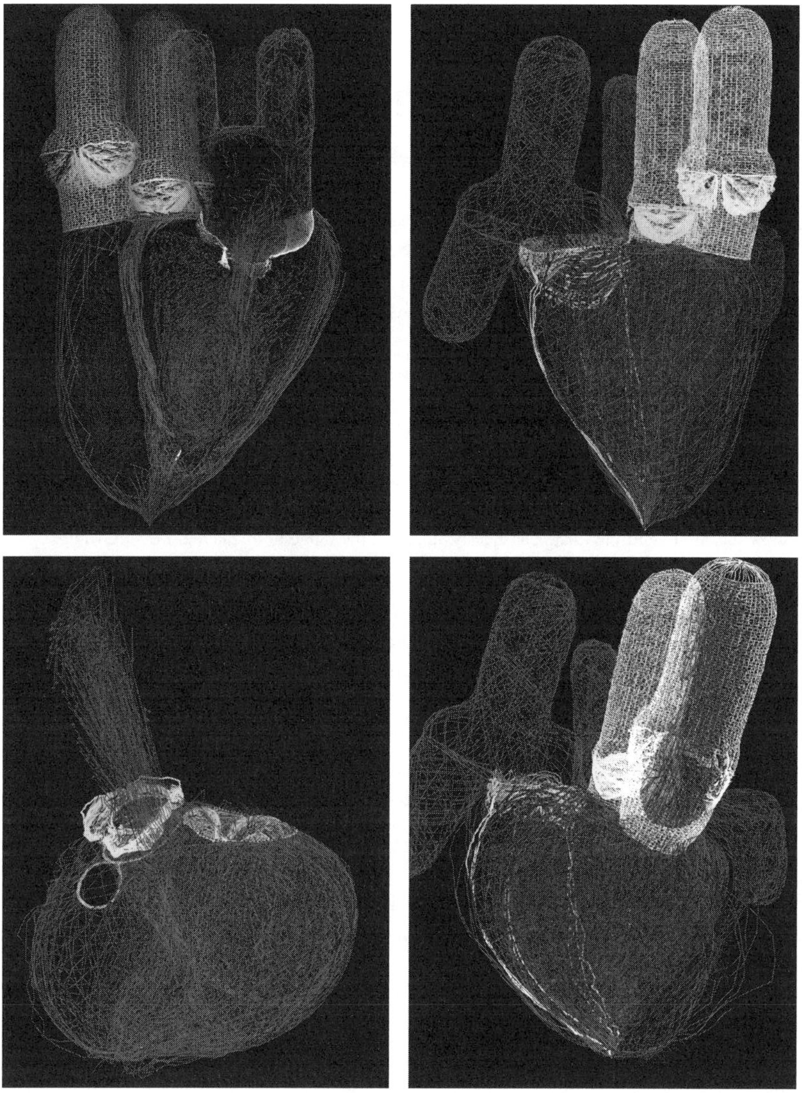

Figure 7.3 Results from an adaptive and distributed-memory parallel simulation of cardiac fluid dynamics in a three-dimensional model of the human heart. *Top row*: diastolic filling in the left ventricle and the right ventricle. *Bottom row*: systolic ejection into the aorta and the pulmonary artery.

Parallel code timings obtained on MCR are reported in Table 7.1. Notice that in all cases, the wall clock time required to compute a single timestep is significantly decreased by the use of adaptive mesh refinement. Moreover, mesh refinement allows us to obtain good performance on as few as 16 processors, whereas reasonable performance in the uniform grid case is only obtained with 64 processors. Note that the

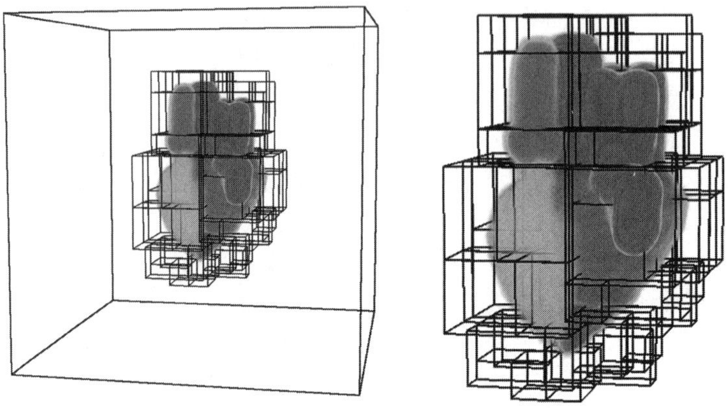

Figure 7.4 Volume rendering of the pressure field prior to systolic ejection from an adaptive and distributed-parallel simulation of cardiac fluid dynamics. Patch boundaries in regions of local refinement are indicated by thick black lines. The entire computational domain is shown on the left of the figure; the portion of the computational domain in the vicinity of the model heart is shown on the right. To allow the right ventricle to appear clearly, note that the range of displayed pressure values does not include the full range of computed values.

large adaptive speedup values obtained in some cases, as well as the deterioration of these values as the number of processors is increased, appear to result from memory cache effects. This is borne out by considering the *parallel* speedup factors (i.e., the wall-clock time per timestep required when employing $2N$ processors divided by the time per timestep required when employing N processors). As the number of

Table 7.1 Average Wall Clock Time (in Seconds) Required to Perform a Single Computed Timestep in the Three-Dimensional Simulations of Cardiac Fluid Mechanics for Uniform and Locally Refined Computations.

# of procs.	uniform		$\mathfrak{r} = 2$		$\mathfrak{r} = 4$	
	Time per timestep	Adaptive speedup	Time per timestep	Adaptive speedup	Time per timestep	Adaptive speedup
8	94.46	—	44.34	2.13	12.53	7.54
16	57.53	—	10.03	5.74	7.61	7.56
32	41.96	—	7.44	5.64	5.81	7.22
64	10.74	—	7.40	1.45	6.74	1.59

All computations were performed on the Multiprogrammatic Capability Cluster (MCR) at Lawrence Livermore National Laboratory, a 1152 node Linux cluster with two Intel 2.4 GHz Pentium 4 Xeon processors and 4 GB of memory per node. Adaptive speedup is computed as the wall clock time required by the nonadaptive computation divided by the time required by the adaptive computation. Note that these speedup numbers do not account for the effect of parallelization; that is, adaptive speedup should not be confused with parallel speedup.

processors is doubled, we generally observe parallel speedup factors ranging from 1.35 to 1.60, at least until the workload per processor is sufficiently small. In the uniform grid case, however, the performance enhancement obtained by increasing the number of processors from 32 to 64 is nearly four. A slightly larger performance bump occurs when the number of processors is increased from 8 to 16 in the adaptive case in which $\tau = 2$. Such parallel performance increases indicate transitions from poor to good cache utilization, resulting from, for example, reductions in the amount of data assigned to each processor. Note that similarly dramatic performance increases do not occur for the adaptive computations in which $\tau = 4$, indicating that good cache performance is obtained in this case on as few as eight processors. When we employ 64 processors, we appear to obtain good cache utilization in all cases, and the corresponding adaptive speedup factors are 1.45 for $\tau = 2$ and 1.59 for $\tau = 4$. Similarly, when we employ eight processors, neither the uniform grid simulation nor the $\tau = 2$ adaptive simulation appears to obtain good cache performance, and in this case, the adaptive speedup is 2.13. On the other hand, in the same eight processor case, the adaptive speedup is 7.54 for $\tau = 4$. Note that we anticipate that the effect of adaptivity on performance would be even more dramatic for a subcycled timestepping scheme, in which the timestep duration is refined locally along with the spatial meshwidth. Even with the present nonsubcycled timestepping scheme, however, it is clear that we are able to obtain simulation results more rapidly and with fewer processors by using adaptive mesh refinement.

7.5 CONCLUSIONS AND FUTURE WORK

In this chapter, we have described the immersed boundary approach to problems of fluid–structure interaction and its adaptive and parallel implementation. Initial results from the application of this technology to the simulation of cardiac mechanics demonstrate the potential for adaptive mesh refinement and distributed-memory parallelism to reduce the computational resources required by such simulations, although there is still work to be done regarding the optimization of the software and numerical methods. In future work, we plan to use this software framework to perform simulations where highly refined grids are deployed only in the vicinity of the heart valve leaflets and the vortices shed from those leaflets. Carrying out such detailed simulations will necessitate some modifications to the present version of the immersed boundary method, however. In particular, the semi-implicit timestepping scheme we presently employ suffers from a severe timestep restriction that rapidly becomes untenable, even when the Cartesian grid is refined in a highly localized manner. Two complementary approaches that we shall take to overcome this difficulty are the use of implicit discretization methods [41] and the use of subcycled timestepping, in which the timestep is refined locally along with the spatial grid [29, 30]. The former approach will allow for substantially larger timesteps than we are able to take presently, whereas the latter will allow us to confine the use of small timesteps to regions of high spatial refinement. We anticipate that modifying the present adaptive scheme to include more advanced timestepping methods will allow us to perform highly resolved simulations that will reveal many fine-scale features of the flow that do not appear in the present results. Such features include the structure of the aortic sinus vortex. This flow pattern, first described by Leonardo da Vinci, allows the aortic valve to close following systolic ejection without leak. The numerical methods and parallel implementation we have described in this chapter will serve as the foundation for this future research.

ACKNOWLEDGMENTS

Portions of this work were done by BEG during the completion of his PhD thesis [17]. This research was supported by the Department of Energy Computational Science Graduate Fellowship Program of the Office of Scientific Computing and Office of Defense Programs in the United States Department of Energy under Contract no. DE-FG02-97ER25308 and by a New York University Graduate School of Arts and Science Dean's Dissertation Fellowship. BEG was also supported by National Science Foundation VIGRE Grant DMS-9983190 to the Department of Mathematics at the Courant Institute of Mathematical Sciences at New York University and is presently supported by an award from the American Heart Association.

Portions of this work were performed under the auspices of the United States Department of Energy by University of California Lawrence Livermore National Laboratory under Contract no. W-7405-Eng-48 and is released under UCRL-JRNL-214559.

REFERENCES

1. C.S. Peskin. The immersed boundary method. *Acta Numer.*, 11:479–517, 2002.
2. C.S. Peskin. Flow patterns around heart valves: a digital computer method for solving the equations of motion. PhD thesis, Albert Einstein College of Medicine, 1972.
3. C.S. Peskin. Numerical analysis of blood flow in the heart. *J. Comput. Phys.*, 25(3):220–252, 1977.
4. J.D. Lemmon and A.P. Yoganathan. Three-dimensional computational model of left heart diastolic function with fluid–structure interaction. *J. Biomech. Eng.*, 122(2):109–117, 2000.
5. J.D. Lemmon and A.P. Yoganathan. Computational modeling of left heart diastolic function: examination of ventricular dysfunction. *J. Biomech. Eng.*, 122(4):297–303, 2000.
6. C.S. Peskin and D.M. McQueen. Fluid dynamics of the heart and its valves. In H.G. Othmer, F.R. Adler, M.A. Lewis, and J.C. Dallon, editors, *Case Studies in Mathematical Modeling: Ecology, Physiology, and Cell Biology*, Prentice-Hall, Englewood Cliffs, NJ, 1996, pp. 309–337.
7. D.M. McQueen and C.S. Peskin. A three-dimensional computer model of the human heart for studying cardiac fluid dynamics. *Comput. Graph.*, 34(1):56–60, 2000.
8. A.L. Fogelson. Continuum models of platelet aggregation: formulation and mechanical properties. *SIAM J. Appl. Math.*, 52(4):1089–1110, 1992.
9. N.T. Wang and A.L. Fogelson. Computational methods for continuum models of platelet aggregation. *J. Comput. Phy.*, 151(2):649–675, 1999.
10. A.L. Fogelson and R.D. Guy. Platelet–wall interactions in continuum models of platelet thrombosis: formulation and numerical solution. *Math. Med. Biol.*, 21(4):293–334, 2004.
11. C.D. Eggleton and A.S. Popel. Large deformation of red blood cell ghosts in a simple shear flow. *Phys. Fluids*, 10(8):1834–1845, 1998.

12. P. Bagchi, P.C. Johnson, and A.S. Popel. Computational fluid dynamic simulation of aggregation of deformable cells in a shear flow. *J. Biomech. Eng.*, 127(7):1070–1080, 2005.
13. C.C. Vesier and A.P. Yoganathan. A computer method for simulation of cardiovascular flow-fields: validation of approach. *J. Comput. Phys.*, 99(2):271–287, 1992.
14. K.M. Arthurs, L.C. Moore, C.S. Peskin, E.B. Pitman, and H.E. Layton. Modeling arteriolar flow and mass transport using the immersed boundary method. *J. Comput. Phys.*, 147(2):402–440, 1998.
15. M.E. Rosar and C.S. Peskin. Fluid flow in collapsible elastic tubes: a three-dimensional numerical model. *New York J. Math.*, 7:281–302, 2001.
16. K.M. Smith, L.C. Moore, and H.E. Layton. Advective transport of nitric oxide in a mathematical model of the afferent arteriole. *Am. J. Physiol. Renal Physiol.*, 284(5):F1080–F1096, 2003.
17. B.E. Griffith. Simulating the blood-muscle-valve mechanics of the heart by an adaptive and parallel version of the immersed boundary method. PhD thesis, Courant Institute of Mathematical Sciences, New York University, 2005.
18. B.E. Griffith, R.D. Hornung, D.M. McQueen, and C.S. Peskin. An adaptive, formally second order accurate version of the immersed boundary method. *J. Comput. Phys.*, 223(1):10–49, 2007.
19. B.E. Griffith and C.S. Peskin. On the order of accuracy of the immersed boundary method: higher order convergence rates for sufficiently smooth problems. *J. Comput. Phys.*, 208(1):75–105, 2005.
20. A.M. Roma. A multilevel self adaptive version of the immersed boundary method. PhD thesis, Courant Institute of Mathematical Sciences, New York University, 1996.
21. A.M. Roma, C.S. Peskin, and M.J. Berger. An adaptive version of the immersed boundary method. *J. Comput. Phys.*, 153(2):509–534, 1999.
22. S. Gottlieb, C.-W. Shu, and E. Tadmor. Strong stability-preserving high-order time discretization methods. *SIAM Rev.*, 43(1):89–112, 2001.
23. A.J. Chorin. Numerical solution of the Navier–Stokes equations. *Math. Comput.*, 22(104):745–762, 1968.
24. A.J. Chorin. On the convergence of discrete approximations to the Navier–Stokes equations. *Math. Comput.*, 23(106):341–353, 1969.
25. J.B. Bell, P. Colella, and H.M. Glaz. A second-order projection method for the incompressible Navier–Stokes equations. *J. Comput. Phys.*, 85(2):257–283, 1989.
26. P. McCorquodale, P. Colella, and H. Johansen. A Cartesian grid embedded boundary method for the heat equation on irregular domains. *J. Comput. Phys.*, 173(2):620–635, 2001.
27. M.L. Minion. On the stability of Godunov-projection methods for incompressible flow. *J. Comput. Phys.*, 123(2):435–449, 1996.
28. M.L. Minion. A projection method for locally refined grids. *J. Comput. Phys.*, 127(1):158–178, 1996.
29. D.F. Martin and P. Colella. A cell-centered adaptive projection method for the incompressible Euler equations. *J. Comput. Phys.*, 163(2):271–312, 2000.
30. A.S. Almgren, J.B. Bell, P. Colella, L.H. Howell, and M.L. Welcome. A conservative adaptive projection method for the variable density incompressible Navier–Stokes equations. *J. Comput. Phys.*, 142(1):1–46, 1998.
31. A.S. Almgren, J.B. Bell, and W.Y. Crutchfield. Approximate projection methods: Part I. Inviscid analysis. *SIAM J. Sci. Comput.*, 22(4):1139–1159, 2000.
32. L. Zhu and C.S. Peskin. Simulation of a flapping flexible filament in a flowing soap film by the immersed boundary method. *J. Comput. Phys.*, 179(2):452–468, 2002.
33. Y. Kim, L. Zhu, X. Wang, and C.S. Peskin. On various techniques for computer simulation of boundaries with mass. In K.J. Bathe, editor, *Proceedings of the Second MIT Conference on Computational Fluid and Solid Mechanics*. Elsevier, 2003, pp. 1746–1750.
34. C.S. Peskin and D.M. McQueen. A three-dimensional computational method for blood flow in the heart. I. Immersed elastic fibers in a viscous incompressible fluid. *J. Comput. Phys.*, 81(2):372–405, 1989.
35. R.E. Ewing, R.D. Lazarov, and P.S. Vassilevski. Local refinement techniques for elliptic problems on cell-centered grids. I. Error analysis. *Math. Comput.*, 56(194):437–461, 1991.
36. A.S. Almgren, J.B. Bell, and W.G. Szymczak. A numerical method for the incompressible Navier–Stokes equations based on an approximate projection. *SIAM J. Sci. Comput.*, 17(2):358–369, 1996.

37. M.F. Lai. A projection method for reacting flow in the zero mach number limit. PhD thesis, University of California at Berkeley, 1993.
38. F.H. Harlow and J.E. Welch. Numerical calculation of time-dependent viscous incompressible flow of fluid with free surface. *Phys. Fluids*, 8(12):2182–2189, 1965.
39. A.M. Wissink, D. Hysom, and R.D. Hornung. Enhancing scalability of parallel structured AMR calculations. In *Proceedings of the 17th ACM International Conference on Supercomputing (ICS'03)*. ACM Press, 2003, pp. 336–347. Also available as LLNL Technical Report UCRL-JC-151791.
40. M.J. Berger and I. Rigoutsos. An algorithm for point clustering and grid generation. *IEEE Trans. Syst. Man Cybern.*, 21(5):1278–1286, 1991.
41. Y. Mori and C.S. Peskin. Implicit second-order immersed boundary methods with boundary mass. *Comput. Methods Appl. Mech. Engrg.*, 197(25–28):2049–2067, 2008.
42. E. Givelberg and K. Yelick. Distributed immersed boundary simulation in Titanium. *SIAM J. Sci. Comput.*, 28(4):1361–1378, 2006.
43. R.D. Hornung and S.R. Kohn. Managing application complexity in the SAMRAI object-oriented framework. *Concurrency Comput. Pract. Exper.*, 14(5):347–368, 2002.
44. R.D. Hornung, A.M. Wissink, and S.R. Kohn. Managing complex data and geometry in parallel structured AMR applications. *Eng. Comput.*, 22(3–4):181–195, (2006).
45. S. Balay, K. Buschelman, V. Eijkhout, W.D. Gropp, D. Kaushik, M.G. Knepley, L.C. McInnes, B.F. Smith, and H. Zhang. *PETSc Users Manual*. Technical Report ANL-95/11 - Revision 2.1.5, Argonne National Laboratory, 2004.
46. S. Balay, V. Eijkhout, W.D. Gropp, L.C. McInnes, and B.F. Smith. Efficient management of parallelism in object oriented numerical software libraries. In E. Arge, A.M. Bruaset, and H.P. Langtangen, editors, *Modern Software Tools in Scientific Computing*. Birkhäuser Press, 1997, pp. 163–202.
47. M. Pernice and R.D. Hornung. Newton-Krylov-FAC methods for problems discretized on locally-refined grids. *Comput. Vis. Sci.*, 8(2):107–118, 2005.
48. S.A. Niederer, P.J. Hunter, and N.P. Smith. A quantitative analysis of cardiac myocyte relaxation: a simulation study. *Biophys. J.*, 90(5):1697–1722, 2006.
49. C.S. Peskin and D.M. McQueen. Mechanical equilibrium determines the fractal fiber architecture of aortic heart valve leaflets. *Am. J. Physiol. Heart Circ. Physiol.*, 266(1):H319–H328, 1994.
50. J.V. Stern and C.S. Peskin. Fractal dimension of an aortic heart valve leaflet. *Fractals*, 2(3):461–464, 1994.

Chapter 8

Quantum Chromodynamics on the BlueGene/L Supercomputer

Pavlos M. Vranas and Gyan Bhanot

QCD is our most perfect physical theory.

—F. Wilczek, Physics Nobel Laureate [1]

8.1 INTRODUCTION: FROM VHDL TO QUARKS OR THE OTHER WAY AROUND

Traditionally, theoretical physicists develop and use powerful mathematics to describe nature. Most theoretical physicists not only do not use supercomputers but might also consider their use a weakness. Most great breakthroughs in theoretical physics have come from inspired thinking using paper and pencil. And this tradition is very much alive today as witnessed by the explosion of progress in string theory. This triumph of human ingenuity has, to date, absolutely no use for supercomputers.

However, supercomputers are absolutely necessary to make progress in a branch of theoretical particle physics that attempts to simulate, from first principles, the theory of the strong force. This theory describes how quarks and gluons interact to form protons, neutrons, pi-mesons, and the many resonances that make up the subnuclear world. The effort of designing, creating, and using powerful supercomputers to perform these simulations requires a focused, integrated approach. In

Advanced Computational Infrastructures For Parallel and Distributed Adaptive Applications. Edited by Manish Parashar and Xiaolin Li

this field, supercomputing influences theoretical physics as much as it is influenced by it.

Supercomputers themselves are enormously expensive and complex systems. The architecture design and construction of these machines involves many intricate steps and an astronomical number of components (elementary gates imprinted in silicon). Sophisticated tools have been developed over the years for the architecture and design of these machines and dedicated software languages such as VHDL (very high density language) take the designer's instructions and convert them to gates. Extensive tests are run on every level of the design to ensure that the system would operate as intended. Given the complexity, it is almost magical that the final complicated structure works at all, and even more astonishing that it improves on previous machines.

This chapter tells the story of how the two disciplines of theoretical physics and supercomputer design come together in helping to understand the strong nuclear force. The theory of how quarks and gluons interact to form stable nuclear particles (protons and neutrons), which, in their turn, combine to form atomic nuclei, is called quantum chromodynamics (QCD). It is briefly described in Section 8.2. It was recognized early on that most of the interesting properties of QCD cannot be calculated with pencil and paper. In 1974, a breakthrough article, published by Wilson [2, 3], described a way to define QCD on a lattice, which opened up the possibility of simulating it on a computer. This method has come to be called lattice gauge theory.

However, even though solving the theory by computer simulation is theoretically possible, the computer would have to perform an unbelievable number of floating point operations per second (flop/s) to yield interesting result in a few years time. A single CPU at 2.4 GHz running at full speed today falls short of this speed by several orders of magnitude. However, lattice QCD can be split up in a way that allows the calculation to be distributed on several processors requiring only simple local communication requirements. It was realized in the mid-1980s that massively parallel supercomputers are a natural fit for QCD and since then, lattice QCD has always used a large fraction of the CPU cycles on many worldwide supercomputers. Lattice gauge theory and its implementation on massively parallel supercomputers is described in Section 8.3.

Physicists who worked in lattice gauge theory in the 1980s and 1990s were not content to wait until supercomputers became powerful enough to do the calculations they wanted to do. On the one hand, they invented numerical methods to speed up the calculation and analytic methods that led to a deeper understanding of the underlying physics and refinements of the underlying theory. Some physicists also got involved in the race to design and build massively parallel supercomputers. Indeed, some of the world's fastest supercomputers (such as Fermi256, GF11, APE, QCDSP, QC-DOC and QCDPAX) were built by lattice gauge theorists. The BlueGene/L (BG/L) is one such supercomputer and is described in Section 8.4. In fact, BG/L is a general purpose computers and can do much more than just QCD. However, the mapping of lattice QCD on BG/L is natural and is described in Section 8.5.

For the implementation of the QCD algorithm to be useful, the code must execute at a substantial fraction of the peak speed of the machine. The QCD code contains a small kernel that consumes a large fraction of the cycles, sometimes as much as

90%. Optimizing this kernel for the BG/L hardware was critical. This kernel is very sensitive to latencies and meticulous coding is necessary to keep the CPU busy. In Section 8.6, we describe the development of this kernel for BG/L. Its performance is described in Section 8.7. Given its importance in the design of supercomputers, the QCD kernel has become a powerful tool for hardware and software architecture design, verification, and validation. This is discussed in Section 8.8. Finally, QCD can serve as an effective HPC benchmark to evaluate supercomputers. This is discussed in Section 8.9. The intimate relationship of QCD and massively parallel supercomputers is summarized in Section 8.10.

Parts of the work described here have appeared in Refs [4–7].

8.2 QUANTUM CHROMODYNAMICS

A brief description of QCD, "...our most perfect physical theory" [1], is presented in this section. For more details on quantum field theory and QCD, the reader is referred to Refs [8, 9] and references therein.

All the matter that surrounds us is made of atoms. Atoms have a size of about 10^{-10} th of a meter (one-tenth of one-billionth of a meter). Atoms are further subdivisible into a small nucleus of size about 1/100,000 the size of the atom (10^{-15} th of a meter—also called a Fermi). The nucleus contains most of the mass of the atom and is made from particles called nucleons that are mainly of two types, protons and neutrons. The nucleons themselves are made from yet smaller particles called quarks and gluons, which are held together by a force called the strong nuclear force. This force is the strongest force in nature (the other three being electromagnetism, weak nuclear force, and gravity). It operates only at very short distances and is mediated by gluons that carry the so-called color charge. Color can be thought of in a way similar to electromagnetic charge (e.g., on electrons). It is believed that quarks and gluons are elementary particles, and there is no experimental evidence that they are made up of smaller particles. The theory that describes the quarks and gluons and their interactions is called quantum chromodynamics.

QCD is a relativistic quantum field theory that describes nature at very small distances. In such a theory, particles are represented as complex waves (fields) in space–time. The wave amplitude is a probability that describes, for example, the location of the particle. There is a finite probability for it to be anywhere (in the past or the future) and to follow every possible trajectory. There is also a finite probability for pairs of particles to appear or disappear out of the vacuum. In this sense, the vacuum of quantum field theories is a busy place.

A field is defined by assigning a complex number to all points of space and time. In fact, the correct formulation is that at each space–time point, there is a distinct independent degree of freedom for the quantum field. Because space–time has four dimensions (three for space and one for time) and is continuous, it has an infinite number of degrees of freedom. However, computers can only represent a finite number of variables. In Section 8.3, we will see how this problem is resolved. An important property of QCD is that the interaction between fields is local; the field interactions at a given point of space–time only involve the field values around that point. In Sections 8.3 and 8.5, we will see that this property dictates the communication patterns in a massively parallel supercomputer.

Quarks come in six types (flavors), whimsically named up, down, strange, charm, top, and bottom. In addition to flavor, quarks carry a "color" charge that is the origin of the strong nuclear force. Gluons, which mediate the force, also have color but no flavor. Unlike the electric charge that can take only two values (positive/negative), there are three values for "color." Physicists use the shorthand notation of "red, green, and blue" to represent the three colors of the strong force. Gluons carry pairs of colors (red/blue, green/blue, etc.). In keeping with tradition in physics, where important ideas are given Greek names, the quantum theory of the interaction of these "colored" quarks and gluons is called quantum chromodynamics since the Greek word for color is chroma.

There are many nuclear particles that can be made by combining the six flavors and three colors. There are two broad categories of nuclear particles. Those made from two quarks are called mesons and those made from three quarks are called baryons. The former includes the pi- rho-, and K-mesons and the latter includes the proton and neutron. However, all of these particles eventually either decay into protons via the strong interaction or into electrons and neutrons via the weak and electromagnetic interaction. Nevertheless, most of these particles do exist long enough to significantly influence the properties of nuclear matter.

One of the amazing properties of QCD is the behavior of quarks inside nuclear particles. Using powerful accelerators, it has been possible to take the equivalent of an "X-ray" of nuclear particles and see what is going on inside. It turns out that the quarks inside nuclear particle behave like free particles, with no force acting on them. The nuclear force seems to vanish at very small distances. This property of the nuclear force is called "asymptotic freedom." However, if one tries to "pull out" a quark, a tube of gluons forms (flux tube) that exerts a very strong force to pull the quark back into the particle. It takes so much energy to pull the quark out of the nucleus that it is energetically favorable to create a quark/antiquark pair from the vacuum to break the gluon tube. One of the particles in the pair goes back into the original particle and the other pairs with the quark being pulled out to create a meson. This property of the strong force, which does not allow free quarks to be seen outside nuclear particles, is called infrared slavery or confinement. It guarantees that the quarks can never exist by themselves. They are slaves of the enormous strong nuclear force and are kept permanently inside nuclear particles.

These properties of asymptotic freedom and confinement are very useful for numerical computation. They imply that one can describe nuclear particles by focusing only in the small region of space–time that contains them. With an appropriate definition of the quark and gluon fields, the interactions between them can be represented as local interactions in space–time (see Section 8.3).

Experimentally, isolated quarks have never been observed. It is believed that the only time when quarks existed as free objects was until 10 μs after the "big bang" when the universe was small and temperatures were high enough to overcome the strong color force. Simulations show that when nuclear particles are subjected to these conditions, there is an abrupt change of state from stable nuclear particles to a "soup" of quarks and gluons called the quark–gluon–plasma. The theory predicts that this abrupt change (called a phase transition) occurs at about 2 trillion Kelvin. At present, an experiment is underway at the Brookhaven National Laboratory, which collides gold nuclei at enormous speeds to briefly "melt" the nuclei, create a quark–gluon–plasma and study its properties. This exciting state of matter has not existed in the universe since 10 μs after the big bang. Its properties are too complex to be studied by pencil and paper using our current analytic abilities. They can only be studied by experiment or by numerical simulations.

In a recent article, Wilczek [1], a 2004 corecipient of the Nobel Prize in Physics, lists the key properties of QCD as follows:

(1) embodies deep and beautiful principles (it is a relativistic quantum field theory);

(2) provides algorithms to answer questions (one such algorithm is described in what follows);

(3) has a wide scope (from nuclear physics to the genesis of the cosmos);

(4) contains a wealth of phenomena (asymptotic freedom, confinement, and many others);

(5) has few parameters (and is therefore simple to describe);

(6) is true (has been verified experimentally); and

(7) lacks flaws (it is fully described by its definition).

8.3 LATTICE GAUGE THEORY AND MASSIVELY PARALLEL SUPERCOMPUTERS

Calculating physical predictions from QCD in the region where the force becomes strong is quite challenging. An important formulation that is particularly suited to computer simulations on massively parallel supercomputers is called lattice gauge theory. We describe it briefly in this section. For a more detailed exposure to lattice gauge theory, the reader is referred, for example, to Refs [10–12].

A computer is a finite machine. It stores a finite amount of information and executes a finite set of instructions in a given time interval. On the other hand, as discussed in Section 8.2, QCD is defined on an infinity of points. How then is it possible to numerically simulate this theory? The answer was discovered by Wilson in 1974 [2, 3].

In Wilson's formulation, continuous space–time is replaced by a discrete 4D hypercubic grid of sites with links between neighboring sites. Figure 8.1 shows a 2D representation of such a lattice. The distance between sites is fixed and is called the "lattice spacing" (denoted by a). As discussed in Section 8.2, we only need to describe the small region of space–time that contains the nuclear particles of interest. Hence, the lattice can be finite in size. The quark field is represented as 24 real numbers on each site of the lattice, while the gluon field (also called gauge field) is described by

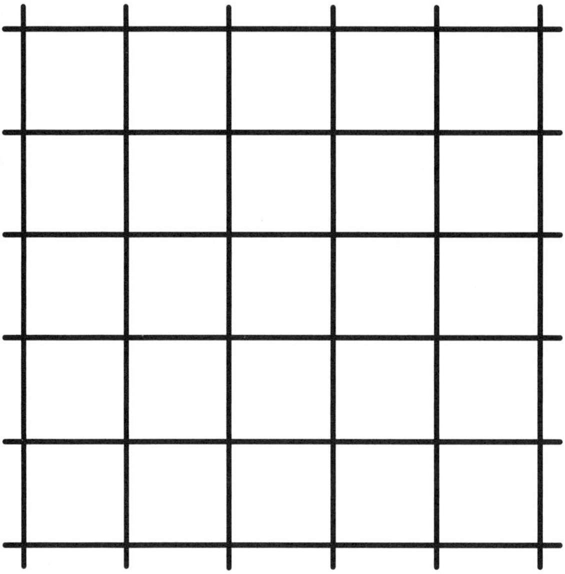

Figure 8.1 A two-dimensional square lattice.

18 real numbers assigned to the links between sites. The reason the gluon field is defined on a link rather than on a site is connected to a deep symmetry of the color interaction. However, it makes intuitive sense. The gluon field on a link "connects" quarks on two neighboring sites. This is what one expects from a field that mediates the force between these quarks.

The field amplitudes representing quark and gluon fields change during the simulation. The probability that the quark/gluon fields (Q and U) are in a given state is given by a probability function called the "Boltzman weight" or the "partition function," which has the form $Z\,\mathrm{e}^{-S(Q,U,\beta)}$ where the function S is computable from the site and link values of Q, U, and β represents the interactions between the fields. Although all possible values for the numbers on each site and link are allowed, Z determines which field values are most likely. Simulating QCD amounts to generating field configurations with the correct weight (as defined by Z) and interesting quantities are computed by averaging over these field configurations generated on the computer.

The configurations themselves are generated using standard simulation techniques. Starting from any configuration, new field configurations are generated by making small changes to the field values. Field configurations that increase Z are always accepted, while those that decrease Z are accepted with probability equal to the ratio of the proposed to the original Z.

A typical computer algorithm consists of an outer loop that generates new fields from the previous fields with probability determined by the Boltzman weights. Once the equilibrium distribution is obtained, physical (measurable) quantities can be calculated from these field values. Some examples of physical quantities are the average energy and its derivatives and the field correlation functions, from which one can determine the masses of the particles.

The core of the algorithm that updates the field values is a conjugate gradient computation that inverts a very large matrix, which is spread out over many nodes. Its size is proportional to $V \times V$, where V is the number of lattice sites. For a "typical" calculation on a 4D lattice with 32 sites per dimension, this matrix is approximately $32^4 \times 32^4$ or about $10^6 \times 10^6$. Inverting such a matrix would be impossible if the matrix was dense. However, since the interactions are local, the matrix is sparse and typically has entries only for nearest neighbor points on the 4D grid. Because of the sparse nature of the matrix, the conjugate gradient algorithm only requires the multiplication of a column vector by this matrix. This operation needs to be performed for every iteration of the conjugate gradient algorithm and forms the innermost kernel of the QCD algorithm. On most computers and algorithms, it consumes about 90% of the CPU compute cycles. The routine that performs this calculations is usually called the "QCD kernel" or "the lattice Dirac operator," or simply "D-slash." Optimizing D-slash for a given computer is the heart of the effort of implementing the QCD algorithm and will be discussed in detail in Section 8.6.

Because the D-slash matrix involves only nearest neighbor entries, it maps well on any massively parallel supercomputer that provides nearest neighbor communication between computing nodes. One simply splits the lattice into smaller sublattices and assigns each sublattice to a computing node. For example, if the massively parallel supercomputer is wired as a connected 4D grid with 8^4 processors, then the original problem on a 32^4 lattice can be implemented by putting 4^4 sites on each node. For illustration purposes, Figure 8.2 shows a two-dimensional 8×8 square lattice split into a 2×2 grid of compute nodes. Each node contains a 4×4 sublattice. The sublattice "surface" data are communicated to the nearest neighbor nodes via the supercomputers communication links (shadowed arrows).

If the massively parallel machine is not a four-dimensional grid of compute nodes, one would have to "map" the problem appropriately. However, most interestingly, the design of parallel supercomputers is also constrained by the requirement of locality. The cables that connect compute nodes need to be as short and as few as possible. The particular map needed for QCD on BG/L is discussed in Section 8.5.

Although the lattice formulation makes it possible to simulate a relativistic quantum field theory like QCD, what we are really after is the continuum properties of the theory. These are obtained by taking the limit $a \to 0$; that is, by reducing the lattice spacing a while keeping a "physical scale," such as the confinement scale, fixed. However, a cannot be made too small because this would result in too many lattice points. In actual practice, one monitors how physical quantities change as a decreases and the results are extrapolated to $a = 0$. For a simulation of a region with a given "physical size," the lattice spacing is carefully controlled so that it is not too small (this would mean more grid points and too much computing), or too large (this would make the nuclear particles smaller than the lattice spacing). Because of these limitations, one must compute variables on many different lattice sizes and then extrapolate to $a = 0$.

Early simulations used rather modest lattices 4^4–8^4. Today, lattice sizes are in the range of 32^4 to 64^4. As anecdotal reference has it that Wilson made an early

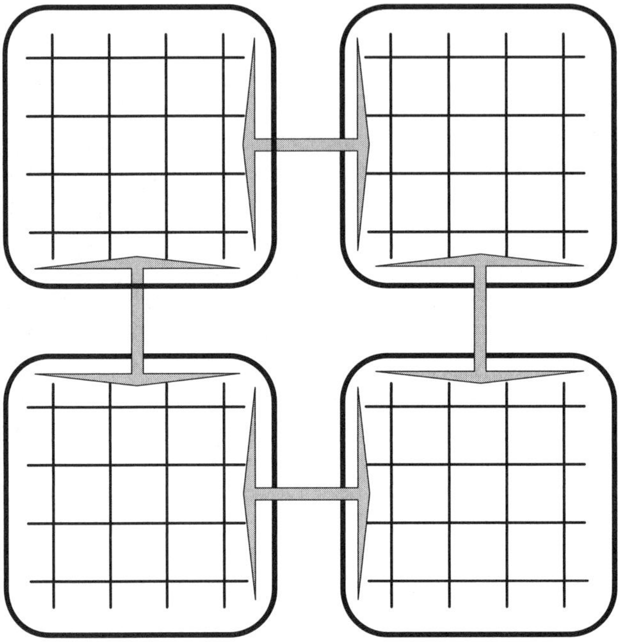

Figure 8.2 A two-dimensional 8 × 8 square lattice split into a 2 × 2 grid of compute nodes. Each node contains a 4 × 4 sublattice. The sublattice "surface" data are communicated to the nearest neighbor nodes via the supercomputers communication links (shadowed arrows).

and quite prescient estimate that a 128^4 lattice would be necessary to adequately simulate the theory and get results that would match experimental numbers. This estimate was based on the parameters of QCD and has proven to be quite accurate. The computing capability needed to simulate such large lattices is almost within our grasp. If supercomputer speed continues to follow Moore's law, such simulations should be possible in the next few years with the advent of multipetaflops size supercomputers.

8.4 THE IBM BLUEGENE/L SUPERCOMPUTER

The fastest supercomputer in the world as of the time of this writing is IBM's BlueGene/L supercomputer installed at Lawrence Livermore National Laboratory (LLNL). This computer has 131,072 CPU units and a peak speed of 370 Tflop/s. Although this speed will undoubtedly be outdated soon, the basic ideas behind implementing QCD on BG/L will apply to any future parallel supercomputer. In what follows, we give a brief description of BG/L focusing on the features that relate to the QCD simulations. For more details, the reader is referred to Ref. [6].

The BG/L massively parallel supercomputer consists of compute nodes that are connected with each other via a 3D cubic network. A schematic picture of the BG/L compute node and its components is shown in Figure 8.3. The compute node is

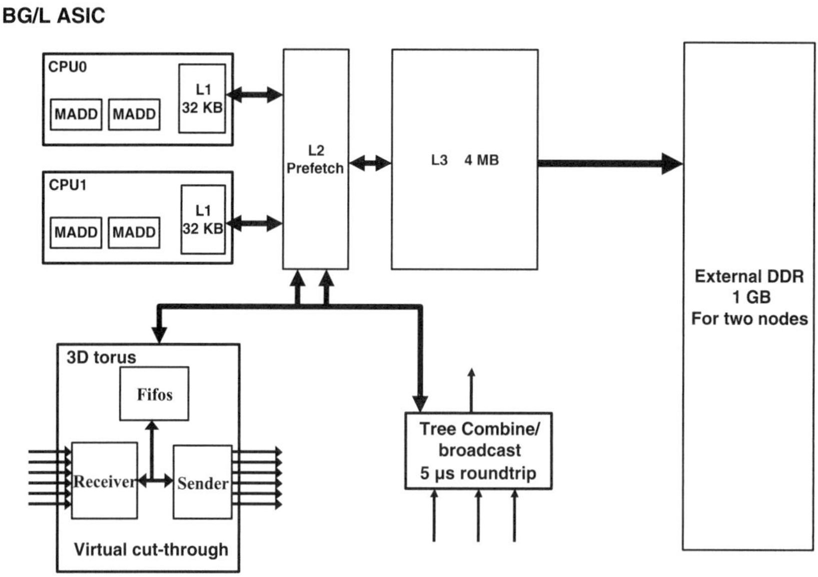

Figure 8.3 The main components of the BG/L ASIC as they relate to QCD and the external DRAM memory.

built using a single ASIC chip. Two chips are attached to a single board that also contains external DRAM. Sixteen such boards are connected to a larger board using dim sockets. These larger boards in turn are connected to a large vertical midplane board using large connectors. A total of 1024 nodes are housed in a "refrigerator-size" cabinet. Cabinets are connected with cables to form a larger system. Systems with different numbers of cabinets are possible. The largest such system (at LLNL) has 64 cabinets. This system contains a total of $32 \times 32 \times 64$ nodes connected as a three-dimensional cubic grid with the topology of a torus. Physical wires connect nearest neighbor nodes on the grid.

Although only nearest neighbors of the three-dimensional grid are physically connected, the network component inside each ASIC is a sophisticated router that allows any node to exchange hardware packets with any other node without any CPU intervention. To be precise, the network is a hardware-packet-based virtual cut-through network implemented entirely on the hardware. When one node decides to send some amount of data to another node, it first attaches a header to each payload to form a packet. This header, among other things, contains the coordinates of the destination node. Then, the CPU writes this packet to specific hardware addresses that correspond to on-node hardware FIFOS (first in first out memory storage). At that point, the network hardware takes over and automatically routes the packet through other nodes to its destination. When the packet is received at the destination node, the hardware deposits it into a reception fifo. The CPU of that node reads the packet from the fifo's hardware address and stores it to memory. Therefore, the network component of each node not only sends and receives packets but also routes packets through it from some input wire to the appropriate output wire. This happens entirely in the network hardware and no CPU intervention is required. The packets can have various sizes that are multiples of 32 byte and range from 32 byte to 256 byte. This size includes an 8 byte hardware header. The payload is the packet size minus 8 byte. It is important to note that the CPU core has to load/unload the packets between the torus fifos and the memory as well as construct and attach the header routing information. This requires CPU cycles that could have been used for calculations. There is no network DMA engine to allow overlap. The network component just described is indicated in Figure 8.3 as the 3D torus. A completely separate tree network is also present that allows fast global reductions such as global sums and broadcasts. In addition, other boot and control networks are also integrated into the ASIC but are not shown in Figure 8.3.

The on-node local environment consists of two standard IBM-440 CPU cores. However, each core is equipped with a custom floating point unit that is capable of executing two multiply–add (MADD) instructions per cycle. There are two floating point register files and a set of new machine instructions that allow a multitude of operations. The custom unit is particularly useful for complex number arithmetic. Therefore, the peak speed of a single chip is 8 instructions per CPU cycle.

Each CPU has its own 32 kB L1 cache. The two L1 caches interface with a very thin L2 cache that is a sequential multistream prefetcher. The L2 connects to a large chip eDRAM 4 MB L3 cache. The L3 interfaces with DRAM memory that is external to the ASIC via a DDR controller. The external DRAM size is 1 GB and is shared between the two ASICs on the board. The memory is not coherent at the L1 level but is coherent at the L2 level end beyond. In addition, there is a small SRAM that can be accessed in a fast way from the two CPU cores.

A popular way to use BG/L is in virtual node mode. In this mode, the system software treats each CPU core as a separate entity with its own private memory footprint. Some part of the memory is commonly mapped to allow data transfers between the cores. Each core is assigned half the network fifos and the cores access the network independently. In some sense, the two cores act as independent "virtual nodes."

8.5 MAPPING QCD ON BLUEGENE/L

As we have discussed in Sections 8.2 and 8.3, locality is a property of QCD as well as of many massively parallel supercomputers, including BlueGene/L. In QCD, locality is a requirement for the theory to have the correct properties to describe the strong force. In the case of BlueGene/L, locality is a requirement that is forced by design and cost considerations. These facts and the 4D and 3D nature of QCD and BG/L, respectively, dictate the natural low communication latency mapping, which is described in this section.

The three-dimensional nearest neighbor grid of BG/L nodes must be mapped to the four-dimensional nearest neighbor lattice grid of QCD. Although BG/L is a 3D grid, the BG/L node itself has an internal fourth dimension. This corresponds to the two CPU cores that can be thought of as two points in the fourth dimension. As a result, the natural mapping of QCD on BG/L uses virtual node mode. Each CPU core is assigned the same size sublattice of the full four-dimensional lattice. The sublattices communicate along the three dimensions of space using the torus network. To communicate along the time dimension, the two cores send each other messages via the common memory on the same node.

8.6 THE QCD KERNEL FOR BLUEGENE/L

As discussed in Section 8.3, the innermost loop of the QCD simulation has a small kernel (about 1000 lines) that consumes the majority of the machine's cycles. Therefore, highly optimizing this kernel is of primary importance to get good performance from the QCD code. In this section, we present the implementation of the QCD kernel, including the limitations and opportunities provided by the specifics of the hardware and software designs.

The kernel we describe uses one popular way of placing quarks on the lattice. It was invented by Wilson [3]. The kernel is called the Wilson fermion D-slash kernel. From here on, we will simply refer to as D-slash. The D-slash kernel describes the kinematics of quarks and their interaction with the gluon fields. It is given by the following equation:

$$D(x, y) = \frac{1}{2} \sum_{\mu=1,\ldots,4} [U_\mu(x)(1 + \gamma_\mu)\delta(x + \mu, y) - U_\mu^\dagger(x - \mu)(1 - \gamma_\mu)\delta(x - \mu, y)]. \tag{8.1}$$

During the CG inversion, the matrix $D(x, y)$ acts on an input quark field to produce an output quark field:

$$\Psi(x) = D(x, y)\Psi(y). \tag{8.2}$$

The gluon field in each of the four directions μ is represented by U_μ. The U_μ fields are link variables that are 3×3 complex unitary matrices. These are represented by 72 real numbers per site (9 complex numbers $\times$ 4 directions). The γ_μ are constant 4×4 complex matrices that act on an internal degree of freedom of the quark field called spin. The gluon fields also have a color index that takes three values. Therefore, the quark field needs 24 real numbers per site. $\delta(a, b)$ is 1 if $a = b$ and 0 otherwise. These δ functions enforce only nearest neighbor interactions. The space–time lattice coordinates are represented by x and y.

It turns out that the matrices $(1 + \gamma_m u)/2$ and $(1 - \gamma_m u)/2$ are projection operators. They project the four spin components of the quark fields down to two spin components. In practice, we first project the quark field using these matrices from 24 numbers down to 12 numbers, do all calculations and communications, and then reconstruct the full quark fields. This procedure saves computation and communication time and is called spin projection and spin reconstruction. The quark indices are in the following sequence: real/imaginary, spin, color, and space–time coordinates, the fastest changing being the leftmost one. The gluon and quark fields are stored in memory as double precision numbers and all calculations are done in double precision. One usual way to code the above equation for $D(x, y)$ that also allows the possibility of overlap between computations and communications is as follows:

(1) Use the "upper" projection operators $(1 + \gamma_\mu)/2$ $(\mu = 1, 2, 3, 4)$ to spin project Ψ into four temporary half spinors χ^u_μ for all local lattice sites, and store them to memory.

(2) Start the "backward" communications by communicating each χ^u_μ that is on the surface of the local lattice with the neighbor nodes along the negative direction μ. Because each half spinor has 12 numbers in double precision, this amounts to 96 byte. This needs to be communicated for each site that is on the surface of the lattice along the negative directions.

(3) Use the lower spin projectors $(1 - \gamma_\mu)/2$ $(\mu = 1, 2, 3, 4)$ to project Ψ and then multiply the result with $U^\dagger_\mu$. This results to four half spinors χ^l_μ for all lattice sites that are then stored to memory.

(4) Start the "forward" communications by communicating each χ^l_μ that is on the surface of the local lattice with the neighbor nodes along the positive direction μ. Because each half spinor has 12 numbers in double precision, this amounts to 96 byte. This needs to be communicated for each site that is on the surface of the lattice along the positive directions.

(5) Now wait for the "backward" communications of the χ^u_μ spinors to complete. For example, this can be done by polling the appropriate network registers.

(6) At this point all needed χ^u_μ spinors are on the local node. Multiply them with U_μ and then convert them back into full spinors. Add the full spinors on each site and store the resulting full spinor into memory.

(7) Now wait for the "forward" communications of the χ^l_μ spinors to complete. Again, for example, this can be done by polling the appropriate network registers.

(8) At this point, all needed χ^l_μ spinors are on the local node. Convert them back into full spinors and add them together on each site. Then load the full spinor of step (7) from memory and add to it the result for each site. This is the final full spinor result for each site.

It is important to note that in the above code, the U fields are not sequential in memory. Although they are sequential for the first four and last four terms in equation (8.2), they are not sequential between the two "sets." Furthermore, the loops over sites are over a four-dimensional lattice and, therefore, accesses to linear memory are typically not sequential in the space–time indices. As mentioned above, the memory accesses per site for a full spinor involves 24 real numbers, for a half spinor 12, and for a gauge field 72. Also, the communication messages are very small. Because the half spinors that need to be communicated are located on the surface of the four-dimensional lattice, they are typically not sequential in memory and cannot be grouped together into large messages. Therefore, each half spinor is communicated as a single message. This message has only $12x8 = 96$ byte in double precision and in BG/L, it cannot be overlapped with computations or memory accesses. In addition, the memory accesses and communications can not be rearranged because they are in-between computations. Furthermore, the computations are short and execute fast. For example, the multiplication of the gluon field with a half spinor on a site requires 72 multiply–add operations that execute in only 36 cycles in the double floating point unit. These properties make the calculation very sensitive to network and memory latencies. As a result of these complexities, QCD can serve as a powerful HPC benchmark. This is discussed in Section 8.9. But, it also means that it has to be coded with extreme care if it is to sustain a significant percent of the peak speed.

We have coded this kernel for BG/L. Although our implementation is particular to BG/L, it serves to show how important it is to "mold" the application to hardware features of the machine. Layers of software abstraction would make the implementation ineffective and performance would degrade significantly. The coding we have implemented is directly on the "metal." It uses in-line assembly and direct accesses instructions to hardware components. We list below the most important optimizations involved in the implementation.

(1) All floating point operations use the double multiply–add instructions (four floating point operations) by pairing all additions with multiplications in sets of two. Because QCD uses complex numbers, this is natural.

(2) All computations are carefully arranged to avoid pipeline conflicts that have to do with register access rules.

(3) The storage of the gauge and gluon fields is chosen to maximize the size of sequential accesses.

(4) All load and store operations are carefully arranged to take advantage of the cache hierarchy and the fact that the 440-CPU is capable of three outstanding load operations.

(5) Load and store operations can proceed in parallel with floating point computations. We take maximal advantage of this to reduce any memory access latencies.

(6) Each CG iteration requires two global sums over the entire machine. We do those using the tree collective network.

(7) BG/L does not have a network DMA engine. The CPU is responsible both for loading/unloading data from the network and preparing and attaching the packet headers. Given the small size of transfers that need to be completed between calculations, care should be taken to avoid introducing latencies. To achieve this, we developed a very fast communications layer directly on the hardware. This layer takes advantage of the nearest neighbor nature of the communication. Since the communication pattern is "persistent" (does not change during the run), the packet headers only need to be calculated once at program initialization. All communications are coded as direct transfers from/to memory without intermediate copying. And finally, since communication along the fourth direction is in the common memory of the two cores, we overlap the necessary memory copy time with the time it takes for the network packets to be fully received.

At the beginning of this section, we mentioned that on BG/L as on most computers, D-slash consumes more than 90% of the cycles. As a result, D-slash was written in the highly optimized in-line assembly code described above. But what about the remaining 10% of the cycles that are spent in other parts of the QCD code. In most implementations of QCD, this code is tens of thousands of lines long, written in a high-level language, including complex algorithms and using sophisticated syntax to allow collaboration between groups. To create a bridge between the kernel implementation of D-slash and such complex codes, we have created a library function for D-slash that can be called from a general C++ program. To test this function, we used the C++ code base of the CPS physics system that originated at Columbia University (Columbia Physics System) [13].

8.7 PERFORMANCE AND SCALING

The performance and scaling of QCD is traditionally given for the D-slash operator and the full CG inverter. As mentioned earlier, this is because they so heavily dominate the execution time. In many cases, more than 90% of the cycles are consumed by them.

All of our performance measurements are done in virtual-node-mode as described in Section 8.6. In Table 8.1, we give the percent of peak sustained on a single node (two CPUs) for different sizes of the local lattice on a CPU. These are strong scaling data since the local size of the problem changes, which is equivalent to strong scaling where the global size is kept fixed while the number of nodes is changed. The performance of D-slash with and without communication is given as well as the performance of the CG inverter. Note that for small local lattice, the performance without communications is larger. This is because the problem almost fits into the L1 cache. However, when the communications are included, the performance drops dramatically because for this small lattice, the surface to volume ratio is large. For larger local lattices, the performance without communications is not as good because the problem does not fit in L1. However, the degradation due to communications is smaller because the surface–volume ratio is smaller.

The QCD kernel can also be tested as a weak scaling application where the local problem size is kept fixed while the machine size is increased. Because of the nearest

Table 8.1 The Percent of Peak Performance for Various Local-Size Lattices on a Single Node (Akin to Strong Scaling)

Lattice size	2^4	4×2^3	4^4	8×4^3	$8^2 \times 4^2$	16×4^3
D-slash, no communications	31.5	28.2	25.9	27.1	27.1	27.8
D-slash, with communications	12.6	15.4	15.6	19.5	19.7	20.3
CG inverter	13.1	15.3	15.4	18.7	18.8	19.0

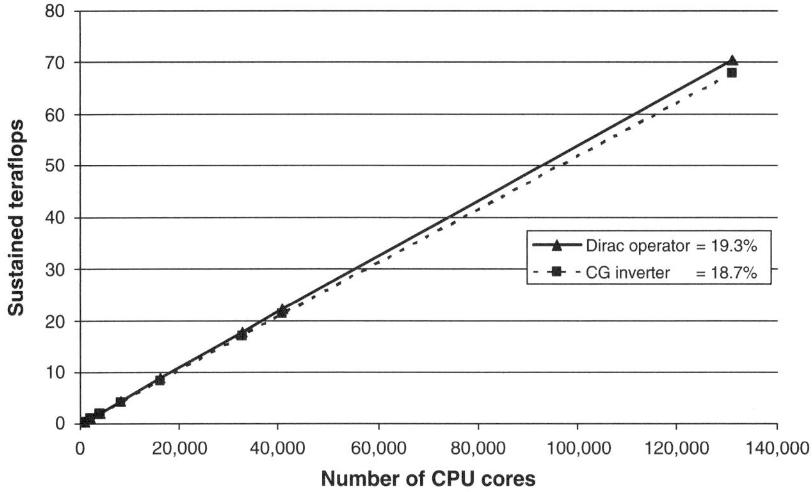

Figure 8.4 The QCD kernel and conjugate gradient inverter speed up on the BG/L supercomputer as the number of compute nodes is increased up to 131,072 CPU cores. The largest sustained speed in this graph is 70.5 Tflop/s. The total lattice has size $128 \times 128 \times 256 \times 32$. The CPU cores form a grid with size $32 \times 32 \times 64 \times 2$ and, therefore, the local lattice on a CPU has size $4 \times 4 \times 4 \times 16$. This figure is from Ref. [5].

neighbor nature of the communication patterns and the fast global sum reduction, the weak scaling is almost perfect. This scaling is shown in Figure 8.4.

The work described above was awarded the Gordon Bell Special Achievement Award in 2006 [5].

8.8 A POWERFUL TOOL TO TEST SUPERCOMPUTERS

The QCD code makes complex requirements on the balance between CPU speed, memory, and network latencies and bandwidths that are useful in making critical architectural decisions and identify software functionality issues. The QCD application code described above can be used in hardware verification as well as in system-level validation and fault isolation. Further, it can be used for performance evaluation both before and after the computer is built. The QCD code described above was used in this way for the designing, bringing up, and benchmarking of BlueGene/L at IBM. Also, it was used for performance evaluation at several customer sites.

During the architecture phase, decisions must be made about the network and memory systems. QCD demands a low-latency, high-bandwidth local neighbor network. This includes neighboring nodes up to a distance of two node–grid hops. Although most QCD implementations only need nearest neighbor communications, some variants of the code need higher order corrections that involve more distant communications—up to two node–grid hops. Further, since the QCD kernel can take advantage of the possibility of overlapping communications and computations, a DMA-driven network could offer significant advantages.

At the level of the single node, low-latency, high-bandwidth memory access is critical, as is the ability to overlap memory accesses with computations as well as communications. This implies that a CPU with separate load/store and compute hardware would provide significant benefits. Also, a DMA or a "smart-prefetch" engine that brings the data closer to the CPU would be beneficial since the QCD-kernel has exactly predictable and repeatable memory access patterns. Prefetching (into memory or cache) the data that the kernel will need further down the code pipeline would reduce memory access latencies significantly.

Note that the above architecture indications are such that they would also benefit a large class of simulations of physical systems. This is because many applications (aircraft simulation, CFD, weather modeling, etc.) have local interactions and, therefore, make similar demands on the computer architecture and software as does QCD.

When designing supercomputer hardware, cost/benefit decisions are made that increase/decrease the latencies of hardware components. It is clear that a design that can meet the hardware architecture demands we have described must be nimble. It would also have to be simple and modular so that it can respond to the demands of the CPU with minimum delays. It must also have short pipelines to meet the stringent latency criteria.

During software design, communication layers and application libraries need to be developed. Again, the architectural criteria described above apply. To maintain low latency and high bandwidth, the network software must also be very "thin," simple, modular, and nimble. In general, software tends to be designed to be able to satisfy "every possible case." However, software "branches" may need to be deployed to serve the specific needs of applications such as QCD. As discussed in Section 8.6, we developed a specialized communications layer molded around the hardware to achieve significant performance. Heavier communication layers such as MPI would simply introduce very large latencies and performance degradation. The specialized memory accesses requirements of QCD may not be optimizable by a compiler. In this case, special implementation of commonly used memory access functions that may be used by many applications may make the difference between good and poor performances. These arguments clearly suggest the need for the development of high-performance libraries that involve functions written directly on the hardware without layers of abstraction, which can achieve a high percentage of the peak speed.

During hardware verification, the QCD kernel can be used to expose otherwise unreachable "bugs." This is because it uses all the hardware at high efficiency and (when possible) at high overlap. The floating point unit can be operating at full performance while the network is transferring packets at maximum bandwidth and the memory system is delivering data, all in a well-orchestrated and repeatable way. This is invaluable because all system components are not only exercised but are also exercised at the same time allowing testing of intercomponent dependencies.

At the system assembly and validation level, one needs to be able to efficiently isolate faulty nodes or network connections. Because QCD is a nearest neighbor application and has high regularity, it can be used to effectively pinpoint faults. For example, each node of the system can be given the same parameters and initial data. Then each node should produce identical answers, including communications, since the data sent in, say, the $+x$ direction would have to be the same as the data received from the $-x$ direction. If a node gets a different answer from the rest of them, the problem has to be isolated to that node's neighborhood.

Finally, as discussed in Sections 8.6 and 8.9, the QCD kernel is very sensitive to performance degradation effects. Paper studies for a given architecture can be done before the machine is built. Performance measurements, such as were presented in Section 8.7, can continue to be done during bringing up of architecture and software and, finally, can be done to benchmark the full system.

8.9 QCD AS AN HPC BENCHMARK

The QCD code performance is very sensitive to latencies. This indicates that QCD can be used to define a strict HPC benchmark that would expose inefficiencies in the hardware memory and network systems as well as in the system and library software components. A possible way in which QCD can be used as an HPC benchmark is to measure the sustained speed as a percent of peak for QCD as follows:

Measure the number of operations per site it takes to execute one application of the QCD Wilson even/odd preconditioned D-slash operator on a sublattice (even or odd) with 0.5 K sites per CPU core including communications. The sustained percent of peak is 1296 divided by this measurement times 100%.

For BG/L, this number is 20.3% (see last column of Table 8.1).

8.10 AN INTIMATE RELATIONSHIP

The relationship of QCD and supercomputing is long-standing and natural. It is important for both theoretical physics and supercomputing to realize the enormous benefits that this relationship has generated for both disciplines. This is especially true now that both fields have entered a new era where new experimental physics efforts (LHC at CERN, the DZero experiment at Fermilab, and the RHIC experiment at BNL) are poised to discover fresh results whose mysteries must be resolved by theoretical physics. Supercomputing is also entering a brave new era where the capabilities of these machines are only a few orders of magnitude away from biological systems and we are on the verge of breakthroughs in understanding global weather and climate change using these new computing capabilities.

To conclude, the reader may find interesting the fact that Richard Feynmann, one of the most celebrated theoretical physicists of the last century and a Physics Nobel Laureate, helped to develop the communication protocol for the connection machine and benchmarked the machine by writing a code for QCD [14].

REFERENCES

1. F. Wilczek. What QCD tells us about nature—and why we should listen. *Nucl. Phys. A.*, 663:3, 2000. http://xxx.lanl.gov/ps/hep-ph/9907340.
2. K.G. Wilson. Confinement of quarks. *Phys. Rev. D*, 10:2445, 1974.
3. K.G. Wilson. Quarks and strings on a lattice. In A. Zichichi, editor, *New Phenomena in Subnuclear Physics*, Part A. Plenum Press, New York, 1975, p. 69.
4. G. Bhanot, D. Chen, A. Gara, J. Sexton, and P. Vranas. QCD on the blueGene/L supercomputer. *Nucl. Phys. B.* 140, (Proc. Suppl.):823, 2005. http://xxx.lanl.gov/ps/hep-lat/0409042.
5. P. Vranas, G. Bhanot, M. Blumrich, D. Chen, A. Gara, M. Giampapa, P. Heidelberger, V. Salapura, J.C. Sexton, and R. Soltz. The blueGene/L supercomputer and quantum chromodynamics, 2006 Gordon Bell Special Achievement Award. *Proceedings of the 2006 ACM/IEE Conference on Supercomputing*, Tampa, FL, USA. http://sc06.supercomputing.org/schedule/pdf/gb110.pdf., 2006.
6. The blueGene/L. IBM *J. Res. Dev.*, 49 (2–3): full issue, 2005.
7. P. Vranas, G. Bhanot, M. Blumrich, D. Chen, A. Gara, M. Giampapa, P. Heidelberger, V. Salapura, J.C. Sexton, and R. Soltz. Massively parallel QCD. IBM *J. Res. Dev.*, 52(1–2):189, 2007.
8. T.-P. Cheng and L.-F. Li. *Gauge Theory and Elementary Particle Physics*. Oxford University Press, 1984.
9. M.E. Peskin and D.V. Schroeder. *An introduction to quantum field theory*. Perseus Books Publishing, 1995.
10. M. Creutz. *Quark, Gluons and Lattices*. Cambridge University Press, 1983.
11. I. Monvay and G. Munster. *Quantum Fields on a Lattice*. Cambridge University Press, 1994.
12. J. Kogut. *Milestones in Lattice Gauge Theory*. Kluwer Academic Publishers, 2004.
13. CPS: Columbia Physics System. http://www.epcc.ed.ac.uk/ ukqcd/cps.
14. W.D. Hillis. Richard Feynman and the connection machine. http://www.kurzweilai.net/articles/art0504.html?printable=1

Part II

Adaptive Computational Infrastructures

Chapter 9

The SCIJump Framework for Parallel and Distributed Scientific Computing

Steven G. Parker, Kostadin Damevski, Ayla Khan, Ashwin Swaminathan, and Christopher R. Johnson

9.1 INTRODUCTION

In recent years, software component technology has been a successful methodology for large-scale commercial software development. Component technology combines a set of frequently used functions in an easily reusable component and makes the implementation transparent to the users or other components. Developers create new software applications by connecting groups of components. Component technology is becoming increasingly popular for large-scale scientific computing to help tame software complexity resulting from coupling multiple disciplines, multiple scales, and/or multiple physical phenomena.

In this chapter, we discuss our SCIJump problem solving environment (PSE) that builds on its successful predecessor SCIRun and the DOE common component architecture (CCA) scientific component model. SCIJump provides distributed computing, parallel components, and the ability to combine components from several component models in a single application. These tools provide the ability to use a larger set of computing resources to solve a wider set of problems. For even larger applications that may require thousands of computing resources and tens of thousands of component instances, we present our prototype scalable distributed component framework technology called CCALoop.

Advanced Computational Infrastructures For Parallel and Distributed Adaptive Applications. Edited by Manish Parashar and Xiaolin Li

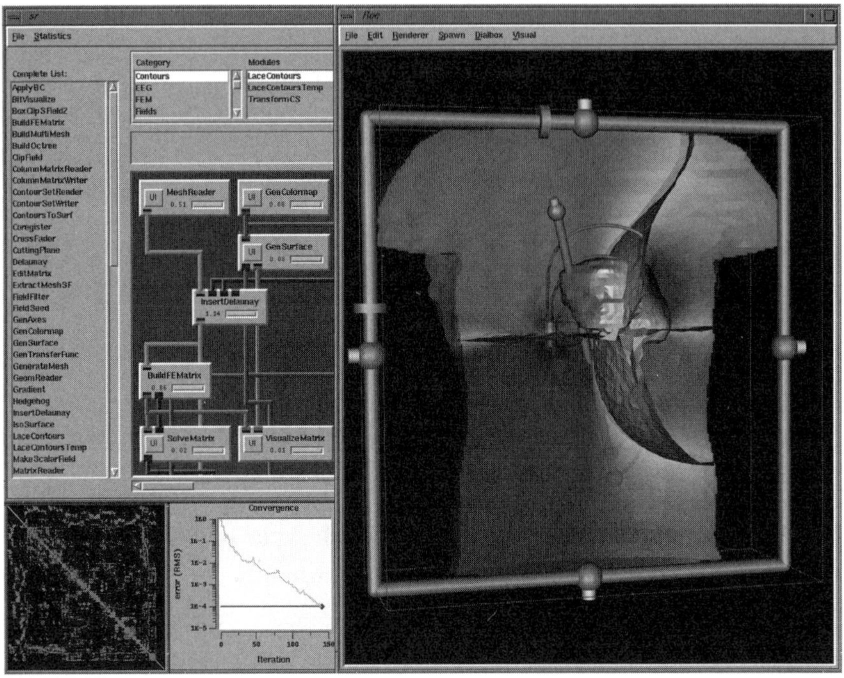

Figure 9.1 The SCIRun PSE, illustrating a 3D finite element simulation of an implantable cardiac defibrillator.

When the technology described in CCALoop matures, it will be included in SCIJump.

SCIRun is a scientific PSE that allows interactive construction and steering of large-scale scientific computations [17–19, 25–27]. A scientific application is constructed by connecting computational elements (modules) to form a program (network), as shown in Figure 9.1. The program may contain several computational elements as well as several visualization elements, all of which work together in orchestrating a solution to a scientific problem. SCIRun is designed to facilitate large-scale scientific computation and visualization on a wide range of architectures from the desktop to large supercomputers. Geometric inputs and computational parameters may be changed interactively, and the interface provides immediate feedback to the investigator.

The CCA model consists of a framework and an expandable set of components. The framework is a workbench for building, connecting, and running components. A component is the basic unit of an application. A CCA component consists of one or more ports, and a port is a group of method call-based interfaces. There are two types of ports: *uses* and *provides*. A provides port (or callee) implements its interfaces and waits for other ports to call them. A uses port (or caller) issues method calls that can be fulfilled by a type compatible provides port on a different component. A CCA port is represented by an interface, which is specified through the scientific interface definition language (SIDL). SIDL is compiled to specific language bindings using compilers such as Babel [12], which supports a number of languages such as C/C++, Java, Fortran, Python, and so on.

SCIJump is a framework built on SCIRun [11] infrastructure that combines CCA compatible architecture with hooks for other commercial and academic component models. It provides a broad approach that will allow scientists to combine a variety of tools for solving a particular problem. The overarching design goal of SCIJump is to provide the ability for a computational scientist to use the right tool for the right job. SCIJump utilizes parallel-to-parallel remote method invocation (RMI) to connect components in a distributed memory environment and is multithreaded to facilitate shared memory programming. It also has an optional visual programming interface. A few of the design goals of SCIJump are

1. SCIJump is fully CCA compatible, thus any CCA components can be used in SCIJump and CCA components developed from SCIJump can also be used in other CCA frameworks.
2. SCIJump accommodates several useful component models. In addition to CCA components and SCIRun dataflow modules, CORBA components and visualization toolkit (Vtk)[20] modules are supported in SCIJump, which can be utilized in the same simulation.
3. SCIJump builds bridges between different component models, so that we can combine a disparate array of computational tools to create powerful applications with cooperative components from different sources.
4. SCIJump supports distributed computing. Components created on different computers can be networked to build high-performance applications.
5. SCIJump supports parallel components in a variety of ways for maximum flexibility. This support is not constrained to only CCA components, because SCIJump employs a M process to N process method invocation and data redistribution ($M \times N$) library [5] that can potentially be used by many component models.

Figure 9.2 shows a SCIJump application that demonstrates bridging multiple component models. SCIJump is currently released under the MIT license and can be obtained at http://www.sci.utah.edu.

As scientific computing experiences continuous growth of the size of simulations, component frameworks intended for scientific computing need to handle more components and execute on numerous hardware resources simultaneously. Our distributed component framework CCALoop presents a novel design that supports scalability in both number of components in the system and distributed computing resources. CCALoop also incorporates several other beneficial design principles for distributed component frameworks such as fault tolerance, parallel component support, and multiple user support.

Section 9.2 discusses meta-components, while Section 9.3 and 9.4 explain the support SCIJump provides for distributed computing and parallel components.

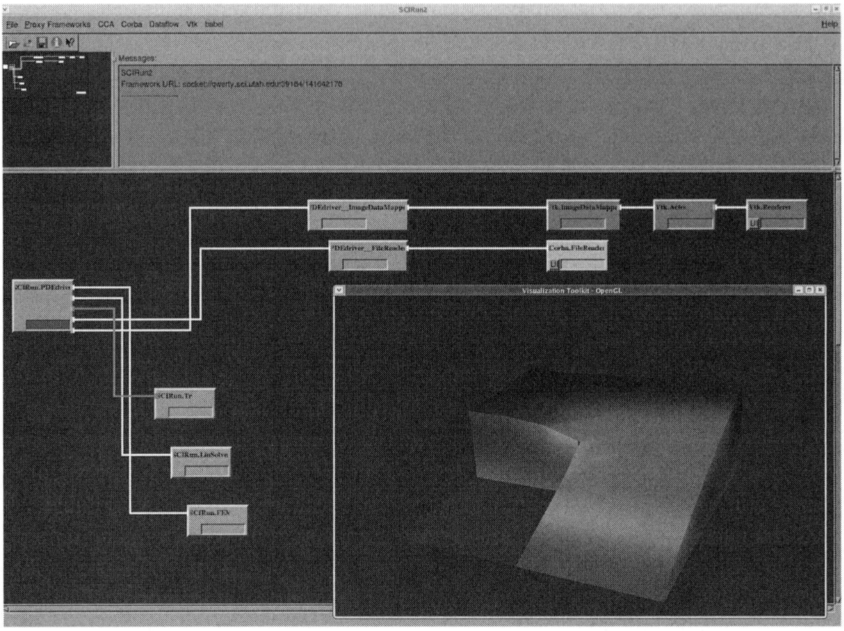

Figure 9.2 Components from different models cooperate in SCIJump.

The design of our highly scalable component framework CCALoop is discussed in Section 9.5. We present conclusions and future work in Section 9.6.

9.2 META-COMPONENT MODEL

Component software systems for scientific computing provide a limited form of interoperability, typically working only with other components that implement the same underlying component model. As such, we propose a next-generation concept of meta-components where software components can be manipulated in a more abstract manner, providing a plug-in architecture for component models and bridges between them, allowing for interoperability between different component models. These abstract, meta-components are manipulated and managed by the SCIJump framework, while concrete, standard component models perform the actual work. Thus, components implemented with disparate component models can be orchestrated together. As an example of a multicomponent system, we have used this system to connect components from SCIRun, the visualization toolkit, and the CCA into a single application (see Figure 9.2).

The success of Java Beans, COM, CORBA, and CCA stems from allowing users to rapidly assemble computational tools from components in a single environment. However, these systems typically do not interact with one another in a straightforward manner, and it is difficult to take components developed for one system and redeploy them in another. Software developers must *buy in* to a particular model and produce components for one particular system. Users must typically select a single system or face the challenges of manually managing the data transfer between multiple (usually) incompatible systems. SCIJump addresses these shortcomings through the meta-component model, allowing support for disparate component-based systems to be incorporated into a single environment and managed through a common user-centric visual interface. Furthermore, many systems that are not traditionally thought of as component models, but that have well-designed, regular structures, can be mapped to a component model and manipulated dynamically.

Figure 9.3 demonstrates a simple example of how SCIJump bridges different component models. Two CCA components (*driver* and *integrator*) and one CORBA component (*function*) are created in the SCIJump framework. In this simple example, the driver is connected to the both function and integrator. Inside SCIJump, two frameworks are hidden: the CCA framework and the CORBA object request broker (ORB). The CCA framework creates the CCA components, driver and integrator. The CORBA framework creates the CORBA component, function. The two CCA components can be connected in a straightforward manner through the CCA component model. However, the components driver and function cannot be connected directly because neither CCA nor CORBA allows a connection from a component of a different model, so a bridge component is created instead. Bridges belong to a special internal component model used to build connections between components of different component models. In this example, bridge has two ports, one CCA port and one CORBA port, allowing it to be connected to the both CCA and CORBA components. The CORBA invocation is converted to a request to the CCA port inside the bridge component.

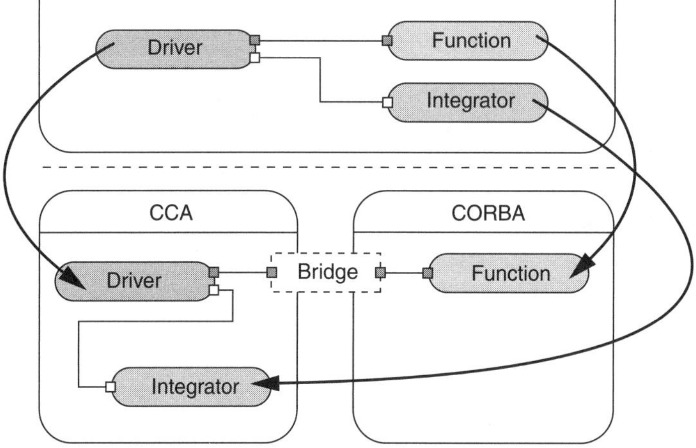

Figure 9.3 Bridging components from different models in SCIJump.

Bridge components can be manually or automatically generated. In situations where interfaces are easily mapped between one interface and another, automatically generated bridges can facilitate interoperability in a straightforward way. More complex component interactions may require manually generated bridge components. Bridge components may implement heavyweight transformations between component models, and therefore have the potential to introduce performance bottlenecks. For scenarios that require maximum performance, reimplementation of both components in a common, performance-oriented component model may be required. However, for rapid prototyping or for components that are not performance critical, this is completely acceptable.

A generalized translation between the component models is needed to automatically generate a bridge component. Typically, a software engineer determines how two particular component models will interact; this task can require creating methods of data and controlling translation between the two models, which can be quite difficult in some scenarios. The software engineer implements the translation as a compiler plug-in, which is used as the translation specification as it abstractly represents the entire translation between the two component models. It is specified by an eRuby (embedded Ruby) template document. eRuby templates are text files that can be augmented by Ruby [13] scripts. Ruby scripts are useful for situations where translation requires more sophistication than regular text (such as control structures or additional parsing). The scripted plug-in provides us with better flexibility and more power with the end goal of supporting translation between a wider range of component models.

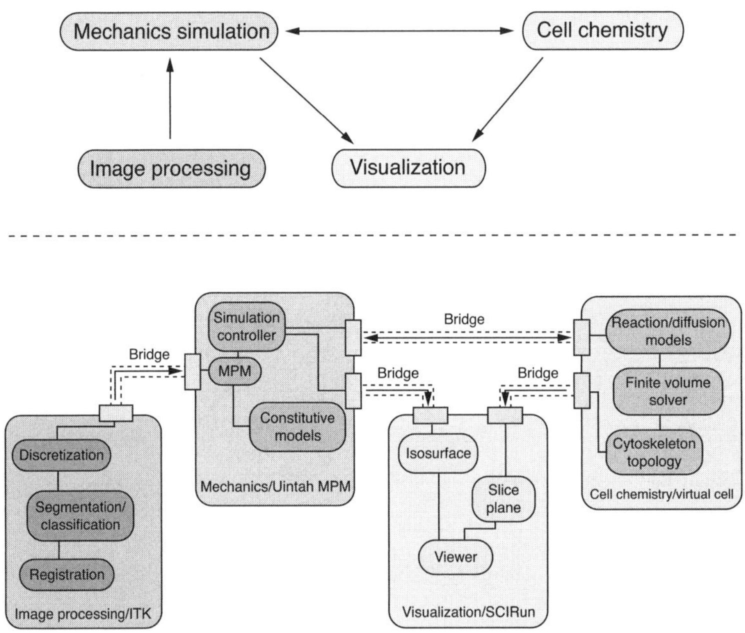

Figure 9.4 A more intricate example of how components of different models cooperate in SCIJump. The application and components shown are from a realistic (albeit incomplete) scenario.

The only other source of information is the interface of the ports we want to bridge (usually expressed in an IDL file). The bridge compiler accepts commands that specify a mapping between incompatible interfaces, where the interfaces between the components differ in member names or types but not functionality. Using a combination of the plug-in and the interface augmented with mapping commands, the compiler is able to generate the specific bridge component. This component is automatically connected and ready to broker the translation between the two components of different models.

Figure 9.4 shows a more complex example that is motivated by the needs of a biological application. This example works very much like the previous one: the framework manages components from several different component models through the meta-model interface. Components from the same model interact with each other natively and interact with components in other models through bridges. Allowing components to communicate with each other through native mechanisms ensures that performance bottlenecks are not introduced and that the original semantics are preserved.

9.3 DISTRIBUTED COMPUTING

SCIJump provides support for RMI-based distributed objects. This support is utilized in the core of the SCIRun framework in addition to distributed components. This section describes the design of the distributed object subsystem.

A distributed object implements a set of interfaces defined in SIDL that can be referenced remotely. The distributed object is similar to the C++ object, it utilizes similar inheritance rules, and all objects share the same code. However, only methods (interfaces) can be referenced, and the interfaces must be defined in SIDL. We implemented a straightforward distributed object system by extending the SIDL language and building upon this system for implementing parallel-to-parallel component connections, which will be demonstrated in the next section.

A distributed object is implemented by a concrete C++ class and referenced by a proxy class. The proxy class is a machine-generated class that associates a user-made method call to a call by the concrete object. The proxy classes are described in a SIDL file, which is parsed by a compiler that recognizes the SIDL extensions to generate the proxy classes. The proxy classes are defined as abstract classes with a set of pure virtual functions. The concrete classes extend those abstract proxy classes and implement each virtual functions.

There are two types of object proxies. One is called server proxy, and the other is called client proxy. The server proxy (or skeleton) is the object proxy created in the same memory address space as the concrete object. When the concrete object is created, the server proxy starts and works as a server, waiting for any local or remote method invocations. The client proxy (or stub) is the proxy created on a different memory address space. When a method is called through the client proxy, the client proxy will package the calling arguments into a single message and send the message to the server proxy, and then wait for the server proxy to invoke the methods and return the result and argument changes.

We created the data transmitter, which is a communication layer used by generated proxy code for handling messaging. We also employ the concept of a data transmission point (DTP), which is similar to the start and end points used in nexus [8]. A DTP is a data structure that contains a object pointer pointing to the context of a concrete class. Each memory address space has only one data transmitter, and each data transmitter uses three communication ports (sockets): one listening port, one receiving port, and one sending port. All the DTPs in the same address space share the same data transmitter. A data transmitter is identified by its universal resource identifier (URI): IP address plus listening port. A DTP is identified by its memory address together with the data transmitter URI, because DTP addresses are unique in the same memory address space. Optionally, we could use other types of object identifiers.

The proxy object package method calls into messages by marshaling objects and then waiting for a reply. Nonpointer arguments, such as integers, fixed-sized arrays and strings (character arrays), are marshaled by the proxy into a message in the order that they are presented in the method. After the server proxy receives the message, it unmarshals the arguments in the same order. An array size is marshaled in the beginning of an array argument so that the proxy knows how to allocate memory for the array. SIDL supports a special opaque data type that can be used to marshal pointers if the two objects are in the same address space. Distributed object references are marshaled by packaging the DTP URI (data transmitter URI and object ID). The DTP URI is actually marshaled as a string and when it is unmarshaled, a new proxy of the appropriate type is created based on the DTP URI.

C++ exceptions are handled as special distributed objects. In a remote method invocation, the server proxy tries to catch an exception (also a distributed object) before it returns. If it catches one, the exception pointer is marshaled to the returned message. Upon receiving the message, the client proxy unmarshals the message and obtains the exception. The exception is then rethrown by the proxy.

9.4 PARALLEL COMPONENTS

This section introduces the CCA parallel component design and discusses issues arising from the implementation. Our design goal is to make the parallelism transparent to the component users. In most cases, the component users can use a parallel component as the way they use sequential component without knowing that a component is actually parallel component.

Parallel CCA component (PCom) is a set of similar components that run in a set of processes. When the number of processes is one, the PCom is equivalent to a sequential component. We call each component in a PCom a *member component*. Member components typically communicate internally with MPI [15] or an equivalent message passing library.

PComs communicate with each other through CCA-style RMI ports. We developed a prototype parallel component infrastructure [3] that facilitates connection of parallel components in a distributed environment. This model supports two types of methods calls, *independent* and *collective*, and as such our port model supports both independent and collective ports.

An independent port is created by a single component member, and it contains only independent interfaces. A collective port is created and owned by all component members in a PCom, and one or more of its methods are collective. Collective methods require that all member components participate in the collective calls in the same order.

As an example of how parallel components interact, let pA be a uses port of component A, and and pB be a provides port of component B. Both pA and pB have the same port type, which defines the interface. If pB is a collective port and has the following interface:

```
collective int foo(inout int arg);
```

then getPort("pA") returns a collective pointer that points to the collective port pB. If pB is an independent port, then getPort("pA") returns a pointer that points to an independent port.

Component A can have one or more members, so each member might obtain a (collective/independent) pointer to a provides port. The component developer can decide what subset (one, many, or all components) should participate in a method call *foo*(*arg*). When any member component registers a uses port, all other members can share the same uses port. But for a collective provides port, each member must call addProvidesPort to register each member port.

The $M \times N$ library takes care of the collective method invocation and data distribution. We repeat only the essentials here, and one can refer to Ref. [5] for details.

If a M-member PCom A obtains a pointer *ptr* pointing to a N-member PCom's B collective port pB, then *ptr*→ *foo*(*args*) is a collective method invocation. The $M \times N$ library index PCom members with rank 0,1, ... , $M-1$ for A and 0,1, ... ,$N-1$ for B. If $M = N$, then the ith member component of A calls *foo*(*args*) on the ith component of B. But if $M < N$, then we "extend" the A's to 0,1,2, ... , M, 0, 1,2, ... M, ... $N-1$ and they call *foo*(*args*) on each member component of B like the $M = N$ case, but only the first M calls request returns.

The left panel of Figure 9.5 shows an example of this case with $M = 3$ and $N = 5$. If $M > N$, we "extend" component B's set to 0, 1, ... , N, 0, 1, ... , N, ... , $M-1$ and only the first N member components of B are actually called, and the rest are not called but simply return the result. We rely on collective semantics from the components to ensure consistency without requiring global synchronization. The right panel of Figure 9.5 shows an example of this case with $M = 5$ and $N = 3$.

The $M \times N$ library also does most of the work for the data redistribution. A multidimensional array can be defined as a distributed array that associates a distribution scheduler with the real data. Both callers and callees define the distribution schedule before the remote method invocation, using a first-stride-last representation for each dimension of the array. The SIDL compiler creates the scheduler and scheduling is done in the background.

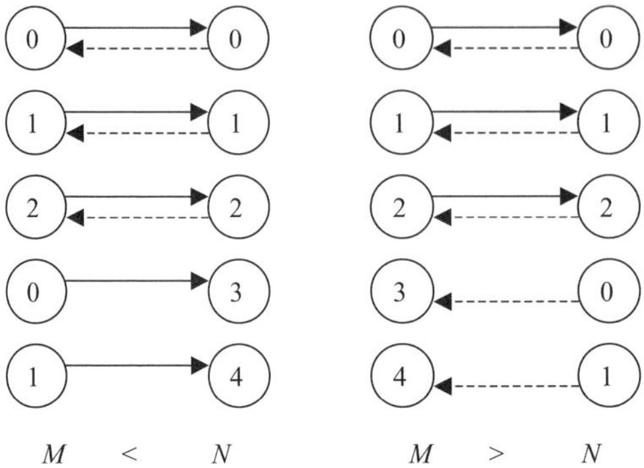

Figure 9.5 $M \times N$ method invocation, with the caller on the left and the callee on the right. In the left scenario, the number of callers is fewer than the numbers of callees, so some callers make multiple method calls. In the right, the number of callees is fewer, so some callees send multiple return values.

With independent ports and collective ports, we cover the two extremes. Ports that require communication among a subset of the member components present a greater challenge. Instead, we utilize a subsetting capability in the $M \times N$ system to produce ports that are associated with a subset of the member components, and then utilize them as collective ports.

SCIJump provides the mechanism to start a parallel component on either shared memory multiprocessors computers or clusters. SCIJump consists of a main framework and a set of parallel component loaders (PCLs). A PCL can be started with ssh on a cluster, where it gathers and reports its local component repository and registers to the main framework. The PCL on a N-node cluster is essentially a set of loaders, each running on a node. When the user requests to create a parallel component, the PCL instantiates a parallel component on its processes (or nodes) and passes a distributed pointer to the SCIJump framework. PCLs are responsible for creating and destroying components running on their nodes, but they do not maintain the port connections. The SCIJump framework maintains all component instances and port connections.

Supporting threads and MPI together can be difficult. MPI provides a convenient communication among the processes in a cluster. However, if any process has more than one thread and the MPI calls are made in those threads, the MPI communication may break because MPI distinguishes only processes, not threads. The MPI interface allows an implementation to support threads but does not require it, allowing most MPI implementations not to be threadsafe. We provide support for both threadsafe and non-threadsafe MPI implementations so that users can choose any available MPI.

To address variability of MPI implementations and to optimize parallel-to-parallel component communication performance, we provide three different locking behaviors, "synchronous," "nonblocking asynchronous," and "one-way asynchronous," as shown in Figure 9.6. These are currently provided only in conjunction with the Babel [12] SIDL compiler, whose facilities are integrated within SCIJump as a separate component model. When Babel uses a wire protocol without threads, we conservatively allow only "synchronous" parallel remote method invocation (PRMI).

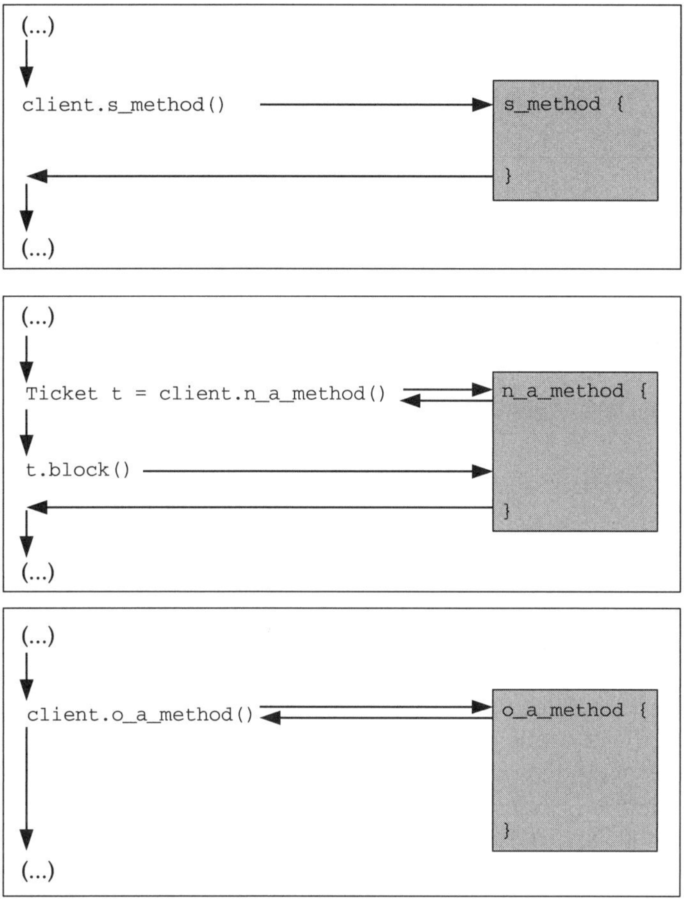

Figure 9.6 The synchronization options given for (top to bottom) synchronous (s_method), nonblocking asynchronous (n_a_method), and one-way asynchronous (o_a_method) parallel remote method invocation.

Similarly, to allow asynchronous PRMI, we require a version of the parallel library (e.g., MPI, PVM) that is threadsafe. An example of the progression of the thread of execution for each type of method is given in Figure 9.6 and an explanation of the types of PRMI synchronization option we provide follows:

- *Synchronous*: These parallel invocations should work in all system environments so they are built to work without any thread support. Even if threads exist in the wire protocol, the parallel library may not be threadsafe, so we synchronize conservatively in order to get the right behavior in all scenarios. The conservative synchronization style of these parallel invocation comes at a significant performance cost.

- *Nonblocking Asynchronous*: Nonblocking methods in Babel return immediately when invoked, and each method returns a ticket that can be used to wait until the call finishes or to periodically check its status. We extend this existing ticket mechanism from Babel nonblocking calls to additionally control our nonblocking asynchronous calls. This enables the caller to use a ticket to check the status of an invocation. For parallel objects receiving invocations from multiple proxies, we provide a guarantee that two method calls coming from the same proxy (caller) will execute in order and will be nonovertaking on the callee.
- *One-Way Asynchronous*: These methods are defined not to return any variable or error condition to the caller, making them least synchronized. Only "in" arguments are allowed so the only guarantee we provide for these calls is ordering and nonovertaking behavior of invocations coming from the same caller.

When designing PRMI, it is crucial to provide the user with a consistent set of guarantees. In the case of most programming languages, execution order is something that a programmer relies on for program correctness. When programming in a middleware that is multithreaded and offers support for an operation such as PRMI, the invocation order given by a user should be preserved. In the past, we have identified situations when some reordering may take place [4] with user awareness. However, in implementing general PRMI, we choose not to reorder any invocations and ensure that calls made on the proxy execute in order on the server. An object may receive calls from multiple proxies, and we see no reason why synchronization should preserve interproxy order. Therefore, our implementation does not guarantee invocation order from more than one proxy.

Some synchronization is necessary to provide single proxy invocation ordering. Another choice we make is to synchronize on the object (callee) side and never on the caller side. Previous implementations have synchronized on the proxy (caller) side, but in a threaded environment this is not necessary. We eliminate any proxy synchronization for all but the conservative "collective" invocations that have to be deadlock free in the absence of threads.

9.5 CCALoop

Component frameworks aimed at scientific computing need to support a growing trend in this domain toward larger simulations that produce more encompassing and accurate results. The CCA component model has already been used in several domains, creating components for large simulations involving accelerator design, climate modeling, combustion, and accidental fires and explosions [14]. These simulations are often targeted to execute on sets of distributed memory machines spanning several computational and organizational domains [1]. To address this computational paradigm, a collection of component frameworks that are able to cooperate to manage a large, long-running scientific simulation containing many components are necessary.

In each of the CCA-compliant component frameworks, facilities are provided to support the collaboration among several distributed component frameworks. However, existing designs do not scale to larger applications and multiple computing resources. This is due to a master–slave (server–client) communication paradigm. In these systems, the master framework manages all the components and their meta-data while also handling communication with the user through the GUI. The slave frameworks act only as component containers that are completely controlled by the master. This centralized design is simple to implement and its behavior is easy to predict. As component and node numbers grow, however, the master framework is quickly overburdened with managing large quantities of data and the execution time of the entire application is affected by this bottleneck. Moreover, as simulation size grows even further, the master–slave design can inhibit the efficiency of future scientific computing applications. We present an alternative design that is highly scalable and retains its performance under high loads. In addition to the scalability problem, the master framework presents a single point of failure that presents an additional liability for long-running applications and simulations.

A component framework's data may be queried and modified by a user through provided user interfaces and by executing components. In both cases, it is imperative that the framework is capable of providing quick responses under heavy loads and high availability to long-running applications. The goal of our work is to present distributed component framework design as the solution to several key issues. The system described in this study is architected to

1. Scale to a large number of nodes and components.
2. Maintain framework availability when framework nodes are joining and leaving the system and be able to handle complete node failures.
3. Facilitate multiple human users of the framework.
4. Support the execution and instantiation of SPMD parallel components. Our distributed component framework, CCALoop, is self-organizing and uses an approach that partitions the load of managing the components to all of the participating distributed frameworks.

The responsibility for managing framework data is divided among framework nodes by using a technique called distributed hash tables (DHT) [9]. CCALoop uses a hash function available at each framework node that maps a specific component type to a framework node in a randomly distributed fashion. This operation of mapping each component to a node is equally available at all nodes in the system. Framework queries or commands require only one-hop routing in CCALoop. To provide one-hop lookup of framework data, we keep perfect information about other nodes in the system, all the while allowing a moderate node joining/leaving schedule and not impacting scalability. We accommodate the possibility that a framework node may fail or otherwise leave the system by creating redundant information and replicating this information onto other frameworks.

9.5.1 Design

Current distributed framework design is inappropriate in accommodating component applications with numerous components that use many computing resources. We implemented a CCA-compliant distributed component framework called CCALoop that prototypes our design for increased framework scalability and fault tolerance. CCALoop scales by dividing framework data storage and lookup responsibilities among its nodes. It is designed to provide fault-tolerance and uninterrupted services on limited framework failure. CCALoop also provides the ability to connect multiple GUIs in order for users to monitor an application from multiple points. While providing these capabilities, CCALoop does not add overwhelming overhead or cost to the user and satisfies framework queries with low latency. In this section, we will examine the parts that form the structure of this framework. We begin by looking more closely at the tasks and roles of a CCA-compliant component framework.

The main purpose of a component framework is to manage and disseminate data. Some frameworks are more involved, such as Enterprise Java Beans [7], but in this study we focus on the ones in the style of CORBA [16] that do not interfere with the execution of every component. This kind of a component framework performs several important tasks in the staging of an application, but gets out of the way of the actual execution. Executing components may access the framework to obtain data or to manage other components if they choose to, but it is not usually necessary. CCA-compliant frameworks also follow this paradigm as it means low overhead and better performance.

CCA-compliant frameworks store two types of data: static and dynamic. The majority of the data is dynamic, which means that it changes as the application changes. The relatively small amount of static data describes the available components in the system. In a distributed setting, static data consist of the available components on each distributed framework node. The dynamic data range from information on instantiated components and ports to results and error messages. A significant amount of dynamic data is usually displayed to the user via a GUI. In our design, we distribute management of framework data without relocating components or forcing the user to instantiate components on a specific resource. The user is allowed to make his or her own decisions regarding application resource usage.

One of the principal design goals of CCALoop is to balance the load of managing component data and answering queries to all participating frameworks. This is done by using the DHT mechanism where each node in the system is assigned a unique identifier in a particular identifier space. This identifier is chosen to ensure an even distribution of the framework identifiers across the identifier space. We provide an operation that hashes each component type to a number in the identifier space. All metadata for a given component is stored at the framework node whose identifier is the successor of the component hash as shown in Figure 9.7(b). Given a random hash function, the component data are distributed evenly across the framework nodes. The lookup mechanism is similar to the storage one: to get information about a component, we compute its hash and query the succeeding framework node.

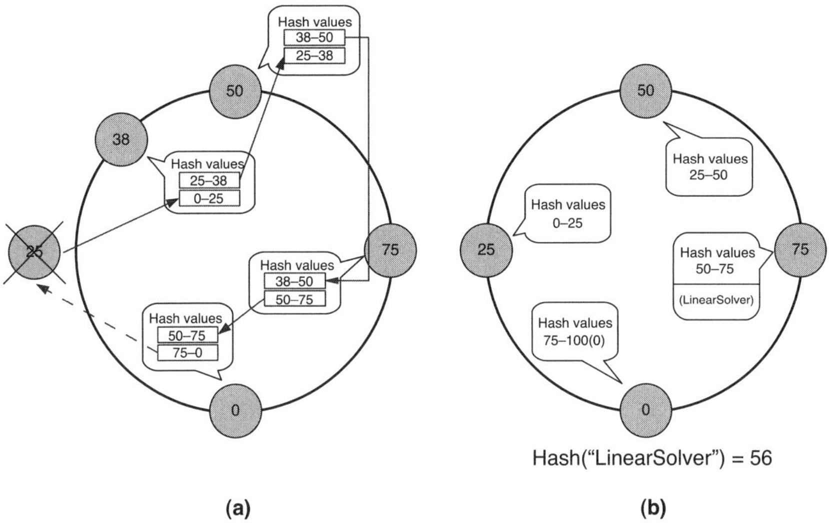

Figure 9.7 (**a**) Framework data replication across node's two successors. Shown as node 25 is leaving the system and before any data adjustments have been made. (**b**) The data responsibilities of the CCALoop framework with four nodes.

Loop Structure CCALoop's framework nodes are organized in a ring structure in topological order by their identifier numbers. Each framework node has a pointer to its successor and predecessor, allowing the ring to span the identifier space regardless of how the system may change or how many nodes exist in a given time. CCALoop also facilitates a straightforward way of recovering from node failure, by naturally involving the successor of the failed node to become new successor to the queried identifier. Use of a loop structure with a DHT lookup is commonly found in several peer-to-peer systems such as Chord [21].

Adding framework nodes to the system splits the responsibility for framework data between the joining node and its current owner. It is a two-step process that begins at any already connected node in the system. The first step is assigning an identifier to the joining node that best distributes the nodes across the identifier space. The identifier in the middle of the largest empty gap between nodes is selected based on the queried framework node's information. Later, we will explain how every node in the system contains perfect information about the existence of other nodes in the distributed framework. Apart from a well-chosen identifier, the node is given the address of its predecessor and successor. The second step is for the joining node to inform the predecessor and successor that it is about to join the network so that they can adjust their pointers. This step also resolves conflicts that may occur if two joining frameworks are assigned the same identifier in the first step by two separate nodes. If this conflict occurs, one of the nodes is assigned a new identifier and forced to repeat the second step. Removing nodes in the system has the opposite effect as adding nodes: the successor of the leaving node becomes responsible for the vacated identifier space and associated framework data.

Periodically, nodes invoke a *stabilize()* method that ensures that the successor and predecessor of that node are still alive. If one or both have failed, the node adjusts its predecessor or successor pointer to the next available node. Since perfect loop membership information is kept at every node, finding the next node in the loop is straightforward. The process of updating predecessor and successor pointers ensures that the loop structure is preserved, even when framework nodes leave the system. When a node leaves and this readjustment takes place, the identifier distribution may become unbalanced. This will last until a new framework joins; when it will be instructed to fill the largest current gap in the identifier space.

In order to enable seamless functioning of CCALoop during framework node failure, we replicate the data across successor nodes, so that if a framework fails, its successor is able to assume its responsibilities. To be able to handle multiple simultaneous failures, we can increase the number of successors to which we replicate the framework data. This incurs a bandwidth cost proportional to the number of replicas. If a node joins or leaves the system, some data readjustment is performed to ensure that the replication factor we have chosen is restored. CCALoop targets the high-performance scientific computing domain, which uses dedicated machines with high availability. Machine failures or intermittent network failures are possible, but infrequent. Because of this, we are content with providing two or three replicas for a particular framework node's data. Figure 9.7(a) shows an example of data replication across two successors as a node leaves the framework.

One-Hop Lookup An advantage of our distributed framework design is the ability for nodes to contact other nodes directly, or through "one hop." The one-hop mechanism was initially designed as an alternative to Chord's multihop query design [10]. One-hop lookup enables low latency querying, which is important in maximizing performance to components in a distributed framework. In order to support one-hop lookups, full membership awareness is required in the framework; every node needs to keep updated information about all other nodes in the system. There is certainly a cost to keeping this information current in the framework, and it is proportional to the joining and leaving (turnover) rate. As with data replication, our expectation is that framework nodes comprising a CCA-compliant distributed framework will not have the same framework turnover rate as one of the popular file sharing networks, where turnover is an issue. Therefore, our design is unlikely to encounter very high levels of node turnover. When node turnover does occur, our distributed framework would provide graceful performance degradation.

CCALoop uses a multicast mechanism to provide easy and quick dissemination of membership information. This mechanism creates a tree structure to propagate node leaving and joining information to all nodes in the system. We divide our loop structure into a number of slices and assign a "slice leader" node to each slice. In CCALoop, the slice leader is the node with the smallest identifier in the slice. When a node joins the framework, its successor contacts the slice leader. The slice leader distributes this information to all other slice leaders as well as all the other nodes in the slice. Finally, each slice leader that received the message propagates it to all members of its slice. This hierarchy enables faster membership propagation that in turn enables CCALoop to reach a steady state faster. In addition, this reduces errant queries as well as providing the means for low-latency access to framework node.

Multiple GUIs Providing a graphical user interface is an important role of a scientific component framework. A framework's user is interested in assembling a simulation, steering it, and analyzing intermediate and final results. In large, cross-organizational simulations, several users may need to manage a simulation, and several others may be interested in viewing the results. State-of-the-art CCA-compliant scientific computing frameworks provide the capability to attach multiple GUIs and users. However, each of these frameworks provides that capability only at the master node, which hinders scalability as previously discussed. One of the opportunities and challenges of a scalable distributed framework like CCALoop is to handle multiple GUIs.

CCALoop allows a GUI to attach to any cooperating framework node. A user is allowed to manage and view the simulation from that node. When multiple GUIs are present, we leverage the slice leader multicast mechanism to distribute information efficiently to all frameworks with GUIs. We establish a general event publish–subscribe mechanism with message caching capability and create a specific event channel for GUI messages. Other channels may be created to service other needs. GUIs on which some state is changed by the user are event publishers, while all the other GUIs in the system are subscribers. We route messages from publishers to subscribers through the system by passing them through slice leaders while ensuring that we are not needlessly wasting bandwidth. All messages are cached on the slice leader of the originating slice of nodes.

The reason we use the hierarchical mechanism to transfer GUI messages over a more direct approach is to cache the GUI state of the framework. CCALoop provides a mechanism that is able to update a GUI with the current state when this GUI joins after some user operations have already occurred. To prepare for this scenario, we continuously cache the contribution to the GUI state from each slice at its slice leader. This is advantageous since we expect GUIs to often join at midstream, then leave the system, and possibly return.

An additional concern with multiple distributed GUIs is the order of state-changing operations. We use a first come first serve paradigm and allow every GUI to have equal rights. A more complex scheme is possible and would be useful, but that is outside the scope of this study.

Parallel Frameworks To support CCA's choice of SPMD-style parallel components, a framework needs to be able to create a communicator, such as an *MPI Communicator*, which identifies the set of components that are executing in parallel and enables their internal communication. This internal (interprocess) communication is embedded in the algorithm and it is necessary for almost any parallel computation. To produce this communicator a framework itself needs to be executing in parallel: In order to execute the component in parallel, we first execute the framework in parallel.

A parallel framework exists as a resource onto which parallel components can execute. Parallel component communication and specifically parallel remote method invocation can be quite complex and it has been studied extensively [2].

A concern of this work is the inclusion of parallel frameworks in a distributed framework environment involving many other parallel and nonparallel frameworks. The parallel framework can be handled as one framework entity with one identifier or it can be considered as a number of entities corresponding to the number of parallel framework processes. We choose to assign one identifier to the entire parallel framework to simplify framework-to-framework interaction. This needs to be done carefully, however, to ensure that communication to all parallel cohorts is coordinated. By leveraging previous work in the area of parallel remote method invocation, we gain the ability to make collective invocations. We use these collective invocations to always treat the parallel framework as one entity in a distributed framework.

Even though we choose to treat all parallel framework processes as one parallel instance, the component's data that the framework stores are not limited to one entry per parallel component. To enable a more direct communication mechanism, we need to store an amount of data that is proportional to the number of parallel processes of the parallel component. Large parallel components are a significant reason that more attention should be directed toward scalable distributed component frameworks.

9.6 SUMMARY

We presented the SCIJump problem-solving environment for scientific computing. SCIJump employs components that encapsulate computational functionality into a reusable unit. It is based on DOE's CCA component standard but it is designed to be able to combine different component models into a single visual problem solving environment.

Several features of SCIJump were discussed: multiple component models, distributed computing support, and parallel components. SCIJump integrates multiple component models into a single visual problem solving environment and builds bridges between components of different component models. In this way, a number of tools can be combined into a single environment without requiring global adoption of a common underlying component model. We have also described a parallel component architecture with several synchronization options and utilizing the common component architecture, combined with distributed objects and parallel $M \times N$ array redistribution that can be used in SCIJump. Finally, we presented our novel design for scalability in component frameworks through our prototype framework CCALoop.

A prototype of the SCIJump framework has been developed, and we are using this framework for a number of applications in order to demonstrate SCIJump's features. Future applications will rely more on the system and will facilitate joining many powerful tools, such as the SCI Institutes' interactive ray-tracing system [22, 23] and the Uintah [6, 24] parallel, multiphysics system. Additional large-scale computational applications are under construction and are beginning to take advantage of the capabilities of SCIJump. The design prototyped by CCALoop, which will greatly increase the scalability of SCIJump to support the future generation application, will be added in the future.

ACKNOWLEDGMENTS

The authors gratefully acknowledge support from NIH NCRR and the DOE ASCI and SciDAC programs. SCIJump is available as open source software at www.sci.utah.edu.

REFERENCES

1. G. Bell and J. Gray. What's next in high-performance computing? *Commun. ACM*, 45(2):91–95, 2002.
2. F. Bertrand, R. Bramley, A. Sussman, D. E. Bernholdt, J. A. Kohl, J.W. Larson, and K. Damevski. Data redistribution and remote method invocation in parallel component architectures. In *Proceedings of the 19th International Parallel and Distributed Processing Symposium (IPDPS)*, 2005. (Best Paper Award).
3. K. Damevski. Parallel component interaction with an interface definition language compiler. Master's thesis, University of Utah, 2003.
4. K. Damevski and S. Parker. Imprecise exceptions in distributed parallel components. In *Proceedings of 10th International Euro-Par Conference (Euro-Par 2004 Parallel Processing)*, Vol. 3149, *Lecture Notes in Computer Science*. Springer, 2004.
5. K. Damevski and S. Parker. $M \times N$ data redistribution through parallel remote method invocation. *Int. J. High Perform. Comput. Appl.*, 19(4):389–398, 2005. (Special issue).
6. J.D. de St. Germain, J. McCorquodale, S.G. Parker, and C.R. Johnson. Uintah: a massively parallel problem solving environment. In *Proceedings of the 9th IEEE International Symposium on High Performance and Distributed Computing*, August 2000.
7. Enterprise Java Beans. http://java.sun.com/products/ejb, 2007.
8. I. Foster, C. Kesselman, and S. Tuecke. The Nexus approach to integrating multithreading and communication. *J. Parallel Distrib. Comput.*, 37:70–82, 1996.
9. S. Gribble, E. Brewer, J. Hellerstein, and D. Culler. Scalable, distributed data structures for Internet service construction. In *Proceedings of the Symposium on Operating Systems Design and Implementation*, 2000.
10. A. Gupta, B. Liskov, and R. Rodrigues. One hop lookups for peer-to-peer overlays. In *9th Workshop on Hot Topics in Operating Systems (HotOS-IX)*, Lihue, Hawaii, 2003, pp. 7–12.
11. C. Johnson and S. Parker. The SCIRun parallel scientific compouting problem solving environment. In *Proceedings of the 9th SIAM Conference on Parallel Processing for Scientific Computing*, 1999.
12. S. Kohn, G. Kumfert, J. Painter, and C. Ribbens. Divorcing language dependencies from a scientific software library. In *Proceedings of the 10th SIAM Conference on Parallel Processing*, Portsmouth, VA, March 2001.
13. The Ruby Language. http://www.ruby-lang.org/en, 2004.
14. L. C. McInnes, B.A. Allan, R. Armstrong, S.J. Benson, D.E. Bernholdt, T.L. Dahlgren, L.F. Diachin, M. Krishnan, J.A. Kohl, J.W. Larson, S. Lefantzi, J. Nieplocha, B. Norris, S.G. Parker, J. Ray, and S. Zhou. Parallel PDE-based simulations using the Common Component Architecture. In A.M. Bruaset and A. Tveito, editors, *Numerical Solution of PDEs on Parallel Computers*, Vol. 51 of *Lecture Notes in Computational Science and Engineering (LNCSE)*. Springer-Verlag, 2006, pp. 327–384.
15. Message Passing Interface Forum. MPI: A Message-Passing Interface Standard, June 1995.
16. OMG. The Common Object Request Broker: Architecture and Specification. Revision 2.0, June 1995.
17. S.G. Parker. The SCIRun Problem Solving Environment and Computational Steering Software System. PhD thesis, University of Utah, 1999.

18. S.G. Parker, D.M. Beazley, and C.R. Johnson. Computational steering software systems and strategies. *IEEE Comput. Sci. Eng.*, 4(4):50–59, 1997.
19. S.G. Parker and C.R. Johnson. SCIRun: a scientific programming environment for computational steering. In *Supercomputing '95*. IEEE Press, 1995.
20. W. Schroeder, K. Martin, and B. Lorensen. *The Visualization Toolkit: An Object-Oriented Approach to 3-D Graphics, 2nd edition.* Prentice Hall PTR, 2003.
21. I. Stoica, R. Morris, D. Karger, M.F. Kaashoek, and H. Balakrishnan. Chord: a scalable peer-to-peer lookup service for internet applications. In *SIGCOMM '01: Proceedings of the 2001 conference on Applications, Technologies, Architectures, and Protocols for Computer Communication*, New York. ACM Press, 2001, pp. 149–160.
22. S. Parker, M. Parker, Y. Livnat, P. Sloan, and P. Shirley. Interactive ray tracing for volume visualization. *IEEE Transactions on Visualization and Computer Graphics*, July–September 1999.
23. J. Bigler, A. Stephens and S.G. Parker. Design for parallel interactive ray tracing systems. In *Proceedings of The IEEE Symposium on Interactive Ray Tracing*, 2006, pp. 187–196.
24. S.G. Parker. A component-based architecture for parallel multi-physics PDE simulation. *Future Generation Comput. Syst.*, 22(1–2):204–216, 2006.
25. SCIRun: a scientific computing problem solving environment. Scientific Computing and Imaging Institute (SCI), University of Utah, 2007. http://software.sci.utah.edu/scirun.html.
26. C.R. Johnson, S. Parker, D. Weinstein, and S. Heffernan. Component-based problem solving environments for large-scale scientific computing. *Concurrency & Comput: Pract. and Exper.*, 14:1337–1349, 2002.
27. D.M. Weinstein, S.G. Parker, J. Simpson, K. Zimmerman, and G. Jones. Visualization in the SCIRun problem-solving environment. In C.D. Hansen and C.R. Johnson, editors, *The Visualization Handbook*. Elsevier, 2005, pp. 615–632.

Chapter 10

Adaptive Computations in the Uintah Framework

Justin Luitjens, James Guilkey, Todd Harman, Bryan Worthen, and Steven G. Parker

10.1 INTRODUCTION

The University of Utah Center for the Simulation of Accidental Fires and Explosions (C-SAFE) [15] is a Department of Energy ASC center that focuses on providing state-of-the-art, science-based tools for the numerical simulation of accidental fires and explosions. The primary objective of C-SAFE has been to provide a software system in which fundamental chemistry and engineering physics are fully coupled with nonlinear solvers, visualization, and experimental data verification, thereby integrating expertise from a wide variety of disciplines. The primary target scenario for C-SAFE is the full simulation of metal containers filled with a plastic-bonded explosive (PBX) subject to heating from a hydrocarbon pool fire, as depicted in Figure 10.1. In this scenario, a small cylindrical steel container (4" outside diameter) filled with PBX-9501 is subjected to convective and radiative heat fluxes from a fire to heat the outside of the container and the PBX. After some amount of time, the critical temperature in the PBX is reached and the explosive begins to rapidly decompose into a gas. The solid→gas reaction pressurizes the interior of the steel container causing the shell to rapidly expand and eventually rupture. The gaseous products of reaction form a blast wave that expands outward along with pieces of the container and the unreacted PBX. The physical processes in this simulation have a wide range in time and length scales from microseconds and microns to minutes and meters. An example of this simulation is depicted in Figure 10.2.

Advanced Computational Infrastructures For Parallel and Distributed Adaptive Applications. Edited by Manish Parashar and Xiaolin Li

Figure 10.1 Depiction of a typical C-SAFE scenario involving hydrocarbon fires and explosions of energetic materials.

The Uintah computational framework, developed as the main computational workhorse of the C-SAFE center, consists of a set of parallel software components and libraries that facilitate the solution of partial differential equations (PDEs) on structured AMR (SAMR) grids. Uintah is applicable to a wide range of engineering

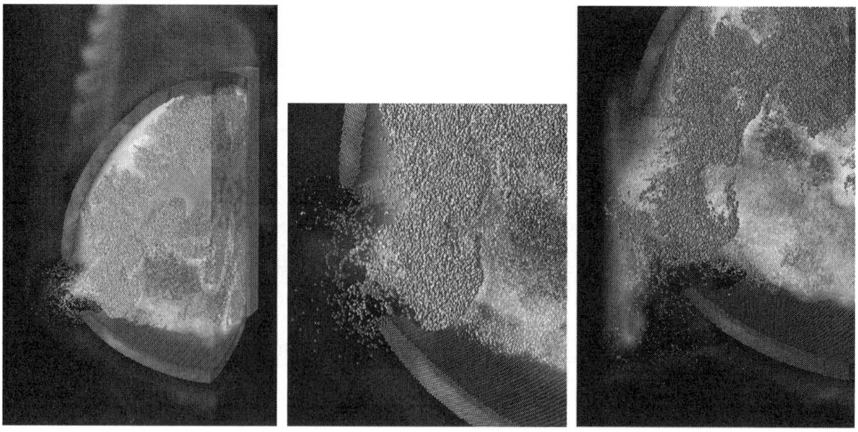

Figure 10.2 Cross section of an energetic device at the point of rupture.

domains that require fluid–structure interactions and highly deformable models. Uintah contains several simulation algorithms, including a general-purpose fluid-structure interaction code that has been used to simulate a wide array of physical systems, including stage separation in rockets, the biomechanics of microvessels [12], the effects of wounding on heart tissue [17, 18], the properties of foam under large deformation [7], and evolution of transportation fuel fires [25], in addition to the scenario described above.

The heart of Uintah is a sophisticated computational framework that can integrate multiple simulation components, analyze the dependencies and communication patterns between them, and efficiently execute the resulting multiphysics simulation. Uintah employs an abstract task graph representation to describe computation and communication. Through this mechanism, Uintah components delegate decisions about parallelism to a scheduler component, which determines communication patterns and characterizes the computational workloads, needed for global resource optimization. These features allow parallelism to be integrated between multiple components while maintaining overall scalability and allow the Uintah runtime to analyze the structure of the computation to automatically enable load balancing, data communication, parallel I/O, and checkpointing.

We describe how these simulations are performed in the Uintah framework, beginning with a discussion of the Uintah framework (Section 10.2) and the techniques to support structured AMR in this framework (Section 10.3). We will then discuss the adaptive ICE (implicit, continuous fluid Eulerian) hydrodynamics solver employed (Section 10.5) and the particle-based material point method (Section 10.5.2) that are used in this computation. Subsequently, we will discuss the results achieved in these computations (Section 10.6). Finally, we will discuss the status of Uintah and its future (Section 10.7).

10.2 UINTAH OVERVIEW

The fundamental design methodology in Uintah is that of software components that are built on the DOE common component architecture (CCA) component model. Components are implemented as C++ classes that follow a very simple interface to establish connections with other components in the system. The interfaces between components are simplified because the components do not explicitly communicate with one another. A component simply defines the steps in the algorithm that will be performed later when the algorithm is executed, instead of explicitly performing the computation tasks. These steps are assembled into a dataflow graph, as described below.

The primary advantage of a component-based approach is that it facilitates the separate development of simulation algorithms, models, and infrastructure, such that components of the simulation can evolve independently. The component-based architecture allows pieces of the system to be implemented in a rudimentary form at first and then evolve as the technologies mature. Most important, Uintah allows the aspects of parallelism (schedulers, load balancers, parallel input/output, and so forth) to evolve independent of the simulation components. This approach allows the computer science support team to focus on these problems without waiting for the completion of the scientific applications or vice versa.

Uintah uses a nontraditional approach to achieving high degrees of parallelism, employing an abstract task graph representation to describe computation and communication that occur in the coarse of a single iteration of the simulation (typically, a timestep or nonlinear solver iteration). Components, by definition, make local decisions. Yet parallel efficiency is only obtained through a globally optimal domain decomposition and scheduling of computational tasks. Consequently, Uintah components delegate decisions about parallelism to a scheduler component through a description of tasks and variable dependencies that describe communication patterns, which are subsequently assembled in a single graph containing all of the computation in all components. This task graph representation has a number of advantages, including efficient fine-grained coupling of multiphysics components, flexible load balancing mechanisms, and a separation of application concerns from parallelism concerns. However, it creates a challenge for scalability that we overcome by creating an implicit definition of this graph and representing the details of the graph in a distributed fashion.

This underlying architecture of the Uintah simulation is uniquely suited to taking advantage of the complex topologies of modern HPC platforms. Multicore processors in SMP configurations combined with one or more communication networks are common petascale architectures, but applications that are not aware of these disparate levels of communication will not be able to scale to the large CPU counts for complex problems. The explicit task graph structure enables runtime analysis of communication patterns and other program characteristics that are not available at runtime in typical MPI-only applications. Through this representation of parallel structure, Uintah facilitates adapting work assignments to the underlying machine topology based on the bandwidth available between processing elements.

Tensor Product Task Graphs: Uintah enables integration of multiple simulation algorithms by adopting an execution model based on coarse-grained "macro" dataflow. Each component specifies the steps in the algorithm and the data dependencies between those steps. These steps are combined into a single graph structure (called a *taskgraph*). The task graph represents the computation to be performed in single-timestep integration and the data dependencies between the various steps in the algorithm. Graphs may specify numerous exchanges of data between components (fine–grained coupling) or few (coarse–grained coupling), depending on the requirements of the underlying algorithm. For example, the MPM–ICE fluid–structure algorithm implemented in Uintah (referenced in Section 10.5) requires several points of data exchange in a single timestep to achieve the tight coupling between the fluid and solids. This contrasts with multi–physics approaches that exchange boundary conditions at fluid–solid interfaces. The task graph structure allows fine-grained interdependencies to be expressed in an efficient manner.

The task graph is a directed acyclic graph of tasks, each of which produces some output and consumes some input (which is in turn the output of some previous task).

These inputs and outputs are specified for each patch in a structured, possibly AMR, grid. Associated with each task is a C++ method that is used to perform the actual computation.

A task graph representation by itself works well for coupling of multiple computational algorithms, but presents challenges for achieving scalability. A task graph that represents all communication in the problem would require time proportional to the number of computational elements to create. Creating this on a single processor, or on all processors would eventually result in a bottleneck. Uintah addresses this problem by introducing the concept of a "tensor product task graph." Uintah components specify tasks for the algorithmic steps only, which are independent of problem size or number of processors. Each task in the task graph is then implicitly repeated on a portion of patches in the decomposed domain. The resulting graph, or tensor product task graph, is created collectively; each processor contains only the tasks that it owns and those that it communicates with. The graph exists only as a whole across all computational elements, resulting in a scalable representation of the graph. Communication requirements between tasks are also specified implicitly through a simple dependency algebra.

Each execution of a task graph integrates a single timestep, or a single-nonlinear iteration, or some other coarse algorithm step. A portion of the MPM timestep graph is shown in Figure 10.3. Task graphs may be assembled recursively, with a typical Uintah simulation containing one for time integration and one for nonlinear integration. An AMR simulation may contain several more for implementing time subcycling and refinement/coarsening operators on the AMR grid.

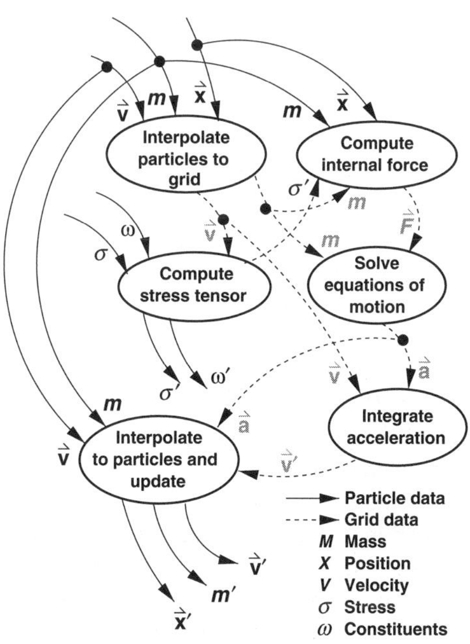

Figure 10.3 An example Uintah task graph for MPM.

The idea of the dataflow graph as an organizing structure for execution is well known. The SMARTS [34] dataflow engine that underlies the POOMA [2] toolkit shares similar goals and philosophy with Uintah. The SISAL language compilers [10] used dataflow concepts at a much finer granularity to structure code generation and execution. Dataflow is a simple, natural, and efficient way of exposing parallelism and managing computation, and is an intuitive way of reasoning about parallelism. What distinguishes implementations of dataflow ideas is that each caters to a particular higher level presentation. SMARTS caters to POOMA's C++ implementation and stylistic template-based presentation. Uintah's implementation supports dataflow (task graphs) of C++ and Fortran-based mixed particle/grid algorithms on a structured adaptive mesh.

Particle and Grid Support: Tasks describe data requirements in terms of their computations on node, cell, and face-centered quantities. A task that computes a cell-centered quantity from the values on surrounding nodes would establish a requirement for one layer of nodes around the cells at the border of a patch. This is termed "nodes around cells" in Uintah terminology. Likewise, a task that computes a node-centered quantity from the surrounding particles would require the particles that reside within one layer of cells at the patch boundary. The region of data required is termed the "halo region." Similarly, each task specifies the nonhalo data that it will compute. By defining the halo region in this way, one can specify the communication patterns in a complex domain without resorting to an explicit definition of the communication needed. These "computes and requires" lists for each task are collected to create the full task graph. Subsequently, the specification of the halo region is combined with the details of the patches in the domain to create the tensor product task graph. Data dependencies are also specified between refinement levels in an AMR mesh using the same approach, with some added complexity. This can often result in complex communication, but is still specified using a simple description of data dependencies.

Executing Task Programs: Each component specifies a list of tasks to be performed and the data dependencies between them. These tasks may also include dependencies on quantities from other components. A scheduler component in Uintah sets up MPI communication for data dependencies and then executes the tasks that have been assigned to it. When the task completes, the infrastructure will send data to other tasks that require that task's output.

On a single processor, execution of the task graph is simple. The tasks are simply executed in the topologically sorted order. This is valuable for debugging, since multipatch problems can be tested and debugged on a single processor. In most cases, if the multipatch problem passes the task graph analysis and executes correctly on a single processor, then it will execute correctly in parallel.

In a multiprocessor machine, the execution process is more complex. There are a number of ways to utilize MPI functionality to overlap communication and computation. In Uintah's current implementation, we process each task in a topologically sorted order. For each task, the scheduler posts nonblocking receives (using MPI_Irecv) for each of the data dependencies. Subsequently, we call

MPI_Waitall to wait for the data to be sent from neighboring processors. After all data has arrived, we execute the task. When the task is finished, we call MPI_Isend to initiate data transfer to any dependent tasks. Periodic calls to MPI_Waitsome for these posted sends ensure that resources are cleaned up when the sends actually complete.

To accommodate software packages that were not written using the Uintah execution model, we allow tasks to be specially flagged as "using MPI." These tasks will be gang scheduled on all processors simultaneously and will be associated with all of the patches assigned to each processor. In this fashion, Uintah applications can use available MPI-based libraries, such as PETSc [3] and Hypre [9].

Infrastructure Features: The task graph representation in Uintah enables compiler-like analysis of the computation and communication steps in a timestep. This analysis is performed at runtime, since the combination of tasks required to compute the algorithm may vary dramatically based on problem parameters. Through analysis of the task graph, Uintah can automatically create checkpoints, perform load balancing, and eliminate redundant communication. This analysis phase, which we call "compiling" the task graph, is what distinguishes Uintah from most other component-based multi-physics simulations. The task graph is compiled whenever the structure of the communication changes resulting from changes to the grid, the load balance, or the nature of the algorithm. Uintah also has the ability to modify the set of components in use during the course of the simulation. This is used to transition between solution algorithms, such as a fully explicit or semi-implicit formulation, triggered by conditions in the simulation.

Data output is scheduled by creating tasks in the task graph just like any other component. Constraints specified with the task allow the load balancing component to direct those tasks (and the associated data) to the processors where data I/O should occur. In typical simulations, each processor writes data independently for the portions of the data set that it owns. This requires no additional parallel communication for output tasks. However, in some cases this may not be ideal. Uintah can also accommodate situations where disks are physically attached to only a portion of the nodes, or a parallel file system where I/O is more efficient when performed by only a fraction of the total nodes.

Checkpointing is obtained by using these output tasks to save all of the data at the end of a timestep. Data lifetime analysis ensures that only the data required by subsequent iterations will be saved automatically. During a restart, the components process the XML specification of the problem that was saved with the data sets and then Uintah creates input tasks that load data from the checkpoint files. If necessary, data redistribution is performed automatically during the first execution of the task graph. As a result, change in the number of processors occurs when restarting is possible.

10.3 AMR SUPPORT

Adaptive Mesh Refinement: Many multiphysics simulations require a broad span of space and timescales. Uintah's primary target simulation scenario includes a

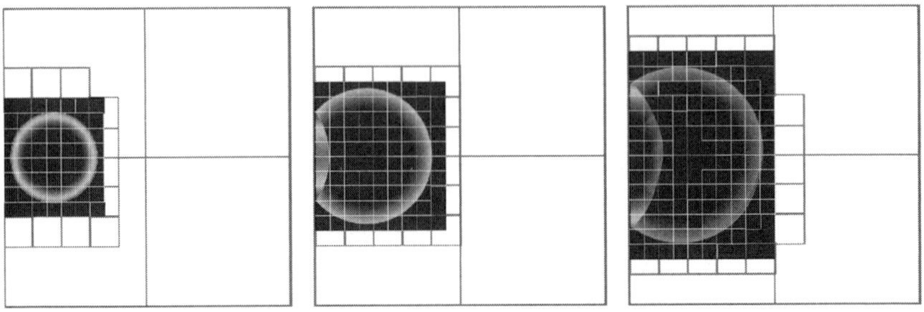

Figure 10.4 A pressure blast wave reflecting off of a solid boundary.

large-scale fire (size of meters, time of minutes) combined with an explosion (size of microns, time of microseconds). To efficiently and accurately capture this wide range of time and length scales, the Uintah architecture has been designed to support AMR in the style of Berger and Colella [6], with great initial success. Figures 10.4 shows a blast wave reflecting off a solid boundary with an AMR mesh using the explicit ICE algorithm and refinement in both space and time.

The construction of the Uintah AMR framework required two key pieces: multilevel grid support and grid adaptivity. A multilevel grid consists of a coarse grid with a series of finer levels. Each finer level is placed on top of the previous level with a spacing that is equal to the coarse-level spacing divided by the refinement ratio, which is specified by the user. A finer level only exists in a subset of the domain of the coarser level. The coarser level is used to create boundary conditions for the finer level.

The framework supports multilevel grids by controlling the interlevel communication and computation. Grid adaptivity is controlled through the use of refinement flags. The simulation components generate a set of refinement flags that specify the regions of the level that need more refinement. As the refinement flags change, a regridder uses them to produce a new grid with the necessary refinement.

Whenever the grid changes, a series of steps must be taken prior to continuing the simulation. First, the patches must be distributed evenly across processors through a process called load balancing. Second, all patches must be populated with data either by copying from the same level of the previous grid, or by interpolating from a coarser level of the previous grid. Finally, the task graph must be recompiled. These steps can take a significant amount of runtime [28, 36] and affect the overall scalability at large numbers of processors.

Multilevel Execution Cycle: There are two styles of multilevel execution implemented in Uintah: the lockstep (typically used for implicit or semi-implicit solvers) and the W-cycle (typically used for explicit formulations) time integration models. The lockstep model, as shown in Figure 10.5, advances all levels simultaneously. After executing each timestep, the coarsening and boundary conditions are applied. The W-cycle, as shown in Figure 10.6, uses larger timesteps on the coarser levels than the finer levels. On the finer levels, there are at least n subtimesteps on the finer

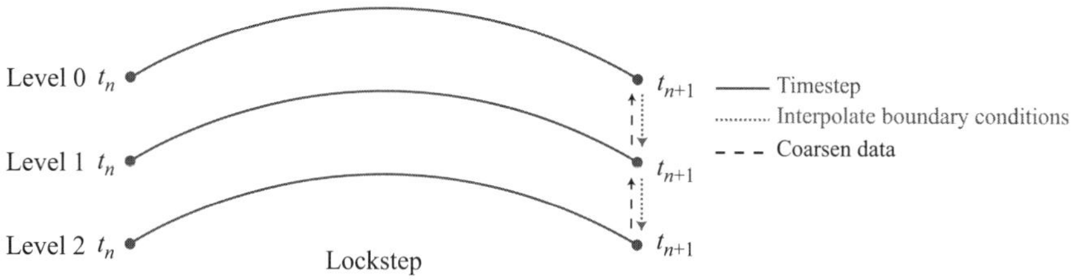

Figure 10.5 The lockstep time integration model.

level for every subtimestep on the coarser level, where n is equal to the refinement ratio. This provides the benefit of performing less computation on the coarser levels, but also requires an extra step of interpolating the boundary conditions after each subtimestep. In both cycles, at the end of each coarse-level timestep, the data on a finer level are interpolated to the coarser levels ensuring that the data on the coarser level reflect the accuracy of the finer level. In addition, the boundary conditions for the finer level are defined by the coarser levels by interpolating the data on a coarse level to the domain boundaries of the finer level [6]. These interlevel operations are described in detail in Section 10.5.1.

Refinement Flags: After the execution of a timestep, the simulation runs a task that marks cells that need refinement. The criteria for setting these flags are determined by the simulation component and are typically determined by a gradient magnitude of a particular quantity or other error metrics.

Regridding: When using AMR, the areas of the domain that need refinement can change every timestep necessitating a full recomputation of the grid. A regrid occurs whenever the simulation components produce flags that are outside of the currently refined regions. Regridding creates a new grid over the refinement flags.

Regridding is a necessary step in AMR codes. The grid must move to fully resolve moving features. A good regridder should produce large patches, whenever possible. If the regridder produces small patches the number of patches will be higher than necessary and can cause significant overhead in other components leading to large

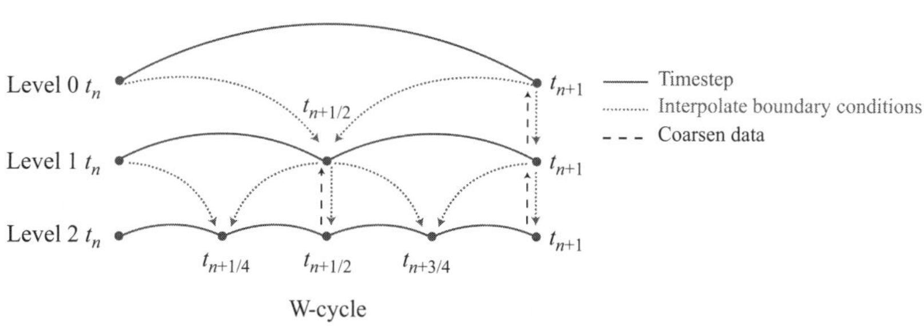

Figure 10.6 The W-cycle time integration model.

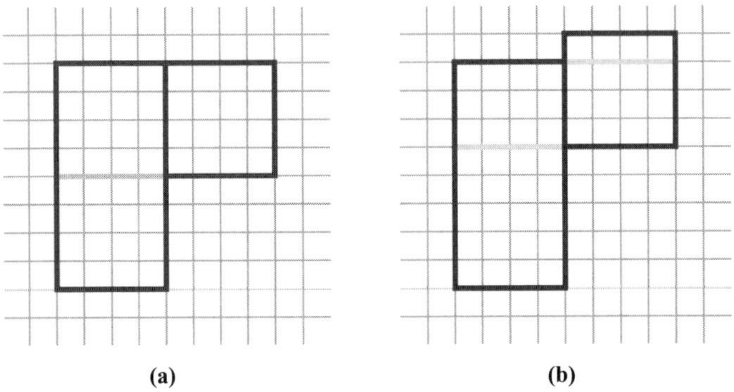

Figure 10.7 The black patches are invalid; in (a) they can be split by the gray line to produce a valid patch set, but in (b) they cannot.

inefficiencies. However, it is also important that the regridder does not produce too large patches because large patches cannot be load balanced effectively. Thus, an ideal regridder should produce patches that are large enough to keep the number of patches small but small enough to be effectively load balanced.

A common algorithm used in AMR codes for regridding is the Berger–Rigoutsos algorithm [5]. The Berger–Rigoutsos algorithm uses edge detection methods on the refinement flags to determine decent areas to place patches. The patch sets produced by the Berger–Rigoutsos algorithm contains a mix of both large and small patches. Regions are covered by patches as large as possible and the edges of those regions are covered by small patches producing tight covering of the refinement flags. In addition, the Berger–Rigoutsos algorithm can be run quickly in parallel [13, 37], making it an ideal algorithm for regridding.

However, the current implementation of Uintah has two constraints on the types of patches that can be produced that prevent direct usage of the Berger–Rigoutsos algorithm. First, patch boundaries must be consistent, that is, each face of the patch can contain only coarse–fine boundaries or neighboring patches at the same level of refinement, not a mixture of the two. Second, Uintah requires that all patches be of at least four cells in each direction. One way around the neighbor constraint is to locate patches that violate the neighboring constraint and split them into two patches, thus eliminating the constraint violation. Figure 10.7a shows an example of fixing a constraint violation via splitting. Unfortunately, splitting patches can produce patches that violate Uintah's size constraint, as shown in Figure 10.7b.

To make the Berger–Rigoutsos algorithm compatible with Uintah, a minimum patch size of at least four cells in each dimension is specified. The minimum patch size is used to coarsen the flag set by dividing every flag's location by the minimum patch size and rounding down producing a coarse flag set. The Berger–Rigoutsos algorithm is then run on the coarse flag set producing a coarse patch set. Next, the patch set is searched for neighbor constraint violations and patches are split until the neighbor constraints are met. An additional step is then taken to help facilitate a decent load balance. Large patches do not load balance well, thus splitting patches larger than a specified threshold helps maintain load balance. The threshold used is equal to the average number of cells per processor multiplied by some percentage. We have found through experimentation that a threshold of 6.25% works well. Finally, the coarse patches are projected onto the fine grid by multiplying the location of patches by the minimum patch size, producing a patch set that does not violate the neighbor constraint or the size constraint.

10.4 LOAD BALANCING

A separate load balancer component is responsible for assigning each detailed task to one processor. In patch-based AMR codes, the load balance of the overall calculation can significantly affect the performance. Cost models are derived from the size of the patches, the type of physics, and in some cases the number of particles within the patch. A load balancer component attempts to distribute work evenly while minimizing communication by placing patches that communicate with each other on the same processor. The task graph described above provides a mechanism for analyzing the computation and communication within the computation to distribute work appropriately. One way to load balance effectively is by using this graph directly, where the nodes of the graph are weighted by the amount of work a patch has and the edges are weighted by the cost of the communication to other processors. Graph algorithms or matrix solves are then used to determine an optimal patch distribution. These methods do a decent job of distributing work evenly while also minimizing communication, but are often too slow to run.

Another method that has been shown to work well for load balancing computations is the use of space-filling curves [8, 31, 32]. The curve is used to create a linear ordering of patches. Locality is maintained within this ordering by the nature of the space-filling curve. That is, patches that are close together on the curve are also close together in space and are likely to communicate with each other. Once the patches are ordered according to the space-filling curve, they are assigned a weight according to how the cost model. Then the curve is split into segments by recursively splitting the curve into two equally weighted segments until there is an equal number of curve segments as processors. Then each segment is assigned to a processor.

With AMR, space-filling curves are preferable to the graph-based and matrix-based methods because the curve can be generated in $O(N \log N)$. In addition, the curve can be generated quickly in parallel using parallel sorting algorithms [27]. Figure 10.8 shows the scalability of the curve generation up to thousands of processors for various problem sizes.

Data Migration: After a new grid is created and load balanced, the data must be migrated to the owning processors. The data are migrated by creating a task graph for the copying data from the old grid to the new grid. If a patch in the new grid is covering a region that does not exist in the old grid, then a refinement task is scheduled that performs the interpolation from the coarser level to populate the data in the patch. The next task is to copy data from the old grid. Any patches within the old grid that

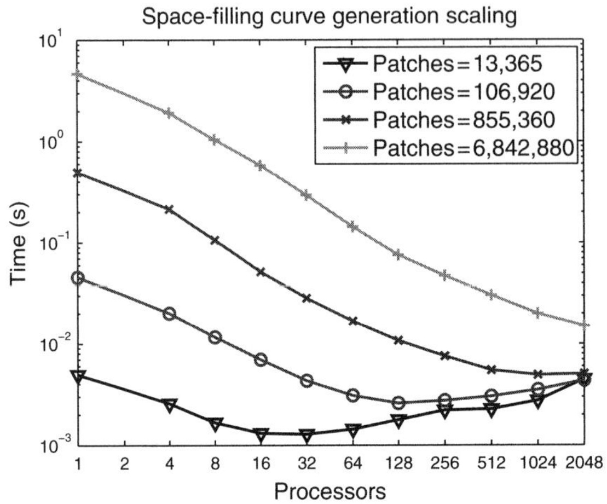

Figure 10.8 The scalability of the SFC curve generation for multiple problem sizes.

overlap the new grid are copied to the new grid. The infrastructure handles copying data between processors whenever needed.

Task Graph Compilation: As discussed earlier, the task graph is responsible for determining the order of task execution and communication that needs to occur between them. This information changes whenever the grid changes, so the task graph needs to be recompiled. Compiling the task graph can take a significant amount of time. In the case of the W-cycle, the compile time can be reduced by reusing redundant sections of the task graph. Each subtimestep has the same data dependencies as the previous subtimestep and thus only needs to be compiled once. This was done by creating task subgraphs for each level. Each level then executes its task subgraph multiple times. This dramatically reduces the compile time for the W-cycle.

Grid Reuse: Changing the grid and the corresponding steps that follow is expensive and does not scale to the computation. Regridding too often can greatly impact the overall scalability and performance. One way to reduce the overhead associated with changing the grid is to generate grids that can be used for multiple timesteps. This can be done by predicting where refinement will be needed and adding refinement before it is needed. In Uintah this is done by dilating the refinement flags prior to regridding. The refinement flags are modified by applying a stencil that expands the flags in all directions. The regridder then operates on the dilated refinement flags producing a grid that is slightly larger than needed but can be reused for multiple timesteps. Prior to the dilation and regridding each timestep, the undilated refinement flags are compared to the grid. If the refinement flags are all contained within the current grid, regridding is not necessary.

Dilation can have a large impact on performance when using large numbers of processors. The time to compute on the grid scales better than the time for changing the

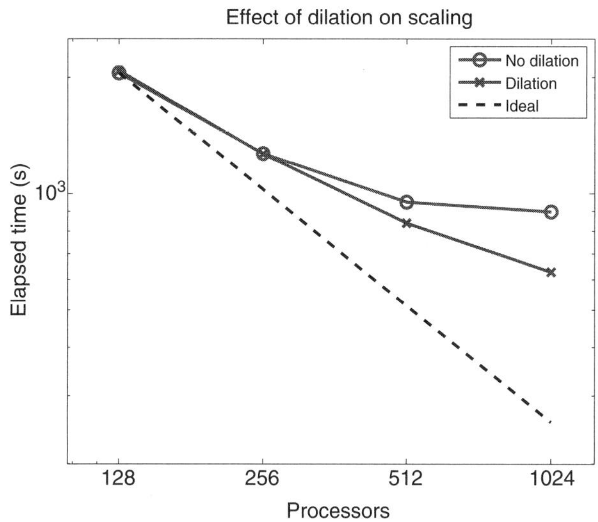

Figure 10.9 The effect of dilation on scalability.

grid. As the number of processors is increased, the time to change the grid becomes the dominant component preventing further scalability. By dilating the refinement flags prior to regridding, the time spent in changing the grid can be significantly reduced keeping the computation on the grid the dominant component. The amount of dilation is controlled at runtime by measuring how much time is spent computing on the grid versus how much time is spent changing the grid. If the percentage of time spent changing the grid is not within a target range, the dilation is either raised or lowered. Figure 10.9 shows the scalability with and without dilation for an expanding blast wave similar to the problem seen in Figure 10.4. In this simulation, the regridder was configured to produce more patches than would typically be used to simulate the overhead due to patches that would be expected when running with larger numbers of processors.

10.5 AMR APPLIED TO A MULTIMATERIAL EULERIAN CFD METHOD

Uintah contains four main simulation algorithms: (1) the Arches incompressible fire simulation code, (2) the ICE [24] compressible (both explicit and semi-implicit versions), (3) the particle-based material point method (MPM) for structural modeling, and (4) a fluid–structure interaction method achieved by the integration of the MPM and ICE components, referred to locally as MPM–ICE. In addition to these primary algorithms, Uintah integrates numerous subcomponents, including equations of state, constitutive models, reaction models, radiation models, and so forth. Here we provide a high-level overview of our approach to "full physics," simulations of fluid–structure interactions involving large deformations and phase change. By "full physics," we refer to problems involving strong coupling between the fluid and solid phases with a full Navier–Stokes representation of fluid-phase materials and the transient, nonlinear response of solid-phase materials, which may include chemical or phase transformation between the solid and fluid phases. Details of this approach, including the model equations and a description of their solution, can be found in Ref. [11].

Multimaterial Dynamics: The methodology upon which our software is built is a full "multimaterial" approach in which each material is given a continuum description and defined over the computational domain. Although at any point in space the material composition is uniquely defined, the multimaterial approach adopts a statistical viewpoint where the material (either fluid or solid) resides with some finite probability. To determine the probability of finding a particular material at a specified point in space, together with its current state (i.e., mass, momentum, and energy), multimaterial model equations are used. These are similar to the traditional single material Navier–Stokes equations, with the addition of two intermaterial exchange terms. For example, the momentum equation has, in addition to the usual terms that describe acceleration due to a pressure gradient and divergence of stress, a term that governs the transfer of momentum between materials. This term is typically modeled by a drag law, based on the relative velocities of two materials at a point. Similarly, in the energy equation, an exchange term governs the transfer of enthalpy between materials based on their relative temperatures. For cases involving the transfer of mass between materials, such as a solid explosive decomposing into product gas, a source/sink term is added to the conservation of mass equation. In addition, as mass is converted from one material to another, it carries with it its momentum and enthalpy, and these appear as additional terms in the momentum and energy equations, respectively. Finally, two additional equations are required due to the multimaterial nature of the equations. The first is an equation for the evolution of the specific volume, which describes how it changes as a result of physical process, primarily temperature and pressure change. The other is a multimaterial equation of state, which is a constraint equation that requires that the volume fractions of all materials in a cell sum up to unity. This constraint is satisfied by adjusting the pressure and specific volume in a cell in an iterative manner. This approach follows the ideas previously presented by Kashiwa and colleagues [20–22, 24].

These equations are solved using a cell-centered, finite volume version of the ICE method [14], further developed by Kashiwa and others at Los Alamos National Laboratory [23]. Our implementation of the ICE technique invokes operator splitting in which the solution consists of a separate Lagrangian phase, where the physics of the conservation laws, including intermaterial exchange, is computed, and an Eulerian phase, where the material state is transported via advection to the surrounding cells. The method is fully compressible, allowing wide generality in the types of scenarios that can be simulated.

Fluid–Structure Interaction Using MPM–ICE: The fluid–structure interaction capability is achieved by incorporating the material point method (described briefly in the following section) within the multimaterial CFD formulation. In the multimaterial formulation, no distinction is made between solid or fluid phases. Where distinctions do arise, it is in the computation of the material stress and material transport or advection. In the former, the use of a particle description for the solid provides a convenient location upon which to store the material deformation and any relevant history variables required for, say, a plasticity model. Regarding the latter, Eulerian advection schemes are typically quite diffusive, and would lead to an unacceptable smearing of a fluid–solid interface. Thus, performing advection by moving particles according to the local velocity field eliminates this concern.

At the beginning of each timestep, the particle state is projected first to the computational nodes and then to the cell centers. This colocates the solid and fluid data and allows the multimaterial CFD solution to proceed unaware of the presence of distinct phases. As stated above, the constitutive models for the solid materials are evaluated at the particle locations, and the divergence of the stress at the particles is computed at the cell centers. The Lagrangian phase of the CFD calculation is completed, including exchange of mass, momentum, and enthalpy. At this point, *changes* to the solid materials' state are interpolated back to the particles and their state, including position, is updated. Fluid-phase materials are advected using a compatible advection scheme such as that described in Ref. [35]. Again, a full description can be found in Ref.[11].

10.5.1 Structured AMR for ICE

In addition to solving the multimaterial equations on each level, there are several basic operators or steps necessary to couple the solutions on the various levels. These steps include the following:

- *Refine*: The initial projection of the coarse-level data onto to the fine level.
- *Refine Coarse–Fine Interface*: Projection of the coarse-level solution to the fine level, only in the ghost cells at the coarse–fine interface.
- *Coarsen*: Projection of the fine-level solution onto the coarse level at the end of the timestep.
- *Refluxing*: Correction of the coarse-level solution due to flux inconsistencies.
- *Refinement Criteria*: Flagging cells that should be refined.

Refine: When a new fine-level patch is generated, data from the coarse level are projected onto the new patch using either a trilinear or triquadratic interpolation. Figure 10.10 shows the computational footprint or stencil used during a triquadratic interpolation in one plane. The dashed lines show the edges of the fine-level ghost cells along the coarse–fine interface. The large open circles show the underlying coarse-level cells used during the projection of data to the pink diamond. Note that multifield CFD algorithm requires one layer of ghost cells on all patch sides that do not have an adjacent neighbor. These ghost cells provide boundary conditions for the fine-level solution.

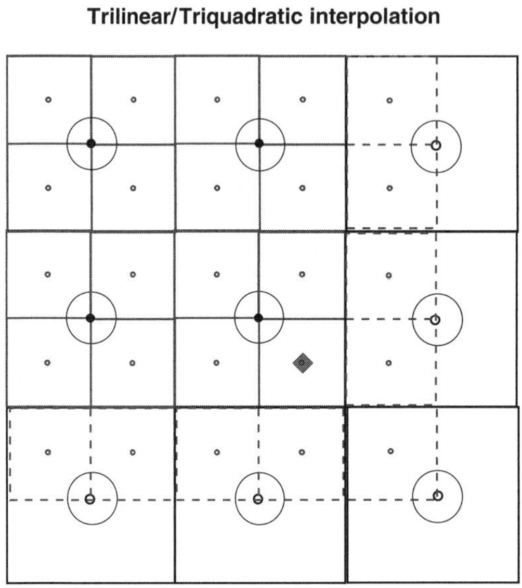

Figure 10.10 Triquadratic interpolation stencil used during the projection of coarse-level data onto a fine level.

Refine coarse–fine Interface: At the end of each timestep, the boundary conditions or ghost cells on the finer levels are updated by performing both a spatial and a linear temporal interpolation. The temporal interpolation is required during the W-cycle on all finer levels, shown as dotted lines in Figure 10.6. When the lockstep cycle is used, there is no need for temporal interpolation. Spatially, either a trilinear or triquadratic interpolation method may be used. Details on the quadratic interpolation method are described in Ref. [30].

Coarsen: At the end of each timestep, the conserved quantities are conservatively averaged from the fine to coarse levels using

$$Q_{\text{coarse level}} = \frac{1}{Z} \sum_{c=1}^{\text{refinement ratio}} Q_{\text{fine level}} \tag{10.1}$$

Refluxing: As mentioned above, the solution to the governing equations occurs independently on each level. During a timestep, at the coarse–fine interfaces, the computed fluxes on the fine level may not necessary equal the corresponding coarse-level fluxes. In Figure 10.11, the length of the arrows indicate a mismatch.

To maintain conservation of the conserved quantities, a correction, as described in Ref. [6], is added to all coarse-level cells that are adjacent to the coarse–fine interfaces. For the W-cycle, the fluxes of mass, momentum, energy, and any number of conserved

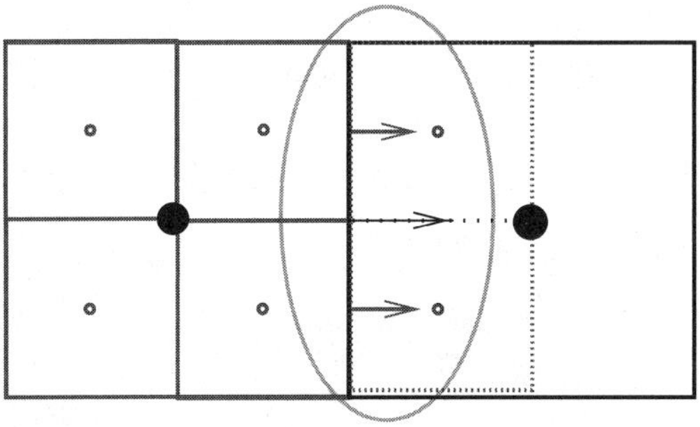

Figure 10.11 Illustration of a flux mismatch at the coarse–fine interface.

scalars are corrected using

$$Q_{\text{correction}} = Q^{C}_{\text{flux}} - \frac{1}{Z} \sum_{t=1}^{\text{subtimesteps}} \sum_{f=1}^{\text{faces}} Q_{\text{flux}} F, \tag{10.2}$$

where superscripts C and F represent the coarse and fine levels, respectively. For the lockstep execution cycle, the correction is given by

$$Q_{\text{correction}} = Q^{C}_{\text{flux}} - \frac{1}{Z} \sum_{f=1}^{\text{faces}} Q^{F}_{\text{flux}}. \tag{10.3}$$

Experience has shown that the most difficult part of computing the correction fluxes lies in the bookkeeping associated with the summation terms in equations (10.2) and (10.3). For each coarse-level cell, there are n_x, n_y, and n_z overlying fine-level cells with faces that overlap the coarse cell face. Keeping track of these faces and fluxes, on multiple levels, in a highly adaptive 3D mesh, where new fine-level patches are constantly being generated, has proven to be difficult (see Figure 10.12).

Regridding Criteria: A cell on a coarser level is flagged to be refined whenever a user-defined threshold has been exceeded. At Present, for fluid calculations, the magnitude of the gradient—density, temperature, volume fraction, pressure, or a passive scalar—may be used. More sophisticated techniques for flagging cells are available, but have not been implemented, an example is described in Ref. [1]. In Figure 10.13, the red squares show cells that have exceeded a user-specified threshold for the magnitude of the gradient of the pressure and are flagged.

Pressure Field: There are two methods implemented for solving for the change in pressure (ΔP) that is used to evolve the multimaterial governing equations. The explicit formulation, used for compressible calculations, uses the W-cycle where ΔP is computed in a pointwise fashion on each of the individual levels, without interlevel communication. The governing equations evolve on each of the levels independently with interlevel communication only taking place at the end of a timestep or whenever a new patch is generated. The price paid for this simplicity is the small timestep that is

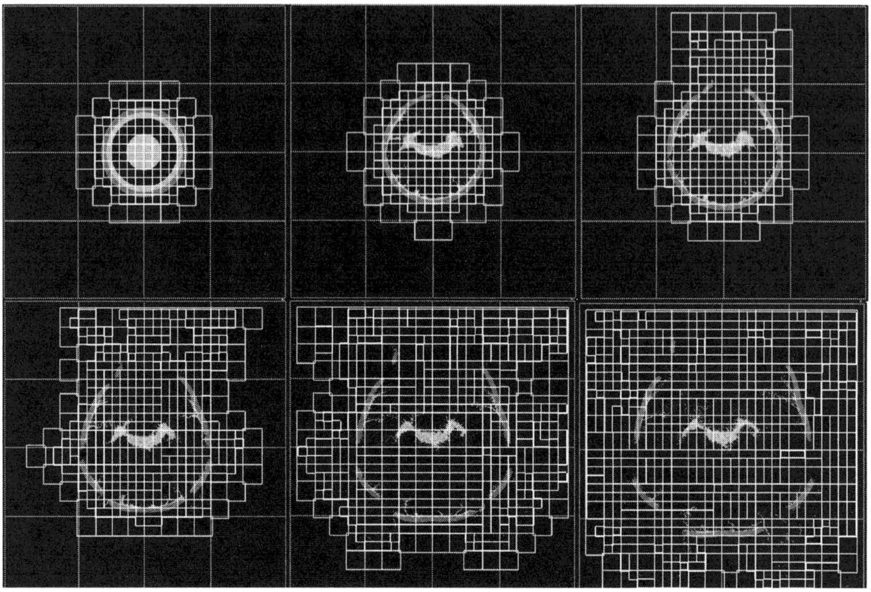

Figure 10.12 Simulation of an exploding container on a three-level adaptive mesh. The solid lines outline patches on the individual levels, red: level 0, green: level 1, and yellow: level 2.

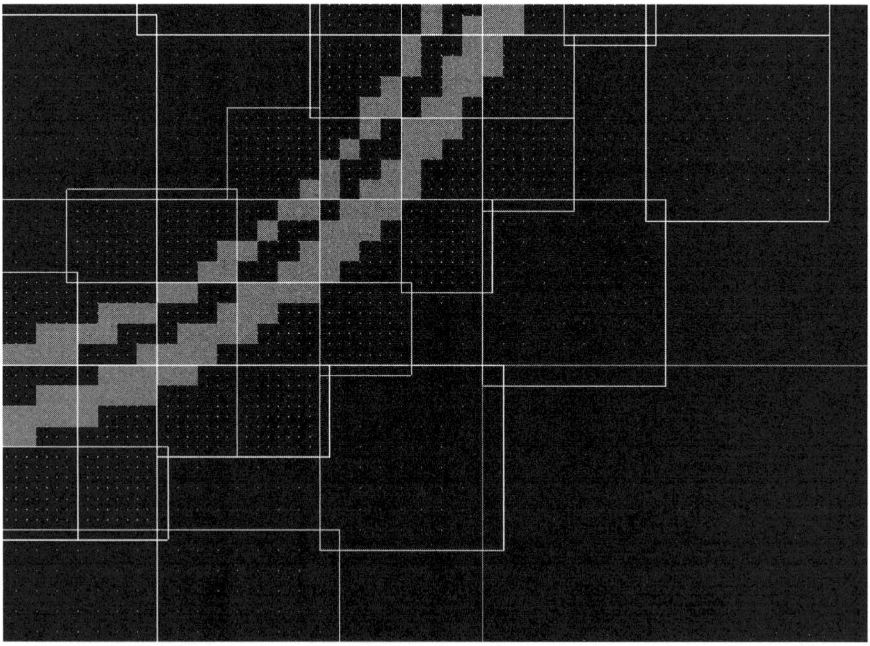

Figure 10.13 Close-up of a three level adaptive grid. The colored lines show the outline of the individual patches, red: level 0, green: level 1, and yellow: level 2. The solid red squares show cells that have been flagged for refinement.

required to guarantee stability. The timestep size is computed based on the convective *and* acoustic velocities.

The semi-implicit technique, which is still being actively developed for multi-level grids, utilizes the lockstep execution cycle. A Poisson equation for ΔP is first solved on a composite grid and then the solution is projected onto the underlying coarse-level cells. Experience has shown that any mismatch in the pressure gradient at the coarse–fine interfaces will produce nonphysical velocities, thereby creating a feedback mechanism for polluting the pressure field in the subsequent timestep. The potential benefit of this method is the larger timestep. In this case, the timestep required to remain stable is computed based on *only* the convective velocity.

10.5.2 MPM with AMR

Uintah contains a component for solid mechanics simulations known as the material point method [33]. MPM is a particle-based method that uses a (typically) Cartesian mesh as a computational scratch pad upon which gradients and spatial integrals are computed. MPM is an attractive computational method in that the use of particles simplifies initial discretization of geometries and eliminates problems of mesh entanglement at large deformations [7], while the use of a Cartesian grid allows the method to be quite scalable by eliminating the need for directly computing particle–particle interactions. A graphical description of MPM is shown in Figure 10.14. Here, a small region of solid material, represented by four particles, overlayed by a portion of grid is shown in panel (a). The particles, or material points, carry minimally, mass, volume, velocity, temperature, and state of deformation. Panel (b) reflects that this particle information is projected to the nodes of the overlying grid or scratch pad. Based on the nodal velocity, a velocity gradient is computed at the particles, and is used to update the state of deformation of the particle, and the particle stress. Based on the internal force (divergence of the stress) and external forces, as well as the mass, acceleration is computed at the nodes, as is an updated velocity. This is shown in panel (c), where the computational nodes have been deformed based on the new velocity and the current timestep size. Note that the deformation of the grid is never explicitly performed. Panel (d) reflects that the changes to the field quantities, specifically velocity and position in the case, are interpolated back to the particles. Once the particle state has been updated, the grid is reset in preparation for the next timestep (e).

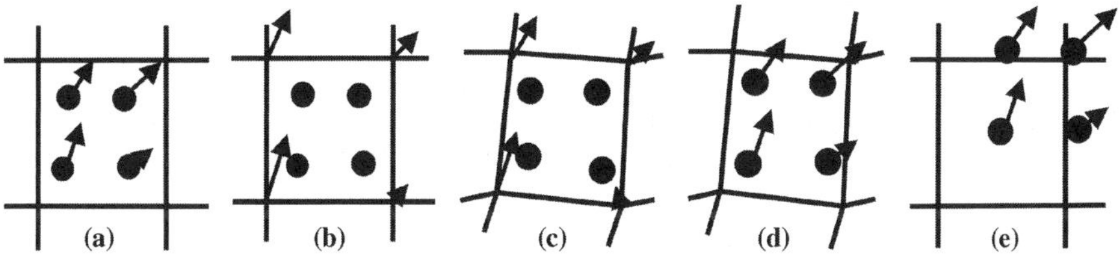

Figure 10.14 Graphical depiction of the steps in the MPM algorithm.

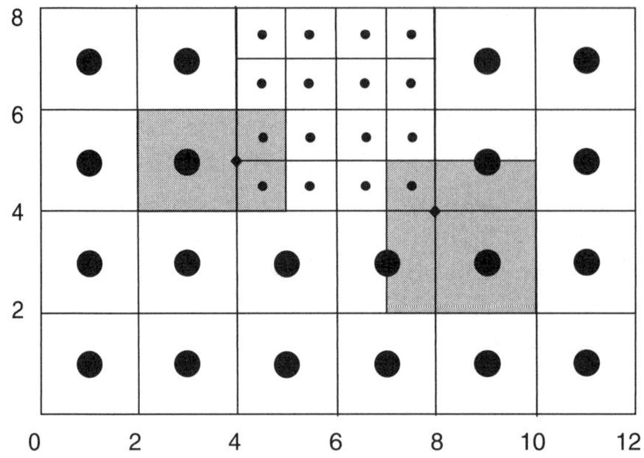

Figure 10.15 Sample region of a multilevel MPM grid.

Development of multilevel MPM is an active area of research that is still in the early stages. Ma et al. [29] reported the first implementation, in which they used the structured adaptive mesh application interface (SAMRAI) [16] as a vehicle to handle the multilevel grid information. While the Ma et al. approach makes a huge step toward realizing general-purpose, multilevel MPM, it does so in a manner that is quite different from standard SAMR algorithms. The brief description of their work, given below, will highlight some of these differences and illustrate some of the remaining challenges ahead.

A region of a simple two-level grid, populated with one particle in each cell, is shown in Figure 10.15. Two of the nodes at the coarse-fine interface, denoted by filled diamonds, are highlighted for discussion. First, consider the node at (4, 5). The work of Ma et al. describes a treatment of these nodes, which could be considered midside nodes on the coarse mesh, using what they term "zones of influence." This refers to the region around each node, within which particles both contribute to nodal values and receive contributions from the nodal values. The zones of influence for the node at (4, 5) and (8, 4) are highlighted. What these are meant to indicate is that the data values at fine-level nodes and particles depend on coarse-level nodes and particles, and vice versa. This is further complicated by the fact that interactions between particles and grid occur multiple times each timestep (projection to grid, calculation of velocity gradient at particles, calculation of divergence of particle stress to the nodes, and update of particle values from nodes).

The result of this is that the multilevel MPM algorithm behaves much more as if it exists on a composite grid than on a traditional SAMR grid. For instance, there is no coarse-level solution in regions where a finer level exists. In addition, dataflow across the coarse-fine interface is much less hierarchical. That is, the solution on one level depends equally on data contributions from both finer and coarser levels. This loss of hierarchy has thus far also frustrated efforts at developing a W-cycle-type approach to temporal refinement. To date, no temporal refinement approaches have been described in the literature.

Finally, the approach described in Ref. [29] did not address adaptivity, but only a static, multilevel solution. An adaptive technique would require further considerations, including particle splitting and merging. Work by Lapenta and Brackbill [26] provides a starting point for this task, although quantities such as history-dependent plasticity variables are not addressed here.

Given the significant challenges associated with a general adaptive material point method, its development within Uintah is at the early stages. The strategy of the Uintah developers has been to maintain particles only at the finest level in the solution. In simulations involving only MPM, this strategy does not provide substantial time savings, given that computational cost is most strongly a function of number of particles and only weakly depends on the number of computational cells/nodes. Where this strategy does prove to be advantageous is in the fluid–structure interaction simulations carried out within Uintah, in which MPM is incorporated within the multimaterial CFD code, described in Section 10.5.1 [11]. For the Eulerian CFD code, cost is entirely dependent upon the number of computational cells, so refining only in the vicinity of the solid objects allows large regions of the domain to be at lower resolutions. This strategy also makes sense from a physical point of view in that regions near the solid object generally demand the highest resolution to capture the fluid–solid interaction dynamics. In addition, for the types of simulations that Uintah was built to address, resolution requirements *within* the solid are usually the most demanding to capture phenomena such as solid-phase reactions and metal failure. Normal error cell flagging still occurs within the rest of the domain, such that regions of the domain that contain only fluid will be refined as well should they require it. Examples of success with this strategy are provided in Section 10.6.

10.6 RESULTS

Within the C-SAFE project, we utilize Uintah to perform simulations of both fires and explosions using hundreds to a few thousand processors. One scenario of two containers stored in proximity is shown in Figure 10.16. In this simulation, the adaptive grid (not shown) was comprised of three levels, with a refinement ratio of four in each direction. The results from this simulation are counterintuitive in that the container with a smaller initial explosive charge (right) produced a more violent explosion. This is due to the rapid release of energy that results from the structural collapse of the explosive into the hollow bore.

Figure 10.17 shows another 2D simulation of one quarter of two steel (red) containers filled with burning explosive (blue). Symmetry boundary conditions are applied on all sides. The containers and contents are preheated to the ignition temperature at $t = 0$. As the explosive decomposes, the containers are pressurized and break apart shortly thereafter. Eventually, the container fragments collide in the center. This simulation demonstrates how AMR allows us to efficiently simulate arrays of explosive devices separated by a significant distance. For multiple 3D containers the cost of such simulations would be prohibitive if the whole domain required the finest resolution everywhere during the entire simulated time.

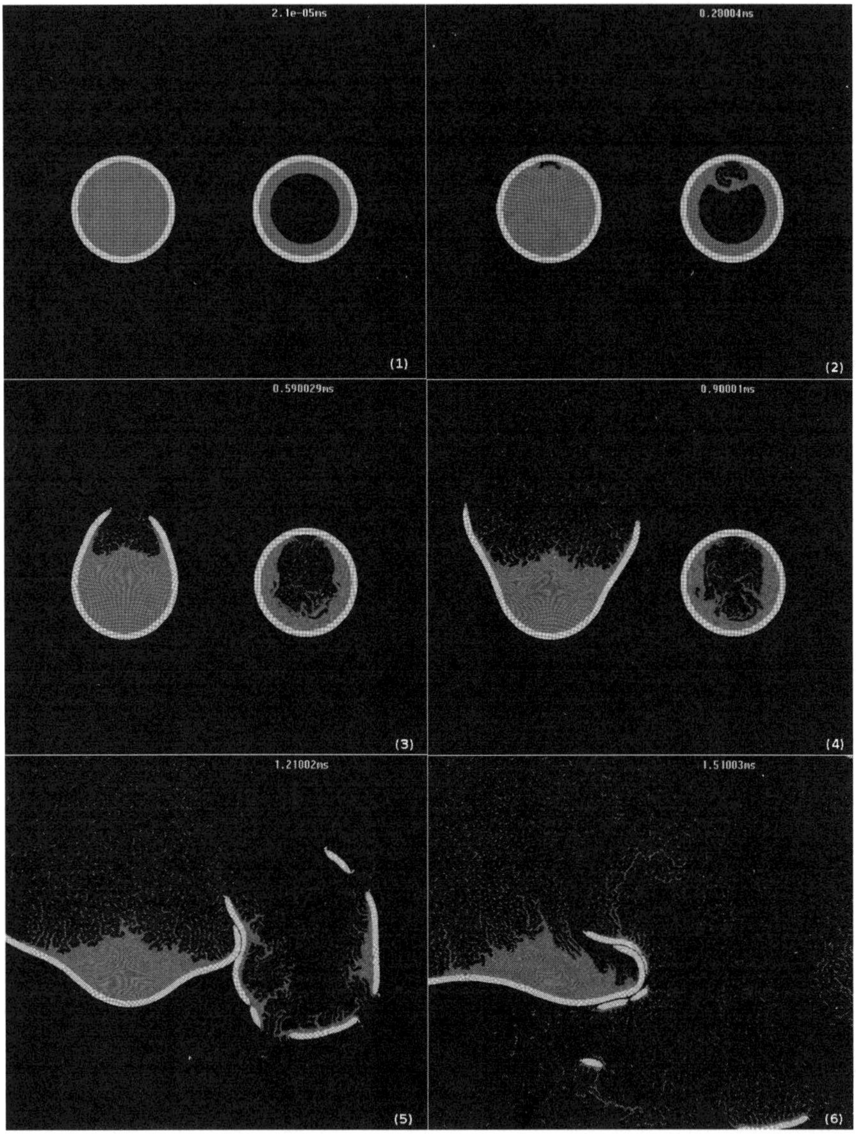

Figure 10.16 Simulation of two exploding containers with different initial configurations of the explosive. The left container was initially full of explosive while the right container had a hollow core.

Figure 10.18 depicts a rigid 20° wedge, represented by MPM particles moving through initially still air. Contours indicate pressure, while the pink boxes reflect regions of refinement in the two level solution. In addition to refinement near the wedge, regions of large-pressure gradient around the leading shock and trailing expansion fan are also automatically refined. This simulation also served as an early validation of ICE method and the fluid–structure interaction formulation, as the

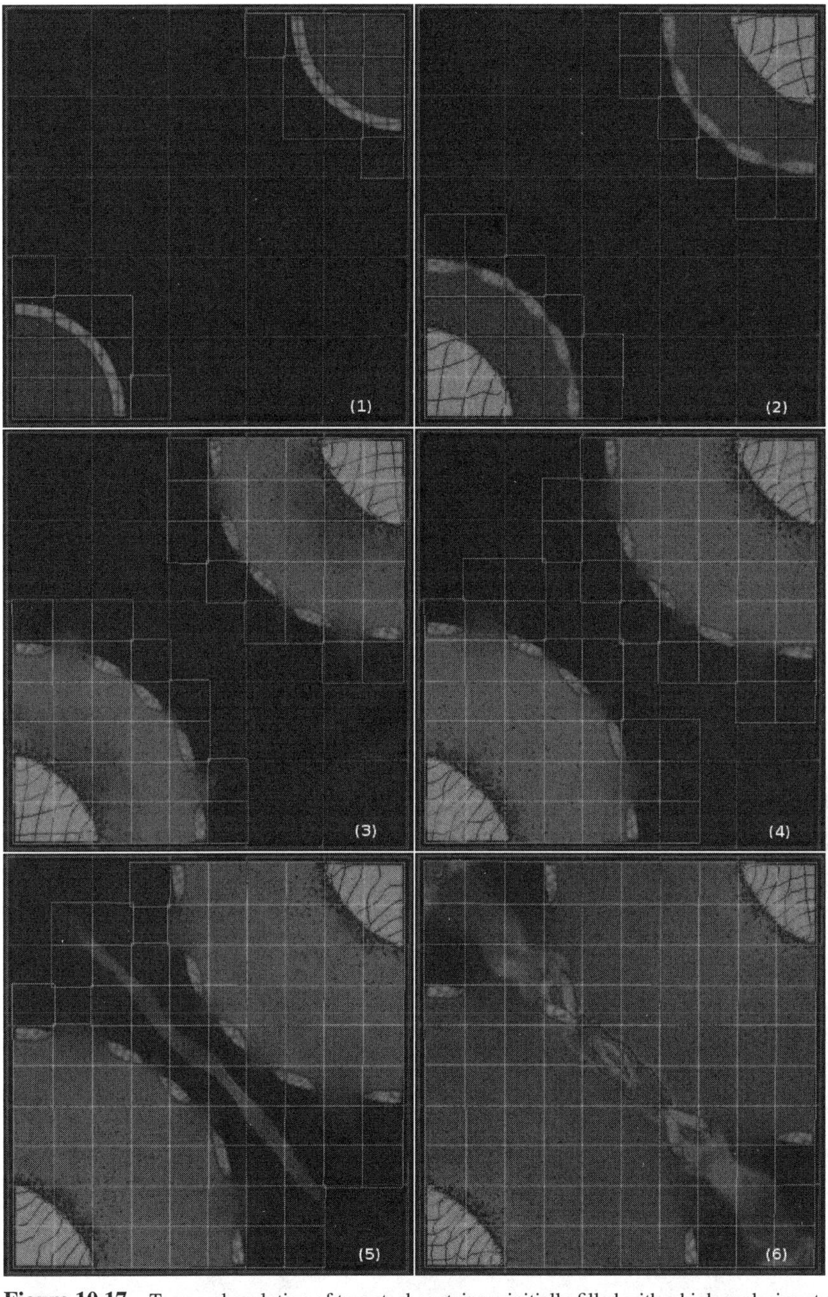

Figure 10.17 Temporal evolution of two steel containers initially filled with a high explosive at a temperature above the threshold ignition temperature. The background contour plot shows the magnitude of pressure and the particles are colored by mass. The solid green lines show the outline of the fine-level patches and the red lines correspond to the coarse-level patches.

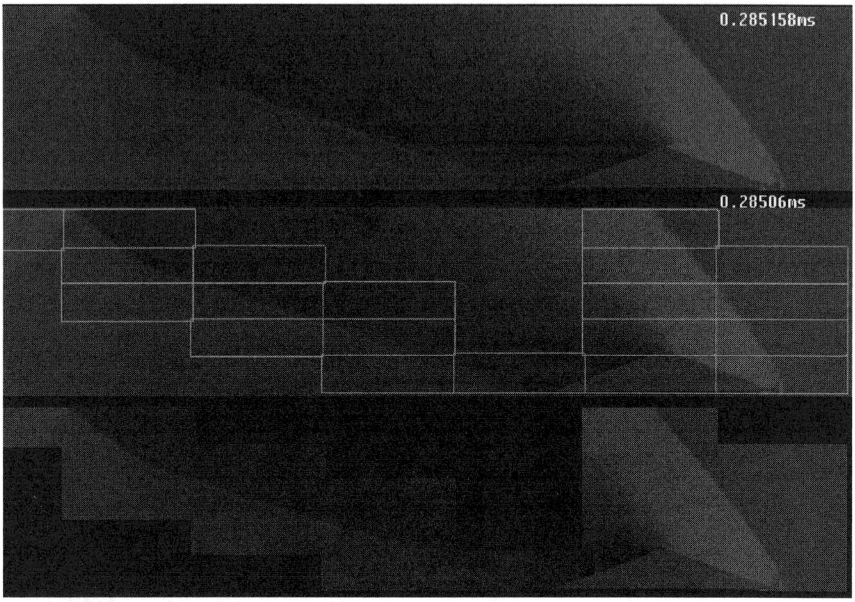

Figure 10.18 A 2D wedge traveling at Mach 2, contour plot of the pressure field. Results from a single-level and a two-level simulations are shown. Top: single-level solution, middle: coarse-level pressure field, and bottom: fine-level pressure field.

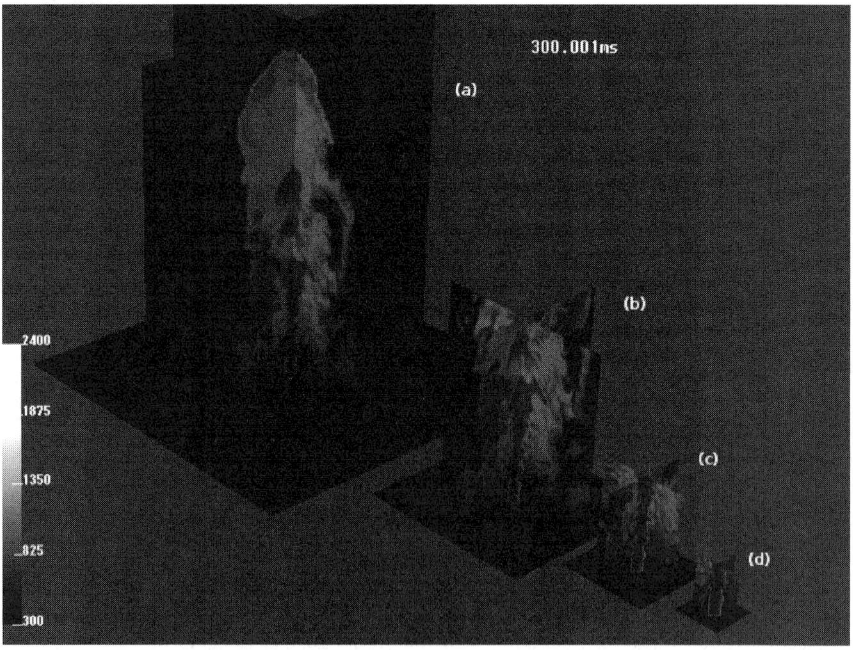

Figure 10.19 Temperature distribution of a JP8 jet flame on four static levels, 128^3 cells per level. (a) L1: 12.8 m^3. (b) L2: 6.4 m^3. (c) L3: 3.2 m^3, (d) L4: 1.6 m^3.

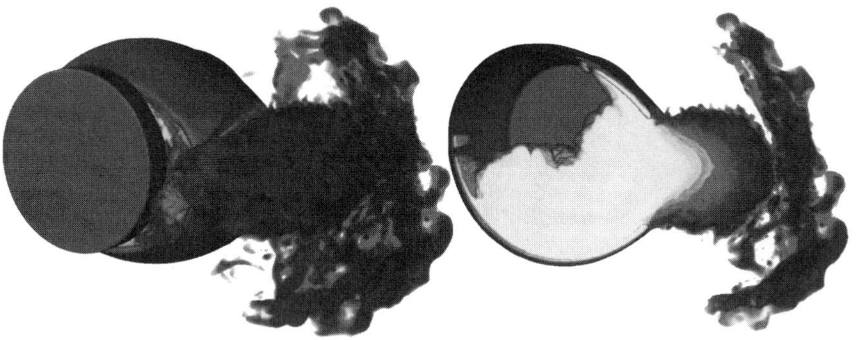

Figure 10.20 Full adaptive 3D simulation of an explosive device subjected to a hydrocarbon fire, shown just as the pressure is release through a rapture in the steel container. The view on the left shows the outside of the container, while the view on the right shows a cross section of the same data.

expected shock angle for this configuration is known, and very favorably compared to the computed result.

Figure 10.19 shows slices of the temperature field, from a simulation of a JP8 jet flame, issuing at 50 m/s from a 0.2 m hole in the floor of the computational domain. The grid consisted of four static levels with 128^3 cells on each level and the computational domain spanned 12.8 m in each direction. This simulation was performed on 600 processors.

One of the scientific questions that Uintah is at present being used to address is to predict how the response of an explosive device that is heated by a jet fuel fire changes with a variety of conditions. These include fire size, container location relative to the fire, and the speed and direction of a cross wind. A total of 12 simulations are being performed to investigate this question. The current state of one of those cases is shown

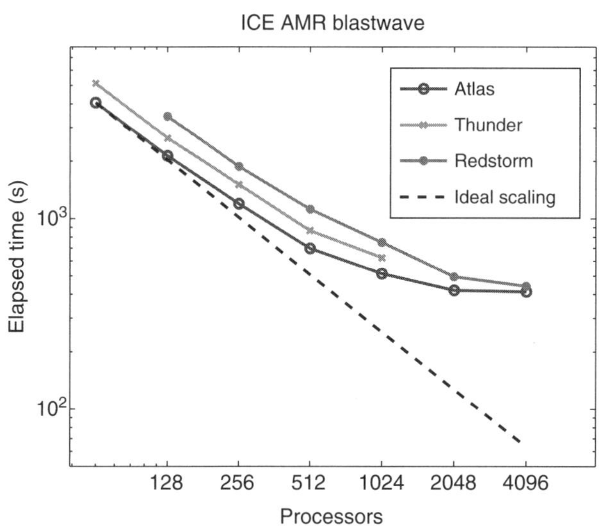

Figure 10.21 The scalability of AMR ICE.

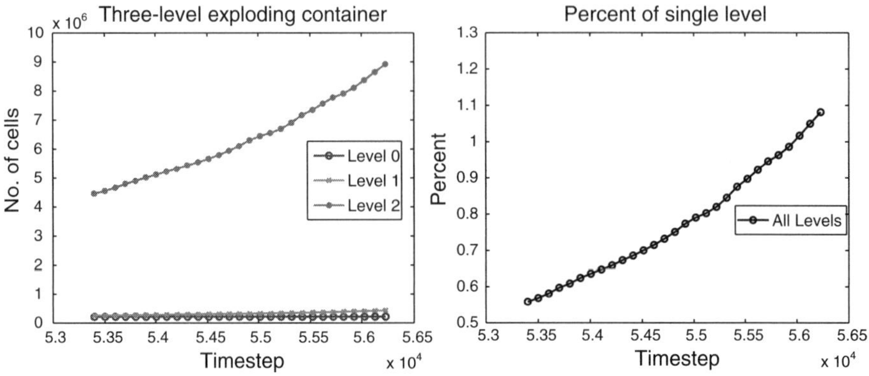

Figure 10.22 *Left*: Number of cells at each level of refinement for the exploding container shown in Figure 10.20, shown just as the container begins to rupture, *Right*: Total number of cells at all refinements levels, expressed as a percentage of the cells required for a nonadaptive simulation.

in Figure 10.20. This simulation is being carried out on 500 processors of the Atlas cluster at LLNL. The grid utilizes four levels of refinement with a refinement ratio of four, with the finest level at 1 mm. The figure shows a cut-away view of an isosurface of the steel container (blue) that has partially ruptured. The density of the products of reaction is volume rendered, and the void space inside the container is where the remaining unburned explosive lies. It was not explicitly shown in this view for the sake of clarity. As these simulations come to completion, data analysis of fragment size and velocity will be used as an indicator of violence of explosion.

Figure 10.21 shows the scalability of Uintah running a three level 3D ICE problem similar to the problem seen in Figure 10.4 on multiple architectures. Thunder is a Linux cluster located at LLNL with 1024 quad processor Intel Xeon nodes, connected via a Quadrics switch. Atlas is also Linux cluster located at LLNL with 1152 nodes each with eight AMD Opteron processors, also connected via a Quadrics switch. Red storm is an Opteron-based supercomputer located at Sandia with 12,920 dual-core CPUs, connected with a proprietary Cray interconnect. Although the code does not scale perfectly for AMR problems, it still dramatically outperforms the non-AMR equivalents. Figure 10.22 (left) illustrates another challenge—that as the container expan ds, the number of refined cells increases consistently. However, the performance gain is still substantial as indicated by the right side of Figure 10.22 as the total number of cells over all levels is just over 1% of the number required by a single-level grid. A non-AMR version of the explosion simulations shown in Figure 10.20 would impose unacceptable limitations on the domain size and grid resolution, or would require nearly a two orders of magnitude increase in computational resources.

10.7 CONCLUSIONS AND FUTURE WORK

We have presented a framework and application for using adaptive methods for complex multiphysics simulations of explosive devices. This framework uses an explicit representation of parallel computation and communication to enable integration of parallelism across multiple simulation methods.

We have also discussed several simulations that are performed routinely using this framework, including the heat up, pressurization, and consequent rupture of an incendiary device. Using adaptive methods, we are able to perform simulations that would otherwise be inaccurate or computationally intractable.

In addition to the adaptive explosion simulations described above, Uintah is a general-purpose simulation capability that has been used for a wide range of applications. MPM has been used to simulate a penetrating wound in a comprehensive cardiac/torso model [17–19], with the goal of understanding mechanics of wounding in an effort to improve the chances of recovery from projectile wounds. It has also been used to study biomechanical interactions of angiogenic microvessels with the extracellular matrix on the microscale level, by developing and applying novel experimental and computational techniques to study a 3D *in vitro* angiogenesis model [12]. The Uintah fluid–structure interaction component (MPM–ICE) is being employed in a study of phonation, or the production of sound, in human vocal folds. This investigation has determined the ability of Uintah to capture normal acoustical dynamics, including movement of the vocal fold tissue, and will consider pathological laryngeal conditions in the future. Uintah has also been used by collaborators at Los Alamos National Laboratory to model the dynamic compaction of foams [4, 7], such as those used to isolate nuclear weapon components from shock loading.

Achieving scalability and performance for these types of applications is an ongoing challenge. We are continuing to evaluate scalability on larger number of processors, and will reduce scaling bottlenecks that will appear when using these configurations. Intertask communication is at present a known bottleneck on large numbers of processors. We aim to reduce this by using the task graph to transparently trade off redundant computation with fine-grained communication. We also have a few situations where extra data are sent, which may improve scalability for large processor counts. Finally, we are exploring methods to reduce communication wait time by dynamically reordering the execution of tasks as their MPI dependencies are satisfied leading to more overlap of communication and computation.

This work was supported by the U.S. Department of Energy through the Center for the Simulation of Accidental Fires and Explosions, under grant W-7405-ENG-48. We thank each of the members of the interdisciplinary C-SAFE team at the University of Utah for their contributions to the Uintah software.

REFERENCES

1. M.J. Aftosmis and M.J. Berger. Multilevel error estimation and adaptive h-refinement for cartesian meshes with embedded boundaries. In *40th AIAA Aerospace Sciences Meeting and Exhibit*, No. AIAA 2002-0863, Calagary, AB, Canada 2002.
2. S. Atlas, S. Banerjee, J.C. Cummings, P.J. Hinker, M. Srikant, J.V.W. Reynders, and M. Tholburn. POOMA: A high-performance distributed simulation environment for scientific applications. In *Proceedings of Supercomputing '95*, San Diego, CA, December 1995.

3. S. Balay, W.D. Gropp, L. Curfman McInnes, and B.F. Smith. Efficient management of parallelism in object oriented numerical software libraries. In E. Arge, A.M. Bruaset, and H.P. Langtangen, editors, *Modern Software Tools in Scientific Computing*. Birkhäuser Press, 1997, pp. 163–202.
4. S.G. Bardenhagen, A.D. Brydon, and J.E. Guilkey. Insight into the physics of foam densification via numerical solution. *J. Mech. Phys. Solids*, 53:597–617, 2005.
5. M. Berger and I. Rigoutsos. An algorithm for point clustering and grid generation. *IEEE Trans. Sys. Man Cybernet.*, 21(5):1278–1286, 1991.
6. M.J. Berger and P. Colella. Local adaptive mesh refinement for shock hydrodynamics. *J. Comput. Phys.*, 82:64–84, 1989.
7. A.D. Brydon, S.G. Bardenhagen, E.A. Miller, and G.T. Seidler. Simulation of the densification of real open-celled foam microstructures. *J. Mech. Phys. Solids*, 53:2638–2660, 2005.
8. K.D. Devine, E.G. Boman, R.T. Heaphy, B.A. Hendrickson, J.D. Teresco, J.Faik, J.E. Flaherty, and L.G. Gervasio. New challanges in dynamic load balancing. *Appl. Numer. Math.*, 52(2-3):133–152, 2005.
9. R.D. Falgout, J.E. Jones, and U.M. Yang. The design and implementation of hypre, a library of parallel high performance preconditioners. In A.M. Bruaset and A. Tveito, editors, *Numerical Solution of Partial Differential Equations on Parallel Computers*. Springer-Verleg, 2006, 267–294.
10. J.T. Feo, D.C. Cann, and R.R. Oldehoeft. A report on the sisal language project. *J. Parallel Distrib. Comput.*, 10:349–366, 1990.
11. J.E. Guilkey, T.B. Harman, and B. Banerjee. An Eulerian-Lagrangian approach for simulating explosions of energetic devices. *Comput. Struct.*, 85:660–674, 2007.
12. J.E. Guilkey, J.B Hoying, and J.A. Weiss. Modeling of multicellular constructs with the material point method. *J. Biomech.*, 39:2074–2086, 2007.
13. B.T.N. Gunney, A.M. Wissink, and D.A. Hysom. Parallel clustering algorithms for structured AMR. *J. Parallel Distrib. Comput.*, 66(11):1419–1430, 2006.
14. F.H. Harlow and A.A. Amsden. Numerical calculation of almost incompressible flow. *J. Comput. Phys.*, 3:80–93, 1968.
15. T.C. Henderson, P.A. McMurtry, P.G. Smith, G.A. Voth, C.A. Wight, and D.W. Pershing. Simulating accidental fires and explosions. *Comput. Sci. Eng.*, 2:64–76, 1994.
16. R.D. Hornung and S.R. Kohn. Managing application complexity in the SAMRAI object-oriented framework. *Concurrency Comput: Pract. Exper.*, 14:347–368, 2002.
17. I. Ionescu, J. Guilkey, M. Berzins, R.M. Kirby, and J. Weiss. *Computational Simulation of Penetrating Trauma in Biological Soft Tissues Using the Material Point Method.* IOS Press, Amsterdam, 2005.
18. I. Ionescu, J. Guilkey, M. Berzins, R.M. Kirby, and J. Weiss. *Ballistic Injury Simulation Using the Material Point Method.* IOS Press, Amsterdam, 2006.
19. I. Ionescu, J.E. Guilkey, M. Berzins, R.M. Kirby, and J.A. Weiss. Simulation of soft tissue failure Using the material point method. *J. Biomech. Eng.*, 128:917–924, 2006.
20. B.A. Kashiwa. A multifield model and method for fluid–structure interaction dynamics. Technical Report LA-UR-01-1136, Los Alamos National Laboratory, Los Alamos, 2001.
21. B.A. Kashiwa and E.S. Gaffney. Design basis for CFDLIB. Technical Report LA-UR-03-1295, Los Alamos National Laboratory, Los Alamos, 2003.
22. B.A. Kashiwa, M.L. Lewis, and T.L. Wilson. Fluid–structure interaction modeling. Technical Report LA-13111-PR, Los Alamos National Laboratory, Los Alamos, 1996.
23. B.A. Kashiwa and R.M. Rauenzahn. A cell-centered ICE method for multiphase flow simulations. Technical Report LA-UR-93-3922, Los Alamos National Laboratory, Los Alamos, 1994.
24. B.A. Kashiwa and R.M. Rauenzahn. A multimaterial formalism. Technical Report LA-UR-94-771, Los Alamos National Laboratory, Los Alamos, 1994.
25. G. Krishnamoorthy, S. Borodai, R. Rawat, J.P. Spinti, and P.J. Smith. *Numerical Modeling of Radiative Heat Transfer in Pool Fire Simulations.* ASME International Mechanical Engineering Congress (IMECE), Orlando, FL. 2005.
26. G. Lapenta and J.U. Brackbill. Control of the number of particles in fluid and MHD particle in cell methods. *Comput. Phys. Commun.*, 87:139–154, 1995.
27. J. Luitjens, M. Berzins, and T. Henderson. Parallel space-filling curve generation through sorting: research articles. *Concurrency Comput. Pract. Exper.*, 19(10):1387–1402, 2007.

28. J. Luitjens, B. Worthen, M. Berzins, and T. Henderson. Scalable parallel AMR for the Uintah multi-physics code. *Petascale Computing Algorithms and Applications.* Chapman and Hall/CRC, 2007.
29. J. Ma, H. Lu, and R. Komanduri. Structured mesh refinement in generalized interpolation material point (GIMP). *Comput. Model. Eng. Sci.*, 12:213–227, 2006.
30. D. Martin. An adaptive cell-centered projection method for the incompressible Euler equations. PhD thesis, University of California, Berkeley, 1998.
31. M. Shee, S. Bhavsar, and M. Parashar. Characterizing the performance of dynamic distribution and load-balancing techniques for adaptive grid hierarchies. In *IASTED: International Conference on Parallel and Distributed Computing and Systems*, Calagary, AB, 1999.
32. J. Steensland, S. Söderberg, and M. Thuné. A comparison of partitioning schemes for blockwise parallel SAMR algorithms. In *PARA '00: Proceedings of the 5th International Workshop on Applied Parallel Computing, New Paradigms for HPC in Industry and Academia.* Springer-Verlag, London, UK, 2001, pp. 160–169.
33. D. Sulsky, Z. Chen, and H.L. Schreyer. A particle method for history dependent materials. *Comput. Methods Appl. Mech. Eng.*, 118:179–196, 1994.
34. S. Vajracharya, S. Karmesin, P. Beckman, J. Crotinger, A. Malony, S. Shende, R. Oldehoeft, and S. Smith. SMARTS: Exploiting temporal locality and parallelism through vertical execution. In *Proceeding of the 1999 Internationl Conference on Supercomputing*, Rhodes, Greece, June 20–25, 1999, pp. 302–310. 1999.
35. W.B. VanderHeyden and B.A. Kashiwa. Compatible fluxes for van leer advection. *J. Comput. Phys.*, 146:1–28, 1998.
36. A.M. Wissink, R.D. Hornung, S.R. Kohn, S.S. Smith, and N. Elliott. Large scale parallel structured AMR calculations using the SAMRAI framework. In *Supercomputing '01: Proceedings of the 2001 ACM/IEEE Conference on Supercomputing (CDROM)*, ACM Press, New York, NY, 2001, p. 6.
37. A.M. Wissink, D. Hysom, and R.D. Hornung. Enhancing scalability of parallel structured AMR calculations. In *ICS '03: Proceedings of the 17th Annual International Conference on Supercomputing*, ACM Press, New York, NY, 2003, pp. 336–347.

Chapter 11

Managing Complexity in Massively Parallel, Adaptive, Multiphysics Finite Element Applications

Harold C. Edwards

How do you create something that provides the core of an application and does it in way that can be used to build many applications? Object oriented skills are a great start, but they just aren't enough to create a successful framework.

—Carey and Carlson in *Framework Process Patterns* [1]

11.1 INTRODUCTION

Sandia National Laboratories (SNL) has developed a new generation of engineering analysis codes that utilize advanced capabilities such as massively parallel processing, dynamic adaptive discretizations, and multiphysics coupling. The success of these development efforts has been predicated upon managing complexity and minimizing redundancy among these analysis codes through a *framework* approach. In a framework approach, capabilities that are common to a breadth of applications are identified and consolidated into a collection of shared components. These components define a separation of concerns from the application-specific physics components and the more broadly usable/reusable framework components.

Advanced Computational Infrastructures For Parallel and Distributed Adaptive Applications. Edited by Manish Parashar and Xiaolin Li

The Sierra framework [2–11] supports a diverse set of finite element and finite volume engineering analysis codes. These SNL codes include

- Fuego and Syrinx [12]—fire environment simulations with low Mach number fluid mechanics with heat and mass transport coupled to participating media radiation;
- Calore [13]—thermal analysis simulations;
- Presto [14]—three-dimensional explicit dynamics simulation with large deformation contact;
- Adagio [15]—three-dimensional, implicit, nonlinear quasi-statics and dynamics simulation;
- Premo [16]—compressible fluid dynamics for aerothermodynamics simulations;
- Aria [17]—tightly coupled multiphysics simulation including incompressible Navier–Stokes, energy transport, species transport, non-Newtonian fluid rheology, linear elastic solid mechanics, and electrostatics, as well as generalized scalar, vector, and tensor transport equations.

These applications deliver significant engineering analysis capabilities and are being used to simulate SNL's extremely challenging, real-world problems with millions of degrees of freedom on massively parallel computers. Elaboration of this broad set of problems and analysis capabilities is outside of the scope of this chapter. Such application-specific information is available through referenced and future publications, as well as numerous conference presentations.

The impact of the presented research and its implementation in the Sierra framework is demonstrated by the employment of the framework's physics-independent capabilities across SNL's diverse set of engineering analysis codes. Each of these applications utilizes core components of distributed mesh data structures, parallel input/output/restart, and parallel execution control. In addition, these applications selectively utilize advanced components for transparent interfacing to equation solver packages, transfer of field data between dissimilar and independently distributed meshes, and several forms of discretization adaptivity. This chapter documents the theory, abstractions, and software design that enabled the successful development and utilization of these complex framework components.

11.1.1 Frameworks for Scientific and Engineering Simulation Codes

A framework has been defined as "a set of cooperating classes that make up a reusable design for a specific class of software" [18]. A framework is said to (1) take a team of individual components and define how they work together, (2) define reusable abstractions for the components *and* how they are integrated, and (3) address a specific target domain [1]. In addition to the Sierra framework at SNL, other active research and development efforts for scientific and engineering parallel computing frameworks include

- SAMRAI [19, 20] and Overture [21] at Lawrence Livermore National Laboratories,
- Unstructured Grid (UG) [22–24] at the University of Heidelberg,
- ParFUM [25] and Roccom [26] at the University of Illinois at Urbana-Champaign,
- AOMD [27, 28] and Trellis [29] at Rensselaer Polytechnic Institute,
- Uintah [30, 31] at University of Utah,
- Cactus [32] at Louisiana State University,
- libMesh [33, 34] and IPARS [35] at the University of Texas at Austin, and
- STAPL at Texas A&M University [36].

11.1.2 Managing Complexity via Conceptual Modeling

The success of the Sierra framework has been predicated for managing the extension and integration of complex capabilities through a conceptual modeling approach. In this approach, the components' capabilities and interactions are formally modeled and analyzed at a high level of abstraction. The resulting model is then mapped to a software design. When subsequent enhancements or new capabilities are required, the conceptual model is extended and reanalyzed, leading to a revised software design.

The formal conceptual model underlying the development of the Sierra framework is based upon abstractions from set theory. These abstractions include sets, subsets, relations, maps, classes (a set of sets, not the C++ language construct), and set topology (a set of sets with certain properties). Fundamental sets in a parallel adaptive multiphysics application include physics models, algorithms, parts of the problem domain (e.g., materials), fields, discretization/mesh entities, and processors. Similarly, relations express connectivity within a mesh, associations of mesh entities with fields, or whether a particular physics model acts upon a given field. Subsets include the portion of a mesh stored on a particular processor, parts of a mesh (e.g., materials and boundary conditions) that a physics model acts upon, and fields that are used by a particular physics model.

It is not sufficient to merely define the sets and relations, that is, to just define a data model. Analysis of how these sets and relations interact and are modified has a significant impact on the translation of these abstractions to a software design. For example, a software design that supports a static mesh on a single processor can be much simpler than is required to support a parallel distributed and dynamically changing mesh.

An essential element of the conceptual model presented here is the idea of an *extension point* within the framework. An extension point is a place in a framework where the core architecture can be extended or customized to fit the needs of different (and potentially unanticipated) uses [1]. Extension points of the Sierra framework include both points at which application code modules can be "plugged in" to the framework and points at which flexibility has been designed into the core framework.

11.1.3 Organization

Presentation of the flexible and extensible conceptual model for the Sierra framework begins with an introduction of the fundamental sets (e.g., mesh entities) and relations (e.g., connectivity) in Section 11.2. From these fundamentals, a model for defining types and roles of mesh entities is given in Section 11.3. A model for efficiently managing mesh complexity due to heterogeneities from mesh entity types, multiple physics, and multiple parts is presented in Section 11.4. The nonparallel/local mesh representation conceptual model is completed in Section 11.5 with a description of connectivity relations. Given the conceptual model of a mesh, a model for managing the complexity from the parallel execution of algorithms is described in Section 11.6. Scalable parallel execution of a nontrivial set of algorithms requires parallel domain decomposition and dynamic load balancing. The conceptual model for a mesh is extended in Section 11.7 to address the parallel distribution of a dynamically adapting mesh and its implications to the runtime performance of parallel algorithms.

The conceptual model of a parallel distributed, adaptive, multiphysics mesh defines the core of the Sierra framework. This core is elaborated in Section 11.8 with a model for interfacing to external equation solver libraries. The Sierra framework's advanced capabilities of intermesh coupling and mesh adaptivity are described in terms of the core conceptual model in Section 11.9 and Section 11.10, respectively.

11.2 SETS AND RELATIONS

A formal conceptual model based upon set theory has been used in the development of the Sierra framework. A brief overview of the set theory nomenclature and fundamental sets and relations used in this model is given.

11.2.1 Nomenclature

- A *set*, $A = \{a_i\}$, is a collection of identifiable member entities. Furthermore, the identification of a member is persistent for the lifetime of that member.
- Sets have well-defined relationships ($= \; \neq \; \subset \subseteq \in$) and operators ($\cap \; \cup \; \backslash$).
- The *cardinality* of a set, denoted by $\#A$, is the number of members in the set.
- A *class* is a set of sets.
- A *partition* of a set A is a class C such that the union of members of C is equal to the set A, $A = \bigcup_{X \in C} X$, and intersection of any two different members of the class C is an empty set, $\emptyset = X \cap Y \; \forall X \neq Y \in C$.

- A *topology* on a set A is a class C such that the sets A and $\emptyset$ are members of C, the union of any members of C is a member of C, and the intersection of any two members of C is also a member of C.
- The *Cartesian product* of two sets A and B, denoted by $A \times B$, is the set of ordered pairs $\{(a, b) : a \in A, b \in B\}$.
- A *relation* is a set R of ordered pairs $\{(a, b)\}$ where the set of the first coordinates $\{a\}$ is the *domain* of R and the set of the second coordinates $\{b\}$ is the *range* of R. Note that $R \subseteq domain\,(R) \times range\,(R)$.
- The *converse* of a relation R^c is the relation defined by reversing the coordinates of the members, $R^c = \{(b, a) : (a, b) \in R\}$.
- A *symmetric relation* is equal to its converse, $R^c = R$.
- A *map* is a relation R such that no two members have the same first coordinate (if $(a, b) \in R$ and $(a, c) \in R$ then $b = c$). A map may be denoted by $a \mapsto b$. Note that the converse of a map is not necessarily a map.

11.2.2 Fundamental Sets

Mesh and Mesh Entity: A mesh is a set of mesh entities $M = \{m_i\}$ that represent the fundamental units within a discretization of the problem domain. In an unstructured finite element mesh, these can include nodes, elements, faces, and edges. Each member mesh entity is uniquely identifiable within the "universal" set of the mesh.

Mesh Part: A nontrivial problem domain will have subsets of mesh entities, or mesh parts, that are associated with a mesh-independent specification of the problem domain. Consider the simple, illustrative problem in Figure 11.1 of a fluid flow through a pipe with localized heating.

This multiphysics problem has a set of mesh parts $\{M_\iota \subseteq M\}$ for which different equations are solved. For example, heat transfer is solved over both solid and fluid parts; fluid flow is solved only within the fluid part; elastic deformation is solved

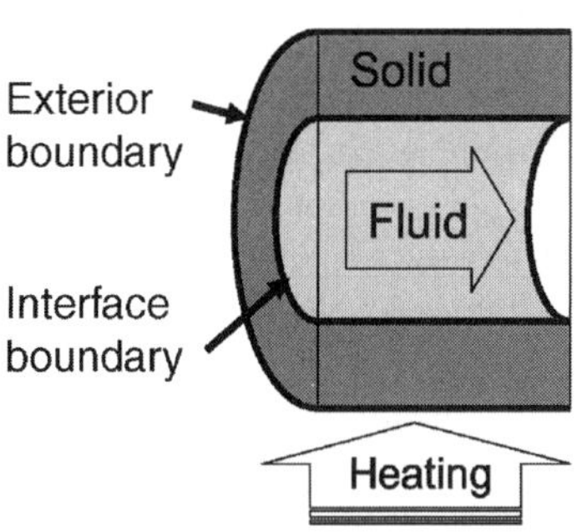

Figure 11.1 Illustrative problem: fluid flow through a pipe with localized heating.

only over the solid part; and different boundary conditions are applied to the exterior, inflow, and outflow boundaries.

A mesh is generated from a geometric representation of the problem domain. For nontrivial problem domains, this representation is typically constructed from a collection of simpler geometric components. These component parts could be carried through the meshing process to define subsets of the generated mesh entities. The resulting mesh parts are artifacts of the original specification of the problem domain.

Mesh parts will also be defined by the discretization scheme. For example, a traditional simple finite element discretization may partition a three-dimensional problem domain into hexahedron mesh entities and node mesh entities at the vertices. This descretization scheme induces two mesh parts: a set of hexahedrons and a set of nodes.

Field: The set of fields $F = \{f_\iota\}$ *describes* the independent, dependent, or scratch variables that are (1) required by the equations and (2) associated with mesh entities. Fields are defined with respect to the equations to be solved and the discretization method use to solve those equations. Thus, the definition of a field is independent of the actual discretization of the problem domain so that changes to the discretization (different mesh or adapting mesh) do not effect the specification for a field.

Field Value: A field *defines* and *describes* the variables required to solve a given set of equations with a given method. A set of values for the field, for example, basis function coefficients, are defined when a field is associated with one or more mesh entities. Each member of the set of field values $\{v_{ij}\}$ is associated with a unique pairing of a mesh entity and field, $v_{ij} \mapsto (m_i, f_j)$.

Algorithm: The computations performed by a scientific or engineering simulation code can be, and should be, decomposed into a set of components. These component algorithms $\{A_\iota\}$ are sequenced or iterated to obtain a solution to a given problem. The concept of an algorithm is flexible in that an algorithm could correspond to a single equation, an integrated set of equations, solution of a system of equations, adaptation of the discretization, and so on. The key concept for an algorithm is that it *acts* upon a well-defined set of mesh entities and fields.

Parallel Processors: A parallel execution environment is defined by a set of processors $\{P_j\}$. Each processor is assumed to be a resource that has exclusive ownership of a finite quantity of memory and can communicate data with other processors. An algorithm typically executes on all processors; however, the execution of algorithm on a given processor necessarily acts upon data that reside on that processor. Algorithms utilize interprocessor communications to access or exchange data among processors. The execution of an algorithm on a given processor is denoted as $A_\iota|_{P_j}$.

Given that per-processor memory is finite, in-memory storage of a large mesh requires that the set of mesh entities and associated field values be distributed among processors, as illustrated in Figure 11.2. The partitioning and distribution of a mesh among parallel processors is commonly defined through a domain decomposition approach. Domain decomposition of an unstructured mesh typically results in portions of the mesh, and corresponding subsets of mesh entities, being shared among processors as illustrated in Figure 11.2.

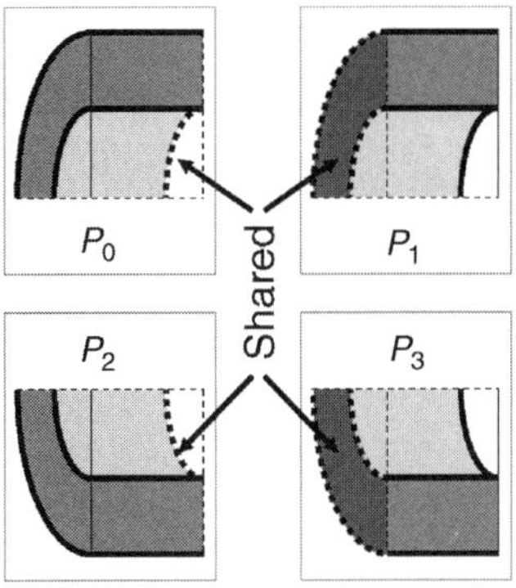

Figure 11.2 Parallel domain decomposition of the illustrative problem.

11.2.3 Fundamental Relations

Connectivity Relation: A mesh is defined by a set of mesh entities and the connections among those mesh entities. Connectivity is defined by a relation over the set of mesh entities $\{(m_i, m_j)\}$. This simple, fundamental relation provides the foundation for more complex models of connectivity that take into account connectivity for geometric entities (e.g., finite elements) and connectivity in a parallel distributed mesh.

Algorithm Action Relations: An algorithm may act upon a subset of mesh entities and use a subset of the defined fields. These action associations are defined by an algorithm–mesh entity relation $\{(A_\iota, m_i)\}$ and an algorithm–field relation $\{(A_\iota, f_j)\}$. The action, or computations, of an algorithm reads and updates field values.

Field Value Relation: A field value v_{ij} is associated with the unique pairing of a mesh entity and field, $v_{ij} \mapsto (m_i, f_j)$. This map is *one-to-one* over the subset of $M \times F$ for which field values are defined. Not every pairing of a mesh entity and a field has a field value. For example, in the illustrative problem (Figure 11.1) the fluid velocity field will not have values in the solid part. The converse of the field value map is the *field value relation* $\{((m_i, f_j), v_{ij})\}$.

$$M \times F \supset \text{range}(v_{ij} \mapsto (m_i, f_j)) \ni (m_i, f_j) \mapsto v_{ij}.$$

11.3 MESH ENTITY TYPES AND ROLES

A complex discretization scheme can define mesh entities of multiple geometric shapes, parametric coordinate frames, interpolation functions, numerical integration schemes, refinement strategies, and so on. These (and other) shared characteristics of mesh entities define the types of mesh entities in a discretization. In a traditional finite element method, a *master element* is an example of a mesh entity type.

11.3.1 Mesh Entity Type: Component Specifications and Kernels

A discretization scheme defines a set of mesh entity types $\{T_i\}$, where each mesh entity type is a collection of specifications and computational kernels $T_i = \{\phi_{ki}\}$. For finite element mesh entities, specifications and computational kernels include the geometric shape, parametric coordinate system, number of basis functions, parametric to physical coordinate mappings, and basis function evaluations. The set of mesh entity types is partitioned according to the *role* of those types in the discretization scheme. It is common to partition mesh entity types according to their association with volumes, areas, curves, and points, or from a finite element point of view separating the elements, sides, edges, and nodes. In the Sierra framework, the element types are further partitioned into volume elements, shell elements, and bar elements.

Mesh entity types of a given role are expected to provide components commensurate with their role. For example, a master element is expected to have a geometric shape, parametric coordinate frame, mapping to physical coordinates, interpolation functions, and integration rules. Each expected component ϕ_{ki} conforms to a defined interface ϕ_{k0} for that specification or computational kernel. A given mesh entity type is expected to provide components with interfaces commensurate with the role of that type, as summarized in equation (11.1). These component interfaces enable algorithms to act on mesh entities of a given role independently of the specific mesh entity type within that role.

$$
\begin{array}{ll}
T_i & \text{mesh entity type,} \\
T_i = \{\phi_{ki}\} & \text{component specifications and computational kernels,} \\
\{\{T_i\}_{\text{role}}\} & \text{types partitioned by role,} \\
\phi_{ki} \mapsto \phi_{k0} & \text{component's interface,} \\
\{\phi_{k0}\}_{\text{role}} & \text{components' interfaces expected for a role.}
\end{array}
\tag{11.1}
$$

New and advanced algorithms often require new, nontraditional specifications and computational kernels from a mesh entity type. For example, the geometric intersection of different meshes requires the inverse of the parametric to physical coordinate transformation, hierarchical mesh refinement requires a kernel for splitting mesh entities, and dynamic load balancing requires kernels supporting the parallel communication of mesh entities. Through the lifetime of the Sierra framework, the set of mesh entity types, components of those types, and roles has been extended, and it is expected to continue to be extended. For example, the traditional finite element roles of nodes and elements was first extended to include edges and sides, and again extended to include arbitrary constraints among mesh entities. Thus, the set of mesh entity types $\{T_i\}$, component interfaces $\{\phi_{k0}\}$, and roles are *extension points* in the conceptual model.

11.3.2 Sierra Master Element: Component Aggregation

A Sierra framework master element is a realization of the mesh entity type concept. Each component of a master element is defined by a generalized interface and is specialized for specific types of mesh entities (e.g., quadrilateral with linear basis and 4-point quadrature rule).

A master element is an aggregation of these components where new components can be added without impacting existing components. An example class diagram of this master element component aggregation design is given in Figure 11.3. This master element design is implemented with C++ virtual base classes defining the component interfaces and C++ derived classes implementing the components.

11.3.3 Field Association and Polymorphism

A field, $f \in F$, is a specification for a variable that is (1) required by one or more algorithms and (2) associated with mesh entities. Each field is typically associated with mesh entities of a particular role in a discretization, for example, associated with the nodes of a mesh. This association defines a partition for the set of fields by roles, $\{F_{\text{role}} \subset F\}$. Consider the illustrative problem of a flow in a heated pipe (Figure 11.1). A discretized temperature field could be defined as a C^0 nodal interpolation where its field values are strictly associated with nodal basis functions. In contrast, a stress field could be defined as a piecewise constant function where each field value is associated with the mean value of stress within an element.

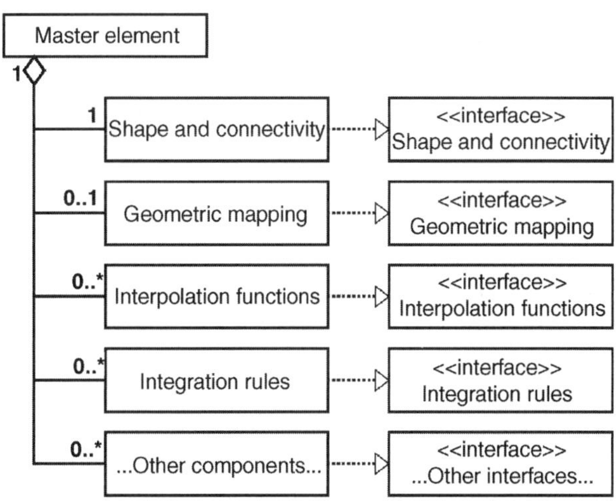

Figure 11.3 UML class diagram for master element component aggregation concept.

In the Sierra framework, a field describes a two-dimensional array of some scalar type (e.g., integer or floating point value). For example, let a field f_j describe an array of double precision values using FORTRAN notation.

$$f_j \rightarrow \text{double precision FIELD (nTensor, nCoefficient)}.$$

The "nTensor" dimension describes a field's size independent of the discretization, for example, a 3D vector valued field has nTensor = 3. The "nCoefficient" dimension describes a field's size that is dependent upon the discretization, for example, the number of Gauss quadrature points on an element. This discretization dependent dimension "nCoefficient" varies with some integer-valued specification ψ_{k0}, which is an expected member of a mesh entity type, $\psi_{ki} \in T_i$. In the example where "nCoefficient" is the number of Gauss quadrature points, this dimension will vary in a mesh with a heterogeneous set of elements.

$$f_j(T_i) \rightarrow \text{FIELD (nTensor, nCoefficient}(\psi_{k0})).$$

Thus, a field's definition can be polymorphic with respect to the mesh entity type.

11.4 HETEROGENEOUS COLLECTION OF MESH ENTITIES

A discretization scheme usually defines a heterogeneous collection of mesh entities, for example, nodes and elements in a finite element mesh. A complex discretization scheme may define numerous different types of mesh entities; for example, it may have a mixture of elements of different shapes and uses. Heterogeneities also result from multiphysics and multiple algorithms that are not uniformly applied throughout the problem domain. More heterogeneities are introduced when considering in which mesh part(s) a given mesh entity is a member. Finally, parallel execution introduces heterogeneities due to the parallel domain decomposition. Modeling these heterogeneities is essential to managing complexity and performance.

11.4.1 Multiple Types, Physics, and Parts

Each mesh entity type T_ι has an associated collection of mesh entities of that type; that is, it defines a mesh part M_{T_ι} $(m_i \mapsto T_\iota \Rightarrow m_i \in M_{T_\iota})$. The number of mesh entity types can be nontrivial for a discretization scheme that allows a mix of geometric shapes, interpolation functions, integration rules, and other components. These mesh entity types and their induced mesh parts can be a significant source of heterogeneity and complexity.

A multiphysics application may solve different sets of physics or material models on different parts of a problem domain. The subdomains over which each model's computations are performed and the fields that each model uses define subsets of the overall mesh and fields. In the illustrative problem of flow in a heated pipe (Figure 11.1), heat transfer computations are applied throughout the entire problem, fluid flow computations are applied inside the pipe, and elastic deformation computations are applied within the solid pipe. This relatively simple illustrative problem defines numerous physics induced subsets of the mesh and fields, for example,

Interface mesh	$M_{\text{interface}} = M_{\text{fluid}} \cap M_{\text{solid}}$,
Interface fields	$F_{\text{interface}} \supseteq F_{\text{fluid}} \cup F_{\text{solid}}$,
Exterior mesh	$M_{\text{exterior}} \subset M_{\text{solid}}$,
Exterior fields	$F_{\text{exterior}} \supseteq F_{\text{solid}}$,
Fluid inflow mesh	$M_{\text{inflow}} \subset M_{\text{fluid}}$, and
Fluid outflow mesh	$M_{\text{outflow}} \subset M_{\text{fluid}}$.

The specification of a problem domain may also identify multiple mesh parts over which the same set of physics models are applied. These mesh parts may reflect parts of the "real" problem. For example, the illustrative problem could have been defined as two pipes joined by an 90° elbow, all of the same material.

11.4.2 Managing Complexity: Finding the Homogeneous Kernels

The numerous and complex sources of heterogeneity can introduce a significant amount of irregularity in data structures and subsequent conditional branching within computations. For example, in the illustrative problem the association of fields with nodes varies across the mesh, so conditional branching is needed by the fluid flow calculations to avoid solid nodes and by the elastic deformation calculations to avoid fluid nodes. Two fundamental precepts for high-performance computational kernels are to minimize the number of operations (especially branching operations) and to ensure memory locality of the data. Thus, the need to support heterogeneous physics, parts, and discretizations is at odds with enabling the use of high-performance computational kernels. Both these needs have been satisfied in the Sierra framework by managing complexity due to heterogeneities through the concept of generating a set topology for the mesh. This set topology is used to partition data into regular homogeneous blocks that are ideally suited for high-performance computational kernels.

Set Topology: The set of mesh parts induced by multiple physics, meshing parts, mesh entity types, and parallel subdomains (Section 11.7.1) defines a class of mesh parts on the mesh, $\{M_\iota \subset M\}$. A set topology $\mathcal{T} \supset \{M_\iota\}$ is generated for a mesh M from its class of mesh parts $\{M_\iota\}$ by extending the class of mesh parts according to equation (11.2).

$$\tilde{\mathcal{T}} = \{\emptyset, M\} \cup \{M_i\}, \cup \left\{ \bigcap_{\beta \in \mathcal{B}} \beta \right\} \quad \forall \mathcal{B} \subseteq \{M_i\}$$
$$\mathcal{T} = \tilde{\mathcal{T}} \cup \left\{ \bigcup_{\beta \in \mathcal{B}} \beta \right\} \quad \forall \mathcal{B} \subset \tilde{\mathcal{T}}. \tag{11.2}$$

The cardinality of generated set topology $\mathcal{T}$ grows exponentially with the number of explicitly defined parts $\{M_\iota\}$. Therefore, an implementation $\mathcal{T}$ must only explicitly generate members that are used within the application; that is, those members that are not empty. Thus, this set topology defines the complete class of *potentially* needed mesh parts.

Homogeneous Kernels: The generated set topology $\mathcal{T}$ contains a subset of members that define a partitioning of the mesh into homogeneous subsets. The members of this homogeneous partition, denoted as $\mathcal{H}$, are identified by equation (11.3).

$$\mathcal{H} = \{H_\iota \in \mathcal{T} : H_\iota \cap M_* = H_\iota \text{ or } \emptyset \quad \forall M_* \in \mathcal{T}\}. \tag{11.3}$$

Members of the homogeneous partition $\mathcal{H} = \{H_\iota\}$ are referred to as the homogeneous *kernels* of the set topology $\mathcal{T}$.

Each member H_ι of the homogeneous partition $\mathcal{H}$ contains mesh entities that are of the same mesh entity type, are acted upon by the same algorithms, are members of the same problem-specific parts, and are members of the same parallel subdomains. Thus, the identical set of computations is performed on all members of a given kernel H_i. Furthermore, all members of such a kernel are associated with the same fields.

A similar homogeneous partitioning of the set of fields, $\mathcal{G} = \{G_\iota\} \supset \{F_j\}$, can be generated. However, the class from which such a partition is generated contains subsets defined by mesh entity types and the algorithms' required fields. Mesh parts from the problem specification (e.g., CAD model) and parallel decomposition do not induce corresponding subsets of fields.

11.4.3 Managing Performance: Homogeneous Blocks of Field Values

Partitioning of the mesh and fields into homogeneous kernels enables algorithms to use computational kernels with minimal branching operations and data structures with guaranteed memory locality. This is accomplished by aggregating mesh entities and associated field values into homogeneous blocks.

Existence of Field Values: A field value exists for a particular mesh entity and field if and only if (1) the mesh entity and field are associated with the same mesh entity type and (2) there exists at least one algorithm that acts upon both the mesh entity and the field.

$$\exists\left(\left(m_i, f_j\right), v_{ij}\right) \Leftrightarrow \exists A_k, T_l : m_i \in M_{A_k} \cap M_{T_l} \quad \texttt{and} \quad f_j \in F_{A_k} \cap F_{T_l}. \tag{11.4}$$

An implementation of this concept efficiently manages resources for field values by allocating only memory for field values that are needed and used by the application. Consider again the illustrative problem of flow in a heated pipe (Figure 11.1), this time with a thin-walled pipe. Let the solid part have only a few high-order elements through the thickness, the fluid part be meshed with significantly more low-order elements to resolve localized flow conditions, and every element (both solid and fluid) be given a stress tensor field value at every quadrature point for the elastic deformation computations. In this scenario, the elastic deformation stress tensor field values would be unused on the fluid elements and unnecessarily consume memory.

Blocks of Field Values: Given a member of the homogeneous partition of the mesh $H_\kappa \in \mathcal{H}$ and a member of the homogeneous partition of the fields $G_\lambda \in \mathcal{G}$, members of these sets will collectivity satisfy, or not, the existence condition.

$$\begin{aligned} &\text{If} \quad \exists\, A_k, T_l : H_\kappa \subset M_{A_k} \cap M_{T_l} \quad \text{and} \quad G_\lambda \subset F_{A_k} \cap F_{T_l}, \\ &\text{then}\ \exists \left(\left(m_i, f_j \right), v_{ij} \right)\ \forall\, m_i \in H_\kappa \quad \text{and} \quad \forall\, f_j \in G_\lambda. \end{aligned} \tag{11.5}$$

Equation (11.5) leads to a *blocking* relationship for field values. In this relationship, the association of a homogeneous kernel subset of the mesh H_κ with a corresponding kernel subset of the fields G_λ defines a block of field values, $V_{\kappa\lambda} \mapsto H_\kappa \times G_\lambda$, which are ideal for high-performance computational kernels.

Performance and Software Design: In the Sierra framework, the concept for blocks of field values $V_{\kappa\lambda}$ is exploited to (1) minimize the number of branching operations within a computational kernel and (2) manage memory in contiguous multidimensional arrays. Each block $V_{\kappa\lambda}$ is associated with the Cartesian product of a homogeneous set of mesh entities and homogeneous set of fields. An obvious data structure for the field values associated with a single field and a homogeneous block of mesh entities is multidimensional array (`nMeshEntity` $= \#H_\kappa$).

$$\texttt{FIELD(nTensor,nCoefficient,nMeshEntity)} \mapsto \left(H_\kappa, f_j \right).$$

The set of multidimensional field value arrays associated with the block $V_{\kappa\lambda}$ is aggregated into a contiguous block of memory. Every member of a kernel H_κ is homogeneous with respect to the computations performed on those mesh entities. As such branching decisions based upon mesh parts (physics induced, parallel induced, etc.) can be performed once for each kernel. Thus, computations of an algorithm A_k can be structured to loop over the class of kernels $\{H_\kappa\}$ and apply one or more high-performance computational kernels (e.g., $\phi_{ki} \in T_i$) to the corresponding block of field values.

```
Algorithm A_k:
  foreach H_κ ⊂ M
    if H_κ ⊂ M_{A_k}
      A_k acts on (H_κ, V_κλ) with array-based computations
    end if
  end foreach
```

11.5 CONNECTIVITY RELATIONS

A discretization strategy results in mesh entities that are geometrically adjacent to, and share a portion of their boundary with, other mesh entities. In a classical three-dimensional unstructured discretization, the elements are simple polyhedrons (e.g., tetrahedron, hexahedron) that are defined by a set of points (a.k.a. nodes) that are associated with the vertices of the simple polyhedrons. Other less conventional types of connectivity can represent actions at a distance or large deformation contact between different mesh entities within the same deforming mesh. The potential use of connectivity represents an extension point in this conceptual model. The connectivity attribute relation is a concept for managing traditional geometric adjacency connectivities, and for extensibility to other less conventional connectivities.

11.5.1 Flexibility and Extensibility: Connectivity Attributes

The simple connectivity relation $\{(m_i, m_j)\}$ introduced in Section 11.2.3 is not sufficient to fully describe the connectivity between an element and its nodes. In an unstructured mesh, a particular element–node pair may exist to denote a particular vertex of the element's polyhedral representation; however, such a pairing does not identify *which* vertex of the polyhedron the node represents. In addition, a simple pairing of mesh entities does not identify the intent of such a pairing; for example, does a face–node pair denote a vertex of the face or a face–node contact condition?

$$\text{Connectivity attribute relation:} \quad \{((m_i, m_j), \alpha_{ij})\}. \qquad (11.6)$$

The connectivity attribute relation equation (11.6) provides additional information to resolve these potential ambiguities and enables the connectivity concept to be easily extended. This relation associates an attribute α_{ij} with each local connection (m_i, m_j), compactly denoted as $m_i \xrightarrow{\alpha_{ij}} m_j$. In the Sierra framework, the connectivity attribute α_{ij} includes a local identifier (illustrated in Figure 11.4), purpose, and orientation.

- The *identifier* differentiates among similar connections. The example element, face, and node connectivity relationships illustrated in Figure 11.4 have a local node numbering convention that provides such identifiers. The identifier attribute is used to clarify the vertex-to-node associations for the correct geometric mapping between the element and problem domain coordinate systems. Similarly, identification of which side of the six possible sides is connected to the element is required for any side-element computations.

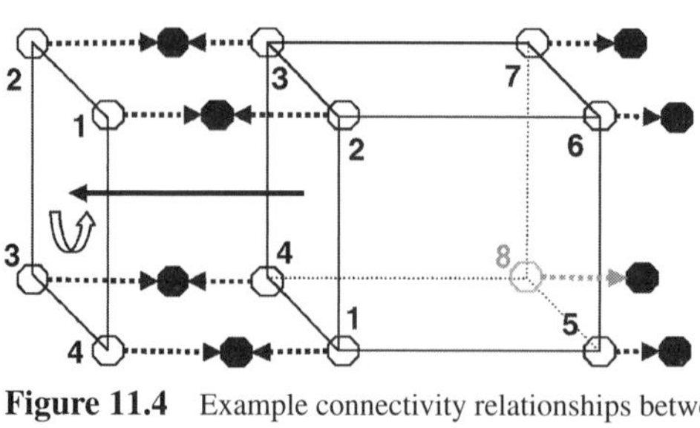

Figure 11.4 Example connectivity relationships between element, face, and node mesh entities.

- The *purpose* categorizes how the connection is used. For example, an *element* $\stackrel{uses}{\longrightarrow}$ *node* relationship defines the vertices or other points of the element. For some algorithms, the converse *node* $\stackrel{usedBy}{\longrightarrow}$ *element* relationships are supported to efficiently query the elements that are connected to a node.
- The *orientation* describes the relative geometric orientation between mesh entities, such as between an element and a face in Figure 11.4. In this example, the face mesh entity is rotated 90° with respect to the "expected" orientation in the *element* $\stackrel{uses:i}{\longrightarrow}$ *face* connection. For some connections, such as the *element* $\stackrel{i}{\longrightarrow}$ *node*, the orientation is unnecessary.

Extensibility: Connectivity has been extended within the Sierra framework on several occasions since its inception. For hierarchical mesh refinement (Section 11.10.1), the purpose attribute is extended from the traditional "uses" and "usedBy" to include "child" and "parent" relationships. This extension supports traversal of hierarchically refined elements through *element* $\stackrel{child}{\longrightarrow}$ *element* and the converse *element* $\stackrel{parent}{\longrightarrow}$ *element* relations. Other extensions include *element* $\stackrel{child}{\longrightarrow}$ *node* to capture the constrained node relationship from h-adaptivity, *element* $\stackrel{auxiliary}{\longrightarrow}$ *node* to capture particle-in-element relationships, and arbitrary connectivity between a conventional volume mesh and level set mesh intersecting the interior of the volume mesh. All these extensions fit within the existing connectivity attribute concept, and therefore existing software design. As such these extensions were introduced without any modifications to the underlying connectivity data structures.

Software Design: The predominant use case for the connectivity relation is that given domain mesh entity should obtain a subset of range mesh entities with a given attribute. For example, given an element obtains the nodes that the element uses. This use case motivates a permutation of the connectivity attribute relation as follows:

$$\left\{\left(\left(m_i, m_j\right), \alpha_{ij}\right)\right\} \Rightarrow m_i \mapsto \left\{\left(\alpha_{ij}, m_j\right)\right\}.$$

In the Sierra framework's software design, the domain mesh entity m_i owns a collection of attributes paired with a reference to the range mesh entity.

11.5.2 Connectivity Topology

A mesh entity of a given type T_i can be expected to have a specified set of connectivity relations. For example, an element is expected to be connected to nodes that define its vertices. These expectations are specified by a *connectivity topology* component of a mesh entity type (recall $\phi_{ki} \in T_i$). A connectivity topology specifies a set of required relationships for a given entity, for example, *element* $\stackrel{uses:j}{\longrightarrow}$ *node*, and set of optional relationships, for example, *element* $\stackrel{uses:j}{\longrightarrow}$ *face*.

$$T_i \mapsto \left\{\left(\alpha_{ij}, T_j\right)\right\}_{\text{required,}}$$
$$T_i \mapsto \left\{\left(\alpha_{ij}, T_j\right)\right\}_{\text{optional,}}$$

The *required* connectivity topology specification states that

$$\begin{aligned}&\text{Given } m_k \mapsto T_i \quad \text{and} \quad T_i \mapsto \left\{\left(\alpha_{ij}, T_j\right)\right\}_{\text{required}},\\&\text{then} \quad \exists\left(\left(m_k, m_l \mapsto T_j\right), \alpha_{ij}\right) \ \forall\, j\,.\end{aligned} \tag{11.7}$$

A connectivity topology includes the following information:

- A set of required relationships for *entity* $\xrightarrow{uses:j}$ *node* is needed to minimally represent an unstructured finite element polyhedron.
- A set of optional relationships for higher dimensional entities connecting to lower dimensional mesh entities; that is, *element* $\xrightarrow{uses:j}$ *face*, *element* $\xrightarrow{uses:j}$ *edge*, and *face* $\xrightarrow{uses:j}$ *edge*. The intermediate mesh entities of faces and edges are generated and maintained on an as-needed basis, for example, to support the definition of a boundary.
- Mappings to define the expected alignment of nodes between a higher dimensional entity to a connected lower dimensional entity. For example, an element–node connectivity identifier k paired with a face–node connectivity identifier j is mapped to an expected element–node connectivity identifier i.

$$\left(\text{elem} \xrightarrow{(k)} \text{face}\,,\ \text{face} \xrightarrow{(j)} \text{node}\right) \mapsto \left(\text{elem} \xrightarrow{(i)} \text{node}\right).$$

11.5.3 Imprinting: Mesh Part Membership Induced through Connectivity

A mesh entity may indirectly be a member of a mesh part due to its relationship with another mesh entity. Consider once again the fluid in pipe illustrative problem from Figure 11.1. An element m_{e} is explicitly a member of the solid (or fluid) mesh part $M_{\text{solid}} \ni m_{\text{e}}$. The element m_{e} has a “uses” relation to a node m_{n}, $m_{\text{e}} \xrightarrow{uses} m_{\text{n}}$. Thus, the node m_{n} is also a member of the solid mesh part M_{solid}, as long as the element m_{e} is a member of M_{solid} and uses the node m_{n}.

$$m_{\text{n}} \in M_{\text{solid}} \Leftarrow m_{\text{e}} \in M_{\text{solid}} \ \text{ and } \ m_{\text{e}} \xrightarrow{uses} m_{\text{n}}.$$

In this example, membership in M_{solid} is said to be *imprinted* on node m_{n} through the *uses* connectivity relation. In general, an imprinting condition is defined for a pairing of a mesh part and connection purpose, (M_*, α).

$$m_i \in M_* \Leftarrow m_j \in M_* \quad \text{and} \quad m_j \xrightarrow{\alpha} m_i. \tag{11.8}$$

A given mesh entity may have more than one imprinting condition, as defined by equation (11.8). However, for a mesh entity to be imprinted there must exist at least one such imprinting condition. Thus the full, per-entity, imprinting-existence condition for (M_*, α) is given by equation (11.9)

$$\text{Imprinting}\,(M_*, \alpha; m_i): \quad m_i \in M_* \Leftrightarrow \exists\, m_j : m_j \in M_* \quad \text{and} \quad m_j \xrightarrow{\alpha} m_i. \tag{11.9}$$

Some algorithms act on subsets of mesh entities defined by imprinting. In this solid–element–node example, a kinematic update algorithm acts on just the nodes of the solid, as identified through imprinting. Without imprinting the algorithm would have to access each element and then operate on the set of nodes that the element uses. Such an algorithm would access nearly all of the nodes multiple times, once per connected element. This algorithm would have to provide additional logic and variables to flag when a node had been updated so that multiply-visited nodes are updated only once.

Memberships induced by imprinting are also used when generating the set topology for nodes or other connected mesh entities (recall Section 11.4.2). This allows imprinting-dependent algorithms, such as the example kinematic update, to take advantage of the field value block data structure.

11.6 ALGORITHM EXECUTION

A simulation code is created by integrating its set of algorithms (computational components) into the Sierra framework. Algorithms are sequenced and iterated in a simulation and problem-specific manner in order to solve the given problem. These algorithms are partitioned into two categories according to the data that they act upon (Figure 11.5). *Model algorithms* act upon field values and mesh entities, and typically implement the physics or engineering models of the simulation. *Solver algorithms* contain the logic for obtaining or advancing a simulation's solution. Solver algorithms do not act directly upon field values and mesh entities; however, they do control the execution of model algorithms and act upon "global" data related to field values. For example, an iterative nonlinear solver algorithm would apply a model algorithm to compute the solution residual from a set of field values, but would only act upon a global norm of that residual.

The execution of an integrated set of algorithms defines a hierarchical calling tree for that set of algorithms. In the software design presented in Figure 11.5, each model algorithm has a set of "field value i/o" entities that define the model algorithm's plans for field value input and output. Field value i/o plans inform the

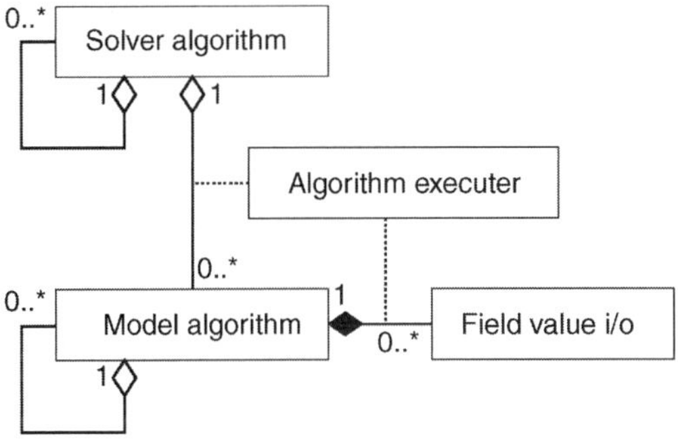

Figure 11.5 UML class diagram for algorithm hierarchy.

algorithm executor of a model algorithm's input needs and output intentions. Output intentions include both what and how field values are to be updated. For example, computations on a finite element typically result in partial sum contributions to field values associated with the nodes of the element. The algorithm executor analyzes these plans to determine what, if any, parallel communication operations are required to complete the model algorithms' updates to field values. For example, partial sum contributions must be communicated and summed among processors that share the element's nodes. This conceptual model and software design for algorithm execution allows the complexity of parallel algorithm execution to be fully separated into a local part and parallel part. Each model algorithm is responsible for its local computations and informing the algorithm executor of its field value i/o requirements. The algorithm executor is then responsible for all parallel operations required by those field value i/o requirements.

11.6.1 Parallel Execution

The parallel execution of solver and model algorithms is illustrated in Figure 11.6. A solver algorithm references a subset of model algorithms $\{A_k\}$ that it intends to execute (Fig. 11.5). On a given processor P_i, each model algorithm A_k acts upon the associated subset of mesh entities M_{A_k} and field values that reside on that processor, $A_k|_{P_i}$ acts on $M_{A_k}\big|_{P_i}$.

A solver algorithm invokes the framework's algorithm executer with its subset of model algorithms. The algorithm executer queries each model algorithm for its field value input/output plans. These plans are analyzed to determine how shared field values must be synchronized after the model algorithms have performed their actions. It is assumed that these field values are in a consistent state before the subset of model algorithms is invoked. After the algorithm executer invokes these model

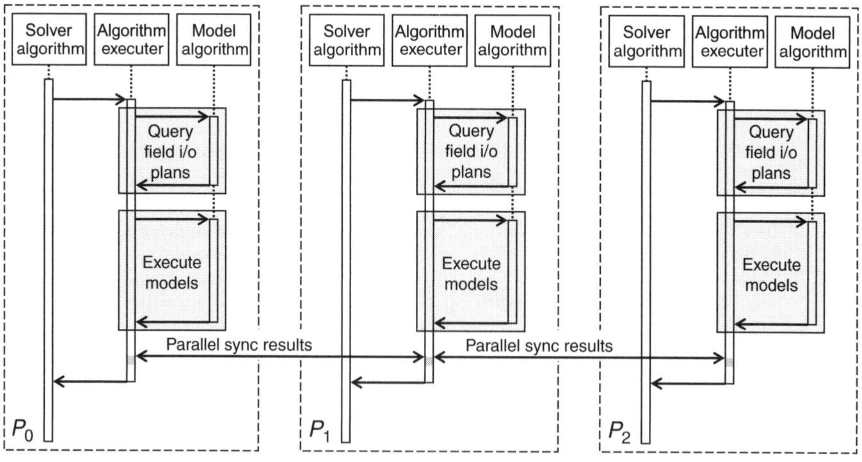

Figure 11.6 UML sequence diagram for algorithm execution.

algorithms it synchronizes the previously identified shared and modified field values among processors.

The parallel execution of model algorithms and subsequent synchronization of effected field values has three major challenges.

1. The model algorithms' changes to field values and mesh entities must be synchronizable. For the given field value v_{ij} residing on more than one processor, there must exist a function F that synchronizes those modified values to a consistent state. Let $v_{ij}\big|_{P_k}$ be a field value residing on processor P_k, then $\exists F$ such that $v_{ij} = F\left(\left\{ v_{ij}\big|_{P_k} \right\}\right)$. The predominant synchronization function is a simple summation of the set of field values, where individual processor's contributions are partial sums of the final value, $v_{ij} = \sum_k v_{ij}\big|_{P_k}$. A model algorithm specifies an appropriate synchronization function F for each field that it intends to update.
2. A model algorithm's subset of field values or mesh entities may not be evenly distributed (i.e., balanced) among processors. In this situation, a model algorithm could have significantly more computational work to perform on a small subset of processors, resulting in the remaining processors being idle during much of that model algorithm's execution.
3. An error condition may occur in one model algorithm on one processor that must be acted upon by all processors. The challenge is to minimize or avoid performance impacts to normal computations and communications while insuring that such error conditions are robustly handled.

11.6.2 Parallel Synchronization

Synchronizing field values to a consistent state is essential. When a parallel duplicated mesh entity has a different field value (for the same field) on two or more processors, then that field value is parallel inconsistent, and it is ambiguous as to which processor has the correct value. Furthermore, such parallel inconsistent data could be given to the calling solver algorithm—potentially leading to parallel processing deadlocks, livelocks, or other undesired behavior. For example, an iterative equation solver algorithm uses the norm of a residual to determine whether the solution has converged; if it has not converged, then the algorithm performs another iteration. If the norm of the residual is parallel inconsistent and near the convergence threshold, then some processors would exit the iteration loop while others would attempt to continue in the loop. At this point, the processors are desynchronized with respect to their computations and communications, leading to undesirable parallel processing behavior.

Model Algorithms Never Communicate: All parallel synchronization required by a model algorithm must be performed by either the framework's algorithm executer or by the solver algorithm invoking the model algorithm. This restriction is intended to address two concerns. First, consistent and deterministic (i.e., repeatable) parallel synchronization is nontrivial and can be complex and difficult to optimize. Second, the parallel synchronization requirements for a collection of model algorithms can be aggregated to improve parallel performance.

Consistency and Repeatability: A parallel synchronization must be repeatable; that is, if the operation were to be identically repeated *as far as the simulation is concerned,* then identical results must be obtained. Repeatable parallel synchronization assures that the same results are obtained given an unmodified simulation code, unchanged operating system and communication services, and stable parallel computer. Unfortunately, the underlying parallel communication service (e.g., a Message Passing Interface (MPI) implementation) is not guaranteed to perform in a deterministic manner—the ordering of received individual processor-to-processor (point-to-point) messages may change unpredictably from one execution to the next. Thus, a parallel synchronization must manage the assimilation of shared field values to insure that $F\left(\left\{\left[v_{ij}\right]_{P_k}\right\}\right)$ is a repeatable even when the underlying communication service is not.

In the Sierra framework, consistency and repeatability are achieved by accepting messages containing field values $v_{ij}\big|_{P_k}$ in any order, and then buffering these received messages until the complete set can be assembled in a prescribed order (e.g., processor rank order). A synchronization function F is given a repeatably and consistently ordered set of field values on each processor. This approach protects the parallel synchronization function F from operating on field values in the unpredictable order in which they are received. However, this approach limits the ability to overlap communication and the synchronization computations. To date this constraint on performance optimization has not impeded scalability and has not been a concern for simulations using the Sierra framework. On the other hand, consistency and repeatability have been a significant benefit to simulations users when analyzing their own complex problems, models, and algorithms.

11.6.3 Aggregation of Model Algorithms

When a processor arrives at a synchronization point, it will block (be idle) until that synchronization event completes. It is typically desirable for every processor to arrive at the synchronization point at the same time—for the computational work to be roughly equal or balanced among processors. However, the computational work performed by an individual model algorithm is dependent upon the resident field values and mesh entities, $M_{A_k}\big|_{P_i}$, which may not be equally sized for each processor. This potential for work imbalance is addressed in the Sierra framework in two ways: dynamic load balancing (Section 11.7) and aggregation of model algorithms.

A solver algorithm invokes the algorithm executer with its subset of model algorithms. The subset of model algorithms is aggregated such that their parallel synchronization communication requirements are merged into a single collective operation. This aggregation approach minimizes the number of synchronization points associated with the solver algorithm's subset of model algorithms.

If work imbalance is defined as the difference between an algorithm's maximum work and mean work over the set of processors, then the aggregation of model algorithms' computations will be no more imbalanced than the sum of the individual algorithms' computations.

$$\text{Let imbalance}(A) = \max_{P_i}\left[\text{work}\left(A|_{P_i}\right)\right] - \text{mean}_{P_i}\left[\text{work}\left(A|_{P_i}\right)\right],$$
$$\text{then imbalance}\left(\bigcup_k A_k\right) \leq \sum_k \text{imbalance}(A_k).$$

This result is reinforced when parallel synchronization operations required by each model algorithm are aggregated into a single parallel operation, as opposed to individual parallel operations performed after each model algorithm executes.

11.6.4 Local to Parallel Error Propagation

A model algorithm may encounter an error condition as it acts upon its local subset of mesh entities or field values. For example, a deforming finite element could invert to have a negative volume or an element-wise Newton iteration could fail to converge. In a parallel execution, these local error conditions are problematic in that the other processors need to be informed of the error condition, which requires communication. However, bringing in an extra parallel communication specifically to check for local error conditions introduces synchronization points in the simulation that are unnecessary for nominal operation.

The Sierra framework's algorithm executor provides an error propagation capability embedded within the normal parallel synchronization operation. This error propagation capability communicates a local error condition to all processors without an extra synchronization and negligible overhead to the normal synchronization. In addition, error propagation is implemented to interoperate with the C++ exception handling such that when a C++ exception is thrown from a model algorithm on a single processor, it is caught by the framework's algorithm executer on that processor and then rethrown on all processors after the parallel synchronization, as illustrated in Figure 11.7.

11.7 PARALLEL DOMAIN DECOMPOSITION AND LOAD BALANCING

A mesh is partitioned among processors according to a domain decomposition algorithm. A model algorithm executes on each processor and acts upon the mesh entities and field values residing on that processor. The work performed by algorithms on a particular processor determines the computational load on that processor. A major motivation for parallel processing is to minimize the time required to arrive at a solution. The traditional approach to minimizing this time is to balance the

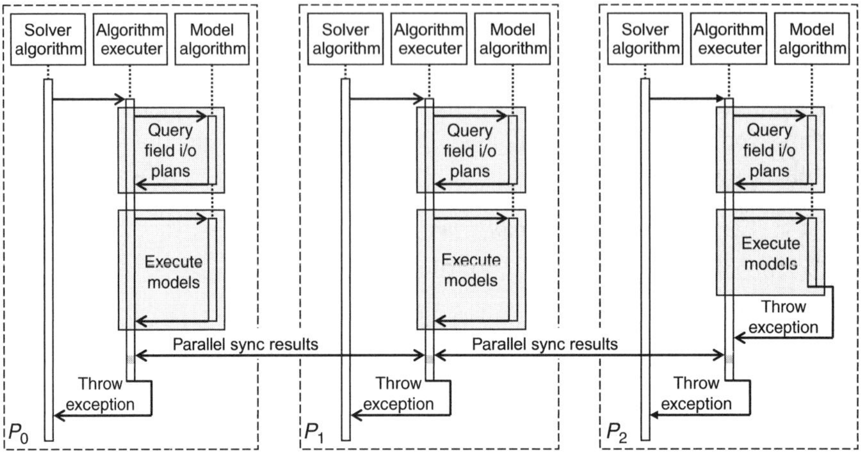

Figure 11.7 UML sequence diagram for local to parallel error propagation.

computational load among processors, typically requiring the domain decomposition to divide the work associated with mesh entities equally among processors.

11.7.1 Parallel Domain Decomposition

In a domain decomposition approach to parallel execution, a mesh is divided among processors (Figure 11.2) according to a selected domain decomposition algorithm. In this approach, subdomains, or mesh parts, are defined for each processor M_{P_k}. These mesh parts define which mesh entities reside within the memory of a given processor.

$$\text{Reside}_{P_i} \equiv \left\{ m_j : m_j \text{ resides-on } P_i \right\}. \tag{11.10}$$

A domain decomposition algorithm may define some amount of overlap between subdomains. When subdomains overlap, the mesh entities within that intersection are duplicated between the corresponding subset of processors.

An algorithm's action over a subset of mesh entities may need to process each mesh entity in that subset exactly once. For example, the 2-norm of a field value should only accumulate one contribution from each mesh entity. If a mesh entity resides on more than one processor, then such a algorithm is required to choose just one of the duplicates for processing. The concept of unique processor ownership for mesh entities is invaluable for resolving this access-once requirement and for defining a mediating processor for changes to shared mesh entities.

$$\text{Owned}_{P_i} \equiv \left\{ m_j : m_j \text{ ownership-assigned-to } P_i \right\}. \tag{11.11}$$

$$\text{Owned}_{P_i} \subseteq \text{Reside}_{P_i},$$

$$M = \bigcup_i \text{Owned}_{P_i} \quad \text{and} \quad \emptyset = \text{Owned}_{P_i} \cap \text{Owned}_{P_k} \; \forall \, i \neq k.$$

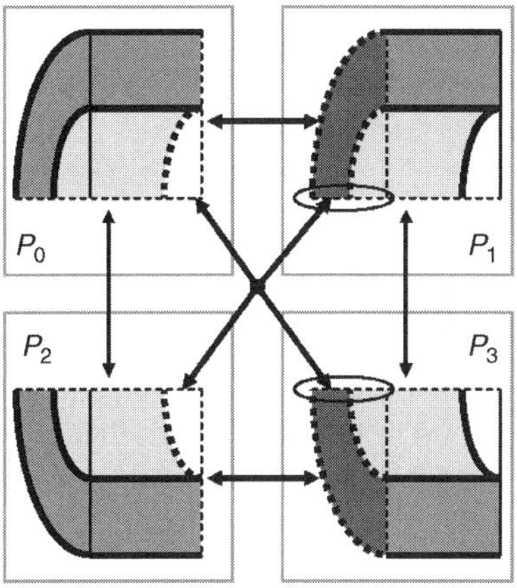

Figure 11.8 Shared mesh entities on subdomain boundaries.

Each mesh entity is designated to be "owned" by exactly one processor, even when that mesh entity is duplicated on several processors.

Mesh entities (or their associated field values) that reside on more than one processor typically require periodic synchronization. The parallel domain decomposition of the illustrative problem (Fig. 11.8) defines processor subdomains with intersecting boundaries. Any mesh entity residing within such an intersection resides on each processor and is shared by those processors. For efficient synchronization, processors should communicate data associated with only those mesh entities that they share, and only with those processors with which they share mesh entities.

In the illustrative problem there are five distinct subdomain intersections, as illustrated in Figure 11.8. Four of these intersections are between distinct pairs of subdomains; however, an interior intersection spans all four subdomains. The vertical and horizontal subdomain intersections ($P_0 \leftrightarrow P_2$, $P_1 \leftrightarrow P_3$, $P_0 \leftrightarrow P_1$, and $P_2 \leftrightarrow P_3$) include mesh entities within their respective unique intersection (illustrated by vertical and horizontal arrows) and the four-way intersection. Similarly, the "diagonal" intersections ($P_0 \leftrightarrow P_3$ and $P_1 \leftrightarrow P_2$) include only the mesh entities from the four-way intersection.

The sharing of mesh entities between two processors is defined by the intersection of those processors' *Reside* subsets. The *Shared* subsets identify the mesh entities for which data must be exchanged in a synchronization operation.

$$\begin{aligned} \text{Shared}_{P_i:P_j} &\equiv \text{Reside}_{P_i} \bigcap \text{Reside}_{P_j}, \;\; P_i \neq P_j, \qquad (11.12) \\ \text{Shared}_{P_i:P_j} &= \text{Shared}_{P_j:P_i}, \;\; \text{is symmetric.} \end{aligned}$$

Note that the *Shared* subsets are symmetric so the corresponding data exchanges are also symmetric.

Each processor's *Reside* mesh entities are partitioned into shared and local subsets.

$$\text{Shared}_{P_i:*} \equiv \bigcup_{j \neq i} \text{Shared}_{P_i:P_j}, \tag{11.13}$$

$$\text{Local}_{P_i} \equiv \text{Reside}_{P_i} \setminus \text{Shared}_{P_i:*}. \tag{11.14}$$

This per-processor *Local* subset identifies those mesh entities for which parallel synchronization is not a concern.

The *Reside*, *Owned*, *Shared*, or *Local* mesh entity subsets are integrated into the conceptual model as distribution-induced mesh parts. The data structure design is no different when accommodating these mesh parts as any other discretization-induced mesh part. However, mesh entities' membership in these mesh parts can change even when the problem's discretization does not. For example, dynamic load rebalancing of a mesh changes the processors on which mesh entities reside but does not change the total number of elements.

11.7.2 Globally Unique Identifiers

The identification of a member of a set must be persistent for the lifetime of that member (recall the definition of a set in Section 11.2.1). A traditional approach for managing and identifying mesh entities within a simple, static, single physics, and single processor mesh has been to maintain mesh entity and field value data in arrays and identify mesh entities by their index into one or more of these arrays. This approach is not extensible for a dynamically changing distributed mesh where mesh entities are created, destroyed, or relocated among processors. In such an identification approach, removing a mesh entity creates a hole in the associated arrays that disrupts any computations operating on those arrays.

The identification strategy used in the Sierra framework is to define a persistent and globally unique integer identifier for each mesh entity. The set of identifiers $\mathcal{I}$ is not necessarily dense over a range of natural integers $\mathcal{N}$; that is, it is not required to be $[1 : n] \subset \mathcal{N}$, where n is the number of mesh entities. Given a set of identifiers $\mathcal{I}$ for existing mesh entities, a new integer identifier ι is selected for a new mesh entity as $\iota = \min_\iota (\mathcal{N} \setminus \mathcal{I})$. This simple algorithm guarantees that a *selected* identifier is never greater than the cardinality of the set of mesh entities. Thus, the Sierra framework has easily implemented globally unique identifiers with simple 32-bit integers.

Persistent globally unique identifiers have been beneficial for users of simulation codes based upon the Sierra framework. When the domain decomposition of a problem changes, the processors on which a specific mesh entity resides change accordingly. If the identifier is also allowed to change (e.g., mesh entities are "renumbered"), then observing a specific mesh entity becomes problematic as continuity of identification would require maintaining an identification history for each mesh entity. A dominant use case for observing specific mesh entities is verifying that results are consistent when running the same simulation with different numbers of processors or different domain decompositions.

The Resident, Owned, and Shared subsets of a mesh change as the parallel decomposition of the mesh changes (dynamic load balancing) or problem's discretization changes (adaptivity). When a mesh entity is communicated among two processors for the first time, the receiving processor must resolve whether the received mesh entity is associated with an already resident mesh entity, or whether the received mesh entity is being added to the processor's resident subset. This use case becomes more complex when a processor receives the same mesh entity from more than one processor, but that mesh entity was not initially in that processor's resident subset. Resolution of received mesh entities is achieved through a simple comparison of their persistent globally unique identifiers.

11.7.3 Distributed Connectivity

A member of a connectivity relation (m_i, m_j) is ambiguous if the domain or range mesh entity is duplicated among processors. The reference to a mesh entity (m_i or m_j) could be to all duplications of that mesh entity, or to just one instance residing on a specific processor. This ambiguity is addressed in two ways: (1) through an enriched distributed connectivity relation referred to in the Sierra framework as a *communication specification* or *CommSpec* and (2) by the convention that in the absence of distribution information a connectivity relation refers to mesh entities residing on the same processor.

Members of a CommSpec are references to mesh entities residing on a specified processor. This relation is constrained such that all mesh entities referenced in the domain and range of the relation must be members of the same *domain mesh* and *range mesh*, respectively.

$$\begin{aligned} \text{CommSpec} &\equiv \left\{ \left((m_i, P_k) \left(m_j, P_l \right) \right) \right\}, \\ m_i &\in \text{Reside}_{P_k} \subseteq M_{\text{domain}}, \\ m_j &\in \text{Reside}_{P_l} \subseteq M_{\text{range}}. \end{aligned} \tag{11.15}$$

Communications: As implied by the name, a CommSpec is used to perform interprocessor communications. A CommSpec defines a *structure* for exchanging information between specified pairs of processors. Let CS be a CommSpec, then the messages to be sent among processors are associated with the mesh entity pairs identified in equation (11.16).

$$P_k \xrightarrow{\text{CS}} P_l \equiv \left\{ \left(m_i, m_j \right) : \left((m_i, P_k), \left(m_j, P_l \right) \right) \in \text{CS} \right\}. \tag{11.16}$$

For example, messages required to synchronize the shared subsets of a mesh are defined by a shared-CommSpec.

$$\text{CS}_{\text{shared}} = \left\{ \left((m_i, P_k), (m_i, P_l) \right) : m_i \in \text{Shared}_{P_k : P_l} \right\}. \tag{11.17}$$

A given message $P_k \xrightarrow{\text{CS}} P_l$ can be empty. For example, a "good" domain decomposition over a large number of processors will have relatively few nonempty messages defined by its shared-CommSpec. Thus, a CommSpec defines an "all-to-all" communication $\left\{ P_k \xrightarrow{\text{CS}} P_l \right\}$ where many of the point-to-point messages may be empty; that is, it defines a *sparse* all-to-all collective communication operation.

Consider an example of the global assembly or "swap add" sparse all-to-all operation. This operation sums field values associated with shared mesh entities such that all duplicate instances of a shared mesh entity have the same resulting value. Let $v_{ij}\big|_{P_k}$ be a field value associated with the instance of mesh entity m_i residing on P_k, then

$$v_{ij} = \sum_{P_k \in \mathcal{P}(m_i)} v_{ij}\big|_{P_k}, \quad \mathcal{P}(m_i) = \left\{ P_k : \left((m_i, P_k), \left(m_i, P_j\right) \right) \in \text{CS}_{\text{shared}} \right\} .$$

In an efficient global assembly algorithm, a $P_k \xrightarrow{\text{CS}} P_l$ message contains values associated with only the mesh entities shared by P_k and P_l. These values are summed on the receiving processor in a consistent and repeatable order so that an identical value for $v_{ij}\big|_{P_k}$ is computed on each processor in which m_i resides.

Software Design: The mesh entities referenced within a CommSpec are distributed among processors and as such a CommSpec is necessarily distributed among processors. Given a CommSpec's member, $\left((m_i, P_k), \left(m_j, P_l\right)\right)$, the domain mesh entity m_i residing on processor P_k must be associated with the range mesh entity m_j residing on a different processor P_l. A CommSpec is distributed among processors by permuting and then partitioning its members as in equation (11.18).

$$\begin{aligned} \left\{ \left((m_i, P_k), \left(m_j, P_l\right)\right)_n \right\}, &\rightarrow \left(\{(m_i, P_l)_n\}, \left\{ \left(m_j, P_k\right)_n \right\} \right), \\ (m_i, P_l)_n &\mapsto P_k, \quad m_i \in \text{Reside}_{P_k}, \\ \left(m_j, P_k\right)_n &\mapsto P_l, \quad m_j \in \text{Reside}_{P_l}. \end{aligned} \tag{11.18}$$

The association of CommSpec members is preserved by ordering the partitioned members $(m_i, P_l)_n$ and $\left(m_j, P_k\right)_n$ conformally on each processor according to the ordinal "n". This ordering is simply defined by comparing the domain mesh entities' global identifiers and the ranks of the range processors.

11.7.4 Imprinting in Parallel

Recall the imprinting scenario defined in Section 11.5.3 and equation (11.9) where a mesh entity's membership in mesh part may be induced by some connectivity relation α.

$$m_i \in M_* \Leftrightarrow \exists\, m_j : m_j \in M_* \quad \text{and} \quad m_j \xrightarrow{\alpha} m_i \;\; ; \;\; \text{recall equation (11.9).}$$

This imprinting scenario is required to hold for mesh entities that are shared among processors. Thus, all instances of m_i must be members of M_* even when the mesh entity m_j, and thus the relation $m_j \xrightarrow{\alpha} m_i$, exists only on one processor.

A mesh that is dynamically modified may introduce or remove relations or mesh entities on one or more processors. Such modifications may result in new imprinting conditions, or invalidate existing imprinting conditions. Enforcement of the imprinting condition (equation (11.9)) in a dynamically changing parallel distributed mesh requires that the existence condition (or lack thereof) be communicated among all processors for which the dependent mesh entity resides.

11.7.5 Dynamic Load Balancing

The Sierra framework provides two types of dynamic load balancing capabilities: rebalancing the entire mesh and creating temporary balanced subsets of a mesh. Both of these capabilities utilize the Zoltan library [37, 38] to determine a new domain decomposition partitioning for a mesh or subset of a mesh. The Zoltan library provides two groups of domain decomposition algorithms: graph based and geometry based. For the graph-based algorithm, mesh entities (typically elements) are mapped to graph nodes and adjacencies (typically element neighbors) are mapped to graph edges, and then the graph is partitioned among processors. For the geometry-based algorithms, mesh entities are mapped to coordinates or bounding boxes and then the spatial domain is partitioned among processors. In both domain decomposition algorithms, mesh entities are partitioned to balance the mesh entities' computational load among processors.

A dynamic load balancing (DLB) function takes a mesh (or subset of a mesh) and a corresponding associated set of work estimates to generate a communication specification.

$$\text{DLB}\left(\overline{M_\star},\ \left\{(m_i, \text{work}_i) : m_i \in \overline{M_\star}\right\}\right) \rightarrow \text{CommSpec}_{\text{DLB}}. \tag{11.19}$$

The input mesh $\overline{M_\star}$ consists of a collection of mesh entities, connectivity relations, current domain decomposition, and geometric information, depending upon which domain decomposition algorithm is used. The output CommSpec is used to communicate mesh entities and field values from the resident processor to the range processor specified in the CommSpec.

Dynamic load rebalancing updates the class of resident subsets as in equation (11.20).

$$\begin{aligned} \text{Reside}_{P_j}^{\text{new}} &= \left(\text{Reside}_{P_j}^{\text{old}} \cup X\right) \setminus Y, \\ X &= \left\{m_i : \left(m_i, P_j\right) \in \text{range}\left(\text{CommSpec}_{\text{DLB}}\right)\right\}, \\ Y &= \text{Reside}_{P_j}^{\text{old}} \setminus X. \end{aligned} \tag{11.20}$$

Mesh entities are communicated according to the DLB CommSpec and added to the resident subsets. Entities that are not part of the new decomposition are then removed from the resident subsets. Rebalancing also updates the symmetric subsets $\text{Shared}_{P_i:P_j}$ according to the new domain decomposition.

$$\text{Shared}^{\text{new}}_{P_j:P_k} = \left\{ m_i : \left(m_i , P_j \right) \in Z \quad \text{and} \quad (m_i , P_k) \in Z \right\} , \qquad (11.21)$$

$$Z = \text{range}\left(\text{CommSpec}_{\text{DLB}} \right) .$$

An algorithm may act upon a subset of the mesh that is severely imbalanced. For example, a localized heating boundary algorithm could be applied to just one processor of the illustrative problem, as in Figure 11.9. In this illustrative problem, the boundary condition algorithm would be completely idle on three of the four processors. The boundary condition's mesh part $M_{A_{BC}}$ is partitioned among processors by applying the DLB function to just that mesh part. The range of the resulting CommSpec defines a domain decomposition of the boundary mesh entities that should balance the work of the boundary condition algorithm among processors. The boundary mesh entities could be added to the resident subsets as indicated by the DLB CommSpec.

$$\text{Reside}^{\text{new}}_{P_j} = \text{Reside}^{\text{old}}_{P_j} \cup X,$$

$$X = \left\{ m_i : \left(m_i , P_j \right) \in \text{range}\left(\text{CommSpec}_{\text{DLB}} \right) \right\} .$$

A second option is for the boundary mesh entities to be copied to a secondary scratch mesh $M_{A_{BC}} \mapsto M^{\text{scr}}$ and then the algorithm acts on this scratch mesh.

$$M^{\text{scr}} \supset \text{Reside}^{\text{scr}}_{P_j} = \left\{ m_i : \left(m_i , P_j \right) \in \text{range}\left(\text{CommSpec}_{\text{DLB}} \right) \right\} .$$

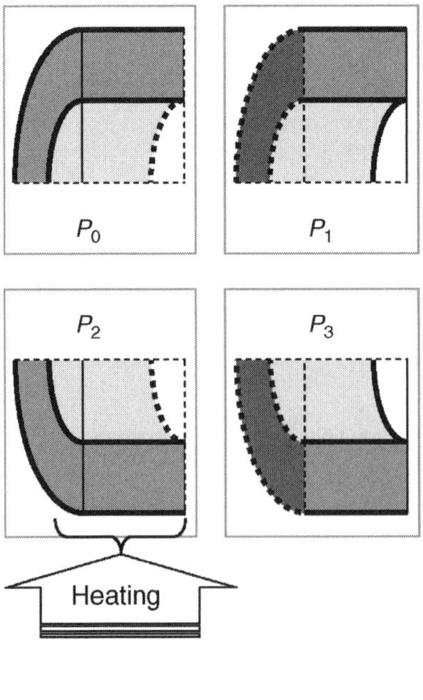

Figure 11.9 Example imbalanced boundary computation.

11.7.6 Dynamic Load Balance Versus Minimizing the Maximum Load

The objective of dynamic load balancing is, as the name implies, to balance the computational work among the set of available processors. However, the objective for optimal utilization of parallel resources is to minimize the maximum execution time over that set of processors.

$$\min\left(\max_k\left[\text{Time}_{P_k}\right] - \text{mean}_k\left[\text{Time}_{P_k}\right]\right), \quad \text{balancing},$$

$$\min\left(\max_k\left[\text{Time}_{P_k}\right]\right), \qquad \text{min–max}.$$

For parallel algorithms dominated by local computation time, dynamic load balancing can be equivalent to minimizing the maximum load. However, for a communication-dominated parallel algorithms, it may be possible that a smaller maximum time can be achieved by distributing work among a subset of processors. Such a situation could have a severe load imbalance, but smaller maximum execution time.

Reduction in execution time of an algorithm is achieved through reducing the sum of (1) the maximum time that each processor spends on its computations, (2) the time required for communications, and (3) the time required to determine a new DLB partitioning and migrate data. All three terms must be considered concurrently; for example, it is counterproductive for a DLB operation to reduce the computation time by Δt, while increasing the communication time by $10\Delta t$. This discussion of the interface for DLB is intended to frame concepts for the analysis of an application's use of DLB; however, this discussion is not intended to be that analysis.

Per-Processor Computational Time: It is assumed that an application predominantly follows an "owner computes" rule, where the processor that owns a mesh entity (equation (11.11)) is responsible for the computations associated with that mesh entity. Thus, the variation in the processors' computational times can be approximated by the sum of the per-mesh entity computational times. However, work on mesh entities may not be equivalent. For example, an algorithm A_n may require per-element solution of an ordinary differential equation or have per-element timestepping. Thus, the computational time, or work of a given computation A_n for a given processor P_k, is a function of the mesh entities being computed on.

$$T_{\text{comp}}\left(P_k\right) \sim \sum_{A_n}\left(\sum_{m_i \in \text{Owned}_{P_k}} \text{work}_{A_n}\left(m_i\right)\right). \tag{11.22}$$

Per-Processor Communication Time: Some communications' costs are insensitive to the domain decomposition, such as the parallel reduction operations associated with the computation of norms and inner products. Communications that are impacted by the domain decomposition can be defined by communication specifications, such as the CommSpec for shared mesh entities (equation (11.17)). A CommSpec defines a set of messages (equation (11.16)) that contain information related to a subset of a distributed connectivity relation. Assuming that the volume of information is approximately the same for each mesh entity, measures for messages can be defined as follows:

$$
\begin{aligned}
\text{SendSize}\,(CS,\,P_k) &= \sum_{P_*} \#\left(P_k \xrightarrow{CS} P_*\right), \\
\text{RecvSize}\,(CS,\,P_k) &= \sum_{P_*} \#\left(P_* \xrightarrow{CS\,P_k}\right), \\
\text{SendCount}\,(CS,\,P_k) &= \sum_{P_*} \begin{cases} 1 & \text{if } \emptyset \neq P_k \xrightarrow{CS} P_*, \\ 0 & \text{otherwise}, \end{cases} \\
\text{RecvCount}\,(CS,\,P_k) &= \sum_{P_*} \begin{cases} 1 & \text{if } \emptyset \neq P_* \xrightarrow{CS} P_k, \\ 0 & \text{otherwise}. \end{cases}
\end{aligned}
\tag{11.23}
$$

Communication cost has several factors affected by the domain decomposition. Let α be the startup cost of sending (or receiving) a message and β be the cost per unit of information communicated. Then a possible measure for communication time, assuming the sending and receiving of multiple messages is not concurrent, is as follows:

$$
\begin{aligned}
T_{\text{comm}}\,(P_k) \sim\ & \alpha * \text{SendCount}\,(CS,\,P_k) + \beta * \text{SendSize}\,(CS,\,P_k) \\
& + \alpha * \text{RecvCount}\,(CS,\,P_k) + \beta * \text{RecvSize}\,(CS,\,P_k)\,.
\end{aligned}
$$

Cost of Performing DLB: Dynamic load balancing consists of generating a new partition and migrating mesh entities from the old to the new partition. Thus, the cost of performing DLB is the sum of the time to determine the partition and the time to migrate (communicate) the mesh. The objective for dynamically load balanced algorithm is to minimize the sum of the time to determine the new decomposition, time to migrate the mesh entities, and time of the algorithm itself (equation (11.24)).

$$
\min\left(T_{\text{DLB}} + \max_{P_k}\left(T_{\text{migrate}}\,(P_k) + T_{\text{algorithms}}\,(P_k)\right)\right). \tag{11.24}
$$

In an evolving, dynamic simulation (e.g., integrating through time and with an adaptive mesh) the mesh entities, per-mesh entity work, and communication times can change from one step to the next. In such a simulation, DLB could be applied at every step, or only applied at selected steps. As such minimization of equation (11.24) spans the computations and communications that occur between DLB operations, and the frequency of DLB becomes a factor in this minimization. Thus, a simulation should elect to accept small degradations in computational and communication efficiency in order to postpone DLB until such a time when the cost of performing DLB is comparable to the gain in post-DLB efficiency. The challenge for such simulations is to determine when this “break-even” point occurs.

Other Desired Properties: Dynamic load balance is used to evolve a mesh or mesh part from its current domain decomposition to a new domain decomposition.

$$\text{DLB}\left(\overline{M_\star^{\text{old}}}, \left\{(m_i, \text{work}_i) : m_i \in \overline{M_\star^{\text{old}}}\right\}\right) \rightarrow \text{CommSpec}_{\text{DLB}} \overset{\text{migrate}}{\longrightarrow} \overline{M_\star^{\text{new}}}.$$

It is desired that this DLB operation be a projection, be bounded, and be repeatable. When a projection is applied to its own output, then the same output should be obtained

$$\text{DLB}\left(\overline{M_\star^{\text{new}}}, \left\{(m_i, \text{work}_i) : m_i \in \overline{M_\star^{\text{new}}}\right\}\right) \rightarrow \text{CommSpec}_{\text{identity}} \overset{\text{migrate}}{\longrightarrow} \overline{M_\star^{\text{new}}}.$$

A stronger desired property is that the operation be bounded such that a small change to the input results in a comparably small migration of mesh entities.

$$\|\text{DLB}\,(\Phi + \delta) - \text{DLB}\,(\Phi)\,\| < \mu\|\delta\|.$$

If a DLB operation is a both projection and bounded, then that operation is incremental—small changes to the mesh or weights results in small changes to the domain decomposition. As with any parallel operation, the *implementation* of a DLB operation should be repeatable or deterministic in that given the same inputs the same result is obtained.

11.8 INTERFACE WITH EQUATION SOLVERS

Numerous equation solver research and development efforts exist and release software libraries, for example, Trilinos [39, 40], PETSc [41], FETI [42, 43], Hypre [44], and Prometheus [45]. Each of these equation solver libraries has its own unique application programmer interface (API) that typically reflects the semantics of linear algebra, as opposed to the semantics of mesh entities and fields. A single mesh-oriented interface to a diverse set of equation solver libraries is defined in the Sierra framework [11] by mapping the abstractions of mesh entities and fields to the equation solver abstractions of equations and unknowns.

A discretization method (e.g., finite element, finite volume) generates a set of equations that are to be solved for a set of degrees of freedom.

$$\text{Given } A : X \mapsto Y \text{ and } y \in Y, \text{ find } x \in X \text{ such that } y = A(x). \quad (11.25)$$

The degrees of freedom, defined by the domain space X, correspond to the set of field values to be solved. The range space Y may match the domain space and thus have an identical correspondence to the set of field values to be solved. While it is *not* assumed that the range space matches the domain space, it is assumed that the range space and domain space have a similar substructuring.

11.8.1 Substructuring

The domain space X is defined by a specified subset of *field values* to be solved. In a finite element application, these unknowns are typically coefficients for solution basis functions and constraint Lagrange multipliers.

$$X \equiv \left\{ v_{ij} \mapsto \left(m_i, f_j \right) \right\}. \tag{11.26}$$

The domain space X has subspaces induced from the associated mesh entities, mesh parts, and field subsets.

$$\begin{aligned} \text{Each mesh entity } m_i : X_{m_i} &\equiv \{ v_{i*} \mapsto (m_i, f_*) \}, \\ \text{Each mesh part } M_k : X_{M_k} &\equiv \bigcup_{m_i \in M_k} X_{m_i}, \\ \text{Each field } f_j : X_{f_j} &\equiv \left\{ v_{*j} \mapsto \left(m_*, f_j \right) \right\}, \\ \text{each field subset } F_l : X_{F_l} &\equiv \bigcup_{f_j \in F_l} X_{f_j}. \end{aligned} \tag{11.27}$$

The class of mesh part and field-induced subspaces ($\left\{X_{M_k}\right\}$, $\left\{X_{f_j}\right\}$, and $\left\{X_{F_l}\right\}$) define course-grained substructuring of the domain space. The class of mesh entity subspaces $\left\{X_{m_i}\right\}$ define a fine-grained partitioning of the domain space.

It is assumed that the range space Y has subspaces similar to those defined for the domain space. However, instead of an association with a set of fields $\left\{f_j\right\}$, there exists a similar association with a set of equations $\left\{e_j\right\}$. For example, a system of equations A is defined to solve a set of N partial differential equations (PDEs) for M fields.

$$\begin{aligned} \text{Each mesh entity } m_i \colon Y_{m_i} &\equiv \{ y_{i*} \mapsto (m_i, e_*) \}, \\ \text{Each mesh part } M_k \colon Y_{M_k} &\equiv \bigcup_{m_i \in M_k} Y_{m_i}, \\ \text{Each equation } e_j \colon Y_{e_j} &\equiv \left\{ y_{*j} \mapsto \left(m_*, e_j \right) \right\}, \\ \text{Each equation subset } E_l \colon Y_{E_l} &\equiv \bigcup_{e_j \in E_l} Y_{e_j}. \end{aligned} \tag{11.28}$$

The equations have a substructure defined by the Cartesian product of the domain space and range space substructuring.

$$\begin{aligned} \text{Mesh entity: } & \left\{X_{m_i}\right\} \times \left\{Y_{m_\iota}\right\}, \\ \text{Field/equation: } & \left\{X_{f_j}\right\} \times \left\{Y_{e_J}\right\}, \\ \text{Mesh part: } & \left\{X_{M_k}\right\} \times \left\{Y_{M_K}\right\}, \\ \text{Field/equation subset: } & \left\{X_{F_l}\right\} \times \left\{Y_{E_\lambda}\right\}. \end{aligned} \tag{11.29}$$

If the same partitioning is defined for the both domain and range spaces, then the equations will have a *symmetric* substructuring, as illustrated by the six-node and two-field problem of Figures 11.10 and Figure 11.11. Note that structural symmetry does not imply a numeric symmetry.

11.8.2 Construction

In a finite element application, a system of equations is constructed element by element. That is, for each element in the mesh a corresponding submatrix contribution

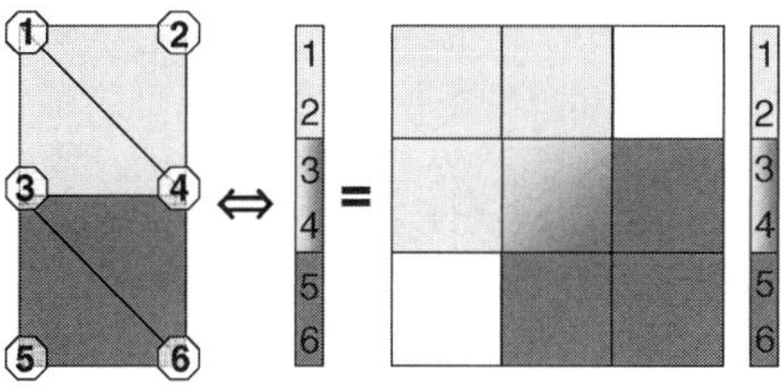

Figure 11.10 Matrix substructuring via grouping by mesh entities.

is made to the equations. For example, the element-by-element construction of a set of linear equations is given in equation (11.30);

$$y = A\,x \quad \leftrightarrow \quad \sum_e B_e^T\, y_e = \left(\sum_e B_e^T\, A_e\, C_e \right) x, \tag{11.30}$$

where A_e and y_e are an element's contribution to the global matrix and right-hand side, and B_e and C_e map the element's contribution from an element-wise numbering scheme to a global numbering scheme.

The matrices B_e and C_e project the global system of equations to a local element contribution, or conversely map an element contribution from its local equation numbering into the global equation numbering. For example, in Figures 11.10 and 11.11 the lower left-hand element (nodes {3, 5, 6}) could have a mapping matrix as follows:

$$B_e = C_e = \left[\begin{array}{cc|cc|cc|cc|cc|cc} \circ & \circ & \circ & \circ & 1 & \circ & \circ & \circ & \circ & \circ & \circ & \circ \\ \circ & \circ & \circ & \circ & \circ & 1 & \circ & \circ & \circ & \circ & \circ & \circ \\ \hline \circ & \circ & \circ & \circ & \circ & \circ & \circ & \circ & 1 & \circ & \circ & \circ \\ \circ & \circ & \circ & \circ & \circ & \circ & \circ & \circ & \circ & 1 & \circ & \circ \\ \hline \circ & \circ & \circ & \circ & \circ & \circ & \circ & \circ & \circ & \circ & 1 & \circ \\ \circ & \circ & \circ & \circ & \circ & \circ & \circ & \circ & \circ & \circ & \circ & 1 \end{array} \right].$$

In this example, the global matrix A and local element matrix A_e are both substructured into 2×2 *field* blocks. Alternatively, the global matrix could remain substructured by 2×2 *field* blocks but the local matrix could be substructured into 3×2 *node*

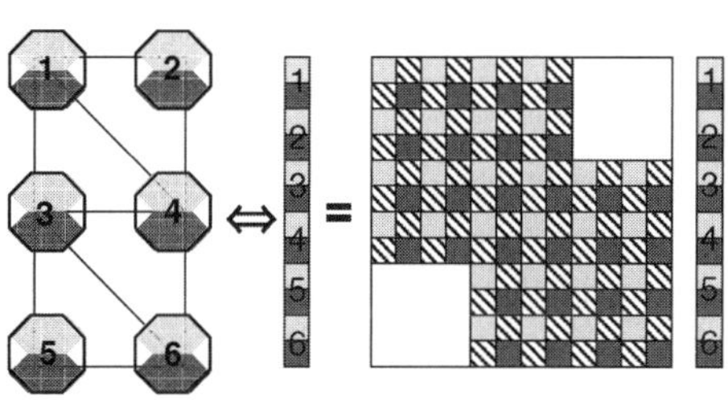

Figure 11.11 Matrix substructuring via grouping by fields.

blocks, resulting in the following mapping matrix.

$$B_e = C_e = \left[\begin{array}{cc|cc|cc|cc|cc|cc} \circ & \circ & \circ & \circ & 1 & \circ & \circ & \circ & \circ & \circ & \circ & \circ \\ \circ & \circ & \circ & \circ & \circ & \circ & \circ & \circ & \circ & 1 & \circ & \circ \\ \circ & \circ & \circ & \circ & \circ & \circ & \circ & \circ & \circ & \circ & 1 & \circ \\ \hline \circ & \circ & \circ & \circ & \circ & 1 & \circ & \circ & \circ & \circ & \circ & \circ \\ \circ & \circ & \circ & \circ & \circ & \circ & \circ & \circ & \circ & \circ & 1 & \circ \\ \circ & \circ & \circ & \circ & \circ & \circ & \circ & \circ & \circ & \circ & \circ & 1 \end{array}\right].$$

Note that the *concept* for B_e and C_e is a mapping or projection matrix. However, an obvious and efficient software design for this concept is an integer array or similar local-to-global table.

The set of projection or mapping matrices $\{(B_e, C_e)\}$ defines the sparse structure of the global matrix A as well as potential substructurings of this matrix. Such mapping matrices can be simply defined by an ordered set of mesh entity–field pairs.

$$B_\mathrm{e} \rightarrow \left\{ \left(m_i, f_j \right) \right\}_\mathrm{e}. \tag{11.31}$$

Each unique mesh entity–field entry in the global set is associated with a specific equation or unknown; however, the ordering of these global equations and unknowns is not defined. It is left to the equation solver library to exploit this global substructuring information.

The mapping abstractions of equations (11.26)–(11.31) provide a well-defined interface between the discretization and equation solver. These abstractions uniquely identify equations and unknowns, dense submatrices, subspaces with potentially exploitable properties such as solution smoothness, and submatrices with potentially exploitable properties such as association with elliptic or hyperbolic subequations.

11.8.3 Solver Opportunities

The mesh entity partitioning of a matrix, as illustrated in Figure 11.10, identifies the dense blocks within a sparse matrix. A solver algorithm may exploit this knowledge, for example, to apply block Jacobi preconditioning within an iterative solver. Similarly, the field substructuring, as illustrated in Figure 11.11, identifies large submatrices of potentially different types of equations (e.g., elliptic or hyperbolic). A solver algorithm may also exploit field substructuring; for example, different preconditioners may be applied to the different field submatrices [46].

A collection of mesh parts may also define an exploitable substructuring of the matrix. For example, a solution may smooth (e.g., $> C^0$ continuity) within each material mesh part but have jumps at the boundaries between mesh parts. Knowledge of such a substructuring can be used to ensure that multilevel or other model reduction solution methods coarsen the mesh conformally with the mesh part submatrices.

The key to a rich interface between a discretization and an equation solver algorithm is the translation of field, mesh entity, and mesh part substructuring information to equation solver semantics of sparse matrices, dense blocks, submatrices, and submatrix properties. Any problem-specific information that can be retained through this translation operation could be exploited to improve the performance of the equation solution operation.

11.9 INTERMESH COUPLING

A multiphysics simulation may define two or more distinct meshes and solve a different set of physics on each mesh. Consider a variant of illustrative problem (Fig. 11.1) where the fluid and solid parts are meshed independently such that the discretizations do not align at the fluid–solid interface. Consistent solution of such a multiple mesh problem requires coupling the solution fields (e.g., temperature) among the respective meshes.

The algorithm for intermesh coupling depends upon the solution method. If the meshes are to be solved in single linear system, then constraint equations must be generated to tie the solution fields together, such as through a mortar space method. Alternatively, an operator splitting (or loose coupling) method could be used where each mesh's physics is solved independently and coupling fields are transferred between coupled meshes.

11.9.1 Transfer Algorithm for Loose Coupling

A loose coupling transfer operation maps one or more fields from a source mesh to a corresponding set of fields in a destination mesh. These meshes can have different discretizations, different parallel domain decompositions, and no guarantee of geometric alignment among processors; that is the processor subdomains of each mesh are not guaranteed to geometrically overlap. For example, Figure 11.12 has a 12-element source mesh indicated by the shaded parallelograms and a 6-element destination mesh indicated by the wireframe trapezoids. Elements of the source (shaded) mesh reside on four different processors as indicated by the shading of elements. Nodes of the destination (wireframe) mesh reside on four different processors as indicated by the *P#* values within each node. In this example, most of the nodes in the destination mesh lie within the geometric boundaries of elements in the source mesh. However,

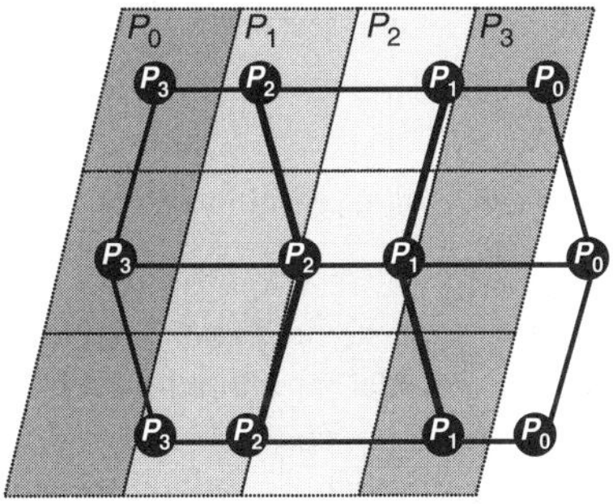

Figure 11.12 Geometrically overlapping but processor misaligned meshes.

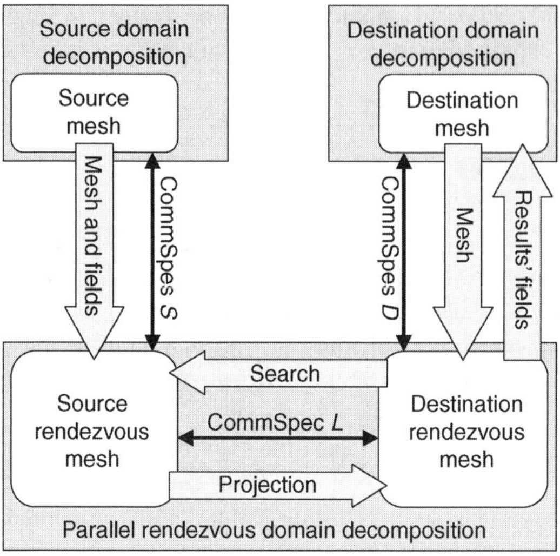

Figure 11.13 Data flow and supporting communication specifications for the transfer operation.

the destination nodes and their geometrically aligned source elements do not reside on the same processors. In this trivial example, an intermesh transfer operation must first determine the geometric alignment between mesh entities in the source and destination mesh and then *rendezvous* information about those entities to a common processor for subsequent transfer computations.

The transfer operation, as illustrated in Figure 11.13, consists of the following steps:

- Identify the mesh parts and fields of the source and destination mesh to be transferred.
- Determine a shared parallel rendezvous domain decomposition, currently supported in the Sierra framework via the Zoltan library [37, 38].
- Create the rendezvous CommSpecs *S* and *D*.
- Use the rendezvous CommSpecs to copy the designated subsets of the source and destination mesh to the rendezvous domain decomposition.
- Perform an on-processor geometric search to match mesh entities in the destination rendezvous mesh with mesh entities in the source rendezvous mesh.
- Perform an on-processor mapping of the source field values to the destination field values.
- Communicate resulting field values from the rendezvous destination mesh to the original destination mesh.

The on-processor mapping operation is dependent upon the field and discretization. This operation could be a simple evaluation of a C^0 nodal interpolation field at specified points in the destination mesh. However, the operation could be as complex as determining the volume overlap between different geometric discretizations and then performing a mass fraction or energy conserving mapping from source volume to the destination volume.

11.9.2 Parallel Geometric Rendezvous

The *parallel geometric rendezvous algorithm* [47] determines how to bring different meshes (or specified mesh subsets) with different parallel domain decompositions into a single, geometrically aligned domain decomposition (see Figure 11.13). In this algorithm, the shared geometry-based domain decomposition is determined from a combination of both the source mesh and the destination mesh. This geometric domain decomposition partitions the spatial region that contains the geometric intersection of the two meshes, as illustrated in Figure 11.14. Each geometric subdomain is "owned" by a processor; thus, the geometric domain decomposition maps each mesh entity in the identified subsets of the source and destination mesh to one or more processors, $\text{GeomDD}(m_i) \rightarrow \{P_g\}$. In this example, the nodes of the destination mesh are mapped to the processor owning the geometric region indicated in Figure 11.14. Each element of the source mesh is mapped to each processor owning a geometric region that intersects with that element.

Given the mapping of mesh entities to processors, a *rendezvous* communication specification (equation (11.15)) is defined for the source mesh and for the destination mesh. The two *Rendezvous CommSpecs*, denoted CommSpec S and CommSpec D in Figure 11.13, are constructed as per equation (11.32).

$$\text{CS}_{\text{rdzvs}} = \left\{ \left((m_i, P_k), \left(m_i, P_g \right) \right) \right\} \; : \; \text{GeomDD}\left(m_i \in \text{Owned}_{P_k} \right) \mapsto \left\{ P_g \right\}. \tag{11.32}$$

11.9.3 Field Mapping

The rendezvous communication specifications define how source and destination mesh entities are to be communicated for geometric alignment. As illustrated in Figure 11.13, the source mesh entities are *copied* (not migrated) to the source

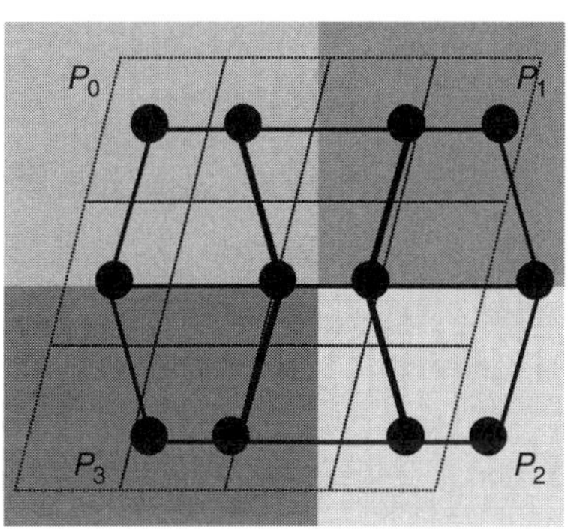

Figure 11.14 A geometric rendezvous domain decomposition partitions space among processors.

rendezvous mesh along with the field values that are to be transferred. The destination mesh entities are similarly copied to a destination rendezvous mesh. Thus, geometrically aligned mesh entities in the destination rendezvous mesh and source rendezvous mesh are now resident on the same processor.

Given this on-processor geometric alignment, a local (nonparallel) search is performed to match each destination mesh entity with the source mesh entity with which it geometrically overlaps. This local search results in a communication specification, denoted by CommSpec L in Figure 11.13. Thus, the three transfer CommSpecs S, D, and L in Figure 11.13 could be composed to define a relation directly between the source mesh M_{src} and destination mesh M_{dst} as follows:

$$\begin{aligned} S &: M_{\text{src}} \mapsto M_{\text{rdzvs-src}}, \\ L &: M_{\text{rdzvs-dst}} \mapsto M_{\text{rdzvs-src}}, \\ D &: M_{\text{dst}} \mapsto M_{\text{rdzvs-dst}}, \\ S^c \circ L \circ D &: M_{\text{dst}} \mapsto M_{\text{src}}. \end{aligned}$$

The local CommSpec L defines the connectivity required to support a local field mapping operation. This operation can be a simple interpolation of a discretized source field to a point (e.g., node) in a destination field or could involve complex computations such as determining the intersection of discrete volumes between source and destination mesh entities. Such a complex mapping operation can require a geometrically larger "patch" of mesh entities than is provided by the geometric rendezvous algorithm. These operations are supported by extending the rendezvous communication specifications, CommSpec S and D, to include mesh entities sufficient to provide the required "patch" coverage.

$$\bar{S} = S \cup \left\{ \begin{array}{l} \left(\left(m_j, P_k\right), \left(m_j, P_l\right)\right) : \\ \left(\left(m_i, P_k\right), \left(m_i, P_l\right)\right) \in S \text{ and } m_j \in \text{Patch}\left(m_i\right) \cap \text{Owned}_{P_k} \end{array} \right\}.$$

The field values resulting from the field mapping operation on the destination rendezvous mesh are finally communicated back to the original destination mesh. This final communication operation is simply defined by the converse of CommSpec D from the original destination mesh to the rendezvous destination mesh.

11.10 ADAPTIVITY

A mesh may be dynamically adapted to more efficiently resolve the discretization required for a solution to a given problem. Types of mesh adaptation currently supported by the Sierra framework include

- dynamic load balancing to improve utilization of parallel resources,
- local refinement and unrefinement (h-adaptivity) to control the local spatial resolution of the mesh, and
- element erosion (a.k.a. element death) to model destruction or phase change of materials.

Dynamic load balancing is the simplest form of mesh adaptivity in that it merely migrates mesh entities among processors. In contrast, h-adaptivity and element death modify the global mesh by creating and destroying mesh entities. Other forms of adaptivity being considered include patch remeshing for severely distorted regions in a mesh and local enrichment of the discretization's interpolation functions (p-adaptivity).

11.10.1 Hierarchical Mesh Refinement

The objective of h-adaptivity is to locally modify the spatial discretization of a mesh in order to more efficiently resolve features of the problem's solution. Hierarchical h-adaptivity involves splitting elements into nested elements (refinement) or merging previously refined elements (unrefinement). A typical solution feature to be resolved is the error due to the spatial discretization, in which case the h-adaptivity objective is to efficiently obtain a solution of a specified discretization error tolerance.

Support for hierarchical h-adaptivity is a collaboration between the Sierra framework and the application, summarized in Figure 11.15. In this collaboration, an application is responsible for

- solving the problem on the current discretization,
- evaluating whether the solution's discretization is satisfactory,
- marking elements for refinement or unrefinement,
- estimating the elements' computational work for DLB,
- restricting fields from the to be unrefined nested "child" mesh entities to the "parent" mesh entities, and
- prolonging the fields from the "parent" mesh entity to the newly created "child" mesh entities.

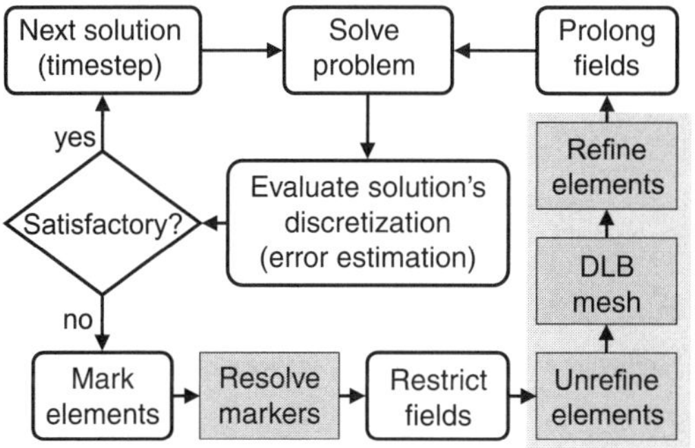

Figure 11.15 Control flow of the h-adaptivity driver algorithm.

The Sierra framework is responsible for the following steps, as indicated by the four gray boxes in Figure 11.15:

- Resolving an application's markers for refinement propagation and unrefinement constraints
- Deleting mesh entities for unrefinement
- Dynamically load balancing the modified mesh, and
- Creating new mesh entities for refinement.

The sequence of unrefinement → DLB → refinement is performed as a group so that DLB can occur when the mesh is at its smallest, that is, after selected elements are unrefined and before selected elements are refined. Such a sequence requires that the estimated work for the to be refined elements reflects the work associated with the to be created child elements. The estimated work for DLB is adjusted assuming that each child element has the same work as the parent element, and thus each to-be-refined element's work estimate is scaled by the number of child elements that will be created.

11.10.2 Hierarchical Refinement: in Parallel

Two hierarchical refinement strategies, illustrated in Figure 11.16, are supported in the Sierra framework: (1) the classical hanging node refinement illustrated by the upper sequence of quadrilateral meshes and (2) longest edge refinement [48] illustrated by the lower sequence of triangle meshes. In both strategies, an application selects and marks elements for refinement or unrefinement.

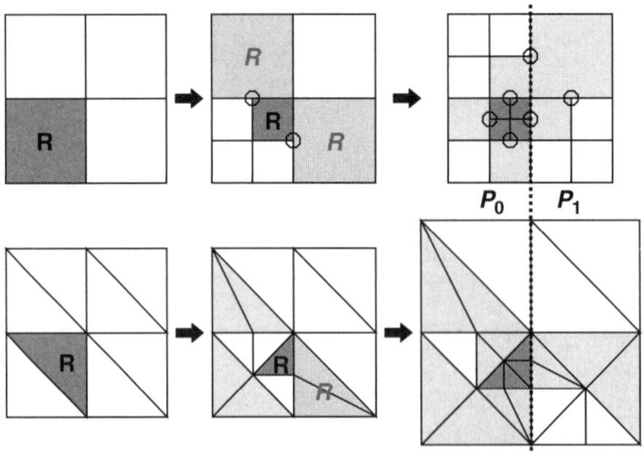

Figure 11.16 Illustrations of hanging node refinement for quadrilaterals and longest edge refinement for triangles.

Refinement and unrefinement selections are processed as follows:

- Requests for refinement always cause an element to be refined
- Requests for unrefinement will only be accepted if (1) all "children" of a given element are marked for unrefinement and (2) deletion of any of those children will not violate a two-to-one refinement rule

The two-to-one refinement rule states that elements that share a common edge cannot be refined more than one generation or level different from a neighboring element. Enforcement of this two-to-one refinement rule varies according to the hierarchical refinement strategy.

Hanging Node Refinement: In the classical hanging node refinement strategy, a marked element (dark gray in Figure 11.16) is split into child elements and a "hanging node" is created on boundaries where the neighboring element is not similarly refined. In Figure 11.16, the location of these hanging nodes is indicated by open circles. Basis functions associated with hanging nodes are typically constrained for continuity with the basis functions of the larger, less refined neighboring element. Subsequent refinement of an element may force neighboring elements to be refined to satisfy the two-to-one rule, as illustrated by the two light gray elements at the center mesh of Figure 11.16. Thus the combination of the "always refine application-marked elements" and the two-to-one rule may cause more elements to be refined than the application had originally requested. Currently, the hanging node refinement strategy is supported in the Sierra framework for hexahedral, wedge, pyramid, and tetrahedral elements.

Longest Edge Refinement: In the edge-based refinement strategy, a marked element is split into child elements. However, instead of creating a hanging node between the refined element and its neighbor, the neighbor element is *partially* refined by splitting only the shared edge. These partially refined elements are indicated by the light gray triangles in Figure 11.16. Subsequent refinement of a partially refined element could (but does not) lead to subsequent partial refinement of an already partially refined element. Instead, such a partially refined element is first unrefined from its partial refinement and then fully refined, as illustrated by the rerefinement of the lower right partially refined triangle in Figure 11.16. This rerefinement algorithm is applied to insure that a sequence of nested refinements conforms to the longest edge algorithm for triangles and tetrahedrals. The edge-based strategy is currently supported in the Sierra framework only for tetrahedral elements.

Parallel Resolution of Two-to-One: The two-to-one rule is enforced across processor boundaries, as illustrated by the rightmost meshes in Figure 11.16. Edges may not explicitly exist in the mesh data structure; however, edges are implicitly defined by two end point nodes that will exist. Processors apply the enforcement algorithm by structuring collective communications according to the shared node CommSpec. Let $\tilde{e}_{ij}$ be an edge implicitly defined by the pair of nodes (m_i, m_j) and let CS be the shared node CommSpec (equation (11.17)), then the induced CommSpec for *potentially* shared edges is constructed as follows:

$$\{((\tilde{e}_{ij}, P_k), (\tilde{e}_{ij}, P_l)) : ((m_i, P_k), (m_i, P_l)) \in \text{CS}, \quad \text{and} \\ ((m_j, P_k), (m_j, P_l)) \in \text{CS}\}.$$

An edge, $\tilde{e}_{ij} \equiv \langle m_i, m_j \rangle$, may not exist on a processor identified by the constructed CommSpec. A final condition requires the existence of an element m_E on a processor P_k that implicitly defines an edge conformal to the pair of nodes.

$$\exists\, m_\text{E} : m_\text{E} \in \text{Reside}_{P_k} \text{ and } m_\text{E} \xrightarrow{uses} \{m_i, m_j\}.$$

11.10.3 Smoothing the Geometry

Mesh refinement generates new mesh entities with new vertices. The geometric location of these vertices should conform to the geometry of the actual problem, otherwise solution accuracy can degrade. For example, in Figure 11.17 two concentric circles are meshed with quadrilaterals and then the top half of the mesh is refined. If the new vertices were placed along the existing edges, as in the left mesh, then

- material associated with the outer gray circle and inner white circle would not be correctly modeled by the elements, and
- artificial corners would be introduced where the exterior and intermaterial boundaries should be smooth.

Geometrically conformal placement of new vertices, or other nodes, requires two operations: (1) sufficiently resolving the problem's geometry and (2) projecting the new nodes to that geometry. In the Sierra framework, the problem's geometry is approximated by recovering smooth boundaries from the mesh [49], as opposed to maintaining a CAD model of the problem. This approach is used so that geometry recovery can occur even when the mesh is deformed from its original CAD geometry.

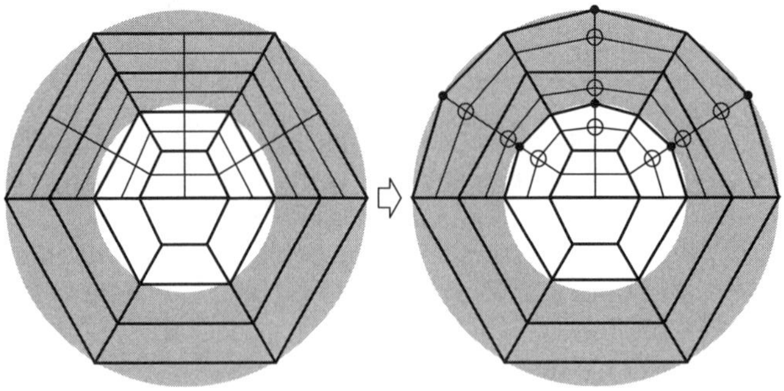

Figure 11.17 Example of geometry recovery improving the placement of new nodes.

In the right-hand mesh of Figure 11.17, there are six vertices on the exterior and intermaterial boundaries (denoted by solid dots). These vertices would be projected to a smooth geometry recovered for these boundaries. In addition, nine new interior vertices (denoted by open circles) are also shifted to smooth the transition between new boundary vertices and existing interior vertices.

11.10.4 Refinement Pattern

The hierarchical refinement of an element is not unique. For example, triangles in Figure 11.16 are either fully refined into four child triangles or partially refined into two child triangles. Flexible hierarchical refinement is supported by defining a refinement pattern that conforms to the refinement of one or more of the element's edges. For three-dimensional mesh entities (hexahedrals, wedges, pyramids, and tetrahedrals), the set of possible refinement patterns is large and complex.

This complexity is managed by extending the abstraction of $\textit{element} \xrightarrow{uses} \textit{node}$ relationship to nodes that may be created to support refinement of the element. The relationship for such a new node is $\textit{element} \xrightarrow{child} \textit{node}$. Thus, a refinement pattern defines

- all potential parent-$\textit{element} \xrightarrow{child} \textit{node}$ relationships resulting from any supported refinement all of an element,
- a set of child-elements for a full or partial refinements, and
- the mapping of child-$\textit{element} \xrightarrow{uses} \textit{node}$ relations to the parent element's *uses* and *child* nodes.

The example refinement pattern for a triangle illustrated in Figure 11.18 defines three *uses* nodes, numbered 1–3, and three potential *child* nodes, numbered 4–6. The combination of *uses* and *child* nodes defines the complete set of nodes that could be needed for refinement. In this example, one of the three potential *child* nodes (node 6) is not needed by this particular set of child elements.

Child mesh entities are related to their parent mesh entities through their nodal connectivity relations, child-$\textit{element} \xrightarrow{uses} \textit{node} \xleftarrow{uses/child}$ parent-*element*. The refinement pattern specification for these relations is similar to the connectivity topology (Section 11.5.2) in that the local element-node identifiers are used to map child-element nodes to corresponding parent-element nodes. For example, in Figure 11.18 child–element #2 node #3 maps to parent-element node #1.

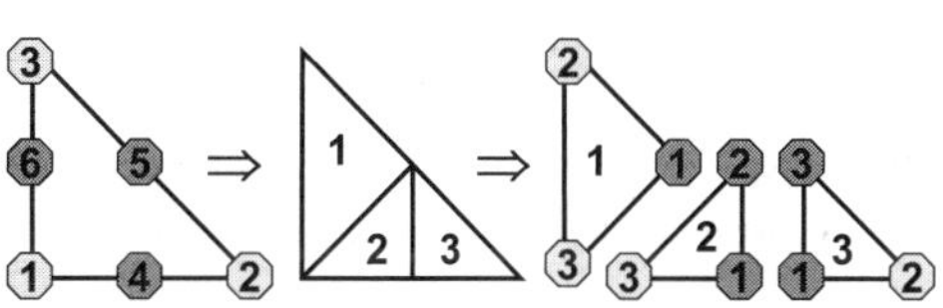

Figure 11.18 Example hierarchical refinement pattern based upon *child* node connectivity.

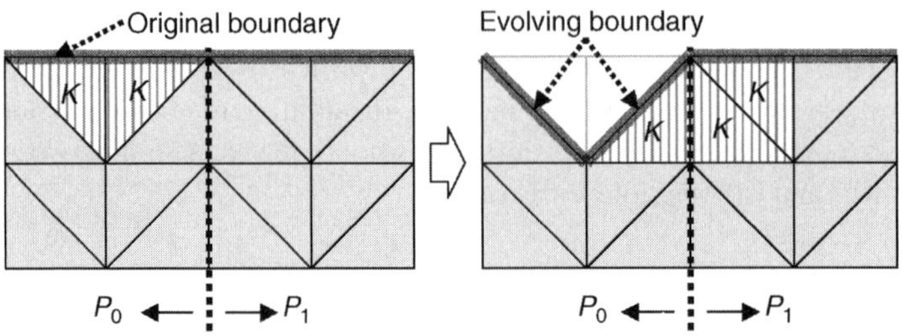

Figure 11.19 Example element death and evolution of the boundary.

11.10.5 Element Death

An application may include physics that models destruction of a material, for example, phase change or chemical reaction. Such an application can remove the elements associated with the destroyed material from the computations. These mesh entities may be deleted from the mesh or simply deactivated with respect to the application's computations. In either case, when an element is destroyed, the boundary of the problem must be updated accordingly, as illustrated in Figure 11.19.

The mesh management challenge for element death is the efficient evolution of boundaries in a distributed mesh. In Figure 11.19, two triangles are "killed" and the boundary is evolved such that sides that were originally in the interior of the mesh become part of the boundary. In the second (right-hand) mesh, three additional triangles are marked to be killed; however, the resulting patch of to-be-killed triangles now crosses processor boundaries. Resolution of the patch of to-be-killed mesh entities is similar to the enforcement of the two-to-one rule in h-adaptivity where processors communicate patch information via implicitly defined edges (or faces in three dimensions).

An application's computations on an evolving boundary are supported by adding sides to, and removing sides from, the corresponding boundary mesh part. Such changes can result in imprinting changes (equation (11.9)), creation and deletion of field values (equation (11.4)), creation and deletion of the sides themselves, and dynamic load balancing if the number of "killed" mesh entities becomes significant.

11.10.6 Patch Remeshing

The capability to remesh a patch of elements has been prototyped in the Sierra framework. This capability is planned to enable applications that have large mesh motion, such as Lagrangian explicit dynamics, to remesh severely distorted patches of elements. For example, in Figure 11.20 a patch containing five severely distorted triangles is remeshed with eight acute triangles.

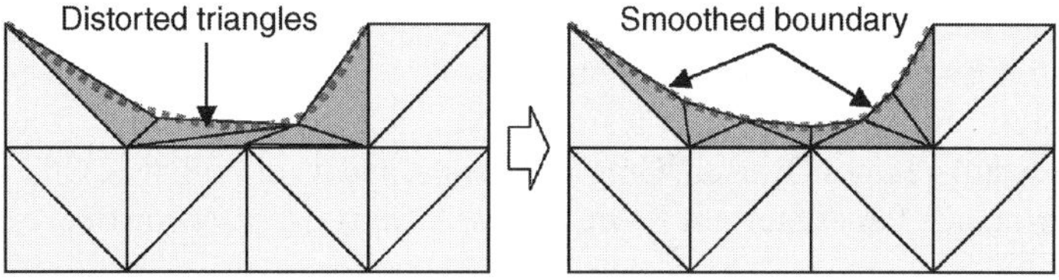

Figure 11.20 Example remeshing of a severely distorted patch of elements.

The following planned parallel patch remeshing algorithm integrates most of the advanced capabilities that Sierra framework provides:

- An application marks elements that are to be remeshed.
- Patches are identified by traversing neighboring elements, similar to h-adaptivity two-to-one and element death traversals.
- A new domain decomposition is dynamically generated to consolidate each patch on a single processor.
- A smooth geometric representation is recovered for mesh boundaries.
- New elements are created that conform to the boundary of the patch, as defined by neighboring elements or smoothed boundary representation.
- Fields are transferred from the existing elements to the new elements.
- The elements that have been replaced are deleted.
- The resulting mesh is load balanced.

11.11 CONCLUSION

Complex capabilities such as massively parallel execution, dynamically adaptive discretizations, and multiphysics coupling have been successfully integrated within the Sierra framework and are being shared by engineering simulation codes at Sandia National Laboratories. Successful development and integration of these capabilities is predicated upon well-defined mathematical abstractions for the mesh, fields, models, algorithms, and parallel environment of these applications. This approach to managing complexity through a conceptual model based upon mathematical abstractions is broadly applicable and will be fundamental to the emerging discipline of frameworks for scientific and engineering simulation codes.

ACKNOWLEDGMENTS

This work was performed at Sandia National Laboratories (SNL), a multiprogram laboratory operated by Sandia Corporation, a Lockheed-Martin Company, for the United States Department of Energy (DOE) National Nuclear Security Administration

(NNSA) under Contract No. DE-AC-94AL85000. It was sponsored by DOE-NNSA Advanced Simulation and Computing (ASC) program.

The current Sierra framework project team at SNL includes David Baur, Noel Belcourt, Carter Edwards, James Overfelt, Greg Sjaardema, and Alan Williams. Other recent contributors include James Stewart, Kevin Copps, Alfred Lorber, Aaron Becker, and Isaac Dooley.

REFERENCES

1. J. Carey and B. Carlson. *Framework Process Patterns: Lessons Learned Developing Application Frameworks*. Addison-Wesley, 2002.
2. H. C. Edwards. Managing complexity in massively parallel, adaptive, multiphysics applications. *Eng. Comput.*, 22:135–155, 2006.
3. J. R. Stewart and H. C. Edwards. A framework approach for developing parallel adaptive multiphysics applications. *Finite Elem. Anal. Des.*, 40:1599–1617, 2004.
4. H. C. Edwards. Sierra framework for massively parallel adaptive multiphysics applications. In *Proceedings from the NECDC 2004*, Livermore, CA. Lawrence Livermore National Laboratory, October 2004.
5. H. C. Edwards, J. R. Stewart, and John D. Zepper. Mathematical abstractions of the SIERRA computational mechanics framework. In H. A. Mang, F. G. Rammerstorfer, and J. Eberhardsteiner, editors, *Proceedings of the 5th World Congress on Computational Mechanics*, Vienna, Austria, July 2002.
6. H. C. Edwards and J. R. Stewart. Sierra, a software environment for developing complex multiphysics applications. In K. J. Bathe, editor, *Computational Fluid and Solid Mechanics. Proceedings of the First MIT Conference*, Cambridge, MA. Elsevier, Oxford, UK, 2001, pp. 1147–1150.
7. H. C. Edwards. Sierra framework version 3: core services theory and design. Technical report SAND2002-3616, Sandia National Laboratories, Albuquerque, NM, November 2002.
8. J. R. Stewart. Sierra framework version 3: master element subsystem. Technical report SAND2003-0529, Sandia National Laboratories, Albuquerque, NM, February 2003.
9. J. R. Stewart. Sierra framework version 3: transfer services design and use. Technical report SAND2003-0249, Sandia National Laboratories, Albuquerque, NM, January 2003.
10. J. R. Stewart and H. C. Edwards. Sierra framework version 3: h-adaptivity design and use. Technical report SAND2002-4016, Sandia National Laboratories, Albuquerque, NM, December 2002.
11. A. B. Williams. Sierra framework version 4: solver services. Technical report SAND2004-6428, Sandia National Laboratories, Albuquerque, NM, February 2005.
12. S.P. Domino, C. D. Moen, S. P. Burns, and G. H. Evans. Sierra/fuego: a multimechanics fire environment simulation tool. In *41st Aerospace Sciences Meeting*, Reno, NV. AIAA Paper No. 2003-0149, January 2003.
13. S. W. Bova and R. Lober. An approach to coupled, multiphysics thermal analysis. In K. J. Bathe, editor, *Computational Fluid and Solid Mechanics. Proceedings of the First MIT Conference*, Cambridge, MA. Elsevier, Oxford, UK, 2001.
14. J. R. Koteras, A. S. Gullerud, V. L. Porter, W. M. Scherzinger, and K. H. Brown. Presto : impact dynamics with scalable contact using the sierra framework. In K. J. Bathe, editor, *Computational Fluid and Solid Mechanics. Proceedings of the First MIT Conference*, Cambridge, MA. Elsevier, Oxford, UK, 2001.
15. J. A. Mitchell, A. S. Gullerud, W. M. Scherzinger, J. R. Koteras, and V. L. Porter. Adagio: non-linear quasi-static structural response using the sierra framework. In K. J. Bathe, editor, *Computational Fluid and Solid Mechanics. Proceedings of the First MIT Conference*, Cambridge, MA. Elsevier, Oxford, UK, 2001.
16. T. Smith, C. Ober, and A. Lorber. Sierra/premo—a new general purpose compressible flow simulation code. In *32nd AIAA Fluid Dynamics Conference and Exhibit*, AIAA St. Louis, Missouri. AIAA-2002-3292, 2002.

17. P. K. Notz, S. R. Subia, M. H. Hopkins, and P. A. Sackinger. A novel approach to solving highly coupled equations in a dynamic, extensible and efficient way. In M. Papadrakakis, E. Onate, and B. Schrefler, editors, *Computation Methods for Coupled Problems in Science and Engineering. International Center for Numerical Methods in Engineering (CIMNE)*, Barcelona, Spain, April 2005, p. 129.
18. E. Gamma, R. Helm, R. Johnson, and J. Vlissides. *Design Patterns: Elements of Reusable Object-Oriented Software*. Addison-Wesley Publishing Company, 1995.
19. R. D. Hornung, A. M. Wissink, and S. R. Kohn. Managing complex data and geometry in parallel structured AMR applications. *Eng. Comput.*, 22(3):181–195, 2006.
20. SAMRAI home page. http://www.llnl.gov/CASC/SAMRAI/samrai_home.html, July 2005.
21. Overture home page. http://www.llnl.gov/CASC/Overture/, July 2005.
22. S. Lang. Parallel-adaptive simulation with the multigrid-based software framework UG. *Eng. Comp.*, 22(3):157–179, 2006.
23. S. Lang and G. Wittum. Large-scale density-driven flow simulations using parallel unstructured grid adaptation and local multigrid methods. *Concurrency Comput. Pract. Exper.*, 17(11):1415–1440, 2005.
24. UG home page. http://cox.iwr.uni-heidelberg.de/~ug/, July 2005.
25. O. S. Lawlor, S. Chakravorty, T. L. Wilmarth, N. Choudhury, I. Dooley, G. Zheng, and L. Kalé. ParFUM: a parallel framework for unstructured meshes for scalable dynamic physics applications. *Eng. with Comput.*, 22(3):215–235, 2006.
26. X. Jiao, G. Zheng, P. A. Alexander, M. T. Cambell, O. S. Lawlor, J. Norris, A. Haselbacher, and M. T. Heath. A system integration framework for coupled multiphysics simulations. *Eng. Comput.*, 22(3):293–309, 2006.
27. E. S. Seol and M. S. Shepard. Efficient distributed mesh data structure for parallel automated adaptive analysis. *Eng. Comput.*, 22(3):197–213.
28. AOMD home page. http://www.scorec.rpi.edu/AOMD/, July 2005.
29. Trellis home page. http://www.scorec.rpi.edu/Trellis/, July 2005.
30. Steven G. Parker, James Guilkey, and Todd Harman. A component-based parallel infrastructure for the simulation of fluid–structure interaction. *Eng. Comput.*, 22(3):277–292, 2006.
31. Uintah home page. http://software.sci.utah.edu/uintah.html, July 2005.
32. Cactus home page. http://www.cactuscode.org/, July 2005.
33. B. S. Kirk, J. W. Peterson, R. H. Stogner, and G. F. Carey. libMesh: a C++ library for parallel adaptive mesh refinement/coarsening simulations. *Eng. Comput.*, 22(3)237–254, 2006.
34. libMesh home page. http://libmesh.sourceforge.net/, July 2005.
35. IPARS home page. http://www.ices.utexas.edu/CSM/software_csm-ipars.php, July 2005.
36. STAPL home page. http://parasol.tamu.edu/groups/rwergergroup/research/stapl/, July 2005.
37. K. Devine, E. Boman, R. Heaphy, B. Hendrickson, and C. Vaughan. Zoltan data management services for parallel dynamic applications. *Comput. Sci. Eng.*, 4(2):90–97, 2002.
38. K. Devine, B. Hendrickson, E. Boman, M. St. John, and C. Vaughan. Zoltan: a dynamic load balancing library for parallel applications; user's guide guide. Technical report SAND99-1377, Sandia National Laboratories, Albuquerque, NM, 1999.
39. M. A. Heroux and J. M. Willenbring. Trilinos user's guide. Technical report SAND2003-2952, Sandia National Laboratories, Albuquerque, NM, August 2003.
40. M. A. Heroux et al. An overview of trilinos. Technical report SAND2003-2927, Sandia National Laboratories, Albuquerque, NM, August 2003.
41. S. Balay, K. Buschelman, W. Gropp, D. Kaushik, M. Knepley, L. C. McInnes, B. Smith, and H. Zhang. Petsc 2.0 user's manual. Technical report ANL-95/11-Revision 2.1.6, Argonne National Laboratory, August 2003.
42. C. Farhat and K. Pierson. The second generation of feti methods and their application to the parallel solution of large-scale linear and geometrically nonlinear structural analysis problems. *Comput. Meth. Appl. Mech. Eng.*, 184:333–374, 2000.
43. M. Lesoinne and K. Pierson. Feti-dp: an efficient, scalable and unified dual-primal feti method. *12th International Conference on Domain Decomposition Methods*, 2001.
44. R.D. Falgout and U. M. Yang. Hypre: a library of high performance preconditioners. Technical Report UCRL-JC-146175, Lawrence Livermore National Laboratory, Livermore, CA, 2002.

45. Prometheus home page. http://www.columbia.edu/~ma2325/prometheus/, July 2005.
46. H. C. Edwards. A parallel multilevel-preconditioned GMRES solver for multiphase flow models in the implicit parallel accurate reservoir simulator (ipars). Technical Report 98-04, University of Texas at Austin, Austin, Tx, 1998.
47. S. J. Plimpton, B. Hendrickson, and J. R. Stewart. A parallel rendezvous algorithm for interpolation between multiple grids. *J. Parallel Distrib. Comput.*, 64:266–276, 2004.
48. Á. Plaza and M. Rivara. Mesh refinement based on the 8-tetrahedra longest-edge partition. In *Proceedings of the 12th International Meshing Roundtable*. Sandia National Laboratories, 2003, pp. 67–78.
49. S. J. Owen and D. R. White. Mesh-based geometry. *Int. J. Numer. Methods Eng.*, 58(2):375–395, 2003.

Chapter 12

GrACE: Grid Adaptive Computational Engine for Parallel Structured AMR Applications*

Manish Parashar and Xiaolin Li

12.1 INTRODUCTION

Many scientific applications that use differential equations to model physical and chemical phenomena exhibit localized intensive activities [1, 2]. Study of these localized phenomena requires high resolution in both time and space dimensions to yield meaningful understanding and subtle insights. In such situations, conventional numerical techniques based on uniform discretization typically apply high resolution on the entire domain to achieve the required resolution in a very small region, lacking the ability to dynamically zoom into the localized regions only. In contrast, structured adaptive mesh refinement (SAMR) techniques [3, 4] provide an effective means for dynamically concentrating computational effort and resources on localized regions in multidimensional scientific simulation applications. SAMR applies high resolution to only the subregions that require it; similarly, SAMR applies high resolution of

*This chapter is based on the paper "System engineering for high performance computing software: the HDDA/DAGH infrastructure for implementation of parallel structured adaptive mesh refinement," Ó M. Parashar and J. C. Browne: *Structured Adaptive Mesh Refinement (SAMR) Grid Methods*, S.B. Baden, N.P. Chrisochoides, D.B. Gannon, and M.L. Norman, editors, AMA Vol. 117, Springer-Verlag, 2000, pp. 1–18.

Advanced Computational Infrastructures For Parallel and Distributed Adaptive Applications. Edited by Manish Parashar and Xiaolin Li

timescale to only the time intervals that require it. SAMR is based on block-structured refinements overlaid on a structured coarse grid, and provide an alternative to the general, unstructured AMR approach [5, 6]. SAMR techniques have been widely used to solve complex systems of PDEs that exhibit localized features in varied domains, including computational fluid dynamics, numerical relativity, combustion simulations, subsurface modeling, and oil reservoir simulation [1, 2, 7, 8]. However, due to their dynamism and space–time heterogeneity, scalable parallel implementation of SAMR applications remains a challenge.

This chapter presents the requirement analysis, design, and implementation of the GrACE (grid adaptive computational engine) framework and its associated runtime management strategies for SAMR applications. GrACE provides easy-to-use application programming interfaces (API) and libraries for parallel programming, execution, visualization, and simulation. Furthermore, it offers a suite of extensible features and algorithms to support parallel and efficient runtime management of large-scale SAMR applications in thousands of processors. The development of GrACE follows a *system engineering* approach. The term *system engineering* was carefully chosen to distinguish the development process we propose as appropriate for the development of high-performance computing software from the conventional *software engineering* development process.

High-performance systems are typically quite different from these information management systems. They are often of only modest size by commercial standards but often have a high degree of internal complexity. HPC applications are usually developed by small teams or even individuals. There is no commodity implementation infrastructure to be used. The execution environments are state-of-the-art, rapidly changing, frequently parallel computer system architectures. The hardware execution environments are often novel architectures and for which there is little "conventional wisdom" concerning building programs that execute efficiently. These execution environments change much more rapidly than is the case for large commercially oriented systems. The end-user requirements for HPC software systems typically evolve much more rapidly because they are used in research environments rather than in production environments. There are often many variants of solution algorithms. Time for end-to-end execution (absolute performance) is usually the most critical property with adaptability to a multiplicity of applications and portability across the rapidly evolving platforms being other important issues. Reuse of previously written code is also often desired. The complexity of HPC systems primarily arises from the requirements of the applications for data management. If HPC is to become an effective discipline, we must document good practice so that best practice can be identified. This is particularly true for developers in infrastructure systems that are intended to be used by a broad community of users. This chapter uses the development of GrACE as a vehicle to put forward what we think is one example of good design/development process for HPC software systems.

The rest of the chapter is organized as follows. We first give a brief introduction to the structured adaptive mesh refinement technique. We then present an overview of the GrACE conceptual architecture, followed by the design and implementation of GrACE. Following the design and implementation, applications supported by

GrACE are summarized. Related work is then briefly presented and compared with our approach. Finally, we conclude the chapter.

12.2 STRUCTURED ADAPTIVE MESH REFINEMENT

The targeted applications are large-scale dynamic scientific and engineering applications, such as scientific simulations that solve sophisticated partial differential equations (PDEs) using adaptive mesh refinement (AMR) [3] techniques. Partial differential equations are widely used for mathematically modeling and studying physical phenomena in science and engineering, such as heat transfer in solids, interacting black holes and neutron stars, electrostatics of conductive media, formations of galaxies, combustion simulation, wave propagation, and subsurface flows in oil reservoirs [1, 2, 7]. One numerical method to solve PDEs is to compute approximate solutions for discrete points by uniformly discretizing the physical domain. This approach results in a homogeneous grid system with a uniform resolution over the entire physical domain. However, many physical phenomena exhibit shocks, discontinuities, or steep gradients in localized regions of the physical domain. In these cases, to achieve acceptable resolution in these small regions, uniform resolution methods will result in a very fine discretization of the entire domain. Consequently, it requires a significant amount of unnecessary computation and storage.

Instead of using uniform discretization or refinement to obtain finer resolution, SAMR techniques dynamically apply nonuniform refinement on different regions according to their local resolution requirements. SAMR techniques track regions in the domain, which require additional resolution and dynamically overlay finer grids over these regions. This technique concentrates computational efforts (finer grids with finer integration time steps) on regions that exhibit higher numerical errors. These methods start with a base coarse grid with minimum acceptable resolution that covers the entire computational domain. As the solution progresses, regions in the domain requiring additional resolution are tagged and finer grids are overlaid on these tagged regions of the coarse grid. Refinement proceeds recursively so that regions on the finer grid requiring more resolution are similarly tagged and even finer grids are overlaid on these regions. The resulting grid structure for the structured Berger–Oliger AMR is a dynamic adaptive grid hierarchy [3], as shown in Figure 12.1.

12.3 THE GrACE ARCHITECTURE

GrACE is based on the DAGH/HDDA architecture, which address some core underlying application and system requirements [9]. For example, at the application level, the desired application programming interface requirements include the ability to reuse existing Fortran or C modules, to make both dynamic data structuring and distribution of data across multiple address spaces transparent and, at the same time, to lose nothing in the way of efficiency over a very low-level, detailed application-specific implementation. The secondary requirements are that the resulting system should be

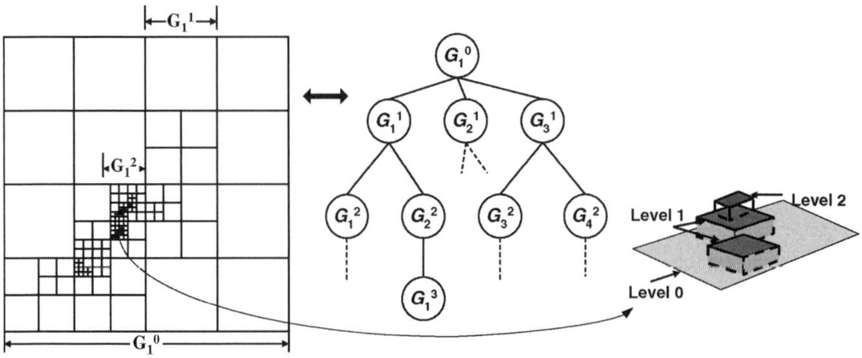

Figure 12.1 Adaptive grid hierarchy for 2D Berger–Oliger SAMR [3]. The left figure shows a 2D physical domain with localized multiple refinement levels. The right figure represents the refined domain as a grid hierarchy.

portable across a wide variety of experimental platforms and that it should scale from solving small to very large problems. Figure 12.2 illustrates the conceptual architecture of DAGH/HDDA, which the GrACE package has inherited and refined. Each layer can be thought of as a set of abstract data types, which implements operations against instances of the structures they define.

The lowest level of the abstraction hierarchy defines a hierarchical dynamic distributed array (HDDA), which is a generalization of the familiar static array of programming languages. The HDDA is purely an array data type, which has defined on it only the operations of creation, deletion, expansion and contraction of arrays, and

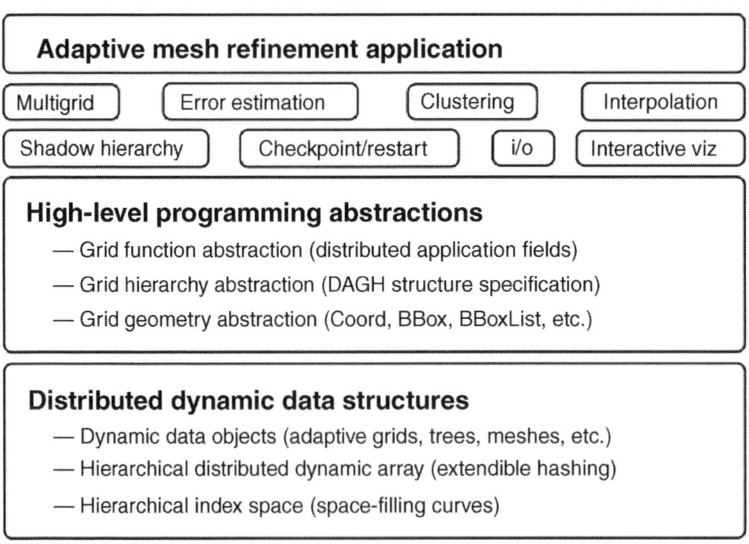

Figure 12.2 Conceptual architecture of GrACE [9].

accessing and storing of values in the elements of the arrays. Further, since the use of computational kernels written in C and Fortran is a requirement, partitioning, communication, expansion, and contraction must be made transparent to these computational kernels. Separation of concerns is illustrated by the fact that we define a separate level in the hierarchy to implement grids and/or meshes. We shall see defining the HDDA as a separate abstraction layer gives material benefit by making definition of multiple types of grids and meshes simple and straightforward.

The next abstraction level implements grids by instantiating arrays as a component of a larger semantic concept, that of a grid. A grid adds definition of a coordinate system and computational operators defined in the coordinate system. The definition of a grid includes the operations of creation, deletion, expansion, and contraction, which are directly translated to operations on instances of the HDDA and also defines computational (stencil) operators, partitioning operators, geometric region operators and refinement and coarsening operators, and so on. Creation of a hierarchical grid is directly mapped to creation of a set of arrays. Since arrays are implemented separately from grids, it is straightforward to separately implement many different variants of grids using the array abstractions that are provided. Thus, separation of concerns spreads vertically across higher levels of the abstraction hierarchy leading to simpler, faster, and more efficient implementations.

If the HDDA maintains locality and minimizes overheads, then the high-level programming abstractions level can be focused on implementing a wide span of grid variants. Since each grid variant can be defined independent of the other grid types without redundancy and can implement only the computational operations unique to the specific grid type, each grid variant can have a simple and efficient implementation. Hierarchical abstractions are a recursive concept. The HDDA is itself a hierarchy of levels of abstractions.

The critical requirement for the HDDA/GrACE package is to maximize performance at the application level. Performance at the application level requires locality of data at the storage operation level. Locality minimizes communication cost on parallel systems and also maximizes cache performance within processors. Since the operators of the application (the grids) are defined in an n-dimensional application space, it is critical that the locality of the data in the one-dimensional and distributed physical storage space maintain the locality defined by the geometry of the problem in the n-dimensional coordinate space in which the solution is defined. Therefore, we must choose or define storage management algorithms that lead to preservation of the geometric locality of the solution in the physical layout of data and storage. A second factor in obtaining high performance is the minimization of such overhead copying of data, communication, and so on. Therefore, our algorithm choices for the HDDA must focus on minimizing these overheads.

The implementation model must preserve the structure and properties of the design model clearly in the implementation. The implementation model that we chose is a C++ class hierarchy where a judicious integration of composition and inheritance is used to lead to a structure that captures and accurately reflects the hierarchical abstractions in the design model. This structure will be seen in Section 12.4 to closely follow the design model.

12.4 DESIGN AND IMPLEMENTATION OF GrACE

GrACE has been designed and implemented to meet a wide spectrum of requirements of applications and systems. The original design of GrACE as well as its evolution over the years is discussed below.

12.4.1 Requirement Analysis

The design and implementation of GrACE was driven by the needs from applications, domain scientists, available HPC systems, and available communication mechanisms. In this section, we present a requirement analysis based on application, communication, and system-level perspectives. GrACE and its predecessor, the DAGH infrastructure, were initially developed to support the computational requirements of the binary black hole (BBH) NSF grand challenge project. GrACE has been extended and expanded to support a wide range of applications, including computational fluid dynamics, numerical relativity, combustion simulations, subsurface modeling, and oil reservoir simulation [1, 2, 7, 8]. These applications are based on the Berger–Oliger AMR algorithm. To enable high-performance parallel implementation of such a class of applications, GrACE (and DAGH) was designed through a set of generic interfaces and templates. In particular, the application requirements are as follows: (1) High-performance parallel implementation of Berger–Oliger structured AMR algorithm. (2) GrACE should be highly portable to support the wide range of applications and hardware architectures due to different needs and different system setups in this diverse application base. (3) Visualization, checkpointing, and restart should be supported to aid visualized analysis, fault tolerance, data logging, and debugging. (4) Shadow hierarchy should be supported to enable error analysis. (5) Dynamic and distributed data management should be designed and implemented efficiently with minimal communication overheads. (6) Multiple different grid types and computational operators must be supported. (7) Reuse of existing Fortran and C heritage codes should be supported.

Communication requirements of parallel SAMR applications primarily consist of four components: (1) *Interlevel communications*, defined between component grids at different levels of the grid hierarchy and consist of prolongations (coarse to fine transfer and interpolation) and restrictions (fine to coarse transfer and interpolation). (2) *Intralevel communications*, required to update the grid elements along the boundaries of local portions of a distributed component grid, consisting of near-neighbor exchanges. (3) *Synchronization cost*, which occurs when the load is not balanced among processors. (4) *Data migration cost*, which occurs between two successive regridding and remapping steps.

12.4.2 Design Overview

Figure 12.3 illustrates the overall design of GrACE. At the bottom layer is the data management substrate, providing fundamental data communication, migration,

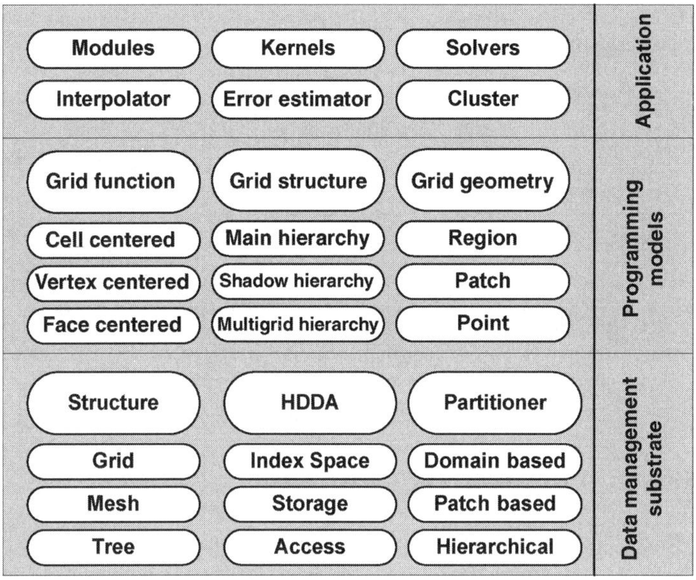

Figure 12.3 Overall design of GrACE.

indexing, and storage mechanisms on parallel and distributed systems. On the top of data management substrate, we define a set of programming models to be used by application developers. Built on the top of these programming abstractions and templates, application developers design their own application-specific components (stencil operators, solvers, interpolation operators, and error estimator).

Specifically, the layer of programming models provides means to operate on geometrical objects, organize domain structure, and manage physical functions (PDEs) on these geometries and structures. With this set of programming interfaces, templates, and instantiated objects, users of GrACE can define and develop domain-specific applications by defining physical grid functions, initializing grid hierarchy, and then evolving the underlying domains to perform scientific simulations.

The bottom layer is the focus of our further research and performance optimization due to its flexible and broad operation and parameter space. We follow the design principle of separation of concerns to design the HDDA data structure. The first one is the separation of logical structure from physical structure. Partitioning, expansion and contraction, and access are defined on the logical structure (the index space) and mapped to the physical structure implementing storage. The HDDA is composed from three abstractions: index spaces, storage, and access. Index spaces define the logical structure of the hierarchical array while storage defines the layout in physical memory. Access virtualizes the concept of accessing the value stored at a given index space location across hierarchy and partitioning. In parallel implementations, the index space is typically distributed across multiple computers. This layer is described in more detail in the Section 12.4.3.

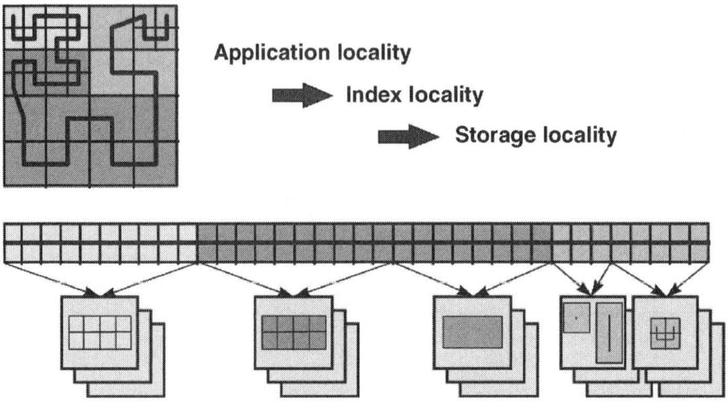

Figure 12.4 HDDA/GrACE distributed dynamic storage [9].

12.4.3 Indexing, Mapping, and Storage

We use the space-filling curve to map n-dimensional space (application domains) to one-dimensional space (index space) (Figure 12.4) [10]. The index space is derived from the discretization of the midpoints of the segments in solution space. Space filling mapping encodes application domain locality and maintains this locality through expansion and contraction. The self-similar or recursive nature of these mappings can be exploited to represent a hierarchical structure and to maintain locality across different levels of the hierarchy.

The mapping from the multidimensional index space to the one-dimensional physical address space is accomplished by mapping the positions in the index space to the order in which they occur in a traversal of the space-filling curve. This mapping can be accomplished with simple bit-interleaving operations to construct a unique ordered key. Data storage is implemented using extendible hashing techniques to provide a dynamically extendible, globally indexed storage. The HDDA data storage provides a means for efficient communication between GrACE blocks. To communicate data to another GrACE blocks, the data are copied to appropriate locations in the HDDA. This information is then asynchronously shipped to the appropriate processor. Similarly, data needed from the remote GrACE blocks are received on the fly and inserted into the appropriate location in the HDDA. Storage associated with the HDDA is maintained in ready-to-ship buckets. This alleviates overheads associated with packing and unpacking. An incoming bucket is directly inserted into its location in the HDDA. Similarly, when data associated with a GrACE block entry are ready to ship, the associated bucket is shipped as is.

12.5 PARTITIONING AND RUNTIME MANAGEMENT ALGORITHMS

The overall behavior and performance of SAMR applications depends on a large number of system and application parameters. Consequently, optimizing the execution of SAMR applications requires identifying an optimal set and configuration of these parameters. Furthermore, the relationships between the contributing factors might be highly intricate and depend on current application and system state. Built in the GrACE framework, we designed and implemented a suite of partitioning algorithms and autonomic runtime management strategies to reactively and proactively manage and optimize the execution of SAMR applications.

12.5.1 Domain-Based SFC Partitioners

The bottom layer of the partitioner stack is a set of domain-based SFC partitioners that partition the entire SAMR domain into subdomains that can be mapped by the ARM on to application computational units, which are then partitioned and balanced among available processors. The partitioners include SFC+CGDS from GrACE-distributed AMR infrastructure [11, 12] and G-MISP+SP and pBD-ISP that belong to the Vampire SAMR partitioning library [13]. Their characteristics [14] are as follows:

- *SFC+CGDS:* The SFC+CGDS scheme is fast, has average load balance, and generates low overhead, low communication, and average data migration costs. This scheme is suited for application states associated with low-to-moderate activity dynamics and more computation than communication.
- *G-MISP+SP:* The G-MISP+SP scheme is aimed toward speed and simplicity and favors simple communication patterns and partitioning speed over amount of data migration. Sequence partitioning used by G-MISP+SP significantly improves the load balance but can be computationally expensive.
- *pBD-ISP:* The pBD-ISP scheme is fast and the coarse granularity partitioning generated results in low overheads and communication costs. However, the overall load balance is average and may deteriorate when refinements are strongly localized. This scheme is suited for application states with greater communication and data requirements and lesser emphasis on load balance.

12.5.2 Binpack-Based Partitioning Algorithm

The Binpack-based partitioning algorithm (BPA) attempts to improve the load balance during the SAMR partitioning phase, where the computational workload associated with patches at different levels of the SAMR hierarchy is distributed among available processors. The distribution is performed under constraints such as the minimum patch size and the aspect ratio. BPA distributes the workload among processors as long as the processor work threshold is not exceeded. Patches with a workload larger than the threshold limit are split into smaller patches. Unallocated work is first distributed using a "best-fit" approach. If this fails, the "most-free" approach is adopted. BPA technique improves the load balance between partitions and, hence, the execution time for a SAMR application. However, as a result of multiple patch divisions, a large number of patches may be created.

12.5.3 Level-Based Partitioning Algorithm

The computational workload for a certain patch of the SAMR application is tightly coupled to the refinement level at which the patch exists. The computational workload at a finer level is considerably greater than that at coarser levels. The level-based partitioning algorithm (LPA) [15] attempts to simultaneously balance load and minimize synchronization cost. LPA essentially preprocesses the global application computational units represented by a global grid unit list (GUL), disassembles them according to refinement levels of the grid hierarchy, and feeds the resulting homogeneous units at each refinement level to GPA. The GPA scheme then partitions this list to balance the workload. Due to preprocessing, the load on each refinement level is also balanced. LPA benefits from the SFC+CGDS technique by maintaining parent–children relationship throughout the composite grid and localizing interlevel communications, while simultaneously balancing the load at each refinement level.

12.5.4 Hierarchical Partitioning Algorithm

In the hierarchical partitioning algorithm (HPA), the partitioning phase is divided into two subphases: local partitioning phase and global partitioning phase. In the local partitioning phase, the processors within a group partition the group workload based on a local load threshold and assign a portion to each processor within the group. Parent groups iteratively partition among their children groups in a hierarchical manner. In the global partitioning phase, the root group coordinator decides if a global repartitioning has to be performed among its children groups according to the group threshold.

The HPA scheme attempts to exploit the fact that given a group with adequate number of processors and an appropriately defined number of groups, the number of global partitioning phases can be greatly reduced, thereby eliminating unnecessary communication and synchronization overheads. The prototype implementation has two variants of the HPA scheme, namely, static HPA (SHPA) and adaptive HPA (AHPA) [16].

In the SHPA scheme, the group size and group topology are defined at startup based on available processors and size of the problem domain. The group topology then remains fixed for the entire execution session. To account for application runtime dynamics, the AHPA scheme proposes an adaptive strategy. AHPA dynamically partitions the computational domain into subdomains to match the current adaptations. The subdomains created may have unequal workloads. The algorithm then assigns the subdomains to corresponding nonuniform hierarchical processor groups that are constructed at runtime. More recent algorithms based on hybrid runtime management strategies (HRMS) have been proposed in Ref. [17].

12.5.5 Application Aware Partitioning and Mapping

The application aware partitioning and mapping mechanism is an adaptive strategy on top of the basic partitioners. It uses the state of the application and its current requirements to select and tune partitioning algorithms and parameters. It is composed of three components: application state characterization component, partitioner selection component and policy engine, and runtime adaptation (meta-partitioner) component. The state characterization component implements mechanisms that abstract and characterize the current application state in terms of the computation/communication requirements, application dynamics, and the nature of the adaptation. The policy engine defines the associations between application state and partitioner behavior. Based on the state characterization and defined policies, the appropriate partitioning algorithm and associated partitioning parameters (such as granularity) are selected at runtime from the available repository of partitioners. The partitioners include a selection from broadly used software tools such as GrACE [11, 12, 18] and Vampire [13]. The runtime adaptation component dynamically configures partitioning granularity and invokes the appropriate partitioner, thus adapting and optimizing application performance. Experimental studies of the application aware adaptive partitioning [19] have shown that it can significantly improve the efficiency and performance of parallel/-distributed SAMR applications. Performance functions can be used in conjunction with system-sensitive partitioning [20] to predict the application execution time based on current loads, available communication bandwidth, current latencies, and available memory. These performance estimates are then used to adjust the relative capacity associated with each processor.

12.6 APPLICATIONS OF GrACE

Three different infrastructures targeting computational grand challenges have used GrACE (and/or its predecessor DAGH) as their foundation: (1) a computational infrastructure for the binary black hole grand challenge, (2) a computational infrastructure for the neutron star grand challenge, and (3) IPARS: a problem-solving environment for parallel oil reservoir simulation. Application codes developed using the HDDA/GrACE data structures and programming abstractions include general relativity codes for black hole, boson star, and neutron star interactions, coupled hydrodynamics and general-relativity codes, laser plasma codes, and geophysics codes for adaptive modeling of the whole earth. GrACE is also used to design a multiresolution database for storing, accessing, and operating on satellite information at different levels of detail. Finally, base HDDA objects have been extended with visualization, analysis, and interaction capabilities. The capabilities are then inherited by application objects derived from HDDA objects and provide support for a framework for interactive visualization and computational steering where visualization, analysis, and interaction are directly driven from the actual computational objects.

To further aid the analysis and visualization of applications based on GrACE, we developed the GridMate simulator, which is capable to represent computing resources in both clusters and multisite grids [21].

12.7 RELATED WORK

There are a number of infrastructures that support parallel and distributed implementations of structured and unstructured AMR applications. Each of these systems represents a combination of design choices. Table 12.1 summarizes these systems and their features.

GrACE is an object-oriented adaptive computational engine with pluggable domain-based partitioners. HRMS built on GrACE consists of an adaptive hierarchical multi-partitioner scheme and other hybrid schemes. Charm++ [22] is a comprehensive parallel C++ library that supports processor virtualization and provides an intelligent runtime system. Its AMR module offers flexible representation and communication for implementing the AMR algorithm. It uses the domain-based decomposition method and a quadtree structure to partition and index the computational domain and supports coarse-grained partitioning. Chombo [23] consists of

Table 12.1 Parallel and Distributed AMR Infrastructures

System	Execution mode	Granularity	Partitioner organization	Decomposition	Institute
GrACE/ HRMS	Comp intensive	Fine grained, coarse grained	Adaptive hierarchical multipartitioner, hybrid strategies	Domain based, hybrid	Rutgers/OSU
Charm	Comp intensive	Coarse grained	Static single partitioner	Domain based	UIUC
Chombo	Comp intensive	Fine grained, coarse grained	Static single partitioner	Domain based	LBNL
Nature+ fable	Comp intensive	Coarse grained	Single meta-partitioner	Domain based, hybrid	Sandia
ParaMesh	Comp intensive	Fine grained, coarse grained	Static single partitioner	Domain based	NASA
ParMetis	Comp intensive, comm intensive	Fine grained	Static single partitioner	Graph based	Minnesota
PART	Comp intensive	Coarse grained	Static single partitioner	Domain based	Northwestern
SAMRAI	Comp intensive, comm intensive	Fine grained, coarse grained	Static single partitioner	Patch based	LLNL

four core modules: BoxTools, AMRTools, AMRTimeDependent, and AMRElliptic. Its load balance strategy follows Kernighan–Lin multilevel partitioning algorithm. Nature+Fable formulates a meta-partitioner approach by characterizing both partitioners and application domains [24]. ParaMesh [25] uses octree representation of the adaptive grid structure with predefined block sizes and uses this representation to partition the SAMR domain. ParMetis [26] applies multilevel hypergraph partitioning and repartitioning techniques to balance the load. PART [27] considers heterogeneities in the application and the distributed system. It uses simulated annealing to perform the backtracking search for desired partitions. Nevertheless, simplistic partitioning schemes are used in the PART system. SAMRAI [28–30] is an object-oriented framework (based on LPARX). It uses a patch-based decomposition scheme. In the SAMRAI library, after the construction of computational patches, patches are assigned to processors using a greedy bin-packing procedure. SAMRAI uses the Morton space-filling curve technique to maintain spatial locality for patch distribution. To further enhance the scalability of SAMR applications using the SAMRAI framework, Wissink et al. [30] proposed a *recursive binary box tree* algorithm to improve communication schedule construction. A simplified point clustering algorithm based on Berger–Regoutsos algorithm [31] has also been presented. The reduction of runtime complexity using these algorithms substantially improves the scalability of parallel SAMR applications on up to 1024 processors. As mentioned above, the SAMRAI framework uses patch-based partitioning schemes, which result in good load balance but might cause considerable interlevel communication and synchronization overheads.

12.8 CONCLUSION

Following a system engineering approach, this chapter presented the design, implementation, and management algorithms of the GrACE package consisting of library, pluggable modules and programming models and interfaces (APIs). The GrACE package represents more than 10 years of efforts to engineer a high-performance software framework with wide user bases in academia and national labs, featuring open source, open platform, multiple programming languages compatibility, high scalability (over 1000 processors), and friendly programming interfaces for developing the large-scale parallel software of hundreds of complex PDE systems. The built-in partitioning and runtime management algorithms provide a flexible suite to address different needs in a wide spectrum of application and system scenarios. In addition, GrACE provides the flexibility for users to customize the partitioning algorithms, scientific equation templates, heterogeneous workload density, and visualization tools.

ACKNOWLEDGMENTS

The authors would like to thank James C. Browne for his many contributions to the original HDDA/DAGH design. We would also like to thank Sumir Chandra and Johan Steensland for many insightful research discussions. The research presented in this chapter is supported in part by National Science Foundation via Grant Nos ACI

9984357, EIA 0103674, EIA 0120934, ANI 0335244, CNS 0709329, CNS 0305495, CNS 0426354, and IIS 0430826, and by the Department of Energy via the Grant No. DE-FG02-06ER54857.

REFERENCES

1. S. Hawley and M. Choptuik. Boson stars driven to the brink of black hole formation. *Phys. Rev. D*, 62:10(104024), 2000.
2. J. Ray, H.N. Najm, R.B. Milne, K.D. Devine, and S. Kempka. Triple flame structure and dynamics at the stabilization point of an unsteady lifted jet diffusion flame. *Proc. Combust. Inst.*, 25(1):219–226, 2000.
3. M. Berger and J. Oliger. Adaptive mesh refinement for hyperbolic partial differential equations. *J. Comput. Phys.*, 53:484–512, 1984.
4. M. Berger and P. Colella. Local adaptive mesh refinement for shock hydrodynamics. *J. Comput. Phys.*, 82:64–84, 1989.
5. K. Devine, E. Boman, R. Heaphy, B. Hendrickson, and C. Vaughan. Zoltan data management services for parallel dynamic applications. *Comput. Sci. Eng.*, 4(2):90–97, 2002.
6. S.K. Das, D.J. Harvey, and R. Biswas. Parallel processing of adaptive meshes with load balancing. *IEEE Trans. Parallel Distrib. Syst.*, 12(12):1269–1280, 2001.
7. J. Cummings, M. Aivazis, R. Samtaney, R. Radovitzky, S. Mauch, and D. Meiron. A virtual test facility for the simulation of dynamic response in materials. *J. Supercomput.*, 23:39–50, 2002.
8. Ipars. http://www.cpge.utexas.edu/new_generation/.
9. M. Parashar and J.C. Browne. System engineering for high performance computing software: the HDDA/DAGH infrastructure for implementation of parallel structured adaptive mesh refinement. *Structured Adaptive Mesh Refinement (SAMR) Grid Methods*, 2000, IMA Vol. 117, pp. 1–18.
10. H. Sagan. *Space-Filling Curves*. Springer-Verlag, 1994.
11. M. Parashar and J. Browne. Distributed dynamic data-structures for parallel adaptive mesh-refinement. In *Proceedings of the International Conference for High Performance Computing*, Trivandrum, India, December 1996, pp. 22–27.
12. M. Parashar and J. Browne. A common data management infrastructure for adaptive algorithms for PDE solutions. *Proceedings of the 1997 ACM/IEEE Conference on Supercomputing*. San Jose, CA, 1997, pp. 1–22.
13. J. Steensland. Vampire. http://www.tdb.uu.se/~johans/research/vampire/vampire1.html., 2000.
14. S. Chandra and M. Parashar. An evaluation of partitioners for parallel SAMR applications. In R. Sakellariou, J. Keane, J. Gurd, and L. Freeman, editors, *Euro-Par 2001*, Vol. 2150. Springer-Verlag, 2001, pp. 171–174.
15. X. Li and M. Parashar. Dynamic load partitioning strategies for managing data of space and time heterogeneity in parallel SAMR applications. In *Proceedings of the 9th International Euro-Par Conference (Euro-Par 2003)*, Klagenfurt, Austria, 2003.
16. X. Li and M. Parashar. Hierarchical partitioning techniques for structured adaptive mesh refinement applications. *J. Supercomput.*, Kluwer Academic Publishers, 2004, Vol. 28(3), pp. 265–278.
17. X. Li and M. Parashar. Hybrid runtime management of space–time heterogeneity for parallel structured adaptive applications. *IEEE Trans. Parallel Distrib. Syst.*, 18(9):1202–1214, 2007.
18. M. Parashar. GrACE: grid adaptive computational engine. http://www.caip.rutgers.edu/~parashar/TASSL/Projects/GrACE.
19. S. Chandra, J. Steensland, M. Parashar, and J. Cummings. An experimental study of adaptive application sensitive partitioning strategies for SAMR applications. In *2nd Los Alamos Computer Science Institute Symposium (also Best Research Poster at Supercomputing Conference 2001)*, Santa Fe, NM, October 2001.
20. S. Chandra, Y. Zhang, S. Sinha, J. Yang, M. Parashar, and S. Hariri. Adaptive runtime management of SAMR applications. In S. Sahni, V. K. Prasanna, U. Shukla, editors, *Proceedings of the 9th*

International Conference on High Performance Computing (HiPC), Lecture Notes in Computer Science, Vol. 2552. Springer-Verlag, Bangalore, India, 2002.
21. X. Li and M. Parashar. Gridmate: a portable simulation environment for large-scale adaptive scientific applications. In *The 8th IEEE International Symposium on Cluster Computing and the Grid (CCGrid 2008)*, Lyon, France, 2008.
22. L.V. Kale. Charm. http://charm.cs.uiuc.edu/research/charm/.
23. P. Colella, et. al. Chombo, 2003. http://seesar.lbl.gov/anag/chombo/.
24. J. Steensland. Efficient partitioning of structured dynamic grid hierarchies. PhD thesis, Uppsala University, 2002.
25. P. MacNeice. ParaMesh. http://esdcd.gsfc.nasa.gov/ESS/macneice/paramesh/paramesh.html.
26. G. Karypis. Parmetis. http://www-users.cs.umn.edu/~karypis/metis/parmetis/index.html., 2003.
27. J. Chen and V. Taylor. Mesh partitioning for efficient use of distributed systems. *IEEE Trans. Parallel Distrib. Syst.*, 13(1):67–79, 2002.
28. S. Kohn. SAMRAI: structured adaptive mesh refinement applications infrastructure. Technical report, Lawrence Livermore National Laboratory, 1999.
29. R.D. Hornung and S.R. Kohn. Managing application complexity in the SAMRAI object-oriented framework. *Concurrency Comput. Pract. Exper.*, 14(5):347–368, 2002.
30. A. Wissink, D. Hysom, and R. Hornung. Enhancing scalability of parallel structured AMR calculations. *The 17th ACM International Conference on Supercomputing (ICS03)*, 2003, pp. 336–347.
31. M. Berger and I. Regoutsos. An algorithm for point clustering and grid generation. *IEEE Trans. Syst., Man, Cyber.*, 21(5):1278–1286, 1991.

Chapter 13

Charm++ and AMPI: Adaptive Runtime Strategies via Migratable Objects

Laxmikant V. Kale and Gengbin Zheng

13.1 INTRODUCTION

Parallel programming is certainly more difficult than sequential programming because of the additional issues one has to deal with in a parallel program. One has to decide what computations to perform in parallel, which processors will perform which computations, and how to distribute the data, at least in the predominant distributed memory programming models. To alleviate this difficulty, one should try to automate a parallel programming effort as much as possible. But which aspects of parallel programming should be automated? A reasonable strategy is to automate what the "system" can do well, while leaving what the programmers can do well to them. This "optimal division of labor between the system and the programmer" is a guiding principle behind Charm++. In particular, we believe that the programmers can decide *what* to do in parallel, while the runtime system should decide the assignment of data and computations to processors, and the order in which processors will execute their assigned work. This approach has led to Charm++, an intuitive parallel programming system, with a clear cost model, and a highly adaptive, intelligent runtime system (RTS), along with an ambitious research agenda for runtime optimization.

In this study, we first briefly describe Charm++ and Adaptive MPI (AMPI)—an implementation of MPI that leverages the adaptive RTS of Charm++. We then describe multiple adaptive aspects of Charm++/AMPI, including adaptive overlap

Advanced Computational Infrastructures For Parallel and Distributed Adaptive Applications. Edited by Manish Parashar and Xiaolin Li

of communication and computation, dynamic measurement-based load balancing, communication optimizations, adaptations to available memory, and fault tolerance. We then present an overview of a few applications and describe some recent higher level parallel programming abstractions built using Charm++.

13.2 THE PROGRAMMING MODEL

The basic unit of parallelism in Charm++ is a *chare*, a C++ object containing entry methods that may be invoked asynchronously from other such objects (which may reside on other processors). Chares are medium-grained entities. Typically, average entry method execution times are in the tens of microseconds or larger and a single processor core may house tens of chares. (Although there are applications where each processor houses thousands of chares.)

Execution on a chare is triggered when another chare sends a message targeting the recipient chare's entry point or a specially registered function for remote invocation. Note that the remote invocation is asynchronous: it returns immediately after sending out the message, without blocking or waiting for the response. Since each physical processor may house many chares, the runtime has a scheduler to decide which chare will execute next. This scheduler is message driven; only chares with a pending message can be chosen to execute.

Although Charm++ supports important constructs such as specifically shared variables, prioritized execution, and object groups, from the point of view of this study, the most important construct in Charm++ is a chare array [25, 30]. A chare array is an indexed collection of chares. It has a single global ID and consists of a number of chares, each indexed by a unique index within the array. Charm++ supports one-dimensional through six-dimensional, sparse as well as dense, chare arrays. In addition, users may define a variety of other index types on their own (for instance, an oct-tree might be represented by a chare array, where the index is a bit vector representing the position of a node in the tree).

As shown in Figure 13.1, the programmer thinks of the array as a set of objects, and the code in these objects may invoke methods of other array members

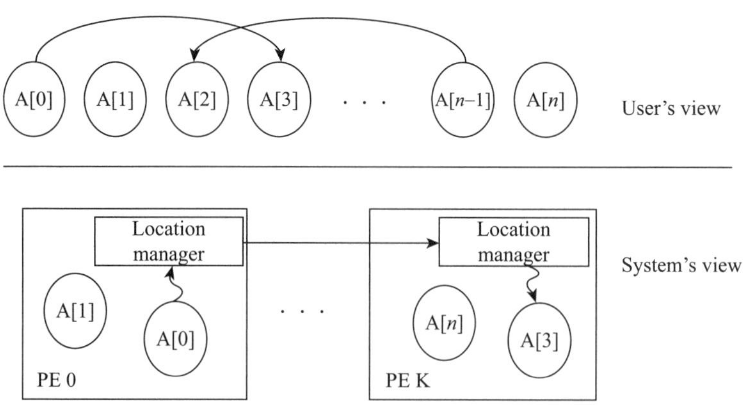

Figure 13.1 Object arrays.

asynchronously. However, the system mediates the communication between the objects. As a result, if an object moves from one processor to another, other objects do not need to know this. The system has automatic mechanisms that efficiently forward messages when needed, and it caches location information so as to avoid forwarding costs in most situations [25]. In addition to method invocation, chare arrays support broadcast ("invoke this method on all live array members") and reductions, which work correctly and efficiently in the presence of dynamic creation and deletions of array members, as well as their dynamic migration between processors.

Chare kernel, the C-based version of Charm, was developed before 1989 [22], while the C++-based version (Charm++) was created in 1992 [23]. The C-based version (with its notion of object encoded as a global pointer, with a function to execute on the destination processor) has similarities to nexus [8], except that nexus entities were not migratable. Active messages and message-driven execution (MDE) in Charm++ are quite similar, although the original notion of active messages was interrupt based (and akin to an implementation of inexpensive interrupts on CM-5). Also, message driven-objects of Charm++ are similar to the Actors model [1]. The Actor's work precedes chare kernel, whereas active messages and nexus [8] are after chare kernel. However, Charm++ arose from our work on parallel prolog, and the intellectual progenitors for our work included the RediFlow project of Bob Keller [24]. Our approach can also be considered a macro-data-flow approach [2]. Other research with overlapping approaches include work on Percolation and Earth multithreading system [16], work on HTMT and Gilgamesh projects [9], and work on Diva [11].

13.2.1 Adaptive MPI

Adaptive MPI [13, 15] is an adaptive implementation and extension of MPI built on top of the Charm++ runtime system. AMPI implements virtualized MPI processes (VPs) using lightweight migratable user-level threads [32], several of which may be mapped to one physical processor as illustrated in Figure 13.2.

In 1994, we conducted extensive studies [10], and demonstrated that Charm++ had superior performance and modulartity properties compared to MPI. However, it

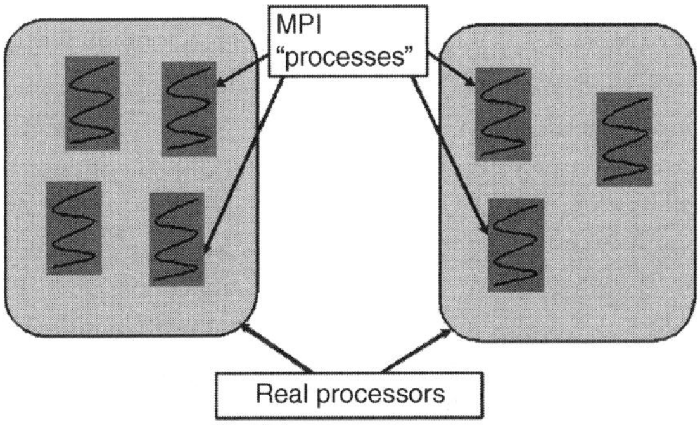

Figure 13.2 AMPI implements MPI processes as user-level migratable threads.

became clear that MPI is the prevalent and popular programming model. Although virtualization in Charm++ was useful, the split-phase programming engendered by its asynchronous method invocation was difficult for many programmers, especially in science and engineering. MPI's model had certain anthropomorphic appeal. A processor sends a message, waits for a message, does some computation, and so on. The program specifies the sequence in which a processor does these things.

Given this fact, we examined what we considered to be the main advantages of Charm++: the C++-based aspect of asynchronous method invocation was seen as less important than the ability to separate decomposition and mapping by allowing programmers to decompose their problem into a large number of work and data units, and allowing an intelligent runtime system to map them to processors. The work units thus may communicate using MPI-style messages and still benefit from the Charm++ RTS. These observations led to the development of Adaptive MPI. In AMPI, as in Charm, the user programs in terms of a large number of MPI "processes," independent of the number of processors. AMPI implements each "process" as a user-level lightweight and *migratable* thread as shown in Figure 13.2. This should not be confused with a Pthreads-style MPI implementation. We can have tens of thousands of such MPI threads on each processor, if needed, and the context switching time is of the order of 1 μs on most of today's machines. Migrating user-level threads, which contain their own stacks and heaps, and may contain pointers to stack and heap data, is technically challenging but has been efficiently implemented [4], based in part on the *isomalloc* technique developed in PM^2 [26].

Porting existing MPI codes to AMPI can be done automatically on most machines. On some machines, codes may have to be modified somewhat to encapsulate references to global variables. AMPI has been used to parallelize several applications, including codes at the DOE-supported Rocket Simulation Center at Illinois, and early versions of a computational cosmology code (which was converted to AMPI within one afternoon, sans the optimizations that followed).

13.2.2 Charm++/AMPI in Use

Charm++ and AMPI have been used scalably as mature runtime systems for a variety of real-world applications.

NAMD (nanoscale molecular dynamics) is a molecular dynamics application designed to facilitate the study of biological molecules via simulation on parallel computers. Since its initial release (free for noncommercial use since 1995), NAMD has grown to become one of the most widely used and fastest molecular dynamics applications for the study of biologically important systems. Its hybrid spatial decomposition and implementation on top of Charm++ are the keys to NAMD's speed and scalability. By decomposing problem domain into many cells, and interacting cell pairs, the computational work can be load balanced automatically by Charm++'s intelligent runtime system. Charm++'s asynchronous model is exploited by choosing the number of cell pairs to be significantly greater than the number of processors. This "overdecomposition" allows the communication of data between cell pairs to overlap with computation using data that have already arrived. NAMD is currently used by thousands of scientists, scales single system simulation for hundreds of thousands of atoms to over 32,000 processors, and won the Gordon Bell award in 2002.

OpenAtom (formerly known as LeanCP) is an implementation of the Car–Parrinello method for *ab initio* molecular dynamics using Charm++. Many important problems, such as the study of chemical reactions, require that the electronic structure be modeled explicitly using quantum mechanical principles rather than approximated as is done in classical model molecular dynamics. Despite the computational intensity, it is critical that systems be studied for sufficiently long timescales to capture interesting events, which motivates the use of parallel computers to minimize the time required for each computation step. Each timestep of this computation, using Kohn–Sham density functional theory and a finite basis set of plane waves, requires the computation of multiple concurrent 3D FFTs and matrix matrix multiplies with a variety of data dependencies and integration steps whose order must be strictly enforced to maintain correctness. The aforementioned correctness constraints vie with performance optimizing techniques that maximize overlap and simultaneous execution. A fine-grained implementation, using arrays of Charm++ objects to contain portions of electronic state, allows all the inherent parallelism of computation to be expressed. As data dependencies are met and integration correctness checks are satisfied, each successive phase of the computation can begin even though the previous phase is not yet finished. The complexity of managing these data dependencies is delegated to the Charm++ intelligent runtime system, which allows for network topology aware placement of objects to optimize communication performance. This fine-grained approach has led to remarkable scalability, effectively scaling systems up to 30 times the number of electronic states. Benchmark systems as small as 128 molecules of water with a 70 rydberg cutoff have been studied using 40960 BlueGene/L processor cores.

ChaNGa (Charm N-body Gravity solver) is a code to perform collisionless N-body simulations. It can perform cosmological simulations with periodic boundary conditions in comoving coordinates or simulations of isolated stellar systems. ChaNGa uses a Barnes–Hut tree to calculate gravity, with quadrapole expansion of nodes and Ewald summation for periodic forces. Timestepping is done with a leapfrog integrator with individual timesteps for each particle. By leveraging the object-based virtualization and the data-driven execution model inherent in the Charm++ runtime system, ChaNGa obtains automatic overlapping of communication and computation time. The Charm++ runtime also provides automatic measurement-based load balancing. These capabilities have been used to successfully scale ChaNGa to more than 32,000 processors, with data sets consisting of hundreds of millions of particles. ChaNGa is freely available for noncommercial use, and its first public release occurred in February 2007.

AMPI has also been used in applications such as fractography [15], a dynamic 3D crack propagation simulation program to simulate pressure-driven crack propagation in structures, and rocket simulation [3, 15].

We have also demonstrated that virtualization has minimal performance penalty [20], due to the low scheduling overheads of user-level threads. In fact, cache performance is often significantly improved by its blocking effect.

13.3 AUTOMATIC ADAPTIVE OVERLAP: ADAPTING TO COMMUNICATION LATENCIES AND RESPONSE DELAYS

One of the issues in MPI programs is that of overlapping communication with computation. When a program calls a receive statement, one would like the message one is waiting for to have already arrived. To achieve this, one tries to move `send` ahead and `receive` down, so that between sends and receives one can get some computation done, giving time for communication to complete. When multiple data items are to be received, one has to make guesses about which will arrive sooner, or use wildcard receives, which often break the flow of the program [10].

With message-driven execution, adaptive overlap between communication and computation is automatically achieved, without programmer intervention. The object or thread whose message has already arrived will be automatically allowed to continue, via the message-driven scheduler (Section 13.2).

This advantage is all the more stronger when one considers multiple parallel modules (Figure 13.3). A, B, and C are each parallel modules spread across all processors. A must call B and C, but there is no dependence between B and C. In traditional MPI-style programming, one must choose one of the modules (say B) to call first, on all the processors. The module may contain sends, receives, and barriers. Only when B returns can A call C on each processor. Thus, idle time (which arises for a variety of reasons including load imbalance and critical paths) in each module cannot be overlapped with useful computation from the other, even though there is no depenendence between the two modules.

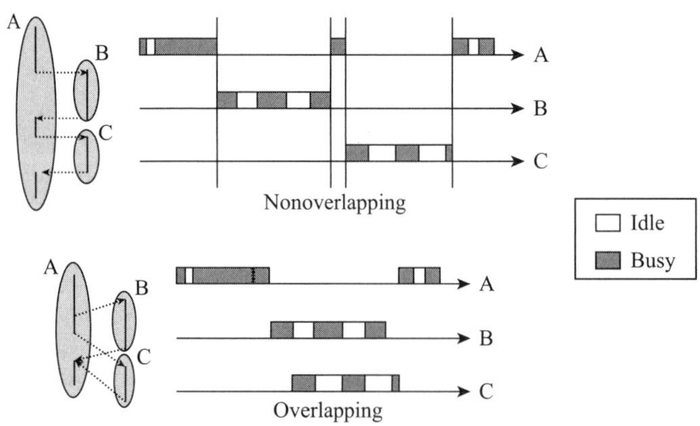

Figure 13.3 Modularity and adaptive overlapping.

In contrast, with Charm++, A invokes B on each (virtual) processor, which computes, sends initial messages, and returns to A. A then starts off module C in a similar manner. Now B and C interleave their execution based on availibility of data (messages) they are waiting for. This automatically overlaps idle time in one module with computation in the other, as shown in the figure. One can attempt to achieve such overlap in MPI, but at the cost of breaking the modularity between A, B, and C. The code in B does not have to know about that in A or C, and vice versa.

13.4 ADAPTING TO LOAD VARIATIONS IN THE APPLICATION

Many parallel applications involve simulations with dynamic behaviors, leading to application load imbalance. For example, some finite element method (FEM) simulations involve dynamic geometry and use adaptive techniques to solve highly irregular problems. In these applications, load balancing is required to achieve the desired high performance on large parallel machines. It is especially needed for applications where the amount of computation can increase significantly as the simulation evolves.

The load balancing problem involves making decisions on placing newly created computational tasks on processors, or migrating existing tasks among processors uniformly. Finding an optimal solution to balance the load is an NP-complete problem. However, many heuristic algorithms have been developed that find a reasonably good approximate solution [7, 17, 24, 29, 31]. In order for the load balancing algorithms to make better load balancing decisions, it is essential for the RTS to provide most up-to-date application and system load information. The Charm++ RTS exploits a simple heuristic called *principle of persistence* to achieve automated load instrumentation. The *principle of persistence* is a heuristic that can be thought of as the parallel analogue to the principle of locality.

Principle of Persistence: Once an application is expressed in terms of its natural objects (as virtual processors) and their interactions, the object computation times and communication patterns (number and sizes of messages exchanged between each communicating pair of objects) *tend to* persist over time [19].

This principle arises from the fact that most parallel applications are iterative in nature, and the physical system being simulated changes gradually, due to numerical constraints. For example, some applications such as those using adaptive mesh refinement may involve abrupt but infrequent changes in these patterns. Other applications such as molecular dynamics may involve slow changes in these patterns. Therefore, the correlation between recent past and near future, expressed in terms of interacting virtual processors, holds, which makes it possible to use recent history load data to predict the near future. This allows for measurement-based load balancing and optimization algorithms that can adapt to application behavior.

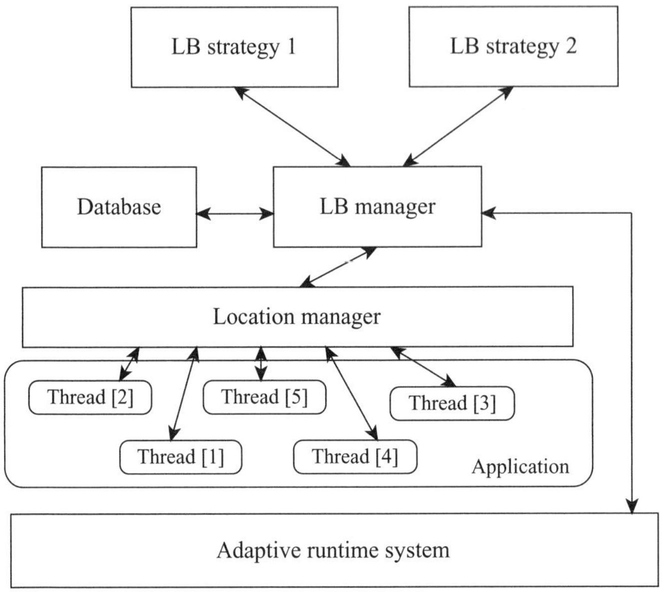

Figure 13.4 Components of the load balancing framework.

13.4.1 Measurement-Based Load Balancing

Relying on the principle of persistence, the Charm RTS employs a measurement-based load balancing scheme. The load balancer automatically collects statistics on each object's computational load and communication patterns into a load database. Using the collected load database, the load balancer decides on when and where to migrate objects.

Figure 13.4 illustrates the components of the load balancing framework on a single processor. At the top level of the figure are the load balancing strategies, from which the runtime can choose one to plug in and use. At the center is the LB manager that plays a key role in load balancing. When informed by LB manager to perform load balancing, strategies on each processor may retrieve information from the local LB manager database about the current state of the processor and the objects currently assigned to it. Depending on the specific strategy, there may be communication with other processors to gather state information. With all information available, strategies determine when and where to migrate the object (and any thread embedded in it) and provide this information to the LB manager, which supervises the movements of the objects, informing the strategies as objects arrive. When the moves are complete, the strategies signal the LB manager to resume the objects.

A suite of dynamic load balancing strategies (some centralized, some fully distributed, some incremental, and others periodic and comprehensive) can tap into this database to make decisions about when and where to migrate the objects.

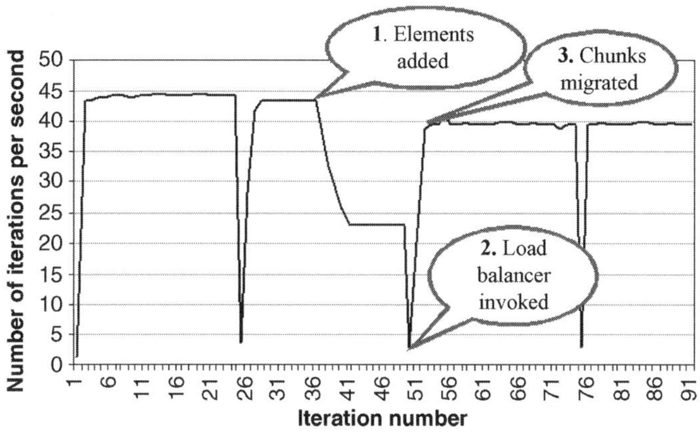

Figure 13.5 Automatic load balancing in crack propogation.

An example of dynamic load balancing in action is shown in Figure 13.5. An FEM-based structural dynamics application is running on a parallel computer. The y-axis shows its throughput (i.e., the number of iterations completed per second), while the x-axis shows the iteration number. At timestep 37, the application experiences an adaptive event (some new elements are added as a result of a crack propagating into the domain). At the next load balancing event (the system is using a periodic load balancer), the performance is brought back to almost the original level, by migrating objects precisely from the overloaded processors to others, based on the measurement of load each object presents.[1]

13.5 ADAPTING TO CHANGING NUMBER OF AVAILABLE PROCESSORS

Probably one of the most dramatic uses of virtualization is in changing the number of processors used by application at runtime. Consider a parallel machine with a thousand processors running a job on 800 processors. If a new job that needs 400 processors arrives, it will have to wait for the first job to finish, while the system wastes 200 processors. With virtualization, our runtime system is capable of shrinking the first job to 600 processors, by migrating objects away from the 200 additional processors needed by the second job. Further, when the second job finishes, the system can expand the set of processors allocated to the first job to the original 800 again. We have already demonstrated a cluster scheduler [21] that makes use of this capability to optimize its utilization and response time. This is especially useful for interactive parallel jobs, which are slowly becoming popular (for example, interactive molecular dynamics, or cosmology analysis and visualization).

[1]This experiment used an artificial refinement event. Real applications will take much longer to induce the refinement and insertion of new elements.

This capability is also useful for jobs that themselves know when they need more or fewer processors, based on their application's dynamic structure, as well as jobs that are perpetually "hungry" for more processors, and are willing to run in the background at a lower priority.

13.6 ADAPTIVE COMMUNICATION OPTIMIZATIONS

Charm++ runtime provides adaptive communication optimizations for both point-to-point and collective communication operations. It improves communication performance in applications by adaptively overlapping communication with computation automatically (as described in Section 13.3).

On a large number of processors, all-to-all communication can take several milliseconds to finish. With synchronous collectives defined in MPI, the processor idles while the collective messages are in flight. Therefore, the Charm++ runtime provides an asynchronous collective communication framework to let the CPU compute while the all-to-all messages are in flight. The best strategy for all-to-all communication depends on the message size [27]. Different techniques are needed to optimize all-to-all communication for small and large messages. For small messages, the cost of the collective operation is dominated by the software overhead of sending the messages. For large messages, the cost is dominated by network contention, which can be minimized by smart sequencing of messages based on the underlying network topology [27]. This suggests that parameters including application communication pattern and properties of actual communication hardware can be observed at runtime and used to choose the optimal strategy for all-to-all communication. The Charm++ runtime implements an adaptive strategy switching for all-to-all communication.

13.7 ADAPTING TO AVAILABLE MEMORY

Petascale supercomputers tend to have low memory-to-processor ratio; exemplar machines include BlueGene/L and next-generation machines based on the Cell Broadband Engine Architecture (CBEA). Applications running on such machines have to deal with such memory constraints while achieving desirable performance. CHARM++'s virtualization idea has been exploited to adapt to the memory availability.

13.7.1 Automatic Out-of-Core Execution

Running applications that require a large amount of memory on a parallel machine with relatively smaller per-node memory is challenging. Our out-of-core execution technique [28] has been designed to solve this problem by temporarily moving the data in memory to disk when it is not needed immediately. Out-of-core execution can suffer from large disk I/O latencies. However, CHARM++ provides several features that can hide the high latencies. First, CHARM++ uses a prioritized scheduling queue that can be used for peeking ahead for prefetching, and hence overlapping I/O with computation. Second, CHARM++ supports object migration; therefore, moving an object to disk simply means migrating an object to disk. An automatic out-of-core execution can be supported at runtime without the knowledge of the applications.

13.7.2 Exploiting the Cell Processor

The CBEA, or "Cell" for short, has been jointly designed by IBM, Sony, and Toshiba. Compared to other commodity processors, the Cell has tremendous processing power (especially for single-precision floating-point arithmetic). However, it also presents several challenges including ease of programming. There are a total of nine cores on each Cell chip. There is a single *main* core called the power processor element (PPE). This core can be thought of as a *standard commodity* processor. It is a two-way SMT and can access the main system memory just like a typical processor. In addition to the PPE, there are eight synergistic processor elements (SPEs). The SPEs are specialized cores specifically designed to do large amounts of number crunching through the use of SIMD instructions. The SPEs cannot access main memory. Instead, each SPE has a local store (LS) on chip (currently 256 kB in size). All data needed by the SPE must be present in the LS including stack, code, and data. To move data between the LS and main system memory, direct memory access (DMA) transactions must be used. This allows the programmer to explicitly control the contents of the LS. However, this also means that the programmer must explicitly manage several aspects of the LS and its contents.

There are several aspects of the Charm++ runtime system that will allow it to take advantage of the Cell processor. The following paragraphs discuss some of these points. To use the SPEs, the Charm++ RTS uses the Offload API. The Offload API has been developed with the Charm++ RTS in mind. However, it is independent of the Charm++ RTS and can be used by C/C++-based programs in general. The Offload API allows the PPE code to send chunks of computation called *work requests* to the SPEs. A work request specifies the code to be executed along with the buffers containing the data to be operated on (read-only, read/write, and write-only buffers are possible). Each SPE has an SPE runtime that schedules the work requests passed to that SPE and takes care of transferring the data between the SPE's LS and main memory.

First, in the Charm++ model, data are already divided and encapsulated into migratable objects called chares. For the most part, each chare contains the data it needs. Through the use of pack/unpack (PUP) routines, each chare can be migrated between processors. In addition, the messages already encapsulate their data. As a message arrives, the entry method associated with it is executed. Typically, an entry method needs data from the message (input), modifies the contents of the chare (input/output), and creates new messages (output).

Second, since Charm++ is a message-driven model, each processor is constantly receiving messages. These messages are queued by the RTS as they arrive and are then executed one by one. The Charm++ RTS can take advantage of this by *peaking ahead* in the message queue. Each message is associated with a particular chare (object containing data) and a specific entry method for that chare (member function containing code to execute in reaction to receiving the message). By *peaking ahead* in the queue, the RTS *knows* what code and data will be needed in the near future (when the message reaches the head of the queue). This allows the RTS to preemptively start transferring the code and data to the SPE's LS through a DMA transaction while the SPE is still processing a previous message.

Third, Charm++ uses a technique called processor virtualization. The idea is to have the number of chares be much greater than the number of processors (e.g., 16 processors and 128 total chares). This allows the RTS to hide the latency of messages passing through the interconnect. As chare A is waiting for a message to arrive, at least one of the other chares, B, on the same processor is likely to already have a message waiting for it. B can then be *executed* while A waits for its message to arrive, thus helping to ensure that the processor is always performing useful computation. This technique can be applied to the SPEs as well. Since there are several chares on each processor, different chares with messages waiting in the message queue can be preemptively pushed down to the SPEs. When an SPE is finished executing its current entry method, it can immediately start at the next entry method as the data and/or code has already been placed in the SPE's LS. This technique can help hide the overheads caused by having to pass messages between processors and having to DMA code/data between the PPE and SPE.

13.7.3 Minimizing Transient Memory Usage Due to Messages

Many scientific applications consume large amount of transient memory due to communications. It is often found that this transient consumption of memory may lead to significant performance problems for the following reasons: one is that large transient memory might drive the program into disk swapping zone where performance will be dismal due to the severe overhead of disk swapping; another is that a large memory footprint might potentially bring poor cache performance. Furthermore, applications might fail to run as a result of insufficient swapping space. An extreme architecture case is the IBM BlueGene/L machine, where there is no virtual memory, with only 512 MB of physical memory available. With a object-oriented model of programming and a fine-grained computation, this transient memory may increase even more as the number of parallel entities increases. The Charm++ runtime provides a memory-aware control for such bursty memory usage patterns caused by communication, which helps applications with large memory footprint to keep within the bounds of physical memory and avoid disk swapping.

13.8 "ADAPTING" TO FAULTS

Current supercomputers already have tens of thousands of processors and even larger machines are planned for the future. The large number of components in these systems makes partial failures unavoidable. So, any application running for a significant time needs to be fault tolerant. The Charm++ runtime system provides multiple schemes for fault tolerance. These can be divided into two main categories: *proactive* and *reactive*.

Modern hardware and fault prediction schemes that can predict failures with a good degree of accuracy make proactive fault tolerance possible. Proactive fault tolerance [6] reacts to fault predictions for computation nodes by adapting the Charm++ run time system such that an application can continue even if the warned nodes fail. When a node is warned that it might crash, the Charm++ objects on it are migrated away. The runtime system is changed so that message delivery can continue seamlessly even if the warned node crashes. Reduction trees are also modified to remove the warned node from the tree so that its crash does not cause the tree to become disconnected. A node in the tree is replaced by one of its children. If the tree becomes too unbalanced, the whole reduction tree can be recreated from scratch. The proactive fault tolerance protocol does not require any extra nodes; it continues working on the remaining ones. It can deal with multiple simultaneous warnings, which is useful for real-life cases when all the nodes in a rack are about to go down. Evacuating objects due to a warning can lead to load imbalance. The measurement-based load balancing system described in Section 13.4 can be used to balance the load among the remaining processors after some processors are evacuated due to warnings.

Reactive fault tolerance is used when fault prediction for the proactive scheme is not available or has failed to predict a failure. Charm++ provides a number of reactive fault-tolerant schemes that help an application recover after a processor has crashed:

1. An automated traditional disk-based coordinated checkpoint protocol that allows an application to restart on a different number of processors
2. An in-remote-memory double checkpointing protocol
3. A message logging-based scalable fault tolerance protocol with fast restart

13.8.1 Automatic Checkpoint and Restart

The simplest fault tolerance protocol is a disk-based checkpoint and restart protocol for Charm++ and AMPI [12]. The user code calls a checkpoint method periodically to save the state of the computation to the parallel file system. In the case of AMPI, this is a collective call that all MPI threads in an application must call. Once all the threads have made the call, the runtime system packs the application’s state and sends it to the parallel file system. If some processors crash, the entire application is restarted from the previous checkpoint. Since AMPI and Charm++ code are independent of the physical location of Charm++ objects, the application can be restarted on a different number of processors than on which it was running earlier. This approach provides more flexibility to the scheduler of a large machine in the event of a crash.

13.8.2 Scalable Fault Tolerance with Fast Restart

The Charm++ runtime system provides a scalable fault tolerance protocol with fast restart by combining the ideas of processor virtualization and sender side message logging [5]. The messages and the sequence in which they are processed by the receiving virtual processors are stored on the sending virtual processor. Each physical processor also periodically takes checkpoints. If a processor crashes, the state of the crashed processor is restored on a fresh processor and recovery is started. During recovery, messages to the virtual processors on the restarted processor are sent again. After a crash a virtual processor re-executes messages in the same sequence as before and can thus recover its exact precrash state.

Processors other than the crashed ones are not rolled back to old checkpoints in our protocol, unlike checkpoint-based methods. This means that in the case of weakly coupled applications, the execution can continue on some processor while the crashed processor recovers. Though this is not possible for strongly coupled applications, not having to redo work on all processors prevents wastage of power and keeps the interconnect network free for the recovering processor. Moreover, the recovery of the crashed processor can be speeded up by distributing the virtual processors on it among other physical processors that are waiting for the crashed processor to catch up.

Virtualization affords us a number of potential benefits with respect to our message logging protocol. It is the primary idea behind faster restarts since it allows us to spread the work of the restarting processor among other processors. The facility of runtime load balancing can be utilized to restore any load imbalances produced by spreading the work of a processor among other processors. Virtualization also makes applications more latency tolerant by overlapping communication of one object with the computation of another. This helps us hide the increased latency caused by the sender-side message logging protocol. Although combining virtualization with message logging provides a number of advantages, it requires significant extensions to a basic sender-side message logging protocol. These extensions are primarily required for the case where a virtual processor sends a message to another one on the same physical processor.

13.9 LANGUAGE EXTENSIONS

13.9.1 MSA

Multiphase shared array (MSA) is a shared address space programming model motivated by the observation that a general shared variable that any thread can read or write is rarely needed and inefficient to support. MSA is not a complete model and is intended to be used in conjunction with other data exchange paradigms such as message passing.

MSA supports shared arrays of data elements that can be globally accessed by parallel entities such as objects, processes, or threads. The elements of an MSA can be one of the standard C++ intrinsic types, or a user-defined class with certain operations. In any phase, an MSA element can be accessed only in one of the following modes: *read-only*, *write* (updated by one writer), or *accumulate* (multiple commutative associative updates). Each array is in one mode at a time, and the mode can be changed dynamically over the life of the array. The mode is set implicitly by the first read, write, or accumulate operation on it after a sync point.

To achieve adaptivity in MSA, we use data virtualization by organizing MSA arrays into pages implemented as Charm++ migratable objects. We employ a software check of the page table at each access as the default mechanism. The cost of such checks on modern machines is low and may be tolerable in some parts of the application. To avoid this overhead, the compiler or user will insert page prefetches, and loops will be strip mined to match page boundaries.

13.9.2 Charisma++

A Charm++ program divides the computation into multiple independent arrays of chares. This enables automatic runtime optimizations, as well as modularity. However, for complex programs with a large number of object arrays, this comes at a cost of obscuring the overall flow of control. The class code for each object specifies, in a reactive manner, what the object will do when presented with a particular message. The overall behavior of the program, then, is an emergent property of this reactive specification. This clearly hurts the clarity of expression of the program, both for the programmer and its future reader.

In Charisma++ [18], which is a wrapper around Charm++, we make the communication more symmetric, with both sends and receives outside the object's class code. Each asynchronous method invocation is now seen to consume some data, *published* by other objects, and publishes some data itself, without specifying to whom it goes. The orchestration "script" then connects the produced and consumed data. With this notation, the programmer can describe the interaction among the parallel tasks in a producer-consumer fashion, as illustrated in the example in Figure 13.6 with a 5-point stencil calculation with 1D decomposition.

`J[i]` is an array of parallel objects, and `lb[i] and rb[i]` are the corresponding border data arrays. In each iteration, `J[i].compute` consumes the border columns from its right and left neighbors, and generates its left and right border information. Here, the values generated from one iteration are used in the next iteration, with a loop-carried data dependence. This is compiled to Charm++ style asynchronous method invocation. The notation can specify collectives such as multicast, reduction (e.g., maxError), and all-to-all.

Thus, Charisma++ allows expression of locality of data access and explicit communication (à la Charm++), along with global flow of control (à la HPF). As Charisma++ generates standard Charm++ programs, all the benefits of virtualization supported by Charm++ will be available to Charisma++ programmers.

```
while (maxError > threshold)
  foreach i in J
    <+maxError,lb[i],rb[i]> := J[i].compute(rb[i-1],lb[i+1]);
```

Figure 13.6 Charisma++ code for stencil calculation in producer–consumer notation.

13.9.3 Virtualizing Other Paradigms and Multiparadigm Programming

Different programming paradigms suite different types of algorithms and applications. Also, the programmer proficiency and preference may result in the variety of choice in programming languages and models. Especially, there are already many parallel libraries and applications developed with prevalent paradigms. Beyond the message passing paradigm (AMPI), we are providing adaptivity support for a broader spectrum of paradigms, for example, global address space (GAS) languages such as Global Array via a virtualized ARMCI implementation [14]. With multiparadigm programming supported on the adaptive runtime system, we aim at offering interoperability among these paradigms.

13.10 SUMMARY

We have painted a broad-brush sketch of our approach for supporting adaptivity in parallel programming. We showed that a relatively simple idea, that of over-decomposing a computation and allowing the runtime system to assign work and data units to processors, empowers the runtime system to adapt to a variety of exigencies. This idea of migratable objects has been implemented in Charm++, which sports indexed collections of migratable (C++) objects, interacting with each other via asynchronous method invocations and being scheduled in a message-driven manner. It has also been implemented in adaptive MPI, which provides the familiar MPI model, but implements MPI processes as migratable user-level threads. Newer programming models are being built atop these abstractions.

Once the RTS has been given a collection of such migratable entities, it can use introspection to adapt, to the application behavior as well as to the environment presented by the parallel machine. It can migrate them across processors for load balancing, migrate them to disk for automatic checkpointing or out-of-core execution, and double buffer them for exploiting scratchpad memories on Cell-like processors or prefetching into caches. It can shrink or expand the sets of processors used and tolerate faults without requiring all processors to run back to their checkpoints. It can automatically overlap communication and computation, adapting to communication latencies and response delays.

Of course, migratable objects only create a potential for the RTS to achieve this. Much research is needed on developing highly adaptive runtime techniques and strategies. Although we have demonstrated many such techniques, most of them may be considered low hanging fruit once we followed the basic idea of migratable objects. We think the Charm++ RTS represents a framework for experimenting with ever more advanced adaptation strategies, and we invite researchers to contribute such strategies, leveraging the framework and application base represented by Charm++/AMPI.

REFERENCES

1. G. Agha. *Actors: A Model of Concurrent Computation in Distributed Systems*. MIT Press, 1986.
2. Arvind and S. Brobst. The evolution of dataflow architectures: from static dataflow to P-RISC. *Int. J. High Speed Computing*, 5(2):125–153, 1993.
3. Milind Bhandarkar and L. V. Kalé. A parallel framework for explicit FEM. In M. Valero, V. K. Prasanna, and S. Vajpeyam, editors, *Proceedings of the International Conference on High Performance Computing (HiPC 2000)*, Vol. 1970, *Lecture Notes in Computer Science*. Springer Verlag, December 2000, pp. 385–395.
4. M. Bhandarkar, L. V. Kale, E. de Sturler, and J. Hoeflinger. Object-based adaptive load balancing for MPI programs. In *Proceedings of the International Conference on Computational Science*, San Francisco, CA, Vol. 2074, *Lecture Notes in Computer Science*, May 2001, pp. 108–117.
5. S. Chakravorty and L. V. Kale. A fault tolerant protocol for massively parallel machines. In *FTPDS Workshop for IPDPS 2004*. IEEE Press, 2004.
6. S. Chakravorty, C. L. Mendes, and L. V. Kalé. Proactive fault tolerance in MPI applications via task migration. In *HiPC*, Vol. 4297, *Lecture Notes in Computer Science*. Springer, 2006, pp. 485–496.
7. A. K. Ezzat, R. D. Bergeron, and J. L. Pokoski. Task allocation heuristics for distributed computing systems. In *Proceedings of International Conference on Distributed Computing Systems*, 1986, pp. 337–346.
8. I. Foster, C. Kesselman, R. Olson, and S. Tuecke. Nexus: an interoperability layer for parallel and distributed computer systems. Technical Report ANL/MCS-TM-189, Argonne National Laboratory, May 1994.
9. G. Gao, K. Theobald, A. Marquez, and T. Sterling. The HTMT program execution model, 1997.
10. A. Gursoy. Simplified expression of message driven programs and quantification of their impact on performance. PhD thesis, University of Illinois at Urbana-Champaign, June 1994. Also, Technical Report UIUCDCS-R-94-1852.
11. M. Hall, P. Kogge, J. Koller, P. Diniz, J. Chame, J. Draper, J. LaCoss, J. Granacki, A. Srivastava, W. Athas, J. Brockman, V. Freeh, J. Park, and J. Shin. Mapping irregular applications to DIVA, a PIM-based data-intensive architecture. In *Proceedings of the High Performance Networking and Computing Conference (SC'99)*, 1999.
12. C. Huang. System support for checkpoint and restart of Charm++ and AMPI applications. Master's thesis, Department of Computer Science, University of Illinois, 2004.
13. C. Huang, O. Lawlor, and L. V. Kalé. Adaptive MPI. In *Proceedings of the 16th International Workshop on Languages and Compilers for Parallel Computing (LCPC 2003)*, Vol. 2958, *Lecture Notes in Computer Science*, College Station, Texas, October 2003, pp. 306–322.
14. C. Huang, C. W. Lee, and L. V. Kalé. Support for adaptivity in ARMCI using migratable objects. In *Proceedings of Workshop on Performance Optimization for High-Level Languages and Libraries*, Rhodes Island, Greece, 2006.
15. C. Huang, G. Zheng, S. Kumar, and L. V. Kalé. Performance evaluation of adaptive MPI. In *Proceedings of ACM SIGPLAN Symposium on Principles and Practice of Parallel Programming 2006*, March 2006.
16. H. Hum. A design study of the earth multiprocessor, 1995.
17. L. V. Kalé. Comparing the performance of two dynamic load distribution methods. In *Proceedings of the 1988 International Conference on Parallel Processing*, St. Charles, IL, August 1988, pp. 8–11.
18. L. V. Kalé, M. Hills, and C. Huang. An orchestration language for parallel objects. In *Proceedings of 7th Workshop on Languages, Compilers, and Runtime Support for Scalable Systems (LCR 04)*, Houston, TX, October 2004.
19. L. V. Kalé. The virtualization model of parallel programming: runtime optimizations and the state of art. In *Los Alamos Computer Science Institute Symposium (LACSI 2001)*, Albuquerque, October 2002.

20. L. V. Kalé. Performance and productivity in parallel programming via processor virtualization. In *Proceedings of the First International Workshop on Productivity and Performance in High-End Computing (at HPCA 10)*, Madrid, Spain, February 2004.
21. L. V. Kalé, S. Kumar, and J. DeSouza. A malleable-job system for timeshared parallel machines. In *2nd IEEE/ACM International Symposium on Cluster Computing and the Grid (CCGrid 2002)*, May 2002.
22. L.V. Kale. The Chare Kernel parallel programming language and system. In *Proceedings of the International Conference on Parallel Processing*, Vol. 2, August 1990, pp. 17–25.
23. L.V. Kalé and S. Krishnan. CHARM++: a portable concurrent object oriented system based on C++. In A. Paepcke, editor, *Proceedings of OOPSLA'93*, ACM Press, September 1993, pp. 91–108.
24. R.M. Keller, F.C.H. Lin, and J. Tanaka. Rediflow Multiprocessing. *Digest of Papers COMPCON, Spring'84*, February 1984, pp. 410–417.
25. O. Lawlor and L. V. Kalé. Supporting dynamic parallel object arrays. In *Proceedings of ACM 2001 Java Grande/ISCOPE Conference*, Stanford, CA, Jun 2001, pp. 21–29.
26. R. Namyst and J.-F. Méhaut. PM^2: parallel multithreaded machine. A computing environment for distributed architectures. In *Parallel Computing: State-of-the-Art and Perspectives*, Vol. 11, *Advances in Parallel Computing, Proceedings of the Conference ParCo'95*, September 19–22 1995, Ghent, Belgium, Amsterdam. Elsevier, North-Holland, February 1996, pp. 279–285.
27. S. Paranjpye. A checkpoint and restart mechanism for parallel programming systems. Master's thesis, University of Illinois at Urbana-Champaign, 2000.
28. M. Potnuru. Automatic out-of-core exceution support for Charm++. Master's thesis, University of Illinois at Urbana-Champaign, 2003.
29. V. A. Saletore. A distributed and adaptive dynamic load balancing scheme for parallel processing of medium-grain tasks. In *Proceedings of the 5th Distributed Memory Computing Conference (5th DMCC'90)*, Vol. II, *Architecture Software Tools and Other General Issues*, Charleston, SC. IEEE, April 1990, pp. 994–999.
30. S. Krishnan and L. V. Kale. A parallel array abstraction for data-driven objects. In *Proceedings of Parallel Object-Oriented Methods and Applications Conference*, Santa Fe, NM, February 1996.
31. W. W. Shu and L. V. Kalé. A dynamic load balancing strategy for the Chare Kernel system. In *Proceedings of Supercomputing '89*, November 1989, pp. 389–398.
32. G. Zheng, O. S. Lawlor, and L. V. Kalé. Multiple flows of control in migratable parallel programs. In *2006 International Conference on Parallel Processing Workshops (ICPPW'06)*, Columbus, OH. IEEE Computer Society, August 2006, pp. 435–444.

Chapter 14

The Seine Data Coupling Framework for Parallel Scientific Applications

Li Zhang, Ciprian Docan, and Manish Parashar

14.1 INTRODUCTION

Scientific and engineering simulations are becoming increasingly sophisticated as they strive to achieve more accurate solutions to realistic models of complex phenomena. A key aspect of these emerging simulations is the modeling of multiple interacting physical processes that make up the phenomena being modeled. This leads to challenging requirements for coupling between multiple physical models and associated parallel codes, which may execute independently and in a distributed manner. For example, in plasma science, an integrated predictive plasma edge simulation couples an edge turbulence code with a core turbulence code through common "mortar" grids at the spatial interface [17]. Similarly, in geosciences, multiple scales in the domain and multiple physics models are coupled via shared boundaries between neighboring entities (grid blocks) [18]. These coupled systems provide the individual models with a more realistic simulation environment, allowing them to be interdependent on and interact with other physics models in the coupled system and to react to dynamically changing boundary conditions.

As mentioned above, individual modules in a coupled system interact with each other by sharing data on shared regions of the domain, such as a 1D boundary, a 2D interface, or a 3D volume. The interactions between individual modules on these shared regions depend on different factors for different application domains. For

Advanced Computational Infrastructures For Parallel and Distributed Adaptive Applications. Edited by Manish Parashar and Xiaolin Li

example, the interactions can be based on relative physical positions of the interacting entities and affected by other physical features represented by various parameters, such as velocity or temperature. These parameters represent the degrees of freedom, based on which the interactions must proceed. Therefore, the interactions can be viewed as occurring in an abstract multidimensional space that represents the degrees of freedom, that is, each dimension of the abstract space corresponds to a degree of freedom and the number of dimensions corresponds to the number of degrees of freedom. Entities may "move" around within the multidimensional abstract space and interactions may happen between entities in the space when certain criteria are satisfied.

Data coupling in scientific computing refers to the sharing of data between coupled modules during their interactions. To provide the desirable support for interactions in a coupled system, the coupling mechanism is required to provide the appropriate level of abstraction in order to be able to handle the complexity that arises from the code coupling and model coupling requirements, to use the right coupling level (in terms of tight coupling or loose coupling) between individual modules, and to present a friendly interface to user applications.

Existing coupling research has divided the coupling problem into distinct parts. At a higher level, model or code coupling deals with how to couple individual models (and their implementations) together and what parameters should be coupled. This level involves domain-specific aspects and information. At a lower level, research has focused on issues such as parallel data redistribution, which addresses the problem of transferring data between individual models running on systems with different numbers of processors. Although addressing these two issues as separate problems may make them easier to tackle, it can also limit the effectiveness and flexibility of the overall solution.

This is because the low level is formulated as a generic data redistribution support, which is supposed to provide general parallel data redistribution support to various coupling scenarios for different fields of applications. However, when the low-level data redistribution can handle only coupling scenarios with limited complexity level, the flexibility achievable by this approach is limited by the low-level support.

Clearly, forcibly separating the coupling problem may not be the optimum way to approach the problem. As mentioned, code/model coupling requirements call for data coupling support that (1) can handle the complexity raised from the interactions between individual models, (2) provides the appropriate cohesion level between models, and (3) presents a user-friendly interface. Furthermore, conceptually the interactions occur in an abstract space mapped from the degree of freedom of the interaction. It is then spontaneous to use a multidimensional abstract space to facilitate the interaction. The idea is to create a geometry-based shared space abstraction to emulate the abstract degree of freedom interaction space. Since the interactions are based on the degree of freedom, they can be described using tuples with each tuple field corresponding to one degree or dimension in the abstract space. Interactions will be based on the tuples described in such manner. Because of the expressiveness of tuple, the complexity level of interactions will be much less limited because given the expressiveness of tuples, they are capable of describing complex interactions. Furthermore, in a shared space model, the interactions are automatically decoupled so that the producer and the consumer of tuples do not need to know of each other or synchronize with each other either temporarily or spatially. Therefore, it provides a loose coupling between individual models. Loose coupling is desirable in a coupled system because one module does not have to be concerned with the internal implementation of another module. With loose coupling, a change in one module will not require a change in the implementation of another module. This is important especially in coupled systems that usually involve cooperative efforts, each focusing on one module. Consequently, loose coupling offers more flexibility to individual modules. Finally, the shared space abstraction presents an extremely simple set of space access primitives for reading or writing data from/to the shared space.

The geometry-based shared space is based on the tuple space model, in which processes interact by sharing tuples in an associatively shared tuple space. However, implementation of generic and global tuple spaces remains a challenge. The overheads are caused by the generic tuple sharing that requires pattern matching on tuple fields and global tuple sharing that requires operations to be potentially on the entire system. In order to make the model practical for parallel scientific applications, customizations are made to specialize the generic and global tuple sharing into domain-specific tuple sharing, that is, the geometry-based shared space. The geometry-based shared space is able to extract the domain-specific information necessary for coupling from the application by using tuples to describe the degree of freedom. And interactions are usually localized to subspaces of the entire shared space, therefore, avoiding global tuple sharing that impedes scalability of the system.

We present a coupling framework that realizes the geometry-based shared space abstraction, which is able to capture the conceptual essence of data coupling, that is, module interactions proceed in an abstract degree of freedom space, and provide such an abstract space to facilitate the interactions. The framework is based on the Seine geometry-based interaction model [12, 20], which is motivated by two observations about parallel scientific applications: (1) formulations of these scientific and engineering applications are based on multidimensional geometric discretizations of the problem domain (e.g., grid or mesh) and (2) couplings and interactions in these applications can be defined based on geometric relations in this discretization (e.g., intersecting or adjacent regions). When targeting at data coupling, these observations are extended to the following: (1) model interactions in data coupling are based on an abstract degree of freedom space, (2) the abstract degree of freedom space can be emulated by a geometry-based space, and (3) module interactions are typically localized to a subspace of the abstract space. Seine provides a geometry-based virtual shared space interaction abstraction. This abstraction derives from the tuple space model. However, instead of implementing a general and global interaction space (as in the tuple model), Seine presents an abstraction of transient geometry-based interaction spaces, each of which is localized to a subregion of the overall geometric domain. This allows the abstraction to be efficiently and scalably implemented and allows interactions to be decoupled at the application level. A Seine interaction space is defined to cover a closed region of the application domain described by an interval of coordinates in each dimension and can be identified by any set of coordinates contained in the region.

The Seine geometry-based coupling framework differs from existing approaches in several ways. First, it provides a simple but powerful abstraction for interaction and coupling in the form of the virtual geometry-based shared space. Processes register geometric regions of interest and associatively read and write data associated with the registered regions from/to the space in a decoupled manner. Second, it supports efficient local computation of communication schedules using lookups into a directory implemented as a distributed hash table. The index space of the hash table is directly constructed from the geometry of the application using Hilbert space-filling curves (SFC) [14]. Processes register their regions of interest with the directory layer, and the directory layer automatically computes communication schedules based on overlaps between the registered geometric regions. Registering processes do not need to know of or explicitly synchronize with other processes during registration and the computation of communication schedules. Finally, it supports efficient and low-overhead processor-to-processor socket-based data streaming and adaptive buffer management. The Seine model and the Seine-based coupling framework are designed to complement existing parallel programming models and can work in tandem with systems such as MPI, PVM, and OpenMP.

We present in this chapter the design, implementation, and experimental evaluation of the Seine-based coupling framework. The implementation is based on the DoE common component architecture (CCA) [5] and enables coupling within and across CCA-based simulations. The experimental evaluation measures the performance of the framework for various data redistribution patterns and different data sizes. The results demonstrate the performance and overheads of the framework.

14.2 BACKGROUND AND RELATED WORK

Code or model coupling consists of numerical, algorithmic, and computational aspects. As mentioned, the computation aspect has been separated out from the rest of the problem to be solved by computer scientists, that is, the parallel data redistribution (or the $M \times N$ problem). The goal is to provide a general support for parallel data redistribution to various applications fields. The $M \times N$ support has been formulated as a concrete problem, that is, to move parallel data among coupled processes. Underlying this concreteness is the simplification of the problem: it is assumed that the coupled sides have the same domain definition and domain decomposition, or the same numerical grids and grid naming scheme. A number of recent projects have investigated the problem. These include model coupling toolkit (MCT) [7], InterComm [4], parallel application workspace (PAWS) [3], collaborative user migration, user library for visualization and steering (CUMULVS) [2], distributed component architecture (DCA) [9], and SciRun2 [11], each with different foci and approach. In the context of component-based systems such as CCA, parallel data redistribution support is typically encapsulated into a standard component that can then be composed with other components to realize different coupling scenarios. An alternate approach embeds the parallel data redistribution support into a parallel remote method invocation (PRMI) [10] mechanism. This PRMI-based approach addresses issues other than just data redistributions, such as remote method invocation semantic for nonuniformly distributed components.

The projects based on these two approaches are summarized into (1) common component architecture and (2) parallel remote method invocations as follows. Projects such as MCT, InterComm, PAWS, CUMULVS, and DDB (distributed data broker) use the component-based approach. Some of these systems have only partial or implicit support for parallel data redistribution and can support only a limited set of data redistribution patterns. Projects such as PAWS and InterComm fully address the parallel data redistribution problem. These systems can support random data redistribution patterns. PRMI-based projects include SciRun2, DCA, and XCAT.

While all these existing coupling frameworks address the parallel data redistribution problem, they differ in the approaches they use to compute communication schedules, the data redistribution patterns that they support, and the abstractions they provide to the application layer. Some of the existing systems gather distribution information from all the coupled models at each processor and then locally compute data redistribution schedules. This implies a global synchronization across all the coupled systems, which can be expensive and limit scalability. Furthermore, abstractions provided by most existing systems are based on message passing, which requires explicitly matching sends and receives and sometimes synchronous data transfers. Moreover, expressing very general redistribution patterns using message passing-type abstractions can be quite cumbersome. Existing systems are briefly described below:

InterComm [4]: InterComm is a framework that couples parallel components and enables efficient communication in the presence of complex data distributions for multidimensional array data structures. It provides the support for direct data transfer between different parallel programs. InterComm supports parallel data redistribution in several steps: (1) locating the data to be transferred within the local memories of each program, (2) generating communication schedules (the patterns of interprocessor communication) for all processes, and (3) transferring the data using the schedules. Note that these are three common steps in various data coupling frameworks. But different frameworks may have different ways to compute communication schedules. Furthermore, some have support for only limited data redistribution patterns. InterComm supports data distributions with any complex patterns. It uses a linearization space to find the mapping between two parallel data objects. The Seine–Coupe approach in addressing the parallel data redistribution problem has similarity to InterComm in that Seine–Coupe also uses a linearization space to find the mapping between data objects. The differences between them include how the linearization is done, how the communication schedule is computed, and the abstractions they present to the application.

PAWS [3]: PAWS is a framework for coupling parallel applications within a component-like model. It supports redistribution of scalar values and parallel multidimensional array data structures. The shape of a PAWS subdomain can be arbitrarily defined by an application. Multidimensional arrays in PAWS can be generally partitioned and distributed completely. It uses a process as a central controller to link applications and parallel data structures in the applications. PAWS controller establishes a connection between those data structures using information in its registry. The controller organizes and registers each of the applications participating in the framework. Through the controller, component applications ("tasks") register the data structures that should be shared with other components. Tasks are created and connections are established between registered data structures via the script interface of the controller. The controller provides for dynamic data connection and disconnection, so that applications can be launched independently of both one another and the controller. PAWS uses point-to-point transfers to move segments of data from one node to remote nodes directly and in parallel. PAWS uses Nexus to permit communication across heterogeneous architectures.

MCT [7]: MCT is a system developed for the Earth System Modeling Framework (ESMF). The system addresses the general model coupling problem, with the parallel data redistribution tightly integrated into the system. MCT defines a globalSegmentMap to describe each continuous chunk of memory for the data structure in each process. Using globalSegmentMap, MCT can generate a router or a communication scheduler, which tells processes how to transfer data elements between a simulation component and the flux coupler. Note that this indicates that the transfers between two physics components are executed through the flux coupler.

CUMULVS [2]: CUMULVS is a middleware library aimed to provide support for remote visualization and steering of parallel applications and sharing parallel data structures between programs. It supports multidimensional arrays like PAWS; however, arrays cannot be distributed in a fully general way. A receiver program in CUMULVS is not a parallel program. It specifies the data it requires in a request that is sent to the parallel sender program. After receiving the request, the sender program generates a sequence of connection calls to transfer the data. CUMULVS essentially provide $M \times 1$ parallel data redistribution support, not full $M \times N$ support.

DDB [15]: DDB handles distributed data exchanges between ESM (Earth Science Model) components. DDB is a general-purpose tool for coupling multiple, possibly heterogeneous, parallel models. It is implemented as a library used by all participating elements, one of which serves as a distinguished process during a startup phase preceding the main computation. This "registration broker" process correlates offers to produce quantities with requests to consume them, forwards the list of intersections to each of the producers, and informs each consumer of how many pieces to expect. After the initial phase, the registration broker may participate as a regular member of the computation. A library of data translation routines is included in the DDB to support exchanges of data between models using different computational grids. Having each producer send directly to each consumer conserves bandwidth, reduces memory requirements, and minimizes the delay that would otherwise occur if a centralized element were to reassemble each of the fields and retransmit them.

XChange [22]: The XChange project uses the common component approach to embed the communicating applications into components, but it enables the communication between components through an anonymous publish/subscribe model, as opposed to "Ports". To enable the data exchange across components, each component has to initially register the metadata information about the data it has to share with a central service. The system uses a global description of the data distribution that it expresses through the metadata information. The metadata information contains the type, the size, and the distribution of the data for a component, that is, the start index, the length, and the stripe for an array or a matrix. The system computes the communication schedules based on the registered metadata information and sends to each component the schedules it needs. The components exchange the data directly in a peer-to-peer manner. The components can have any data distribution, and the system has full support for the $M \times N$ problem.

MOCCA [23]: The MOCCA project implements a layer for component cooperation that is compatible with the CCA specifications and is based on the H2O framework. H2O is a lightweight sharing resource framework similar with GLOBVS. MOCCA framework enables interaction between components that live on the same host or different hosts, and between components written in different programming languages. The application components are instantiated by a container component that also connects the components ports for communication. The components exchange data through the connected ports in a peer-to-peer manner. For components that live on the same host, MOCCA invokes port methods as local calls, and for remote components, it uses the remote method invocation mechanism of the underlying framework.

Phylospaces [24]: The Phylospaces project uses the tuple space coordination abstraction to implement a parallel and cooperative version of a sequential heuristic algorithm for phylogeny reconstruction. Phylogeny is an evolutionary tree that tries to relate the common ancestors of a set of organisms. The algorithm proposed uses the divide and conquer technique to distribute the searching space across multiple searcher/workers. The workers coordinate and communicate through the logically shared memory, that is, the tuple space. The experimental evaluation of the system shows an order of magnitude improvement over existing sequential implementation of the algorithm.

SCIRun2 [11]: SCIRun2 project implements a combination between components and parallel remote method invocation. It uses the modularization of CCA, and provides a framework for applications to run as components, and provides remote method invocation abstractions for component communication. SCIRun2 framework introduces support for parallel components; that is, components that can run SPMD-type applications. It allows data redistribution between parallel components through remote method invocation calls. The parallel components can have different distributions, for example, two parallel components can run on different number of nodes, and so it provides full support for the $M \times N$ data redistribution problem.

14.3 THE SEINE GEOMETRY-BASED COUPLING FRAMEWORK

Seine is a dynamic geometry-based coupling/interaction framework for parallel scientific and engineering applications. It is derived from the tuple space model and provides the abstraction of a geometry-based virtual shared space, allowing it to support decoupled and extremely dynamic communication and coordination patterns presented during the interaction between coupled processes. It allows couplings and interactions to be defined based on geometric relations in the abstract geometry-based space and utilizes the fact that interaction and coupling are localized to a subspace of the abstract space. This enables efficient and scalable implementations. Seine spaces can be dynamically created and destroyed. Finally, Seine complements existing parallel programming models and can coexist with them during program execution. The Seine interaction/coupling model and framework are described in detail in this section.

14.3.1 The Seine Geometry-Based Coupling Model

Conceptually, the Seine coupling/interaction model is based on the tuple space model where entities interact with each other by sharing objects in a logically shared space. However, there are key differences between the Seine model and the general tuple space model. In the general tuple space model, the tuple space is global, spans the entire application domain, can be accessed by all the nodes in computing environments, and support a very generic tuple-matching scheme. These characteristics have presented several implementation challenges for the general tuple model. In contrast, Seine defines a virtual dynamic shared space that spans a geometric region, which is a subset of the entire problem domain, and is accessible to only the dynamic subset of nodes to which the geometric region is mapped. Furthermore, objects in the Seine space are geometry based; that is each object has a geometric descriptor, which specifies the region in the application domain that the object is associated with. Applications use these geometric descriptors to associatively *put* and *get* objects to/from a Seine space. Interactions are naturally decoupled.

Seine provides a small set of very simple primitives, which are listed in Table 14.1. The *register* operation allows a process to dynamically register a region of interest, which causes it to join an appropriate existing space or a new space to be created if one does not exist. The *put* operator is used to write an object into the space, while the *get* operator reads a matching object from the space, if one exists. The *get* operation is blocking; that is, it blocks until a matching object is *put* into the space. *rd* copies a geometric object from Seine without removing it. It is nonblocking; that is, it returns immediately with an appropriate return code if no matching object exists. The *deregister* operation allows a process to deregister a previously registered region. The operation of Seine is described in more detail in this section.

Table 14.1 Primitives of the Seine Geometry-Based Coupling/Interaction Framework

Primitives	Description
init(bootstrap server IP)	Uses a bootstrap mechanism to initialize the Seine runtime system
register(object geometric descriptor)	Registers a region with Seine
put(object geometric descriptor, object)	Inserts a geometric object into Seine
get(object geometric descriptor, object)	Retrieves and removes a geometric object from Seine This call will block until a matching object is *put*
rd(object geometric descriptor, object)	Copies a geometric object from Seine without removing it Multiple *rd* can be simultaneously invoked on an object. It returns immediately if the object searched for does not exist
deregister(object geometric descriptor)	Deregisters a region from Seine

14.3.2 Design of the Seine Geometry-Based Coupling Framework

A schematic of the Seine architecture is presented in Figure 14.1. The framework consists of three key components: (1) a distributed *directory layer* that enables the registration of spaces and the efficient lookup of objects using their geometry descriptors; (2) *storage layer* consisting of local storage at each processor associated with a shared space and used to store its shared objects; (3) a *communication layer* that provides efficient data transfer between processors.

Directory Layer: The Seine distributed directory layer is used to (1) detect geometric relationships between shared geometry-based objects, (2) manage the creation of shared spaces based on the geometric relationship detected so that all objects

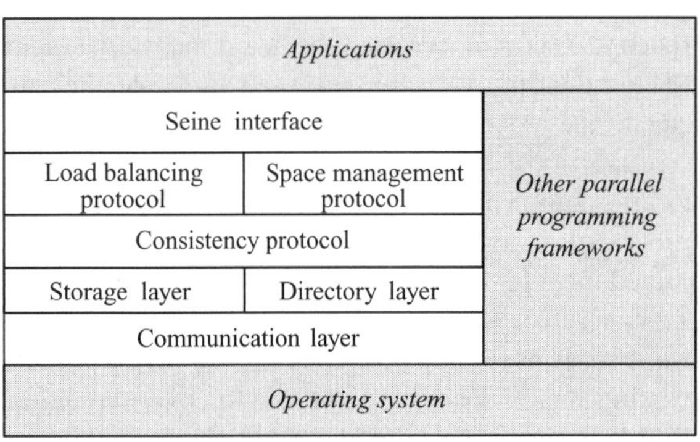

Figure 14.1 Architecture of the Seine geometry-based coupling/interaction framework [13].

associated with intersecting geometric regions are part of a single shared space, (3) manage the operation of geometry-based shared spaces during their lifetimes including the merging of multiple spaces into a single space and the splitting of a space into multiple spaces, and (4) manage the destruction of a shared space when it is no longer needed.

The directory layer is essentially a distributed hash table where the index space of the table is directly constructed from the geometry of the discretized computational domain using the Hilbert SFC. SFC [14] are a class of locality preserving mappings from d-dimensional space to one dimensional space, that is, $N^d \rightarrow N^1$, such that each point in N^d is mapped to a unique point or index in N^1. Using this mapping, a point in the N^d can be described by its spatial or d-dimensional coordinates, or by the length along the one-dimensional index measured from one of its ends. The construction of SFCs is recursive and the mapping functions are computationally inexpensive and consist of bit-level interleaving operations and logical manipulations of the coordinates of a point in multidimensional space. SFCs are locality preserving in that points that are close together in the one-dimensional space are mapped from points that are close together in the d-dimensional space.

The Hilbert SFC is used to map the d-dimensional coordinate space of the computational domain to the one-dimensional index space of the hash table. The index space is then partitioned and distributed to the processors in the system. As a result, each processor stores a span of the index space and is responsible for the corresponding region of the d-dimensional application domain. The processor manages the operation of the shared space in that region, including space creation, merges, splits, memberships, and deletions. As mentioned above, object sharing in Seine is based on their geometric relationships. To share objects corresponding to a specific region in the domain, a processor must first register the region of interest with the Seine runtime. A directory service daemon at each processor serves registration requests for regions that overlap with the geometric region and the corresponding index span mapped to that processor. Note that the registered spaces may not be uniformly distributed in the domain, and as a result, registration load must be balanced while mapping and possibly remapping index spans to processors.

To register a geometric region, the Seine runtime system first maps the region in the d-dimensional coordinate space to a set of intervals in the one-dimensional index space using the Hilbert SFC. The index intervals are then used to locate the processor(s) to which they are mapped. The process of locating corresponding directory processors is efficient and only requires local computation. The directory service daemon at each processor maintains information about currently registered shared spaces and associated regions at the processor. Index intervals corresponding to registered spaces at a processor are maintained in an interval tree. A new registration request is directed to the appropriate directory service daemon(s). The request is compared with existing spaces using the interval tree. If overlapping regions exist, a union of these regions is computed and the existing shared spaces are updated to cover the union. Note that this might cause previously separate spaces to be merged. If no overlapping regions exist, a new space is created.

Storage Layer: The Seine storage layer consists of the local storage associated with registered shared spaces. The storage for a shared space is maintained at each of the processors that has registered the space. Shared objects are stored at the processors that own them and are not replicated. When an object is written into the space, the update has to be reflected to all processors with objects whose geometric regions overlap with that of the object being inserted. This is achieved by propagating the object or possibly corresponding parts of the object (if the data associated with the region is decomposable based on regions, such as multidimensional arrays) to the processors that have registered overlapping geometric regions. Such an update propagation mechanism is used to maintain consistency of the shared space. As each shared space only spans a local communication region, it typically maps to a small number of processors and as a result update propagation does not result in significant overheads. Further, unique tags are used to enable multiple distinct objects to be associated with the same geometric region. Note that Seine does not impose any restrictions on the type of application data structures used. However, the current implementation is optimized for multidimensional arrays.

Communication Layer: Since coupling and parallel data redistribution for scientific application typically involves communicating relatively large amounts of data, efficient communication and buffer management are critical. Furthermore, this communication has to be directly between individual processors. Currently, Seine maintains the communication buffers at each processor as a queue, and multiple sends are overlapped to better utilize available bandwidth [16]. Adaptive buffer management strategies described in Ref. [16] are currently being integrated.

14.3.3 Coupling Parallel Scientific Applications Using Seine

A simple parallel data redistribution scenario shown in Figure 14.2 is used to illustrate the operation of the Seine coupling framework. In this scenario, data associated with two-dimensional computational domain of size 120×120 are coupled between two parallel simulations running on four and nine processors. The data decomposition for each simulation and the required parallel data redistribution are shown in the figure. Simulation M is decomposed into four blocks, for example, $M.1 \cdots M.4$ and

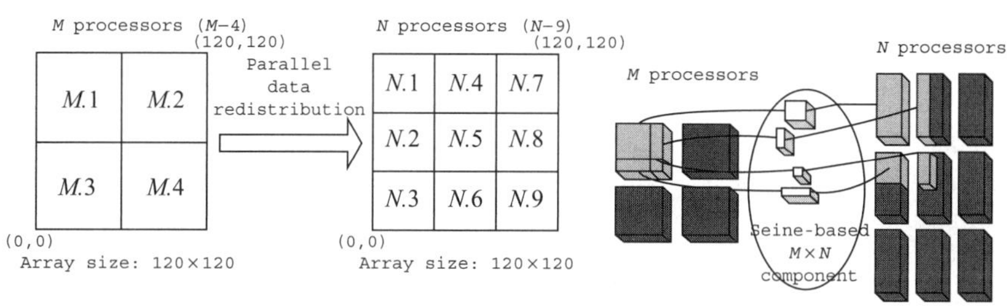

Figure 14.2 An illustrative example [19].

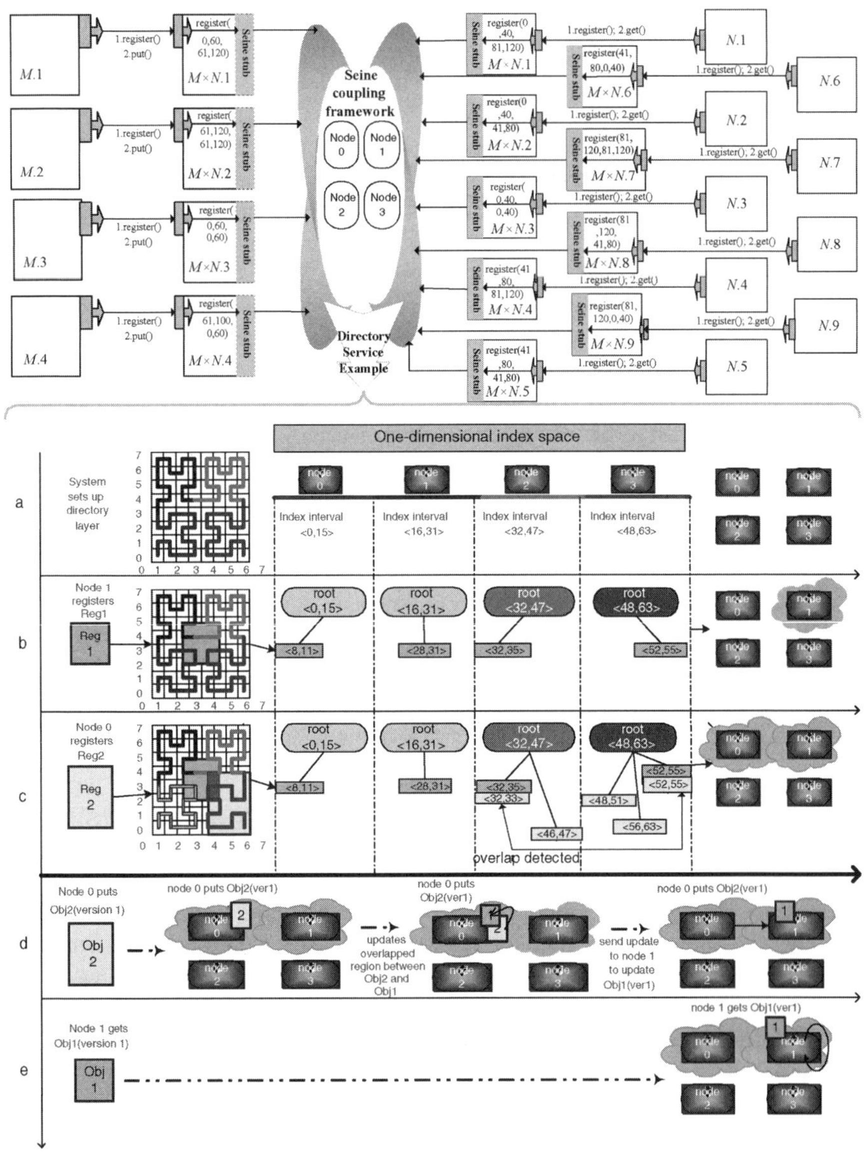

Figure 14.3 Operation of coupling and parallel data redistribution using Seine [19].

simulation N is decomposed into nine blocks, for example, $N.1 \cdots N.9$. The Seine coupling framework coexists with one of the simulations and is also distributed across four processors in this example. This is shown at the top portion of Figure 14.3. Note that the processors running Seine may or may not overlap with the processors running the simulation codes. Figure 14.3 also illustrates the steps involved in coupling and parallel data redistribution using Seine, which are described below.

The initialization of the Seine runtime using the *init* operator is shown in Figure 14.3a. During the initialization process, the directory structure is constructed by mapping the two-dimensional coordinate space to a one-dimensional index using the Hilbert SFC and distributing index intervals across the processors.

In Figure 14.3b, processor 1 registers an interaction region R1 (shown using a darker shade in the figure) at the center of the domain. Since this region maps to index intervals that span all four processors, the registration request is sent to the directory service daemon at each of these processors. Each daemon services the request and records the relevant registered interval in its local interval tree. Once the registration is complete, a shared space corresponding to the registered region is created at processor 1 (shown as a cloud on the right in the figure).

In Figure 14.3c, another processor, processor 0, registers region R2 (shown using a lighter shade in the figure). Once again, the region is translated into index intervals and corresponding registration request is forwarded to appropriate directory service daemons. Using the existing intervals in its local interval tree, the directory service daemons detect that the newly registered region overlaps with an existing space. As a result, processor 0 joins the existing space and the region associated with the space is updated to become the union of the two registered regions. The shared space also grows to span both processors. As more regions are registered, the space is expanded if these regions overlap with the existing region, or new spaces are created if the regions do not overlap.

Once the shared space is created, processors can share geometry-based objects using the space. This is illustrated in Figures 14.3d and e. In Figure 14.3d, processor 0 uses the *put* operation to insert object 2 into the shared space. As there is an overlap between the regions registered by processors 0 and 1, the update to object 2 is propagated from processor 0 to processor 1. The propagated update may only consist of the data corresponding to the region of overlap, for example, a subarray if the object is an array. In Figure 14.3e, processor 1 retrieves object 1 using a local *get* operation.

Building Coupled Simulations Using the Seine Abstractions: Seine provides a virtual dynamic geometry-based shared space abstraction to the parallel scientific applications. Developing coupled simulations using this abstraction consists of the following steps. First, the coupled simulations register their geometric regions of interests in the geometry-based shared space with Seine. The registration phase detects geometric relationships between registered regions and results in the creation of a virtual shared space localized to the region and the derivation of associated communication schedules. Coupling data between simulations consists of one simulation writing the data into the space, along with a geometric descriptor describing the region that it belongs to, and the other simulation independently reading data from the space with an appropriate geometric descriptor. The communication schedule associated with the space and the Seine communication layer is used to set up parallel point-to-point communication channels for direct data transfer between source and destination processors. The associated parallel data redistribution is conceptually illustrated in Figure 14.2.

Computation of Communication Schedules: Communication schedules in the context of coupling and parallel data redistribution refer to the sequence of messages required to correctly move data among coupled processes [10]. As mentioned above, these schedules are computed in Seine during registration using the Hilbert SFC-based linearization of the multidimensional application domain coordinate space. When a region is registered, the Seine directory layer uses the distributed hash table to route the registration request to corresponding directory service node(s). The directory service node is responsible for detecting overlaps or geometric relationships between registered regions efficiently. This is done by detecting overlaps in corresponding one-dimensional index intervals using the local interval tree. Note that all registration requests that are within a particular region of the application domain are directed to the same Seine directory service node(s), and as a result, the node(s) can correctly compute the required schedules. This is in contrast to most existing systems that require information about the distributions of all the coupled processes to be gathered.

Data Transfer: When an object is written into a space, Seine propagates the object (or possibly the appropriate part of the object, e.g., if the object is an array) to update remote objects based on the relationships between registered geometric regions, using the communication layer.

14.4 PROTOTYPE IMPLEMENTATION AND PERFORMANCE EVALUATION

14.4.1 A CCA-Based Prototype Implementation

The first prototype implementation of the Seine coupling framework is based on the DoE common component architecture [5] and enables coupling within and across CCA-based simulations. In CCA, components communicate with each other through *ports*. There are two basic types of *ports*: the *provides* port and the *uses* port. Connections between components are achieved by wiring between a *provides* port on one component and a *uses* port on the other component. The component can invoke methods on the *uses* port once it is connected to a *provides* port. CCA ports are specified using the scientific interface definition language (SIDL) [6]. CCA frameworks can be distributed or direct connected. In a direct connected framework all components in one process live in the same address space. Communication between components, or the port invocation, is local to the process.

The Seine coupling framework was encapsulated as a CCA-compliant component within the CCAFFEINE direct-connected CCA framework and is used to support coupling and parallel data redistribution between multiple instances of the framework, each executing as an independent simulation, as well as within a single framework executing in the multiple component–multiple data (MCMD) mode. The former setup is illustrated in Figure 14.4. In the figure, cohorts of component A1 need to redistribute data to cohorts of component B1; similarly, cohorts of component B2 need to redistribute data to cohorts of component A2. To enable data redistribution between framework instances A and B (executing on M and N processors, respectively), a third framework instance, C, containing the Seine coupling component is first instantiated.

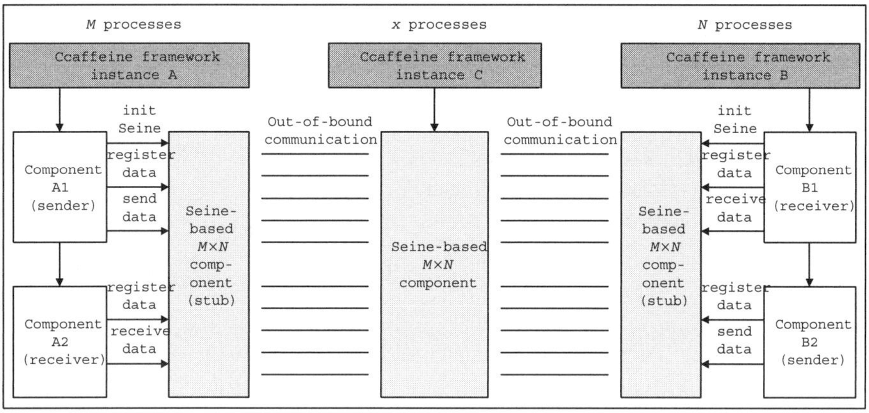

Figure 14.4 $M \times N$ data redistribution between CCA frameworks using the Seine coupling component [19].

This framework executes on X processors, which may or may not overlap with the M and N processors of frameworks A and B. The Seine coupling component handles registrations and maintains the Seine directory. Frameworks A and B initiate Seine stubs, which register with the Seine coupling component. The ports defined by the Seine coupling and stub components are *register*, *put*, and *get*. The operation is as follows. To achieve A1–B1 coupling, component A1 registers its region of interest using the *register* port of its stub and invokes the *put* port to write data. Similarly, component B1 independently registers its region of interest using the *register* port of its stub and invokes the *get* port. The *register* request is forwarded to the Seine coupling component, and if there is an overlap between their registered regions, at the *put* request from A1, the data written by A1 is directly and appropriately forwarded to Seine stubs at B1 by Seine stubs at A1. At the *get* request from B1, the data received by Seine stubs at B1 are copied from Seine's buffer. Note that A1 does not have to be aware of B1 or its data distribution. We have conducted a set of experiments using this prototype implementation. In these experiments, we used three-dimensional array as the data to be redistributed. In other words, the three-dimensional array index space is mapped as the abstract space for the data coupling. When such mapping is used, it is assumed that coupled sides have the same domain definition and decomposition or same grid and grid naming scheme.

Experiment with Different Data Redistribution Scenarios: In this experiment, a three-dimensional array of size $120 \times 120 \times 120$ is redistributed to 27 processors from 2, 4, 8, and 16 processors, respectively, that is, $M = 2, 4, 8$, and 16 and $N = 27$. Data in the array are of type double. The distribution of the array is (block, block, block)[1] on the x-, y-, z-axis, respectively, on both the sender and receiver ends,

[1]Block distribution along each dimension. This notation for distribution patterns is borrowed from High Performance Fortran and is described in Ref. [1].

Table 14.2 Cost in Seconds of Computing Registration and Data Transfer for Different Data Redistribution Scenarios

Array size: 120 × 120 × 120; data type: double
Distribution type (x–y–z):
M side: block–block–collapsed (Cases I and II)
or block–block–block (Cases III and IV)
N side: block–block–block

$M \times N$	Case I 2 × 27	Case II 4 × 27	Case III 8 × 27	Case IV 16 × 27
Registration	5.6725	3.6197	2.7962	2.273
Data transfer	0.6971	0.3381	0.1636	0.1045
M side (put)	0.6971	0.3381	0.1636	0.1045
N side (get)	0.0012	0.0012	0.0012	0.0012

except that for case I and II, (block, block, collapsed) [2] is used at the sender end. The registration, data transfer, and send (put) and receive (get) costs are listed in Table 14.2. The application components do not explicitly compute communication schedules when using Seine. However, from their perspective, the time spent on computing communication schedule is equivalent to the time it takes to register their region of interest, that is, the cost of the *register* operation, which is a one-time cost. Since this cost depends on the region and its overlap, it will be different for different components, and the cost listed in Table 14.2 is the average cost. As the table shows, for a given total data size to be redistributed, the average registration cost decreases as the number of processors involved increases. The reason for this decrease is that as the number of processors involved in registration increases, each processor is assigned a correspondingly smaller portion of the array. As a result, each processor registers a smaller region. Since processing a *register* request involves computing intersections with registered regions, a smaller region will result in lower registration cost. In this experiment, as the number of processors increases, that is, $2 + 27, 4 + 27, 8 + 27$, and $16 + 27$, and the size of the overall array remains constant, the sizes of regions registered by each processor decrease and the average registration cost decreases correspondingly.

This experiment also measured the cost in data send (put) and receive (get) operations. The Seine model decouples sends and receives. In Seine, a push model is used to asynchronously propagate data. As a result, the cost of a data send consists of data marshalling, establishing a remote connection, and sending the data, while the cost of data receive consists of only a local memory copy from the Seine buffer. Consequently, the total data transfer cost is essentially the data send cost and is

[2]The first two dimension are distributed using a block distribution and the third dimension is not distributed.

Table 14.3 Cost in Seconds of Registration and Data Transfer for Different Array Sizes

$M \times N$: 16 × 27; Data type: double
Distribution(x–y–z): block–block–cyclic
M side: number of cycles at z direction = 3
N side: number of cycles at z direction = 4

Array size	60^3	120^3	180^3	240^3
Registration	0.0920	0.9989	6.31	9.987
Data transfer	0.0423	0.1117	0.271	0.8388
M side (put)	0.0423	0.1117	0.271	0.8388
N side (get)	0.0001	0.0008	0.004	0.0136

relatively higher than the data receive cost. We explicitly list the data transfer cost in the table since this metric has been used to measure and report the performance of other coupling frameworks.

Experiment with Different Array Sizes: In this experiment, the size of the array and, consequently, the size of the data redistribution is varied. The distribution of the array is (block, block, cyclic) on the x-, y-, z-axis, respectively, on both the sender and receiver ends. The registration, data transfer, and send (put) and receive (get) costs are listed in Table 14.3. As these measurements show, the registration cost increases with array size. As explained for the experiment above, this is because the registered regions of interest are correspondingly smaller and the computation of intersections is quicker for smaller array sizes. As expected, the costs for send and receive operations also increase with array size.

Scalability of the Seine Directory Layer: In this experiment, the number of processors over which the Seine coupling and parallel data redistribution component is distributed is varied. Distributing this component also distributes the registration process, and registrations for different regions can proceed in parallel. This leads to a reduction in registration times as seen in Table 14.4. The improvement, however, seems to saturate around four processors for this experiment, and the improvement from four to eight

Table 14.4 Scalability of the Directory Layer of the Seine Coupling Component

$M \times N$: 16 × 27; Array size: 120 × 120 × 120; data type: double
Distribution(x–y–z): block–block–block

Number of processors running Seine coupling component	1	4	8
Registration	4.2	2.273	2.089
Data transfer	0.112	0.1045	0.1172
M side (put)	0.112	0.1045	0.1172
N side (get)	0.0012	0.0012	0.0012

processors is not significant. Note that the actual data transfer is directly between the processors and is not affected by the distribution of the Seine component, and remains almost constant.

From the evaluation presented above, we can see that the registration cost ranges from less than a second to a few seconds, and is the most expensive aspect of Seine's performance. However, registration is a one-time cost for each region, which can be used for multiple *get* and *put* operations. Note that registration cost also includes the cost of computing communication schedules, which do not have to be computed repeatedly. Data transfers take place directly between the source and destination processors using socket-based streaming, which does not incur significant overheads as demonstrated by the evaluation. Overall, we believe that the costs of Seine operations are reasonable and not significant when compared to per iteration computational time of the targeted scientific simulations.

14.4.2 Experiment with Wide-Area Data Coupling

The second prototype implementation of the Seine coupling framework simply divides the framework into two parts: Seine-stub and Seine-dir. Seine-stub is the Seine daemon running locally on each process, and Seine-dir is the Seine distributed directory layer running as a separate parallel program to provide directory service exclusively to the Seine-stubs. Different from the previous prototype, this prototype has not encapsulated the Seine coupling framework as a CCA component. We used this prototype implementation to enable wide-area data coupling for the coupling scenario in SciDAC Fusion project.

Overview of SciDAC Fusion Simulation Project The DoE SciDAC Fusion project is developing a new integrated predictive plasma edge simulation code package that is applicable to the plasma edge region relevant to both existing magnetic fusion facilities and next-generation burning plasma experiments, such as the international thermonuclear experimental reactor (ITER). The plasma edge includes the region from the top of the pedestal to the scape-off layer and divertor region bounded by a material wall. A multitude of nonequilibrium physical processes on different spatiotemporal scales present in the edge region demand a large-scale integrated simulation. The low collisionality of the pedestal plasma, magnetic X-point geometry, spatially sensitive velocity-hole boundary, non-Maxwellian nature of the particle distribution function, and particle source from neutrals combine to require the development of a special massively parallel kinetic transport code for kinetic transport code for kinetic transport physics, using a particle-in-cell (PIC) approach. To study the large-scale molecular hydro dynamic (MHD) phenomena, such as edge localized modes (ELMs), a fluid code is more efficient in terms of computing time, and such an event is separable since its timescale is much shorter than the transport time. However, the kinetic and MHD codes must be integrated together for a self-consistent simulation as a whole. Consequently, the edge turbulence PIC code (XGC) will be connected with the microscopic MHD code, based on common grids at the spatial interface, to study the dynamical pedestal–ELM cycle.

Data Coupling in the Fusion Simulation Project In this project, two distinct parallel simulation codes, XGC and MHD, will run on different numbers of processors on different platforms. The overall workflow illustrating the coupling between XGC and MHD codes is shown in Figure 14.5. The coupling begins with the generation of a common spatial grid. XGC then calculates two-dimensional density, temperature, bootstrap current, and viscosity profiles in accordance with neoclassical and turbulence transport, and sends these values to MHD. The input pressure tensor and current information are used by MHD to evolve the equilibrium magnetic field configuration, which it then sends back to XGC to enable it to update its magnetic equilibrium and check for stability. During and after the ELM crash, the pressure, density, magnetic field, and current will be toroidally averaged and sent to XGC. During the ELM calculation, XGC will evaluate the kinetic closure information and kinetic E_r evolution and pass them to MHD for a more consistent simulation of ELM dynamics. Note that most probably XGC and MHD will use a different formulation and domain configuration and decomposition. As a result, a mesh interpolation module (referred to as MI afterward) is needed to translate between the meshes used in the two codes, as shown in Figure 14.5.

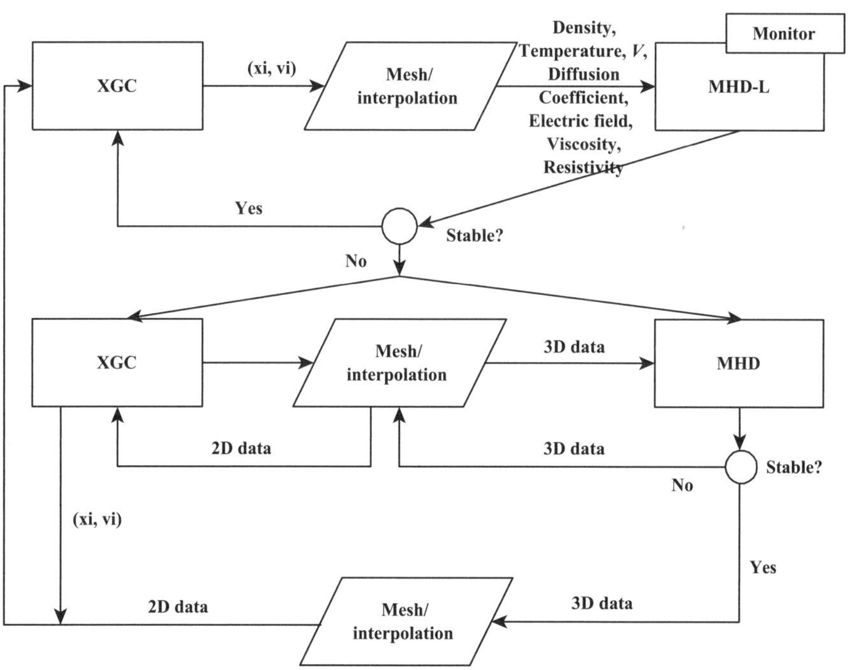

Figure 14.5 Data workflow between XGC and MHD [13].

Challenges and Requirements XGC is a scalable code and will run on a large number of processors. MHD, on the other hand, is not as scalable due to high interprocessor communications and runs on relatively smaller numbers of processors. As a result, coupling these codes will require $M \times N$ parallel data redistribution. In this project, the transfer is $M \times P \times N$, where the XGC code runs on M processors, the interpolation module runs on P processors, and the MHD code runs on N processors.

The fusion simulation application imposes strict constraints on the performance and overheads of data redistribution and transfer between the codes. Since the integrated system is constructed in a way that overlaps the execution of XGC with stability check by MHD, it is essential that the result of the stability check is available by the time it is needed by XGC, otherwise the large number (1000s) of processors running XGC will remain idle offsetting any benefit of a coupled simulation. Another constraints is the overhead of the coupling framework imposed on the simulations. This requires effective utilization of memory and communication buffers, specially when the volume of the coupled data is large. Finally, the data transfer has to be robust and ensure that no data are lost.

A Prototype Coupled Fusion Simulation Using Seine Since the Fusion project is at a very early stage, the scientists involved in the project are still investigating the underlying physics and numerics, and the XGC and MHD codes are still under development. However, the overall coupling behaviors of the codes is reasonably understood. As a result, we use synthetic codes, which emulate the coupling behaviors of the actual codes but perform dummy computation, to develop and evaluate the coupling framework. The goal is to have the coupling framework ready when the project moves to production runs. The configuration of the mock simulation using the synthetic codes is shown in Figure 14.6. In this figure, the coupling consists of two parts, the coupling between XGC and MI and the coupling between MI and MHD.

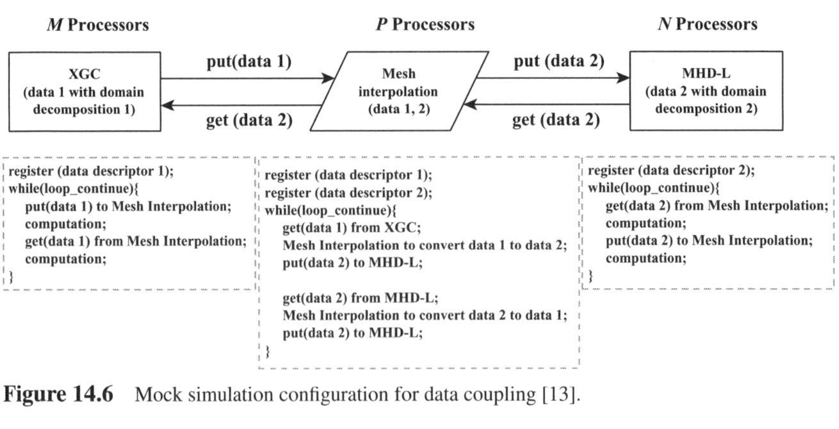

Figure 14.6 Mock simulation configuration for data coupling [13].

Domain Decompositions: The entire problem domain in the coupled fusion simulation is a 3D toroidal ring. The 3D toroidal ring is then sliced to get a number of 2D poloidal planes as the computation domains. Each plane contains a large number of particles, each of which is described by its physical location information via coordinates and a set of physics variables. Each 2D poloidal plane is assigned to and replicated on a group of processors. Since XGC and MHD use different domain decompositions, the numbers of planes in the two codes are different, and MI is used to map the XGC domain decomposition to the MHD domain decomposition.

Coupled Fusion Simulations Using Seine Shared Spaces: Recall that coupling in Seine is based on a spatial domain that is shared between the entities that are coupled. This may be the geometric discretization of the application domain or may be an abstract multidimensional domain defined exclusively for coupling purposes. In the prototype described here, we use the latter.

Given that the first phase of coupling between XGC and MHD is essentially based on the 2D poloidal plane, a 3D abstract domain can be constructed as follows:

- The X-axis represents particles on a plane and is the dimension that is distributed across processors.
- The Y-axis represents the plane id. Each processor has exactly one plane id and may have some or all the particles in the plane.
- The Z-axis represents application variables associated with each particle. Each processor has all the variables associated with each particle that is mapped to it.

Using this abstract domain, coupling using Seine is achieved as follows. Each XGC processor registers its region in the 3D abstract domain based on the 2D poloidal plane and the particles assigned to it, and the variable associated with each particle. The registered region is specified as a six-field tuple and represents a 2D plane in the 3D abstract domain since each processor is assigned with particles on only one poloidal plane. Each processor running MI similarly registers its region in the 3D abstract domain. Note that since MI acts as the "coupler" between XGC and MHD, these processors register regions twice—once corresponding to the XGC domain decomposition and the second time corresponding to the MHD the domain decomposition. Once the registration is complete, the simulations can use the operators provided by Seine, that is, *put* and *get*, to achieve coupling.

Prototype Implementation and Performance Evaluation The Seine coupling framework is used to support coupling and parallel data redistribution between multiple parallel applications, each executing as an independent simulation. A schematic of the prototype implementation of the Seine-based coupled fusion simulation is shown in Figure 14.7. The Seine framework has two key components. The first is the Seine distributed directory layer that deterministically maps the shared abstract domain onto the Seine infrastructure processors. The second is the Seine-proxy, which is a local daemon that resides on each processor that uses Seine. Note that the

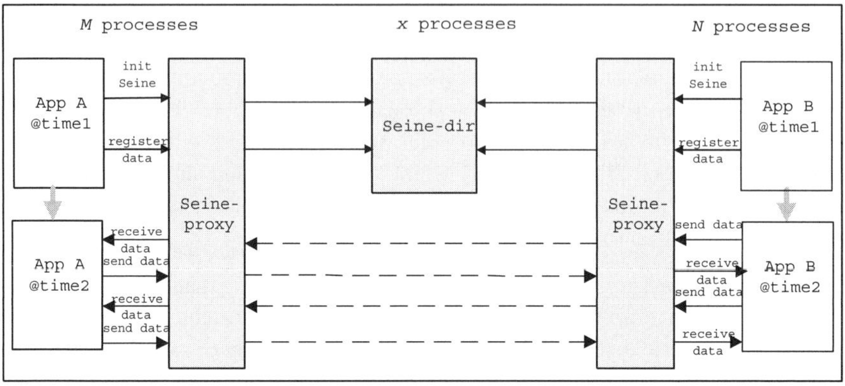

Figure 14.7 $M \times N$ data redistribution between parallel applications using the Seine framework [13].

Seine-Coupe infrastructure runs on *X* processors, which may or may not overlap with the *M*, *P*, and *N* processors running, XGC, MI, and MHD, respectively. The Seine-proxy at each processor is initialized by calling *init* within the application code. Once the Seine-proxy is initialized, it handles all the processor interaction with Seine including registration and *put* and *get* operations. When Seine is initialized, each processor registers its region(s) of interest. Registration request are used to construct the Seine distributed directory and to detect overlaps between regions of interest of different processors. Using this overlap, data *put* by one processor are automatically forwarded to all processors that have overlapping regions of interest and can be read locally using the *get* operation. All interaction are completely decoupled and asynchronous. Details about the implementation and operation of Seine can be found in Ref. [19].

Experiments with Wide-Area Coupling Using the Prototype Seine-Based Fusion Simulation: The experiments presented in this section were conducted between two sites; a 80 nodes cluster with two processors per node at Oak Ridge National Laboratory (ORNL) in Tenessee, and 64-node cluster at the CAIP Center at Rutgers University in New Jersey. The synthetic XGC code is run on the ORNL cluster, and the MI module and the synthetic MHD code are run on the CAIP cluster. That is, site M was at ORNL and sites P and N were are CAIP. The two clusters had different processors, memory and interconnects. Due to security restrictions at ORNL, these experiments were only able to evaluate the performance of data transfer from ORNL to CAIP, that is, XGC pushing data to the MI module that then pushes the data to MHD.

In the experiment, the XGC domain was decomposed into eight 2D poloidal planes, while the MHD problem domain was decomposed into six 2D poloidal planes. The number of particles in each plane was varied in the different experiments. Each particle is associated with nine variables. Since the *get* operation in Seine is local and does not involve data communication, the evaluations presented below focus on the *put* operation, which pushes data over the network. The experiments evaluate the operation cost and throughput achieved by the *put* operation.

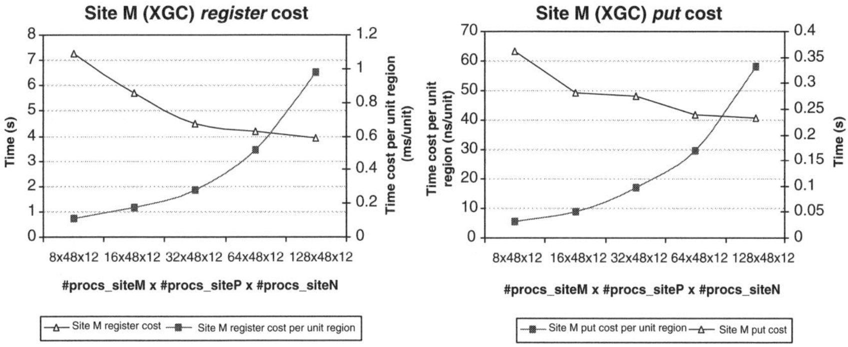

Figure 14.8 Operation cost and normalized operation cost.

Operation Cost: This experiment evaluated the cost of Seine coupling operations. In this experiment, 7200 particles were used in each poloidal plane resulting in an abstract domain of size $7200 \times 8 \times 9$ between XGC and MI and $7200 \times 6 \times 9$ between MI and MHD. The number of processors at site M, which ran the XGC code, was varied and the costs of the *register* and *put* operations were measured and plotted in Figure 14.8. The plot shows the operation cost and the normalized operation cost, that is, the cost per-unit region in the abstract domain. The figure shows that as the number of processors at site M increases, the absolute time costs of the *register* and *put* operations decrease while the normalized time costs for them increase. The decrease in absolute time cost is because the size of the abstract domain is fixed, and as the number of processor increases, each processor *registers/puts* a smaller portion of this domain. Since the operation costs are directly affected by the size of the region, these costs decrease accordingly. The increase in the normalized time cost is due to the increasing communication overhead imposed on each unit region being sent. Detailed analysis of this behavior can be found in Ref. [20].

Throughput Achieved: The goal of this experiment is to measure the effective system throughput that can be achieved during wide-area data coupling for different system and abstract domain sizes. Herein, the effective system throughput refers to the amount of data pushed out by the entire parallel application running on site M during a unit time. Since data transfers issued from different computer nodes can overlap with each other, this effective system throughput is expected to be higher than throughput of a single node. In the experiment, the number of particles per poloidal plane was varied to be 7200, 14400, and 28800, and the number of processors running XGC at site M were varied to be 8, 16, 32, 64, and 128. We measured the per-processor throughput using netperf [21] benchmark. The measurement was conducted by adjusting parameters that determine the different data transfer size at the measurement. The data size used in netperf measurement is set up to be the same as the data size sent out by each processor in the data redistribution experiment. The per-processor throughput on site M is plotted in Figure 14.9a and the effective system throughput is computed by dividing the total data size transferred by the entire system by the duration of time used from the beginning of the transfer that starts the

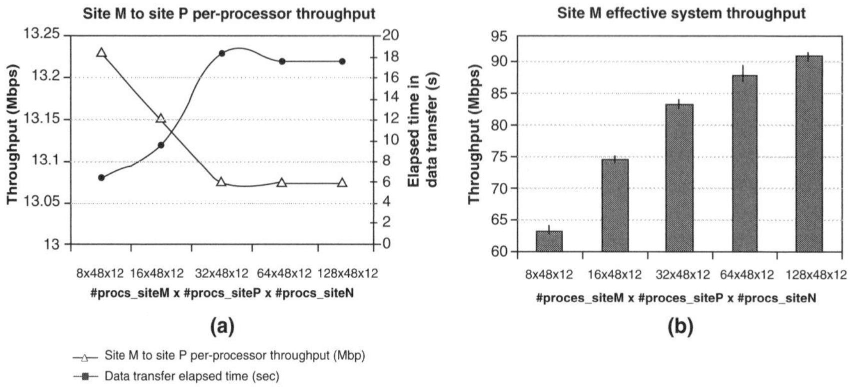

Figure 14.9 XGC site per-processor throughput measured by netperf (plotted in (a)) and effective system throughput (plotted in (b)).

first to the end of the transfer that ends the last. The result is plotted in Figure 14.9b. Error bar in Figure 14.9b shows standard deviation of the set of results measured. Two observations can be made from Figure 14.9a. First, the per-processor throughput at site M measured by netperf has very small amount of fluctuation for all abstract domain sizes tested. And the elapsed time during data transfer is roughly in reverse proportion to the throughput achieved in the same measurement. Second, effective system throughput achieved during the wide-area data coupling experiment, as shown in Figure 14.9b, is much higher than per-processor throughput shown in Figure 14.9a. The higher system throughput is achieved via data transfer overlaps on concurrent systems. Single processor data transfer is not able to take advantage of the concurrency. Furthermore, from Figure 14.9b, we can also observe that the system throughput increases with the system size at site M. Such increasing trend is due to the increased concurrency level of data transfer when the system size of site M becomes large.

In the Fusion project, XGC site throughput is a key requirement that must be met by the coupling framework. An initial conjecture of the transfer rate from XGC to mesh interpolation module is 120 Mbps. By running test in a wide-area environment as in the experiments presented above, one can analyze the feasibility of Seine meeting the requirement. Since in real Fusion production XGC will be running on a large-scale platform with 40 I/O nodes, we look at the results measured for 32 processors in the figures. The estimated effective system throughput is around 84 Mbps . While this figure still does not meet the Fusion throughput requirement, we believe that Seine can meet such requirement when used in the real production run because the experiment conducted here is in a wide-area environment while in real production XGC will be connected with MI with a private and extremely fast interconnection.

Effect of Data Generation Rate: This experiment evaluated the effect of varying the rate at which data were generated by XGC at site M. In this experiment, XGC generates data at regular intervals between which it computes. It is estimated by the physicists that, on average, XGC requires three times the computation as compared to MI and MHD. As a result, we experiment compute time for XGC, MI, and MHD of (1) 0,

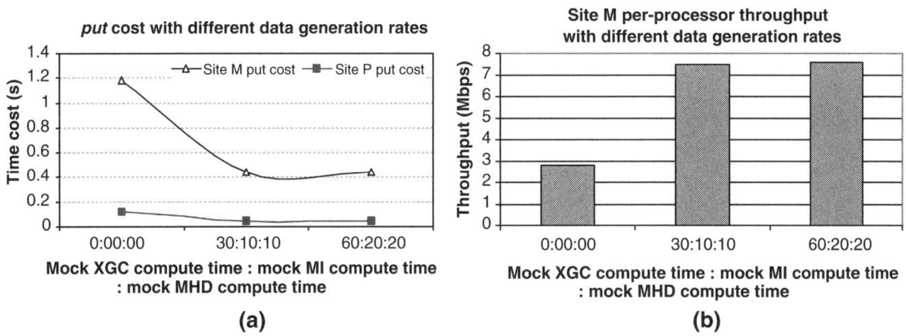

Figure 14.10 *put* operation cost and XGC site per-processor throughput with respect to different data generation rates [13].

0, and 0 s (corresponding to the previous cases), (2) 30, 10, and 10 s, and (3) 60, 20, and 20 s, respectively. The results are plotted in Figure 14.10. As seen from the plots, as the data generation rate reduces from case (1) to (2) to (3), the cost of the *put* operation and the throughput per processor improves, since the network is less congested. The jump is more significant from case (1) to (2) and less significant from case (2) to (3).

14.5 CONCLUSION

This chapter presented the Seine framework for data coupling and parallel data redistribution. Seine addresses the model/code coupling requirements of emerging scientific and engineering simulations, and enables efficient computation of communication schedules. Seine supports low-overhead processor-to-processor data streaming, and provides a high-level programming abstraction for application developers.

The Seine framework decouples the communication process in time and space, and the communicating entities do not need to know about each other or about each other's data distributions. A key component of Seine is a distributed directory layer that is constructed as a distributed hash table from the application domain and enables decentralized computation of communication schedules.

A component-based prototype implementation of Seine using the CAFFEINE CCA framework and its experimental evaluation are also presented. The Seine CCA coupling component enables code coupling and parallel data redistribution between multiple CCA-based applications. The CCA Seine implementation offers an elegant solution to the more general problem of data redistribution, that is, the $M \times N$ problem, for intracomponent communications as well as intercomponent communications. The evaluation demonstrates the performance and low overheads of using Seine.

This chapter also presented experiments and experiences with code coupling for a fusion simulation using the Seine coupling framework over wide-area network. The goal of these experiments was to evaluate the ability of Seine to meet the coupling requirements of the ongoing DoE SciDAC Fusion Simulation Project. The experimental results using a prototype coupled fusion simulation scenario demonstrated the performance, throughput, and low overheads achieved by Seine. The experiments presented here are a proof-of-concept and demonstrate feasibility. As the project progresses and real codes and more detailed requirements become available, the Seine framework and abstractions will have to be tuned to ensure that it can support true production runs.

In summary, the chapter has addressed some of the core computational issues in enabling large-scale coupled simulations. However, there are several issues that need further investigation. For example, optimization of memory usage during data redistribution, especially when data sizes are large. Current research is looking at optimizing the Seine communication layer to use adaptive buffering and maximize utilization of available network bandwidth. For large application runs at supercomputing centers, Seine is also looking at improving the communication layer by leveraging the remote direct memory access communication primitives and by overlapping communications with data transfers.

REFERENCES

1. Distributed Data Descriptor. http://www.cs.indiana.edu/ febertra/mxn/parallel-data/index.html.
2. J.A. Kohl, G.A. Geist. Monitoring and steering of large-scale distributed simulations. In *IASTED International Conference on Applied Modeling and Simulation*, Cairns, Queensland, Australia, September 1999.
3. K. Keahey, P. Fasel, S. Mniszewski. PAWS: collective interactions and data transfers. In *Proceedings of the High Performance Distributed Computing Conference*, San Francisco, CA, August 2001.
4. J.-Y. Lee and A. Sussman. High performance communication between parallel programs. In *Proceedings of 2005 Joint Workshop on High-Performance Grid Computing and High Level parallel Programming Models* (HIPS–HPGC 2005). IEEE Computer Society Press, April 2005.
5. CCA Forum. http://www.cca-forum.org.
6. S. Kohn, G. Kumfert, J. Painter, and C. Ribbens. Divorcing language dependencies from a scientific software library. In *Proceedings of the 11th SIAM Conference on Parallel Processing for Scientific Computing*. SIAM, March 2001.
7. J.W. Larson, R.L. Jacob, I.T. Foster, and J. Guo. The Model Coupling Toolkit. In V.N.Alexandrov, J.J.Dongarra, B.A.Juliano, R.S.Renner, and C.J.K.Tan, editors, *International Conference on Computational Science (ICCS) 2001*, Vol. 2073, *Lecture Notes in Computer Science*, Berlin. Springer-Verlag, 2001, pp. 185–194.
8. S. Zhou. Coupling earth system models: an ESMF-CCA prototype. http://www.nasa.gov/vision/earth/everydaylife/esmf.html, 2003.
9. F. Bertrand and R. Bramley. DCA: a distributed CCA framework based on MPI. In *Proceedings the 9th International Workshop on High-Level Parallel Programming Models and Supportive Environments of HIPS 2004*, Santa Fe, NM. IEEE Press, April 2004.
10. F. Bertrand, D. Bernholdt, R. Bramley, K. Damevski, J. Kohl, J. Larson, and A. Sussman. Data redistribution and remote method invocation in parallel component architectures. In *Proceedings of the 19th International Parallel and Distributed Processing Symposium (IPDPS'05)*, April 2005.
11. K. Zhang, K. Damevski, V. Venkatachalapathy, and S. Parker. SCIRun2: a CCA framework for high performance computing. In *Proceedings of the 9th International Workshop on High-Level Parallel Programming Models and Supportive Environments (HIPS 2004)*, Santa Fe, NM. IEEE Press, April 2004.
12. L. Zhang, M. Parashar: A dynamic geometry-based shared space interaction framework for parallel scientific applications. In *Proceedings of High Performance Computing (HiPC 2004) 11th International Conference*, Bangalore, India, December 19–22, 2004, pp. 189–199.

13. L. Zhang and M. Parashar. Experiments with wide area data coupling using the Seine framework. In *Proceedings of the 13th IEEE International Conference on High Performance Computing (HiPC 2006)*, Bangalore, India, December 2006.
14. T. Bially. A class of dimension changing mapping and its application to bandwidth compression. PhD thesis, Polytechnic Institute of Brooklyn, June 1967.
15. L.A. Drummond, J. Demmel, C.R. Mechoso, H. Robinson, K. Sklower, and J.A. Spahr. A data broker for distributed computing environments. In *Proceedings of the International Conference on Computational Science*, 2001, pp. 31–40.
16. V. Bhat, S. Klasky, S. Atchley, M. Beck, D. McCune, and M. Parashar. High performance threaded data streaming for large scale simulations. In *Proceedings of the 5th IEEE/ACM International Workshop on Grid Computing*, Pittsburgh, PA, November 2004.
17. I. Manuilskiy and W.W. Lee. *Phys. Plasmas* 7: 1381, 2000.
18. Q. Lu, M. Peszynska, and M.F. Wheeler. A parallel multi-block black-oil model in multi-model implementation. *Reservoir Simulation Symposium*, In *2001 SPE* Houston, TX. SPE 66359, 2001.
19. L. Zhang and M. Parashar. Enabling efficient and flexible coupling of parallel scientific applications. In *Proceedings of the 20th IEEE International Parallel and Distributed Processing Symposium*, Rhodes Island, Greece. IEEE Computer Society Press, 2006.
20. L. Zhang and M. Parashar. Seine: a dynamic geometry-based shared space interaction framework for parallel scientific applications. Concurrency Comput. Pract. and Exper. 18(15):1951–1973, 2006.
21. Netperf benchmark. http://www.netperf.org/netperf/NetperfPage.html.
22. H. Abbasi, M. Wolf, K. Schwan, G. Eisenhauer, and A. Hilton. XChange: coupling parallel applications in a dynamic environment. In *Proceedings of the International Parallel and Distributed Processing Symposium*, 2004.
23. M. Malawski, D. Kurzyniec, and V. Sunderam. MOCCA—towards a distributed CCA framework for metacomputing. In *Proceedings of International Parallel and Distributed Processing Symposium*, 2004.
24. M. Smith and T. Williams. Phylospaces: reconstructing evolutionary trees in tuple spaces. In *Proceedings of International Parallel and Distributed Processing Symposium*, 2006.

Part III

Dynamic Partitioning and Adaptive Runtime Management Frameworks

Chapter 15

Hypergraph-Based Dynamic Partitioning and Load Balancing

Umit V. Catalyurek, Doruk Bozdağ, Erik G. Boman, Karen D. Devine, Robert Heaphy, and Lee A. Riesen

15.1 INTRODUCTION

An important component of many scientific computing applications is the *assignment* of computational load onto a set of processors. The distribution of load has an impact on the overall execution time, and an even distribution is usually preferred. The problem of finding a task-to-processor mapping that minimizes the total execution time is known as the *partitioning* or *mapping* problem. Although efficient optimal solutions exist for certain restricted cases, such as chain- or tree-structured programs [21], the general problem is NP-hard [28]. In this chapter, we consider the general problem where any task can potentially be assigned to any processor. In the literature, a two-step approach is commonly employed to solve the problem: first, tasks are *partitioned* into *load balanced* clusters of tasks, then these clusters are mapped to processors. In the partitioning step, the common goal is to minimize the interprocessor communication while maintaining a computational load balance among processors. Partitioning occurs at the start of a computation (*static partitioning*), but often, reassignment of work is done during a computation (*dynamic partitioning* or *repartitioning*) as the work distribution changes over the course of the computation. Dynamic partitioning usually includes both partitioning and mapping. Although distinctions between *partitioning*, *load balancing*, and *mapping* can be made as described, throughout this

Advanced Computational Infrastructures For Parallel and Distributed Adaptive Applications. Edited by Manish Parashar and Xiaolin Li

chapter we will use the terms interchangeably to refer the assignment problem. We will assume that the mapping step of the two-step approach is either trivial or inherent in the partitioning approach.

In parallel adaptive computations, the structure of the computational graph or hypergraph that represents the application changes over time. For instance, a computational mesh in an adaptive mesh refinement simulation is updated between time, steps. Therefore, after several steps, even an initially balanced assignment may suffer serious imbalances. To maintain the balance throughout the computations, a repartitioning procedure needs to be applied; that is, data must be moved among processors periodically.

Repartitioning is a well-studied problem [9, 10, 13, 15, 19, 31, 32, 34, 35, 37, 39, 41, 43, 44] that has multiple objectives with complicated trade-offs among them:

1. balanced load in the new data distribution;
2. low communication cost within the application (as determined by the new distribution);
3. low data migration cost to move data from the old to the new distribution; and
4. short repartitioning time.

Total execution time is commonly modeled [26, 34] as follows to account for these objectives:

$$t_{\text{tot}} = \alpha(t_{\text{comp}} + t_{\text{comm}}) + t_{\text{mig}} + t_{\text{repart}}.$$

Here, t_{comp} and t_{comm} denote computation and communication times, respectively, in a single iteration of the application; t_{mig} is the data migration time and t_{repart} is the repartitioning time. The parameter α indicates how many iterations (e.g., timesteps in a simulation) of the application are executed between each load balance operation. Since the goal of repartitioning is to establish balance, we can safely assume that computation will be balanced and hence ignore t_{comp}. Furthermore, t_{repart} is typically much smaller than αt_{comp} for most applications, thanks to fast state-of-the-art repartitioners. Thus, the objective reduces to minimize $\alpha t_{\text{comm}} + t_{\text{mig}}$.

Diffusive methods have been one of the most studied dynamic load balancing techniques in the literature [9, 19, 20, 32, 33, 41, 43]. In a diffusive load balancing scheme, extra work on overloaded processors is distributed to neighboring processors that have less than average loads. In a simpler approach, called *scratch–remap* method, the graph or hypergraph representing the modified structure of the application is partitioned *from scratch* without accounting for existing part assignments. Then, old and new parts are remapped to minimize the migration cost [35].

Even though scratch–remap schemes achieve low communication volume, they are slow and often result in high migration cost. On the contrary, diffusive schemes are fast and result in low migration cost; however, they may incur high communication volume. Diffusion and scratch–remap methods correspond to two extreme cases, where α is taken to be very small and very large, respectively, while minimizing the objective function $\alpha t_{\text{comm}} + t_{\text{mig}}$. In a dynamic loading scheme, however, it is desirable for an application developer to have more control of α to be able to set it at intermediate values as well. Schloegel et al. introduced such a parallel adaptive repartitioning scheme [34], where relative importance of migration time against communication time is set by a user-provided parameter. Their work is based on the multilevel graph partitioning paradigm, and this parameter is taken into account in the refinement phase of the multilevel scheme. Aykanat et al. [2] proposed a graph-based repartitioning model, called *RM model*, where the original computational graph is augmented with new vertices and edges to account for migration cost. Then, repartitioning with fixed vertices is applied to the graph using RM-METIS, a serial repartitioning tool that the authors developed by modifying the graph partitioning tool METIS [22]. Although the approaches of Schloegel et al. and Aykanat et al. attempt to minimize both communication and migration costs, their applicability is limited to problems with symmetric, bidirectional dependencies. A hypergraph-based model is proposed in a concurrent work of Cambazoglu and Aykanat [5] for the adaptive screen partitioning problem in the context of image–space–parallel direct volume rendering of unstructured grids. Despite the fact that the limitations mentioned above for graph-based models do not apply, their model accounts only for migration cost since communication occurs merely for data replication (migration) in that problem.

In a recent work, Catalyurek et al. [6] introduced a generalized hypergraph model for the repartitioning problem. This chapter provides a detailed description of the model in Ref. [6] and extends the experimental results presented there. As we describe in Section 15.3, this new hypergraph model minimizes the sum of total communication volume in the application and migration cost to move data. Hypergraphs accurately model the actual communication cost and have greater applicability than graphs (e.g., hypergraphs can represent nonsymmetric and/or nonsquare systems) [7]. Furthermore, appropriately combining representations of communication and migration costs in a single hypergraph is more suitable to successful multilevel partitioning schemes than graph-based approaches (see Section 15.2 for details). The new model can be more effectively realized with a parallel repartitioning tool. However, as will be described in Section 15.3, it necessitates hypergraph partitioning with fixed vertices. Although serial hypergraph partitioners with this feature exist (PaToH) [8], to the best of our knowledge Zoltan [3] is the first parallel hypergraph partitioner that can handle fixed vertices.

The remainder of this chapter is organized as follows. In Section 15.2, we present preliminaries for hypergraph partitioning and multilevel partitioning. In Section 15.3, we discuss three approaches for dynamic load balancing using hypergraphs. The parallel repartitioning tool developed within the Zoltan [45] framework is presented in Section 15.4. Section 15.5 includes empirical results of hypergraph-based repartitioning compared to graph-based repartitioning. Finally, we give our conclusions and suggest future work.

15.2 PRELIMINARIES

In this section, we present a brief description of hypergraph partitioning with fixed vertices as well as the multilevel partitioning paradigm.

15.2.1 Hypergraph Partitioning with Fixed Vertices

Hypergraphs can be viewed as generalizations of graphs where an edge is not restricted to connect only two vertices. Formally, a hypergraph $H = (V, N)$ is defined by a set of vertices V and a set of nets (hyperedges) N, where each net $n_j \in N$ is a nonempty subset of vertices. A weight w_i can be assigned to each vertex $v_i \in V$, and a cost c_j can be assigned to each net $n_j \in N$ of a hypergraph. $P = \{V_1, V_2, \ldots, V_k\}$ is called a k-way partition of H if each part $V_p,\ p = 1, 2, \ldots, k$, is a nonempty, pairwise disjoint subset of V and $\cup_{p=1}^{k} V_p = V$. A partition is said to be *balanced* if

$$W_p \leq W_{\text{avg}}(1 + \epsilon) \text{ for } p = 1, 2, \ldots, k, \tag{15.1}$$

where part weight $W_p = \sum_{v_i \in V_p} w_i$ and $W_{\text{avg}} = \left(\sum_{v_i \in V} w_i\right)/k$, and ϵ is a predetermined maximum tolerable imbalance.

In a given partition P, a net that has at least one vertex in a part is considered as connected to that part. The connectivity $\lambda_j(H, P)$ of a net n_j denotes the number of parts connected by n_j for the partition P of H. A net n_j is said to be *cut* if it connects more than one part (i.e., $\lambda_j > 1$).

Let cost(H, P) denote the cost associated with a partition P of hypergraph H. There are various ways to define cost(H, P) [30]. The relevant one for our context is known as connectivity-1 (or k-1) metric, defined as follows:

$$\text{cost}(H, P) = \sum_{n_j \in N} c_j(\lambda_j - 1). \tag{15.2}$$

The standard hypergraph partitioning problem [30] can then be stated as the task of dividing a hypergraph into k parts such that the cost (15.2) is minimized while the balance criterion (15.1) is maintained.

Hypergraph partitioning with fixed vertices is a more constrained version of the standard hypergraph partitioning problem. In this problem, in addition to the input hypergraph H and the requested number of parts k, a *fixed part* function $f(v)$ is also provided as an input to the problem. A vertex is said to be *free* (denoted by $f(v) = -1$) if it is allowed to be in any part in the solution P, and it is said to be fixed in part q ($f(v) = q$ for $1 \leq q \leq k$) if it is required to be in V_q in the final solution P. If a significant portion of the vertices is fixed, it is expected that the partitioning problem becomes easier. Clearly, in the extreme case where all the vertices are fixed (i.e., $f(v) \neq -1$ for all $v \in V$), the solution is trivial. Empirical studies of Alpert et al. [1] verify that the presence of fixed vertices can make a partitioning instance considerably easier. However, to the best of our knowledge, there is no theoretical work on the complexity of the problem. Experience shows that if only a very small fraction of vertices are fixed, the problem is almost as "hard" as the standard hypergraph partitioning problem.

15.2.2 Multilevel Partitioning Paradigm

Although graph and hypergraph partitioning are NP-hard [16, 30], several algorithms based on multilevel paradigms [4, 18, 24] have been shown to compute high-quality partitions in reasonable time. In addition to serial partitioners for graphs [17, 23, 42] and hypergraphs [8, 25], multilevel partitioning paradigm has been recently adopted by parallel graph [26, 42] and hypergraph [12, 38] partitioners.

Multilevel partitioning consists of three phases: *coarsening*, *coarse partitioning*, and *refinement*. Instead of partitioning the original hypergraph directly, a hierarchy of smaller hypergraphs that approximate the original one is generated during the *coarsening* phase. The smallest hypergraph obtained at the end of coarsening phase is partitioned in the *coarse partitioning* phase. Finally, in the *refinement* phase, the coarse partition is projected back to the larger hypergraphs in the hierarchy and improved using a local optimization method. The same procedure applies to graphs as well.

In this chapter, we also describe a technique for parallel multilevel hypergraph partitioning with fixed vertices [6]. The implementation is based on the parallel hypergraph partitioner in Zoltan [12].

15.3 HYPERGRAPH-BASED REPARTITIONING METHODS

A typical adaptive application, for example, timestepping numerical methods with adaptive meshes, consists of a sequence of iterations. At each iteration, the structure of the problem (computation) may change slightly, usually insignificantly. After a certain number of iterations, these changes accumulate and the workload becomes unevenly distributed among the processors. To restore the balance, a load balancer is invoked and some of the data are moved (migrated) to establish a new partition. Then, the computation resumes and this process is repeated until the application is finished.

In dynamic load balancing (repartitioning), communication cost and migration cost are the two main objectives to be minimized. These objectives are typically conflicting, posing a challenge in designing an efficient load balancing algorithm. The majority of the previous work is based on simplifying the problem by setting either of these objectives as a primary one and the other as a secondary, thereby impeding any trade-off between them. Furthermore, none of the previous methods are designed for or applied to hypergraphs. In this section, we first discuss two naive approaches to achieve dynamic load balancing using hypergraph partitioning, and then introduce a new repartitioning hypergraph model that accurately represents the costs associated with the dynamic load balancing problem.

15.3.1 Scratch–Remap-Based Repartitioning

One of the trivial approaches for dynamic load balancing is to repartition the modified hypergraph that models the application from scratch after certain number of iterations. Previous part assignments are ignored during partitioning. However, they are used in a postprocessing step that reorders parts to maximize the overlap between new and previous assignments and, thus, reduce the migration cost [31].

15.3.2 Refinement-Based Repartitioning

Second naive approach is just a simple application of successful move- or swap-based refinement algorithms, such as Kernighan–Lin [29], Schweikert–Kernighan [36], or Fiduccia–Mattheyses [14]. In this approach, vertices initially preserve their previous assignments and new vertices are assigned to existing parts via a simple, possibly random, partitioner. Then, a single refinement is applied to minimize the communication cost. Since vertices are allowed to change parts only during the refinement phase, migration cost is somewhat constrained. However, constrained vertex movement may lead to lower cut quality and, hence, larger communication cost. This approach may be extended to the multilevel partitioning framework to improve cut quality (albeit with increased partitioning time). However, we do not present multilevel refinement results here, as our new model below incorporates both coarsening and refinement in a more accurate way to achieve repartitioning.

15.3.3 A New Repartitioning Hypergraph Model

We present a novel hypergraph model to represent the trade-off between communication and migration costs in the repartitioning problem. Hypergraph partitioning is then directly applied to optimize the composite objective defined in Section 15.1.

We call the period between two subsequent load balancing operations an *epoch* of the application. An epoch consists of one or more computation iterations. The computational structure and dependencies of an epoch can be modeled using a computational hypergraph [7]. Since all computations in the application are of the same type but the structure is different across epochs, a different hypergraph is needed to represent each epoch. We denote the hypergraph that models the jth epoch of the application by $H^j = (V^j, E^j)$ and the number of iterations in that epoch by α_j.

Load balancing for the first epoch is achieved by partitioning H^1 using a static partitioner. For the remaining epochs, data redistribution cost between the previous and current epochs should also be included during load balancing. Total cost should be the sum of the communication cost for H^j with the new data distribution, scaled by α_j, and the migration cost for moving data between the distributions in epoch $j - 1$ and j.

Our new *repartitioning hypergraph model* appropriately captures both application communication and data migration costs associated with an epoch. To model migration costs in epoch j, we construct a repartitioning hypergraph $\bar{H}^j = (\bar{V}^j, \bar{E}^j)$ by augmenting H^j with k new vertices and $|V^j|$ new hyperedges using the following procedure:

- Scale each net's cost (representing communication) in E^j by α_j while keeping the vertex weights intact.

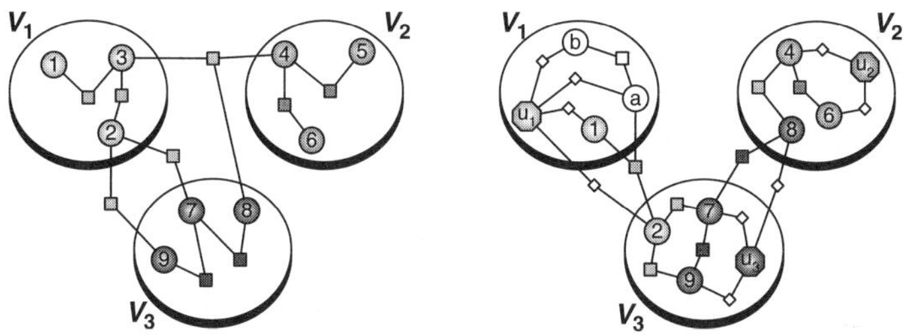

Figure 15.1 *Left*: A sample hypergraph for epoch $j-1$. *Right*: Repartitioning hypergraph for epoch j with a sample partition.

- Add a new *part vertex* u_i with zero weight for each part i, and fix those vertices in respective parts, that is, $f(u_i) = i$ for $i = 1, 2, \ldots, k$. Hence, $\bar{V}^j$ becomes $V^j \cup \{u_i | i = 1, 2, \ldots, k\}$.
- For each vertex $v \in V^j$, add a *migration net* between v and u_i if v is assigned to part i at the beginning of epoch j. Set the migration net's cost to the size of the data associated with v, since this migration net represents the cost of moving vertex v to a different part.

Figure 15.1 illustrates a sample hypergraph H^{j-1} for epoch $j-1$ (left) and a repartitioning hypergraph $\bar{H}^j$ for epoch j (right). A nice feature of our model is that no distinction is required between communication and migration vertices as well as nets. However, for clarity in this figure, we represent computation vertices with circles and part vertices with hexagons. Similarly, nets representing communication during computation are represented with squares, and migration nets representing data to be migrated due to changing vertex assignments are represented with diamonds. In this example, there are nine unit weight vertices partitioned into three parts with a perfect balance at epoch $j-1$. Three cut nets represent data that need to be communicated among the parts. Two of these nets have connectivity of two and one has three. Assuming unit cost for each net, total communication volume is four (equation 15.2). In other words, each iteration of epoch $j-1$ incurs a communication cost of four.

The computational structure changes in epoch j, as shown in Figure 15.1 (right). In H^j, new vertices a and b are added, while vertices 3 and 5 are deleted. To construct the repartitioning hypergraph $\bar{H}^j$ from H^j, three part vertices u_1, u_2, and u_3 are added and net weights in H^j are scaled by α_j. Then, each of the seven computation vertices inherited from H^{j-1} is connected to the part vertex associated with the part to which the computation vertex was assigned in epoch $j-1$, via a migration net.

Once the new repartitioning hypergraph $\bar{H}^j$ that encodes both communication and migration costs is obtained, the repartitioning problem reduces to hypergraph partitioning with *fixed* vertices. Here, the constraint is that vertex u_i must be assigned, or fixed, to part i.

Let $P = \{V_1, V_2, \ldots, V_k\}$ be a valid partition for this problem. Assume that a vertex v is assigned to part V_p in epoch $j-1$ and V_q in epoch j, where $p \neq q$. Then, the migration net between v and u_q that represents the migration cost of vertex v's data is cut (note that u_q is fixed in V_q). Therefore, the cost of moving vertex v from part V_p to V_q is appropriately included in the total cost. If a net that represents a communication during the computation phase is cut, the cost incurred by communicating the associated data in all α_j iterations in epoch j is also accounted for since the net's weight has already been scaled by α_j. Hence, our repartitioning hypergraph accurately models the sum of communication during computation phase plus migration cost due to moved data.

In the example given in Figure 15.1, assume that epoch j consists of five iterations, that is, $\alpha_j = 5$. Then, each of the unit weight communication nets incurs a communication cost of five in epoch j. Further, assume that the size of each vertex is three, that is, moving a vertex across parts adds three units to total communication volume. In the repartitioning hypergraph $\bar{H}^j$, this data movement is represented by migration nets of weight three connecting each vertex to the fixed vertex in its part. In this example, after applying hypergraph partitioning on $\bar{H}^j$, vertices 2 and 8 are assigned to parts V_3 and V_2, respectively. The cost associated with migration of these vertices is captured by associated migration nets being cut with connectivity of two. Total migration cost is then $2 \times 3 \times (2 - 1) = 6$. In this partition, two communication nets ($\{1, 2, a\}$ and $\{7, 8\}$) are also cut with connectivity of two, resulting in a total application communication volume of $2 \times 5 \times (2 - 1) = 10$. Thus, the total cost of epoch j is 16.

15.4 PARALLEL REPARTITIONING TOOL

The dynamic repartitioning model presented in the previous section can be implemented using parallel hypergraph partitioning with fixed vertices. In such an implementation, the multilevel algorithms commonly used for hypergraph partitioning (as described in Section 15.2) are adapted to handle fixed vertices [8]. In each phase of the multilevel partitioning, the fixed part constraints defined by $f(v)$ must be maintained for each vertex v and its resulting coarse vertices. In this section, we describe our approach for parallel multilevel hypergraph partitioning with fixed vertices [6] using the parallel hypergraph partitioner in Zoltan [12]. We first assume that we partition directly into k parts, and later discuss how fixed vertices are handled when recursive bisection is used to obtain k parts.

15.4.1 Coarsening Phase

In the coarsening phase of the multilevel algorithms, we approximate the original hypergraph with a succession of smaller hypergraphs with similar connectivity and equal total vertex and edge weight. Coarsening ends when the coarsest hypergraph is "small enough" (e.g., it has fewer than $2k$ vertices) or when the last coarsening step fails to reduce the hypergraph's size by a specified amount (typically 10%). To reduce the hypergraph's size, we merge *similar* vertices, that is, vertices whose hyperedge connectivity overlaps significantly. We use the *heavy-connectivity matching* metric initially developed in PaToH [7] and later adopted by hMETIS [27] and

Mondriaan [40] (where it is called *inner-product matching*). Pairs of vertices are matched using a greedy first-choice method. An agglomerative matching strategy [7] that produces higher quality decompositions with little additional execution cost is also implemented but not used in this paper.

Parallel matching is performed in rounds. In each round, each processor broadcasts a subset of candidate vertices that will be matched in that round. Then, all processors concurrently compute their best match for those candidates and global best match for each candidate is selected. Readers may refer to Ref. [12] for more details, including implementation for two-dimensional data layouts.

For fixed vertex partitioning, we constrain matching to propagate fixed vertex constraints to coarser hypergraphs so that coarser hypergraphs truly approximate the finer hypergraphs and their constraints. We do not allow vertices to match if they are fixed to different parts. Thus, there are three scenarios in which two vertices match: (1) both vertices are fixed to the same part, (2) only one of the vertices is fixed to a part, or (3) both are not fixed to any parts (i.e., both are free vertices). In cases 1 and 2, the resulting coarse vertex is fixed to the part in which either of its constituent vertices was fixed. In case 3, the resulting coarse vertex remains free.

15.4.2 Coarse Partitioning Phase

In the coarse partitioning phase, we construct an initial partition of the coarsest hypergraph available. If the coarsest hypergraph is small enough, we replicate it on every processor. Each processor then runs a randomized greedy hypergraph growing algorithm to compute a different partition into k parts, and the partition with the lowest cost is selected. If the coarsest hypergraph is not small enough, each processor contributes to the computation of an initial partition using a localized version of the greedy hypergraph algorithm. In either case, we maintain the fixed part constraints by assigning fixed coarse vertices to their respective parts.

15.4.3 Refinement Phase

In the refinement phase, we project our coarse partition to finer hypergraphs and improve it using a local optimization method. Our code is based on a localized version of the successful Fiduccia–Mattheyses [14] method, as described in Ref. [12]. The algorithm performs multiple pass pairs and in each pass, each free vertex is considered to move to another part to reduce the cut metric. We enforce the fixed vertex constraints simply; we do not allow fixed vertices to be moved out of their fixed part.

15.4.4 Handling Fixed Vertices in Recursive Bisection

Zoltan uses recursive bisection (repeated subdivision of parts into two parts) to obtain a k-way partition. This recursive bisection approach can be extended easily to accommodate fixed vertices. For example, in the first bisection of recursive bisection, the fixed vertex information of each vertex can be updated so that vertices that are originally fixed to parts $1 \leq p \leq k/2$ are fixed to part 1, and vertices originally fixed to parts $k/2 < p \leq k$ are fixed to part 2. Then, the multilevel partitioning algorithm with fixed vertices described above can be executed without any modifications. This scheme is recursively applied in each bisection.

15.5 EXPERIMENTAL RESULTS

In this section, we present detailed comparison of graph- and hypergraph-based repartitioning using dynamic data sets that are synthetically obtained using real application base cases. The properties of the real application data sets are shown in Table 15.1. Two different methods are used to generate the synthetic data used in the experiments. The first method represents biased random perturbations that change structure of the data. In this method, a certain fraction of vertices in the original data is randomly deleted along with the incident edges. At each repartitioning iteration, this operation is repeated independently from previous iterations; hence, a different subset of vertices from the original data is deleted. This operation simulates dynamically changing data that can both lose and gain vertices and edges. The results presented in this section correspond to the case where half of the parts lose or gain 25% of the total number of vertices at each iteration. We tested several other configurations by varying the fraction of vertices lost or gained. The results we obtained in these experiments were similar to the ones presented in this section.

The second method simulates adaptive mesh refinement. Starting with the initial data, a certain fraction of the parts at each iteration is randomly selected. Then, the subdomain corresponding to the selected parts performs a simulated mesh refinement, where weight and the size of its each vertex is increased by a constant factor. In our experiments presented in this section, 10% of the parts are selected at each iteration and the weight and size of each vertex in these parts are randomly increased to between 1.5 and 7.5 of their original value. Similar to the previous method, we tested several other configurations by varying the factor that scales the size and weight of vertices. The results obtained in these experiments were similar to the ones presented here.

Table 15.1 Properties of the Test Data Sets $|V|$ and $|E|$ are the numbers of vertices and graph edges, respectively

			Vertex degree			
Name	$\|V\|$	$\|E\|$	min	max	avg	Application area
xyce680s	682,712	823,232	1	209	2.4	VLSI design
2DLipid	4,368	2,793,988	396	1984	1279.3	Polymer DFT
auto	448,695	3,314,611	4	37	14.8	Structural analysis
apoa1-10	92,224	17,100,850	54	503	370.9	Molecular dynamics
cage14	1,505,785	13,565,176	3	41	18.0	DNA electrophoresis

We carried out our experiments using the Zoltan toolkit [11] as our base framework. For graph-based repartitioning, we used ParMETIS version 3.1 [26] through the Zoltan toolkit. For hypergraph-based repartitioning, we used the repartitioning tool implemented in Zoltan version 3.0 [6, 12].[1]

We executed our tests on a 64-node Linux cluster. Each node of the cluster is equipped with dual 2.4 GHz Opteron 250 processors, 8 GB of RAM, and 500 GB of local storage. The nodes are interconnected with switched gigabit Ethernet and Infiniband. In our experiments, we used Infiniband interconnected via MVAPICH v0.9.8 .[2]

We compare five different algorithms:

1. *Z-repart:* Our new method implemented within the Zoltan hypergraph partitioner (Section 15.3.3).
2. *Z-scratch:* Zoltan hypergraph partitioning from scratch (Section 15.3.1).
3. *Z-refine:* Zoltan refinement-based hypergraph repartitioning (Section 15.3.2).
4. *M-repart:* ParMETIS graph repartitioning using the *AdaptiveRepart* option.
5. *M-scratch:* ParMETIS graph partitioning from scratch (*Partkway*).

For the scratch methods, we used a maximal matching heuristic in Zoltan to map part numbers to reduce migration cost. We do not expect the partitioning-from-scratch methods to be competitive for dynamic problems, but include them as a useful baseline.

In Figures 15.2 through 15.13, the parameter α (which corresponds to the ITR parameter in ParMETIS) is varied ranging from 1 to 1000 and total cost is reported for 16, 32, and 64 processors (parts). Each result is averaged over a sequence of 20

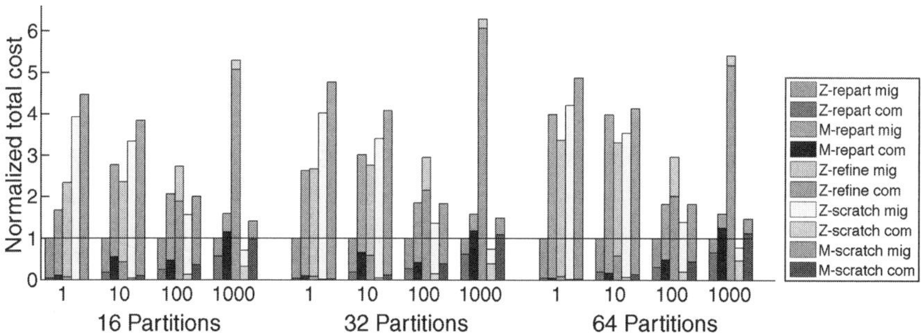

Figure 15.2 Normalized total cost for xyce680s with perturbed data structure with $\alpha = 1, 10, 100, 1000$ on 16, 32, and 64 processors; each bar shows application communication cost on the bottom (darker shade) and migration cost on the top (lighter shade). From left to right, the methods are Z-repart, M-repart, Z-refine, Z-scratch, and M-scratch.

[1] http://www.cs.sandia.gov/Zoltan

[2] MPI over Infiniband and iWARP Project: http://mvapich.cse.ohio-state.edu

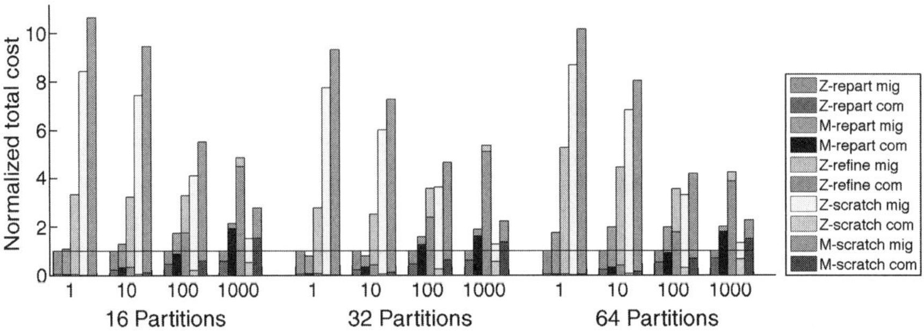

Figure 15.3 Normalized total cost for xyce680s with perturbed weights with $\alpha = 1, 10, 100, 1000$ on 16, 32, and 64 processors; each bar shows application communication cost on the bottom (darker shade) and migration cost on the top (lighter shade). From left to right, the methods are Z-repart, M-repart, Z-refine, Z-scratch, and M-scratch.

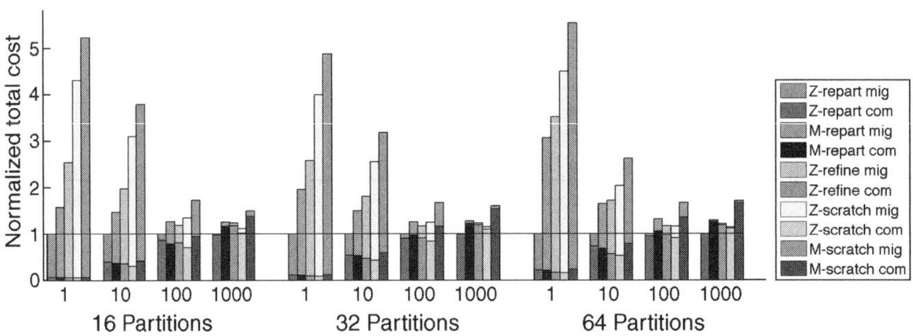

Figure 15.4 Normalized total cost for 2DLipid with perturbed data structure with $\alpha = 1, 10, 100, 1000$ on 16, 32, and 64 processors; each bar shows application communication cost on the bottom (darker shade) and migration cost on the top (lighter shade). From left to right, the methods are Z-repart, M-repart, Z-refine, Z-scratch, and M-scratch.

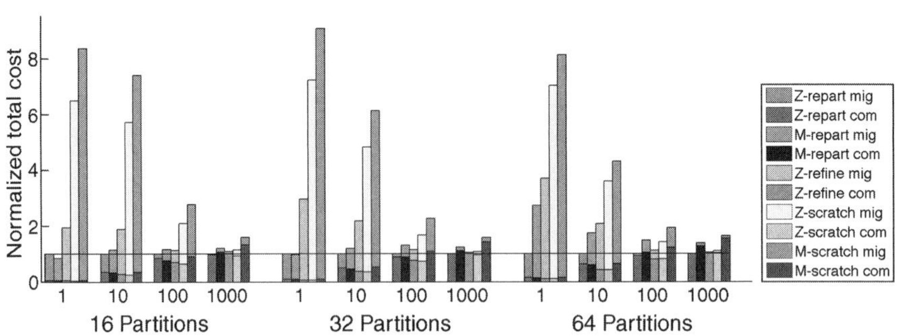

Figure 15.5 Normalized total cost for 2DLipid with perturbed weights with $\alpha = 1, 10, 100, 1000$ on 16, 32, and 64 processors; each bar shows application communication cost on the bottom (darker shade) and migration cost on the top (lighter shade). From left to right, the methods are Z-repart, M-repart, Z-refine, Z-scratch, and M-scratch.

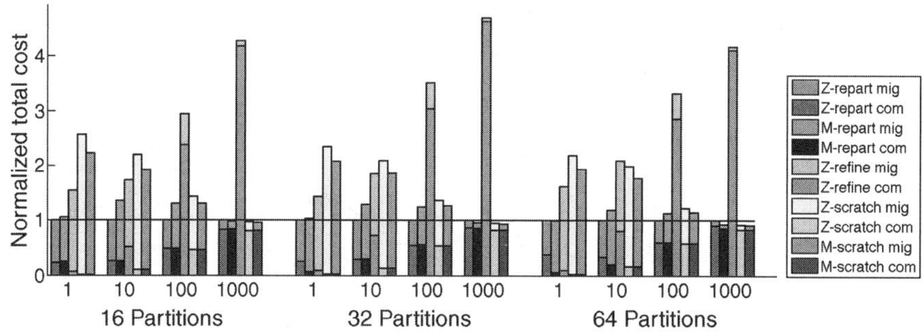

Figure 15.6 Normalized total cost for auto data set with perturbed data structure with $\alpha = 1, 10, 100, 1000$ on 16, 32, and 64 processors; each bar shows application communication cost on the bottom (darker shade) and migration cost on the top (lighter shade). From left to right, the methods are Z-repart, M-repart, Z-refine, Z-scratch, and M-scratch.

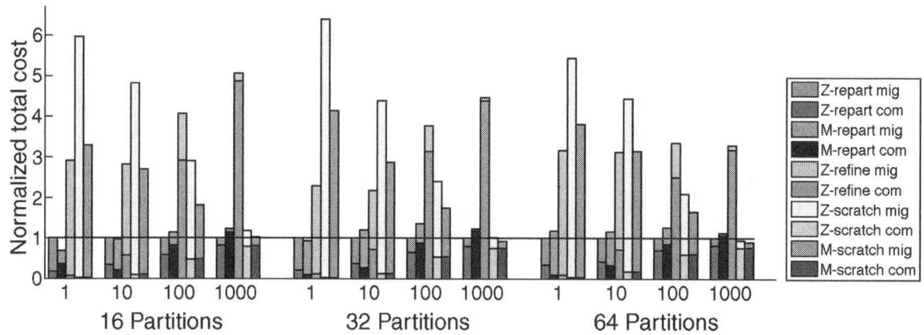

Figure 15.7 Normalized total cost for auto data set with perturbed weights with $\alpha = 1, 10, 100, 1000$ on 16, 32, and 64 processors; each bar shows application communication cost on the bottom (darker shade) and migration cost on the top (lighter shade). From left to right, the methods are Z-repart, M-repart, Z-refine, Z-scratch, and M-scratch.

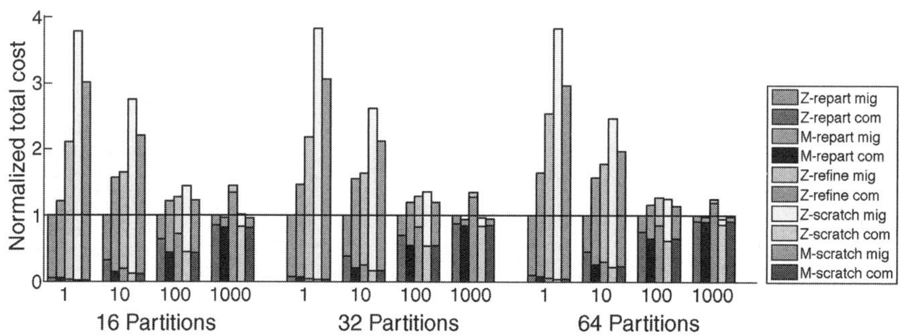

Figure 15.8 Normalized total cost for apoa1-10 with perturbed data structure with $\alpha = 1, 10, 100, 1000$ on 16, 32, and 64 processors; each bar shows application communication cost on the bottom (darker shade) and migration cost on the top (lighter shade). From left to right, the methods are Z-repart, M-repart, Z-refine, Z-scratch, and M-scratch.

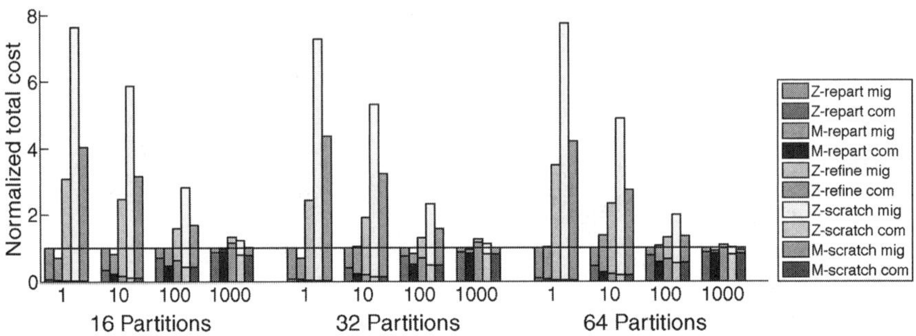

Figure 15.9 Normalized total cost for apoa1-10 with perturbed weights with $\alpha = 1, 10, 100, 1000$ on 16, 32, and 64 processors; each bar shows application communication cost on the bottom (darker shade) and migration cost on the top (lighter shade). From left to right, the methods are Z-repart, M-repart, Z-refine, Z-scratch, and M-scratch.

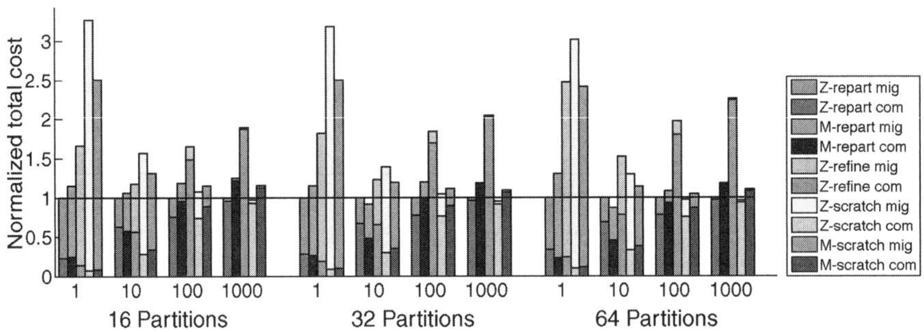

Figure 15.10 Normalized total cost for cage14 with perturbed data structure with $\alpha = 1, 10, 100, 1000$ on 16, 32, and 64 processors; each bar shows application communication cost on the bottom (darker shade) and migration cost on the top (lighter shade). From left to right, the methods are Z-repart, M-repart, Z-refine, Z-scratch, and M-scratch.

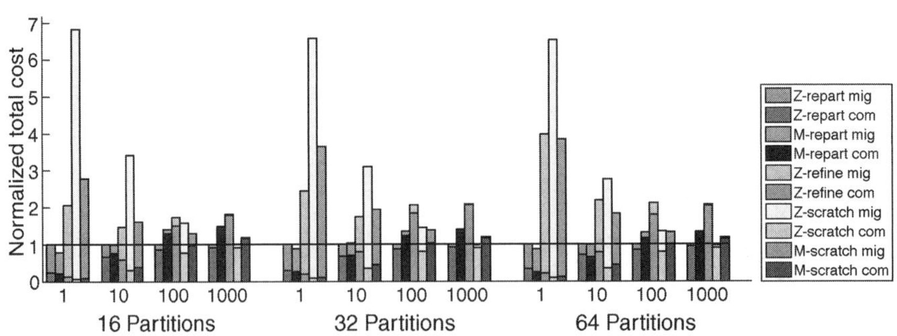

Figure 15.11 Normalized total cost for cage14 with perturbed weights with $\alpha = 1, 10, 100, 1000$ on 16, 32, and 64 processors; each bar shows application communication cost on the bottom (darker shade) and migration cost on the top (lighter shade). From left to right, the methods are Z-repart, M-repart, Z-refine, Z-scratch, and M-scratch.

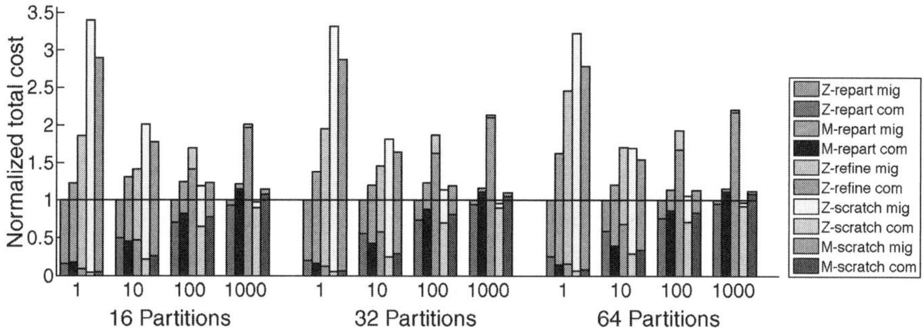

Figure 15.12 Normalized total cost for average of five test graphs with perturbed data structure with $\alpha = 1, 10, 100, 1000$ on 16, 32, and 64 processors; each bar shows application communication cost on the bottom (darker shade) and migration cost on the top (lighter shade). From left to right, the methods are Z-repart, M-repart, Z-refine, Z-scratch, and M-scratch.

trials for each experiment. For each configuration, there are five bars representing total cost for Z-repart, M-repart, Z-refine, Z-scratch, and M-scratch, from left to right, respectively. Total cost in each bar is normalized by the total cost of Z-repart in the respective configuration and consists of two components: communication (bottom) and migration (top) costs. The first 10 figures (Figures 15.2–15.11) display comparisons of the five methods in terms of total cost, for each one of the five test cases, with perturbed data structure and weights. Figures 15.12 and 15.13 display the average quality results for those five test data sets.

The results indicate that our new hypergraph repartitioning method Z-repart performs better than M-repart in terms of minimizing the total cost in the majority of the test cases. This can be explained by the fact that migration cost minimization objective is completely integrated into the multilevel scheme rather than handled only in the refinement phase. Therefore, Z-repart provides a more accurate trade-off between communication and migration costs than M-repart to minimize the total cost.

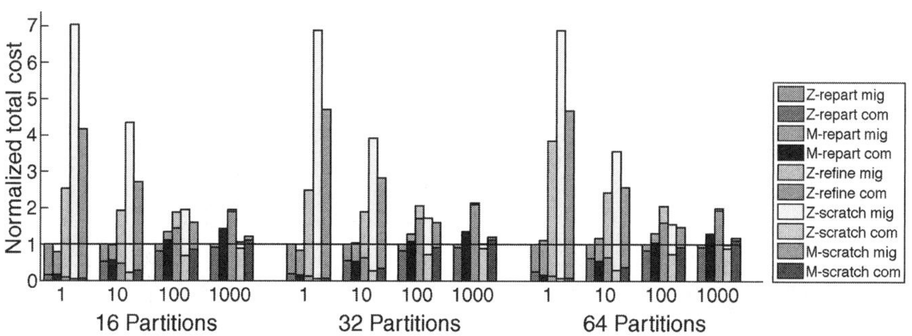

Figure 15.13 Normalized total cost for average of five test graphs with perturbed weights with $\alpha = 1, 10, 100, 1000$ on 16, 32, and 64 processors; each bar shows application communication cost on the bottom (darker shade) and migration cost on the top (lighter shade). From left to right, the methods are Z-repart, M-repart, Z-refine, Z-scratch, and M-scratch.

This is more clearly seen for small and moderate α-values where these two costs are comparable. On the other hand, for large α-values, migration cost is less important relative to communication cost, and the problem essentially reduces to minimizing the communication cost alone. Therefore, in such cases, Z-repart and M-repart behave similarly to partitioners using scratch methods.

Similar arguments hold when comparing Z-repart against scratch–remap repartitioning methods. Since minimization of migration cost is ignored in Z-scratch and M-scratch, migration cost gets extremely large and dominates the total cost as α gets smaller. Total cost with Z-scratch and M-scratch is comparable to Z-repart only when α is greater than 100, where communication cost starts to dominate. Z-repart still performs as well as the scratch methods in this range to minimize the total cost.

In Z-refine, the communication volume is attempted to be minimized with relatively fewer vertex movements due to the constrained initial partition. Therefore, the cut quality of Z-refine is lower than the other partitioners, resulting in a relatively higher total cost for large α-values. On the other hand, it produces lower migration costs compared to scratch methods for small α-values. However, Z-refine is outperformed by Z-repart in all of our test cases.

As the number of parts (processors) increases, there is a noticeable increase in migration cost relative to communication cost when using M-repart. On the other hand, with Z-repart, the increase in migration cost is smaller at the expense of a modest increase in communication cost. This shows that Z-repart achieves a better balance between communication and migration costs, and, consequently, results in a smaller total cost than M-repart with increasing number of parts. This suggests that in addition to minimization of the total cost, Z-repart is superior to M-repart in terms of scalability of the solution quality.

Runtimes of the tested partitioners normalized by that of Z-repart while changing the data's structure are given in Figures 15.14–15.18. Results for changing vertex weights and sizes are omitted here as they were similar to the ones presented. We observed three different runtime profiles in our test cases. The first one is shown in Figure 15.14, where multilevel hypergraph-based methods, Z-repart and Z-scratch,

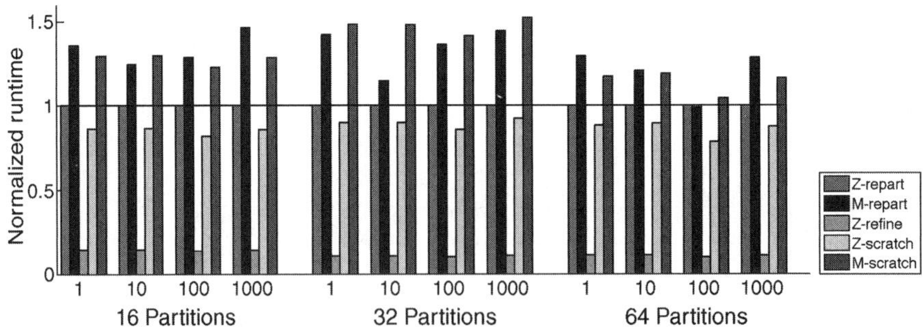

Figure 15.14 Normalized runtime with perturbed data structure for xyce680s with $\alpha = 1, 10, 100, 1000$ on 16, 32, and 64 processors. From left to right, the methods are Z-repart, M-repart, Z-refine, Z-scratch, and M-scratch.

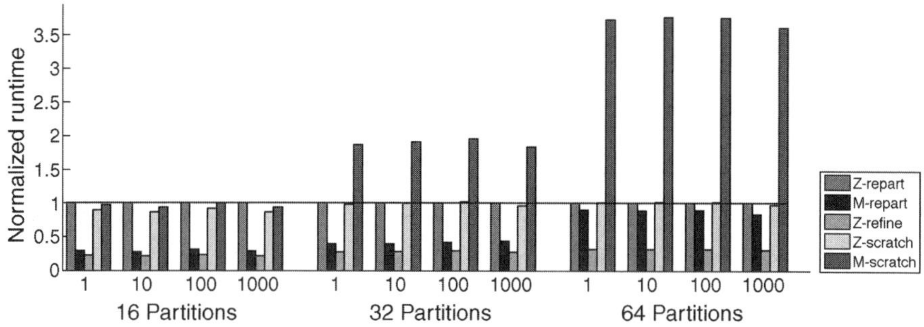

Figure 15.15 Normalized runtime with perturbed data structure for 2DLipid with $\alpha = 1, 10, 100, 1000$ on 16, 32, and 64 processors. From left to right, the methods are Z-repart, M-repart, Z-refine, Z-scratch, and M-scratch.

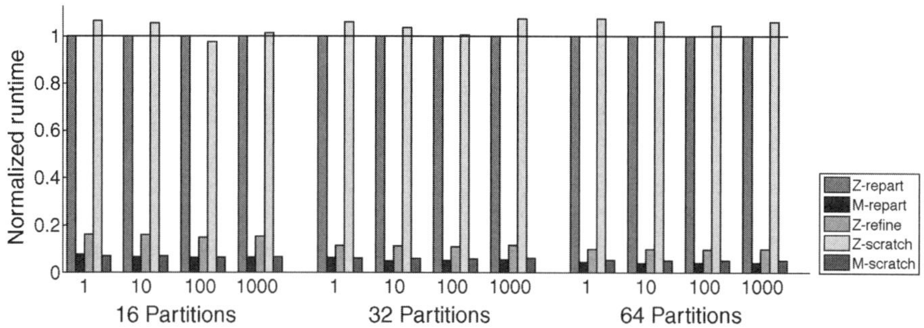

Figure 15.16 Normalized runtime with perturbed data structure for cage14 with $\alpha = 1, 10, 100, 1000$ on 16, 32, and 64 processors. From left to right, the methods are Z-repart, M-repart, Z-refine, Z-scratch, and M-scratch.

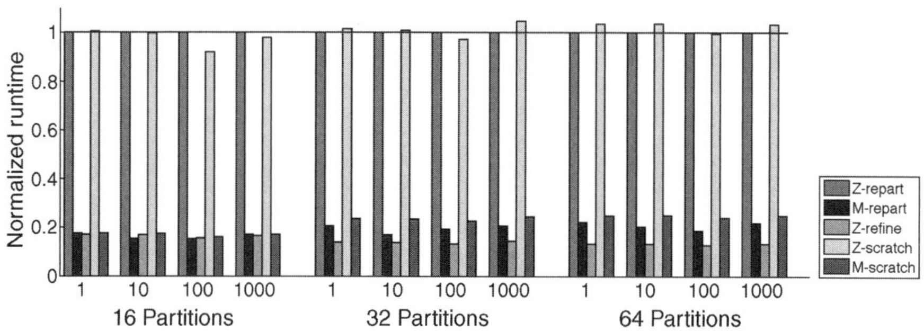

Figure 15.17 Normalized runtime for average of five test graphs with perturbed data structure with $\alpha = 1, 10, 100, 1000$ on 16, 32, and 64 processors. From left to right, the methods are Z-repart, M-repart, Z-refine, Z-scratch, and M-scratch.

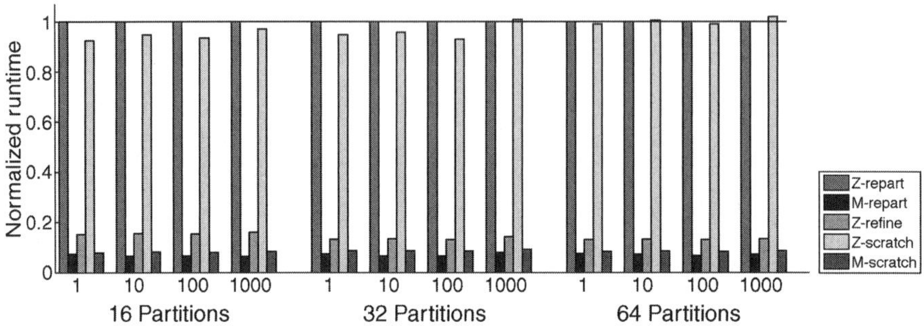

Figure 15.18 Normalized runtime for average of five test graphs with perturbed weights with $\alpha = 1, 10, 100, 1000$ on 16, 32, and 64 processors. From left to right, the methods are Z-repart, M-repart, Z-refine, Z-scratch, and M-scratch.

are at least as fast as their graph-based counterparts, M-repart and M-scratch, on sparse data sets such as xyce680s. Z-refine is significantly faster than all others in this data set; therefore, it becomes a viable option for applications that require a very fast repartitioner for small α-values. The second runtime profile is displayed in Figure 15.15 for 2DLipid. In this case, although graph-based repartitioning runs faster for small number of parts, with increasing number of parts its execution time increases as well and becomes comparable to that of hypergraph-based repartitioning. This behavior is probably due to direct k-way refinement strategies used in the graph partitioner. When a dense graph such as 2DLipid is partitioned, the number of computations done by the partitioner increases with increasing number of parts, since it becomes more likely to have an adjacent vertex on every processor. The last runtime profile is observed for cage14, auto and apoa1-10. We omitted results for auto and apoa1-10 and presented results for only cage14 in Figure 15.16, which is the largest graph in this class. The results show that hypergraph-based repartitioning can be up 10 times slower than graph-based approaches. Runtime results averaged over all graphs in our data set are presented in Figures 15.17 and 15.18. As shown in these figures, hypergraph-based repartitioning is about five times slower than graph-based repartitioning on the average. We plan to improve runtime performance by using local heuristics in Z-repart to reduce global communication (e.g., using local matching instead of global matching).

15.6 CONCLUSION

In this chapter, we presented a new approach to dynamic load balancing based on a single hypergraph model that incorporates both communication volume in the application and data migration cost. Detailed comparison of graph- and hypergraph-based repartitioning using data sets from a wide range of application areas showed that hypergraph-based repartitioning produces partitions with similar or lower cost than the graph-based repartitioning. To provide comparisons with graph repartitioners, in this work, we restricted our tests to square, symmetric problems. The full benefit of hypergraph partitioning is realized on unsymmetrical and nonsquare problems that cannot be represented easily with graph models [7, 12].

Hypergraph-based repartitioning uses a single user-defined parameter α to trade between communication cost and migration cost. Experiments show that the approach works particularly well when migration cost is more important, but without compromising quality when communication cost is more important. Therefore, we recommend the presented approach as a universal method for dynamic load balancing. The best choice of α will depend on the application and can be estimated. Reasonable values are in the range 1–1000.

The experiments showed that the hypergraph-based repartitioning approach implemented in Zoltan is scalable. However, it generally required more time than its graph-based counterpart, mostly due to the greater richness of the hypergraph model. By exploiting locality given by the data distribution, the hypergraph-based repartitioning implementation can be made to run faster without reducing quality. However, since the application runtime is often far greater than the partitioning time, this enhancement may not be important in practice.

REFERENCES

1. C.J. Alpert, A.E. Caldwell, A.B. Kahng, and I.L. Markov. Hypergraph partitioning with fixed vertices [vlsi cad]. *IEEE Trans. Comput. Aid. Des. Integr. Circ. Syst.*, 19(2):267–272, 2000.
2. C. Aykanat, B.B. Cambazoglu, F. Findik, and T. Kurc. Adaptive decomposition and remapping algorithms for object–space–parallel direct volume rendering of unstructured grids. *J. Parallel Distrib. Comput.*, 67(1):77–99, 2007.
3. E. Boman, K. Devine, L.A. Fisk, R. Heaphy, B. Hendrickson, C. Vaughan, U. Catalyurek, D. Bozdag, and W. Mitchell. Zoltan 2.0: data management services for parallel applications: user's guide. Technical Report SAND2006-2958. Sandia National Laboratories, Albuquerque, NM. http://www.cs.sandia.gov/Zoltan/ug_html/ug.html, 2006.
4. T.N. Bui and C. Jones. A heuristic for reducing fill-in sparse matrix factorization. In *Proceedings of the 6th SIAM Conference on Parallel Processing for Scientific Computing*, SIAM, 1993, pp. 445–452.
5. B.B. Cambazoglu and C. Aykanat. Hypergraph-partitioning-based remapping models for image–space–parallel direct volume rendering of unstructured grids. *IEEE Trans. Parallel Distrib. Syst.*, 18(1):3–16, 2007.
6. U.V. Catalyurek, E.G. Boman, K.D. Devine, D. Bozdağ, R. Heaphy, and L. A. Fisk. Dynamic load balancing for adaptive scientific computations via hypergraph partitioning. In *Proceedings of the 21st International Parallel and Distributed Processing Symposium (IPDPS'07)*, IEEE, 2007.
7. Ü. V. Çatalyürek and C. Aykanat. Hypergraph-partitioning based decomposition for parallel sparse–matrix vector multiplication. *IEEE Trans. Parallel Distrib. Syst.*, 10(7):673–693, 1999.
8. Ü. V. Çatalyürek and C. Aykanat. PaToH: A Multilevel Hypergraph Partitioning Tool, Version 3.0. Department of Computer Engineering, Bilkent University, Ankara, Turkey. http://bmi.osu.edu/~umit/software.htm, 1999.
9. G. Cybenko. Dynamic load balancing for distributed memory multiprocessors. *J. Parallel Distrib. Comput.*, 7:279–301, 1989.
10. H.L. deCougny, K.D. Devine, J.E. Flaherty, R.M. Loy, C. Ozturan, and M.S. Shephard. Load balancing for the parallel adaptive solution of partial differential equations. *Appl. Numer. Math.*, 16:157–182, 1994.
11. K. Devine, E. Boman, R. Heaphy, B. Hendrickson, and C. Vaughan. Zoltan data management services for parallel dynamic applications. *Comput. Sci. Eng.*, 4(2):90–97, 2002.

12. K.D. Devine, E.G. Boman, R.T. Heaphy, R.H. Bisseling, and U.V. Catalyurek. Parallel hypergraph partitioning for scientific computing. In *Proceedings of the 20th International Parallel and Distributed Processing Symposium (IPDPS'06),* IEEE, 2006.
13. P. Diniz, S. Plimpton, B. Hendrickson, and R. Leland. Parallel algorithms for dynamically partitioning unstructured grids. In *Proceedings of the 7th SIAM Conference on Parallel Processing for Scientific Computing*, SIAM, 1995, pp. 615–620.
14. C. M. Fiduccia and R. M. Mattheyses. A linear-time heuristic for improving network partitions. In *Proceedings of the 19th IEEE Design Automation Conference, 1982*, pp. 175–181.
15. J.E. Flaherty, R.M. Loy, M.S. Shephard, B.K. Szymanski, J.D. Teresco, and L.H. Ziantz. Adaptive local refinement with octree load-balancing for the parallel solution of three-dimensional conservation laws. *J. Parallel Distrib. Comput.*, 47(2):139–152, 1998.
16. M. R. Garey and D. S. Johnson. *Computers and Intractability*. W.H. Freeman and Co., NY, New York, 1979.
17. B. Hendrickson and R. Leland. The Chaco User's Guide, Version 2.0. Sandia National Laboratories, Albuquerque, NM, 1995.
18. B. Hendrickson and R. Leland. A multilevel algorithm for partitioning graphs. In *Proceedings of Supercomputing '95*. ACM, December 1995.
19. Y. F. Hu and R. J. Blake. An optimal dynamic load balancing algorithm. Technical Report DL-P-95-011. Daresbury Laboratory, Warrington, UK, 1995.
20. Y. F. Hu, R. J. Blake, and D. R. Emerson. An optimal migration algorithm for dynamic load balancing. *Concurrency Pract. Exper.*, 10:467–483, 1998.
21. M.A. Iqbal and S.H. Bokhari. Efficient algorithms for a class of partitioning problems. *IEEE Trans. Parallel Distrib. Syst.*, 6(2):170–175, 1995.
22. G. Karypis and V. Kumar. METIS 3.0: Unstructured graph partitioning and sparse matrix ordering system. Technical Report 97-061, Department of Computer Science, University of Minnesota, Minneabolis. http://www.cs.umn.edu/~metis., 1997.
23. G. Karypis and V. Kumar. *MeTiS A Software Package for Partitioning Unstructured Graphs, Partitioning Meshes, and Computing Fill-Reducing Orderings of Sparse Matrices Version 4.0.* Army HPC Research Center, Department of Computer Science and Engineering, University of Minnesota, Minneapolis, 1998.
24. G. Karypis and V. Kumar. A fast and high quality multilevel scheme for partitioning irregular graphs. *SIAM J. Sci. Comput.*, 20(1), 1999.
25. G. Karypis, V. Kumar, R. Aggarwal, and S. Shekhar. *hMeTiS A Hypergraph Partitioning Package Version 1.0.1.* Army HPC Research Center, Department of Computer Science and Engineering, University of Minnesota, Minneapolis, 1998.
26. G. Karypis, K. Schloegel, and V. Kumar. ParMETIS: parallel graph partitioning and sparse matrix ordering library, version 3.1. Technical report, Department of Computer Science, University of Minnesota, Minneapolis. http://www-users.cs.umn.edu/ karypis/metis/parmetis/download.html, 2003.
27. G. Karypis, R. Aggarwal, V. Kumar, and S. Shekhar. Multilevel hypergraph partitioning: application in VLSI domain. In *Proceedings of the 34th Design Automation Conference*, ACM, 1997, pp. 526–529.
28. H. Kasahara and S. Narita. Practical multiprocessor scheduling algorithms for efficient parallel processing. *IEEE Trans. Comput.*, C-33(11):1023–1029, 1984.
29. B. W. Kernighan and S. Lin. An efficient heuristic procedure for partitioning graphs. *The Bell Syst. Tech. J.*, 49(2):291–307, 1970.
30. T. Lengauer. *Combinatorial Algorithms for Integrated Circuit Layout.* Willey–Teubner, Chichester, UK, 1990.
31. L. Oliker and R. Biswas. PLUM: parallel load balancing for adaptive unstructured meshes. *J. Parallel Distrib. Comput.*, 51(2):150–177, 1998.
32. C.-W. Ou and S. Ranka. Parallel incremental graph partitioning using linear programming. Technical report, Syracuse University, Syracuse, NY, 1992.
33. K. Schloegel, G. Karypis, and V. Kumar. Multilevel diffusion algorithms for repartitioning of adaptive meshes. *J. Parallel Distrib. Comput.*, 47(2):109–124, 1997.
34. K. Schloegel, G. Karypis, and V. Kumar. A unified algorithm for load-balancing adaptive scientific simulations. In *Proceedings of Supercomputing*, Dallas, TX, 2000.

35. K. Schloegel, G. Karypis, and V. Kumar. Wavefront diffusion and LMSR: algorithms for dynamic repartitioning of adaptive meshes. *IEEE Trans. Parallel Distrib. Syst.*, 12(5):451–466, 2001.
36. D. G. Schweikert and B. W. Kernighan. A proper model for the partitioning of electrical circuits. In *Proceedings of the 9th ACM/IEEE Design Automation Conference*, 1972, pp. 57–62.
37. J.D. Teresco, M.W. Beall, J.E. Flaherty, and M.S. Shephard. A hierarchical partition model for adaptive finite element computation. *Comput. Methods Appl. Mech. Eng.*, 184:269–285, 2000.
38. A. Trifunovic and W.J. Knottenbelt. Parkway 2.0: a parallel multilevel hypergraph partitioning tool. In *Proceedings of the 19th International Symposium on Computer and Information Sciences (ISCIS 2004)*, Lecture Notes in Computer Science, Vol. 3280. Springer, 2004, 789–800.
39. R.V. Driessche and D. Roose. Dynamic load balancing with a spectral bisection algorithm for the constrained graph partitioning problem. In B. Hertzberger and G. Serazzi, editors, *High-Performance Computing and Networking*, Lecture Notes in Computer Science, No. 9,9. Springer, 1995, pp. 392–397.
40. B. Vastenhouw and R.H. Bisseling. A two-dimensional data distribution method for parallel sparse matrix-vector multiplication. *SIAM Rev.*, 47(1):67–95, 2005.
41. C. Walshaw, M. Cross, and M. Everett. Parallel dynamic graph-partitioning for adaptive unstructured meshes. *J. Parallel Distrib. Comput.*, 47(2):102–108, 1997.
42. C. Walshaw. *The Parallel JOSTLE Library User's Guide, Version 3.0.* University of Greenwich, London, UK, 2002.
43. M. Willebeek-LeMair and A.P. Reeves. Strategies for dynamic load balancing on highly parallel computers. *IEEE Trans. Parallel Distrib. Syst.*, 4(9):979–993, 1993.
44. R. Williams. Performance of dynamic load balancing algorithms for unstructured mesh calculations. *Concurrency*, 3:457–481, 1991.
45. Zoltan: data management services for parallel applications. http://www.cs.sandia.gov/Zoltan/.

Chapter 16

Mesh Partitioning for Efficient Use of Distributed Systems

Jian Chen and Valerie E. Taylor

16.1 INTRODUCTION

Distributed computing has been regarded as the future of high-performance computing. Nationwide high-speed networks such as vBNS [25] are becoming widely available to interconnect high-speed computers, virtual environments, scientific instruments, and large data sets. Projects such as Globus [16] and Legion [21] are developing software infrastructure that integrates distributed computational and informational resources. In this study, we present a mesh partitioning tool for distributed systems. This tool, called PART, takes into consideration the heterogeneity in processors and networks found in distributed systems as well as heterogeneities found in the applications.

Mesh partitioning is required for efficient parallel execution of finite element and finite difference applications, which are widely used in many disciplines such as biomedical engineering, structural mechanics, and fluid dynamics. These applications are distinguished by the use of a meshing procedure to discretize the problem domain. Execution of a mesh-based application on a parallel or distributed system involves partitioning the mesh into subdomains that are assigned to individual processors in the parallel or distributed system.

Mesh partitioning for homogeneous systems has been studied extensively [2, 3, 15, 28, 34, 35, 39]; however, mesh partitioning for distributed systems is a relatively new area of research brought about by the recent availability of such systems [6, 7]. To ensure efficient execution on a distributed system, the heterogeneities in the processor

Advanced Computational Infrastructures For Parallel and Distributed Adaptive Applications. Edited by Manish Parashar and Xiaolin Li

and network performance must be taken into consideration in the partitioning process; equal size subdomains and small cut set size, which results from conventional mesh partitioning, are no longer desirable. PART takes advantage of the following heterogeneous system features:

1. processor speed,
2. number of processors,
3. local network performance, and
4. wide area network performance.

Furthermore, different finite element applications under consideration may have different computational complexity, different communication patterns, and different element types, which also must be taken into consideration when partitioning.

In this study, we discuss the major issues in mesh partitioning for distributed systems. In particular, we identify a good metric to be used to compare different partitioning results, present a measure of efficiency for a distributed system, and discuss optimal number of cut sets for remote communication. The metric used with PART to identify good efficiency is estimated execution time.

We also present a parallel version of PART that significantly improves performance of the partitioning process. Simulated annealing is used in PART to perform the backtracking search for desired partitions. However, it is well known that simulated annealing is computationally intensive. In the parallel version of PART, we use the asynchronous multiple Markov chain approach of parallel simulated annealing [22]. PART is used to partition six irregular meshes into 8, 16, and 100 subdomains using up to 64 client processors on an IBM SP2 machine. The results show superlinear speedup in most cases and nearly perfect speedup for the rest. The results also indicate that the parallel version of PART produces partitions consistent with the sequential version of PART.

Using partitions from PART, we ran an explicit, 2D finite element code on two geographically distributed IBM SP machines with different processors. We used Globus software for communication between the two SPs. We compared the partitions from PART with that generated using the widely used partitioning tool METIS [26], which considers only processor performance. The results from the regular problems indicate a 33–46% increase in efficiency when processor performance is considered as compared to the conventional even partitioning; the results indicate 5–15% increase in efficiency when network performance is considered as compared to considering only processor performance. This is significant given that the optimal is 15% for this application. The result from the irregular problem indicate up to 36% increase in efficiency when processor and network performance are considered as compared to even partitioning.

The remainder of the study is organized as follows: Section 16.2 discusses issues particular to mesh partitioning for distributed systems. Section 16.3 describes PART in detail. Section 16.4 introduces parallel simulated annealing. Section 16.5 is experimental results. Section 16.6 gives previous work and Section 16.7 gives the conclusions and areas of future work.

16.2 MAJOR ISSUES RELATED TO MESH PARTITIONING FOR DISTRIBUTED SYSTEMS

In this section, we discuss the following major issues related to the mesh partitioning problem for distributed systems: comparison metric, efficiency, and number of cuts between groups.

16.2.1 Comparison Metric

The *de facto* metric for comparing the quality of different partitions for homogeneous parallel systems has been equal subdomains and minimum interface (or cut set) size. Although there have been objections and counter examples [15], this metric has been used extensively in comparing the quality of different partitions. It is obvious that equal subdomain size and minimum interface is not valid for comparing partitions for distributed systems.

One may consider an obvious metric for a distributed system to be unequal subdomains (proportional to processor performance) and small cut set size. The problem with this metric is that heterogeneity in network performance is not considered. Given that the local and wide area networks are used in distributed system, it is the case that there will be a big difference between local and remote communication, especially in terms of latency.

We argue that the use of an estimate of execution time of the application on the target heterogeneous system will always lead to a valid comparison of different partitions. The estimate is used for relative comparison of different partition methods. Hence, a coarse approximation of the execution is appropriate for the comparison metric. It is important to make the estimate representative of the application and the system. The estimate should include parameters that correspond to system heterogeneities such as processor performance, and local and remote communication time. It should also reflect the application computational complexity. For example, with the WHAMS application, which uses explicit methods, the coarse approximation includes a linear function in terms of the number of nodes assigned to a processor and the amount of communication. For implicit methods, one way use a nonlinear function, with the exponent equal to 1.5 assuming a good iterative method is used for the solve step, in addition to the amount of communication. The coefficent of the linear (or nonlinear) function can be determined from previous runs of the application and using a least squares fit to the data.

16.2.2 Efficiency

The efficiency for the distributed system is equal to the ratio of the relative speedup to the effective number of processors, V. This ratio is given below:

$$\text{Efficiency} = \frac{E(1)}{E \times V}, \tag{16.1}$$

where $E(1)$ is the sequential execution time on one processor and E is the execution time on the distributed system. The term V is equal to the summation of each processor's performance relative to the performance of the processor used for sequential execution. This term is as follows:

$$V = \sum_{i=1}^{P} \frac{F_i}{F_k}, \tag{16.2}$$

where k is the processor used for sequential execution and F_i represents the performance of processor i. For example, with two processors having processor performance $F_1 = 1$ and $F_2 = 2$, the efficiency would be

$$\text{Efficiency} = \frac{E(1)}{E \times 3}, \tag{16.3}$$

if processor 1 is used for sequential execution; the efficiency is

$$\text{Efficiency} = \frac{E(1)}{E \times 1.5}, \tag{16.4}$$

if processor 2 is instead used for sequential execution.

16.2.3 Network Heterogeneity

It is well-known that heterogeneity of processor performance must be considered with distributed systems. In this section, we identify conditions for which heterogeneity in network performance must be considered.

For a distributed system, we define a *group* to be a collection of processors that have the same performance and share a local interconnection network. A group can be a symmetric multiprocessor (SMP), a parallel computer, or a cluster of workstations or personal computers. Communication occurs within a group and between groups. We refer to communication within a group as *local* communication; communication between processors in different groups is referred to as *remote* communication. Given that for the execution of the application some processors will require remote and local communication, while others only require local communication, there will be a disparity between the execution times of these processors corresponding to the difference in remote and local communications (assuming equal computational loads).

Ideal Reduction in Execution Time A retrofit step is used with the PART tool to reduce the computational load of processors with local and remote communication to equalize the execution time among the processors in a group. This step is described in detail in Section 16.3.2. The reduction in execution time that occurs with this retrofit is demonstrated by considering a simple case, stripe partitioning, for which communication occurs with at most two neighboring processors. Assume that there exists two groups having the same processor and local network performance; the groups are located at geographically distributed sites requiring a WAN for interconnection. Figure 16.1 illustrates one such case.

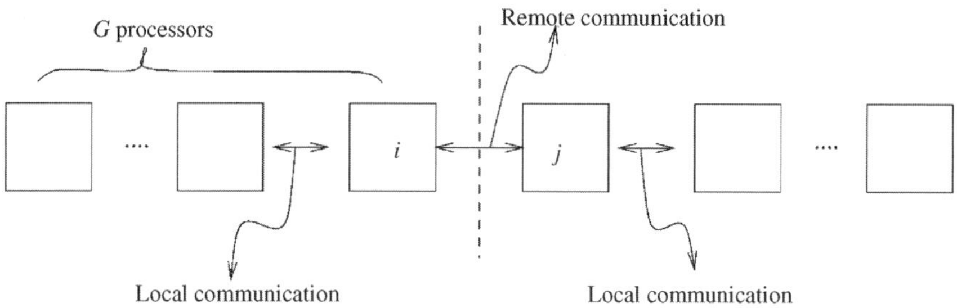

Group 1 Group 2

Figure 16.1 Communication pattern for stripe partitioning.

Processor i (as well as processor j) requires local and remote communication. The difference between the two communication times is

$$C_{\text{R}} - C_{\text{L}} = x\%E, \tag{16.5}$$

where C_{R} and C_{L} are remote and local communication times, respectively, and x is the percentage of the difference of C_{R} and C_{L} in terms of the total execution time, E. Assume that E represents the execution time using a partition that takes into consideration processor performance only. Since it is assumed that all processors have the same performance, this entails an even partition of the mesh. The execution time can be written as

$$E = C_{\text{L}} + C_{\text{R}} + E_{\text{comp}} = 2C_{\text{L}} + x\%E + E_{\text{comp}}, \tag{16.6}$$

where E_{comp} represents the computation time of any given processor that is equal among all processors.

Now, consider the case of partitioning to take into consideration the heterogeneity in network performance. This is achieved by decreasing the load assigned to processor i and increasing the loads of the $G - 1$ processors in group 1. The same applies to processor j in group 2. The amount of the load to be redistributed is $C_{\text{R}} - C_{\text{L}}$ or $x\%E$ and this amount is distributed to G processors. This is illustrated in Fig. 16.5, which is discussed with the retrofit step of PART. The execution time is now

$$E' = 2C_{\text{L}} + \frac{x}{G}\%E + E_{\text{comp}}. \tag{16.7}$$

The difference between E and E' is

$$T_{\text{reduction}} = E - E' = x\%E - \frac{x}{G}\%E = \frac{G-1}{G}x\%E. \tag{16.8}$$

Therefore, by taking the network performance into consideration when partitioning, the percentage reduction in execution time is approximately $x\%E$ (denoted as $\Delta(1, G)$), which includes the following: (1) the percentage of communication in the application and (2) the difference in the remote and local communication. Both factors are determined by the application and the partitioning. If the maximum number of processors among the groups that have remote communication is ν, then the reduction in execution time is as follows:

$$T_{\text{reduction}} = \frac{G - \nu}{G} \Delta(\nu, G). \tag{16.9}$$

For example, for the WHAMS2D application in our experiments, we calculated the ideal reduction to be 15% for the regular meshes with $\nu = 1$ and $G = 8$. For those partitions, only one processor in each group has local and remote communication; therefore, it is relatively easy to calculate the ideal performance improvement.

Number of Processors in a Group with Local and Remote Communication The major issue to be addressed with the reduction is how to partition the domain assigned to a group to maximize the reduction. In particular, this issue entails a trade-off between the following two scenarios: one with many processors in a group having local and remote communication and the other with only one processor in a group having local and remote communication.

1. Many processors in a group, having local and remote communication, result in small message sizes for which the execution time without the retrofit step is smaller than that for case 2. However, given that many processors in a group have remote and local communication, there are fewer processors that are available for redistribution of the additional load. This is illustrated in Figure 16.2, where a mesh of size $n \times 2n$ is partitioned into $2P$ blocks. Each block is $n/\sqrt{P} \times n/\sqrt{P}$ assuming all processors have equal performance. The mesh is partitioned into two groups, each group having P processors. Processors on the group boundary incur remote communication as well as local communication. Part of the computational load of these processors needs to be moved to processors with only local communication to compensate for the longer communication times. Assuming that there is no overlap in communication messages and message aggregation is used for the communication of one node to the diagonal processor, the communication time for a processor

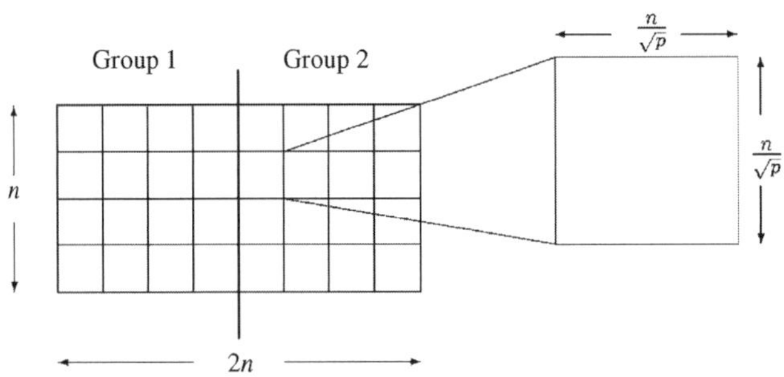

Figure 16.2 A size $n \times 2n$ mesh partitioned into $2P$ blocks.

on the group boundary is approximately

$$T_{\text{comm}}^{\text{local+remote}} = 3\left(\alpha_{\text{L}} + \beta_{\text{L}} \times \frac{n}{\sqrt{P}}\right) + \left(\alpha_{\text{R}} + \beta_{\text{R}} \times \frac{n}{\sqrt{P}}\right). \quad (16.10)$$

For a processor with only local communication, the communication time is approximately (again, message aggregation and no overlapping are assumed)

$$T_{\text{comm}}^{\text{local}} = 4\left(\alpha_{\text{L}} + \beta_{\text{L}} \times \frac{n}{\sqrt{P}}\right), \quad (16.11)$$

where the subscripts denote local and remote communication parameters. Therefore, the communication time difference between a processor with local and remote communication and a processor with only local communication is approximately

$$\begin{aligned} T_{\text{comm}}^{\Delta}(blocks) &= T_{\text{comm}}^{\text{local+remote}} - T_{\text{comm}}^{\text{local}} \\ &= (\alpha_{\text{R}} - \alpha_{\text{L}}) + (\beta_{\text{R}} - \beta_{\text{L}}) \times \frac{n}{\sqrt{P}}. \end{aligned} \quad (16.12)$$

There are a total of $\sqrt{P}$ number of processors with local and remote communication. Therefore, using equation (16.9), the ideal reduction in execution time in group 1 (and group 2) is

$$T_{\text{reduction}}^{\text{blocks}} = \frac{P - \sqrt{P}}{P} T_{\text{comm}}^{\Delta}(\text{blocks}). \quad (16.13)$$

2. Only one processor in a group has local and remote communication, resulting in large message than that for case 1. However, there are more processors that are available for redistribution of additional load. This is illustrated in Figure 16.3, where the same mesh is partitioned into stripes. There is only one processor in each group that has local and remote communication. Following a similar analysis as in Figure 16.3, the communication time difference between a processor with both local and remote communication and a processor with only local communication is approximately

$$\begin{aligned} T_{\text{comm}}^{\Delta}(\text{stripes}) &= T_{\text{comm}}^{\text{local+remote}} - T_{\text{comm}}^{\text{local}} \\ &= (\alpha_{\text{R}} - \alpha_{\text{L}}) + (\beta_{\text{R}} - \beta_{\text{L}}) \times n. \end{aligned} \quad (16.14)$$

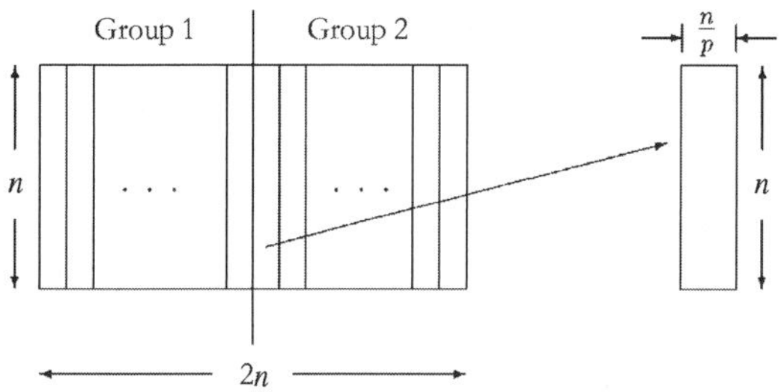

Figure 16.3 A size $n \times 2n$ mesh partitioned into 2P stripes.

There is only one processor with remote communication in each group. Hence, using equation (16.9), the ideal reduction in execution time is

$$T^{\text{stripes}}_{\text{reduction}} = \frac{P-1}{P} T^{\Delta}_{\text{comm}}(\text{stripes}). \tag{16.15}$$

Therefore, the total execution time for stripe and block partitioning are

$$T^{\text{stripes}}_{\text{Total}} = T_{\text{comp}} + (\alpha_{\text{R}} + \beta_{\text{R}} \times n) + (\alpha_{\text{L}} + \beta_{\text{L}} \times n) - T^{\text{stripes}}_{\text{reduction}}. \tag{16.16}$$

$$T^{\text{blocks}}_{\text{Total}} = T_{\text{comp}} + \left(\alpha_{\text{R}} + \beta_{\text{R}} \times \frac{n}{\sqrt{P}}\right) + 3\left(\alpha_{\text{L}} + \beta_{\text{L}} \times \frac{n}{\sqrt{P}}\right) - T^{\text{blocks}}_{\text{reduction}}. \tag{16.17}$$

The difference in total execution time between block and stripe partition is

$$\Delta T^{\text{blocks}-\text{stripes}}_{\text{Total}} = T^{\text{blocks}}_{\text{Total}} - T^{\text{stripes}}_{\text{Total}} \tag{16.18}$$

$$= \underbrace{\frac{2P - \sqrt{P} + 1}{P}\alpha_{\text{L}}}_{A} + \underbrace{\frac{4 - 2\sqrt{P}}{\sqrt{P}} n\beta_{\text{L}}}_{B} + \underbrace{\frac{\sqrt{P} - 1}{P}\alpha_{\text{R}}}_{C} \tag{16.19}$$

Therefore, the difference in total execution time between block and stripe partitioning is determined by P, n, α_{L}, β_{L}, and α_{R}. The terms A and C are positive since $P > 1$, while the term B is negative if $P > 4$. Therefore, if $P \leq 4$, the block partition has a higher execution time; that is, the stripe partitioning is advantageous. If $P > 4$, however, block partitioning will still have a higher execution time unless n is so large that the absolute value of term B is larger than the sum of the absolute values of A and C. Note that α_{L} and α_{R} are one to two orders of magnitude larger than β_{L}. In our experiments, we calculated that block partitioning has a lower execution time only if $n > 127$ KB. In the meshes that we used, however, the largest n is only about 10 KB.

16.3 DESCRIPTION OF PART

PART considers heterogeneities in both the application and the system. In particular, PART takes into consideration that different mesh-based applications may have different computational complexities and the mesh may consist of different element types. For distributed systems, PART takes into consideration heterogeneities in processor and network performance.

Figure 16.4 shows a flow diagram of PART. PART consists of an interface program and a simulated annealing program. A finite element mesh is fed into the interface program and produces the proposed communication graph, which is then fed into a simulated annealing program where the final partitioning is computed. This partitioned graph is translated to the required input file format for the application. This section describes the interface program and the steps required to partition the graph.

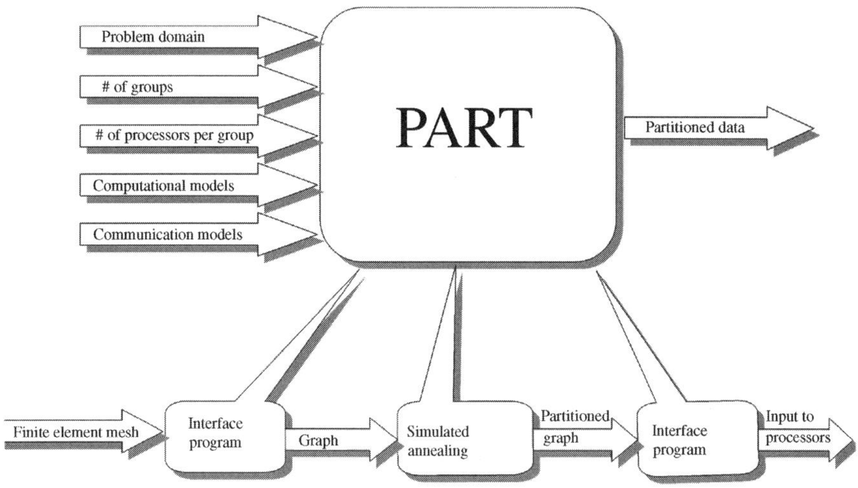

Figure 16.4 PART flowchart.

16.3.1 Mesh Representation

We use a weighted communication graph to represent a finite element mesh. This is a natural extension of the communication graph. As in the communication graph, vertices represent elements in the original mesh. A weight is added to each vertex to represent the number of nodes within the element. Same as in the communication graph, edges represent the connectivity of the elements. A weight is also added to each edge to represent the number of nodes of which information need to be exchanged between the two neighboring elements.

16.3.2 Partition Method

PART entails three steps to partition a mesh for distributed systems. These steps are

1. Partition the mesh into S subdomains for the S groups, taking into consideration heterogeneity in processor performance and element types.
2. Partition each subdomain into G parts for the G processors in a group, taking into consideration heterogeneity in network performance and element types.
3. If necessary, globally retrofit the partitions among the groups, taking into consideration heterogeneity in the local networks among the different groups.

Each of the above steps is described in detail in the following sections. Each section includes a description of the objective function used with simulated annealing.

The key to a good partitioning by simulated annealing is the cost function. The cost function used by PART is the estimate of execution time. For one particular supercomputer, let E_i be the execution time for the ith processor ($1 \leq i \leq p$). The goal here is to minimize the variance of the execution time for all processors.

While running the simulated annealing program, we found that the best cost function is

$$\sum_{1 \leq i \leq p} \left(E^2_{\text{comp}} + \lambda E^2_{\text{comm}} \right) \tag{16.20}$$

instead of the sum of the $E_i{}^2$. So, equation (16.20) is the actual cost function used in the simulated annealing program. In this cost function, E_{comm} includes the communication cost for the partitions that have elements that need to communicate with elements on a remote processor. Therefore, the execution time will be balanced. The term λ is the parameter that needs to be tuned according to the application, such that the communication costs are weighted equally with the computation costs.

Step 1: Group Partition The first step generates a coarse partitioning for the distributed systems. Each group gets a subdomain that is proportional to its number of processors, the performance of the processors, and the computational complexity of the application. Hence, computational cost is balanced across all the groups.

The cost function is given by

$$\sum_{1 \leq i \leq S} \left[E^2_{\text{comp}_\text{i}} + \lambda \left[\sum_j \left(\alpha_j + \beta_j \times L_j \right) \right]^2 \right], \tag{16.21}$$

where S is the number of groups in the system.

Step 2: Retrofit In the second step, the subdomain that is assigned to each group from step 1 is partitioned among its processors. Within each group, simulated annealing is used to balance the execution time. In this step, heterogeneity in network performance is considered. Processors that entail intergroup communication will have reduced computational load to compensate for the longer communication time.

The step is illustrated in Figure 16.5 for two supercomputers, SC1 and SC2. In SC1, four processors are used and two processors are used in SC2. Computational load is reduced for $p3$ since it communicates with a remote processor. The amount of reduced computational load is represented as δ. This amount is equally distributed to the other three processors. Assuming the cut size remains unchanged, the communication time will not change, and hence the execution time will be balanced after this shifting of computational load.

Step 2 entails generating imbalanced partitions in group i that take into consideration the fact that some processors communicate locally and remotely, while other processors communicate only locally. The imbalance is represented with the term Δ_i. This term is added to processors that require local and remote communication. The results in a decrease in E_{comp_i} for processors that require local and remote communication as compared to processors requiring only local communication. The cost

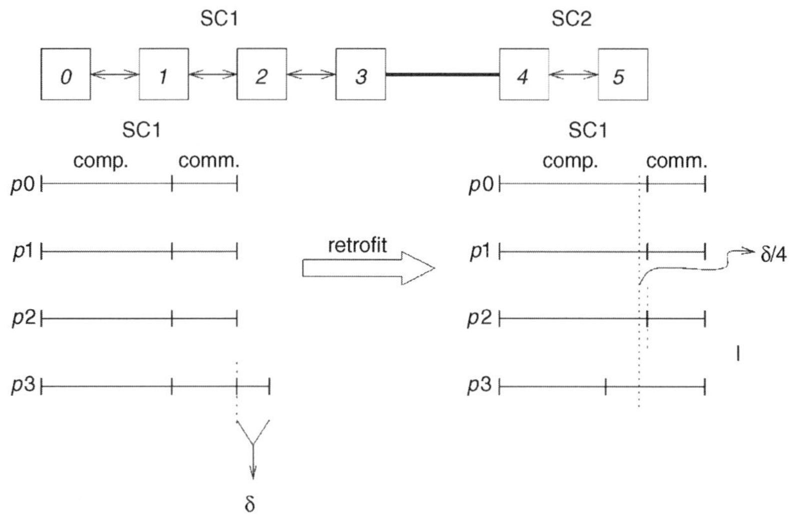

Figure 16.5 An illustration of the retrofit step for two supercomputers assuming only two nearest neighbor communication.

function is given by the following equation:

$$\sum_{1 \leq i \leq p} \left[(E_{comp_i} + \Delta_i)^2 + \lambda \left[\sum_{j,k} \{ (\alpha_j + \beta_j \times L_j) + (\alpha_k + \beta_k \times L_k) \} \right]^2 \right], \quad (16.22)$$

where p is the number of processors in a given group; Δ_i is the difference in the estimation of local and remote communication time. For processors that only communicate locally, $\Delta_i = 0$.

Step 3: Global Retrofit The third step addresses the global optimization, taking into consideration differences in the local interconnect performance of various groups. Again, the goal is to minimize the variance of the execution time across all processors. This step is only executed if there is a large difference in the performance of the different local interconnects. After step 2, processors in each group will have a balanced execution time. However, the execution times of the different groups may not be balanced. This may occur when there is a large difference in the communication time of the different groups. In step 3, elements on the boundaries of partitions are moved according to the execution time variance between neighboring processors. For the case when a significant number of elements are moved between the groups, the second step is executed again to equalize the execution time in a group given the new computational load.

To balance the execution among all the groups, we take the weighted average of execution times E_i $(1 \leq i \leq S)$ from all the groups. The weight for each group is equal to the ratio of the computing power of that group to the total computing power of the distributed system. The computing power for a particular group is the multiplication of the number of processors in the group and the ratio of the processor performance with respect to the slowest processor among all the groups.

We denote the weighted average execution time as $\bar{E}$. Under the assumption that communication time will not change much (i.e., the separators from step 1 will not incur a large change in size), $\bar{E}$ is the optimal execution time that can be achieved. To balance the execution time so that each group will have an execution time of $\bar{E}$, we first compute the difference of E_i with $\bar{E}$:

$$\Gamma_i = E_i - \bar{E}. \tag{16.23}$$

The term Γ_i is then added to each E_{comp_i} in the cost function. The communication cost E_{comm_i} is now the remote communication cost for group i. The cost function is, therefore, given by

$$\sum_{1 \leq i \leq S} \left[(E_{\text{comp}_i} + \Gamma_i)^2 + \lambda \left[\sum_j \left(\alpha_j + \beta_j \times L_j \right) \right]^2 \right], \tag{16.24}$$

where S is the number of groups in the system. For groups whose $\Gamma_i < 0$, the domain will increase; for groups whose $\Gamma_i > 0$, the domain will decrease. If step 3 is necessary, then step 2 is performed again to partition within each group.

16.4 PARALLEL SIMULATED ANNEALING

PART uses simulated annealing to partition the mesh. Figure 16.6 shows the serial version of the simulated annealing algorithm. This algorithm uses the Metropolis criteria (line 8–13 in Figure 16.6) to accept or reject moves. The moves that reduce the cost function are accepted; the moves that increase the cost function may be accepted with probability $e^{-\Delta E/T}$, thereby avoiding being trapped in local minima. This probability decreases when the temperature is lowered. Simulated Annealing is computationally intensive; therefore, a parallel version of simulated annealing is used with PART.

There are three major classes of parallel simulated annealing [20]: serial-like [29, 37], parallel moves [1], and multiple Markov chains [4, 22, 31]. Serial-like algorithms essentially break up each move into subtasks and parallelize the subtasks (parallelizing lines 6 and 7 in Figure 16.6). For the parallel moves algorithms, each processor generates and evaluates moves independently; cost function calculation may be inaccurate since processors are not aware of moves by other processors. Periodic updates are normally used to address the effect of cost function error. Parallel moves algorithms essentially parallelize the loop in Figure 16.6 (line 5–14). For the multiple Markov chains algorithm, multiple simulated annealing processes are started on various processors with *different* random seeds. Processors periodically exchange solutions and the best is selected and given to all the processors to continue their annealing processes. In Ref. [4], the multiple Markov chain approach was shown to be most effective for VLSI cell placement. For this reason, PART uses the multiple Markov chain approach.

```
Get an initial solution S
Get an initial temperature T > 0
While stopping criteria not met {
  M = number of moves per temperature
  for m = 1 to M {
    Generate a random move
    Evaluate changes in cost function: ΔE
   if (ΔE < 0) {
    accept this move, and update solution S
  } else {
    accept with probability P = e^(-ΔE/T)
    update solution S if accepted
  }
} /*end for loop*/
Set T = rT (reduce temperature)
} /*end while loop */
Returns S
```

Figure 16.6 Simulated annealing.

To achieve speedup, P processors perform an independent simulated annealing with a different seed, but performs only M/P moves (M is the number of moves performed by the simulated annealing at each temperature). Processors exchange solutions at the end of each temperature. The exchange of data can occur synchronously or asynchronously. In the synchronous multiple Markov chain approach, the processors periodically exchange solutions with each other. In the asynchronous approach, the client processors exchange solutions with a server processor. It has been reported that the synchronous approach is more easily trapped in a local optima than the asynchronous one [22], therefore, PART uses the asynchronous approach. During solution exchange, if the client solution is better, the server processor is updated with the better solution; if the server solution is better, the client gets updated with the better solution and continues from there. Each processor exchanges its solution with the server processor at the end of each temperature.

To ensure that each subdomain is connected, we check for disconnected components at the end of PART. If any subdomain has disconnected components, the parallel simulated annealing is repeated with a different random seed. This process continues until there are no disconnected subdomains or the number of trials exceeds three times. A warning message is given in the output if there are disconnected subdomains.

16.5 EXPERIMENTS

In this section, we present the results from two different experiments. The first experiment focuses on the speedup of the parallel simulated annealing used with PART. The second experiment focuses on the quality of the partitions generated with PART.

16.5.1 Speedup Results

PART is used to partition six 2D irregular meshes with triangular elements: barth4 (11,451 elem.), barth5 (30,269 elem.), inviscid (6928 elem.), labarre (14,971 elem.), spiral (1992 elem.), and viscous (18,369 elem.). It is assumed that the subdomains will be executed on a distributed system consisting of two IBM SPs, with equal number of processors but different processor performance. Furthermore, the machines are interconnected via vBNS for which the performance of the network is given in Table 16.2 (discussed in Section 16.5.2). The solution quality of using two or more client processors is within 5% of that of using one client processor. In this case, the solution quality is the estimate of the execution time of WHAMS2D.

Figures 16.7 and 16.8 are graphical representations of the speedup of the parallel version of PART relative to one client processor. The figures show that when the meshes are partitioned into 8 subdomains, superlinear speedup occurs in all cases. When the meshes are partitioned into 100 subdomains, superlinear speedup occurs only in the cases of two smallest meshes, spiral and inviscid. Other cases show slightly less than perfect speedup. This superlinear speedup is attributed to the use of multiple client processors conducting a search, for which all the processors benefit from the results. Once a good solution is found by any one of the clients, this information is given to other clients quickly, thereby reducing the effort of continuing to search for a solution. The superlinear speedup results are consistent with that reported in Ref. [30].

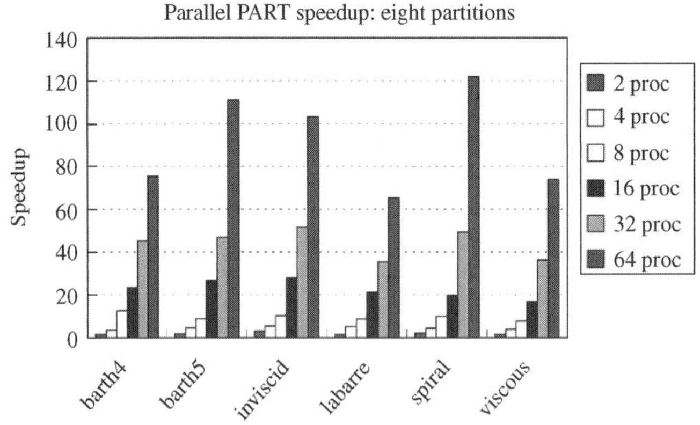

Figure 16.7 Parallel PART speedup for eight partitions.

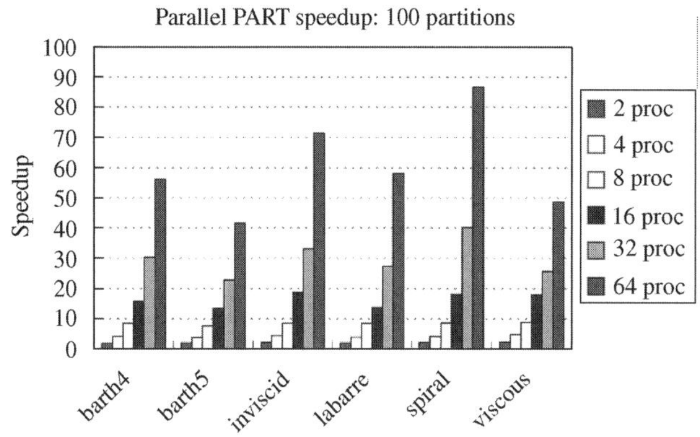

Figure 16.8 Parallel PART speedup for 100 partitions.

16.5.2 Quality of Partitions

Regular Meshes PART was applied to an explicit, nonlinear finite code, called WHAMS2D [5], that is used to analyze elastic–plastic materials. The code uses MPI built on top of Nexus for interprocessor communication within a supercomputer and between supercomputers. Nexus is a runtime system that allows for multiple protocols within an application. The computational complexity is linear with the size of the problem.

The code was executed on the IBM SP machines located at Argonne National Laboratory (ANL) and the Cornell Theory Center (CTC). These two machines were connected by the Internet. Macro benchmarks were used to determine the network and processor performance. The results of the network performance analysis are given in Table 16.1. Furthermore, experiments were conducted to determine that the Cornell nodes were 1.6 times faster than the Argonne nodes.

The problem mesh consists of three regular meshes. The execution time is given for 100 time steps corresponding to 0.005 s of application time. Generally, the application may execute for 10, 000 to 100, 000 timesteps. The recorded execution time represents over 100 runs, taking the data from the runs with standard deviation of less than 3%. The regular problems were executed on a machine configuration of eight processors (four at ANL IBM SP and four at CTC IBM SP).

Table 16.2 presents the results for the regular problems. Column 1 is the mesh configuration. Column 2 is the execution time resulting from the conventional equal partitioning. In particular, we used Chaco's spectral bisection. Column 3 is the result

Table 16.1 Values of α and β for the Different Networks

Argonne SP Vulcan Switch	$\alpha_1 = 0.0009$ s	$\beta_1 = 0.0001$ s/KB
Cornell SP Vulcan Switch	$\alpha_2 = 0.0006$ s	$\beta_2 = 0.0001$ s/KB
Internet	$\alpha_3 = 0.1428$ s	$\beta_3 = 0.0507$ s/KB

Table 16.2 Execution Time Using the Internet 8 Processors; Four at ANL, Four at CTC

Case	Chaco	Proc. Perf.	Local Retrofit
9 × 1152 mesh	102.99 s	78.02 s	68.81 s
Efficiency	0.46	0.61	0.71
18 × 576 mesh	101.16 s	78.87 s	72.25 s
Efficiency	0.47	0.61	0.68
36 × 288 mesh	103.88 s	73.21 s	70.22 s
Efficiency	0.46	0.67	0.70

from the partitioning taken from the end of the first step for which the heterogeneity in processor performance and computational complexity are considered. Column 4 is the execution time resulting from the partitioning taken from the end of the second step of PART for which the heterogeneity in network performance is considered. The results in Table 16.2 shows that approximately 33–46% increase in efficiency can be achieved by balancing the computational cost; another 5–15% efficiency increase can be achieved by considering the heterogeneity in network performance. The small increase in efficiency by considering the network performance was due to communication being a small component of the WHAMS2D application. However, recall that the optimal increase in performance is 15% for the regular problem as described earlier.

The global optimization step, which is the last step of PART that balances execution time across all supercomputers, did not give any increase in efficiency (it is not included in Table 16.2). This is expected since all of the IBM SPs used in our experiments have interconnection networks with very similar performance.

Irregular Meshes The experiments on irregular meshes were performed on the GUSTO testbed, which is not available when we experimented on the regular meshes. This testbed includes two IBM SP machines, one located at Argonne National Laboratory (ANL) and the other located at the San Diego Supercomputing Center (SDSC). These two machines are connected by vBNS (very high speed Backbone Network Service). We used Globus [16, 17] software to allow multimodal communication within the application. Macro-benchmarks were used to determine the network and processor performance. The results of the network performance analysis are given in Table 16.3. Furthermore, experiments were conducted to determine that the SDSC SP processors nodes were 1.6 times as fast as the ANL ones.

Table 16.3 Values of α and β for the Different Networks

ANL SP Vulcan Switch	$\alpha_1 = 0.00069$ s	$\beta_1 = 0.000093$ s/KB
SDSC SP Vulcan Switch	$\alpha_2 = 0.00068$ s	$\beta_2 = 0.000090$ s/KB
vBNS	$\alpha_3 = 0.059$ s	$\beta_3 = 0.0023$ s/KB

PART is used to partition five 2D irregular meshes with triangular elements: barth4 (11,451 elem.), barth5 (30,269 elem.), labarre (14,971 elem.), viscous (18,369 elem.), and inviscid (6928 elem.). Our experiments use two versions of PART. The first version, called PART without restriction, does not impose any restrictions on the number of processors in a group with local and remote communication. The second version, called PART with restriction, partitions the meshes so that only one processor per group has local and remote communication. METIS 3.0 [26] is used to generate partitions that take into consideration processor performance (each processor's compute power is used as one of the inputs). These three partitioners are used to identify the performance impact of considering heterogeneity of networks in addition to that with processors. Furthermore, the three partitioners highlight the difference when forcing remote communication to occur on one processor in a group versus having multiple processors with remote communication in a group.

We consider 6 configurations of the 2 IBM SP machines, 4 at ANL and 4 at SDSC, 8 at ANL and 8 at SDSC, and 20 at ANL and 20 at SDSC. The two groups correspond to the two IBM SPs at ANL and SDSC. We used up to 20 processors from each SP due to limitations in coscheduling computing resources. The execution time is given for 100 timesteps. The recorded execution time represents an average of 10 runs, and the standard deviation is less than 3%.

Tables 16.4–16.6 show the experimental results from the three partitioners. Column 1 identifies the irregular meshes and the number of elements in each mesh (included in parentheses). Column 2 is the execution time resulting from the partitions from PART with the restriction that only one processor per group entails remote communication. For columns 2–4, the number ν indicates the number of processors that has remote communication in a group. Column 3 is similar to column 2 except that the partition does not have the restriction that remote communication be on one processor. Column 4 is the execution time resulting from METIS that takes computing power into consideration (each processor's compute power is used as one of the inputs to the METIS program).

Table 16.4 Execution Time Using the vBNS on Eight Processors; Four at ANL and Four at SDSC

Mesh	PART w/ restriction	PART w/o restriction	Proc. Perf. (METIS)
barth5 (30,269 elem.)	239.0 s (ν=1)	260.0 s (ν=3)	264.0 s ($\nu = 4$)
Efficiency	0.89	0.81	0.80
viscous (18,369 elem.)	150.0 s (ν=1)	169.0 s (ν=3)	170.0 s ($\nu = 3$)
Efficiency	0.86	0.75	0.75
labarre (14,971 elem.)	133.0 s (ν=1)	142.0 s (ν=2)	146.0 s ($\nu = 3$)
Efficiency	0.79	0.73	0.71
barth4 (11,451 elem.)	101.5 s (ν=1)	118.0 s (ν=3)	119.0 s ($\nu = 3$)
Efficiency	0.79	0.68	0.68
inviscid (6928 elem.)	73.2 s (ν=1)	85.5 s (ν=3)	88.5 s($\nu = 3$)
Efficiency	0.66	0.56	0.55

Table 16.5 Execution Time Using the vBNS on 16 Processors: Eight at ANL and Eight at SDSC

Mesh	PART w/ restriction	PART w/o restriction	Proc. perf. (METIS)
barth5 (30,269 elem.)	147.8 s(ν=1)	169.5 s(ν=4)	178.3 s($\nu = 5$)
Efficiency	0.72	0.62	0.59
viscous (18,369 elem.)	82.9 s(ν=1)	100.8 s(ν=4)	106.0 s($\nu = 5$)
Efficiency	0.77	0.64	0.61
labarre (14,971 elem.)	75.8 s(ν=1)	83.7 s(ν=3)	88.6 s($\nu = 3$)
Efficiency	0.69	0.62	0.59
barth4 (11,451 elem.)	54.2 s(ν=1)	79.2 s(ν=2)	83.2 s($\nu = 3$)
Efficiency	0.74	0.50	0.48
inviscid (6928 elem.)	42.2 s(ν=1)	62.8 s(ν=3)	67.2 s($\nu = 4$)
Efficiency	0.57	0.39	0.36

The results show that by using PART without restrictions, a slight decrease (1–3%) in execution time is achieved as compared to METIS. However, by forcing all the remote communication to be on one processor, the retrofit step can achieve more significant reduction in execution time. The results in Tables 16.4–16.6 show that efficiency is increased by up to 36% as compared to METIS, and the execution time is reduced by up to 30% as compared to METIS. This reduction comes from the fact that even on a high-speed network, such as the vBNS, the difference of message startup cost on remote and local communication is very large. From Table 16.3, we see that this difference is two orders of magnitude for message startup compared to approximately one order of magnitude for bandwidth. Restricting remote communication on one processor allows PART to redistribute the load among more processors, thereby achieving close to the ideal reduction in execution time.

16.6 PREVIOUS WORK

The problem of mesh partitioning for finite element meshes is equivalent to partitioning the graph associated with the finite element mesh. Graph partitioning has been

Table 16.6 Execution Time Using the vBNS on 40 Processors: 20 at ANL and 20 at SDSC

Mesh	PART w/restriction	PART w/o restriction	Proc. perf. (METIS)
barth5 (30,269 elem.)	61.6 s(ν=1)	78.3 s(ν=6)	94.2 s($\nu = 7$)
Efficiency	0.69	0.54	0.45
viscous (18,369 elem.)	38.7 s(ν=1)	58.6 s(ν=5)	64.9 s($\nu = 7$)
Efficiency	0.67	0.44	0.40
labarre (14,971 elem.)	33.8 s(ν=1)	51.2 s(ν=3)	53.5 s($\nu = 6$)
Efficiency	0.62	0.41	0.40
barth4 (11,451 elem.)	41.2 s(ν=1)	46.8 s(ν=5)	50.7 s($\nu = 5$)
Efficiency	0.39	0.34	0.32
inviscid (6928 elem.)	33.5(ν=1)	34.7 s(ν=4)	46.8 s($\nu = 5$)
Efficiency	0.29	0.28	0.21

proven to be an NP-complete problem [18]. Many good heuristic static partitioning methods have been proposed. Kernighan and Lin [28] proposed a locally optimized partitioning method. Farhat and Lesoinne [14, 15] proposed an automatic domain decomposer based on the Greedy algorithm. Berger and Bokhari [3] proposed recursive coordinate bisection (RCB) that utilizes spatial nodal coordinate information. Nour-Omid *et al.* [33] and Taylor and Nour-Omid [38] proposed recursive inertial bisection (RIB). Simon [35] proposed recursive spectral bisection (RSB) taht computes the Fiedler vector for the graph using the Lanczos algorithm and then sorts vertices according to the size of the entries in Fiedler vector. Recursive graph bisection (RGB) is proposed by George and Liu [19], uses SPARSPAK RCM algorithm to compute a level structure and then sort vertices according to the RCM-level structure. Barnard and Simon [2] proposed a multilevel version of RSB which is faster. Hendrickson and Leland [23, 24] also reported a similar multilevel partitioning method. Karypis and Kumar [27] proposed a new coarsening heuristic to improve the multilevel method. Legion [32] provided a two-dimensional FileObejct interface that could be used to block partition a data file into multiple subfiles that could be distributed over different disks on different machines.

Most of the aforementioned decomposition methods are available in one of the three automated tools: Chaco [23], METIS [26], and TOP/DOMDEC [36]. Chaco, the most versatile, implements inertial, spectral, Kernighan–Lin, and multilevel algorithms. These algorithms are used to recursively bisect the problem into equal-sized subproblems. METIS uses the method for fast partitioning of the sparse matrices, using a coarsening heuristic to provide the speed. TOP/DOMDEC is an interactive mesh partitioning tool. All these tools produce equal-sized partitions. These tools are applicable to systems with the same processors and one interconnection network. Some tools, such as METIS, can produce partitions with unequal weights. However, none of these tools can take network performance into consideration in the partitioning process. For this reason, these tools are not applicable to distributed systems.

Crandall and Quinn [8–13] developed a partitioning advisory system for network of workstations. The advisory system has three built-in partitioning methods (contiguous row, contiguous point, and block). Given information about the problem space, the machine speed, and the network, the advisory system provides ranking of the three partitioning methods. The advisory system takes into consideration of heterogeneity in processor performance among the workstations. The problem, however, is that linear computational complexity is assumed for the application. This is not the case with implicit finite element problems, which are widely used. Furthermore heterogeneity, in network performance is not considered.

16.7 CONCLUSION AND FUTURE WORK

In this study, we addressed issues in the mesh partitioning problem for distributed systems. These issues include comparison metric, efficiency, and cut sets. We present a tool, PART, for automatic mesh partitioning for distributed systems. The novel feature of PART is that it considers heterogeneities in both the application and the distributed system. The heterogeneities in the distributed system include processor and network performance; the heterogeneities in the application include computational complexity. We also demonstrate the use of a parallel simulated annealing for use with PART. PART uses the asynchronous multiple Markov chain approach. PART was used to partition six irregular meshes into 8, 16, and 100 subdomains using up to 64 client processors on an IBM SP2 machine. Results show superlinear speedup in most cases and nearly perfect speedup for the rest.

We used Globus software to run an explicit, 2D finite element code using mesh partitions from the parallel PART. Our testbed includes two geographically distributed IBM SP machines with different processors. Experimental results are presented for three regular meshes and four irregular finite element meshes for the WHAMS2D application. The results from the regular problems indicate a 33–46% increase in efficiency when processor performance is considered as compared to even partitioning; the results also indicate an additional 5–15% increase in efficiency when network performance is considered. The result from the irregular problem indicate a 38% increase in efficiency when processor and network performance are considered compared to even partitioning. Experimental results from the irregular problems also indicate up to 36% increase in efficiency compared to using partitions that only take processor performance into consideration. This improvement comes from the fact that even on a high-speed network such as the vBNS, there is large difference in the message startup cost on remote versus local communication.

Future work entails extending the concepts of PART to adaptive mesh refinement applications. In particular, we are developing dynamic mesh partitioning techniques for an AMR cosmological application executed on distributed systems. This class of applications require very low overhead of the dynamic mesh partitioning scheme. Furthermore, such applications often require very complex data structures resulting in scratch and repartition methods being inappropriate because of the need to revise the complex data structures.

REFERENCES

1. P. Banerjee, M.H. Jones, and J.S. Sargent. Prallel simulated annealing algorithms for cell placement on hypercube multiprocessors, *IEEE Trans. Prallel. Distrib. Sys.*, 1(1):91–106, 1990.
2. S.T. Barnard and H.D. Simon. A fast multilevel implementation of recursive spectral bisection for partitioning unstructured problems. Technical report, NAS systems Division, Applied Research Branch, NASA systems Division, Applied Research Branch, NASA Ames Research Center, 1993.
3. M. Berger and S. Bokhari. A partitioning strategy for nonuniform problems on multiprocessors. *IEEE Trans. Comput.*, 36(5):570–580, 1987.
4. J.A. Chandy, S. Kim, B. Ramkumar, S. Parkes, and P. Banerjee. An evaluation of parallel simulated annealing strategies with application to standard cell placement. *IEEE Trans. Comput.*, 16(4):398–410, 1997.
5. H.C. Chen, H. Gao, and S. Sarma. WHAMS3D Project Progress Report (PR-2). Technical Report 1112, University of Illinois (CSRD), 1991.
6. J. Chen and V.E. Taylor. Mesh partitioning for distributed systems. *Proceedings of the 7th IEEE International Symposium on High Performance Distributed Computing*, July 1998.
7. J. Chen and V.E. Taylor. Parapart: parallel mesh partitioning tool for distributed systems. *Proceedings of the 6th International Workshop Solving Irregularly Strucured Problems in Parallel*, April 1999.

8. P.E. Crandall and M.J. Quinn. Data partitioning for networked parallel processing, *Proceedings of the 5th IEEE Symposium on Parallel and Distributed Processing*, 1993.
9. P.E. Crandall and M.J. Quinn. Problem decomposition in parallel networks. Technical report, Department of Computer Science, Oregon State University, March 1993.
10. P.E. Crandall and M.J. Quinn. Block data partitioning for partial homogeneous parallel networks. *Proceedings of the 27th Hawaii International Conference on System Science*, 1994.
11. P.E. Crandall and M.J. Quinn. Three-dimensional grid partitioning for network parallel processing. *Proceedings of the ACM 1994 Computer Science Conference*, 1994.
12. P.E. Crandall and M.J. Quinn. Evaluating decomposition techniques for high-speed cluster computing. Technical report, Department of Computer Science, Oregon State University, 1995.
13. P.E. Crandall and M.J. Quinn. A partitioning advisory system for networked data-parallel processing. *Concurrency Pract. Exper.*, 7(5):479–495, 1995.
14. C. Farahat. A simple and efficient automatic FEM domain decomposer. *Comput. Struct.*, 28(5): 579–602, 1988.
15. C. Farahat and M. Lesoinne. Automatic partitioning of unstrucured meshes for the parallel solution of problems in computational mechanincs. *Int. J. Numer. Methods Eng.*, 36:745–764, 1993.
16. I. Foster, J. Geisler, C. Kesselman, and S. Tuecke. Managing multiple communication methods in high-performance networked computing systems. *J. Parallel Distrib. Comput.*, 40:35–48, 1997.
17. I. Foster, J. Geisler, C. Kesselman, and S. Tuecke. Software infrastructure for the I-Way metacomputing experiment. *Concurrency Pract. Exper.*, 10(7):567–581, 1998.
18. M.R. Garey and D.S. Johnson. *Computers and Interactability: A Guide to the Theory of NP-Completeness*. W.H. Freeman and Co., 1979.
19. A. George and J. Liu,. *Computer Solution of Large Sparse Positive Definite Systems*. Prentice-Hall, Englewood Cliffs, NJ, 1981.
20. D.R. Greening. Parallel simulated annealing techniques. *Physica*, 42:293–306, 1990.
21. A.S. Grimshaw, W.A. Wulf, and The Legion Team. The Legion vision of worldwide virtual computer. *comm. ACM*, 40(1):39–45, 1997.
22. G. Hasteer and P. Banerjee. Simulated annealing based parallel state assignment of finite state machines. *J. Paralllel Distribut. Comput.*, 43(1):21–35,1997.
23. B. Hendrickson and R. Leland. *The Chaco User's Guide*, Technical Report SAND93-2339, Sandia National Laboratory, 1993.
24. B. Hendrickson and R. Leland. A multilevel algorithm for partitioning graphs. Technical report, Sandia National Laboratories, June 1993.
25. J. Jamison and R. Wilder. vBNS: the internet fast lane for research and education, *IEEE commun. Mag.*, 35(1):60–63, 1997.
26. G. Karypis and V. Kumar. A fast and high quality multilevel scheme for partitioning irregular graphs. Technical Report TR95-035, Department of Computer Science, University of Minnesota, 1995.
27. G. Karypis and V. Kumar. Multilevel k-way partitioning scheme for irregular graphs. Technical Report TR95-064, University of Minnesota, Department of Computer Science, 1995.
28. B. Kernighan and S. Lin. An effiecient heuristic procedure for partitioning graphs. *Bell Syst. Tech. J.*, 29:291–307, 1970.
29. S.A. Kravitz and R.A. Rutenbar. Placement by simulated annealing on a multiprocessor. *IEEE Transactions on Computer Aided Design*, Vol. 6, July 1987, pp. 534–549.
30. V. Kumar, A. Grama, A. Gupta, and G. Karypis. *Introduction to Parallel Computing: Design and Analysis of Algorithms*. Benjamin/Cummings, 1994.
31. S.Y. Lee and K.G. Lee. Asynchronous communication multiple Markov chain in parallel simulated annealing, *Proceedings of International Conference on Parallel Processing*, Vol. 3, August 1992, pp. 169–176.
32. *Legion 1.7 Developer Manual*. The Legion Group, University of Virginia, Charlottesville, Va, 2000.
33. B. Nour-Omid, A. Raefsky, and G. Lyzenga. Solving finite element equations on concurrent computers. In A.K. Noor editor, *PraralLel Computations and Their Impact on Mechanics, American Society of Mechanical Engineer (ASME)*, 1987.
34. A. Pothen, H.D. Simon, and K.-P. Liou. Partitioning sparse matrices with eigenvectors of graphs. *SIAM J. Matrix Anal. Appl.*, 11(3):430–452, 1990.

35. H.D. Simon. Partitioning of unstructured problems for parallel processing. *Comput. Syst. Eng.*, 2(2–3):135–148, 1991.
36. H.D. Simon and C. Farhat. Top/domdec: a software tool for mesh partitioning and parallel processing. Technical Report RNR-93-011, NASA, July 1993.
37. A. Sohn. Parallel N-ary speculative computation of simulated annealing. *IEEE Trans. Parallel Distrib. Syst.*, 6(10):997–1005, 1995.
38. V.E. Taylor and B. Nour-Omid. A study of the factorization fill-in for a parallel implementation of the finite element method. *Int. J. Numer. Methods Eng.*, 37:3809–3823, 1994.
39. D. Vanderstraeten, C. Farhat, P.S. Chen, R, Keunings, and O. Zone. A Retrofit based methodolgy for the fast generation and optimization of large-scale mesh partitions: beyond the minimum interface size criterion. Technical Report, Center for Aerospace Structures, University of Colorado, September, 1994.

Chapter 17

Variable Partition Inertia: Graph Repartitioning and Load Balancing for Adaptive Meshes

Chris Walshaw

17.1 INTRODUCTION

Graph partitioning is now well established as an important enabling technology for mapping, unstructured meshes, for example, from applications such as computational fluid dynamics (CFD), onto parallel machines. Typically, the graph represents the computational load and data dependencies in the mesh, and the aim is to distribute it so that each processor has an equal share of the load while ensuring that communication overhead is kept to a minimum.

One particularly important variant of the problem arises from applications in which the computational load varies throughout the evolution of the solution. For example, heterogeneity either in the computing resources (e.g., processors that are not dedicated to single users) or in the solver (e.g., solving for fluid flow and solid stress in different regions during a multiphysics solidification simulation [13]) can result in load imbalance and poor performance. Alternatively, time-dependent mesh codes that use adaptive refinement can give rise to a series of meshes in which the position and density of the data points vary dramatically over the course of a simulation and which may need to be frequently repartitioned for maximum parallel efficiency.

Advanced Computational Infrastructures For Parallel and Distributed Adaptive Applications. Edited by Manish Parashar and Xiaolin Li

This dynamic partitioning problem has not been as thoroughly studied as the static problem, but an interesting overview can be found in Ref. [6]. In particular, the problem calls for parallel load balancing (i.e., *in situ* on the parallel machine, rather than the bottleneck of transferring it back to some host processor) and a number of software packages, most notably JOSTLE [26] and ParMETIS [15], have been developed that can compute high-quality partitions, in parallel, using the existing (unbalanced) partition as a starting point. A question arises, however, over data migration—in general, the better the computed partition, the more the data (mesh elements, solution variables, etc.) have to be transferred to realize it. Of course, either a poor partition or heavy data migration slows the solver down and so the trade-off between partition quality and data migration can be crucial. Furthermore, the requirements of this trade-off may change as the simulation continues (see Section 17.3).

In this chapter, we look at a new framework for managing this trade-off. First, however, we establish some notation.

17.1.1 Notation and Definitions

Let $G = G(V, E)$ be an undirected graph of vertices, V, with edges, E, which represent the data dependencies in the mesh. We assume that both vertices and edges can be weighted (with nonnegative integer values) and that $\|v\|$ denotes the weight of a vertex v and similarly for edges and sets of vertices and edges. Given that the mesh needs to be distributed to P processors, define a partition π to be a mapping of V into P disjoint subdomains, S_p, such that $\bigcup_P S_p = V$. The weight of a subdomain is just the sum of the weights of the vertices assigned to it, $\|S_p\| = \sum_{v \in S_p} \|v\|$, and we denote the set of intersubdomain or cut edges (i.e., edges cut by the partition) by E_c. Finally, note that we use the words subdomain and processor more or less interchangeably: the mesh is partitioned into P subdomains; each subdomain, S_p, is assigned to a processor p and each processor p owns a subdomain S_p.

The definition of the graph partitioning problem is to find a partition that evenly balances the load (i.e., vertex weight) in each subdomain, while minimizing the communication cost. To evenly balance the load, the optimal subdomain weight is given by $\overline{S} := \lceil \|V\|/P \rceil$ (where the ceiling function $\lceil x \rceil$ returns the smallest integer greater than x) and the *imbalance* θ is then defined as the maximum subdomain weight divided by the optimal (since the computational speed of the underlying application is determined by the most heavily weighted processor). Note that $\theta \geq 1$ and perfect balance is given by $\theta = 1$. As is usual, throughout this chapter, the communications cost will be estimated by $\|E_c\|$, the weight of cut edges or cut-weight (although see Ref. [23] for further discussion on this point). A more precise definition of the graph-partitioning problem is therefore to find π such that $\|S_p\| \leq \overline{S}$ and such that $\|E_c\|$ is minimized.

The additional objective for dynamic repartitioning is to minimize the amount of data that the underlying application will have to transfer. We model this by attempting to minimize $|V_m|$, the number of vertices that have to migrate (change subdomains) to realize the final partition from the initial one.

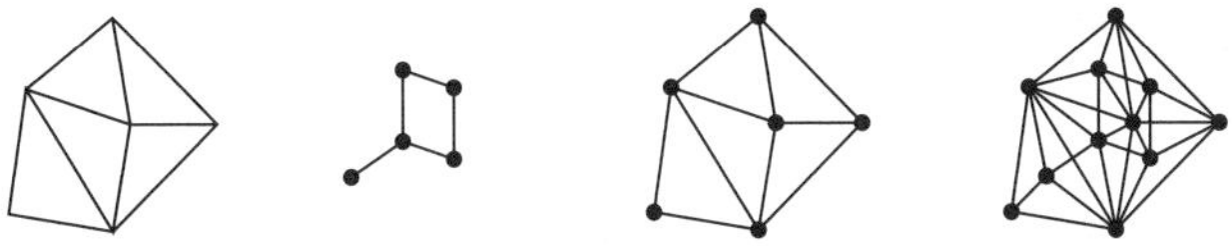

(a) Mesh **(b)** Dual graph **(c)** Nodal graph **(d)** Combined graph

Figure 17.1 An example mesh and some possible graph representations.

17.1.2 Mesh Partitioning

As mentioned above, many of the applications for which partitioning is used involve a parallel simulation, solved on an unstructured mesh that consists of elements, nodes and faces, and so on. For the purposes of partitioning, it is normal to represent the mesh as a graph. Thus, if we consider the mesh shown in Figure 17.1a, the graph vertices can either represent the mesh elements (the dual graph (b)), the mesh nodes (the nodal graph (c)), a combination of both (the full or combined graph (d)), or even some special purpose representation to model more complicated interactions in the mesh. In each case, the graph vertices represent the units of workload that exist in the underlying solver and the edges represent data dependencies (e.g., the value of the solution variable in a given element will depend on those in its neighboring elements).

17.1.3 Overview

In this chapter, we will discuss a new framework for the (re)partitioning and load balancing of adaptive unstructured meshes. In Section 17.2, we first give an overview of the standard graph partitioning and load balancing tools and in particular our implementation. In Section 17.3, we then describe the new approach, variable partition inertia (VPI), and look at how it relates to previous work. We test the new framework in Section 17.4 and illustrate some of the benefits, and finally in Section 17.5, we present some conclusions and suggest some future work.

Note that for the purposes of this chapter, particularly with regard to the results, we tend to concentrate on situations where the changes in load are at discrete points during the evolution of the solution. This is likely to happen when either the mesh changes (as is the case for adaptive refinement) or the computational resources change. However, the techniques discussed apply equally to situations where the load changes are continuous (or at least quasi-continuous) such as the solidification example mentioned above. In this sort of problem, a further issue is *when* to rebalance, the decision being based on a trade-off between the additional overhead for carrying out the repartitioning and resultant data migration, as against the inefficiency of continuing the simulation with an unbalanced solver. We do not address that issue here, but an algorithm for determining whether or not a rebalance is likely to be profitable (and thus for deciding the frequency of repartitioning) can be found in Ref. [1].

17.2 MULTILEVEL REFINEMENT FOR GRAPH REPARTITIONING

In this section, we will give an overview of the standard graph (re)partitioning and load balancing tools and in particular their implementation within JOSTLE, the parallel graph-partitioning software package written at the University of Greenwich [24].

JOSTLE uses a multilevel refinement strategy. Typically, such multilevel schemes match and coalesce pairs of adjacent vertices to define a new graph and recursively iterate this procedure until the graph size falls below some threshold. The coarsest graph is then partitioned (possibly with a crude algorithm) and the partition is successively refined on all the graphs starting with the coarsest and ending with the original. At each change of levels, the final partition of the coarser graph is used to give the initial partition for the next level down. The use of multilevel refinement for partitioning was first proposed by both Hendrickson and Leland [7] and Bui and Jones [4], and was inspired by Barnard and Simon [2], who used a multilevel numerical algorithm to speed up spectral partitioning.

Figure 17.2 shows an example of a multilevel partitioning scheme in action. On the top row (left to right) the graph is coarsened down to four vertices that are (trivially) partitioned into four sets (bottom right). The solution is then successively extended and refined (right to left). Although at each level the refinement is only local in nature, a high-quality partition is still achieved.

The graph partitioning problem was the first combinatorial optimization problem to which the multilevel paradigm was applied and there is now a considerable body of literature about multilevel partitioning algorithms. Initially used as an effective way of speeding up partitioning schemes, it was soon recognized, more importantly, as giving them a "global" perspective [10], and has been successfully developed as a strategy for overcoming the localized nature of the Kernighan–Lin (KL) [12] and other optimization algorithms. In fact, as discussed in Ref. [24, Section 3.2], this coarsening has the effect of *filtering* out most of the poor-quality partitions from the solution space, allowing the refinement algorithms to focus on solving smaller, simpler problems.

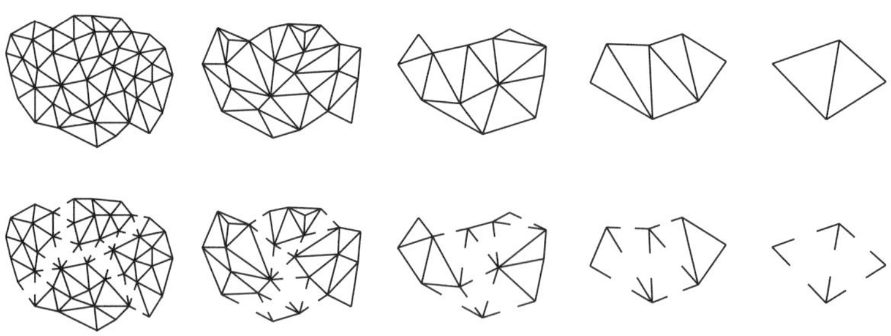

Figure 17.2 An example of multilevel partitioning.

This very successful strategy and the powerful abilities of the multilevel framework have since been extended to other combinatorial problems, such as the traveling salesman problem [19].

17.2.1 Multilevel Framework

Graph Coarsening A common method for creating a coarser graph $G_{l+1}(V_{l+1}, E_{l+1})$ from $G_l(V_l, E_l)$ is the edge contraction algorithm proposed by Hendrickson and Leland [7]. The idea is to find a maximal independent subset of graph edges or a *matching* of vertices and then collapse them. The set is independent if no two edges in the set are incident on the same vertex (so no two edges in the set are adjacent), and maximal if no more edges can be added to the set without breaking the independence criterion. Having found such a set, each selected edge, $(v_1, v_2) \in E_l$ say, is collapsed and the vertices, $v_1, v_2 \in V_l$, are merged to form a new vertex, $v \in V_{l+1}$, with weight $\|v\| = \|v_1\| + \|v_2\|$. Edges that have not been collapsed are inherited by the child graph G_{l+1} and where they become duplicated, they are merged with their weight combined. This occurs if, for example, the edges (v_1, v_3) and (v_2, v_3) exist when edge (v_1, v_2) is collapsed. Because of the inheritance properties of this algorithm, it is easy to see that the total graph weight remains the same, $\|V_{l+1}\| = \|V_l\|$ and the total edge weight is reduced by an amount equal to the weight of the collapsed edges.

Figure 17.3 shows an example of this; on the left, two pairs of vertices are matched (indicated by dotted rings). On the right, the graph arising from the contraction of this matching is shown with numbers illustrating the resulting vertex and edge weights (assuming that the original graph had unit weights).

A simple way to construct a maximal independent subset of edges is to create a randomly ordered list of the vertices and visit them in turn, matching each unmatched vertex with an unmatched neighbor (or with itself if no unmatched neighbors exist). Matched vertices are removed from the list. If there are several unmatched neighbors, the choice of which to match with can be random, but it has been shown by Karypis and Kumar [10] that it can be beneficial to the optimization to collapse the most heavily weighted edges.

JOSTLE uses a similar scheme, matching across the heaviest edges, or in the event of a tie, matching a vertex to the neighbor with the lowest degree (with the aim of trying to avoid highly connected vertices).

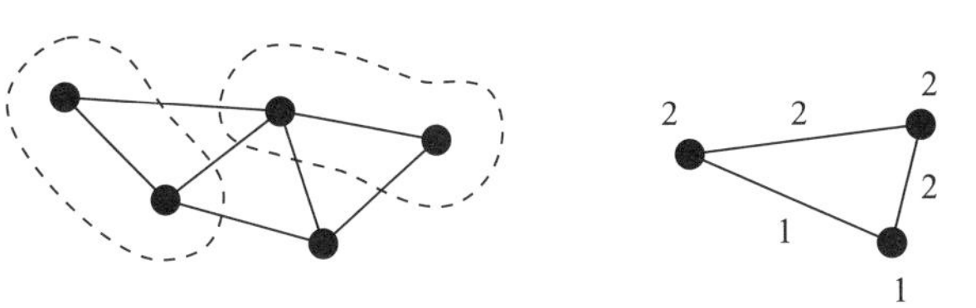

Figure 17.3 An example of coarsening via matching and contraction.

In the case of *repartitioning*, an initial partition already exists and it is quite common to restrict the coarsening to use only *local matching* (i.e., vertices are only allowed to match with other vertices in the same subdomain). It has been shown that on its own, this can help reduce vertex migration [26], and when combined with modifications to the refinement algorithms, can be used to help control the trade-off between migration and cut weight [15]. However, in Section 17.3.1 and following, we shall see that this is not necessarily the most effective strategy.

Note that even if nonlocal matching is allowed, an initial partition of each graph level can still be maintained by migrating one of each pair of nonlocally matched vertices to the other's subdomain (the choice of which to migrate being based on relative subdomain weights or even random). JOSTLE allows either local or nonlocal matching to take place (chosen by the user at runtime).

The Initial Partition The hierarchy of graphs is constructed recursively until the number of vertices in the coarsest graph is smaller than some threshold and then an initial partition is found for the coarsest graph. Since the vertices of the coarsest graph are generally inhomogeneous in weight, some mechanism is then required for ensuring that the partition is balanced, that is, each subdomain has (approximately) the same vertex weight. Various methods have been proposed for achieving this, often by terminating the contraction so that the coarsest graph G_L still retains enough vertices, $|V_L|$, to achieve a balanced initial partition (i.e., so that typically $|V_L| \gg P$) [7, 10]. Alternatively, if load balancing techniques are incorporated alongside the refinement algorithm, as is the case with JOSTLE [20], the contraction can be terminated when the number of vertices in the coarsest graph is the same as the number of subdomains required, P, and then vertex v_p is assigned to subdomain S_p, $p = 1, \ldots, P$.

In the case of repartitioning, even this is unnecessary. If only local matching is allowed, then the vertices of the coarsest graph will already be assigned to their original subdomain and the partition cut-weight of the coarsest graph will match that of the initial partition. It has also been shown [22, 26] that a simple scheme for trading-off vertex migration against cut-weight is to terminate the coarsening early, such as when the number of vertices in the graph falls below some threshold (e.g., in experiments in Ref. [22], $20P$ was chosen as an appropriate threshold, where P is the number of processors/subdomains). The reason for this is simple: each vertex in the coarsest graphs may represent hundreds or even thousands of vertices in the original graph and so moving them from subdomain to subdomain may give rise to very high data migration in the application. Conversely, since coarsening provides a continuum that affords a global perspective [10, 19] to the refinement algorithms (with single-level refinement having almost no global abilities), the more the coarsening occurs, the better the cut-weight.

For the methods described here, however, we use our standard technique of coarsening the graph down to P vertices, one per subdomain.

Partition Extension Having refined the partition on a graph G_{l+1}, the partition must be extended onto its parent G_l. The extension algorithm is trivial;

if a vertex $v \in V_{l+1}$ is in subdomain S_p, then the matched pair of vertices that it represents, $v_1, v_2 \in V_l$, are also assigned to S_p.

17.2.2 Refinement

At each level, the new partition extended from the previous level is refined. Because of the power of the multilevel framework, the refinement scheme can be anything from simple greedy optimization to a much more sophisticated one, such as the Kernighan–Lin algorithm. Indeed, in principle, any iterative refinement scheme can be used and examples of multilevel partitioning implementations exist for simulated annealing, tabu search, genetic algorithms, cooperative search, and even ant colony optimization (see Ref. [19] for references).

Greedy Refinement Various refinement schemes have been successfully used, including greedy refinement, a steepest descent approach, which is allowed a small imbalance in the partition (typically 3–5%) and transfers border vertices from one subdomain to another if the move either improves the cost without exceeding the allowed imbalance, or improves the balance without changing the cost. Although this scheme cannot guarantee perfect balancing, it has been applied to very good effect [11] and is extremely fast.

Although not the default behavior, JOSTLE includes a greedy refinement scheme, accessed by turning off the hill-climbing abilities of the optimization (see below).

The k-Way Kernighan–Lin Algorithm A more sophisticated class of refinement method is based on the Kernighan–Lin bisection optimization algorithm [12], which includes some limited hill-climbing abilities to enable it to escape from local minima. This has been extended to the k-way partitioning (here k is the same as P, the number of processors/subdomains) in different ways by several authors [7, 11, 20] and recent implementations almost universally use the linear time complexity improvements (e.g., bucket sorting of vertices) introduced by Fiduccia and Mattheyses [5].

A typical KL-type algorithm will have inner and outer iterative loops with the outer loop terminating when no vertex transfers take place during an inner loop. It is initialized by calculating the *gain*—the potential improvement in the cost function (the cut-weight)—for all border vertices. The inner loop proceeds by examining candidate vertices, highest gain first, and if the candidate vertex is found to be acceptable (i.e., it does not overly upset the load balance), it is transferred. Its neighbors have their gains updated and, if not already tested in the current iteration of the outer loop, join the set of candidate vertices.

The KL hill-climbing strategy allows the transfer of vertices between subdomains to be accepted even if it degrades the partition quality and later based on the subsequent evolution of the partition, the transfers are either rejected or confirmed. During each pass through the inner loop, a record of the best partition achieved by transferring vertices within that loop is maintained, together with a list of vertices that have been transferred since that value was attained. If a better partition is found during subsequent transfers, then the transfer is confirmed and the list is reset.

This inner loop terminates when a specified number of candidate vertices have been examined without improvement in the cost function. This number (i.e., the maximum number of continuous failed iterations of the inner loop) can provide a user-specified intensity for the search, λ. Note that if $\lambda = 0$, then the refinement is purely greedy in nature (as mentioned in Section "Greedy Refinement"). Once the inner loop is terminated, any vertices remaining in the list (vertices whose transfer has not been confirmed) are transferred back to the subdomains they came from when the best cost was achieved.

JOSTLE uses just such a refinement algorithm [20], modified to allow weighted graphs (even if the original graph is not weighted, coarsened versions will always have weights attached to both vertices and edges). It incorporates a balancing flow of vertex weight calculated by a diffusive load balancing algorithm [9], and indeed, by relaxing the balance constraint on the coarser levels and tightening it up gradually as uncoarsening progresses, the resulting partition quality is often enhanced [20].

Further details of the diffusive load balancing and how it is incorporated into the refinement can be found in Ref. [22]. However, since we regard it as only incidental to the framework described below and, in particular, since we do not consider the partition inertia scheme to be diffusive load balancing in its classical sense, we do not discuss it further.

17.2.3 Parallelization

Although not necessarily easy to achieve, all the techniques above have been successfully parallelized. Indeed, the matching, coarsening, and expansion components of the multilevel framework are inherently localized and hence straightforward to implement in parallel. The refinement schemes are more difficult, but, for example, by treating each intersubdomain interface as a separate problem and then using one of the two processors that shares ownership of the region to run the (serial) refinement scheme above, parallel partitioning has not only been realized but has also been shown to provide almost identical results (qualitatively speaking) as the serial scheme. More details can be found in Ref. [21], and parallel runtimes for dynamic diffusive repartitioning schemes appear in Ref. [26].

17.2.4 Iterated Multilevel Partitioning

The multilevel procedure usually produces high-quality partitions very rapidly, and if extra time is available to the algorithm, then one possibility is to increase the search intensity, λ (see Section 17.2.2). However, this has limited effect and it has been shown [19] that an even more effective, although time-consuming, technique is to iterate the multilevel process by repeatedly coarsening and uncoarsening and, at each iteration, using the current solution as a starting point to construct the next hierarchy of graphs.

When used with local matching, the multilevel refinement will find a new partition that is no worse than the initial one. However, if the matching includes a random factor, each coarsening phase is very likely to give a different hierarchy of graphs to previous iterations and hence allow the refinement algorithm to visit different solutions in the search space.

We refer to this process, which is analogous to the use of V-cycles in multigrid, as an *iterated multilevel* (IML) algorithm.

17.3 VARIABLE PARTITION INERTIA

A considerable body of work has now arisen on repartitioning schemes for adaptive meshes [3, 15, 17, 22, 26] and tends to resolve into two different approaches. If the mesh has not changed too much, then it is generally held that the best way of minimizing data migration is to spread the load out diffusively from overloaded to underloaded processors [17, 22]. However, if the mesh has changed dramatically, then diffusion may not only severely compromise partition quality (since migrating vertices are channeled through certain processors [17]) but may also result in heavy data migration. In such cases, it seems more natural to repartition from scratch and then use heuristics to map the new subdomains so as to maximize overlaps with current subdomains as far as possible. This idea, known as *scratch–remapping* has been investigated by Biswas and Oliker [3], who devised appropriate mapping heuristics, and improved by Schloegel et al. [16], who modified the strategy to use the remapping heuristics on the coarsest graphs of the multilevel process (rather than the final partition).

However, a question arises from this choice of procedures: How does the solver know which approach to use *a priori*, and, if it chooses the diffusive route, how does it manage the trade-off between cut-weight and data migration? (*NB* Since the scratch–remapping is two-phase optimization/assignment approach, there is no possibility for a trade-off and the migration is purely a function of the partition found.)

Furthermore, consider a typical situation in which a CFD solver simulates the build up of a shock wave–initially, the mesh will change frequently and so data migration may be of prime concern; however, as the solution approaches a steady state, remeshes become infrequent and so the emphasis should perhaps be on finding the very best quality partition to minimize the cost of repeated halo updates of solution variables. In other words, the correct trade-off is not even fixed.

17.3.1 Motivation

In this chapter, we attempt to answer the question raised above by deriving a general framework that can handle both large and small changes in the partition balance and can elegantly manage the migration/cut-weight trade-off. To motivate the ideas, we first consider some related work and then discuss the issue of local matching.

Related Work In developing the fairly simple ideas behind this chapter, we borrowed from a selection of previous works, and three papers in particular, all of which have attempted to address the trade-off between cut-weight and data migration. For example, in an early attempt, Walshaw and Berzins [28] condensed internal vertices (i.e., those at some chosen distance from subdomain borders) to form "supervertices," one per subdomain, and then employed the standard recursive spectral bisection (RSB) algorithm [18] on the resulting graph. Not only did this considerably reduce the computational expense of RSB but it also prevented excessive data migration since the supervertices and their contents were fixed in their home subdomain. However, it results in rather an inflexible strategy—once condensed, vertices that make up the supervertices cannot ever migrate, even if necessary to balance the load or improve partition quality.

Another strategy for controlling the migration/cut-weight trade-off is to use local matching, but to terminate the graph coarsening early (once the graph size falls below some threshold), and then use diffusive load balancing in conjunction with the refinement phase [22, 26]. As mentioned in Section "The Initial Partition," this works because the more the coarsening occurs, the more "global" the partition quality and hence, in principle, the smaller the cut-weight and the larger the data migration. The threshold can thus serve as a parameter to manage the migration/cut-weight trade-off. However, although it works reasonably well (at least in situations where the graph has not changed too much), this parameter is rather crude and hence affords little control over the trade-off.

Perhaps most closely related to the work here, however, is the multilevel-directed diffusion (MLDD) algorithm of Schloegel et al. [15]. They used the observation that if only the local matching is allowed, *every* vertex, both those in the original graph and those in the coarsened graph, has a home processor/subdomain. (Recall from Section "Graph coarsening," local matching means that vertices are allowed to match only with those in the same subdomain, and so any coarsened vertex is purely made up of vertices from one subdomain.) They then classified vertices as *clean* if they were still assigned to their home processor, or *dirty* if they had moved away. This meant that they could modify the refinement algorithm, a similar variant of KL to that described in Section 17.2.2, to prefer the migration of dirty vertices to clean ones (since they do not increase migration any further). Furthermore, they defined a cleanness factor (CF) that allowed the algorithm to control the movement of clean vertices—for example, with the CF set to a small value, clean vertices were *only* allowed to migrate if they reduced the cut-weight. However, they found that the modified algorithm only worked if the graph had not changed too much, and they also found that in certain situations, the diffusive load balancing could compromise the partition quality (hence, the introduction of their wave front diffusion scheme in Ref. [17]).

In all of these schemes, although the intent to control data migration is evident, there are still some issues that arise. First, as mentioned above, it is not clear when to use the scratch–remap scheme rather than diffusive load balancing and, indeed, when using diffusive load balancing, it does seem that it can sometimes damage the partition quality by forcing vertices to move according to the balancing flow computed by the load balancing algorithm (see Section17.2.2). For example, if two subdomains with very different loads are adjacent, then the balancing flow may require that a large number of vertices flow across their common border. However, if that border is very short (a factor that the load balancer does not take into account), then this flow can seriously distort the partition and hence increase cut-weight.

Local Matching All three schemes mentioned above use a form of local matching. Although this does seem to result in lower data migration, we have noticed that sometimes it may inhibit the multilevel algorithm from doing the best job it can, since it places artificial restrictions on the multilevel coarsening.

To see this, consider the coarsenings shown in Figure 17.4, where the dashed line indicates an initial partition. Clearly, there are a number of ways that this tiny graph could be coarsened, but if only local matching is allowed, then that indicated by the rings in Figure 17.4a is quite likely. In particular, vertices on the subdomain borders are forced to match with each other or with internal vertices. When such a matching is used for coarsening, the graph shown in Figure 17.4b results (here the larger vertices now have weight 2 and the thicker line indicates an edge of weight 2). The second coarsening is more straightforward; if the heavy-edge heuristic is used (see Section "Graph coarsening"), it is very likely that the matching shown by the single ring will occur, resulting in the coarsened graph shown in Figure 17.4c. Unfortunately, however, neither graph in (b) or (c) is much good for finding the optimal partition (since the optimal edges to cut have been hidden by the coarsening) and so the multilevel partitioner must wait until the original graph before it can solve the problem. In other words, edges close to the subdomain borders are very likely to be collapsed early on by local matching and yet these edges are often the very ones that the partitioner is likely to want to cut.

Conversely, suppose we do not restrict the matching of vertices to others in the same subdomain and the matching shown in Figure 17.4d is chosen. This results in the graph in Figure 17.4e and indeed if this graph were coarsened using the heavy-edge

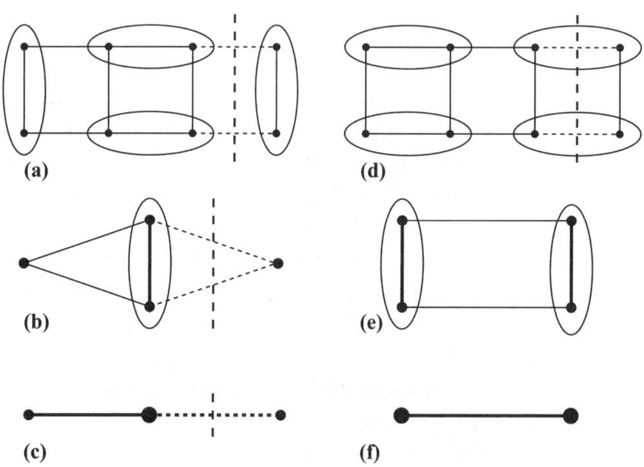

Figure 17.4 An example partitioned graph being coarsened via local matching (a–c) and nonlocal matching (d–f).

heuristic, the graph in Figure 17.4f would inevitably result. Unlike the previous case, however, the optimal partition can now be found from the coarsest graph!

To summarize, the local matching, although a heuristic that certainly reduces vertex migration, may actually act against the needs of the partitioner.

Of course, this is only a tiny example in which we have deliberately chosen bad and good matchings. However, although coarsening is typically a very randomized process (since, even with the heavy-edge heuristic in place, the vertices are usually visited in random order), once certain initial matching choices have been made, many others are forced on the graph. For example, in Figure 17.4d, once the vertex in the top left-hand corner has matched with the next vertex along horizontally, then the vertex in the bottom left-hand corner is also forced to match horizontally. Indeed, in Figure 17.4e, the matching shown is the *only* one that the heavy-edge heuristic would compute.

Nonetheless, it is interesting to see that the issue can be demonstrated in such a small graph, and it seems quite possible that an accumulation of many suboptimal coarsening choices, forced by local matching, could have deleterious effects on the partition quality. This is also borne out by experimentation (see below).

17.3.2 The Inertia Graph

To overcome the issues raised in Section 17.3.1, we borrow ideas from the papers mentioned above. First, we want a consistent strategy that can be employed whether or not the graph has changed dramatically, and this mitigates against the use of diffusive load balancing. Furthermore, we want to give the coarsening complete freedom to create the hierarchy of graphs and, in particular, allow nonlocal matching (i.e., the matching of vertices in different subdomains). However, we also need to control the vertex migration explicitly.

Building the Graph In fact, a simple solution presents itself: We first add P zero-weighted vertices to the graph, $\{\overline{v}_1, \ldots, \overline{v}_P\}$, one for each subdomain, which we refer to as subdomain vertices. We then attach every ordinary vertex v to its home subdomain vertex using a weighted edge $(v, \overline{v}_p)$, where v is in subdomain S_p in the initial partition. The weight on these edges will reflect in some way how much we wish to restrict vertex migration.

We refer to this new graph, an augmented version of the original, as the *inertia graph*, $\overline{G}(\overline{V}, \overline{E})$, so called because it encourages an inertia against vertex migration. Here, the number of vertices is given by $|\overline{V}| = |V| + P$ and since we add one edge for every existing vertex, the number of edges is given by $|\overline{E}| = |V| + |E|$.

Figure 17.5a shows an example of a small partitioned graph and Figure 17.5b the corresponding inertia graph. Figure 17.5c and d then shows the first and second coarsenings of this graph. A number of nonlocal matchings, indicated by a coarsened vertex having edges to two (or potentially more) subdomain vertices, can be seen in both of these figures, for example, center top of Figure 17.5d.

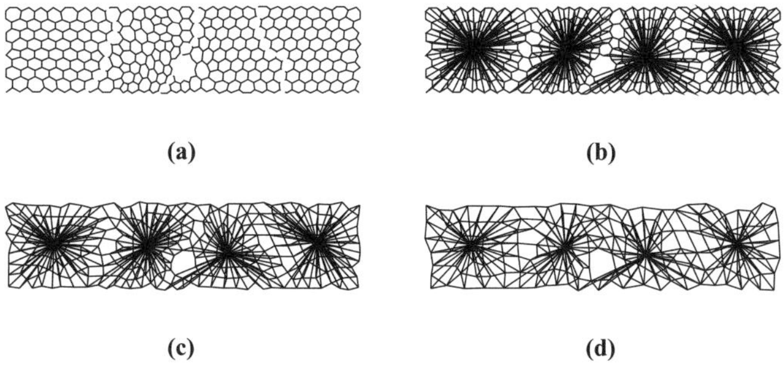

Figure 17.5 An example graph showing (a) the initial partition, (b) the corresponding inertia graph, (c) the first coarsening, and (d) the second coarsening.

An important point is that the inertia graph represents exactly the same problem as the original graph in terms of load balance, since the subdomain vertices are zero weighted. However, every vertex that migrates away from its original subdomain results in an additional contribution to the partition cost, the impact of which is determined by the ratio of ordinary edge weights to inertial edge weights.

We can then use exactly the same multilevel partitioning techniques on the graph as described in Section 17.2, provided we ensure that none of the subdomain vertices are ever allowed to migrate. We also want to leave the matching essentially unchanged, so we never allow the ordinary vertices to match with subdomain vertices. These two features are achieved by implementing the subdomain vertices as *fixed* vertices that are not allowed to migrate, nor to match with other vertices. (In fact, fixed vertices were already implemented in JOSTLE as part of an approach to the multiphase partitioning problem [27].)

Weighting the Edges The question then arises, what weight should be put on the new inertial edges between vertices and subdomain vertices? We want the weights to control the vertex migration, and indeed, as mentioned in the introduction to Section 17.3, the priorities may change as the solver progresses. It is, therefore, more useful to think about the ratio between ordinary and inertial weights.

Consider first the simplest case, where the original graph edges are unweighted, that is, they all have a weight of 1. If the ratio is 1:3, then we could simply set every inertial weight to 3. Conversely, if we required a ratio of 3:1, it suggests setting the weight of the inertial edges to 1/3. However, noninteger weights complicate the partition refinement algorithms (although they can be achieved—see Ref. [25]) and so instead we could set every inertia weight to 1 and then adjust every ordinary edge by giving it an additional weight of 2. (Note that adding a constant weight to every ordinary edge does not in itself change the partitioning problem, since the change in the cost function of moving a vertex from one subdomain to another is calculated as a relative quantity.)

In our initial experiments, we then found that the results for different ratios were rather dependent on the type of graph being employed. Consider, for example, the case where the weights on the inertial edges are all set to 1. A 2D dual graph that represents a mesh formed of triangles (see Section 17.1.2) will have a maximum vertex degree of 3 and so an inertial edge of weight 1 has quite a large effect. Conversely, in a 3D nodal graph representing a mesh formed of tetrahedra, a vertex might have a degree of 20 or 30 and so the effect of the inertial edge is negligible.

To counteract this, we calculated the average vertex edge weight $\overline{e} = \|E\|/|V|$, the average weight of edges incident on each vertex (rounded to the nearest integer value). Then, if we require a ratio of w_{e}:w_{i} between ordinary and inertial weights, where, without much loss of generality w_{e} and w_{i} are positive integers, we simply set the inertia edges to have the weight $w_{\mathrm{i}} \times \overline{e}$ and add $(w_{\mathrm{e}} - 1)$ to the ordinary edge weights. This also covers the case of graphs with weighted edges.

To give two examples from the test graphs in Section 17.4.1, brack2, a 3D nodal graph, has 62,631 vertices and 366,559 edges, each of weight 1, so the average vertex edge weight is 5.85, rounded up to $\overline{e} = 6$. Thus, for a ratio of 1:1, we set the inertial edge weights to 6 and leave the ordinary edge weights at 1, whereas for a ratio of 5:1, we set the inertial edge weights to 6 and add $4 = (5 - 1)$ to the ordinary edge weights. Meanwhile, mesh100, a 3D dual graph, has 103,081 vertices and 200,976 edges, each of weight 1, so the average vertex edge weight is 1.94, rounded up to $\overline{e} = 2$. Thus, for a ratio of 1:1, we set the inertial edge weights to 2 and leave the ordinary edge weights at 1, whereas for a ratio of 5:1, we set the inertial edge weights to 2 and again add $4 = (5 - 1)$ to the ordinary edge weights. With this scheme in place, experimentation indicates that a given ratio produces similar effects across a wide range of graph types.

Discussion As mentioned, the partition inertia framework borrows from existing ideas and the strategy of modifying the graph and then using standard partitioning techniques has been successfully employed previously [25, 27]. Indeed, in a very similar vein, both Hendrickson et al. [8] and Pellegrini and Roman [14] used additional graph vertices, essentially representing processors/subdomains, although in these cases the aim was to enhance data locality when mapping onto parallel machines with nonuniform interconnection architectures (e.g., a grid of processors or a metacomputer).

Superficially, the partition inertia framework is most similar to the multilevel-directed diffusion algorithm of Schloegel et al. [15], as described in Section "Related Work," with the ratio of inertia edge weights to ordinary edge weights (the parameter that controls the trade-off of cut-weight and migration) mirroring the cleanness factor.

However, it differs in three important aspects. First, the MLDD scheme relies on local matching—indeed, without the local matching, there is no means to determine whether a coarsened vertex is "clean" or "dirty." Second, MLDD uses diffusion in the coarsest graphs to balance the load, whereas the partition inertia framework uses a more general multilevel partitioning scheme that is not diffusive in nature (indeed, since nonlocal matching is allowed, the initial partition is completely ignored throughout the coarsening and the coarsest graph is likely to be better balanced than the initial one since the nonlocal matching may result in migrations that can be chosen to improve the balance). It is true that a balancing flow, calculated via a diffusive algorithm, is incorporated into JOSTLE's refinement algorithm to adjust partitions that become imbalanced, but this is simply a standard tool in JOSTLE's armory, which is frequently never used. Third, and most important, the MLDD scheme is implemented by restricting the matching and then modifying the refinement algorithm, whereas partition inertia is a much more general framework that works by modifying the input graph and, in principle, could use any high-quality partitioning scheme (with the minor requirement that the P fixed vertices never migrate from their home subdomain).

17.3.3 Setting the Ratio: A Self-Adaptive Framework

Of course, it is not easy to judge what ratio to choose for the inertial and ordinary weights. Even with extensive experimentation, it would be hard to predict for any given problem. In addition, as has been mentioned, the relative weighting is quite likely to change throughout the simulation.

As a result, we propose the following simple scheme. Initially, the ratio is set to something reasonable, chosen empirically. In the experiments below, Section 17.4, an appropriate ratio seems to be around 5:1 in favor of the ordinary edge weights. However, this depends on the characteristics of the simulation.

Subsequently, all that is required from the solver is that it monitor the parallel overhead due to halo updates of solution variables and estimate the data migration time at each remesh. It then simply passes an argument to the partitioner, expressing whether halo updates take more, less, or about the same time. If the halo updates are taking longer time, the ratio is increased (e.g., 6:1, 7:1, and so on) in favor of ordinary edge weights, with the aim of improving cut-weight. Conversely, if the data migration time is longer, the partitioner decreases the ratio (e.g., 4:1, 3:1, and so on) and if this trend continues beyond 1:1, it is increased in the other direction (e.g., 2:1, 1:1, 1:2, 1:3, and so on). Not only is this extremely simple, it also requires little monitoring on the part of the solver.

Note that although this idea is very straightforward and could easily have been implemented in the previous work [22], where the trade-off was controlled by the coarsening threshold, in fact, the problem with that was that the threshold parameter is rather a crude one that gives relatively a little control over migration. However, the experimental results indicate that with variable partition inertia, the correlation between the parameter settings (the edge weight ratio) is much more stable and hence provides a much more robust method for managing the trade-off.

17.4 EXPERIMENTAL RESULTS

As discussed in Section 17.2, the software tool written at Greenwich and which we use to test the variable partition inertia concept is known as JOSTLE. It is written in C and can run in both serial and parallel, although here we test it in serial.

In the following experiments, we use two metrics to measure the performance of the algorithms—the cut-weight percentage, $\|E_c\|/\|E\|$, and the percentage of vertices that need to be migrated, $|V_m|/|V|$. We do not give runtimes since, essentially, the partition inertia scheme is running exactly the same algorithms as JOSTLE-MS. It is true that the input graph is extended by having subdomain vertices and inertial edges, but since these are excluded from most calculations, the runtimes are broadly similar.

17.4.1 Sample Results

We first provide some sample results from fairly well-known mesh-based graphs,[1] often used for benchmarking partitioners. For each of the three meshes, we have generated three high-quality, but imbalanced, partitions calculated by JOSTLE with the permitted imbalance set to approximately 25%, 50%, and 100% (although JOSTLE was never written to hit these relaxed constraints exactly, so some of the imbalances vary a little). We then test each configuration using these partitions as a starting point.

First, to compare with our previous work and the algorithms discussed in Ref. [22], it is run in three previous configurations, dynamic (JOSTLE-D), multilevel dynamic (JOSTLE-MD), and multilevel static (JOSTLE-MS). The two dynamic configurations primarily use diffusive load balancing: JOSTLE-D reads in the existing partition and uses the single-level refinement algorithm outlined in Section 17.2.2 to balance and refine the partition, whereas JOSTLE-MD, uses the same procedure but incorporated within the multilevel framework (Section 17.2.1) to improve the partition quality. JOSTLE-MD also uses local matching and, as discussed in Section "The Initial Partition," a coarsening threshold to control the trade-off between cut-weight and vertex migration (set to $20P$ for all the experiments below). Finally, the static version, JOSTLE-MS, uses the same core algorithms, but ignores the initial partition entirely and hence provides a set of control results.

To demonstrate the variable partition inertia framework, we employ three different settings. Recall from Section 17.3.2 that the paradigm involves modifying the input graph by attaching an inertial edge between every vertex and its home subdomain. The graph edges are then weighted according to a ratio, $w_{\mathrm{e}}:w_{\mathrm{i}}$, which expresses the difference between ordinary and inertial edge weights.

After some preliminary experimentation, we chose the ratios 10:1, 5:1, and 1:1 for the results presented here. A ratio of 1:1 gives approximately equal weighting to inertial and ordinary edges and hence puts a lot of emphasis on minimizing vertex migration. Meanwhile, a ratio of 10:1 makes the inertial edges very much weaker than any ordinary edge and hence puts the emphasis on minimizing cut-weight (although still preventing too much migration).

The migration and cut-weight results are presented in Tables 17.1 and 17.2 respectively. The averages for each partitioning scheme over the nine results are shown at the bottom and it is instructive to focus on these. First, and as should be expected, the trend lines of the two different approaches show how migration can be traded-off against cut-weight. Because JOSTLE-MS takes no account of the existing partition, it results in a vast amount of data migration (94.3%). However, and as shown in

[1] Available from `http://staffweb.cms.gre.ac.uk/~c.walshaw/partition.`

Table 17.1 Migration Results for the Sample Graphs

	JOSTLE			JOSTLE(VPI)		
Graph/imbalance	MS	MD	D	10:1	5:1	1:1
4elt/1.25	96.5%	11.6%	10.0%	8.8%	7.4%	7.7%
4elt/1.49	96.8%	28.1%	27.7%	22.1%	23.9%	19.7%
4elt/1.98	92.5%	47.1%	44.5%	36.8%	34.7%	34.8%
brack2/1.22	95.9%	14.7%	14.8%	16.2%	11.3%	9.8%
brack2/1.55	96.7%	29.6%	30.8%	26.7%	24.3%	21.5%
brack2/1.99	93.0%	41.5%	44.3%	43.8%	37.2%	36.7%
mesh100/1.30	87.4%	16.2%	17.0%	15.7%	14.4%	13.5%
mesh100/1.50	96.9%	48.1%	43.3%	34.9%	28.0%	22.8%
mesh100/1.89	92.6%	50.9%	49.3%	44.8%	42.7%	38.0%
Average	94.3%	32.0%	31.3%	27.8%	24.9%	22.7%
Local				28.0%	24.2%	23.3%
IML				25.0%	22.4%	22.1%

Ref. [22], the dynamic diffusive partitioners are able to make a considerable difference and reduce this to just over 30%. The cut-weight results increase accordingly (from 2.77% up to 3.27%) and if less migration takes place (JOSTLE-D), the partitioner cannot refine as well and the cut-weight driven up. Interestingly, however, and as suggested in Ref. [15], with these very unbalanced initial partitions, the diffusive

Table 17.2 Cut-Weight Results for the Sample Graphs

	JOSTLE			JOSTLE(VPI)		
Graph/imbalance	MS	MD	D	10:1	5:1	1:1
4elt/1.25	2.32%	2.21%	2.31%	2.25%	2.30%	2.42%
4elt/1.49	2.32%	2.26%	2.48%	2.43%	2.52%	3.02%
4elt/1.98	2.32%	2.35%	2.71%	2.58%	2.60%	3.92%
brack2/1.22	3.59%	3.60%	3.84%	3.54%	3.57%	3.82%
brack2/1.55	3.59%	3.85%	3.97%	3.57%	3.72%	4.45%
brack2/1.99	3.59%	3.87%	4.41%	3.60%	3.74%	3.89%
mesh100/1.30	2.38%	2.42%	2.73%	2.36%	2.41%	2.97%
mesh100/1.50	2.38%	2.61%	3.65%	2.62%	2.83%	3.41%
mesh100/1.89	2.38%	2.33%	3.29%	2.58%	2.78%	3.37%
Average	2.77%	2.83%	3.27%	2.84%	2.94%	3.47%
Local				2.93%	3.00%	3.48%
IML				2.70%	2.80%	3.24%

partitioners may not be the method of choice and JOSTLE-D does little better in terms of migration than its multilevel counterpart JOSTLE-MD.

The same trends are in evidence with the VPI results—as the edge weight ratio decreases from 10:1 to parity (thus putting increasing emphasis on minimizing migration), the migration certainly decreases, but at the cost of increasing cut-weight. However, comparing the two, JOSTLE(VPI) does much better than the diffusive partitioners. For example, with the ratio 10:1, JOSTLE(VPI) has almost identical cut-weight to JOSTLE-MD (2.84% against 2.83%) but considerably better migration (27.8% against 32.0%) and with the ratio 1:1, JOSTLE(VPI) even reduces migration down to 22.7%. Perhaps most important, however, the VPI framework appears to offer much finer control over the migration/cut-weight trade-off.

At the bottom of the tables, we also present averages for two other flavors of the VPI scheme. The row marked "local" uses local matching (and hence should produce very similar results to the MLDD scheme, as discussed in Section "Discussion"). However, as suggested in Section "Local Matching," it does seem that the local matching results in worse partition quality (2.93–3.48% against 2.84–3.47%) without improving the migration (28.0–23.2% against 27.8–22.7%).

Finally, the row marked IML uses iterated multilevel refinement (Section 17.2.4), repeatedly coarsening and uncoarsening to find better results. Although not a serious contender in a time-critical application such as the repartitioning of parallel adaptive meshes, it does indicate very well the flexibility of the VPI framework. Indeed, since we have just modified the input graph, we can, in principle, use any partitioning scheme to attack the problem, and here, by using a very high-quality one, albeit much more time consuming, we can find even better results. For example, the ratio 10:1 used in iterated JOSTLE(VPI) finds the best cut-weight results (2.70%) in combination with very good migration results (25.0%).

17.4.2 Laplace Solver Adaptive Mesh Results

To give a fuller flavor of the VPI framework, we carried out further experiments on two sets of adaptive unstructured meshes.

The first set of test meshes have been taken from an example contained in the DIME (distributed irregular mesh environment) software package [29]. This particular application solves Laplace's equation with Dirichelet boundary conditions on a square domain with an S-shaped hole and using a triangular finite element discretization. The problem is repeatedly solved by Jacobi iteration, refined based on this solution and then load-balanced. Similar sets of meshes have previously been used for testing repartitioning algorithms [17, 22, 26] and details of DIME can be found in Ref. [30].

For the test configurations, the initial mesh is partitioned with the static version—JOSTLE-MS. Subsequently, at each refinement, the existing partition is interpolated onto the new mesh using the techniques described in Ref. [28] (essentially, new elements are owned by the processor that owns their parent) and the new partition is then refined.

As for the sample graphs, the experiments have been run using JOSTLE-MS as a control, two example diffusive partitioners, JOSTLE-MD and JOSTLE-D, and a

Table 17.3 Migration Results for the Laplace Graphs

	JOSTLE			JOSTLE(PI)			JOSTLE(VPI)	
G	MS	MD	D	10:1	5:1	1:1	10↓:1	1↑:1
1	90.3%	17.3%	10.6%	23.2%	14.8%	9.2%	23.2%	9.2%
2	93.6%	18.5%	12.9%	20.4%	15.7%	10.4%	17.4%	11.4%
3	98.2%	13.3%	5.8%	10.7%	9.2%	6.7%	12.2%	10.2%
4	86.5%	9.3%	6.7%	12.8%	8.6%	5.6%	7.4%	8.7%
5	97.8%	6.4%	2.5%	8.6%	5.0%	1.5%	5.7%	4.8%
6	98.2%	5.5%	3.1%	9.3%	4.9%	1.6%	4.1%	6.3%
7	92.7%	6.8%	1.9%	3.7%	4.0%	0.6%	2.1%	0.0%
8	100.0%	4.0%	1.3%	3.7%	2.1%	0.6%	2.1%	3.2%
9	96.6%	4.9%	1.3%	3.2%	2.7%	0.7%	0.5%	3.9%
Average	94.9%	9.6%	5.1%	10.6%	7.5%	4.1%	8.3%	6.4%
Local				5.9%	5.4%	4.2%	5.4%	5.5%
IML				7.6%	5.9%	4.0%	7.2%	5.4%

number of partition inertia variants. In particular, we use the same three edge weight ratio settings as above, 10:1, 5:1, and 1:1, and two variable schemes that we discuss below. Note that we now distinguish between the schemes where the edge weight ratios are fixed, JOSTLE(PI), and the variable ones, JOSTLE(VPI).

The migration and cut-weight results are presented in Tables 17.3 and 17.4 respectively, and, once again, looking at the averages, the trend lines are in the same

Table 17.4 Cut-Weight Results for the Laplace Graphs

	JOSTLE			JOSTLE(PI)			JOSTLE(VPI)	
G	MS	MD	D	10:1	5:1	1:1	10↓:1	1↑:1
1	5.19%	5.73%	5.86%	5.77%	5.86%	6.27%	5.77%	6.27%
2	4.04%	4.59%	5.34%	4.95%	4.88%	5.92%	4.72%	5.14%
3	3.57%	3.74%	4.86%	3.95%	3.98%	5.10%	3.91%	4.26%
4	3.35%	3.13%	4.12%	3.30%	3.49%	4.37%	3.13%	3.51%
5	2.86%	2.40%	3.33%	2.72%	2.78%	3.50%	2.77%	2.85%
6	2.31%	2.00%	3.00%	2.24%	2.45%	3.07%	2.31%	2.48%
7	1.94%	1.74%	2.53%	1.91%	1.96%	2.55%	1.96%	2.20%
8	1.71%	1.48%	2.19%	1.59%	1.69%	2.25%	1.70%	1.73%
9	1.40%	1.34%	1.92%	1.37%	1.46%	1.95%	1.51%	1.47%
Average	2.93%	2.91%	3.68%	3.09%	3.17%	3.88%	3.09%	3.32%
Local				3.17%	3.52%	3.91%	3.30%	3.43%
IML				2.96%	3.06%	3.75%	3.04%	3.30%

directions. From left to right, as the vertex migration decreases, the cut-weight increases. In fact, for this set of results, the best average cut-weight is found by JOSTLE-MD and the VPI scheme is unable to match this. However, JOSTLE-MD results in 9.6% migration and if vertex migration is the most important factor, then the VPI scheme 1:1 manages to find the minimum value of 4.1%.

As mentioned in the introduction to Section 17.3, however, as the simulation progresses, the needs of the solver may change with respect to the migration/cut-weight trade-off. To test this, we looked at the trend of the results and tried two schemes, indicated by 10↓:1 and 1↑:1, in which the edge weight ratio changes with each mesh. For example, if we look at the cut-weight results for individual meshes, we can see that they decrease from between 5–6% down to 1–2% as the simulation progresses. In other words, the cut-weight plays a more important role at the beginning of the simulation than at the end. This suggests a VPI scheme that does the same and so we tested the 10↓:1 scheme where the ratio starts at 10:1 for the first mesh and then decreases toward parity with every successive mesh (i.e., 10:1, 9:1, 8:1, and so on). The average results indicate the success of this strategy—when compared with 10:1, it achieves the same cut-weight (3.09%) but improves on the migration (8.3% against 10.6%).

Similarly, we looked at the migration, which also plays a more important role at the beginning of the simulation than at the end, and tried to match this with the scheme 1↑:1 (with ratios of 1:1, 2:1, 3:1, and so on). Once again, this improved on the 1:1 scheme and fits well into the trade-off curve of migration versus cut-weight.

In summary, these two variable schemes give some indication of how the VPI framework can track the needs of the solver. In this particular case, it is not clear which of the two schemes to use, but this would depend heavily on the relative costs of data migration and halo updates of solution variables.

Finally, we used these graphs to test local matching and iterated multilevel refinement in combination with the VPI framework (the two rows at the bottom of the table). Once again, the results demonstrate that local matching can harm partition quality, and that the VPI framework is not dependent on a particular partitioner—if given more time for searching, such as with the iterated multilevel algorithm, it can find considerably better results (e.g., iterated JOSTLE(PI) with 10:1 ratio).

Overall then, for this set of test meshes, the results are inconclusive in the comparison of diffusive repartitioners against VPI-based schemes. However, the VPI framework does give a lot more control over the trade-off, particularly when we employ the variable version.

17.4.3 CFD Adaptive Mesh Results

Our second set of test meshes come from a CFD simulation in which a shock wave builds up rapidly. Commercial sensitivity prevents us from giving details of the meshes, but they are of medium size and consist of 2D triangular elements.

As above, we use JOSTLE-MS as a control, two example diffusive partitioners, JOSTLE-MD and JOSTLE-D, and the same partition inertia variants as above, 10:1,

Table 17.5 Migration Results for the CFD Graphs

	JOSTLE			JOSTLE(PI)			JOSTLE(VPI)	
G	MS	MD	D	10:1	5:1	1:1	10↓:1	1↑:1
1	73.4%	7.0%	0.5%	3.8%	3.0%	0.5%	3.8%	0.5%
2	46.7%	9.1%	5.9%	4.9%	5.5%	4.0%	4.8%	3.8%
3	53.3%	12.5%	7.0%	9.7%	8.5%	5.9%	12.2%	7.6%
4	53.7%	16.0%	4.6%	7.8%	5.6%	3.5%	6.9%	8.3%
5	93.5%	18.4%	4.8%	21.0%	17.2%	7.4%	12.1%	12.2%
6	57.4%	19.0%	8.8%	12.3%	14.1%	5.9%	9.8%	9.9%
7	68.6%	24.2%	14.1%	22.6%	15.6%	12.9%	18.1%	18.7%
8	55.2%	7.4%	6.5%	8.5%	6.5%	6.1%	9.3%	9.1%
9	91.5%	7.4%	5.6%	6.8%	5.8%	2.4%	4.3%	8.3%
Average	65.9%	13.5%	6.4%	10.8%	9.1%	5.4%	9.0%	8.7%
Local				14.4%	7.1%	5.3%	7.5%	16.9%
IML				7.8%	7.3%	5.4%	7.2%	7.4%

5:1, 1:1, and the variable schemes 10↓:1 and 1↑:1. The migration and cut-weight results are presented in Tables 17.5 and 17.6 respectively.

As before, the average trend lines are in the right directions; from left to right, as the vertex migration decreases, the cut-weight increases. However, for this set of results, the VPI strategy finds the best results. For example, the 10:1 weighting finds

Table 17.6 Cut-Weight Results for the CFD Graphs

	JOSTLE			JOSTLE(PI)			JOSTLE(VPI)	
G	MS	MD	D	10:1	5:1	1:1	10↓:1	1↑:1
1	3.24%	3.16%	3.09%	3.01%	3.01%	3.09%	3.01%	3.09%
2	2.86%	2.86%	2.86%	3.10%	3.10%	3.10%	3.19%	3.27%
3	3.01%	3.01%	5.02%	3.18%	3.60%	4.10%	3.51%	3.43%
4	2.90%	3.49%	4.86%	3.49%	3.49%	4.00%	2.98%	3.49%
5	3.10%	3.63%	7.79%	3.19%	4.60%	5.40%	4.34%	4.16%
6	3.28%	3.56%	6.10%	3.00%	3.47%	5.72%	3.66%	4.03%
7	3.02%	2.87%	7.92%	3.09%	2.94%	5.51%	3.47%	3.32%
8	2.76%	2.76%	6.49%	2.99%	3.21%	4.63%	3.06%	3.21%
9	3.86%	2.78%	6.87%	2.93%	3.24%	5.95%	3.17%	3.01%
Average	3.11%	3.13%	5.67%	3.11%	3.41%	4.61%	3.38%	3.45%
Local				3.51%	3.33%	5.23%	3.53%	3.39%
IML				2.95%	3.06%	4.64%	3.08%	3.20%

the best cut-weight (matched by JOSTLE-MS), better than JOSTLE-MD in this case, and also manages to improve on the vertex migration, as compared with JOSTLE-MD. Similarly, the 1:1 weighting beats JOSTLE-D in both cut-weight and migration.

Considering the variable schemes, the choice of whether to increase or decrease the edge weight ratio is not as clear as in Section 17.4.2; the cut-weight seems more or less constant throughout the simulation, and the migration has no obvious trend. Nevertheless, the 10↓:1 scheme improves slightly on the 5:1 weighting, while the 1↑:1 provides very similar results.

Finally, and once again, the local matching and iterated multilevel results support the same results as before, that local matching can harm the partition quality and that the VPI framework is both robust and flexible.

17.5 SUMMARY AND FUTURE WORK

We have presented a new framework, variable partition inertia, for the repartitioning of adaptive unstructured meshes. It is simple to implement, since it merely involves manipulation of the input graph (plus the minor requirement that the partitioner can handle fixed vertices). In principle, it can therefore be used with any partitioner and the results indicate that it is robust and flexible. Above all, VPI seems to afford much greater control over the repartitioning problem than diffusive load balancing and the edge weighting ratio gives a powerful parameter for managing the trade-off between cut-weight and migration.

We have also indicated a scheme for varying the edge weight ratio, based solely on runtime instrumentation within the solver.

As part of the work, we have also demonstrated, both by example and empirically, that the well-accepted local matching can damage partition quality (albeit only a little).

In the future, it would be of interest to validate the variable edge weight scheme by running tests alongside a genuine parallel adaptive simulation. It would also be instructive to test the VPI framework against the scratch–remapping schemes (see Section 17.3), currently held to be the best approach when the mesh has undergone dramatic changes.

REFERENCES

1. V. Aravinthan, S.P. Johnson, K. McManus, C. Walshaw, and M. Cross. Dynamic load balancing for multi-physical modelling using unstructured meshes. In C.-H. Lai, et al., editors, *Proceedings of the 11th International Conference on Domain Decomposition Methods*. Greenwich, UK, 1998, pp. 380–387. www.ddm.org, 1999.
2. S.T. Barnard and H.D. Simon. A fast multilevel implementation of recursive spectral bisection for partitioning unstructured problems. *Concurrency Pract. Exper.*, 6(2):101–117, 1994.
3. R. Biswas and L. Oliker. Experiments with repartitioning and load balancing adaptive meshes. Technical Report NAS-97-021, NAS, NASA Ames, Moffet Field, CA, USA, 1997.
4. T.N. Bui and C. Jones. A heuristic for reducing fill-in in sparse matrix factorization. In R.F. Sincovec et al., editors, *Parallel Processing for Scientific Computing*. SIAM, Philadelphia, 1993, pp. 445–452.

5. C.M. Fiduccia and R.M. Mattheyses. A linear time heuristic for improving network partitions. In *Proceeding of the 19th IEEE Design Automation Conference*, IEEE, Piscataway, NJ, 1982, pp. 175–181.
6. B. Hendrickson and K. Devine. Dynamic load balancing in computational mechanics. *Comput. Methods Appl. Mech. Eng.*, 184(2–4):485–500, 2000.
7. B. Hendrickson and R. Leland. A multilevel algorithm for partitioning graphs. In S. Karin, editor, *Proceedings of Supercomputing '95, San Diego*. ACM Press, New York, 1995.
8. B. Hendrickson, R. Leland, and R. Van Driessche. Enhancing data locality by using terminal propagation. In *Proceedings of the 29th Hawaii Intnational Conference on System Science*, 1996.
9. Y.F. Hu, R.J. Blake, and D.R. Emerson. An optimal migration algorithm for dynamic load balancing. *Concurrency Pract. Exper.*, 10(6):467–483, 1998.
10. G. Karypis and V. Kumar. A fast and high quality multilevel scheme for partitioning irregular graphs. *SIAM J. Sci. Comput.*, 20(1):359–392, 1998.
11. G. Karypis and V. Kumar. Multilevel k-way partitioning scheme for irregular graphs. *J. Parallel Distrib. Comput.*, 48(1):96–129, 1998.
12. B. W. Kernighan and S. Lin. An efficient heuristic for partitioning graphs. *Bell Syst. Tech. J.*, 49:291–308, 1970.
13. K. McManus, C. Walshaw, M. Cross, P. F. Leggett, and S. P. Johnson. Evaluation of the JOSTLE mesh partitioning code for practical multiphysics applications. In A. Ecer et al., editors, *Parallel Computational Fluid Dynamics: Implementations and Results Using Parallel Computers*. Elsevier, Amsterdam, 1996, pp. 673–680. (*Proceedings of the Parallel CFD'95*, Pasadena, 1995).
14. F. Pellegrini and J. Roman. Experimental analysis of the dual recursive bipartitioning algorithm for static mapping. TR 1038-96, LaBRI, URA CNRS 1304, University of Bordeaux I, 33405 TALENCE, France, 1996.
15. K. Schloegel, G. Karypis, and V. Kumar. Multilevel diffusion schemes for repartitioning of adaptive meshes. *J. Parallel Distrib. Comput.*, 47(2):109–124, 1997.
16. K. Schloegel, G. Karypis, and V. Kumar. Wavefront diffusion and LMSR: algorithms for dynamic repartitioning of adaptive meshes. TR 98-034, Department of Computer Science, University of Minnesota, Minneapolis, MN, 1998.
17. K. Schloegel, G. Karypis, and V. Kumar. Wavefront diffusion and LMSR: algorithms for dynamic repartitioning of adaptive meshes. *IEEE Trans. Parallel Distrib. Syst.*, 12(5):451–466, 2001.
18. H.D. Simon. Partitioning of unstructured problems for parallel processing. *Comput. Syst. Eng.*, 2:135–148, 1991.
19. C. Walshaw. Multilevel refinement for combinatorial optimisation problems. *Annals Oper. Res.*, 131:325–372, 2004.
20. C. Walshaw and M. Cross. Mesh partitioning: a multilevel balancing and refinement algorithm. *SIAM J. Sci. Comput.*, 22(1):63–80, 2000.
21. C. Walshaw and M. Cross. Parallel optimisation algorithms for multilevel mesh partitioning. *Parallel Comput.*, 26(12):1635–1660, 2000.
22. C. Walshaw and M. Cross. Dynamic mesh partitioning and load-balancing for parallel computational mechanics codes. In B.H.V. Topping, editor, *Computational Mechanics Using High Performance Computing*. Saxe-Coburg Publications, Stirling, 2002, pp. 79–94 (Invited Chapter, *Proceedings of the Parallel & Distributed Computing for Computational Mechanics*, Weimar, Germany, 1999).
23. C. Walshaw and M. Cross. Parallel Mesh partitioning on distributed memory systems. In B.H.V. Topping, editor, *Computational Mechanics Using High Performance Computing*. Saxe-Coburg Publications, Stirling, 2002, pp. 59–78. (Invited Chapter, *Proceeding of the Parallel & Distributed Computing for Computational Mechanics*, Weimar, Germany, 1999).
24. C. Walshaw and M. Cross. JOSTLE: parallel multilevel graph-partitioning software: an overview. In C.-H. Lai and F. Magoules, editors, *Mesh Partitioning Techniques and Domain Decomposition Techniques*. Civil-Comp Ltd., 2007.
25. C. Walshaw, M. Cross, R. Diekmann, and F. Schlimbach. Multilevel mesh partitioning for optimising domain shape. *Intl. J. High Perform. Comput. Appl.*, 13(4):334–353, 1999.

26. C. Walshaw, M. Cross, and M. G. Everett. Parallel dynamic graph partitioning for adaptive unstructured meshes. *J. Parallel Distrib. Comput.*, 47(2):102–108, 1997.
27. C. Walshaw, M. Cross, and K. McManus. Multiphase mesh partitioning. *Appl. Math. Model.*, 25(2):123–140, 2000.
28. C.H. Walshaw and M. Berzins. Dynamic load-balancing for PDE solvers on adaptive unstructured meshes. *Concurrency Pract. Exper.*, 7(1):17–28, 1995.
29. R. D. Williams. DIME: distributed irregular mesh environment. Caltech Concurrent Computation Report C3P 861, 1990.
30. R. D. Williams. Performance of dynamic load balancing algorithms for unstructured mesh calculations. *Concurrency Pract. Exper.*, 3:457–481, 1991.

Chapter 18

A Hybrid and Flexible Data Partitioner for Parallel SAMR

Johan Steensland

18.1 INTRODUCTION: WHY REALISTIC SAMR SIMULATIONS REQUIRE HYBRID PARTITIONING

With thousands of processors, million-dollar supercomputers have a theoretical performance measured in Tera FLOPS. This computing power translates into being able to execute thousands of billion arithmetical operations per second. In practice, though, the performance is typically just a fraction of the theoretical. The actual execution speed for an adaptive scientific application might be reduced to Giga FLOPS. This poor use of expensive resources is caused by an inability to cope with inherent dynamics. To make important three-dimensional simulations practical, more sophisticated methods for efficient use of hardware resources are needed.

The major parts of a supercomputer are the *processing units*, the *memory hierarchy*, and the *interconnect*. Digital traffic flows in the interconnect between the processing units much like vehicle traffic flows on the freeways between cities. For both infrastructures, the result of significant traffic imbalance is overloaded parts and congestion (Figure 18.1). Expensive resources are wasted, severely limiting the infrastructure's capability. For the supercomputer, poor use of resources limits what kind of physical phenomena can realistically be simulated.

With better technology for coping with data traffic dynamics, more advanced simulations will be possible. For instance, direct numerical simulations of turbulent reactive flows that resolve all relevant continuum flow and flamescales cannot still be done for industrial-scale problems [15]. Even though mathematical models exist, the demand for computing power is huge. To enable such multiphysics simulations,

Advanced Computational Infrastructures For Parallel and Distributed Adaptive Applications. Edited by Manish Parashar and Xiaolin Li

Figure 18.1 Significant data traffic imbalance in a supercomputer leads to overloaded parts and congestion.

more research is needed in efficient runtime computer resource allocation as well as application and system adaptive data partitioning.

Structured adaptive mesh refinement (SAMR) is widespread and established as one of the most efficient approaches to scientific simulations based on partial differential equations (PDE) [31]. Despite its efficiency, SAMR is far from the point where scientists can routinely use it for arbitrary realistic three-dimensional simulations. Current application domains include climate modeling [13], computational fluid dynamics [4], numerical relativity [8], astrophysics [7], subsurface modeling, oil reservoir simulation [33], electromagnetic field simulations [11], and flame simulations [12]. Independently, both the huge data sets involved and the demand for reasonable execution times require these simulations to be executed in parallel. Although parallelization of SAMR applications is straightforward, achieving high performance is not. The parallel performance is dictated by the ability to simultaneously trade-off and balance computing load, optimize communication and synchronization, minimize data migration costs, maximize grid quality, and expose and exploit available parallelism. Addressing all that is the task of the data partitioner.

Partitioning techniques for SAMR have traditionally been classified as either *domain based* or *patch based*. Both techniques have significant inherent shortcomings. For realistic simulations with complex refinement patterns and many levels of refinements, domain-based partitioners generate intractable load imbalances, while patch-based partitioners generate significant communication bottlenecks. Moreover, because of the dynamics present in adaptive simulations, a key requirement for the partitioner is to be flexible and configurable. Domain-based and patch-based techniques both have a narrow scope: they both have a limit beyond which they cannot perform with acceptable results. As a consequence, neither technique can by itself provide good scalability for a broad spectrum of computer-application combinations.

This chapter presents an alternative to the traditional partitioning techniques. `Nature+Fable` [28] is a hybrid, dedicated SAMR partitioning tool that brings together the advantages of both domain-based and patch-based techniques while avoiding their drawbacks. Designed on fundamental SAMR principles, `Nature+Fable` is a framework of modules designed for flexibility and configurability to accommodate the dynamics inherent in adaptive scientific applications.

18.2 PARALLEL SAMR—RELATED WORK

18.2.1 Parallel SAMR

The SAMR algorithm [6] starts with a coarse base grid that covers the entire computational domain and has the minimum acceptable resolution for the given required numerical accuracy of the PDE solution. As the simulation progresses, local features in the simulation will cause regions in the domain to exhibit unacceptable numerical errors. By identifying these regions and overlaying grid patches with higher resolution, the magnitude of the errors is reduced. Because the refinement process is recursive, the refined regions requiring higher resolution are similarly identified and even higher resolution patches are overlaid on these regions [4]. The result is a dynamic adaptive grid hierarchy. Software infrastructures for parallel SAMR include Paramesh [19], a FORTRAN library for parallelization of and adding adaption to existing serial structured grid computations, SAMRAI [34], a C++ object-oriented framework for implementing parallel structured adaptive mesh refinement simulations, and GrACE [22], AMROC [9], and CHOMBO[1], all of which are adaptive computational and data management engines for parallel SAMR.

18.2.2 Partitioning SAMR Grid Hierarchies

Parallel implementations of SAMR methods present challenges in dynamic resource allocation and runtime management. The parallel performance is dictated by the ability to simultaneously trade-off and balance computing load, optimize communication and synchronization, minimize data migration costs, maximize grid quality, and expose and exploit available parallelism. Maintaining logical locality is critical—both across different refinement levels under expansion and contraction of the hierarchy, and within collections of grid patches at all levels when the patches are decomposed and mapped across processors. The former enables efficient computational access to grid patches and minimizes the parent–child communication overheads, while the latter minimizes overall communication and synchronization overheads. Because application adaptation results in grid patches being dynamically created, moved, and deleted at runtime, repeated repartitioning is necessary to ensure an efficient use of computer resources.

Traditionally, partitioners for SAMR grid hierarchies have been classified as either *patch based* or *domain based*. For patch-based partitioners [3, 18], distribution decisions are made independently for each newly created grid. A grid may be kept on the local processor or entirely moved to another processor. If the grid is too large, it may be split. The SAMR framework SAMRAI [17, 34] (based on the LPARX [2] and KeLP [14] model) fully supports patch-based partitioning. Domain-based techniques [21, 25, 27, 32] partition the physical domain, rather than operating on the hierarchy and its patches. Using rectilinear cuts through the domain along with all overset grids on all refinement levels, the hierarchy is cut like a cake.

A common approach to patch-based partitioning is to distribute each patch in equal portions over all processors. Independently of the depth and complexity of the grid hierarchy, this approach results in good load balance. Moreover, it enables incremental partitioning: complete redistribution when grids are created or deleted is not required. However, patches that are too small need to be treated as special cases. This adds complexity to the algorithms as well as communication and imbalance to the application [32]. Patch-based techniques often lead to substantial "depthwise" parent–child communication overheads. A fine grid patch typically corresponds to a relatively small region of the underlying coarser grid patch. If both the fine and coarse grids are distributed over the entire set of processors, all processors will communicate with the small set of processors assigned to the underlying coarse grid region, thereby causing a serialization bottleneck (see Figure 18.2a). In addition, parallelism in SAMR applications primarily comes from operating on grid patches at a level in parallel. In the figure, grids G_1^1, G_2^1, and G_3^1 are distributed across the same set of processors and have to be integrated sequentially.

Domain-based partitioners (Figure 18.2b) eliminate "depthwise" communication by strictly preserving parent–child locality. These partitioners exploit the available parallelism at each refinement level in the grid hierarchy. However, when grid patches are created or deleted, domain-based partitioners require complete repartitioning. To avoid the overhead involved with creating a partitioning from scratch and remapping it onto the existing partitioning for minimizing data redistribution, domain-based repartitioning can be done incrementally [21]. The major shortcoming inherent in domain-based partitioning is the deteriorating load balance for deep SAMR hierarchies with strongly localized regions of refinement. Consider, for example, the overloaded partitions P_0 and P_3 in Figure 18.2b. Because of minimal size constraints on the coarsest level, these partitions cannot be further divided. Another problem is the occurrence of "bad cuts," leading to unnecessarily small and numerous patches, and patches with bad aspect ratios. For instance, the greatest part of a patch is assigned to one processor, and a tiny part is assigned to another processor.

18.3 DESIGNING A FLEXIBLE AND HYBRID PARTITIONER

This section discusses how to use the inherent shortcomings in the traditional partitioning techniques as the basis for a new design [28].

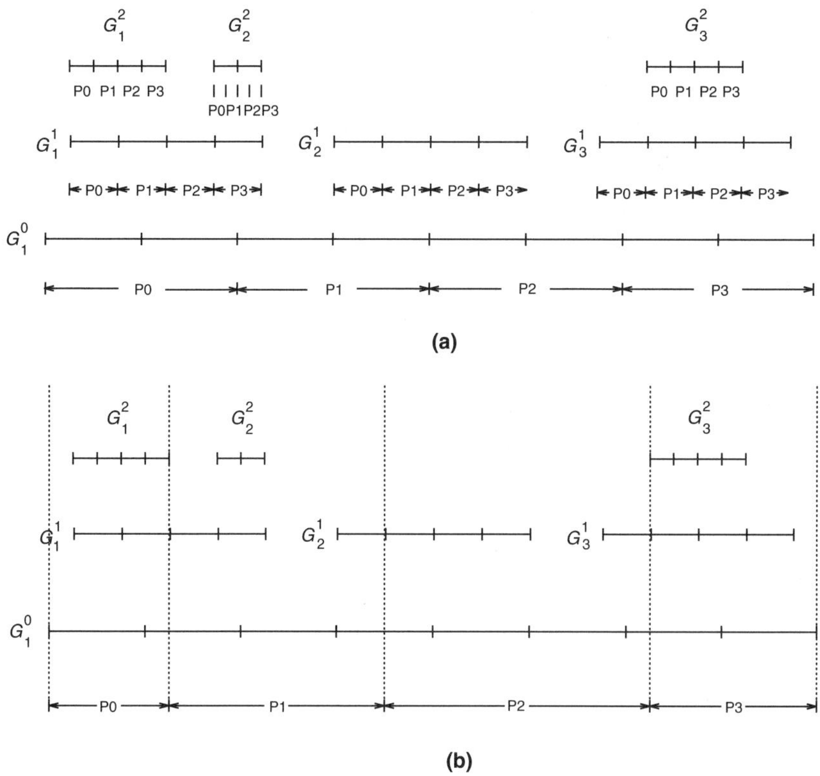

Figure 18.2 (a) A patch-based partitioning of a 1D SAMR grid hierarchy. Each patch is divided into P patches. Note that a restriction from grid G_2^2 to grid G_1^1 requires all processors to communicate with processor P_3. Furthermore, grids G_1^1, G_2^1, and G_3^1 are distributed across the same set of processors and have to be integrated sequentially. Courtesy: M. Parashar. (b) A domain-based partitioning of a 1D SAMR grid hierarchy. By maintaining parent–child locality, interlevel communications are eliminated. Note that the partitions for P_0 and P_3 due to constraints on the smallest allowed patch size cannot be further divided. For deep hierarchies, this leads to significant load imbalances. Courtesy: M. Parashar.

Recall that there are two basic problems with traditional techniques. First, both domain-based and patch-based techniques suffer from their own set of inherent shortcomings. Second, because of the dynamics inherent in adaptive physical simulations, no partitioning technique works best for all grid hierarchies [25]. The functional scope of the two separate techniques is too narrow to allow for the required degree of configurability. Thus, both domain-based and patch-based techniques are too limited to be considered viable alternatives for a scalable solution.

To address the problems with traditional techniques, our design for a new partitioning tool starts with two ideas:

1. With a hybrid approach, we can combine the advantages of both patch-based and domain-based techniques while still avoiding their shortcomings.

2. With a parameterized framework of expert algorithms that can be applied to specific portions of the grid hierarchy, we can achieve a high degree of flexibility and configurability.

The above two ideas constitute the cornerstone for the design of our new partitioning tool. Refining and expanding the two ideas, we identify the following design requirements:

A prepartitioning algorithms that divides the grid hierarchy into parts with fundamentally different properties. Because it allows expert algorithms to operate exclusively on preferred classes of input, identifying and separating regions without refinements from regions with (multilevel) refinements is a powerful division. The separation must be efficient and the unit must allow for parameters to dictate the overall behavior of how the regions are created. Dividing the hierarchy into structurally different regions can also be naturally extended to hierarchical partitioning. Each natural region could be assigned to a unique processor group, thereby allowing for further parallel partitioning within the group and synchronizing only processor groups needing repartitioning.

Expert algorithms for different parts of the hierarchy. A set of fast, flexible, and high-quality blocking algorithms needs to be designed for homogeneous, unrefined portions of the hierarchy. A hybrid core needs to be designed for handling the complex, refined parts of the hierarchy. For these parts of the hierarchy, it is desired that the fast and high-quality blocking schemes for the unrefined regions could be reused.

An organizer that provides the application program interface and supervises the partitioning procedure. It should call the prepartitioner, feed the result to the expert algorithms, and gather the final result for returning to the application. Mapping blocks to processors is also the organizer's responsibility.

We present the partitioning tool `Nature+Fable` (natural regions + fractional blocking and bi-level partitioning) [28, 29, 30], designed and implemented in accordance with the design requirements discussed above. `Nature+Fable` is depicted in Figure 18.3 and it consists of the following software units (described in the

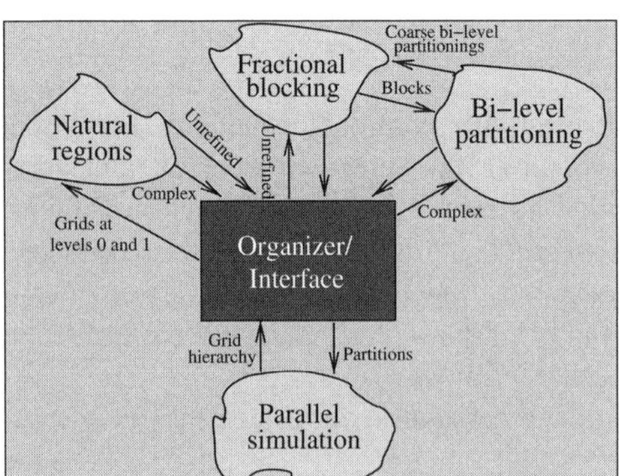

Figure 18.3 `Nature+Fable`, a partitioning tool designed to provide good scalability for realistic SAMR applications with deep and complex grid hierarchies.

following sections):

1. *A prepartitioning unit* Nature, which divides the domain into *natural regions*, suitable for expert algorithms.
2. *A set of expert algorithms for blocking homogeneous and unrefined parts of a grid*, which is implemented as one part of Fable.
3. *A hybrid expert algorithm for partitioning complex and multilevel refined portions of a grid*, implemented as the other part of Fable.
4. *An Organizer*, which functions as the brain of, and interface to, Nature+Fable.

With the components listed above, Nature+Fable is a hybrid and flexible partitioner. Nature+Fable is the result of our research and the reasoning above. It is designed to cope with the scenarios known to cause problems for traditional techniques. The aim is that Nature+Fable will provide good scalability for realistic large-scale SAMR applications with deep and complex hierarchies. Moreover, the generality and configurability of Nature+Fable make it suitable for applications in distributed computing, where resources are heterogeneous and even more dynamic than for regular parallel SAMR.

18.4 PREPARTITIONING WITH NATURAL REGIONS

The natural regions approach [28] is a prepartitioning step striving to optimize partitioning input for each expert algorithm. This section defines the natural regions, discusses the criteria for creating them, and describes the C module Nature (Natural regions), offering efficient, general, and parameterized algorithms based on the discussed criteria.

Definition 18.1 *A natural region in the context of structured grid hierarchies is a physically connected region of bounding boxes. They exist in two kinds: homogeneous/unrefined (Hue) and complex/refined (Core). A Hue covers only parts of the base grid (level 0) where there are no refinements present. A Core is a region with overlaid refined grids with levels 1 and greater. No natural regions overlap and the union of all natural regions equals the computational domain.*

Natural regions could be trivially created by cutting all level 1 grids from the base grid. The remaining parts of the base grid constitute the Hue, and the cutout parts would be the Core. However, this approach offers no way of controlling the result in terms of granularity, number of boxes, aspect ratio, and so forth. To produce prepartitions with properties desired for specific expert algorithms, controlling the result could be vital.

For the natural regions to serve their purpose as optimized input to a partitioning tool, we define the following (conflicting) criteria for creating them: (a) *The natural regions should depict and reflect the current state of the grid hierarchy.* Being "natural regions," they should look naturally superimposed on the base grid and level 1 grids. (b) *The Cores should contain as little unrefined area as possible.* The expert algorithms should preferably operate exclusively on input they were designed for. (c) *The natural regions should have low granularity* in the sense that they should be defined on a coarse (low-resolution) grid. Most expert algorithms for both kinds of natural regions most likely benefit from low granularity, since it implies fewer boxes with better aspect ratio. This criterion may contradict criterion (a) and (b). (d) *There should be as few natural regions as possible.* Expert algorithms may benefit from connected boxes. Considering block connectivity, the algorithms can make better choices for assigning blocks to processors. This criterion may contradict (a) and (b). (e) *The boxes forming a natural region should be as few as possible and avoid bad aspect ratio.* This strives to minimize the overhead involved with many boxes and boxes with bad aspect ratio. It may contradict criteria (a) and (b).

Our implementation must also be general and efficient. Generality is required to control behavior. Because partitioning time is extremely limited, our implementation needs to be efficient. Considering all the criteria discussed above, our design comprises the following steps. Exactly how `nature` implements each step is also described. Note that boxes only on levels 0 and 1 are needed to define natural regions. All other levels are disregarded.

Smoothing of Level 1 Boxes: This step strives to obtain the desired granularity and a smoother shaped structure of the level 1 boxes. Smoothing addresses all of the criteria (a) through (e), except (b). By forming "simpler" level 1 boxes (a)—without violating other constraints such as (d) and (e)—smoothing increases the chances for natural regions that depict the underlying refinement pattern. It reduces resolution at which to construct the natural regions (c). It helps in creating few natural regions (d). It helps in creating natural regions with few and good aspect ratio boxes since it simplifies the structure and reduces granularity (e).

`Nature` implements an optional smoothing operation based on integer arithmetics for maximum speed. The level 1 boxes are aligned to "visible points" defined by a *stepsize*. The lower bounds are moved downward to the nearest visible grid point, and the upper bounds upward to the nearest visible grid point. As a result, the regions are nonshrinking as resolution decreases.

Consider a base grid (level 0) with *stepsize* $= 8$ and thus has its visible points at $8 \times n$ for $n = 1, 2, 3....$ Smoothing is achieved by scaling down, or coarsening, the base grid using the *stepsize*. A smoothing factor of 2 will force the grid patches *on both levels* (0 and 1) to be aligned to the "visible grid" points at $16 \times n$.

Merging of Level 1 Boxes: The purpose of the merging step is twofold. (1) To avoid small and badly shaped boxes by merging level 1 boxes close to each other (hence addressing criteria (c), (d), and (e)) and (2) merge level 1 boxes that overlap as a result of the smoothing.

`Nature`'s *merging strategy* 1 tests each box against all other boxes. Two boxes A and B are merged if *intersect(grow(A, growing),grow(B, growing))*, where the function *grow* grows its input box *growing* visible units in each dimension, and *intersect* is *true* if its box arguments intersect. Growing boxes too much will unnecessarily merge

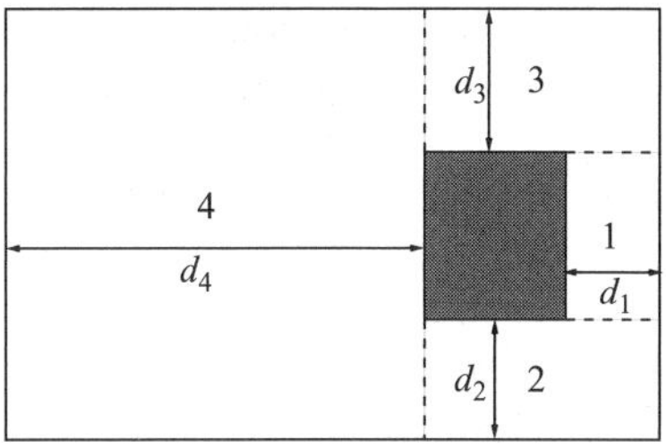

Figure 18.4 The BARAM operator. A Core region is cut out from the base grid by rectilinear cuts. Since $d_1 < d_2 < d_3 < d_4$, the cut order is 1, 2, 3, and 4.

level 1 boxes far from each other. Conversely, growing the boxes too little may cause small and an unnecessarily large number of (bad-quality) boxes. Research is needed to determine a suitable amount of growing.

Many applications exhibit a strongly localized refinement pattern. With *strategy* 1, such a refinement pattern will result in a bounding box around all level 1 boxes. Such a bounding box can be trivially computed in linear, as opposed to quadratic (for *strategy* 1) time (in number of level 1 boxes). These observations justify an alternative, simpler strategy for merging boxes.

Merging strategy 2 simply creates a bounding box around all level 1 boxes.

Subtract the Result from the Domain: The resulting boxes from the smoothing and merging are now subtracted, or "cut," from the base grid (the computational domain). This should be done while avoiding bad aspect ratios (e) and an unnecessarily large number of boxes (e). When all Core natural regions have been cut out from the base grid, the result is a list containing the boxes that define the Hue(s).

`Nature` uses the following proposed bad aspect ratio avoiding minus (*BARAM*) operator for two boxes, for cutting one box out from another. Our simple heuristics are illustrated in Figure 18.4 and do indeed avoid bad aspect ratios [28]. The distances between the Core natural region and the bounds of the computational domain are computed and sorted. The shortest distance is selected first. To minimize aspect ratio, this short distance is not allowed to expand in other dimensions, so as to create a long but narrow box. Instead, the first cut is made so as to minimize the other dimensions of this short side. Recursively, the algorithm continues with the next shortest distance.

The *order* in which the Core boxes are cut from the base grid has significant impact on box quality. For example, tiny boxes residing at the border of the base grid should be cut *after* larger boxes residing in the middle. If those tiny boxes are cut first, they will generate long and narrow boxes (boxes with bad aspect ratio) along the borders. These narrow boxes are unlikely to be further cut/improved by other cuts/boxes since the other boxes reside in the middle of the domain. Conversely, if we cut the big boxes in the middle first, chances are that we cut the domain so these tiny boxes affect only a *part* of the domain. Hence, it *cannot* generate these long and narrow boxes. `Nature` sorts on the greatest distance from the base grid border to the box to be cut. The box with the smallest such distance is cut first and so forth.

Find connected boxes to form regions: Connecting boxes addresses criterion (d) and ensures that each connected region (Core or Hue) is stored in a separate list. This allows expert algorithms to benefit from box connectivity information.

`Nature`'s previous steps do not keep track of which boxes of either kind of natural region are adjacent. The book-keeping and algorithm modification required to obtain such information would be substantial. Since some expert algorithms would rely on this information, while others would operate just as well on "boxes," the connection of boxes into regions is made in a separate (optional) step.

Our simple connection algorithm is based on a triple loop and starts by creating a new empty connected natural region, denoted *current*. Then it puts the first box of the list containing all the boxes (Core *or* Hue), denoted *allBoxes*, in *current*. It loops through all the other boxes in *allBoxes* to check for adjacency with this first box. If a box sharing (a part of) a side is found, this box is deleted from *allBoxes* and inserted in *current*.

Because not all expert algorithms will exploit this information and because of the complexity of the connection algorithm, connectivity information can be turned off in `Nature`. Turning it on increases the execution time for creating natural regions by about 14%.

18.5 FRACTIONAL BLOCKING FOR SPEED AND QUALITY

Recall that natural regions exist in the two categories Hues (homogeneous/unrefined) and Cores (complex/refined). A Hue is a set of bounding boxes, typically defining an irregular but connected part of the computational domain. Given the number of processors assigned to the Hue, the task for an expert algorithm is to compute a distribution of processors over the boxes and to divide the boxes into blocks according to that distribution. The result should conform to all pertinent partitioning metrics, such as load balance, communication pattern, and partitioning time. This section introduces such an expert partitioning algorithm, called *fractional blocking* [28].

Given the uniform workload, a trivial distribution of processors over the Hue is achieved by assigning processors proportional to the relative size (or workload) of each box. Although such a distribution gives perfect load balance in theory, it is often impractical. Consider, for example, a distribution with 7.00234 processors assigned to a box. Because a block suitable for assigning to 0.00234 processors would probably correspond to a block with sides smaller than the smallest side allowed (the atomic unit), creating such a block would often be impossible. Another problem is assembling all these arbitrary decimal-part workload blocks into pieces suitable for one processor. Given these problems, it is more practical to create distributions based on integers.

Previous research has investigated integer distributions of processors over a set of boxes (or workloads) [24]. Like the following example shows, trivial rounding of real-valued processor assignments often results in poor load balance. Consider a Hue with two boxes and an optimal distribution $\{1.4, 22.6\}$. The intuitive integer distribution is $\{1, 23\}$. However, the rounding of 1.4 to 1 results in a 40% load imbalance. The counterintuitive distribution {2, 22} generates approximately only 3% load imbalance. An algorithm that minimizes load imbalance has been proposed by Rantakokko [24]. However, even an optimal integer distribution often results in high imbalances [32]. For example, consider a Hue with four boxes and the optimal distribution {1.75, 1.75, 1.75, 1.75}. This optimal integer distribution generates a 75% load imbalance.

In summary, both integer and real-valued distributions have inherent disadvantages. However, the load balance for integer-based distributions can be improved by using *virtual processors*. In this common approach [24], the number of processors is scaled up by a factor k (where k is an integer larger than 1) to kp virtual processors. After blocking the boxes into kp blocks (with equal workload), each processor receives exactly k blocks.

Combining virtual processors and Rantakokko's integer distribution algorithm results in a simple, effective, and general blocking scheme. This scheme is referred to here as a "conventional method" and is included as a means of comparison to the presented fractional blocking.

For the conventional method, we use binary dissection [5, 20] for the blocking. Each cut splits the workload as evenly as possible. Note that an odd number of processors requires splitting the load in the same fractions as the number of available processors is split.

The shortcomings of the conventional method are as follows. If the current scale factor k produces too much load imbalance, then k is increased for a finer granularity. However, the gained potential for lower imbalance is a trade-off for increased and more complex communication. In addition, the overhead for the solver increases. Depending on the application, too many blocks can be disastrous to execution time [23]. Another disadvantage with conventional methods is that the execution time for the dissection algorithm increases linearly with k.

Fractional blocking addresses all the listed shortcomings in the conventional method by keeping the number of created blocks close to a minimum. Instead of increasing the number of blocks, fractional blocking generally creates exactly one block per physical processor. It creates at most two fractional blocks per box. Matched and paired across neighboring boxes, each fractional pair has a unit workload and is assigned to exactly one processor.

The first step of fractional blocking is identical to that of conventional blocking. Fractional blocking scales up the number of processors by a factor Q (an integer greater than 1). After the integer distribution, the conventional method divides box b_i into p_i equal-sized blocks by binary dissection. Each of these blocks is assigned to exactly one (virtual) processor. Instead, the fractional blocking method computes an integer part P_i and a fractional part f_i for box b_i by

$$P_i = p_i \text{ div } Q,$$
$$f_i = p_i \bmod Q.$$

The box b_i is then divided into P_i "whole" blocks conforming to the unit workload u, and one smaller, fractional block conforming to $u * f_i/Q$. Fractional blocking for the next box b_j starts with creating a match m_j for f_i by setting $m_j = (Q - f_i)$. Note that the pair of blocks corresponding to f_i and m_j now together correspond to u. They will be assigned to the same processor. Fractional blocking then proceeds by computing P_j and f_j for the remains of b_j.

We define fractions and matches in terms of a number of workload *quanta*, dictated by the quantum parameter Q. To gain load balance potential, the quantum size is decreased. This corresponds to increasing k for the conventional methods. The advantages of this new approach over conventional methods are (1) most processors (more than $P - n + 1$) receive exactly one block each, regardless of quantum (2) partitioning runtime does not increase with a smaller quantum, and (3) the communication pattern does not deteriorate as a result of a smaller quantum.

We introduce a fractional binary dissection blocking scheme that operates as follows. For example, consider a box to be divided into 7.4 blocks. We want seven blocks of workload u, and one decimal-part block with workload $0.4u$. This is established by keeping the 0.4 decimal part intact, giving it to one of the blocks in each recursion step until it is the only piece left. In this example, the processors are divided into $p_1 = 3.4$ and $p_2 = 4$, and the box is split so that $3.4/7.4$ of the workload is assigned to block 1 and $4/7.4$ of the load is assigned to block 2. Now, block 2 is further dissected into four blocks by the conventional method. Block 1 is further split by the fractional blocking scheme, giving one block with workload $1.4u$ and one block with workload $2u$. Again, the former block is split by the fractional method, while the latter is split by the conventional method. At this last step, the decimal-part block is cut into one block of workload u and one block with workload $0.4u$. Figure 18.5 illustrates the difference between the fractional scheme and the conventional scheme.

In our experiments, increasing k for the conventional strategy did increase execution times significantly. However, the execution times for Frac(Q) were more or less constant. This constant time was about the same as that obtained by creating exactly one block per processor with the conventional method. Increasing k for the conventional strategy did improve load balance. However, there was no advantage in using the conventional over the fractional method for the same scaling factor ($k = Q$).

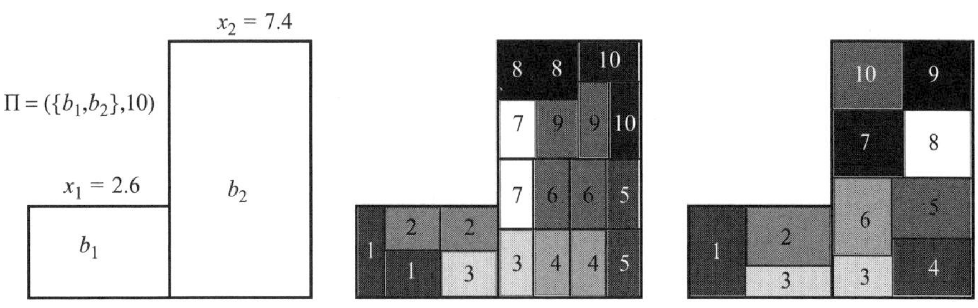

Figure 18.5 The difference between conventional blocking (middle) and fractional blocking (right) of a Hue (left). In this example, $P = 10$ and $k = Q = 2$. The conventional method scales up the problem to $2p$ virtual processors and assigns two blocks/processor. The fractional method splits *one* key block into two pieces with workload $1/2 \times u$, assigning these two pieces to the same processor (processor 3).

Increasing k for the conventional methods did increase the amount of communication. However, for the fractional method, the amount of communication increased only marginally with a larger Q. Data migration was slightly worse for the fractional method. While the number of boxes grew linearly with k for the conventional methods, it grew only marginally for the fractional method. Moreover, the average number of boxes per processor was close to one for all Q.

18.6 HYBRID BI-LEVEL PARTITIONING

Recall that natural regions exist in the two categories Hue (homogeneous/unrefined) and Core (complex/refined). This section presents an expert algorithm for Cores. It is implemented in the software unit `Fable`, where it constitutes the bi-level domain-based part.

We present below a list of observations for partitioning structured grid hierarchies. An expert algorithm for Cores should be able to address each of these observations. We present the hybrid algorithm BLED (bi-level domain based) [28]. BLED is not only designed with the constraint to cope with the observations listed below, but BLED is also designed on the very basis of these observations. We present below the observations and outline how BLED addresses each of them.

Desirable Domain-Based Properties: The main advantages with domain-based techniques are better exploitation of inherent parallelism and elimination of interlevel communication. It is desirable to maintain these properties.

BLED *maintains desirable domain-based properties* by (a) dividing the grid hierarchy in the refinement dimension into distinct level groups and (b) using the same numbering scheme for mapping all level groups. These groups are illustrated in Figure 18.6 and consist of all grids at ν adjacent refinement levels. The level groups are considered as "domains" and are partitioned by domain-based techniques. Hence, we expect to see advantages inherent in domain-based techniques. Using the same numbering scheme for all level groups increases the probability for the

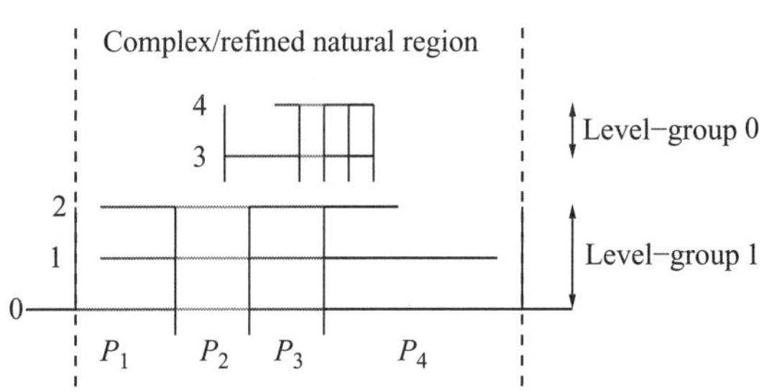

Figure 18.6 A 1D, four-processor example illustrating the group-level approach with max $\nu = 3$. Note (a) the grouping into two levelgroups, (b) how the finest grids within each levelgroup are dictating the cuts, and (c) that interlevel communication is needed between processors 1 through 3 between refinement levels 2 and 3 only, since a "domain-based-like" communication pattern is present between grids on levels 2 and 3 assigned to processor 4 as a result of the numbering scheme.

type of beneficial communication pattern that occurs for domain-based techniques, also illustrated in Figure 18.6. As a result of this numbering, a parent and a child grid, belonging to different level groups, could share the same processor for parts of their extents, and (c) using a heuristic remapping algorithm for decreasing interlevel communication.

Undesirable domain-based properties: The greatest disadvantages with domain-based techniques are deterioration of load imbalance for deep hierarchies and the occurrence of "bad cuts." These undesirable properties should be avoided.

BLED *avoids undesirable domain-based properties* by restricting the number of levels ν in each level group to a maximum of 2 (hence the name *bi-level*). This restriction makes the algorithm able to deal with arbitrarily deep hierarchies without deterioration of load balance. Furthermore, it eliminates "bad cuts."

We use a static value of $\nu = 2$ for the following two reasons. First, $\nu > 1$ will improve the strictly patch-based approach, giving it advantages inherent in domain-based techniques while the algorithm will still be able to deal with arbitrarily deep hierarchies without deterioration of load balance. Second, $\nu > 2$ would substantially increase the potential for bad cuts. In general, $\nu = 2$ implies bi-level domains, which are relatively easy to reshape and cut. A tri-level domain contains an "invisible" middle refinement layer, which would suffer from any reasonably simple cutting regime.

Prioritizing the Finer Refinement Levels: The PDE solver typically spends the major part of its time advancing the solution on grid patches at the finer refinement levels. As a consequence, we can tolerate some imbalance and even some idle processors for the coarsest levels, given that this benefits the partitioning in general.

BLED *prioritizes the partitioning quality of the finer refinement levels* by (a) letting the finest level patch in a bi-level block dictate the partitioning cuts (see Figure 18.6) and (b) assigning all processors assigned to a Core to each bi-level group in that particular Core. As a consequence of (a), the finest grid patches take priority in the partitioning, and as a consequence of (b), the finest levels will be distributed "perfectly," while the arithmetic load for the coarsest levels in a deep hierarchy might not be enough to keep all processors busy.

Reusing Fast and High-Quality Blocking Schemes: For Hues, there exist fast blocking schemes generating one (or few) blocks per processor. However, for complex hierarchies the existing partitioning strategies are often more complex and lead to a number of grid blocks assigned to each processor. It is desirable to design partitioning strategies for Cores with the same beneficial features as for Hues.

BLED *reuses the fast and high-quality blocking schemes* used for Hues by (a) creating a coarse partitioning containing blocks suitable for attack by the fast and high-quality blocking schemes presented, and (b) employing a modified variant of the proposed numbering scheme. The choice of $\nu = 2$ allows for simple algorithms, modifying the level groups into "sandwich" pieces suitable for blocking. Moreover, the proposed numbering scheme based on a partial SFC ordering allows for ordering the blocks without a complete sorting of all blocks in the Core.

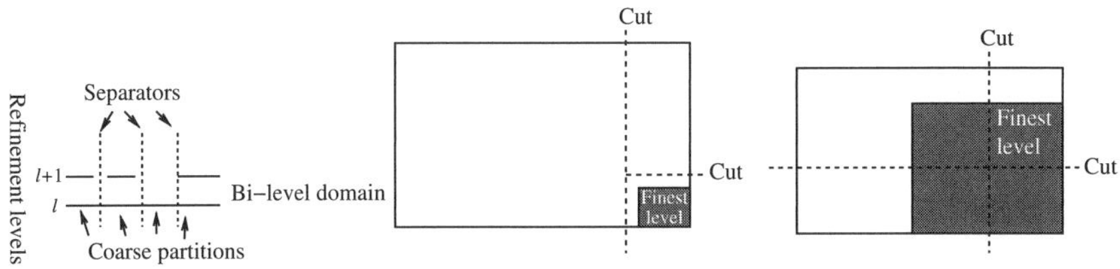

Figure 18.7 The three steps of the original approach (CDA): (1) separation, (2) cleaning, and (3) blocking.

BLED Groups Refinement Levels Two by Two: A *bi-level* is a patch—a parent—at the lower level in a group together with all its children. Bi-levels are transformed into coarse partitions, suitable for blocking. BLED implements two bilevel approaches side by side. By using a customized classification method, BLED switches automatically between the two approaches [30]. The first approach is called the *child-driven approach* (CDA) and its steps are as follows:

Separation: Separate the children patches from each other: Without cutting any of the children, split up the parent in a domain-based fashion so that each piece gets a maximum of one child (Figure 18.7, Left). The quality of a cut is determined by comparing the aspect ratios of the two resulting "halves." The better the aspect ratio, the better the quality (see Figure 18.7). BLED finds the best cut by comparing the best cut possible in each of the spatial dimensions. BLED then proceeds recursively in each "half" until all children are separated.

Cleaning: Remove "white space": Cut off excessive parts of the parent if it has a relatively "small" child (Figure 18.7, middle). The purpose of the cleaning step is to further modify the coarse partitions to make them suitable as input to a high-quality blocking scheme. The parameter `whiteSpace`, a real value between 0 and 1, defines how much white space is allowed for each coarse partition. BLED iteratively removes white space from a coarse partition from the side exhibiting the greatest portion of such, until the total amount is lower than `whiteSpace`.

Blocking: Send the coarse partitions to the blocker and *let the child (if there is one) dictate the cuts* (Figure 18.7, right). The coarse partitions belonging to the level group are regarded as the regions and are blocked in the same way as natural regions. However, the blocking unit was designed to operate on Hues. The coarse partitions consist primarily of entities of *two* levels. To handle bi-level coarse partitions, the blocking unit was modified to consider the child patch only. This patch is blocked conventionally by the selected blocking scheme. The parent is "slaved" by receiving exactly the same cuts.

The CDA generally generates high-quality results for all inputs it can possibly handle. Quality does not deteriorate as the inputs get "harder." Rather, there is a hard cutoff beyond where it cannot go. Therefore, the CDA is the cornerstone in the algorithm.

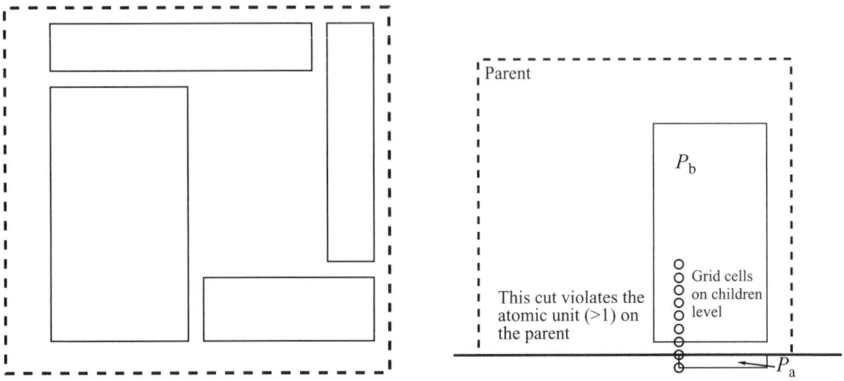

Figure 18.8 Two "impossible" bi-levels. *Left*: The "circular" children pattern. *Right*: A patch of atomic unit size P_a with an immediate neighbor P_b.

The CDA sometimes fails because the children patches are laid out in a way that makes the separation step impossible. For example, if the parent is "cluttered" with children, it is unlikely that there will be any clean cuts for the separation: it will be impossible to cut the parent without simultaneously cutting at least one of the children. Another problem is that the occurrence of children of the smallest possible size—that is, the *atomic unit*—may have the result that the only possible cuts create patches smaller than the atomic unit on the parent.

We can identify two criteria for a complementing approach: (1) it should cope with all possible bi-levels (as it will be fed all bi-levels that the CDA could not handle), and (2) it should generate high-quality results for bi-levels badly suited to the CDA.

To design a successful complementing approach, further analysis of the "impossible" bi-levels is needed. We list the two basic types of impossible bi-levels:

1. *Circular children pattern:* If the children form a "circular pattern" as illustrated by Figure 18.8 (left), there is no possible separation cut that does not cut through at least one of the children.
2. *Children of Atomic Unit Size with Close Neighbor:* If a child of atomic unit size resides at the border of the parent *and* has an immediate neighbor (illustrated by Figure 18.8, right), these two children cannot be separated without creating a piece of the parent smaller than the atomic unit.

Though not exclusively, both of the types listed above occur for many and spread-out children often including small patches. An implication of this observation is that for "impossible" bi-levels, there is a good chance that the children (a) are reasonably spread out, (b) are many, and (c) includes patches of atomic unit size. We design our complementing approach on the basis of this observation.

The complementing approach should be most efficient for exactly the bi-levels described by our observation. For now, we leave (c) for later and focus on (a) and (b) from the paragraph above. We make a further observation: A bi-level having many and spread-out children might not only be impossible to handle for the CDA, but it may also be *unnecessary* to handle such a bi-level with the CDA. There may be a simpler

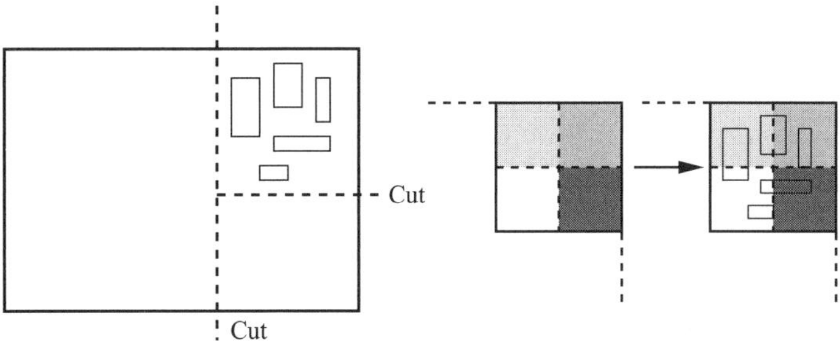

Figure 18.9 The three steps of the complementary approach (PDA): (1) cleaning, (2) blocking, and (3) derive kids.

way, exploiting the given characteristics. If the children are many and spread out, a high-quality result should follow automatically by the following simple approach, which we define as the *parent-driven approach* (PDA) (illustrated in Figure 18.9):

Cleaning: Make a bounding box around the children and reuse the original cleaning algorithm (described in the previous section) with the bounding box as the child (Figure 18.9, left).

Blocking: Block the parent and *let the parent alone dictate the cuts.* In this step, we only regard the children's combined workload. All other aspects of the children—such as position, size, and number—are disregarded (Figure 18.9, middle).

Derive kids: For each block, reuse `Nature+Fable`'s existing functionality for deriving the block's children (Figure 18.9, right).

Letting the parent dictate the cuts is logical considering the class of input: many and spread-out children patches. Statistically, this would produce a reasonably well-balanced partitioning. Note that for the PDA, the result has a different structure compared to the CDA. The PDA generates bi-level blocks with one parent and potentially multiple children, while the CDA generates bi-level blocks with one or zero blocks per parent.

The task is now to design an efficient algorithm that classifies a given bi-level as suitable for either the CDA or the PDA. This algorithm's job is to switch automatically and transparently between the two approaches, always producing a high-quality result.

Because the CDA generally gives high-quality results, a goal for the classification algorithm is to classify as many bi-levels as possible as suitable for the CDA. A crucial constraint is that it should never classify an "impossible" bi-level to the CDA as this will cause `Nature+Fable` to fail. We also want the classification algorithm to conform to the general `Nature+Fable` algorithm policy regarding efficiency; that is, for significantly complex tasks, we prefer powerful heuristics over searching for an exact or optimal solution.

While deriving and computing mathematical quantities for classifying a bi-level might be possible and bears the potential of rigorous results, we considered this prohibitively expensive. Instead, we constructed a conceptually trivial, yet powerful, recursive algorithm that singles out bi-levels that are trivial to classify. If trivial classification fails, the bi-level is split and both resulting parts are classified recursively.

The strength in this classic divide-and-conquer algorithm is that it simultaneously separates and classifies the input bi-level. It reuses the split function used by the CDA, meaning that each split is equivalent to the optimal separation cut. Thus, each recursive call will generate a meaningful breakdown (separation) of the input, effectively decreasing the number of bi-levels that would unnecessarily be classified as impossible.

The challenge inherent in this algorithm is to define the suitable predicates and determine the numerical thresholds associated with each predicate. To be trivially suitable for the PDA, we identify the following sufficient conditions: the children pattern should be very dense, or there should be a lot of children, exhibiting a not-very-sparse pattern, or the children should be on average very small, exhibiting a not-very-sparse pattern. To be trivially suitable for the CDA, we identify the following sufficient conditions: the bi-level has only one child, which is not of atomic unit size, or the bi-level has very few and large children and there is no patch of atomic unit size. Governed by a set of realistic applications, the numerical thresholds were set by trial and error.

In a conventional ISP approach, the SFC ordering of blocks implies that data tend to migrate only little at adaptation and repartitioning of the hierarchy. The natural regions/expert algorithms approach does not allow for implicit indexing and ordering. To obtain an SFC ordering, time-consuming algorithms like (parallel) sorting have to be employed. To avoid this, `Fable` implements a *partial* SFC ordering. Instead of sorting locally within each natural region, we rely on natural regions consisting of a number of boxes. First, these boxes are ordered according to the SFC. Then, a local ordering inside each box is established. The first step orders data roughly, and the second step assures order in critical regions. This scheme has the potential to generate feasible orderings that assure small amounts of data migration caused by grid refinements.

Figure 18.10 (left) displays a communication breakdown for the Richtmyer–Meshkow instability with five levels of refinement for 100 timesteps [29], partitioned

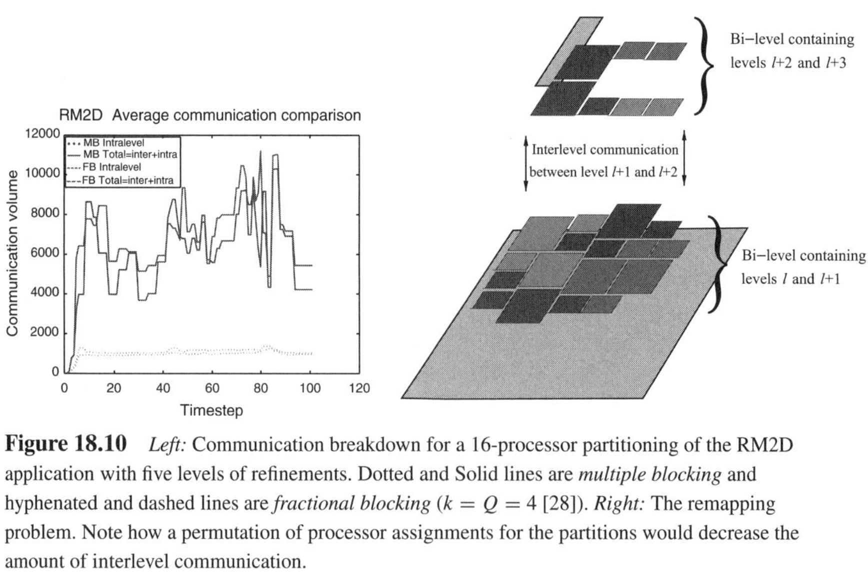

Figure 18.10 *Left:* Communication breakdown for a 16-processor partitioning of the RM2D application with five levels of refinements. Dotted and Solid lines are *multiple blocking* and hyphenated and dashed lines are *fractional blocking* ($k = Q = 4$ [28]). *Right:* The remapping problem. Note how a permutation of processor assignments for the partitions would decrease the amount of interlevel communication.

by `Nature+Fable`. Despite the bi-level partitioning approach, the interlevel component can for some applications account for about 80% of the total communication costs. Consequently, there are potentially huge savings in runtime by explicitly addressing interlevel communication.

Because most work is done at the higher refinement levels, we let the top bi-level be untouched. We recursively move down the refinement levels and operate on bi-level by bi-level. The partially ordered SFC mapping is probably a good initial guess to an acceptable solution. We take advantage of this, which lowers the complexity substantially. Because "greedy approaches" are often successfully used in partitioning contexts, we employ a greedy approach for processor reassignment.

Our heuristic remapping algorithm [29] is composed of the three steps: (1) linearizing/approximation, (2) removing "good-enough" partitions in the default mappings, and (3) remapping of the remaining partitions. The first two steps strive to reduce the data volume and algorithm complexity. The overall complexity is $O(m^2)$ where m is the number of remaining items in the list of boxes after the first two steps.

Linearizing/Approximation: To avoid costly evaluation and nonlinear, highly complex data structures (e.g., arrays of lists of boxes), the first step creates the simpler scenario where each partition consists of exactly one box. For each partition, one box will represent (or approximate) its partition. Depending on the given partitioning scenario, different strategies are useful. We propose two schemes for creating approximating boxes: (1) *Union* is used when *multiple blocking* is used. A bounding box around all the partition's boxes (a box union of them) approximates the partition and (2) *largest* is used when *fractional blocking* is used. *Union* will not approximate the partition when processors are assigned more than one box (most processor are assigned exactly one box). The set of boxes may be spatially spread out over the computational domain. A bounding box will give little information about the partition. We propose to represent/approximate the partition with its largest box. The complexity for both strategies is linear in the number of approximating boxes in either of the lists.

Removing "Good-Enough" Pairs: It is not feasible to search for an optimal solution (it is not even clear what "optimal" means at this point) even for this simplified case established by the linearizing/approximation. We further lower the complexity by acknowledging that the default SFC mapping probably is a good initial guess to a high-quality solution. Given this, we can reduce the required work by reducing the size of the input. We remove pairs of partitions that as a result of the default mapping are already "good-enough."

Consider two lists A and B of approximating boxes representing partitions on level $l + 1$ and level $l + 2$ as in the above example. Let *threshold* $\in [0, 100]$. Intersect the boxes in list A with their counterparts in list B and remove all pairs with an intersection volume greater than *threshold* percent of the box in A. The deleted pairs are regarded as having a good-enough mapping and will not be considered further. The complexity for this step is linear in the number of approximating boxes in either of the lists.

Remapping of Approximating Boxes: We use a greedy approach to remap the partitions remaining in lists A and B after the previous algorithmic steps. We start with the first box in list A and intersect it with all boxes in list B. The greatest intersection volume is considered the best choice, and the box in A is greedily assigned to the processor of the matching box in B. If no best choice was found, we assign it to the processor of the first box in B. Finally, we remove the corresponding box from B. We then continue with the rest of the boxes in A. This algorithm is quadratic in the number of remaining list items.

Viewing the results [29], we list some observations: (a) the proposed remapping algorithm reduced the *total* communication volume by up to 30%, (b) the positive impact of the proposed remapping algorithm was greater for FB than for MB, (c) the result of the parameter *threshold* on total communication was predictable and "well behaved" for FB but unpredictable for MB, (d) MB produced less communication than FB for the unmapped cases for three out of five applications, (e) FB produced less communication than MB for the mapped cases for *all* applications, and (f) FB struggled with data migration and it got a few percent worse as an effect of the mapping.

To lower the complexity of the remapping algorithm, the parameter *threshold* should be set as low as possible. The present results show that a fairly low setting is sufficient for FB to generate good results. Since FB has the two advantages over MB, namely, (1) it generates fewer boxes per processor, and (2) it is significantly faster to compute, the present results support choosing FB over MB when data migration does not have a significant impact on overall application execution time.

18.7 THE ORGANIZER

Given the expert algorithms and natural regions approach presented in the previous sections, the tasks of the `Organizer` [28] are to provide a simple interface to `Nature+Fable` for the application, to call `Nature` for the prepartitioning step, to assign a number of processors to each natural region, to make a first coarse ordering of the natural regions, to call pertinent blocking methods for the Hues, to call the bi-level partitioning for the Cores, to combine the results from the blocking and the bi-level partitioning, and to do the overall mapping of blocks to physical processors. The following sections describe in detail how these tasks are performed.

The interface: The `Organizer` provides a simple interface to `Nature+Fable` for the application. It consists of a single function call. Apart from the parameters modifying partitioning algorithm and behavior, the function takes two arguments: the input hierarchy and the partitioning result. The result is a subdivision of the input hierarchy, where each box has received a processor assignment.

Handling of Natural Regions: The `Organizer` sends refinement levels 0 and 1 to `Nature`, which identifies the natural regions and returns them as lists of bounding boxes. The `Organizer` makes a first coarse ordering of these regions by sorting them on the SFC index corresponding to the lower bound of their first box.

After the ordering, the `Organizer` uses the bounding boxes for the natural regions for building the actual Hues and Cores. Note that a Core is the actual grid hierarchy contained *within* the bounding box. For building the actual natural regions, each grid is checked for overlap with the natural region boxes.

The workload of each natural region is computed. On the basis of the relative workload contribution, the `Organizer` assigns processors to each natural region. Rantakokko's optimal algorithm is used for distributing processors over the natural regions. Because even the optimal integer distribution might generate too much load imbalance, `Nature+Fable` can via the `Organizer` use virtual processors. A parameter `maxNRLoadImb` determines the highest acceptable natural region-induced load imbalance. If the load imbalance generated in this step is greater than `maxNRLoadImb`, then the `Organizer` tries to remedy by using virtual processors.

Partitioning and Mapping: After assigning processors to all natural regions, the entire domain is partitioned into *Pk* partitions. The `Organizer` sends the Hues to the blocking unit and the Cores to the hybrid bi-level partitioner with the pertinent parameters. Each of these calls generates a partial result. The `Organizer` gathers and considers all these partial results.

When each natural region is partitioned, the `Organizer` has a list of all blocks in the final (partial SFC) order. Because each natural region can be partitioned by a different method and have a different number of blocks per partition, the final task for the `Organizer` is to map these blocks onto physical processors. Before combining the partial result for a natural region with the final result, the `Organizer` marks each block with the label of the pertinent processor.

18.8 EXPERIMENTATION

The following experiments show the usefulness of `Nature+Fable` and compare its performance to that of AMROC SFC–DB for two applications [30].

The first application, *Ramp2d*, is a double Mach reflection of a Mach-10 shock wave impinging on a 30° wedge (also used by Berger and Colella [4]). In serial, this application uses 293 grid patches per timestep on average. There are three additional levels of refinement. The second application, *ConvShock2d*, is a converging Richtmyer–Meshkow instability. In this simulation, a spherically converging Mach-5 shock hits an initially perturbed spherical interface between two different gases and drives it inward. The shock is reflected around $t \approx 0.3$ in the origin and inverts the direction of motion of the interface as it hits it again. The simulation is motivated by mixing phenomena related to inertial confinement fusion. As a consequence of this refinement pattern, the application is particularly challenging for the PDA. In serial, this simulation uses 745 grid patches per timestep on average. There are four additional levels of refinement. Both simulations use the second-order accurate multidimensional wave propagation method with MUSCL slope limiting in the normal direction [10] in combination with linearized Riemann-solvers of Roe type.

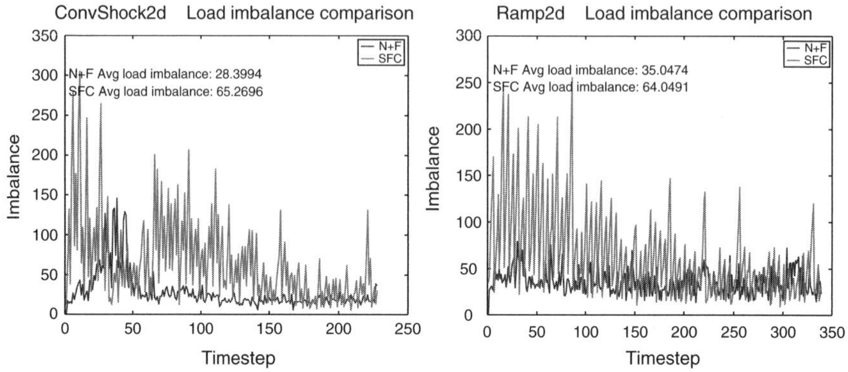

Figure 18.11 Load imbalance: `Nature+Fable` versus AMROC DB/SFC for ConvShock2d (left) and Ramp2d (right) and 16 processors.

Using data from a related study [16], `Nature+Fable` was configured for each application with the goal to generate low average imbalances. Although `Nature+Fable` is highly configurable, there was no attempt to optimize for individual timesteps or for other metrics.

Load imbalance, box count, and communication amount are derived using software [26] developed at Rutgers University in New Jersey by The Applied Software Systems Laboratory that simulates the execution of the Berger–Colella SAMR algorithm. For each coarse timestep, load imbalance is defined as the load of the heaviest loaded processor divided by the average load, box count as the average number of boxes per processor, and communication amount as the maximum number of ghost cells required to be transferred by any single processor.

As can be seen in Figures 18.11–18.13, `Nature+Fable` coped with all grid hierarchies. Load imbalance was significantly lower—about half—compared to AMROC DB–SFC, while box count on average was similar. Communication volume, on the other hand, was from 4 to 4.5 times higher for `Nature+Fable`.

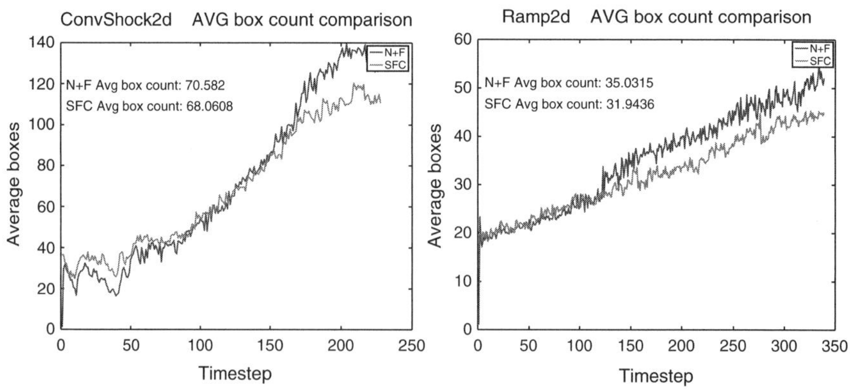

Figure 18.12 Box count: `Nature+Fable` versus AMROC DB/SFC for ConvShock2d (left) and Ramp2d (right) and 16 processors.

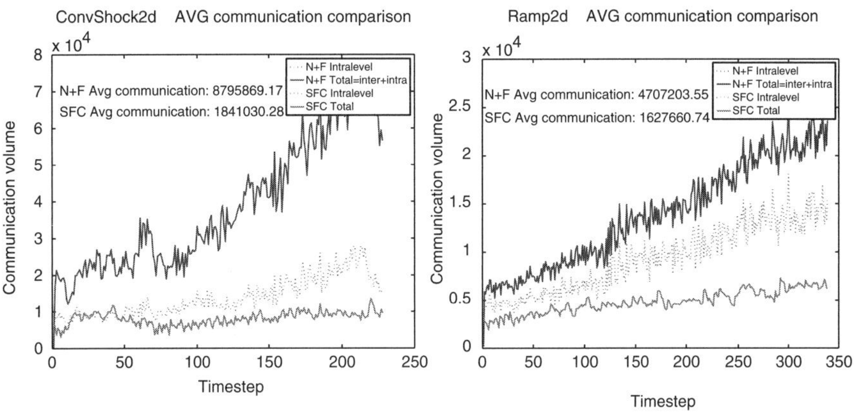

Figure 18.13 Communication volume: `Nature+Fable` versus AMROC DB/SFC for ConvShock2d (left) and Ramp2d (right) and 16 processors.

The combination of perfect load balance and four times more communication for a regular Berger–Collela SAMR application such as Ramp2d can reduce the synchronization costs by up to about 50% [30]. If the fraction of the time spent in synchronization is about 25% as for our applications, this gain will translate to better than a 10% improvement of overall runtime. Conversely, for more complex applications requiring more frequent synchronization and having a higher communication-to-computation demand, the partitioning focus needs to be on the communication volume. An increased communication volume by a factor of 4 would, for these applications, be devastating to parallel performance.

Note, however, that `Nature+Fable` is highly configurable. Communication was not part of the target for the present configurations. A related report [16] shows that `Nature+Fable` can be configured so that it generates even less communication than AMROC DB does, for the applications considered in the present experiments. It is unclear, however, to what extent such a configuration will negatively impact load balance. Regardless of the specific communication versus load balance trade-off, our experiments show that `Nature+Fable` can be configured to generate high-quality partitionings for a variety of targets.

The recursive classification algorithm divides the bi-levels and automatically switches between the parent-driven or the child-driven partitioning approach. As a result, `Nature+Fable` successfully copes with realistic applications.

The conclusion is that the performance of Berger–Collela-type applications, like Ramp2d, can be significantly improved by using `Nature+Fable` . To be considered a general solution to scalability problems for SAMR applications, however, `Nature+Fable` probably needs to generate lower average communication costs.

18.9 SUMMARY, CONCLUSIONS, AND FUTURE WORK

Structured AMR is widely used as a powerful alternative to unstructured AMR in many areas of application. The power of adaptive computational techniques comes from effective use of computer resources. For large-scale SAMR applications, the data sets are huge. It is the task of the data partitioner to divide and distribute the data over the processors so that all resources are used efficiently. Adaptation causes the workload to change dynamically, calling for dynamic repartitioning to maintain efficient resource use. The overall goal of the work presented here was to decrease runtimes for large-scale SAMR applications.

We have presented `Nature+Fable`, a hybrid and flexible partitioning tool dedicated to structured grid hierarchies. `Nature+Fable` successfully copes with demanding, complex, and realistic applications. In the experiments, `Nature+Fable` was configured to generate low average load imbalance. Compared to the native AMROC DB–SFC partitioner, `Nature+Fable` generated significantly less load imbalance, similar box count, but 4–4.5 time more communication. For some computer-application combinations, like the Ramp2d on a 16-processor Linux cluster, `Nature+Fable` with such a configuration is expected to improve performance. For other combinations, another configuration of `Nature+Fable`, the AMROC DB–SFC, or some other technique that better optimizes the pertinent metrics would probably give better performance.

Future work includes addressing the blocks-to-processor mapping in `Nature+Fable`. An optimal mapping in `Nature+Fable` should be such that a strictly domain-based mapping is automatically created for suitable hierarchies. For other hierarchies, `Nature+Fable` should guarantee a minimal amount of parent–child separation given the current bi-level blocks. With a significantly improved mapping scheme, `Nature+Fable` would generate communication patterns comparable to those generated by domain-based techniques. Consequently, `Nature+Fable` would become a complete tool for decreasing runtimes for most SAMR computer-application combinations.

ACKNOWLEDGMENTS

For scientific collaboration, I thank Jaideep Ray at Advanced Software R&D, Sandia National Laboratory, California, Manish Parashar and Sumir Chandra at the Center for Advanced Information Processing, Rutgers University, NJ, USA, and Michael Thuné, Jarmo Rantakokko, and Henrik Johansson at Information Technology, Uppsala University, Sweden, and Ralf Deiterding at California Institute of Technology, CA, USA. For comments and suggestions leading to a significantly improved manuscript, I thank fellow “Sandians” Robert Clay and Joseph Kenny. Sandia is a multiprogram laboratory operated by Sandia Corporation, a Lockheed Martin Company, for the United States Department of Energy under Contract No. DE-AC04-94-AL85000.

REFERENCES

1. CHOMBO. http://seesar.lbl.gov/anag/chombo/, NERSC, ANAG of Lawrence Berkeley National Lab, CA, 2003.
2. S.B. Baden, S.R. Kohn, and S. Fink. Programming with LPARX. Technical Report, University of California, San Diego, CA, 1994.

3. D. Balsara and C. Norton. Highly parallel structured adaptive mesh refinement using language-based approaches. *J. Parallel comput.*, (27):37–70, 2001.
4. M.J. Berger and P. Colella. Local adaptive mesh refinement for shock hydrodynamics. *J. Comput. Phy.*, 82:64–84, 1989.
5. M.J. Berger and S. Bokhari. A partitioning strategy for non-uniform problems on multiprocessors. *IEEE Trans. Comput.*, 85:570–580, 1987.
6. M.J. Berger and J. Oliger. Adaptive mesh refinement for hyperbolic partial differential equations. *J. Comput. Phys.*, 53:484–512, 1984.
7. G. Bryan. Fluids in the universe: adaptive mesh refinement in cosmology. *Comput. Sci. Eng.*, 1(2):46–53, 1999.
8. M.W. Choptuik. Experiences with an adaptive mesh refinement algorithm in numerical relativity. In *Frontiers in Numerical Relativity*, Cambridge University Press, London, 1989, pp. 206–221.
9. R. Deiterding. AMROC. http://amroc.sourceforge.net/ VTF, California Institute of Technology, CA, USA, 2003.
10. R. Deiterding. Parallel adaptive simulation of multi-dimensional detonation structures. PhD thesis, Brandenburgische Technische Universität Cottbus, Germany, 2003.
11. F. Edelvik and G. Ledfelt. A comparison of the GEMS time domain solvers. In F. Edelvik et al., editors, *EMB 01—Electromagnetic Computations—Methods and Applications*, Department of Scientific Computing, Uppasala University, Sweden, November 2001, pp. 59–66.
12. J. Ray et al. Triple flame structure and dynamics at the stabilization point of an unsteady lifted jet diffusion flame. *Proc. Combust. Inst.*, 25(1):219-226, 2000.
13. T. Wilhelmsson et al. Increasing resolution and forecast length with a parallel ocean model. In *Operational Oceanography—Implementation at the European and Regional Scales*. Elsevier, 1999.
14. S.J. Fink, Scott B. Baden, and Scott R. Kohn. Flexible communication mechanisms for dynamic structured applications. In *Proceedings of IRREGULAR '96*, 1996, pp. 203–215..
15. E.R. Hawkes, R. Sankaran, J.C. Sutherland, and J. Chen. Direct numerical simulation of turbulent combustion: fundamental insights towards predictive models. *J. Phys., Conf. Ser.*, 16:65–79, 2005.
16. H. Johansson and J. Steensland. A performance evaluation of load balancing algorithms for parallel SAMR applications. Technical Report 2006-009, Uppsala University, IT, Deptartment of Scientific Computing, Uppsala, Sweden, 2006.
17. S. Kohn. SAMRAI homepage: structured adaptive mesh refinement applications infrastructure. http://www.llnl.gov/CASC/SAMRAI/, 1999.
18. Z. Lan, V. Taylor, and G. Bryan. Dynamic load balancing for structured adaptive mesh refinement applications. In *Proceedings of ICPP 2001*, 2001, pp. 571–579.
19. P. MacNeice et al. PARAMESH: a parallel adaptive mesh refinement community toolkit. *Comput. Phys. Commun.*, (126):330–354, 2000.
20. F. Manne and T. Sørevik. Partitioning an array onto a mesh of processors. In *Proceedings of PARA96 (Workshop on Applied Parallel Computing in Industrial Problems and Optimization)*, 1996.
21. M. Parashar and J.C. Browne. On partitioning dynamic adaptive grid hierarchies. In *Proceedings of the 29th Annual Hawaii International Conference on System Sciences*, 1996.
22. M. Parashar and J. Browne. System engineering for high performance computing software: the HDDA/DAGH infrastructure for implementation of parallel structured adaptive mesh refinement. *IMA Volume on Structured Adaptive Mesh Refinement (SAMR) Grid Methods*, 2000, pp. 1–18.
23. J. Rantakokko. Comparison of partitioning strategies for PDE solvers on multiblock grids. In *Proceedings of PARA98*, Vol. 1541, *Lecture Notes in Computer Sciences*. Springer Verlag, 1998.
24. J. Rantakokko. Partitioning strategies for structured multiblock grids. *Parallel Comput.*, 26(12):1161–1680, 2000.
25. J. Rantakokko. Data partitioning methods and parallel block-oriented PDE solvers. PhD thesis, Uppsala University, 1998.
26. M. Shee. Evaluation and optimization of load balancing/distribution techniques for adaptive grid hierarchies. M.S. Thesis, Graduate School, Rutgers University, NJ. http://www.caip.rutgers.edu/TASSL/Thesis/mshee-thesis.pdf, 2000.
27. J. Steensland. Domain-based partitioning for parallel SAMR applications, 2001. Licentiate thesis. Department of Scientific Computing, Uppsala University, IT, 2001–002.

28. J. Steensland. Efficient partitioning of dynamic structured grid hierarchies. PhD thesis, Uppsala University, 2002.
29. J. Steensland and J. Ray. A heuristic re-mapping algorithm reducing inter-level communication in SAMR applications. In *Proceedings of The 15th IASTED International Conference on Parallel and Distributed Computing and Systems (PDCS03)*, vol. 2, ACTA Press, 2003, pp. 707–712.
30. J. Steensland, J. Ray, H. Johansson, and R. Deiterding. An improved bi-level algorithm for partitining dynamic grid hierarchies. Technical Report SAND2006-2487, Sandia National Laboratory, Livermore, CA, 2006.
31. E. Steinthorsson and D. Modiano. Advanced methodology for simulation of complex flows using structured grid systems. In *Surface Modeling, Grid Generation, and Related Issues in Computational Fluid Dynamic (CFD) Solutions, p 697-710 (SEE N95-28723 10-02)*, March 1995, pp. 697–710.
32. M. Thuné. Partitioning strategies for composite grids. *Parallel Algorithms Appl.*, 11:325–348, 1997.
33. P. Wang, I. Yotov, T. Arbogast, C. Dawson, M. Parashar, and K. Sepehrnoori. A new generation EOS compositional reservoir simulator: Part I—formulation and discretization. *Proceedings of the Society of Petroleum Engineerings Reservoir Simulation Symposium*, Dallas, TX, June 1997, pp. 31–38.
34. A.M. Wissink et al. Large scale parallel structured AMR calculations using the SAMRAI framework. *In Proceedings of Supercomputing 2001*, 2001, pp. 6–6.

Chapter 19

Flexible Distributed Mesh Data Structure for Parallel Adaptive Analysis

Mark S. Shephard and Seegyoung Seol

19.1 INTRODUCTION

An efficient distributed mesh data structure is needed to support parallel adaptive analysis since it strongly influences the overall performance of adaptive mesh-based simulations. In addition to the general mesh-based operations [4], such as mesh entity creation/deletion, adjacency and geometric classification, iterators, arbitrary attachable data to mesh entities, and so on, the distributed mesh data structure must support (1) efficient communication between entities duplicated over multiple processors, (2) migration of mesh entities between processors, and (3) dynamic load balancing.

Issues associated with supporting parallel adaptive analysis on a given unstructured mesh include dynamic mesh load balancing techniques [8, 11, 32, 34] and data structure and algorithms for parallel mesh adaptation [9, 17, 20, 21, 23, 24, 27]. The focus of this chapter is on a parallel mesh infrastructure capable of handling general nonmanifold [19, 35] models and effectively supporting automated adaptive analysis. The mesh infrastructure, referred to as Flexible distributed Mesh DataBase (FMDB), is a distributed mesh data management system that is capable of shaping its data structure dynamically based on the user's requested mesh representation [28, 29].

Advanced Computational Infrastructures For Parallel and Distributed Adaptive Applications. Edited by Manish Parashar and Xiaolin Li

19.1.1 Nomenclature

V	the model, $V \in \{G, P, M\}$ where G signifies the geometric model, P signifies the partition model, and M signifies the mesh model.
$\{V\{V^d\}\}$	a set of topological entities of dimension d in model V. (For example, $\{M\{M^2\}\}$ is the set of all the faces in the mesh.
V_i^d	the ith entity of dimension d in model V. $d = 0$ for a vertex, $d = 1$ for an edge, $d = 2$ for a face, and $d = 3$ for a region.
$\{\partial(V_i^d)\}$	set of entities on the boundary of V_i^d.
$\{V_i^d\{V^q\}\}$	a set of entities of dimension q in model V that are adjacent to V_i^d. (For example, $\{M_3^1\{M^3\}\}$ are the mesh regions adjacent to mesh edge M_3^1.
$V_i^d\{V^q\}_j$	the jth entity in the set of entities of dimension q in model V that are adjacent to V_i^d. (For example, $M_1^3\{M^1\}_2$ is the second edge adjacent to mesh region M_1^3.)
$U_i^{d_i} \sqsubset V_j^{d_j}$	classification indicating the unique association of entity $U_i^{d_i}$ with entity $V_j^{d_j}$, $d_i \leq d_j$, where $U, V \in \{G, P, M\}$ and U is lower than V in terms of a hierarchy of domain decomposition.
$\mathcal{P}[M_i^d]$	set of partition id(s) where entity M_i^d exists.

19.2 REQUIREMENTS FOR A PARALLEL INFRASTRUCTURE FOR ADAPTIVELY EVOLVING UNSTRUCTURED MESHES

The design of a parallel mesh infrastructure is dictated by the type of meshes to be stored, the mesh-level information and functions to be performed by the applications, and the parallel computational environment that will be applied. This chapter considers the parallel representation of adaptively evolving conforming unstructured meshes that can include multiple mesh entity topological types.

The mesh information needed and the functions that must be carried out on the mesh are a strong function of the specific application operations to be performed. In the case of adaptive analysis, the most demanding of operations performed are the mesh modifications associated with adapting the mesh [1, 5, 9, 15, 16, 20]. In the case of curved geometries, the mesh modifications must be performed such that the geometric approximation of the domain is improved as the mesh is modified [15]. This requires that the mesh be related back to the original geometry definition. The most common form of geometric representation is a boundary representation defined in terms of topological entities including vertices, edges, faces, and regions and the adjacencies between the entities [19, 35]. This leads to consideration of a boundary representation for the mesh in which the mesh entities are easily related to geometric model entities, and the topological entities and their adjacencies are used to support the wide range of mesh information in need of mesh modification operations [4, 6, 13, 25]. The three basic functional requirements of a general topology-based mesh data structure are topological entities, geometric classification, and adjacencies between entities.

Topology provides an unambiguous, shape-independent abstraction of the mesh. With reasonable restrictions on the topology [4], a mesh can be effectively represented with only the basic 0- to d-dimensional topological entities, where d is the dimension of the domain of interest. The full set of mesh entities in 3D is $\{\{\mathrm{M}\{M^0\}\}, \{\mathrm{M}\{M^1\}\}, \{\mathrm{M}\{M^2\}\}, \{\mathrm{M}\{M^3\}\}\}$, where $\{\mathrm{M}\{M_i^d\}\}$, $d = 0, 1, 2, 3$, are, respectively, the set of vertices, edges, faces, and regions. Mesh edges, faces, and regions are bounded by the lower order mesh entities.

Geometric classification defines the relation of a mesh to a geometric model. The unique association of a mesh entity of dimension d_i, $M_i^{d_i}$, to the geometric model entity of dimension d_j, $G_j^{d_j}$, where $d_i \leq d_j$, on which it lies is termed as geometric classification and is denoted $M_i^{d_i} \sqsubset G_j^{d_j}$, where the classification symbol, $\sqsubset$, indicates that the left-hand entity, or a set of entities, is classified on the right-hand entity.

Adjacencies describe how mesh entities connect to each other. For an entity of dimension d, adjacency, denoted by $\{M_i^d\{M^q\}\}$, returns all the mesh entities of dimension q, which are on the closure of the entity for a downward adjacency ($d > q$), or for which the entity is part of the closure for an upward adjacency ($d < q$).

There are many options in the design of the mesh data structure in terms of the entities and adjacencies stored [4, 6, 13, 25]. If a mesh representation stores all *0–d*-level entities explicitly, it is a *full* representation, otherwise it is a *reduced* representation. *Completeness of adjacency* indicates the ability of a mesh representation to provide any type of adjacencies requested without involving an operation dependent on the mesh size such as the global mesh search or mesh traversal. Regardless of full or reduced, if all adjacency information is obtainable in $O(1)$ time, the representation is complete, otherwise it is incomplete [4, 6, 25]. In terms of the requirements to be the basic mesh data structure to be used for parallel adaptive computations, it must be able to provide all the mesh adjacencies needed by the operations to be performed and needs to be able to provide them effectively, which does require they be provided in $O(1)$ time since any requirement to provide an adjacency in time at all proportional to the mesh size is not acceptable unless it is only done once. Although this does not strictly require the use of a complete mesh representation, the wide range of adjacencies typically needed by mesh modification will force one to select a complete representation. The implementation of a complete mesh data structure that is not full is more complex, particularly in parallel [28].

The requirements placed on the mesh are a function of the parallel computing environment. To ensure the greatest flexibility, it is desirable to be able to distribute the mesh to the processors in a distributed memory computing environment with the need to store little more than the mesh entities assigned to that processor. It is also a desirable feature that with the exception of possibly added information, the mesh data structure on the individual processors be identical to that of the serial implementation. This way the parallel procedures can easily interoperate with a serial mesh structure implementation.

19.3 STRUCTURE OF THE FLEXIBLE MESH DATABASE

One approach to the implementation of a mesh data structure is to select a fixed representation that meets the full set of needs of the applications to be executed. In those cases where the specific adjacencies needed are not known in advance, one will want to be sure the representation selected is complete so that any adjacency can be obtained with acceptable efficiency. Since explicitly storing all the adjacencies used is typically unacceptable, one wants to select a representation that can efficiently obtain those that are not stored. Even when a complete representations is used, the constant on some of the $O(1)$ time adjacency recovery operations can be quite large [4]. An alternative approach taken recently is to employ a flexible mesh data representation that at the time an application is initiated can select the adjacencies stored to be well suited to the application at hand [24, 25, 28, 29].

This section discusses the design of a flexible mesh database, FMDB, which enables the mesh database to shape its structure based on the representational needs. A mesh representation matrix (MRM), is used to define the mesh entities and adjacency information to be maintained. The initial MRM is input by the user based on their knowledge of the entities and adjacencies to be used where the "user" is an application program that interacts with mesh information in some manner, including changing it. The MRM provided by the user is then modified to optimize its ability to provide the indicated information efficiently without the storage of entities that can be quickly determined based on others that are stored. To ensure the user-requested representation remains correct, even with mesh modification, the mesh entity creation/deletion operators used in the application are set to the proper ones dynamically to maintain the needed representation. The MRM used in Ref. [24] to describe a mesh representation has been extended to be able to represent the equally classified mesh entities and adjacencies available only for the stored entities.

Mesh Representation Matrix: The MRM is a 4×4 matrix where diagonal element $\mathcal{R}_{i,i}$ is equal to 1 if mesh entities of dimension i are present in the representation, is equal to $-$ if only entities of the same order as the geometric model entities they are classified on are stored, and is equal to 0 if not stored. Nondiagonal element $\mathcal{R}_{i,j}$ of MRM is equal to 1 if $\mathcal{R}_{i,i} = \mathcal{R}_{j,j} = 1$ and $\{M^i\{M^j\}\}$ is present, is equal to $-$ if $\{M^i\{M^j\}\}$ is present only for stored $\{M\{M^i\}\}$ and $\{M\{M^j\}\}$, and is equal to 0 if the adjacency is not stored at all, and $i \neq j$ and $0 \leq i, j \leq 3$.

Figure 19.1 gives the MRMs of the circular, one-level, and minimum sufficient representation (MSR). The circular and one-level representation are popular full representations that are complete. The minimum sufficient representation is the minimal representation with no loss of information. In the MSR adjacency graph given in Figure 19.1, $\mathcal{R}_{0,0}$, $\mathcal{R}_{3,3}$, and $\mathcal{R}_{3,0}$ are 1 since all the vertices, regions, and adjacency $\{M^3\{M^0\}\}$ are present in the representation. $\mathcal{R}_{1,1}$ and $\mathcal{R}_{2,2}$ are $-$ since only edges classified on model edges and faces classified on model faces are present. $\mathcal{R}_{1,0}$ and $\mathcal{R}_{2,0}$ are $-$ since the downward adjacencies $\{M^1\{M^0\}\}$ and $\{M^2\{M^0\}\}$ are stored only for the represented edges and faces. The remaining $\mathcal{R}_{i,j}$, $i \neq j$, are 0.

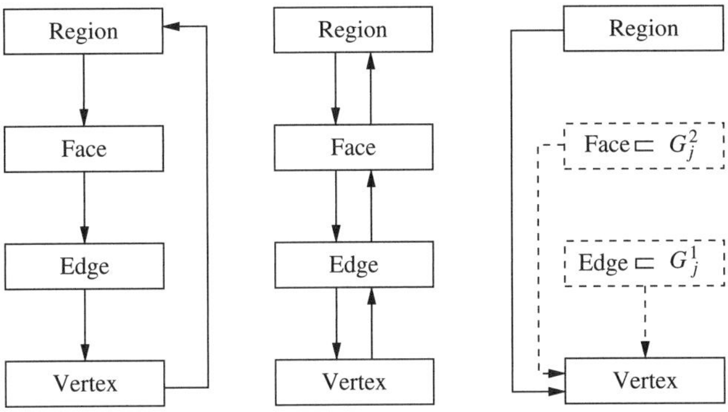

$$\begin{bmatrix} 1 & 0 & 0 & 1 \\ 1 & 1 & 0 & 0 \\ 0 & 1 & 1 & 0 \\ 0 & 0 & 1 & 1 \end{bmatrix} \quad \begin{bmatrix} 1 & 1 & 0 & 0 \\ 1 & 1 & 1 & 0 \\ 0 & 1 & 1 & 1 \\ 0 & 0 & 1 & 1 \end{bmatrix} \quad \begin{bmatrix} 1 & 0 & 0 & 0 \\ - & - & 0 & 0 \\ - & 0 & - & 0 \\ 1 & 0 & 0 & 1 \end{bmatrix}$$

Circular One level MSR

Figure 19.1 3D mesh representation matrices.

The requirements of the flexible mesh data structure are

- The user-requested representation should be properly maintained even with mesh modification such as entity creation/deletion and mesh migration.
- Restoration of implicit entities should produce valid entities in every aspect such as geometrical classification and vertex ordering.
- Any mesh operators, except mesh loading/exporting and query to unrequested adjacencies, should be effective without involving global mesh-level search or traversal to ensure efficiency and scalability in parallel.

To meet the requirements, the mesh database is designed to shape its data structure dynamically by setting mesh modification operators to the proper ones that keep the requested representation correct. Shaping mesh data structure is performed in three steps:

Step 1: Union the user-requested representation with the minimum sufficient representation. Unioning of the user-requested representation with the MSR is performed since the MSR is the minimal representation to be stored in the mesh with no information loss. For two MRMs, R^1 and R^2, the union operation is performed on each pair of $R^1_{i,j}$ and $R^2_{i,j}$, $i, j = 0, 1, 2, 3$, where union of $R^1_{i,j}$ and $R^2_{i,j}$ returns the maximum of $R^1_{i,j}$ and $R^2_{i,j}$, $1 > - > 0$.

Figure 19.2 depicts examples of 3D MRM union. By union, $\mathcal{R}^a$, $\mathcal{R}^d$, and $\mathcal{R}^g$ are, respectively, modified to $\mathcal{R}^b$, $\mathcal{R}^e$ and $\mathcal{R}^h$. In case of $\mathcal{R}^d$, $\mathcal{R}^d_{1,1}$ and $\mathcal{R}^d_{1,0}$ are set to $-$ to store edges classified on model edges with their bounding vertices. $\mathcal{R}^d_{3,0}$ and

	User representation	After union
Case 1:	$\mathcal{R}^a = \begin{bmatrix} 0 & 0 & 0 & 0 \\ 1 & 0 & 0 & 0 \\ 0 & 0 & 0 & 0 \\ 0 & 0 & 0 & 0 \end{bmatrix}$	$\mathcal{R}^b = \begin{bmatrix} 1 & 0 & 0 & 0 \\ 1 & - & 0 & 0 \\ - & 0 & - & 0 \\ 1 & 0 & 0 & 1 \end{bmatrix}$
Case 2:	$\mathcal{R}^d = \begin{bmatrix} 1 & 0 & 1 & 1 \\ 0 & 0 & 0 & 0 \\ 0 & 0 & 1 & 1 \\ 0 & 0 & 1 & 1 \end{bmatrix}$	$\mathcal{R}^e = \begin{bmatrix} 1 & 0 & 1 & 1 \\ - & - & 0 & 0 \\ - & 0 & 1 & 1 \\ 1 & 0 & 1 & 1 \end{bmatrix}$
Case 3:	$\mathcal{R}^g = \begin{bmatrix} 0 & 0 & 0 & 0 \\ 0 & 1 & 1 & 0 \\ 0 & 1 & 1 & 0 \\ 0 & 0 & 0 & 0 \end{bmatrix}$	$\mathcal{R}^h = \begin{bmatrix} 1 & 0 & 0 & 0 \\ - & 1 & 1 & 0 \\ - & 1 & 1 & 0 \\ 1 & 0 & 0 & 1 \end{bmatrix}$

Figure 19.2 Examples of union of 3D mesh representation matrices.

$\mathcal{R}^d_{2,0}$ are, respectively, set to 1 and $-$ since regions and faces are defined in terms of vertices in the MSR. In case of $\mathcal{R}^g$, $\mathcal{R}^g_{0,0}$ and $\mathcal{R}^g_{3,3}$ are set to 1 to store vertices and regions. $\mathcal{R}^g_{1,0}$ and $\mathcal{R}^g_{2,0}$ are set to $-$ and $\mathcal{R}^g_{3,0}$ is set to 1 to store adjacent vertices of edges, faces, and regions.

Step 2: Optimize the representation. The second step alters the MRM to provide the optimal representation that satisfies the user-requested representation at the minimum memory cost. Optimization is performed as follows:

2.1 *Correct MRM:* The first substep corrects the MRM to be consistent in terms of entity existence and adjacency request. If $\mathcal{R}_{i,j} = 1$ but any of $\mathcal{R}_{i,i}$ and $\mathcal{R}_{j,j}$ is not 1, $\mathcal{R}_{i,j}$ is corrected to $-$. If $\mathcal{R}_{i,j} = -$ and both $\mathcal{R}_{i,i}$ and $\mathcal{R}_{j,j}$ are 1, $\mathcal{R}_{i,j}$ is corrected to 1.

2.2 *Determine the level of bounding entities:* A face can be created by vertices or edges, and a region can be created with vertices, edges, or faces. However, to maintain the needed adjacencies efficiently, it is desirable to determine the level of bounding entities for face and region definition, and create face and region only with predetermined level of entities. For example, for a representation that requires adjacencies $\{M^2\{M^3\}\}$ and $\{M^3\{M^2\}\}$, creating a region with faces is more effective than creating a region with vertices in terms of updating adjacencies between regions and faces. Thus, the second step determines the level of bounding entities in face/region creation to expedite the adjacency update. Note that restricting the lower level of entities for face/region creation does not necessarily mean that creating face/region with other lower level of entities is not supported. It does mean creating a face/region with a nonpreferred level of entities will involve more effort to update desired adjacencies.

2.3 *Suppress unnecessary adjacencies:* The third step removes unnecessary adjacencies that are effectively obtainable by local traversal to save the storage. For instance, consider $\mathcal{R}_{1,2}$, $\mathcal{R}_{1,3}$, and $\mathcal{R}_{2,3}$ are equal to 1. Then $\mathcal{R}_{1,3}$ is suppressed to 0 since $\{M^1\{M^3\}\}$ can be effectively obtained by traversing $\{M^1\{M^2\}\}$

Representation after union After optimization

$$\text{Case 1}: \quad \mathcal{R}^b = \begin{bmatrix} 1 & 0 & 0 & 0 \\ 1 & - & 0 & 0 \\ - & 0 & - & 0 \\ 1 & 0 & 0 & 1 \end{bmatrix} \qquad \mathcal{R}^c = \begin{bmatrix} 1 & 0 & 0 & 0 \\ - & - & 0 & 0 \\ - & 0 & - & 0 \\ 1 & 0 & 0 & 1 \end{bmatrix}$$

$$\text{Case 2}: \quad \mathcal{R}^e = \begin{bmatrix} 1 & 0 & 1 & 1 \\ - & - & 0 & 0 \\ - & 0 & 1 & 1 \\ 1 & 0 & 1 & 1 \end{bmatrix} \qquad \mathcal{R}^f = \begin{bmatrix} 1 & 0 & 1 & 0 \\ - & - & 0 & 0 \\ 1 & 0 & 1 & 1 \\ 0 & 0 & 1 & 1 \end{bmatrix}$$

$$\text{Case 3}: \quad \mathcal{R}^h = \begin{bmatrix} 1 & 0 & 0 & 0 \\ - & 1 & 1 & 0 \\ - & 1 & 1 & 0 \\ 1 & 0 & 0 & 1 \end{bmatrix} \qquad \mathcal{R}^i = \begin{bmatrix} 1 & 0 & 0 & 0 \\ 1 & 1 & 1 & 0 \\ 0 & 1 & 1 & 0 \\ 0 & 0 & 1 & 1 \end{bmatrix}$$

Figure 19.3 Example of 3D mesh representation matrix optimization.

and $\{M^2\{M^3\}\}$. This step can be turned off by the user in case the user does not want local traversal for specific adjacency queries.

Figure 19.3 depicts examples of 3D MRM optimization. By optimization, $\mathcal{R}^b_{1,0}$ is corrected to $-$ since $\mathcal{R}^b_{1,1}$ is not 1. $\mathcal{R}^e_{2,0}$ is corrected to 1 since both $\mathcal{R}^e_{0,0}$ and $\mathcal{R}^e_{2,2}$ are 1. $\mathcal{R}^e_{0,3}$ and $\mathcal{R}^e_{3,0}$ are set to 0 since they are obtainable, respectively, by $\{M^0\{M^2\}\{M^3\}\}$ and $\{M^3\{M^2\}\{M^0\}\}$. In case of $\mathcal{R}^h$, first, $\mathcal{R}^h_{1,0}$ and $\mathcal{R}^h_{2,0}$ are corrected to 1 since all $\mathcal{R}^h_{i,i}$, $i = 0, 1, 2$, are 1. Then, $\mathcal{R}^h_{2,0}$ and $\mathcal{R}^h_{3,0}$ are set to 0, and $\mathcal{R}^h_{3,2}$ is set to 1. Regions and faces with $\mathcal{R}^c$ are determined to create with vertices. Regions with $\mathcal{R}^f$ and $\mathcal{R}^i$ are determined to create with faces. Faces with $\mathcal{R}^f$ (resp. $\mathcal{R}^i$) are determined to create with vertices (resp. edges).

Step 3: Shape mesh data structure via setting mesh operators. This step shapes the mesh data structure based on the mesh representation. To keep the user-requested adjacency even with mesh modification efficient and correct, the needed adjacencies should be updated when mesh entities are created or deleted. For example, suppose an application requires adjacency $\{M^0\{M^2\}\}$. To keep $\{M^0\{M^2\}\}$, face creation must be followed by adding M_i^2 into $\{M_i^0\{M^2\}\}$, and face deletion must be followed by deleting M_i^2 from $\{M_i^0\{M^2\}\}$, for each mesh vertex on the boundary of the mesh face, $M_i^0 \in \{\partial(M_i^2)\}$.

The mesh data structure is shaped by setting the mesh operators that create or delete the mesh entities to the proper ones in order to preserve the user-requested representation. Shaping the representations using dynamic setting of mesh operators does not involve any mesh size operation such as search and traversal, and maintains a valid representation under all mesh-level operations.

Consider the adjacency request $\{M^d\{M^p\}\}$ and $\{M^d\{M^q\}\}$, $p < d < q$. The following are the rules for determining mesh entity creation/deletion operators that are declared as function pointers:

1. When M_i^d is created, $\{M_i^d\{M^p\}\}$ is stored for each $M_i^p \in \{\partial(M_i^d)\}$.

2. When M_i^q is created, $\{M_i^d\{M^q\}\}$ is stored for each $M_i^d \in \{\partial(M_i^q)\}$.

3. When M_i^d is deleted, $\{M_i^d\{M^p\}\}$ does not need to be explicitly updated.
4. When M_i^q is deleted, $\{M_i^d\{M^q\}\}$ is updated for each $M_i^d \in \{\partial(M_i^q)\}$ to remove M_i^q.

Rule 1 means that when M_i^d is created, M_i^p is added to the downward adjacency $\{M_i^d\{M^p\}\}$ for each $M_i^p \in \{\partial(V_i^d)\}$. Rule 2 means that when M_i^q is created, M_i^q is added to the upward adjacency $\{M_i^d\{M^q\}\}$ for each $M_i^d \in \{\partial(M_i^q)\}$. In the object-oriented paradigm where a mesh entity stores its adjacency information as the member data of the entity [3, 10, 26], the downward adjacency $\{M_i^d\{M^p\}\}$ is removed automatically when M_i^d is deleted. Thus, rule 3 means that when M_i^d is deleted, the downward adjacencies of M_i^d do not need to be removed explicitly. However, when M_i^q is deleted, M_i^q is not deleted from the upward adjacency of $\{M_i^d\{M^q\}\}$ stored in M_i^d for each $M_i^d \in \{\partial(M_i^q)\}$. Rule 4 means that, when M_i^q is removed, M_i^q should be removed explicitly from all the stored upward adjacency $\{M_i^d\{M^q\}\}$ for each $M_i^d \in \{\partial(M_i^q)\}$.

19.4 PARALLEL FLEXIBLE MESH DATABASE (FMDB)

A *distributed mesh* is a mesh divided into partitions for distribution over a set of processors for parallel computation.

A *partition* P_i consists of the set of mesh entities assigned to i^{th} processor. For each partition, the unique partition id can be given. Each partition is treated as a serial mesh with the addition of mesh partition boundaries to describe groups of mesh entities that are on interpartition boundaries. Mesh entities on partition boundaries are duplicated on all partitions on which they are used in adjacency relations. Mesh entities that are not on the partition boundary exist on a single partition. Figure 19.4 depicts a mesh that is distributed on three partitions. Vertex M_1^0 is common to three

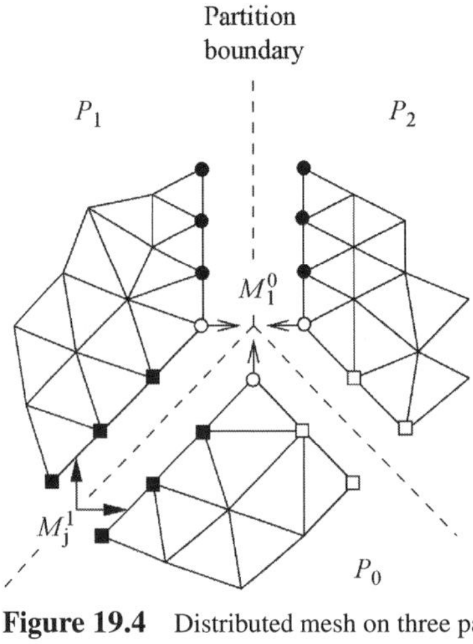

Figure 19.4 Distributed mesh on three partitions P_0, P_1, and P_2 [24].

partitions and on each partition, several mesh edges like M_j^1 are common to two partitions. The dashed lines are *partition boundaries* that consist of mesh vertices and edges duplicated on multiple partitions.

In order to simply denote the partition(s) where a mesh entity resides, we define an operator $\mathscr{P}$ that returns a set of partition id(s) where M_i^d exists. Based on the *residence partition equation* that operates as follows, if $\{M_i^d\{M^q\}\} = \emptyset$, $d < q$, then $\mathscr{P}[M_i^d]$ = $\{p\}$ where p is the id of a partition on which M_i^d exists. Otherwise, $\mathscr{P}[M_i^d] = \cup\, \mathscr{P}[M_j^q \mid M_i^d \in \{\partial(M_j^q)\}]$.

The explanation of the *residence partition equation* is as follows. For any entity M_i^d not on the boundary of any other mesh entities and on partition p, $\mathscr{P}[M_i^d]$ returns $\{p\}$ since when the entity is not on the boundary of any other mesh entities of higher order, its residence partition is determined simply to be the partition where it resides. If entity M_i^d is on the boundary of any higher order mesh entities, M_i^d is duplicated on multiple partitions depending on the residence partitions of its bounding entities since M_i^d exists wherever a mesh entity it bounds exists. Therefore, the residence partition(s) of M_i^d is the union of residence partitions of all entities that it bounds. For a mesh topology where the entities of order $d > 0$ are bounded by entities of order $d - 1$, $\mathscr{P}[M_i^d]$ is determined to be $\{p\}$ if $\{M_i^d\{M_j^{d+1}\}\} = \emptyset$. Otherwise, $\mathscr{P}[M_i^d]$ is $\cup\, \mathscr{P}[M_j^{d+1} \mid M_i^d \in \{\partial(M_j^{d+1})\}]$. For instance, for the 3D mesh depicted in Figure 19.5, where M_1^3 and M_1^2 are on P_0, M_2^3 and M_2^2 are on P_1 (shaded), and M_1^1 is on P_2 (thick line), residence partition ids of M_1^0 (big black dot) are $\{P_0, P_1, P_2\}$ since the union of residence partitions of its bounding edges, $\{M_1^1, M_2^1, M_3^1, M_4^1, M_5^1, M_6^1\}$, are $\{P_0, P_1, P_2\}$.

To migrate mesh entities to other partitions, the destination partition id's of mesh entities must be determined before moving the mesh entities. The residence partition equation implies that once the destination partition id of M_i^d that is not on the boundary of any other mesh entities is set, the other entities needed to migrate are determined by the entities it bounds. Thus, a mesh entity that is not on the boundary of any higher

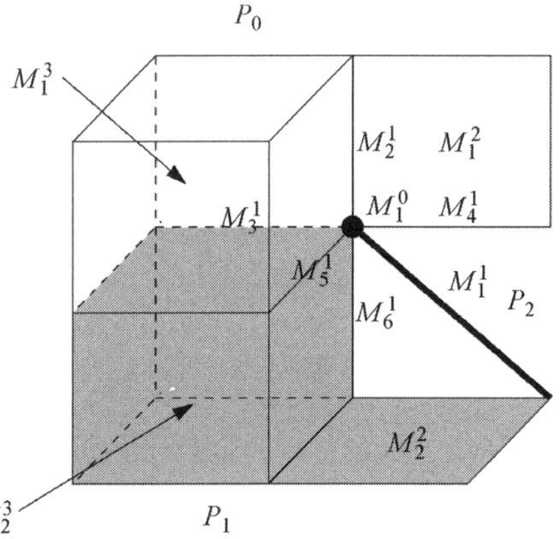

Figure 19.5 Example 3D mesh distributed on three partitions.

order mesh entities is the basic unit to assign the destination partition id in the mesh migration procedure.

The need for a formal definition of the residence partition is due to the fact that unlike manifold models where only the highest order mesh entities need to be assigned to a partition, nonmanifold geometries can have lower order mesh entities not bounded by any higher order mesh that thus must be assigned to a partition. Thus, a *partition object* is the basic unit to which a destination partition id is assigned. The full set of partition objects is the set of mesh entities that are not part of the boundary of any higher order mesh entities. In a 3D mesh, this includes all mesh regions, the mesh faces not bounded by any mesh regions, the mesh edges not bounded by any mesh faces, and mesh vertices not bounded by any mesh edges.

Requirements of the mesh data structure for supporting mesh operations on distributed meshes are

- *Communication Links*: Mesh entities on the partition boundaries (shortly, partition boundary entities) must be aware of where they are duplicated. This is done by maintaining the *remote partition* where a mesh entity is duplicated and the *remote copy* memory location on the remote partition. In a parallel adaptive analysis, the mesh and its partitioning can change thousands of times. Therefore, an efficient mechanism to update mesh partitioning that keeps the links between partitions updated is mandatory to achieve scalability.
- *Entity Ownership*: For entities on partition boundaries, it is beneficial to assign a specific copy as the owner of the others and let the owner be in charge of communication or computation between the copies. For the dynamic entity ownership, there can be several options in determining owning partition of mesh entities. With the FMDB, entity ownership is determined based on the rule of *the poor-to-rich ownership*, which assigns the poorest partition to the owner of entity, where the poorest partition is the partition that has the least number of partition objects among residence partitions of the entity.

19.4.1 A Partition Model

To meet the goals and functionalities of distributed meshes, a partition model has been developed between the mesh and the geometric model. The partition model can be viewed as a part of hierarchical domain decomposition. Its sole purpose is to represent mesh partitioning in topology and support mesh-level parallel operations through interpartition boundary. The specific implementation is the parallel extension of the FMDB, such that standard FMDB entities and adjacencies are used on processors only with the addition of the partition entity information needed to support operations across multiple processors.

A *partition (model) entity*, P_i^d, is a topological entity that represents a group of mesh entities of dimension d that have the same $\mathcal{P}$. Each partition model entity is uniquely determined by $\mathcal{P}$. Each partition model entity stores dimension, id, residence partition(s), and the owning partition. From a mesh entity level, by keeping

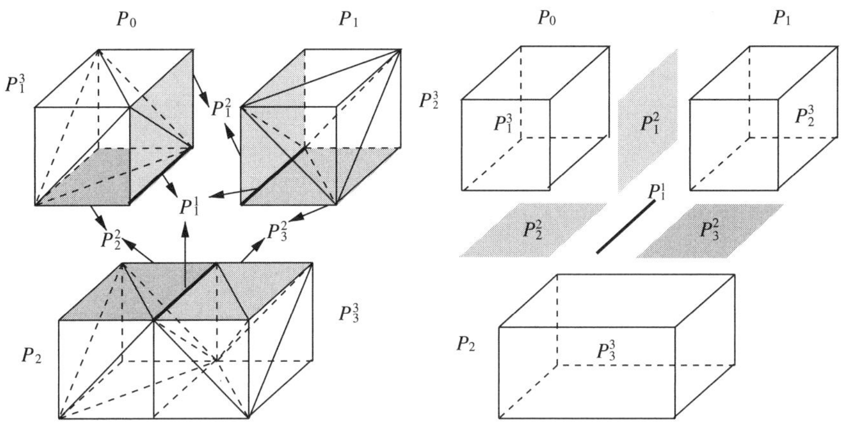

Figure 19.6 Distributed mesh and its association with the partition model via partition classifications.

proper relation to the partition model entity, all needed services to represent mesh partitioning and support interpartition communications are easily supported. Given this the *partition classification* is defined as the unique association of mesh topological entities of dimension d_i, $M_i^{d_i}$, to the topological entity of the partition model of dimension d_j, $P_j^{d_j}$ where $d_i \leq d_j$, on which it lies and is denoted by $M_i^{d_i} \sqsubset P_j^{d_j}$. Figure 19.6 illustrates a distributed 3D mesh with mesh entities labeled with arrows indicating the partition classification of the entities onto the partition model entities and its associated partition model. The mesh vertices and edges on the thick black lines are classified on partition edge P_1^1 and they are duplicated on three partitions P_0, P_1, and P_2. The mesh vertices, edges, and faces on the shaded planes are duplicated on two partitions and they are classified on the partition face pointed with each arrow. The remaining mesh entities are not duplicated; therefore, they are classified on the corresponding partition region.

The following rules govern the creation of the partition model and specify the partition classification of mesh entities:

1. *High-to-Low Mesh Entity Traversal*: The partition classification is set from high-order to low-order entity (residence partition equation).
2. *Inheritance-First*: If $M_i^d \in \{\partial(M_j^q)\}$ and $\mathcal{P}[M_i^d] = \mathcal{P}[M_j^q]$, M_i^d inherits the partition classification from M_j^q as a subset of the partitions it is on.
3. *Connectivity-Second*: If M_i^d and M_j^d are connected and $\mathcal{P}[M_i^d] = \mathcal{P}[M_j^d]$, M_i^d and M_j^d are classified on the same partition entity.
4. *Partition Entity Creation-Last*: If neither of rule 2 nor 3 applies for M_i^d, a new partition entity P_j^d is created.

Rule 2 means if the residence partitions of M_i^d are identical to those of its bounding entity of higher order, M_j^q, it is classified on the partition entity that M_j^q is classified on. For example, in Figure 19.6, any mesh faces, edges, and vertices that are not on shaded planes nor on the thick black line are classified on the partition region by inheriting partition classification from the regions it bounds. Rule 3 is applied when rule 2 is not satisfied. Rule 3 means if residence partitions of M_i^d and M_j^d are the same and they are connected, M_i^d is classified on the same partition entity where M_j^d is classified on. When neither rule 2 nor rule 3 is satisfied, rule 4 applies, thus a new partition entity of dimension d is created for the partition classification of entity M_i^d.

19.5 MESH MIGRATION FOR FULL REPRESENTATIONS

The mesh migration procedure migrates mesh entities from partition to partition. It is performed frequently in parallel adaptive analysis to regain mesh load balance, to obtain the mesh entities needed for mesh modification operators, or to distribute a mesh into partitions. An efficient mesh migration algorithm with minimum resources (memory and time) is the important factor for high performance in parallel adaptive mesh-based simulations. Since the mesh migration process must be able to deal with any partition mesh entity, it can only be efficient with complete representations. The algorithms presented in this section assume a full representation. The next section will indicate the extensions required for migration of reduced representations.

Figure 19.7a and b illustrates the 2D partitioned mesh and its associated partition model to be used as an example in this discussion. In Figure 19.7a, the partition classification of entities on the partition boundaries is denoted with the lines of the same pattern as in Figure 19.7b. For instance, M_1^0 and M_4^1 are classified on P_1^1 and depicted with the dashed lines as P_1^1. In Figure 19.7b. the owning partition of a partition model edge (resp. vertex) is illustrated with thickness (resp. size) of lines (resp. circle). For example, the owning partition of partition vertex P_1^0 is P_0 since P_0 has the least number of partition objects among the three residence partitions of P_1^0. Therefore P_1^0 on P_0 is depicted with a bigger sized circle than P_1^0 on P_1 or P_2 implying that P_0 is the owning partition of P_1^0.

The input of the mesh migration procedure is a list of partition objects to migrate and their destination partition ids, called, for simplicity, *POsToMove*. Given the initial partitioned mesh in Figure 19.7a, we assume that the input of the mesh migration procedure is $\langle (M_1^2,2), (M_7^2,3), (M_8^2,3) \rangle$; M_1^2 will migrate to P_2 and M_7^2 and M_8^2 will migrate to P_3. Partition P_3 is currently empty.

Algorithm 19.1 is the pseudocode of the mesh migration procedure where the pseudocode conventions in Ref. [7] are used.

Step 1: Preparation. For a given list of partition objects to migrate, step 1 collects a set of entities to be updated by migration. The entities collected for the update are maintained in vector *entsToUpdt*, where *entsToUpdt*$[i]$ contains the entities of dimension i, $i = 0, 1, 2, 3$. With a single program multiple data paradigm [22] in parallel, each partition maintains the separate *entsToUpdt*$[i]$ with different contents.

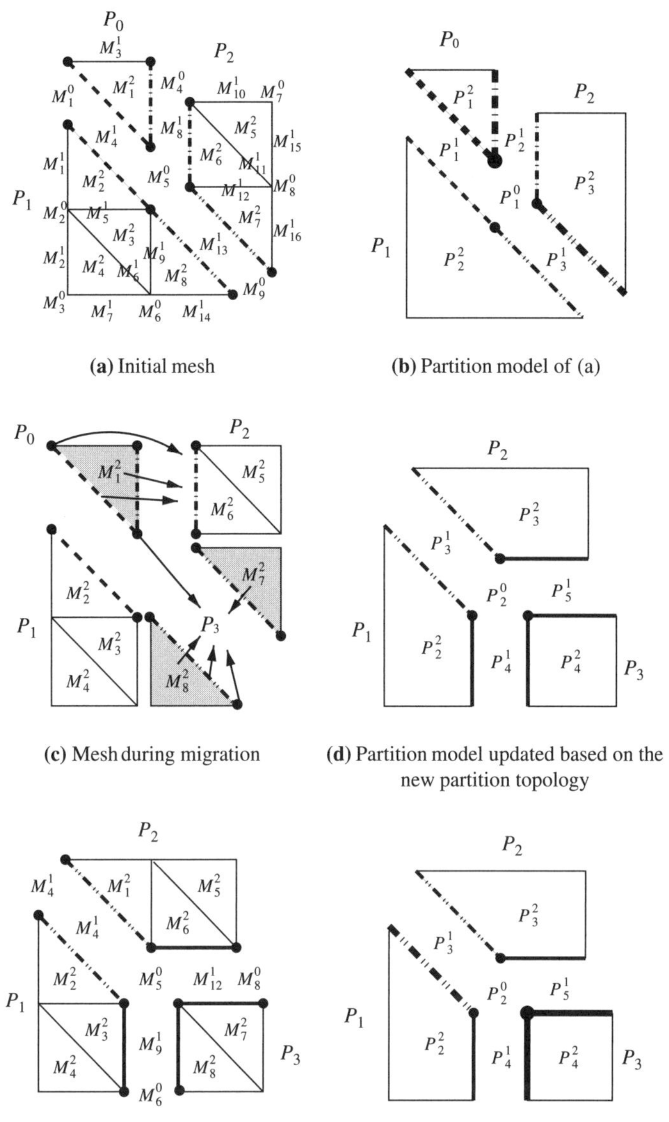

(a) Initial mesh **(b)** Partition model of (a)

(c) Mesh during migration **(d)** Partition model updated based on the new partition topology

(e) Final mesh **(f)** Final partition model with ownership

Figure 19.7 Example of 2D mesh migration.

For the example mesh (Figure 19.7), the contents of *entsToUpdt* by dimension for each partition is given in Table 19.1. Only entities listed in Table 19.1 will be affected by the remaining steps in terms of their location and partitioning related internal data. *entsToUpdt*[2] contains the mesh faces to be migrated from each partition. *entsToUpdt*[1] contains the mesh edges that bound any mesh face in

```
Data   : M, POsToMove
Result : migrate partition objects in POsToMove
begin
    /* Step 1: collect entities to process and clear partitioning data */
    for each M_i^d ∈ POsToMove do
        insert M_i^d into vector entsToUpdt[d];
        reset partition classification and 𝒫;
        for each M_j^q ∈ {∂(M_i^d)} do
            insert M_j^q into entsToUpdt[q];
            reset partition classification and 𝒫;
        endfor
    endfor
    /* Step 2: determine residence partition */
    for each M_i^d ∈ entsToUpdt[d] do
        set 𝒫 of M_i^d;
    endfor
    do one round communication to unify 𝒫 of partition boundary entities;
    /* Step 3: update partition classification and collect entities to remove */
    for d ← 3 to 0 do
        for each M_i^d ∈ entsToUpdt[d] do
            determine partition classification;
            if P_local ∉ 𝒫[M_i^d] do
                insert M_i^d into entsToRmv[d];
            endif
        endfor
    endfor
    /* Step 4: exchange entities */
    for d ← 0 to 3 do
        M_exchngEnts(entsToUpdt[d]); /* Algorithm 19.2 */
    endfor
    /* Step 5: remove unnecessary entities */
    for d ← 3 to 0 do
        for each M_i^d ∈ entsToRmv[d] do
            if M_i^d is on partition boundary do
                remove copies of M_i^d on other partitions;
            endif
            remove M_i^d;
        endfor
    endfor
    /* Step 6: update ownership */
    for each P_i^d in P do
        owning partition of P_i^d ← the poorest partition among 𝒫[P_i^d];
    endfor
end
```

Algorithm 19.1 M_migrate(M, $POsToMove$).

Table 19.1 The contents of vector *entsToUpdt* after step 1

	P_0	P_1	P_2
entsToUpdt[0]	M_1^0, M_4^0, M_5^0	$M_1^0, M_5^0, M_6^0, M_9^0$	$M_4^0, M_5^0, M_8^0, M_9^0$
entsToUpdt[1]	M_3^1, M_4^1, M_8^1	$M_4^1, M_9^1, M_{13}^1, M_{14}^1$	$M_8^1, M_{12}^1, M_{13}^1, M_{16}^1$
entsToUpdt[2]	M_1^2	M_8^2	M_7^2

entsToUpdt[2] and their remote copies. *entsToUpdt*[0] contains the mesh vertices that bound any mesh edge in *entsToUpdt*[1] and their remote copies. The partition classification and $\mathcal{P}$ of entities in *entsToUpdt* are cleared for further update.

Step 2: Determine residence partition(s). Step 2 determines $\mathcal{P}$ of the entities according to the residence partition equation. For each entity that bounds the higher order entity, it should be determined if the entity will exist on the current local partition, denoted as P_{local}, after migration to set $\mathcal{P}$. Existence of the entity on P_{local} after migration is determined by checking adjacent partition objects, that is, checking if there is any adjacent partition object to reside on P_{local}. One round of communication is performed at the end to exchange $\mathcal{P}$ of the partition boundary entities to appropriate neighbors to unify them between remote copies.

Step 3: Update the partition classification and collect entities to remove. For the entities in *entsToUpdt*, based on $\mathcal{P}$, step 3 refreshes the partition classification to reflect a new updated partition model after migration and determines the entities to remove from the local partition, P_{local}. An entity is determined to remove from its local partition if $\mathcal{P}$ of the entity does not contain P_{local}. Figure 19.7d is the partition model updated based on the new partition topology.

Step 4: Exchange entities. Since an entity of dimension > 0 is bounded by lower dimension entities, mesh entities are exchanged from low to high dimension. Step 4 exchanges entities from dimension 0 to 3, creates entities on the destination partitions, and updates the remote copies of the entities created on the destination partitions. Algorithm 19.2 illustrates the pseudocode that exchanges the entities contained in *entsToUpdt*[d], $d = 0, 1, 2, 3$.

Step 4.1 sends the messages to destination partitions to create new mesh entities. Consider entity M_i^d duplicated on several partitions needs to be migrated to P_i. In order to reduce the communications between partitions, only one partition sends the message to P_i to create M_i^d. The partition to send the message to create M_i^d is the partition of the minimum partition id among residence partitions of M_i^d and is called *broadcaster*, denoted as P_{bc}. The broadcaster is in charge of creating as well as updating M_i^d over all partitions. The arrows in Figure 19.7c indicate the broadcaster of each entity to migrate based on minimum partition id. Before sending a message to P_i, M_i^d is checked if it already exists on P_i using the remote copy information and ignored if it exists.

For each M_i^d to migrate, P_{bc} of M_i^d sends a message composed of the address of M_i^d on P_{bc} and the information of M_i^d necessary for entity creation, which consists

Data : $entsToUpdt[d]$
Result : create entities on the destination partitions and update remote copies
begin
  /∗ *Step 4.1: send a message to the destination partitions* ∗/
  for *each* $M_i^d \in entsToUpdt[d]$ **do**
    if $P_{local} \neq$ *minimum partition id where* M_i^d *exists*
      continue;
    endif
    for *each partition id* $P_i \in \mathscr{P}[M_i^d]$ **do**
      if M_i^d *exists on partition* P_i *(i.e.* M_i^d *has remote copy of* P_i*)*
        continue;
      endif
      send message A (address of M_i^d on P_{local}, information of M_i^d) to P_i;
    endfor
  endfor
  /∗ *Step 4.2: create a new entity and send the new entity information to the broadcaster* ∗/
  while P_i *receives message A (address of* M_i^d *on* P_{bc}*, information of* M_i^d*) from* P_{bc} **do**
    create M_i^d with the information of M_i^d;
    if M_i^d *is not a partition object*
      send message B (address of M_i^d on P_{bc}, address of M_i^d created) to P_{bc};
    endif
  end
  /∗ *Step 4.3: the broadcaster sends the new entity information* ∗/
  while P_{bc} *receives message B (address of* M_i^d *on* P_{bc}*, address of* M_i^d *on* P_i*) from* P_i **do**
    $M_i^d \leftarrow$ entity located in the address of M_i^d on P_{bc};
    for *each remote copy of* M_i^d *on remote partition* P_{remote} **do**
      send message C (address of M_i^d on P_{remote}, address of M_i^d on P_i, P_i) to P_{remote};
    endfor
    M_i^d saves the address of M_i^d on P_i as for the remote copy on P_i;
  end
  /∗ *Step 4.4: update remote copy information* ∗/
  while P_{remote} *receives message C (address of* M_i^d *on* P_{remote}*, address of* M_i^d *on* P_i*,* P_i*) from* P_{bc} **do**
    $M_i^d \leftarrow$ entity located in the address of M_i^d on P_{remote};
    M_i^d saves the address of M_i^d on P_i as for the remote copy on P_i;
  end
end

Algorithm 19.2 M_exchngEnts($entsToUpdt[d]$).

of unique vertex id (if vertex), entity shape information, required entity adjacencies, geometric classification information, residence partition(s) for setting partition classification, and remote copy information. For instance, to create M_5^0 on P_3, P_0 sends a message composed of the address of M_5^0 on P_0 and information of M_5^0 including its $\mathcal{P}$ (i.e., P_1, P_2, and P_3) and remote copy information of M_5^0 stored on P_0 (i.e., the address of M_5^0 on P_2 and the address of M_5^0 on P_3).

For the message received on P_i from P_{bc} (sent in step 4.1), a new entity M_i^d is created on P_i (step 4.2). If the new entity M_i^d created is not a partition object, its address should be sent back to the sender (M_i^d on P_{bc}) for the update of communication links. The message to be sent back to P_{bc} is composed of the address of M_i^d on P_{bc} and the address of new M_i^d created on P_i. For example, after M_5^0 is created on P_3, the message composed of the address of M_5^0 on P_0 and the address of M_5^0 on P_3 is sent back to P_0.

In step 4.3, the message received on P_{bc} from P_i (sent in step 4.2) is sent to the remote copies of M_i^d on P_{remote} and the address of M_i^d on P_i is saved as the remote copy of M_i^d. The messages sent are received in step 4.4 and used to save the address of M_i^d on P_i on all the remaining remote partitions of M_i^d. For instance, M_5^0 on P_0 sends the message composed of the address of M_5^0 on P_3 to M_5^0 on P_1 and M_5^0 on P_2.

For the message received on P_{remote} from P_{bc} (sent in step 4.3), step 4.4 updates the remote copy of M_i^d on P_{remote} to include the address of M_i^d on P_i. For instance, when M_5^0's on P_1 and P_2 receive the message composed of the address of M_5^0 on P_3, they add it to their remote copy.

Step 5: Remove unnecessary entities. Step 5 removes unnecessary mesh entities collected in step 3 that will be no longer used on the local partition. If the mesh entity to remove is on the partition boundary, it also must be removed from other partitions where it is kept as for remote copies through one round of communication. As for the opposite direction of entity creation, entities are removed from high to low dimension.

Step 6: Update ownership. Step 6 updates the owning partition of the partition model entities based on the rule of the poor-to-rich partition ownership. The partition model given in Figure 19.7e is the final partition model with ownership.

FMDB is implemented in C++ and uses STL (Standard Template Library) [30], functors [10], templates [33], singletons [12], and generic programming [2] for the purpose of achieving reusability of the software. MPI (message passing interface) [22] and Autopack [18] are used for efficient parallel communications between processors. The Zoltan library [36] is used to make partition assignment during dynamic load balancing.

19.6 MESH MIGRATION FOR REDUCED REPRESENTATIONS

To support flexible mesh representations with distributed meshes, the mesh migration procedure must migrate the needed mesh entities regardless of mesh representation

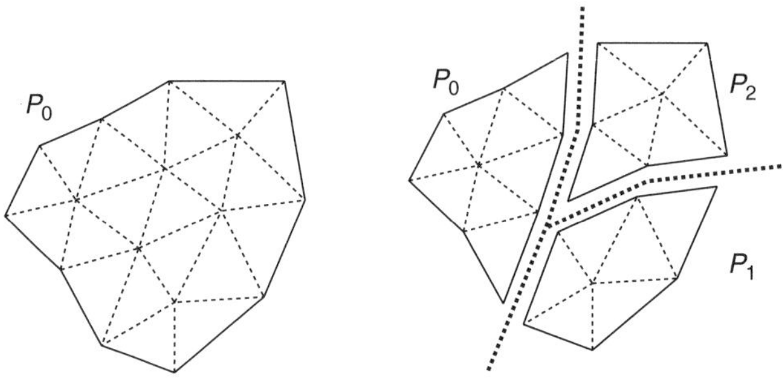

(a) Serial mesh **(b)** Partitioned mesh

Figure 19.8 Example 2D mesh with the MSR.

options while keeping requested mesh representation correct and updating the partition model and communication links based on new mesh partitioning. Figure 19.8a is an example 2D mesh with the minimum sufficient representation where all interior edges are reduced. The reduced edges are denoted with the dotted lines. Figure 19.8b is the partitioned mesh over three partitions with the MSR, where the only interior edges not on the partition boundaries are reduced. After migration, the interior edges on the partition boundaries must be restored in order to represent partitioning topology and support communication links between partitions.

To support mesh migration regardless of mesh representation options, an important question is what is a minimum set of entities and adjacencies necessary for migration. By the analysis of the mesh migration procedure in the previous section, the representational requirements for flexible distributed meshes are the following:

- For each partition object M_i^d, downward adjacent entities on the boundary of that entity, $\in \{\partial(M_i^d)\}$.
- For each downward adjacent entity of M_i^d, M_j^p, the other partition objects adjacent to M_j^p, and the remote copies.

Other partition objects adjacent to M_j^p are necessary in setting $\mathcal{P}$ of M_j^p to check if it will be existing on the local partition even after migration. The representational requirements must be satisfied regardless of representation options to perform migration. In case that the user-requested representation does not satisfy the requirements, the representation is adjusted to meet the representational requirements to support mesh migration.

19.6.1 Mesh Representation Adjustment

To provide communication links between entities on the partition boundaries and represent partitioning topology, nonexisting internal mesh entities must be resurrected if they are located on the partition boundaries after migration. For a reduced representation, checking the existence of downward entities in entity restoration can be efficiently done in $O(1)$ time by maintaining $\{M^0\{M^d\}\}$ for each reduced level d. Therefore, to support efficient downward entity restoration, the first MRM adjustment

$$\begin{bmatrix} 1 & 0 & 0 & 0 \\ - & - & 0 & 0 \\ - & 0 & - & 0 \\ 1 & 0 & 0 & 1 \end{bmatrix} \quad \begin{bmatrix} 1 & - & - & 0 \\ - & - & 0 & 0 \\ - & 0 & - & 0 \\ 1 & 0 & 0 & 1 \end{bmatrix} \quad \begin{bmatrix} 1 & - & - & 1 \\ - & - & 0 & 0 \\ - & 0 & - & 0 \\ 1 & 0 & 0 & 1 \end{bmatrix}$$

(a) Input MSR **(b)** After first adjustment **(c)** After second adjustment

Figure 19.9 MRM adjustments for distributed incomplete meshes.

is to modify the MRM to maintain $\{M^0\{M^d\}\}$ for each reduced level d. For instance, for the 3D user-requested representation given in Figure 19.9a, which is the MSR, $\mathcal{R}_{0,1}$ and $\mathcal{R}_{0,2}$ are set to $-$ as seen in Figure 19.9b. By maintaining the upward adjacencies $\{M^0\{M^1\}\}$ and $\{M^0\{M^2\}\}$ for existing edges and faces, obtaining $\{M_i^3\{M^1\}\}$ and $\{M_i^3\{M^2\}\}$ is done in a constant time by either local searching or restoration.

In mesh migration using a complete representation, checking if an entity will exist on the current partition after migration is done via checking if there is any upward adjacent partition object that is maintained in the local partition. If any upward adjacent partition object remains in the local partition after migration, the current partition id, P_{local}, must be added to $\mathcal{P}$ of the entity.

With flexible mesh representations, especially in case where upward adjacency to the level of partition objects is not available, to determine if an entity will exist on the current partition after migration or not while creating partition object M_i^d, we must store adjacency $\{M_i^0\{M_i^d\}\}$ for each $M_i^0 \in \{\partial(M_i^d)\}$ to avoid the need for global searches.

This process maintains upward adjacency $\{M_i^0\{M_i^d\}\}$ for each vertex M_i^0 on the boundary of partition object M_i^d. The neighboring partition objects of M_i^d is a set of partition objects M_j^{dj} that is bounded by M_j^p where $M_j^p \in \{\partial(M_i^d)\}$. Upward adjacency $\{M_i^0\{M_i^d\}\}$ for each $M_i^0 \in \{\partial(M_i^d)\}$ enables obtaining neighboring partition objects in a constant time. Based on the resident partition equation, for each $M_j^p \in \{\partial(M_i^d)\}$, if the neighboring partition objects of M_i^d is available, existence of M_j^p on the local partition after migration can be checked using downward adjacency of the neighboring partition objects.

This leads to the second step of MRM adjustment that sets $\{M^0\{M^3\}\}$ to 1 in order to support neighboring partition objects of level 3 as seen in Figure 19.9c. The penalty of this option is storing unrequested adjacency information. However, these adjacencies are necessary to avoid mesh-size-dependent operations.

19.6.2 Algorithm of Mesh Migration with Reduced Representations

The mesh migration procedure *M_migrate* based on the use of complete mesh representations is now extended to work with any mesh representation options. Given the *POsToMove*, the overall procedure for the mesh migration is the following:

1. Collect neighboring partition objects.
2. Restore needed downward interior entities.

3. Collect entities to be updated with migration and clear partitioning data ($\mathscr{P}$ and partition classification) of them.
4. Determine residence partition.
5. Update partition classification and collect entities to remove.
6. Exchange entities and update remote copies.
7. Remove unnecessary entities.
8. Update ownership of partition model entities.
9. Remove unnecessary interior entities and adjacencies.

Figure 19.10 depicts the 2D mesh migration procedure with a reduced representation. For the given list of partition objects to migrate, *POsToMove* (Figure 19.10a), first collect the partition objects that are adjacent to any partition object in *POsToMove*

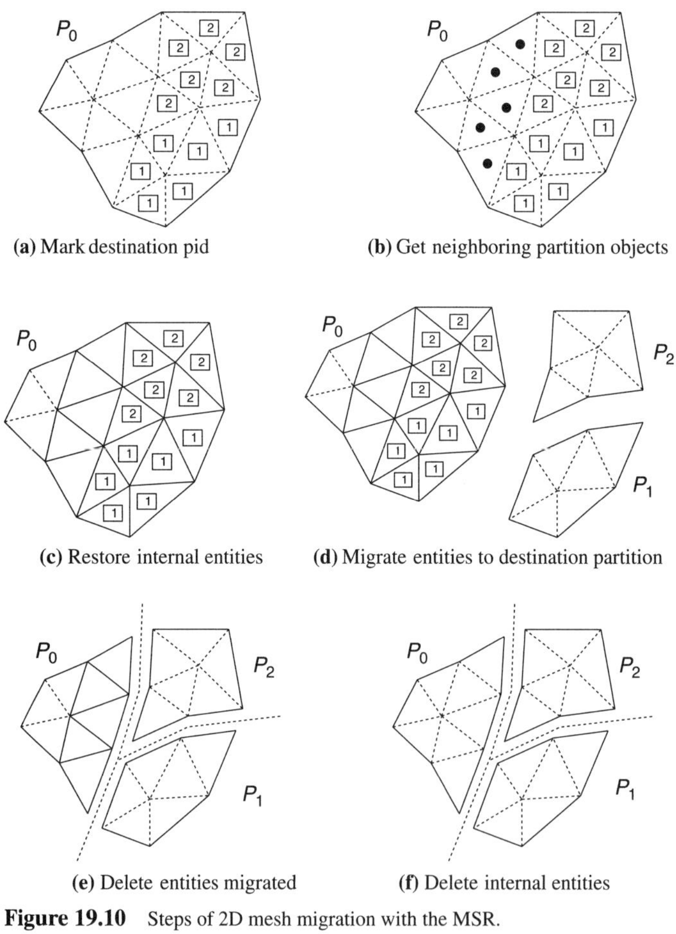

(a) Mark destination pid
(b) Get neighboring partition objects
(c) Restore internal entities
(d) Migrate entities to destination partition
(e) Delete entities migrated
(f) Delete internal entities

Figure 19.10 Steps of 2D mesh migration with the MSR.

and store them in a separate container named *neighborPOs* (Figure 19.10b). Second, for partition objects in *POsToMove* or *neighborPOs*, restore their interior entities and associated downward adjacencies (Figure 19.10c). Collect entities to be updated by migration in terms of their partitioning information such as $\mathscr{P}$, partition classification, and remote copies and save them in a container named *entsToUpdt* for further manipulation. Using downward adjacencies and neighboring partition object information, $\mathscr{P}$ and partition classification of entities in *entsToUpdt* are updated. Based on $\mathscr{P}$ updated, the entities to remove from the local partition after migration are determined among the entities in *entsToUpdt*. After migrating only *necessary* entities to the destination partitions, remote copies of the entities on the partition boundaries are updated (Figure 19.10d). The entities collected to remove are deleted from the local partition (Figure 19.10e). Finally, the interior entities and adjacencies restored in the second step are removed to keep the original requested mesh representation (Figure 19.10f). Algorithm 19.3 is pseudocode that migrates partition objects with reduced mesh representations.

```
Data   : M, POsToMove
Result : migrate partition objects in POsToMove
begin
    /* STEP A: collect neighboring partition objects */
    For each partition object in POsToMove, collect neighboring partition
    objects and store them in neighborPOs;
    /* STEP B: restore downward entities */
    M_buildAdj_URR(M, POsToMove, neighborPOs);
    /* STEP 1: collect entities to process and clear partitioning data */
    Run STEP 1 in Algorithm 19.1;
    /* STEP 2: determine residence partition */
    M_setResidencePartition_URR(POsToMove, neighborPOs);
    /* STEP 3: update p. classification and collect entities to remove */
    Run STEP 3 in Algorithm 19.1;
    /* STEP 4: exchange entities */
    for d ← 0 to 3 do
        M_exchngEnts_URR(entsToUpdt[d]);
    endfor
    /* STEP 5: remove unnecessary entities */
    Run STEP 5 in Algorithm 19.1;
    /* STEP 6: update ownership */
    Run STEP 6 in Algorithm 19.1;
    /* STEP C: remove unnecessary interior entities and adjacencies */
    M_destroyAdj_URR(M, entsToUpdt, neighborPOs);
end
```

Algorithm 19.3 M_migrate_URR(*M*, *POsToMove*).

Step A: Collect neighboring partition objects. For the given list of partition objects to migrate, *POsToMove*, step A collects neighboring partition objects of them, which will be used in step 2 to determine $\mathscr{P}$ of entities. Neighboring partition objects collected are stored in a container named *neighborPOs*. One round of communication is performed to gather neighboring partition objects on remote partitions.

Step B: Restore downward entities. In step B, iterating over *POsToMove* and *neighborPOs*, *M_buildAdj_URR* restores needed nonexisting downward interior entities of each partition object.

Step 1: Preparation. Using downward entities restored in step B, step 1 collects entities to be updated with migration, stores them in *entsToUpdt*, and resets partition classification and $\mathscr{P}$ of those entities.

Step 2: Determine residence partition. Step 2 determines $\mathscr{P}$ of entities collected in *entsToUpdt* (Algorithm 19.4). In step 2.1, according to the resident partition equation, for each partition object M_i^d to migrate to partition p, $\mathscr{P}[M_i^d]$ is set to p, and p is added into $\mathscr{P}[M_j^q]$, where $M_j^q \in \{\partial(M_i^d)\}$. For nonpartition object entity M_j^q, their $\mathscr{P}$ must include local partition id, P_{local}, if it will exist on the

Data : M, *POsToMove*, *entsToUpdt*, *neighborPOs*
Result : determine $\mathscr{P}$ of entities in *entsToUpdt*
begin
  / STEP 2.1: set $\mathscr{P}$ of entities in entitiesToUpdate through downward adjacency of partition objects in POsToMigrate */*
  for *each pair* $(M_i^d, p) \in$ *POsToMove* **do**
    $\mathscr{P}[M_i^d] \leftarrow \{p\}$;
    for *each* $M_j^q \in \{\partial(M_i^d)\}$ **do**
      $\mathscr{P}[M_j^q] \leftarrow \mathscr{P}[M_j^q] \cup \{p\}$;
    endfor
  endfor
  / STEP 2.2: determine if an entity will exist on the local partition after migration */*
  for *each* $M_i^d \in$ *neighborPOs* **do**
    for *each* $M_j^q \in \{\partial(M_i^d)\}$ **do**
      $\mathscr{P}[M_j^q] \leftarrow \mathscr{P}[M_j^q] \cup \{P_{local}\}$;
    endfor
  endfor
  / STEP 2.3: unify $\mathscr{P}$ of partition boundary entities */*
  Do one round of communication to exchange $\mathscr{P}$ of partition boundary entities in *entsToUpdt*;
end

Algorithm 19.4 M_setResidencePartition_URR(*POsToMove*, *entsToUpdt*, *neighborPOs*).

```
Data   : entsToUpdt[d]
Result : create entities on the destination partitions and update remote
         copies
begin
    /* STEP 4.1: send a message to the destination partitions */
    for each M_i^d ∈ entsToUpdt[d] do
        if P_local ≠ minimum partition id where M_i^d exists
            continue;
        endif
        if R_{d,d} ≠ 1
            if M_i^d will not be on p.boundaries or not equally classified
                continue;
            endif
        endif
        for each partition id P_i ∈ 𝒫[M_i^d] do
            if M_i^d exists on partition P_i (i.e. M_i^d has remote copy of P_i)
                continue;
            endif
            send message A (address of M_i^d on P_local, information of M_i^d)
            to P_i;
        endfor
    endfor
    Run STEP 4.2 to 4.4 in Algorithm 19.2;
end
```

Algorithm 19.5 M_exchngEnts_URR(*entsToUpdt*[*d*]).

local partition even after migration. Step 2.2 determines if M_j^q will exist or not on the local partition after migration based on downward adjacency of neighboring partition objects. For partition boundary entities in *entsToUpdt*, step 2.3 performs one round of communication to unify $\mathscr{P}$ of them.

Step 3: Determine partition classification and entities to remove. For each entity in *entsToUpdt*, determine the partition classification and determine if it will be removed from the local partition.

Step 4: Exchange entities and update remote copies. Step 4 exchanges mesh entities from dimension 0 to 3 to create mesh entities on destination partitions. Algorithm 19.2 has been slightly modified to Algorithm 19.5 in order to work with any mesh representation options. Differences from Algorithm 19.2 are the following:

- The dimension of the entities used to create (define) faces and regions are determined based on the MRM.
- Not all interior mesh entities are migrated to the destination partitions. Interior entities are migrated to destination partitions only when they will be on the partition boundaries in new mesh partitioning topology after migration.

Figure 19.10d is an intermediary mesh after step 4 where mesh faces marked for migration are created on destination partitions with reduced interior edges. On the destination partitions, the interior edges on partition boundaries were created to provide communication links. The faces migrated to the destination partitions are not deleted from the original partitions yet.

Step 5: Remove unnecessary entities. Step 5 removes unnecessary mesh entities collected in step 3, which are not used on the local partition any more. Figure 19.10e is an intermediary mesh after step 5, where mesh faces migrated to the destination partitions and their unnecessary adjacent edges and vertices are removed from partition P_0. Note the interior entities of neighboring partition objects restored in step B still exist on partition P_0.

Step 6: Update entity ownership. Step 6 updates the owning partition of the partition model entities based on the rule of the poor-to-rich partition ownership.

Step C: Restore mesh representation. This step restores the mesh representation modified to have interior entities and associated downward adjacencies in step B to the original adjusted MRM. The entities to be considered to remove or update in this step include neighboring partition objects and their downward entities, and entities in *entsToUpdt* not removed in step 5.

19.6.3 Summary

The following are the comparisons of the migration procedures, *M_migrate_URR* in Algorithm 19.3 (steps A, B, 1–6, and C) and *M_migrate* in Algorithm 19.1 (steps 1–6):

- In step A, *M_migrate_URR* collects neighboring partition objects to support computation of $\mathscr{P}$ without upward adjacencies.
- In step B, *M_migrate_URR* restores downward entities and associated downward adjacencies of partition objects to migrate or neighboring.
- Step 1 is identical.
- In step 2, *M_migrate* determines the existence of entities on the local partition after migration based on the existence of adjacent partition objects not to be migrated.
- Step 3 is identical.
- In Step 4, *M_migrate_URR* does not create interior entities on destination partitions if they are not on partition boundaries.
- Step 5 is identical.
- Step 6 is identical.
- In step C, *M_migrate_URR* restores the representation to the original MRM by removing unnecessary downward entities and adjacencies restored in step B.

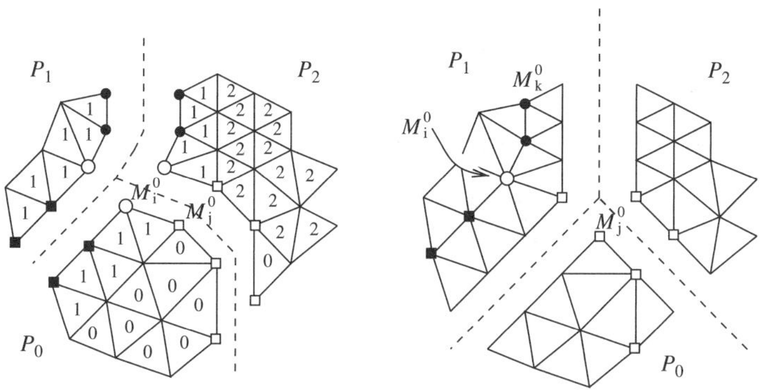

Figure 19.11 Example of 2D mesh load balancing: (left) partition objects are tagged with their destination pids; (right) mesh after load balancing.

It has been noted that step 4 spends most of the migration time among all steps both in *M_migrate* and *M_migrate_URR* because communication for entity exchange is most costly. In case of *M_migrate_URR*, the total migration time varies substantially depending on mesh representation options and partitioning topology due to the varying number of entity exchanges in step 4. Performance results demonstrates that *M_migrate_URR* with reduced representations tends to outperform *M_migrate* with the one-level adjacency representation as the mesh size and the number of partitions increase [28].

During parallel adaptive analysis, the mesh data often needs repartitioning to maintain load balance while keeping the size of the interpartition boundaries minimal [9, 31]. The Zoltan library [36], which is a collection of data management services for parallel, unstructured, adaptive, and dynamic partitioners, is used to assign

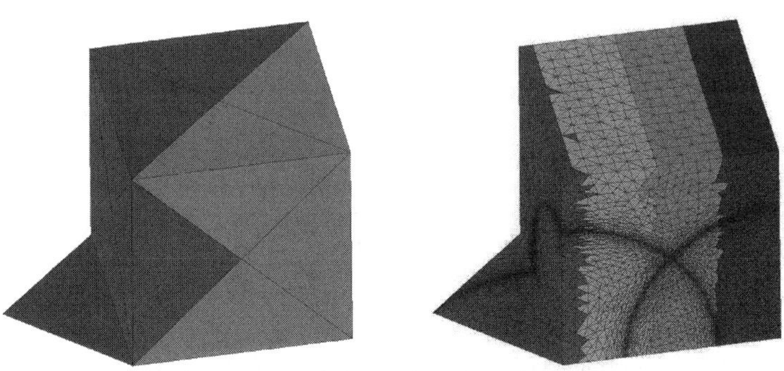

# Proc	2	4	8	16
Speedup	2.23	3.37	5.48	8.40
Relative speedup	2.23	1.50	1.62	1.53

Figure 19.12 Parallel mesh adaptation I: (left) initial 36 tet mesh; (right) adapted approx. 1 million tet mesh.

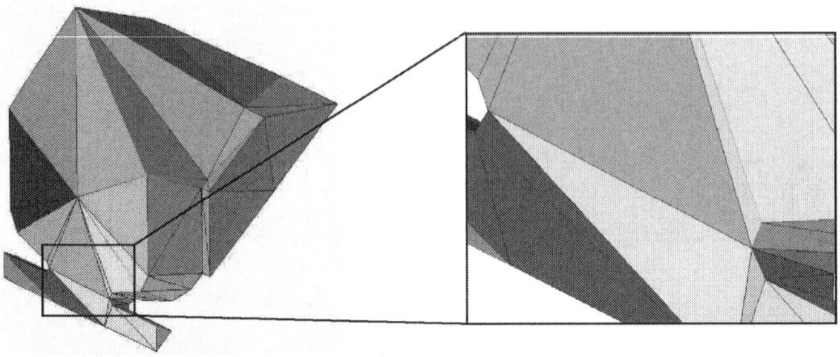

(a) Initial mesh

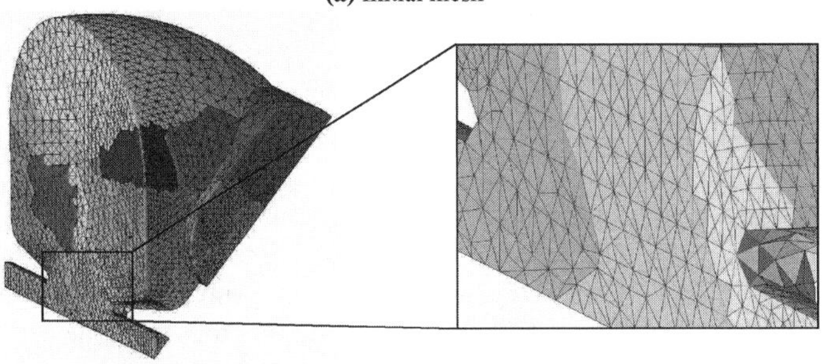

(b) After the second loop

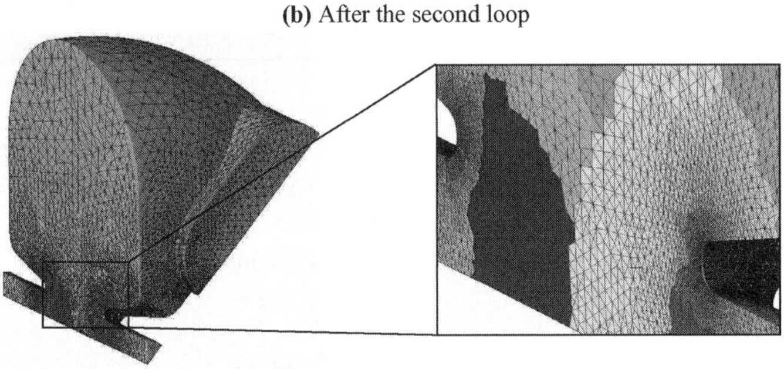

(c) After the eighth loop

# Proc	20	40
Relative speedup	—	1.81

Figure 19.13 Parallel adaptive loop for SLAC I: (a) initial coarse Trispal mesh (65 tets), (b) adapted mesh after the second adaptive loop (approx. 1 million tet), (c) the final mesh converged to the solutions after the eighth adaptive loop (approx. 12 million tets).

partition entities. FMDB computes the input to the Zoltan as a weighted graph or coordinates of partition objects. With the distribution information from Zoltan, the repartitioning or initial partitioning step is completed by calling the mesh migration procedure that moves the appropriate entities from one partition to another. Figure 19.11 illustrates an example of 2D mesh load balancing. In the left, the partition objects (all mesh faces in this case) are tagged with their destination partition ids. The final balanced mesh is given on the right.

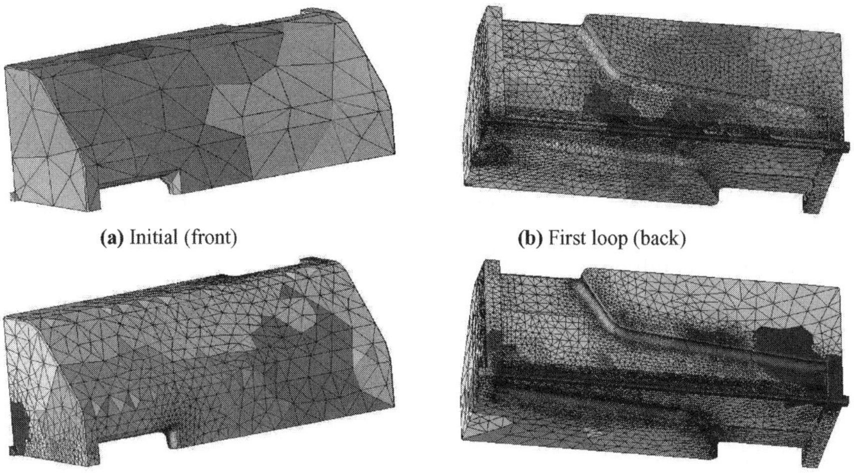

(a) Initial (front) **(b)** First loop (back) **(c)** Second loop (front) **(d)** Second loop (back)

# Proc	28	56
Relative speedup	—	1.97

Figure 19.14 Parallel adaptive loop for SLAC II: (a) initial coarse RFQ mesh (1595 tet), (b) adapted mesh from the first adaptive loop (approx. 1 million tet), (c) the front view of adapted mesh from the second adaptive loop (approx. 24 million tet), and (d) the back view of (c).

19.7 PARALLEL ADAPTIVE APPLICATIONS

The parallel mesh adaptation procedure has been tested against a wide range of models using either analytical or adaptively defined anisotropic mesh size field definitions [16]. The scalability of a parallel program running on p processors is measured as the *speedup* or *relative speedup.*

$$speedup = \frac{\text{runtime on one processor}}{\text{runtime on } p \text{ processors}} \tag{19.1}$$

The relative speedup is the speedup against the program on $p/2$ processors.

$$relative\ speedup = \frac{\text{runtime on } p/2 \text{ processors}}{\text{runtime on } p \text{ processors}} \tag{19.2}$$

Figure 19.12 shows a uniform initial nonmanifold mesh of a $1 \times 1 \times 1$ cubic and triangular surface domain and the adapted mesh with two spherical mesh size fields on four processors. Different color represents different partitions.

Adaptive results have been obtained using the eigenmode solver of Stanford Linear Accelerator Center (SLAC) [14] in conjunction with parallel mesh adaptation. The parallel adaptive procedure has been applied to Trispal model and RFQ model. The speedups given are just for the parallel mesh adaptation portion of the process.

Figure 19.13 shows the Trispal meshes during the parallel adaptive loop. Figure 19.13a gives the initial mesh composed of 65 tetrahedron, (b) is the adapted, approximately 1 million, mesh after the second adaptive loop on 24 processors, and (c) is the adapted, approximately 12 million, mesh after the eighth adaptive loop.

Figure 19.14 gives the RFQ meshes during the parallel adaptive loop. Figure 19.14a gives the initial coarse mesh of 1595 tetrahedron, (b) is the adapted mesh after the first adaptive loop, which is approximately 1 million tetrahedron, and (c) and (d) are the front and back view of the adapted mesh after the second adaptive loop, which contains about 24 million tetrahedron.

19.8 CLOSING REMARK

A flexible mesh database has been defined and implemented for distributed meshes based on the hierarchical domain decomposition providing a partition model as intermediate domain decomposition between the geometric model and the mesh. These procedures build on a carefully defined set of relations with given properties of the mesh and its distribution on a distributed memory computer. The support of partitioning at the partition model level, optimal order algorithms to construct and use it, local mesh entity migration, and dynamic load balancing are supported. These procedures are being actively used to support parallel adaptive simulation procedures.

The FMDB is open source available at http://www.scorec.rpi.edu/FMDB.

REFERENCES

1. F. Alauzet, X. Li, E.S. Seol, and M.S. Shephard. Parallel anisotropic 3D mesh adaptation by mesh modification. *Eng. Comput.*, 21(3):247–258, 2006.
2. A. Alexandrescu. *Modern C++ Design: Generic Programming and Design Patterns Applied.* Addison-Wesley, 2001.
3. M.W. Beall. An object oriented framework for the reliable automated solution of problems in mathematical physics [dissertation]. Rensselaer Polytechnic Institute, Tory, New York, 1999.
4. M.W. Beall and M.S. Shephard. A general topology-based mesh data structure. *Int. J. Numer. Methods Eng.*, 40(9):1573–1596, 1997.
5. R. Biswas and L. Oliker. A new procedure for dynamic adaptation of three-dimensional unstructured grids. *Appl. Numer. Math.*, 13:437–452, 1997.
6. W. Celes, G.H. Paulino, and R. Espinha. A compact adjacency-based topological data structure for finite element mesh representation. *Int. J. Numer. Methods Eng.*, 64(11):1529–1565, 2005.
7. T.H. Cormen, C.E. Leiserson, R.L. Rivest, and C. Stein. *Introduction to Algorithms.*, 2nd edition. MIT Press, 2001.
8. H.L. de Cougny, K.D. Devine, J.E. Flaherty, and R.M. Loy. Load balancing for the parallel solution of partial differential equations. *Appl. Numer. Math.*, 16:157–182, 1995.
9. H.L. de Cougny and M.S. Shephard. Parallel refinement and coarsening of tetrahedral meshes. *Int. J. Numer. Methods Eng.*, 46:1101–1125, 1999.
10. Deitel and Deitel. *C++ How To Program*, 2nd edition. Prentice Hall, 2001.
11. R. Diekmann, R. Preis, F. Schlimbach, and C. Walshaw. Shape-optimized mesh partitioning and load balancing for parallel adaptive FEM. *Parallel Comput.*, 26:1555–1581, 2000.
12. E. Gamma, R. Johnson, R. Helm, and J.M. Vlissides. *Design Pattern: Elements of Reusable Object-Oriented Software.* Addison Wesley, 1994.

13. R.V. Garimella. Mesh data structure selection for mesh generation and FEA applications. *Int. J. Numer. Methods. Eng.*, 55:451–478, 2002.
14. L. Ge, L. Lee, L. Zenghai, C. Ng, K. Ko, Y. Luo, and M.S. Shephard. Adaptive mesh refinement for high accuracy wall loss determination in accelerating cavity design. *IEEE Conference on Electromagnetic Field Computations,* June 2004.
15. X. Li, M.S. Shephard, and M.W. Beall. Accounting for curved domains in mesh adaptation. *Int. J. Numer. Methods Eng.*, 58:247–276, 2002.
16. X. Li, M.S. Shephard, and M.W. Beall. 3D anisotropic mesh adaptation by mesh modifications. *Comput. Methods. Appl. Mech. Eng.*, 194:4915–4950, 2005.
17. libMesh. *http://libmesh.sourceforge.net* 2005.
18. R. Loy, *Autopack User Manual*, 2000.
19. M. Mantyla. *An Introduction to Solid Modeling.* Computer Science Press, Rockville MD, 1988.
20. L. Oliker, R. Biswas, and H.N. Gabow. Parallel tetrahedral mesh adaptation with dynamic load balancing. *Parallel Comput.*, 26:1583–1608, 2000.
21. C. Ozturan, H.L. de Cougny, M.S. Shephard, and J.E. Flaherty. Parallel adaptive mesh refinement and redistribution on distributed memory. *Comput. Methods Appl. Mech. Eng.,* 119:123–127, 1994.
22. P.S. Pacheco. *Parallel Programming with MPI.* Morgan Kaufmann, 1997.
23. Y. Park and O. Kwon. A parallel unstructured dynamic mesh adaptation algorithm for 3-D unsteady flows. *Int. J. Numer. Methods Fluids,* 48:671–690, 2005.
24. J.F. Remacle, O. Klaas, J.E. Flaherty, and M.S. Shephard. A parallel algorithm oriented mesh database. *Eng. Comput.*, 18:274–284, 2002.
25. J.F. Remacle and M.S. Shephard. An algorithm oriented mesh database. *Int. J. Numer. Methods Eng.*, 58:349–374, 2003.
26. M.L. Scott. *Programming Language Pragmatics.* Kaufmann Publisher, 2000.
27. P.M. Selwood and M. Berzins. Parallel unstructured tetrahedral mesh adaptation: algorithms, implementation and scalability *Concurrency Pract. Exper.*, 11(14):863–884, 1999.
28. E.S. Seol. FMDB: Flexible distributed mesh database for parallel automated adaptive analysis [dissertation]. Troy (NY): Rensselaer Polytechnic Institute, Troy, New York, 2005. Available from: *http://www.scorec.rpi.edu/cgi-bin/reports/GetByYear.pl?Year=2005.*
29. E.S. Seol and M.S. Shephard. Efficient distributed mesh data structure for parallel automated adaptive analysis. *Eng. Comput.*, 22:197–213, 2006.
30. Sgi Inc. *http://www.sgi.com/tech/stl/stl_index.html*, 2005.
31. M.S. Shephard, J.E. Flaherty, C.L. Bottasso, and H.L. de Cougny. Parallel automated adaptive analysis. *Parallel Comput.*, 23:1327–1347, 1997.
32. J.D. Teresco, M.W. Beall, J.E. Flaherty, and M.S. Shephard. A hierarchical partition model for adaptive finite element computations. *Comput. Methods Appl. Mech. Eng.*, 184:269–285, 2000.
33. D. Vandevoorde and N.M. Josuttis. C++ Templates. Addison-Wesley, 2003.
34. C. Walshaw and M. Cross. Parallel optimization algorithms for multilevel mesh partitioning. *Parallel Comput.*, 26(12):1635–1660, 2000.
35. K.J. Weiler. The radial-edge structure: a topological representation for non-manifold geometric boundary representations. In *Geometric Modeling for CAD Applications*, Elsevier Amsterdam, 1988, pp. 3–36.
36. Zoltan: data management services for parallel applications. Available from *http://www.cs.sandia.gov/Zoltan*, 2005.

Chapter 20

HRMS: Hybrid Runtime Management Strategies for Large-Scale Parallel Adaptive Applications*

Xiaolin Li and Manish Parashar

20.1 INTRODUCTION

Simulations of complex physical phenomena, modeled by systems of partial differential equations (PDE), are playing an increasingly important role in science and engineering. Furthermore, dynamically adaptive techniques, such as the dynamic structured adaptive mesh refinement (SAMR) technique [1, 2], are emerging as attractive formulations of these simulations. Compared to numerical techniques based on static uniform discretization, SAMR can yield highly advantageous ratios for cost/accuracy by concentrating computational effort and resources on appropriate regions adaptively at runtime. SAMR is based on block-structured refinements overlaid on a structured coarse grid and provides an alternative to the general, unstructured AMR approach [3, 4]. SAMR techniques have been used to solve complex systems of PDEs that exhibit localized features in varied domains, including computational fluid dynamics, numerical relativity, combustion simulations, subsurface modeling, and oil reservoir simulation [5–7].

*This chapter is based on the paper "Hybrid runtime management of space–time heterogeneity for parallel structured adaptive applications," X. Li and M. Parashar, *IEEE Transactions on Parallel and Distributed Systems*, 18(9): 1202–1214, 2007.

Advanced Computational Infrastructures For Parallel and Distributed Adaptive Applications. Edited by Manish Parashar and Xiaolin Li

Large-scale parallel implementations of SAMR-based applications have the potential to accurately model complex physical phenomena and provide dramatic insights. However, while there have been some large-scale implementations [8–13], these implementations are typically based on application-specific customizations, and general scalable implementations of SAMR applications continue to present significant challenges. This is primarily due to the dynamism and space–time heterogeneity exhibited by these applications. SAMR-based applications are inherently dynamic because the physical phenomena being modeled and the corresponding adaptive computational domain change as the simulation evolves. Further, adaptation naturally leads to a computational domain that is spatially heterogeneous, that is, different regions in the computational domain and different levels of refinements have different computational and communication requirements. Finally, the SAMR algorithm periodically regrids the computational domain causing regions of refinement to be created/deleted/moved to match the physics being modeled, that is, it exhibits temporal heterogeneity.

The dynamism and heterogeneity of SAMR applications have been traditionally addressed using dynamic partitioning and load balancing algorithms, for example, the mechanisms presented in Refs [10, 13], which partition and load balance the SAMR domain when it changes. More recently, it was observed in Ref. [14] that for parallel SAMR applications, the appropriate choice and configuration of the partitioning/load-balancing algorithm depend on the application, its runtime state, and its execution context. This leads to the development of meta-partitioners [14, 15], which select and configure partitioners (from a pool of partitioners) at runtime to match the application's current requirements. However, due to the spatial heterogeneity of the SAMR domain, computation and communication requirements can vary significantly across the domain and, as a result, using a single partitioner for the entire domain can lead to decompositions that are locally inefficient. This is especially true for the large-scale simulations that run on over a thousand processors.

The objective of the research presented in this chapter is to address this issue. Specifically, this chapter builds on our earlier research on meta-partitioning [14], adaptive hierarchical partitioning [16], and adaptive clustering [17] and investigates hybrid runtime management strategies and an adaptive hierarchical multipartitioner (AHMP) framework. AHMP dynamically applies multiple partitioners to different regions of the domain, in a hierarchical manner, to match local requirements. This chapter first presents a segmentation-based clustering algorithm (SBC) that can efficiently identify regions in the domain (called *clusters*) at runtime that have relatively homogeneous requirements. The partitioning requirements of these cluster regions are determined and the most appropriate partitioner from the set of available partitioners is selected, configured, and applied to each cluster.

Further, this chapter also presents two strategies to cope with different resource situations in the case of long-running applications: (1) the hybrid partitioning algorithm, which involves application-level pipelining, trading space for time when resources are sufficiently large and underutilized, and (2) the application-level out-of-core strategy (ALOC), which trades time for space when resources are scarce to improve the performance and enhance the survivability of applications. The AHMP framework and its components are implemented and experimentally evaluated using the RM3D application on up to 1280 processors of the IBM SP4 cluster at San Diego Supercomputer Center.

The rest of the chapter is organized as follows. Section 20.2 presents an overview of the SAMR technique and describes the computation and communication behaviors of its parallel implementation. Section 20.3 reviews related work. Section 20.4 describes the AHMP framework and hybrid runtime management strategies for parallel SAMR applications. Section 20.5 presents an experimental evaluation for the framework using SAMR application kernels. Section 20.6 presents a conclusion.

20.2 PROBLEM DESCRIPTION

20.2.1 Structured Adaptive Mesh Refinement

Structured adaptive mesh refinement formulations for adaptive solutions to PDE systems track regions in the computational domain with high solution errors that require additional resolution and dynamically overlay finer grids over these regions. SAMR methods start with a base coarse grid with minimum acceptable resolution that covers the entire computational domain. As the solution progresses, regions in the domain requiring additional resolution are tagged and finer grids are overlaid on these tagged regions of the coarse grid. Refinement proceeds recursively so that regions on the finer grid requiring more resolution are similarly tagged and even finer grids are overlaid on these regions. The resulting SAMR grid structure is a dynamic adaptive grid hierarchy as shown in Figure 20.1.

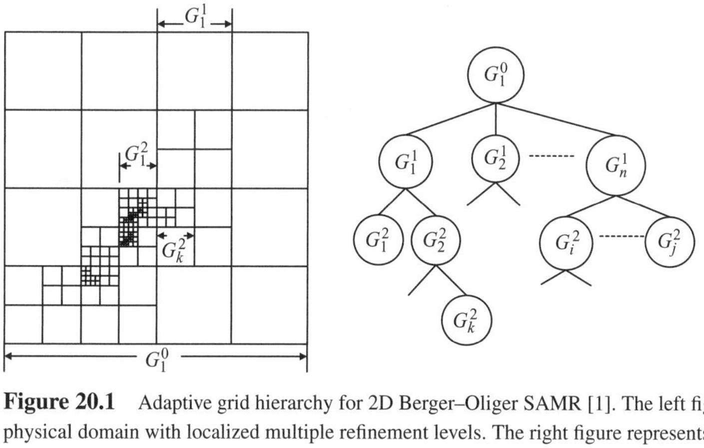

Figure 20.1 Adaptive grid hierarchy for 2D Berger–Oliger SAMR [1]. The left figure shows a 2D physical domain with localized multiple refinement levels. The right figure represents the refined domain as a grid hierarchy.

20.2.2 Computation and Communication Requirements of Parallel SAMR

Parallel implementations of SAMR applications typically partition the adaptive grid hierarchy across available processors, and each processor operates on its local portions of this domain in parallel. The overall performance of parallel SAMR applications is thus limited by the ability to partition the underlying grid hierarchies at runtime to expose all inherent parallelism, minimize communication and synchronization overheads, and balance load.

Communication overheads of parallel SAMR applications primarily consist of four components: (1) *Interlevel communications*, defined between component grids at different levels of the grid hierarchy and consist of prolongations (coarse to fine transfer and interpolation) and restrictions (fine to coarse transfer and interpolation); (2) *Intralevel communications*, required to update the grid elements along the boundaries of local portions of a distributed component grid, consisting of near-neighbor exchanges; (3) *Synchronization cost*, which occurs when the load is not balanced among processors; (4) *Data migration cost*, which occurs between two successive regridding and remapping steps.

Partitioning schemes for SAMR grid hierarchies can be classified as patch based, domain based, and hybrid [14]. A patch, associated with one refinement level, is a rectangular region that is created by clustering adjacent computational grids/cells at that level [18]. In the patch-based schemes, partitioning decisions are made independently for each patch at each level. Domain-based schemes partition the physical domain and result in partitions or subdomains that contain computational grids/cells at multiple refinement levels. Hybrid schemes generally follow two steps. The first step uses domain-based schemes to create partitions, which are mapped to a group of processors. The second step uses patch-based or combined schemes to further distribute the partition within its processor group. Domain-based partitioning schemes have been studied in Refs [13, 14, 19]. Three hybrid schemes are presented in Ref. [13]. In general, pure patch-based schemes outperform domain-based schemes when balancing the workload is the only consideration. However, patch-based schemes incur considerable overheads for communications between refinement levels, for example, prolongation and restriction operations. Typically, boundary information is much smaller than the information in the entire patch. Further, if the patch-based method completely ignores locality, it might cause severe communication bottleneck between refinement levels. In contrast, domain-based schemes distribute subdomains that contain all refinement levels to processors and hence eliminate the interlevel communications. However, for applications with strongly localized and deeply refined regions, domain-based schemes are inadequate to well balance workloads. More detailed description and comparisons of these partitioning schemes can be found in Refs [13, 14, 18]. This chapter mainly focuses on domain-based schemes and also presents a new hybrid scheme.

The timing diagram (note that the figure is not to scale) in Figure 20.2 illustrates the operation of the SAMR algorithm using a three- level grid hierarchy. The process shown in the figure shows a typical parallel SAMR application using a domain-based

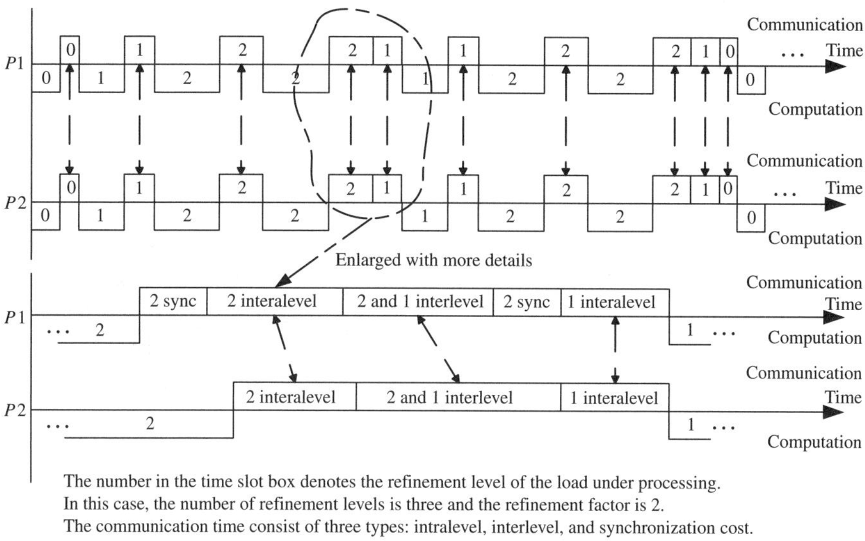

Figure 20.2 Timing diagram for parallel SAMR.

partitioning scheme. For simplicity, the computation and communication behaviors of only two processors, $P1$ and $P2$, are shown. The communication overheads are illustrated in the magnified portion of the time line. This figure illustrates the exact computation and communication patterns for a parallel SAMR implementation. The timing diagram shows that there is one timestep on the coarsest level (level 0) of the grid hierarchy followed by two timesteps on the first refinement level and four timesteps on the second level, before the second timestep on level 0 can start. Further, the computation and communication steps for each refinement level are interleaved. This behavior makes partitioning the dynamic SAMR grid hierarchy to both balance load and minimize communication overheads a significant challenge.

20.2.3 Spatial and Temporal Heterogeneity of SAMR Applications

The space–time heterogeneity of SAMR applications is illustrated using the 3D compressible turbulence simulation kernel solving the Richtmyer–Meshkov (RM3D) instability [5] in Figure 20.3. The figure shows a selection of snapshots of the RM3D adaptive grid hierarchy as well as a plot of its load dynamics at different regrid steps. Since the adaptive grid hierarchy remains unchanged between two regrid steps, the workload dynamics and other features of SAMR applications are hence measured with respect to regrid steps. The workload in this figure represents the computational/storage requirement, which is computed based on the number of grid points in the grid hierarchy. Application variables are typically defined at these grid points and are updated at each iteration of the simulation, and consequently, the

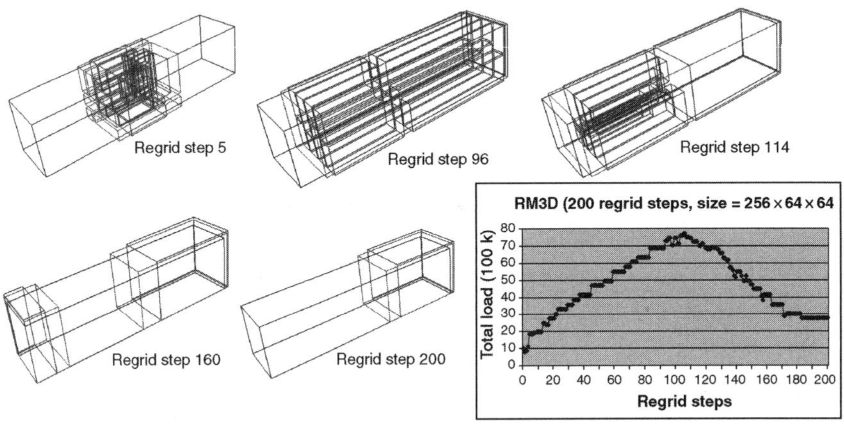

Figure 20.3 Spatial and temporal heterogeneity and load dynamics for a 3D Richtmyer–Meshkov simulation using SAMR.

computational/storage requirements are proportional to the number of grid points. The snapshots in this figure clearly demonstrate the dynamics and space–time heterogeneity of SAMR applications—different subregions in the computational domain have different computational and communication requirements and regions of refinement are created, deleted, relocated, and grow/shrink at runtime.

20.3 RELATED WORK

Parallel SAMR implementations presented in Refs [10, 12, 13] use dynamic partitioning and load balancing algorithms. These approaches view the system as a flat pool of processors. They are based on a global knowledge of the state of the adaptive grid hierarchy, and partition the grid hierarchy across the set of processors. Global synchronization and communication are required to maintain this global knowledge and can lead to significant overheads on large systems. Furthermore, these approaches do not exploit the hierarchical nature of the grid structure and the distribution of communications and synchronization in this structure.

Dynamic load balancing schemes proposed in Ref. [20] involve two phases: *moving-grid phase* and *splitting-grid phase*. The first phase is intended to move load from overloaded processors to underloaded processors. The second phase is triggered when the direct grid movement cannot balance the load among processors. These schemes improve the performance by focusing load balance and are suited for coarse-grained load balancing without considering the locality of patches. Dynamic load balancing schemes have been further extended to support distributed SAMR applications [21] using two phases: global load balancing and local load balancing. The load balancing in these schemes does not explicitly address the spatial and temporal heterogeneity exhibited by SAMR applications. In the SAMRAI library [10, 18], after the construction of computational patches, patches are assigned to processors using a greedy bin packing procedure. SAMRAI uses the Morton space-filling curve technique to maintain spatial locality for patch distribution. To further enhance scalability of SAMR applications using the SAMRAI framework, Wissink et al. proposed a *recursive binary box tree* algorithm to improve communication schedule construction [18]. A simplified point clustering algorithm based on Berger–Regoutsos algorithm [22] has also been presented. The reduction of runtime complexity using these algorithms substantially improves the scalability of parallel SAMR applications on up to 1024 processors. As mentioned above, the SAMRAI framework uses patch-based partitioning schemes, which result in good load balance but might cause considerable interlevel communication and synchronization overheads. SAMR applications have been scaled on up to 6420 processors using FLASH and PARAMESH packages [8, 12]. The scalability is achieved using large domain dimensions ranging from $128 \times 128 \times 2560$ to $1024 \times 1024 \times 20480$. Further, a Morton space-filling curve technique has been applied to maintain spatial locality in PARAMESH. However, the space–time heterogeneity issues are not addressed explicitly.

A recent paper [23] presents a hierarchical partitioning and dynamic load balancing scheme using the Zoltan toolkit [3]. The proposed scheme first uses the multilevel graph partitioner in ParMetis [11] for across node partitioning to minimize the communication across nodes. It then applies the recursive inertial bisection (RIB) method within each node. The approach was evaluated in small systems with eight processors in the paper. The characterization of SAMR applications presented in Ref. [14] is based on the entire physical domain. The research in this paper goes a step further by considering the characteristics of individual subregions. The concept of natural regions is presented in Ref. [24]. Two kinds of natural regions are defined: unrefined/homogeneous and refined/complex. The framework proposed then uses a bi-level domain-based partitioning scheme to partition the refined subregions. This approach is one of the first attempts to apply multiple partitioners concurrently to the SAMR domain. However, this approach restricts itself to applying only two partitioning schemes, one to the refined region and the other to the unrefined region.

20.4 HYBRID RUNTIME MANAGEMENT STRATEGIES

20.4.1 Adaptive Hierarchical Multipartitioner Framework

Figure 20.4 shows the basic operation of the AHMP framework. A critical task is to dynamically and efficiently identify regions that have similar requirements, called *clusters*. A cluster is a region of connected component grids that has relatively homogeneous computation and communication requirements. The input of AHMP is the structure of the current grid hierarchy (an example is illustrated in Figure 20.1), represented as a list of regions, which defines the runtime state of the SAMR application. AHMP operation consists of the following steps. First, a clustering algorithm is used to identify cluster hierarchies. Second, each cluster is characterized and its partitioning requirements identified. Available resources are also partitioned into corresponding

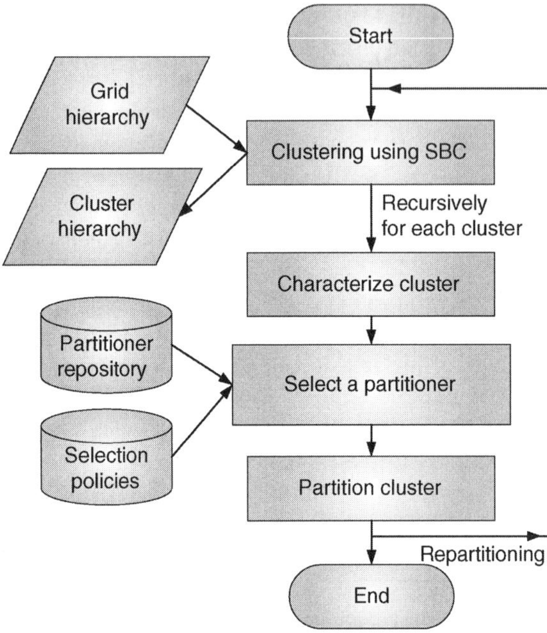

Figure 20.4 A flowchart for the AHMP framework.

resource groups based on the relative requirements of the clusters. A resource group is a set of possibly physically proximal processors that are assigned a coarse-grained partition of the computational workload. A resource group is dynamically constructed based on the load assignment and distribution. Third, these requirements are used to select and configure an appropriate partitioner for each cluster. The partitioner is selected from a partitioner repository using selection policies. Finally, each cluster is partitioned and mapped to processors in its corresponding resource group. The strategy is triggered locally when the application state changes. State changes are determined using the load imbalance metric described below. Partitioning proceeds hierarchically and incrementally. The identification and isolation of clusters uses a segmentation-based clustering scheme. Partitioning schemes in the partitioner repository include greedy partitioning algorithm (GPA), level-based partitioning algorithm (LPA), and others presented in Section 20.4.3. Partitioner selection policies consider cluster partitioning requirements, communication/computation requirements, scattered adaptation, and activity dynamics [14]. This chapter specifically focuses on developing partitioning policies based on cluster requirements defined in terms of refinement homogeneity, which is discussed in Section 20.5.1.

AHMP extends our previous work on the hierarchical partitioning algorithm (HPA) [16], which hierarchically applies a single partitioner, reducing global communication overheads and enabling incremental repartitioning and rescheduling. AHMP additionally addresses spatial heterogeneity by applying the most appropriate partitioner to each cluster based on its characteristics and requirements. As a result, multiple partitioners may concurrently operate on different subregions of the computational domain.

The load imbalance factor (LIF) metric is used as the criteria for triggering repartitioning and rescheduling within a local resource group and is defined as follows:

$$\mathrm{LIF}_A = \frac{\max_{i=1}^{A_n} T_i - \min_{i=1}^{A_n} T_i}{\sum_{i=1}^{A_n} T_i / A_n}, \tag{20.1}$$

where A_n is the total number of processors in resource group A, and T_i is the estimated relative execution time between two consecutive regrid steps for the processor i, which is proportional to its load. In the numerator of the right-hand side of the above equation, we use the difference between maximum and minimum execution times to better reflect the impact of synchronization overheads. The local load imbalance threshold is γ_A. When $\mathrm{LIF}_A > \gamma_A$, the repartitioning is triggered inside the local group. Note that the imbalance factor can be recursively calculated for larger groups as well.

20.4.2 Clustering Algorithms for Cluster Region Identification

The objective of clustering is to identify well-structured subregions in the SAMR grid hierarchy, called clusters. As defined above, a cluster is a region of connected component grids with relatively homogeneous partitioning requirements. This section describes the segmentation-based clustering algorithm, which is based on space-filling curves (SFC) [25]. The algorithm is motivated by the locality-preserving property of SFCs and the localized nature of physical features in SAMR applications. Further, SFCs are widely used for domain-based partitioning for SAMR applications [13, 24–26]. Note that clusters are similar in concept to natural regions proposed in Ref. [24]. However, unlike natural regions, clusters are not restricted to strict geometric shapes, but are more flexible and take advantage of the locality-preserving property of SFCs.

Typical SAMR applications exhibit localized features, and thus result in localized refinements. Moreover, refinement levels and the resulting adaptive grid hierarchy reflect the application runtime state. Therefore, clustering subregions with similar refinement levels is desired.

The segmentation-based clustering algorithm is based on ideas in image segmentation [27]. The algorithm first defines load density factor (LDF) as follows:

$$\begin{aligned}\mathrm{LDF(rlev)} &= (\text{associated workload of patches with } \mathit{levels} \geq \text{rlev on the subregion}) \\ &\quad /(\text{volume of the subregion at rlev}),\end{aligned}$$

where rlev denotes the refinement level and the volume is for the subregion of interest in a 3D domain (it will be area and length in case of 2D and 1D domains, respectively).

The SBC algorithm is illustrated in Figure 20.5. SBC aims to cluster domains with similar load density together to form cluster regions. The algorithm first smoothes out subregions that are smaller than a predefined threshold, which is referred to as the template size. Template size is determined by the stencil size of the finite

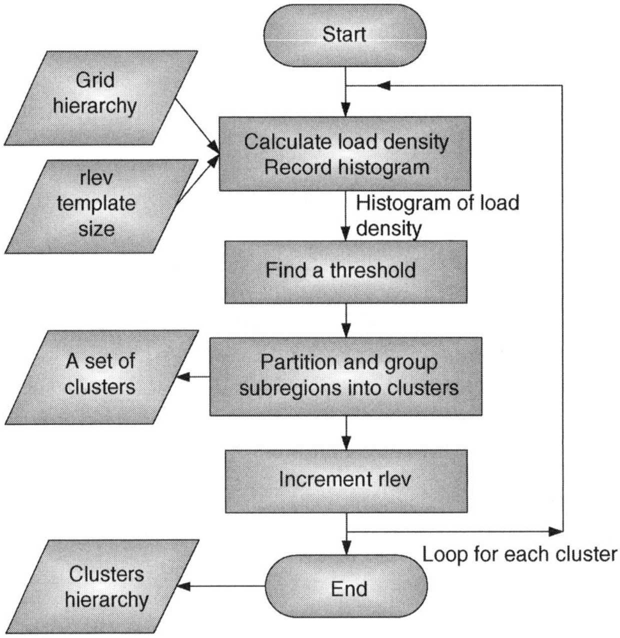

Figure 20.5 Segmentation-based clustering algorithm.

difference method and the granularity constraint, maintaining appropriate computation/communication ratios to maximize performance and minimize communication overheads. A subregion is defined by a bounding box with lower bound and upper bound coordinates and the strides/steps along each dimension. The subregion list input to the SBC algorithm is created by applying the SFC indexing mechanism on the entire domain that consists of patches of different refinement levels. SBC follows the SFC index to extract subregions (defined by rectangular bounding boxes) from the subregion list until the size of the accumulated subregion set is over the template size. It then calculates the load density for this set of subregions and computes a histogram of its load density. SBC continues to scan through the entire subregion list, and repeats the above process, calculating the load density and computing histograms. Based on the histogram of the load density obtained, it then finds a clustering threshold θ. A simplified intermeans thresholding algorithm by iterative selection [27, 28] is used as shown below.

The goal of the thresholding algorithm is to partition the SFC-indexed subregion list into two classes C_0 and C_1 (which may not necessarily be two clusters as shown in Figure 20.7) using an "optimal" threshold T with respect to LDF, so that the LDF of all subregions in $C_0 \leq T$ and the LDF of all subregions in $C_1 > T$. Let μ_0 and μ_1 be the mean LDF of C_0 and C_1, respectively. Initially, a threshold T is selected, for example, the mean of the entire list as a starting point. Then, for the two classes generated based on T, μ_0' and μ_1' are calculated, and a new threshold is computed as $T' = (\mu_0' + \mu_1')/2$. This process is repeated until the value of T converges.

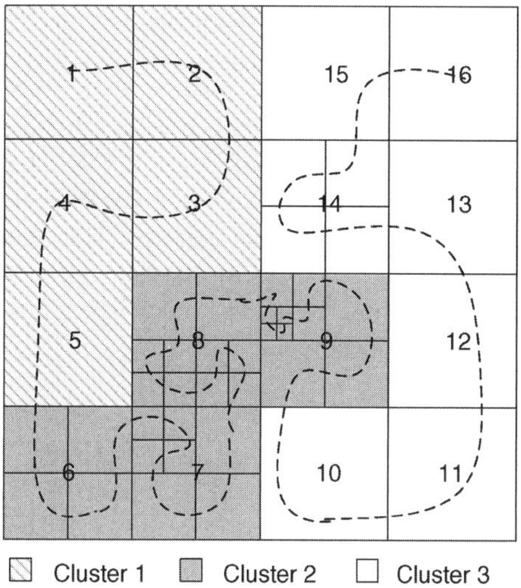

Figure 20.6 Clustering results for the SBC scheme.

Using the threshold obtained, subregions are further partitioned into several cluster regions. As a result, a hierarchical structure of cluster regions is created by recursively calling the SBC algorithm for finer refinement levels. The maximum number of clusters created can be adjusted to the number of processors available. Note that this algorithm has similarities to the point clustering algorithms proposed by Berger and Regoutsos in Ref. [22]. However, the SBC scheme differs from this scheme in two aspects. Unlike the Berger–Regoutsos scheme, which creates fine-grained clusters, the SBC scheme targets coarser granularity clusters. SBC also takes advantage of the locality-preserving properties of SFCs to potentially reduce data movement costs between consecutive repartitioning phases.

The SBC algorithm is illustrated using a simple 2D example in Figure 20.6. In this figure, SBC results in three clusters, which are shaded in the figure. Figure 20.7 shows the load density distribution and histogram for an SFC-indexed subdomain list. For this example, the SBC algorithm creates three clusters defined by the regions

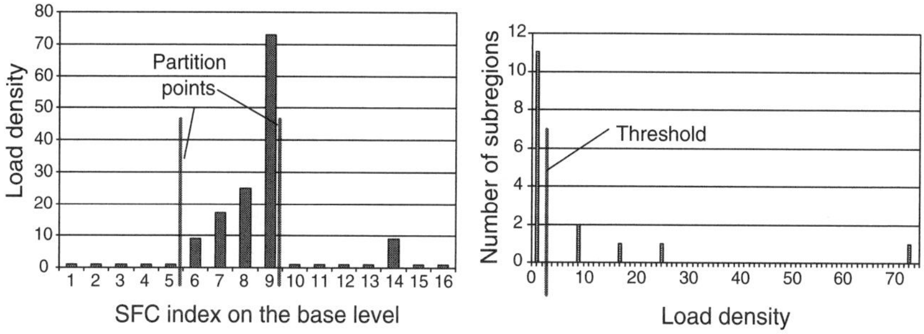

Figure 20.7 Load density distribution and histogram for SBC.

separated by the vertical lines in the figure on the left. The template size in this example is two boxes on the base level. The right figure shows a histogram of the load density. For efficiency and simplicity, this histogram is used to identify the appropriate threshold. For this example, the threshold is identified in between 1 and 9 using the intermeans thresholding algorithm. Although there are many more sophisticated approaches for identifying good thresholds for segmentation and edge detection in image processing [27, 29], this approach is sufficient for our purpose. Note that a predefined minimum size for a cluster region is assumed. In this example, the subregion with index 14 in Figure 20.6 does not form a cluster as its size is less than the template size. It is instead clustered with another subregion in its proximity.

20.4.3 Partitioning Schemes and Partitioner Selection

For completeness, several partitioning algorithms within the GrACE package [30] are briefly described. The greedy partitioning algorithm [13] is the default partitioning algorithm in GrACE. First, GPA partitions the entire domain into subdomains such that each subdomain keeps all refinement levels as a single composite grid unit. Thus, all interlevel communications are local to a subdomain and the interlevel communication time is eliminated. Second, GPA rapidly scans this list only once attempting to equally distribute load among all processors. It helps in reducing partitioning costs and works quite well for a relatively homogeneous computational domain.

For applications with localized features and deep grid hierarchies, GPA can result in load imbalances and hence lead to synchronization overheads at higher levels of refinement. To overcome this problem, the level-based partitioning algorithm [16] attempts to simultaneously balance load and minimize synchronization cost. LPA essentially aims to balance workload at each refinement level among all processors in addition to balancing overall load. To further improve the runtime performance, the hierarchical partitioning algorithm enables the load distribution to reflect the state of the adaptive grid hierarchy and exploit it to reduce synchronization requirements, improve load balance, and enable concurrent communications and incremental redistribution [31]. HPA partitions the computational domain into subdomains and assigns them to hierarchical processor groups. Other partitioners in the partitioner repository include the bin packing partitioner (BPA), the geometric multilevel + sequence partitioner (G-MISP+SP), and p-way binary dissection partitioner (pBD-ISP) [14, 16].

The characterization of clusters is based on their computation and communication requirements, runtime states, and the refinement homogeneity defined in Section 20.5.1. An *octant approach* is proposed in Ref. [14] to classify the runtime states of an SAMR application with respect to (a) the adaptation pattern (scattered or localized); (b) whether runtime is dominated by computations or communications; and (c) the activity dynamics in the solution. A meta-partitioner is then proposed to enable the selection/mapping of partitioners according to the current state of an application in the octant. The mapping is based on an experimental characterization of partitioning techniques and application states using five partitioning schemes and seven applications. The evaluation of partitioner quality is based on a five-component metric, including load imbalance, communication requirements, data migration, partitioning-introduced overheads, and partitioning time. In addition to these characterization and selection policies, we also consider refinement homogeneity. The overall goal of these new policies is to obtain better load balance for less-refined clusters, and to reduce communication and synchronization costs for highly refined clusters. For example, the policy dictates that the GPA and G-MISP+SP partitioning algorithms be used for clusters with refinement homogeneity greater than some threshold and partitioning algorithms LPA and pBD-ISP be used for clusters with refinement homogeneity below the threshold.

20.4.4 Hybrid Partitioning Strategy (HPS)

The parallelism that can be exploited by domain-based partitioning schemes is typically limited by granularity constraints. In cases where a very narrow region has deep refinements, domain-based partitioning schemes will inevitably result in significant load imbalances, especially when using a large-scale system. For example, assume that the predefined minimum dimension of a 3D block/grid on the base level is 4 grid points. In this case, the minimum workload (minimum partition granularity δ) of a composite grid unit with three refinement levels is $4^3 + 2 \times 8^3 + 2 \times 2 \times 16^3 = 17,472$, that is, the granularity constraint is $\delta \geq 17,472$ units. Such a composite block can result in significant load imbalance if domain-based partitioning is used exclusively. To expose more parallelism in these cases, a patch-based partitioning approach must be used. HPS combines domain-based and patch-based schemes. To reduce communication overheads, the application of HPS is restricted to a cluster region that is allocated to a single resource group. Further, HPS is only applied when certain conditions are met. These conditions include (1) resources are sufficient, (2) resources are underutilized, and (3) the gain by using HPS outweighs the extra communication cost incurred. For simplicity, the communication and computation process of HPS are illustrated using three processors in a resource group in Figure 20.8. The cluster has two refinement levels in this example.

HPS has two variants: one is pure hybrid partitioning with pipelining (pure HPS) and the other is hybrid partitioning with redundant computation and pipelining (HPS with redundancy). HPS splits the smallest domain-based partitions into patches at different refinement levels, partitions the finer patches into n partitions, and assigns each partition to a different processor in the group of n processors. When this process extends to many refinement levels, it is analogous to the pipelining process, where the operation at each refinement level represents each pipelining stage. Since the smallest load unit on the base level (level 0) cannot be further partitioned, the pure HPS scheme maps the level 0 patch to a single processor, while the HPS with redundancy scheme redundantly computes the level 0 patch at all processors in the group. Although pure HPS saves redundant computation, it needs interlevel communication from the level 0 patch to the other patches, which can be expensive. In contrast, HPS with redundancy trades computing resource for less interlevel communication overheads. To avoid

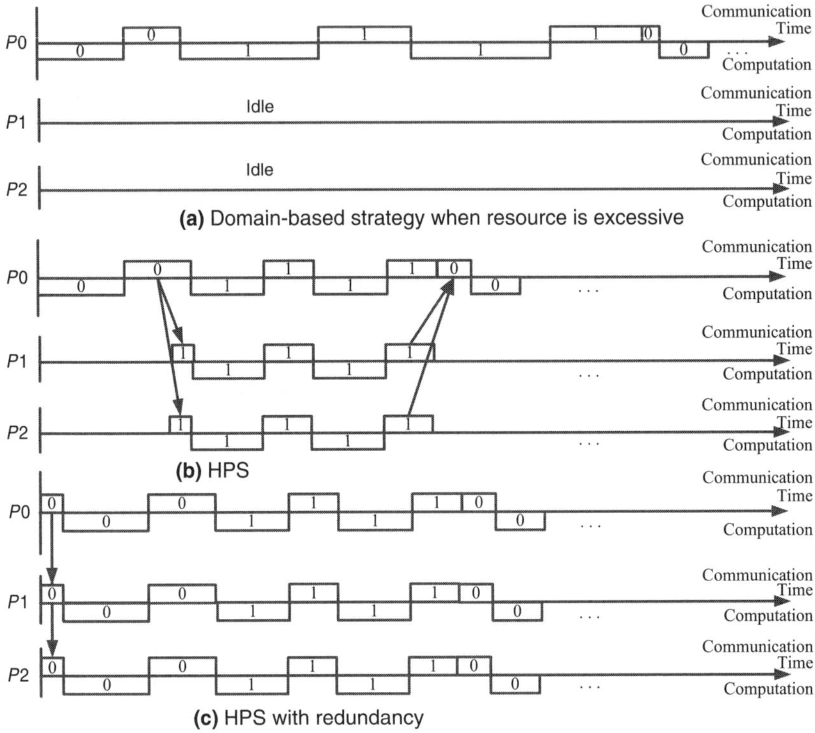

Figure 20.8 Hybrid partitioning strategy.

significant overheads, HPS schemes are applied only to a small resource group, for example, an SMP node with eight processors.

To specify the criteria for choosing HPS, the resource sufficiency factor (RSF) is defined by

$$\mathrm{RSF} = \frac{N_{\mathrm{rg}}}{L_q / L_\delta}, \tag{20.2}$$

where L_q denotes the total load for a cluster region, N_{rg} denotes the total number of processors in a resource group, and L_δ, the granularity, denotes the load on the smallest base-level subregion with the maximum refinement level. In the case of deep refinements, L_δ can be quite large. When RSF $> \rho$, where ρ is the threshold, and resources are underutilized, HPS can be applied to explore additional parallelism. The threshold is determined statistically through sensitivities analysis for a set of applications.

The basic operations of HPS consist of pairing two refinement levels, duplicating the computation on the coarser patch and partitioning the finer patch across the resource group. The operation of HPS is as follows: (1) AHMP generates a set of clusters and assigns each cluster to a resource group; (2) within each resource group, the algorithm checks whether or not to trigger HPS and if the criteria defined above are met, AHMP selects HPS for the cluster and the corresponding resource group;

and (3) HPS splits the cluster into patches at different refinement levels, assigns the patches to individual processors within the resource group, and coordinates the communication and computation as illustrated in Figure 20.8. Note that HPS can be recursively applied to patches of deeper refinement hierarchies.

20.4.5 Application-Level Out-of-Core Strategy

When available physical memory is not sufficient for the application, one option is to rely on the virtual memory mechanism of the operating system (OS). OS handles page faults and replaces less frequently used pages with the required pages from disks. OS however has little knowledge of the characteristics of an application and its memory access pattern. Consequently, it will result in many unnecessary swap-in and swap-out operations, which are very expensive. Data rates from disks are approximately two orders of magnitude lower than those from memory [32]. In many systems, OS sets a default maximum limit on physical and virtual memory allocation. When an application uses up this quota, it cannot proceed and crashes. Experiments show that system performance degrades during excessive memory allocation due to high page fault rates causing memory thrashing [33–35]. As a result, the amount of allocated memory and the memory usage pattern play a critical role in overall system performance.

To address these issues, an application-level out-of-core scheme is designed that exploits the application memory access patterns and explicitly keeps the working set of application patches while swapping out other patches.

The ALOC mechanism proactively manages application-level *pages*, that is, the computational domain patches. It attempts not only to improve performance, but also to enhance survivability when available memory is insufficient. For instance, as shown in Figure 20.3, the RM3D application requires four times more memory during the peak requirements than the average requirements, while the peak time lasts for less than 10% of the total execution time.

As illustrated in Figure 20.9, the ALOC scheme incrementally partitions the local grid hierarchy into temporal virtual computational units (T-VCU) according to

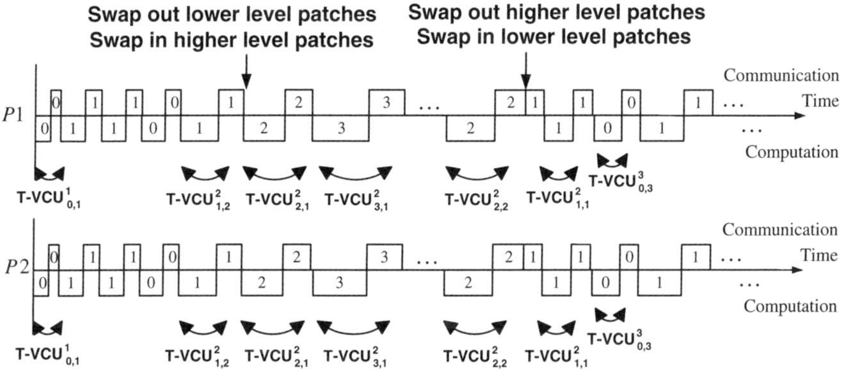

Figure 20.9 Application-level out-of-core strategy.

refinement levels and runtime iterations. In the figure, the notation T-$\text{VCU}^{a}_{b,c}$ denotes the temporal VCU, where a denotes the timestep at the base level, b denotes the current refinement level, and c is the timestep at the current level. To avoid undesired page swapping, ALOC releases the memory allocated by lower level patches and explicitly swaps them out to the disk. The ALOC mechanism is triggered when the ratio between the amount of memory allocated and the size of the physical memory is above a predefined threshold or the number of page faults increases above a threshold. The appropriate thresholds are selected based on experiments. Specifically, each process periodically monitors its memory usage and the page faults incurred. Memory usage information is obtained by tracking memory allocations and de-allocations, while page fault information is obtained using the *getrusage()* system call.

20.5 EXPERIMENTAL EVALUATION

20.5.1 Evaluating the Effectiveness of the SBC Clustering Algorithm

To aid the evaluation of the effectiveness of the SBC clustering scheme, a clustering quality metric is defined. The metric consists of two components: (1) the static quality and (2) the dynamic quality of the cluster regions generated. The static quality of a cluster is measured in terms of its refinement homogeneity and the efficiency of the clustering algorithm. The dynamic quality of a cluster is measured in terms of its communication costs (intralevel, interlevel, and data migration). These criteria are defined as follows.

(1) *Refinement Homogeneity*: This measures the quality of the structure of a cluster. Let $|R_i^{\text{total}}(l)|$ denote the total workload of a subregion or a cluster at refinement level l, which is composed of $|R_i^{\text{ref}}(l)|$, the workload of refined regions, and $|R_i^{\text{unref}}(l)|$, the workload of unrefined regions at refinement level l. Refinement homogeneity is recursively defined between two refinement levels as follows:

$$H_i(l) = \frac{|R_i^{\text{ref}}(l)|}{|R_i^{\text{total}}(l)|}, \tag{20.3}$$

$$H_{\text{all}}(l) = \frac{1}{n}\sum_{i=1}^{n} H_i(l), \quad \text{if } |R_i^{\text{ref}}(l)| \neq 0, \tag{20.4}$$

where n is the total number of subregions that have refinement level $l+1$. A goal of AHMP is to maximize the refinement homogeneity of a cluster as partitioners work well on relatively homogeneous regions.

(2) *Communication Cost*: This measures the communication overheads of a cluster and includes interlevel communication, intralevel communication, synchronization cost, and data migration cost as described in Section 20.2.2. A goal of AHMP is to minimize the communication overheads of a cluster.

(3) *Clustering Cost*: This measures the cost of the clustering algorithm itself. As mentioned above, SAMR applications require regular repartitioning and rebalancing, and as a result clustering cost becomes important. A goal of AHMP is to minimize the clustering cost.

Partitioning algorithms typically work well on highly homogeneous grid structures and can generate scalable partitions with desired load balance. Hence, it is important to have a quantitative measurement to specify the homogeneity. Intuitively, the refinement homogeneity metric attempts to isolate refined clusters that are potentially heterogeneous and are difficult to partition. In contrast, unrefined or completely refined clusters are homogeneous at that refinement level.

The effectiveness of SBC-based clustering is evaluated using the metrics defined above. The evaluation compares the refinement homogeneity of the six SAMR application kernels with and without clustering. These application kernels span multiple domains, including computational fluid dynamics (compressible turbulence: RM2D and RM3D, supersonic flows: ENO2D), oil reservoir simulations (oil–water flow: BL2D and BL3D), and the transport equation (TP2D). The applications are summarized in Table 20.1.

Figure 20.10 shows the refinement homogeneity for the TP2D application with four refinement levels without any clustering. The refinement homogeneity is smooth for level 0 and very dynamic and irregular for levels 1, 2, and 3.

The average refinement homogeneity of the six SAMR applications without clustering is presented in Table 20.2. The refinement homogeneity is calculated for the entire domain and averaged among 100 regridding steps. The table shows that the refinement homogeneity $H(l)$ increases as the refinement level l increases. This observation well reflects the physical properties of SAMR applications, that is, refined regions tend to be further refined. Moreover, these applications typically exhibit intensive activities in narrow regions. Typical ranges of $H(l)$ are $H(0) \in [0.02, 0.22]$, $H(1) \in [0.26, 0.68]$, $H(2) \in [0.59, 0.83]$, and $H(3) \in [0.66, 0.9]$. Several outliers require some explanation. In case of the BL2D application, average $H(2) = 0.4$. However, the individual values of $H(2)$ are in the range $[0.6, 0.9]$ with many scattered zeros. Since the refinement homogeneity on level 3 and above is typically over 0.6 and refined subregions at higher refinement levels tend to be more scattered, the clustering scheme focuses efforts on clustering levels 0, 1, and 2. Furthermore, based on these statistics, we select the thresholds θ for switching between different lower level partitioners as follows: $\theta_0 = 0.4, \theta_1 = 0.6$, and $\theta_2 = 0.8$, where the subscripts denote the refinement level.

Figure 20.11 and Table 20.3 demonstrate the improvements in *refinement homogeneity* using the SBC algorithm. Figure 20.11 shows the effects of using SBC on level 0 for the Transport2D application. The original homogeneity $H(0)$ is in the range $[0, 0.15]$, while the improved homogeneity using SBC is in the range $[0.5, 0.8]$.

The effects of clustering using SBC for the six SAMR applications are presented in Table 20.3. In the table, the gain is defined as the ratio of the improved homogeneity to the original homogeneity at each level. The gains for TP2D, ENO2D, BL3D, and BL2D on level 0 are quite large. The gains for RM3D and RM2D applications

Table 20.1 SAMR Application Kernels

Applications	Dimension	Description	Characteristics
TP	2D	A benchmark kernel for solving transport equation, included in the GrACE toolkit [30].	Intense activity in very narrowly concentrated regions. Key partitioning requirement: minimize partitioning overheads.
RM	2D/3D	A compressible turbulence application solving the Richtmyer–Meshkov (RM) instability. RM is a fingering instability that occurs at a material interface accelerated by a shock wave. This instability plays an important role in studies of supernova and inertial confinement fusion. It is a part of the virtual shock physics test facility (VTF) developed by the ASCI/ASAP Center at Caltech [5].	Intense activity in relatively larger and scattered regions. Key partitioning requirement: minimize communication and balance load at each refinement level.
ENO	2D	A computational fluid dynamics application for studying supersonic flows. The application has several features, including bow shock, Mach stem, contact discontinuity, and a numerical boundary. ENO2D is also a part of the VTF, a suite of computational applications [5].	Intense activity in larger regions. Key partitioning requirement: minimize load imbalance.
BL	2D/3D	An application for studying oil-water flow simulation (OWFS) following the Buckley–Leverette model. It is used for simulation of hydrocarbon pollution in aquifers. This kernel is a part of the IPARS reservoir simulation toolkit (integrated parallel accurate reservoir simulator) developed by the University of Texas at Austin [36].	Intense activity in very narrow and sparse regions, which are highly scattered. Key partitioning requirement: minimize communication and data migration overheads

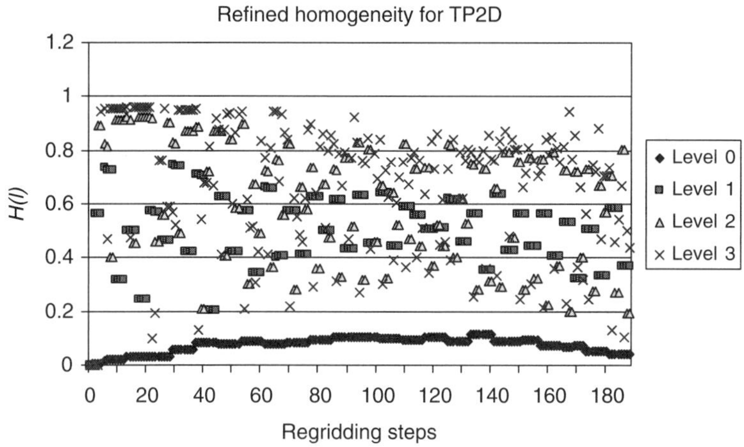

Figure 20.10 Refinement homogeneity for the Transport2D application kernel (four levels of refinement).

Table 20.2 Average Refinement Homogeneity $H(l)$ for Six SAMR Applications

Application	Level0	Level1	Level2	Level3
TP2D	0.067	0.498	0.598	0.6680
RM2D	0.220	0.680	0.830	0.901
RM3D	0.427	0.618		
ENO2D	0.137	0.597	0.649	0.761
BL3D	0.044	0.267		
BL2D	0.020	0.438	0.406	0.316

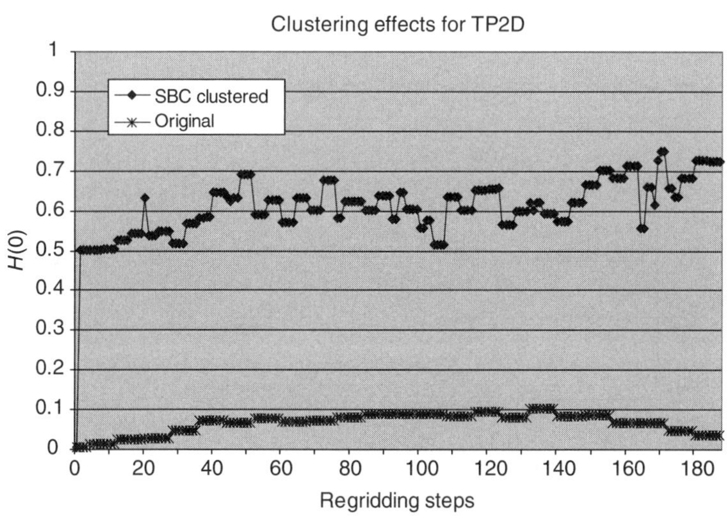

Figure 20.11 Homogeneity improvements using SBC for TP2D.

Table 20.3 Homogeneity Improvements Using SBC for Six SAMR Applications

Application	Level 0	Level 1	Gain on level 0	Gain on level 1
TP2D	0.565	0.989	8.433	1.986
RM2D	0.671	0.996	3.050	1.465
RM3D	0.802	0.980	1.878	1.586
ENO2D	0.851	0.995	6.212	1.667
BL3D	0.450	0.583	10.227	2.184
BL2D	0.563	0.794	28.150	1.813

are smaller because these applications already exhibit high refinement homogeneity starting from level 0, as shown in Table 20.2. These results demonstrate the effectiveness of the clustering scheme. Moreover, clustering increases the effectiveness of partitioners and improves overall performance, as shown in the next section.

Communication Costs The evaluation of communication cost uses a trace-driven simulation. The simulations are conducted as follows. First, a trace of the refinement behavior of the application at each regrid step was obtained by running the application on a single processor. Second, this trace is fed into the partitioners to partition and produce a new partitioned trace for multiple processors. Third, the partitioned trace is then fed into the SAMR simulator, which was developed at Rutgers University [37], to obtain the runtime performance measurements on multiple processors. Figure 20.12 shows the total communication cost for the RM3D application on 64 processors for GPA and AHMP (using SBC) schemes. The figure shows that the overall communication cost is lower for SBC+AHMP. However, in the interval between regrid steps 60 and 100, SBC+AHMP exhibits higher communication costs.

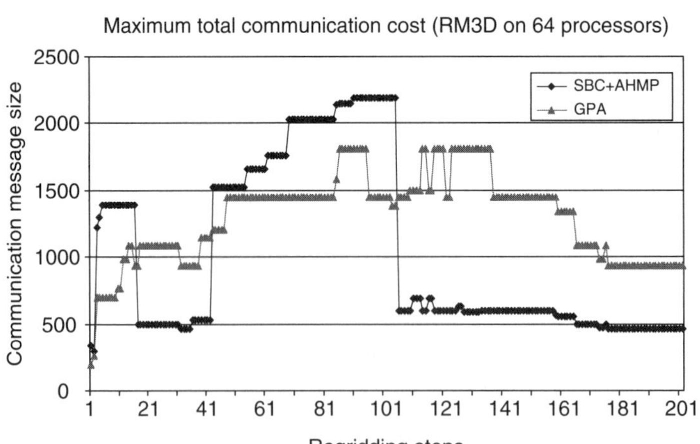

Figure 20.12 Maximum total communication for RM3D on 64 processors.

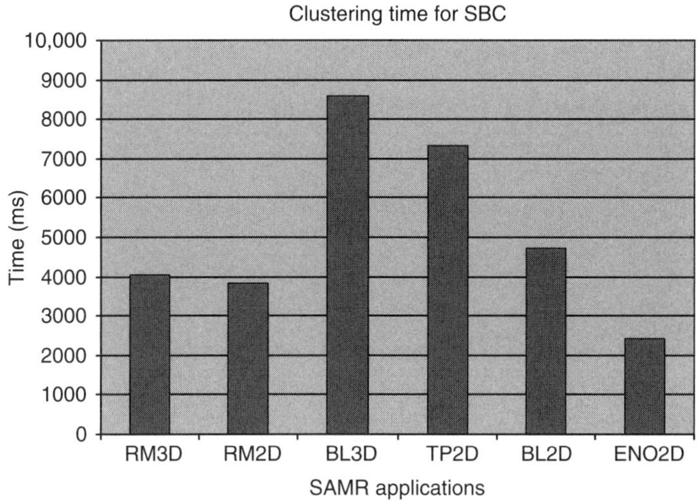

Figure 20.13 Clustering costs for the six SAMR application kernels.

This is because the application is highly dynamic with scattered refinements during this period. The snapshot at the regrid step 96 in Figure 20.3 illustrates the scattered refinements. This in turn causes significant cluster movement during reclustering. Note that the exiting simulator does not measure synchronization costs and thus does not reflect full performance benefits that can be achieved using AHMP. The actual performance gains due to AHMP are seen in Figure 20.15 based on actual runs.

Clustering Costs The cost of the SBC clustering algorithm is experimentally evaluated using the six different SAMR application kernels on a Beowulf cluster (Frea) at Rutgers University. The cluster consists of 64 processors and each processor has a 1.7 GHz Pentium 4 CPU. The costs are plotted in Figure 20.13. As seen in this figure, the overall clustering time on average is less than 0.01 s. Note that the computational time between successive repartitioning/rescheduling phases is typically in the order of tenths of seconds, and as a result the clustering costs are not significant.

20.5.2 Performance Evaluation

This section presents the experimental evaluation of AHMP. The overall performance benefit is evaluated on DataStar, the IBM SP4 cluster at San Diego Supercomputer Center. DataStar has 176 (eight-way) P655+ nodes (SP4). Each node has eight (1.5 GHz) processors, 16 GB memory, and CPU peak performance is 6.0 Gflops. The evaluation uses the RM3D application kernel with a base grid of size $256 \times 64 \times 64$, up to 3 refinement levels, and 1000 base-level timesteps. The number of processors used was between 64 and 1280.

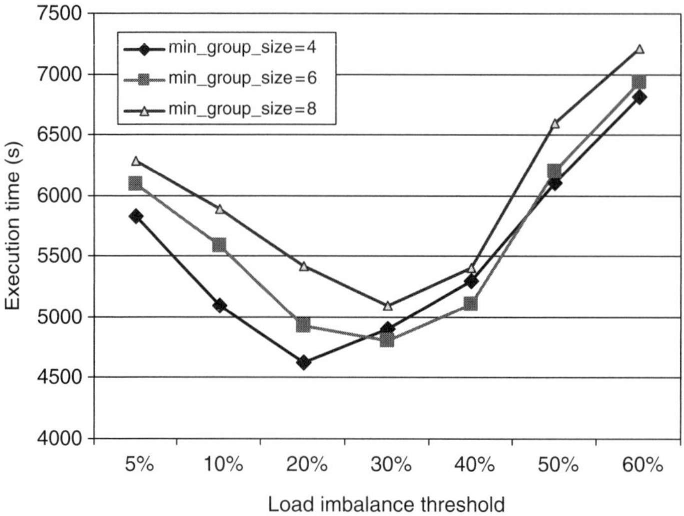

Figure 20.14 Impact of load imbalance threshold for RM3D on 128 processors.

Impact of Load Imbalance Threshold and Resource Group Size

As mentioned in Section 20.3, the load imbalance threshold γ is used to trigger repartitioning and redistribution within a resource group, where *min_group_size* is the minimum number of processors allowed in a resource group when the resource is partitioned hierarchically. This threshold plays an important role because it affects the frequency of redistribution and hence the overall performance. The impact of this threshold for different sizes of resource groups for the RM3D application on 128 processors is plotted in Figure 20.14. When γ increases from 5% to around 20–30%, the execution time decreases. On the other hand, when γ increases from 30% to 60%, the execution time increases significantly. Smaller values of γ result in more frequent repartitioning within a resource group, while larger thresholds may lead to increased load imbalance. The best performance is obtained for $\gamma = 20\%$ and $min\_group\_size = 4$. Due to the increased load imbalance, larger group sizes do not enhance performance. The overall performance evaluation below uses $\gamma = 20\%$ and $min\_group\_size = 4$.

Overall Performance The overall execution time is plotted in Figure 20.15. The figure plots execution times for GPA, LPA, and AHMP. The plot shows that SBC+AHMP delivers the best performance. Compared to GPA, the performance improvement is between 30% and 42%. These improvements can be attributed to the following factors: (1) AHMP takes advantage of the strength of different partitioning schemes matching them to the requirements of each cluster; (2) the SBC scheme creates well-structured clusters that reduce the communication traffic between clusters; (3) AHMP enables incremental repartitioning/redistribution and concurrent communication between resource groups, which extends the advantages of HPA [16].

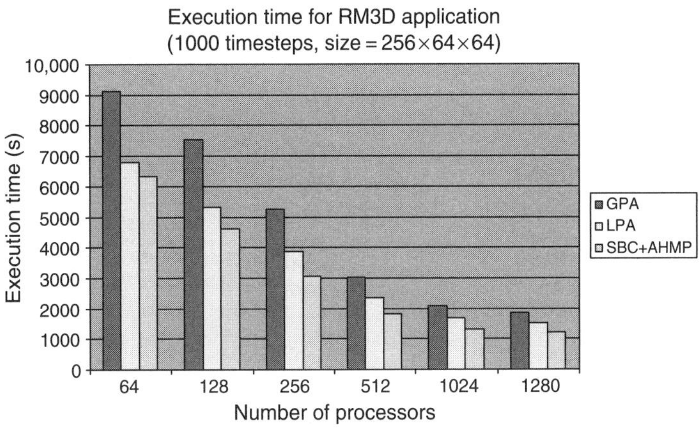

Figure 20.15 Overall performance for RM3D.

Impact of Hybrid Partitioning To show the impact of the hybrid partitioning strategy, we conduct the experiment using RM3D with a smaller domain, 128 × 32 × 32. All the other parameters are same as in the previous experiment. Due to the smaller computational domain, without HPS, the overall performance degrades when the application is deployed on a cluster with over 256 processors (Figure 20.16). The main reason is that without HPS, the granularity constraint and the increasing communication overheads overshadow the increased computing resources. In contrast, with HPS, AHMP can further scale up to 512 processors with performance gains up to 40% compared to the scheme without HPS. Note that the maximum performance gain (40%) is achieved when using 512 processors, where the scheme without HPS results in the degraded performance.

Impact of Out-of-Core The ALOC scheme has been implemented using the HDF5 library [38], which is widely used to store scientific data. The effect of the

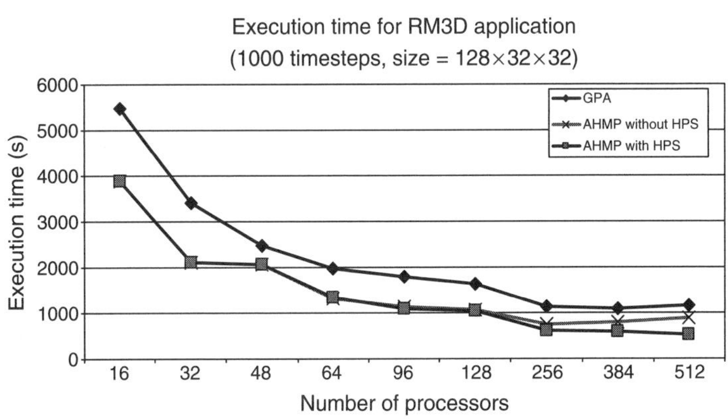

Figure 20.16 Experimental results: AHMP with and without HPS.

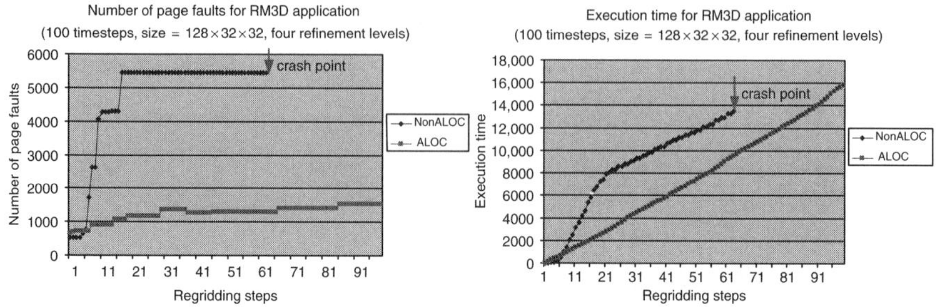

Figure 20.17 Number of page faults: NonALOC versus ALOC.

out-of-core scheme is evaluated using RM3D on the Frea Beowulf cluster. The configuration of RM3D consists of a base grid of size 128 × 32 × 32, four refinement levels, and 100 base-level timesteps (totalling 99 regridding steps). The number of processors used is 64. Without ALOC, it took about 13,507 s to complete 63 regridding steps at which point the application crashed. With ALOC, the application successfully completed the execution of 99 regridding steps. The execution time for the same 63 regridding steps was 9573 s, which includes 938 s for explicit out-of-core I/O operations. Figure 20.17 shows the page faults distribution and the execution time for experiments using NonALOC and ALOC schemes. As seen in the figure, without ALOC, the application incurs significant page faults. With ALOC, the number of page faults is reduced. As a result, the ALOC scheme improves the performance and enhances the survivability.

20.6 CONCLUSION

This chapter presented hybrid runtime management strategies and the adaptive hierarchical multipartitioner framework to address space-time heterogeneity in dynamic SAMR applications. A segmentation-based clustering algorithm was used to identify cluster regions with relatively homogeneous partitioning requirements in the adaptive computational domain. The partitioning requirements of each cluster were identified and used to select the most appropriate partitioning algorithm for the cluster. Further, this chapter presented hybrid partitioning strategy, which involves pipelining process and improves the system scalability by trading space for time, and the application-level out-of-core scheme, which addresses insufficient memory resources and improves overall performance and survivability of SAMR applications. Overall, the AHMP framework and its components have been implemented and experimentally evaluated on up to 1280 processors. The experimental evaluation demonstrated both the effectiveness of the clustering and the performance improvements using AHMP. Future work will consider adaptive tuning of control parameters and will extend the proposed strategies to support workload heterogeneity in multiphysics applications.

ACKNOWLEDGMENTS

The authors would like to thank Sumir Chandra and Johan Steensland for many insightful research discussions. The research presented in this chapter is supported in part by National Science Foundation via Grant Nos ACI 9984357, EIA 0103674, EIA 0120934, ANI 0335244, CNS 0709329, CNS 0305495, CNS 0426354, and IIS 0430826 and by Department of Energy via the Grant No. DE-FG02-06ER54857.

REFERENCES

1. M. Berger and J. Oliger. Adaptive mesh refinement for hyperbolic partial differential equations. *J. Comput. Phys.*, 53:484–512, 1984.
2. M. Berger and P. Colella. Local adaptive mesh refinement for shock hydrodynamics. *J. Comput. Phys.*, 82:64–84, 1989.
3. K. Devine, E. Boman, R. Heaphy, B. Hendrickson, and C. Vaughan. Zoltan data management services for parallel dynamic applications. *Comput. Sci. Engin.*, 4(2):90–97, 2002.
4. S. Das, D. Harvey, and R. Biswas. Parallel processing of adaptive meshes with load balancing. *IEEE Trans. Parallel Distrib. Syst.*, 12(12):1269–1280, 2001.
5. J. Cummings, M. Aivazis, R. Samtaney, R. Radovitzky, S. Mauch, and D. Meiron. A virtual test facility for the simulation of dynamic response in materials. *J. Supercomput.*, 23:39–50, 2002.
6. S. Hawley and M. Choptuik. Boson stars driven to the brink of black hole formation. *Phys. Rev. D*, 62(10):104024, 2000.
7. J. Ray, H.N. Najm, R.B. Milne, K.D. Devine, and S. Kempka. Triple flame structure and dynamics at the stabilization point of an unsteady lifted jet diffusion flame. *Proc. Combust. Inst.*, 25(1):219–226, 2000.
8. A. Calder, H. Tufo, J. Turan, M. Zingale, G. Henry, B. Curtis, L. Dursi, B. Fryxell, P. MacNeice, K. Olson, P. Ricker, R. Rosner, and F. Timmes. High performance reactive fluid flow simulations using adaptive mesh refinement on thousands of processors. in *Proceedings of the 2000 ACM/IEEE Conference on Supercomputing (CDROM)*, 2000.
9. L.V. Kale. Charm. http://charm.cs.uiuc.edu/research/charm/.
10. R.D. Hornung and S.R. Kohn. Managing application complexity in the SAMRAI object-oriented framework. *Concurrency Comput Pract. Exper.*, 14(5):347–368, 2002.
11. G. Karypis and V. Kumar. Parmetis. http://www-users.cs.umn.edu/~karypis/metis/parmetis/index.html., 2003.
12. P. MacNeice. Paramesh. http://esdcd.gsfc.nasa.gov/ESS/macneice/paramesh/paramesh.html.
13. M. Parashar and J. Browne. On partitioning dynamic adaptive grid hierarchies. In *29th Annual Hawaii International Conference on System Sciences*, 1996, pp. 604–613.
14. J. Steensland, S. Chandra, and M. Parashar. An application-centric characterization of domain-based SFC partitioners for parallel SAMR. *IEEE Trans. Parallel Distrib. Syst.*, 13(12):1275–1289, 2002.
15. P.E. Crandall and M.J. Quinn. A partitioning advisory system for networked data-parallel programming. *Concurrency Pract. Exper.*, 7(5):479–495, 1995.
16. X. Li and M. Parashar. Dynamic load partitioning strategies for managing data of space and time heterogeneity in parallel SAMR applications. In *The 9th International Euro-Par Conference (Euro-Par 2003)*, Lecture Notes in Computer Science, Vol. 2790. Springer-Verlag, 2003, pp. 181–188.
17. X. Li and M. Parashar. Using clustering to address the heterogeneity and dynamism in parallel SAMR application. In *The 12th Annual IEEE International Conference on High Performance Computing (HiPC05)*, 2005.
18. A. Wissink, D. Hysom, and R. Hornung. "Enhancing scalability of parallel structured AMR calculations. In *The 17th ACM International Conference on Supercomputing (ICS03)*, 2003, pp. 336–347.

19. M. Thune. Partitioning strategies for composite grids. *Parallel Algorithms Appl.*, 11:325–348, 1997.
20. Z. Lan, V. Taylor, and G. Bryan. Dynamic load balancing for adaptive mesh refinement applications: Improvements and sensitivity analysis. In *The 13th IASTED International Conference on Parallel and Distributed Computing and Systems (PDCS2001)*, 2001.
21. Z. Lan, V. Taylor, and G. Bryan. Dynamic load balancing of SAMR applications on distributed systems. *J. Sci. Program.*, 10(4):319–328, 2002.
22. M. Berger and I. Regoutsos. An algorithm for point clustering and grid generation. *IEEE Trans. Syst. Man Cybern.*, 21(5):1278–1286, 1991.
23. J.D. Teresco, J. Faik, and J.E. Flaherty. Hierarchical partitioning and dynamic load balancing for scientific computation. Technical Report CS-04-04, Williams College Department of Computer Science, 2004, (also in *Proceedings of PARA'04*).
24. J. Steensland. Efficient partitioning of structured dynamic grid hierarchies. PhD dissertation, Uppsala University, 2002.
25. H. Sagan. *Space Filling Curves*. Springer-Verlag, 1994.
26. J. Pilkington and S. Baden. Dynamic partitioning of non-uniform structured workloads with space filling curves. *IEEE Trans. Parallel Distrib. Syst.*, 7(3), 1996.
27. R.C. Gonzalez and R.E. Woods. *Digital Image Processing*, 2nd edition. Prentice Hall, Upper Saddle River, NJ, 2002.
28. T. Ridler and S. Calvard. Picture thresholding using an iterative selection method. *IEEE Trans. Syst. Man Cybern.*, 8:630–632, 1978.
29. N. Otsu. A threshold selection method from gray-level histogram. *IEEE Trans. Syst. Man Cybern.*, 6(1):62–66, 1979.
30. M. Parashar. Grace. http://www.caip.rutgers.edu/~parashar/TASSL/.
31. X. Li and M. Parashar. Hierarchical partitioning techniques for structured adaptive mesh refinement applications. *J. Supercomput.*, 28(3):265–278, 2004.
32. J.L. Hennessy, D.A. Patterson, and D. Goldberg. *Computer Architecture: A Quantitative Approach*. Morgan Kaufmann, 2002.
33. M.S. Potnuru. Automatic out-of-core execution support for CHARM++. Master thesis, University of Illinois at Urbana-Champaign, 2003.
34. N. Saboo and L.V. Kale. Improving paging performance with object prefetching. In *International Conference on High Performance Computing (HiPC'01)*, 2001.
35. J. Tang, B. Fang, M. Hu, and H. Zhang. Developing a user-level middleware for out-of-core computation on grids. In *IEEE International Symposium on Cluster Computing and the Grid*, 2004, pp. 686–690.
36. IPARS. http://www.cpge.utexas.edu/new_generation/.
37. S. Chandra and M. Parashar. A simulation framework for evaluating the runtime characteristics of structured adaptive mesh refinement applications. Technical Report TR-275, Center for Advanced Information Processing, Rutgers University, 2004.
38. Hdf5. http://hdf.ncsa.uiuc.edu/HDF5/.

Chapter 21

Physics-Aware Optimization Method

Yeliang Zhang and Salim Hariri

21.1 MOTIVATION

The development of high-performance computing tools and environments has improved dramatically over the past decade and provided scientists and engineers an easier and more powerful environment to solve the large-scale real-world problems. However, the large-scale scientific applications generally experience different phases at runtime and each phase has different physical characteristics. Most of the current research typically uses one algorithm to implement all the phases of the application execution, but a static solution or numerical scheme for all the execution phase might not be ideal to handle the dynamism of the problem.

Meanwhile, in the past three decades, the numerical methods have been studied actively. There exist various packages, serially or parallelly, for different domain subjects. Provided that different execution phases are identified, the domain scientists are no longer facing the problem of lacking algorithms to use, but are rather facing the problem of too many algorithms to choose from. Special knowledge such as which algorithm is better for which application or which algorithm is better over other algorithm on which platform is highly desired for optimization purposes.

We propose to take a more general methodology: monitoring the execution of the application, identifying the current execution phase, searching the knowledge base to find an optimal numerical scheme and algorithm for current phase, and applying optimal numerical method and algorithm on each application phase. Our method can be applied to finite element method, domain decomposition method, finite volume approximations, and others. To facilitate this research, it is imperative to develop a

Advanced Computational Infrastructures For Parallel and Distributed Adaptive Applications. Edited by Manish Parashar and Xiaolin Li

methodology to identify all sorts of application phases in different domain sciences, such as computational fluid dynamics (CFD), mechanics, hydrology, or chemical, as well as a comprehensive knowledge base from which information of different scientific computing phases, their characteristics, and information on optimal algorithm for such phases can be recorded and retrieved.

21.2 NUMERICAL LIBRARIES

In the past three decades, different numerical libraries have been developed on all sorts of problems. For example, Table 21.1 shows some of the available packages for eigenvalue problems. Though these libraries are all for eigenvalue problems, their

Table 21.1 Eigenvalue Problem Packages Available

Name	Method	Version	Date	Language	Parallel
ARPACK	Implicitly restarted Arnoldi/Lanczos	2	1996	F77	MPI
BLZPACK	Block Lanczos, PO+SO	04/00	2000	F77	MPI
DVDSON	Davidson	—	1995	F77	—
GUPTRI	Generalized upper triangular form	—	1999	F77	—
IETL	Power/RQI, Lanczos–Cullum	2.1	2003	C++	—
JDBSYM	Jacobi–Davidson (symmetric)	0.14	1999	C	—
LANCZOS	Lanczos (Cullum, Willoughby)	—	1992	F77	—
LANZ	Lanczos, PO	1.0	1991	F77	—
LASO	Lanczos	2	1983	F77	—
LOBPCG	Preconditioned conjugate gradient	4.10	2004	C	MPI
LOPSI	Subspace iteration	1	1981	F77	—
MPB	Conjugate gradient / Davidson	1.4.2	2003	C	—
NAPACK	Power method	—	—	F77	—
PDACG	Deflation–acceleration conjugate gradient	—	2000	F77	MPI
PLANSO	Lanczos, PO	.10	1997	F77	MPI
QMRPACK	Nonsymmetric Lanczos with look ahead	—	1996	F77	—
SLEPc	Power/RQI, subspace, Arnoldi	2.2.1	2004	C/F77	MPI
SPAM	Subspace projected approx. matrix	—	2001	F90	—
SRRIT	Subspace Iteration	1	1997	F77	—
SVDPACK	SVD via Lanczos, Ritzit, and Trace Minim	—	1992	C/F77	—
TRLAN	Lanczos, dynamic thick restart	1.0	1999	F90	MPI
Underwood	Block Lanczos	—	1992	F77	—

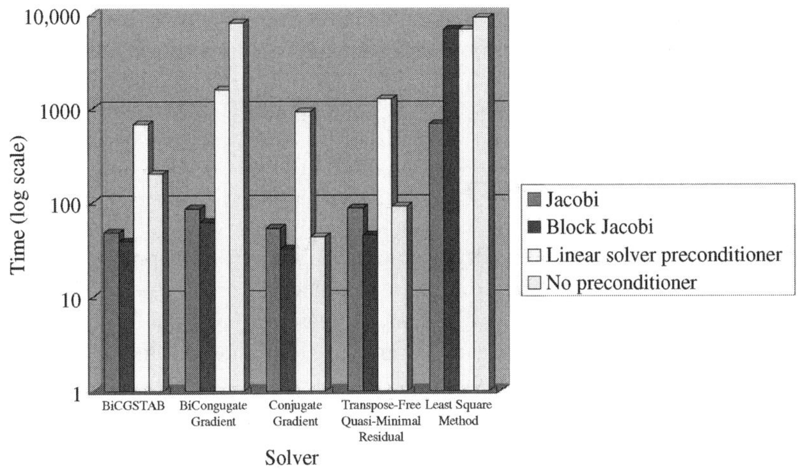

Figure 21.1 Execution time for VSAFT2D on linear solvers and preconditioners.

performance will vary with each application. The same thing holds for linear algebra libraries. In the numerical library PETSc [22], developed by Argonne National Lab, there are 12 different linear solvers and 8 different preconditioners available for the users to select from. Figure 21.1 shows different execution time using different linear solvers and preconditioners for a finite element application kernel, which we extract from variable saturated aquifer flow and transport (VSAFT2D) application [25] used in hydrology underground water research. The execution time could vary at the order of 2 or 3 magnitudes if a wrong solver is selected.

The optimal linear solver algorithm for an application might not be the same for the other applications. Table 21.2 shows three matrices execution time with different best solvers and worst solvers, and we also show the failure rate (failure means the result does not converge) provided we only use 12 solvers available in PETSc. The three matrices are from applications of reaction–diffusion, structural engineering, and bounded finline dielectric waveguide, respectively.

For the matrix rdb32001, if the user has little knowledge of these 12 solvers available in PETSc, his/her application is highly likely to have a nonconverged result if he/she just randomly selects a solver from the library. Therefore, it requires the domain scientists to possess an in-depth knowledge of each of these libraries to

Table 21.2 Performance of Different Solvers on Three Different Applications

Matrix	Automatic selection	Best time	Worst time	% of failures
rdb32001	bicg + none	2.54(bicg + none)	22.16 (bcgs + asm)	56.2%
bcsstk26	cr + bjacobi	1.62 (cr + bjacobi)	11.78 (bicg + none)	43.8%
bfw782b	cr + jacobi	0.0645 (cr + jacobi)	0.0942 (lsqr + asm)	9.3%

make an optimal choice for their application. Otherwise, the application performance either shows a nonoptimal result or, more unfortunately, the application will have a nonconverged result, as we shown in Table 21.2. Yet, most of the domain scientists lack such knowledge or have no time to possess such knowledge.

21.3 PROPOSED PROJECT

To make a maximum use of the available numerical libraries and apply them dynamically on each application execution phase, we need to profile the application characteristics at runtime. At runtime, different application phases can be abstracted as a skeleton in which information, such as optimal algorithm on which platform, what is this phase about, it is an I/O phase or a linear system solving phase, and so on is stored. Though there are unlimited scientific applications in the community, the total number of the skeletons is limited. We need to build a knowledge base to identify classes of applications and store all the skeletons and develop an optimal numerical algorithm for each skeleton. At runtime, we can retrieve information from this knowledge base to instruct the application to switch algorithms based on their current physical phases.

Therefore, to optimize any scientific application using our techniques, the following major steps will be enforced:

1. *Identifying Phases:* At runtime, we monitor the application execution and identify different phases based on the physical properties of the application.
2. *Planning Phase:* The monitored physical phases are fed into planning engine in which corresponding optimization techniques will be decided. Planning

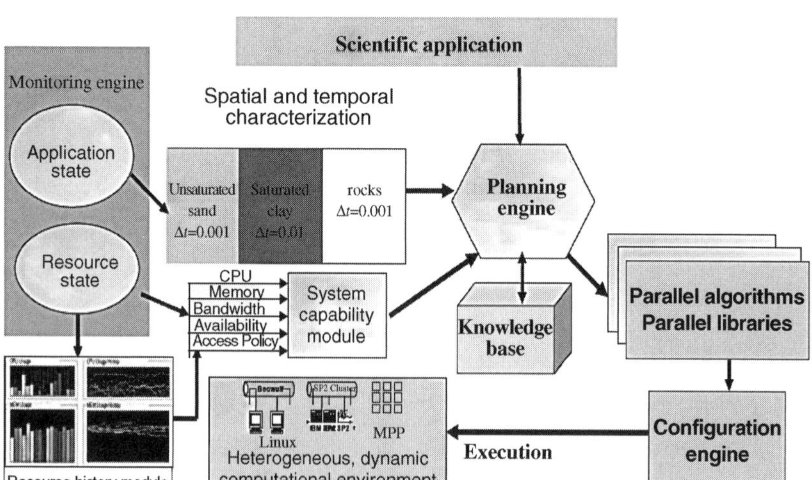

Figure 21.2 Architecture of physics-aware runtime manager (PARM).

engine is connected with knowledge base where different application and optimization historical information is stored. Planning engine will find the optimal spatial and temporal characterization for the application as well as the optimal numerical solvers.

3. *Configuration Phase:* After we decide the optimal algorithm, we need to generate the files needed by the new algorithm based on the previous phase execution result. For example, regenerate a nodal values using interpolation and extrapolation after we change a grid size in a finite element method application.
4. Restart the execution.

A primary architecture of our proposed system is shown in Figure 21.2.

21.4 A RUNNING EXAMPLE

We use a variable saturated aquifer flow and transport finite element hydrodynamics application developed by the researchers at the Hydrology and Water Resources Department at The University of Arizona [25] as a running example to explain the physics-aware runtime manager. This application is developed to simulate water flow and chemical transport through variably saturated porous media. At each timestep, the calculation involves transport through multiple types of media, which lead to disparate resolution requirements across the grid.

21.4.1 Numerical Analysis of VSAFT2D

The following discussion of VSAFT2D focused on a 2D case, but it can be easily applied to a 3D case because of the similarity of the governing equation and application implementation. The VSAFT2D flow in variably saturated media is computed as in equation (21.1):

$$\frac{\partial}{\partial x_i}(K_{ij}\frac{\partial}{\partial x_j}(\Psi + \beta_g x_2)) = (C + \beta_s S_s)\frac{\partial \Psi}{\partial t} - q_s \quad \text{in } \Omega, \tag{21.1}$$

where x_i and x_j are spatial coordinates, K_{ij} is the hydraulic conductivity tensor, Ψ is the pressure head, C is the specific moisture capacity, β_g is the index for gravity, β_s is the index for saturation, S_s is the specific storage, t is time, q_s is the source/sink term, and Ω is the solution domain.

Equation (21.1) is solved using the Galerkin scheme by representing the pressure at any point (x_1, x_2) in the domain at any instant t as

$$\Psi(x_1, x_2, t) = N_I(x_1, x_2)\Psi^I(t), \tag{21.2}$$

where N_I are the shape functions associated with node I and Ψ^I is the value of Ψ at node I with the range of I being from 1 to NN (NN is the total number of nodes).

In a similar way, the hydraulic conductivity tensor and the moisture capacity are represented as

$$[K] = N^I [K]^I \tag{21.3}$$

and

$$C = N^I C^I, \tag{21.4}$$

where K and C are the conductivity tensor and the moisture capacity, respectively, at any point in the domain and at any time and $[K]^I$ and C^I are the nodal values. Equations (21.3) and (21.4) are inconsistent with equations (21.2) because of the nonlinear relations between the pressure head and the unsaturated hydraulic conductivity, and relations between the pressure head and the moisture capacity term. Errors due to this inconsistent approach may however be resolved by using small elements; therefore, we could assign a uniform small element size to all the materials in the problem domain to achieve an accurately approximate result. Since material conductivity K controls the application's accuracy and determine the spatial and temporal attributes, this variable will be monitored to decide the spatial and temporal characteristics at runtime. Considering the different materials have different hydraulic conductivities, we could designate a different element size for each material to make equations (21.3) and (21.4) an accurate approximation according to its hydraulic conductivities at runtime and at the same time preserve the application's accuracy and convergence.

21.4.2 Determination of Numerical Scheme, Spatial Characteristics at Runtime

Given a VSAFT2D problem with a pumping well injecting or extracting water, the physical domain is composed of silt and sand, as shown in Figure 21.3. According to the mass conservation law [19], the volume of water flow through different media in a unit time will be a constant in the steady-state case [19],

$$K_{\text{sand}} J_{\text{sand}} = K_{\text{silt}} J_{\text{silt}}, \tag{21.5}$$

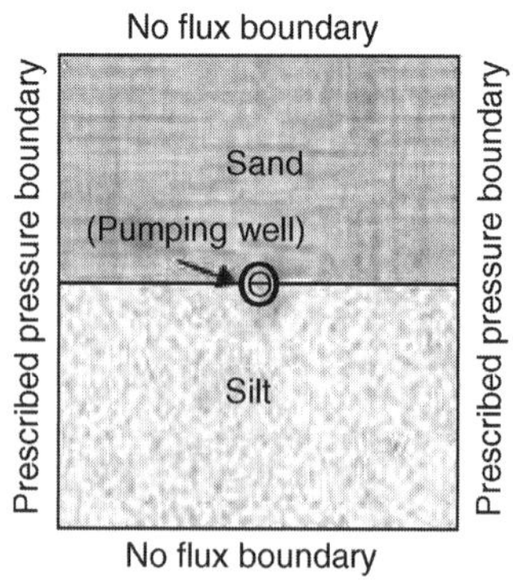

Figure 21.3 VSAFT2D domain with two different materials.

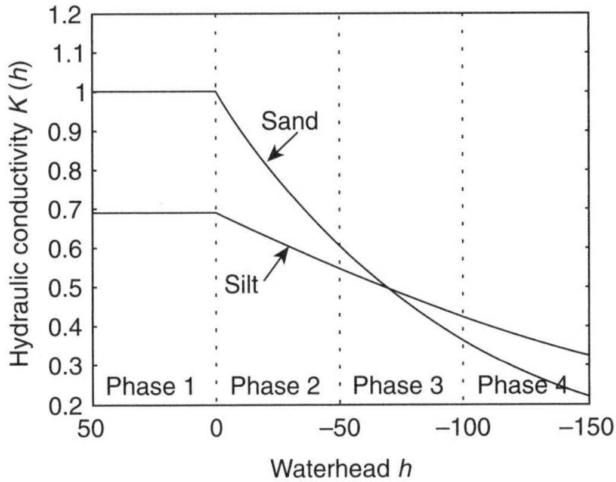

Figure 21.4 Functional relationship between hydraulic conductivity and waterhead.

where K is the hydraulic conductivity and J is the gradient of waterhead. The mass conservation equation of transient case is similar to equation (21.5) but with an addition of a storage change term [19].

At runtime, the application execution can be either in a saturated or unsaturated phase. However, each phase requires different configuration parameters to achieve the desired performance and accuracy requirements as explained below:

1. *Saturated Execution Phase:* K is a constant as shown in phase 1 of Figure 21.4. Provided $K_{\text{silt}} < K_{\text{sand}}$, according to equation (21.5), $J_{\text{silt}} > J_{\text{sand}}$. Since J is the waterhead gradient, that is, J represents how fast the field variable's variation is. The greater the J, the faster the field variable changes, then the finer grid is needed for the fast changing region to achieve the desired accuracy. Hence, at runtime, the PARM approach will exploit the physics properties of the application by making the grid finer in the silt domain (that means when $J_{\text{silt}} > J_{\text{sand}}$, we need to use a smaller Δx, Δy, and Δz on silt subdomain). In a similar way, the grid points will be coarser for the sand region. Note that this step is done at the beginning of the execution and not changed in the middle of the execution because of the steady-state condition. It is also well known that Newton–Raphson method will be a better iterative numerical scheme for saturated problems over Picard iterative scheme [19].
2. *Unsaturated Execution Phase*: The hydraulic conductivity K is a function of waterhead h as shown in phases 2, 3, and 4 of Figure 21.4. At the intersection of curves $K_{\text{sand}}(h)$ and $K_{\text{silt}}(h)$, we have $K_{\text{sand}}(h') = K_{\text{silt}}(h')$.

When $h < h'$, $K_{\text{silt}} > K_{\text{sand}}$ and $J_{\text{silt}} < J_{\text{sand}}$, so we need a finer grid on sand subdomain, that is, reduce Δx, Δy, and Δz for the sand domain and a coarser grid for the silt domain.

However, when $h > h'$, $K_{\text{silt}} < K_{\text{sand}}$ and $J_{\text{silt}} > J_{\text{sand}}$, so we need to apply a coarser grid for the sand region but a finer grid for the silt region. Based on heuristic information, we also know that Picard iterative numerical scheme will be better for unsaturated problems [19].

At each new phase, once a new set of grids is generated (coarse or fine), the solution is transferred from the old grid to the new one with interpolation. As a general rule, solution values on the new grid are interpolated from the values available on the old grid. Though many points on the new grids can be determined as a simple copy from the old grids, the missing points (if Δx, Δy, and Δz are reduced, as we discussed above) need some interpolation steps to ensure accurate values.

By monitoring the hydraulic conductivity and the waterhead at runtime, we will be able to accurately characterize the application state and identify its execution phase (saturated or unsaturated) and by exploiting the physics properties we will be able to adjust the temporal properties Δt and spatial properties (Δx, Δy, Δz) to optimize application performance at runtime. The degree of spatial characteristics restriction and prolongation is also governed by the desired accuracy. To avoid abruptly changing the element size, we divide the application into four phases, as shown in Figure 21.4.

21.4.3 Linear Solver Selection

In addition to exploiting the physics properties of the application, the PARM approach will search for a better solver for the linear system related to the application. Since PDE solving involves sparse matrix computations in general, we focus on linear solvers for sparse matrices. Generally, a sparse matrix can be categorized into diagonalized, tridiagonalized, and band diagonalized. Numerical libraries such as LAPACK [8, 10–12] and PETSc [22] provide various solvers for matrices with different structures. It is a daunting task to select an optimized solver for a particular application from these library pools. Besides, a particular solver will be best for a particular matrix format, but will perform poorly with other matrix formats. Even the same matrix format and the same solver will perform differently on various computer platforms since memory hierarchy plays an important role in linear algebra computations. Figure 21.5 shows the execution time of VSAFT2D for saturated steady cases with a homogeneous grid size for the entire simulation domain with different problem sizes and solver types. The y-axis is on a logarithm scale. When the problem size exceeds 288 elements, the conjugate gradient solver always gives the best performance for a saturated problem. The selection of linear solver is very important because it will be called multiple times in each timestep. Consequently, dramatic performance differences will be observed for various solvers even for the same problem size. Bearing in mind that transient problems like VSAFT2D needs a large number of timesteps to have an accurate approximation of the real-world problem, by choosing the optimal linear solver, a significant performance gain can be achieved. For example, as we shown in Figure 21.5, in the saturated case for a problem size as small as 490,000 elements, the conjugate gradient will save 38% of the time spent solving the linear system when compared with a transpose free QMR (tfqmr) solver.

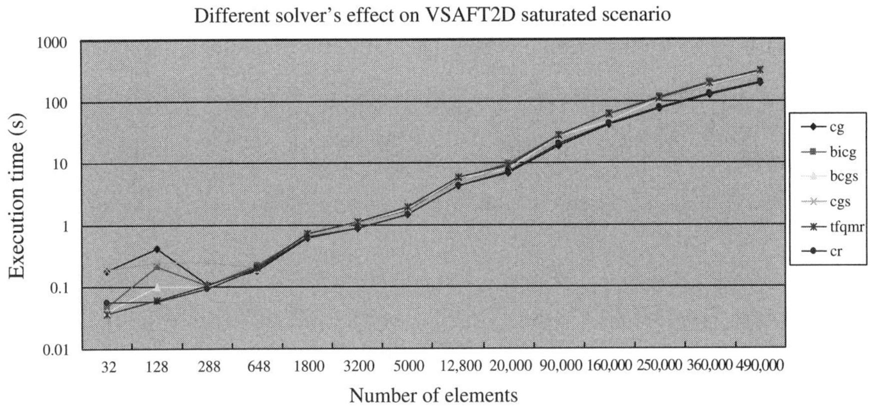

Figure 21.5 Different solvers' performance on various problem sizes.

21.4.4 Experiment Results and Analysis

We integrated the PETSc [22] with our runtime optimization approach. PETSc is a widely used library and provides a uniform interface for many solvers. Other linear solvers such as SuperLU [24] can be easily integrated with our PARM approach. We have evaluated the performance of our approach to optimize VSAFT2D on the Ohio Supercomputing Center Pentium 4 Cluster, a distributed/shared memory hybrid system constructed from commodity PC components running the Linux operating system. The cluster has 112 compute nodes for parallel jobs; approximately, half of them are connected using Infiniband, a switched 8 Gbit/s network [28]. Each compute node is configured with the following features:

1. Four gigabytes of RAM
2. Two 2.4 GHz Intel P4 Xeon processors, each with 512 kB of secondary cache
3. One 80 GB ATA100 hard drive
4. One Infiniband 10 GB interface
5. One 100Base-T Ethernet interface and one 1000Base-T Ethernet interface

The VSAFT2D is solved using the Galerkin finite element technique with either the Picard or the Newton iteration scheme. The convergence is checked by comparing the maximum pressure head difference between two successive iterations and comparing that difference to a prescribed tolerance. We evaluate the performance of the PARM approach with triangle element shape and focus on transient problem setting as shown in Figure 21.3. For simplicity, we let only PARM manipulate the spatial characteristics of the application such as the grid size for each phase switch. However, we do not change the temporal characteristics of the application, although our approach can support both types (spatial and temporal) of adaptations. Furthermore, we assume the area is divided evenly between silt and sand (each represents 50% for the computational domain). In reality, this distribution varies depending on the area being modeled, and our objective here is just to show how PARM approach can exploit the physics properties (silt or sand) to reduce the computational complexity of the solution. Because the analytic solution for such application as VSAFT2D is hard to achieve, we compare our PARM execution result with the finest grid resolution execution result. We first evaluated the PARM solution for the saturated transient case and then for the unsaturated transient case. The correct selection of the numerical scheme, spatial characteristics, and linear solvers are evaluated and summarized below.

Saturated Transient Case In this case, the silt and sand hydraulic conductivity is shown in phase 1 of Figure 21.4. Within each subdomain silt and sand, the water is saturated in each direction and thus the hydraulic conductivity is homogeneous for each sum domain, as shown in Figure 21.3. In the middle of the computation domain, there is a well that is pumping water out at a rate of 52.5 m^3/day and the initial boundary condition is 52.5 m at the X direction and 0 at the Y direction. The pumping test was simulated for 0.2 day with a timestep of 0.0005 day. We execute the code without PARM with finest grid size and with PARM approach that chooses the optimal grid size and record the simulation result at $200\Delta t$ and $400\Delta t$.

We notice that the PARM approach chooses the Newton–Raphson method in this case because it is saturated and instead of using the finest grid on both computational subdomains, it chooses the fine to coarse ratio as 4:1 according to our prescribed error tolerance. If we keep on pumping water from the well, the waterhead will eventually become negative, that is, it becomes an unsaturated case. We increase our total simulation time to make the problem change from saturated to unsaturated and find that once any waterhead become negative, PARM will capture this phase change at runtime. It first halts the computation, save the current execution results, switch from Newton–Raphson to Picard scheme, reselect a spatial characteristic for each subdomain according to their physical properties, generate new node and element file, and then restart the execution with the new scheme. Table 21.3 shows the kernel execution time of a 1.3 million nodes case in one timestep. The speedup is twofold. First, PARM uses different grid size on different hydraulic material. Second, PARM switch the original matrix solver ILUCG to a better preconditioner Block–Jacobi according to the VSAFT2D matrix format.

Unsaturated Transient Case In unsaturated scenario, the computation domain contains at least one node having negative waterhead. Similar to Section "Saturated Transient Case", the hydraulic conductivity is homogeneous at each subdomain.

Table 21.3 Exeuction Time on a 1.3 Million Nodes Case

Processor #	2	4	8	16	32
Execution time (s)	270.4142	199.26	127.13	68.52	42.32

In the middle of the computation domain, there is a well that is injecting water out at a rate of 2.5 m^3/day and the initial boundary condition is -75.5 m at the X direction and 0 at the Y direction. With the water injection, the waterhead of the nodes around the well will increase which means our execution is actually experiencing changes in the application execution phase, which include the changes from phase 4 $\rightarrow$ phase 3 $\rightarrow$ phase 2, as shown in Figure 21.4. As we discussed in Section 21.4.2, phase 3 is used to avoid abrupt change in spatial characteristics, therefore, it shall not occupy a lot of timesteps. In this test case, phase 3 takes 100 timesteps to show perceptible waterhead change. In real simulation, the timesteps for this phase can be set to 2 or 4. Furthermore, because this phase is within a relative small interval around h', we can regard silt and sand have the same hydraulic conductivity in phase 3, therefore, we use 1:1 grid ratio in two materials. As we discussed in Section 21.4.2, upon the switch between phases 4, 3, and 2, the PARM approach chooses the grid size ratio of silt to sand as 3:4, 1:1, and 3:2, respectively, according to their physics property and the user requirement for the error tolerance at runtime.

We execute the code without PARM with finest grid size and with PARM approach will choose the optimal grid size for 0.3 day and record the simulation result at $100\Delta t$, $200\Delta t$, $300\Delta t$, $500\Delta t$, and $600\Delta t$ with a timestep of 0.0005 day. According to the physics properties, phase 4 is from Δt to $200\Delta t$, phase 3 is from $201\Delta t$ to $300\Delta t$, and phase 2 is from $301\Delta t$ to $600\Delta t$.

Phase 4 changed to phase 3 between timestep $200\Delta t$ and $300\Delta t$. By monitoring this change, PARM-based runtime optimization would first help to halt the application execution, save all the current execution results, regenerate the node and element files, interpolate the values for the new grid, and then finally restart the computation with the new node and element files.

Figure 21.6 shows that with PARM, the execution time is reduced massively. The reason is that with runtime physical information, PARM can adjust the spatial characteristics that provide the required accuracy but also reduce the computation needs. Without PARM and lack of runtime information, the finest grid resolution has to be applied that lead to waste of computation power on unnecessary subdomain. On 32 processors, PARM saves 38% execution time compared with the finest grid.

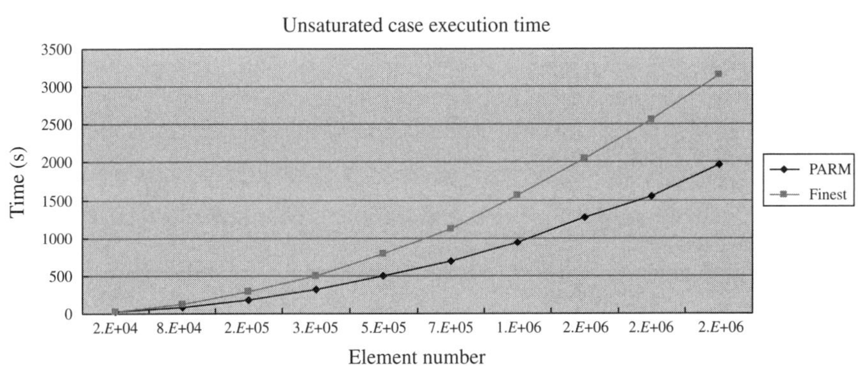

Figure 21.6 Execution time of unsaturated case with 32 processors.

Table 21.4 Absolute and Relative Error on Saturated Case at Different TimeSteps for Problem Size 20,000

Saturated	$200\Delta t$	$400\Delta t$
Absolute error	0.1925	0.1928
Relative error(%)	1.68	1.79

21.4.5 Error, Gain, and Overhead Analysis

The error of using PARM versus the finest grid resolution through all the application phases is shown in Tables 21.4 and 21.5. The error is calculated as absolute error and relative error is shown in the bracket.

$$\text{Absolute error} = \max(h_i' - h_i), \tag{21.6}$$

$$\text{Relative error} = \max(|h_i' - h_i|/h_i), \tag{21.7}$$

where h_i' is PARM calculated value at node i and h_i is the finest grid calculation at node i, $i = 0, \ldots,$ total number of nodes.

The gain from using PARM approach is twofold. Adjusting spatial characteristics at runtime, PARM approach effectively reduces the total number of elements and nodes required for the computation. The total execution time to assemble the global matrix reduces to 8%. On the other hand, the matrix solving time of FEM is governed by square of half-bandwidth b_W [30], which is calculated as

$$b_W = N_{\text{DOF}}(1 + \Delta_{\max}), \tag{21.8}$$

where N_{DOF} is the number of degrees of freedom per node and $\Delta_{\max}$ is the maximum of the maximum differences between node numbers on each element considering all elements one at a time. In VSAFT2D, $N_{\text{DOF}} = 2$, in Table 21.6, we can see b_{W^2} using PARM for a medium problem size with 2,000,000 nodes. The silt and sand element size is a ratio to silt and sand element size in the finest grid configuration.

Table 21.6 shows that using PARM, for a medium size with million nodes, we can roughly save at least 32.9% (silt = 4/3 and sand = 1) of the total matrix solving time versus that of the finest grid. Considering larger silt and sand element size, this saving ratio will be even greater.

Though we reduce b_{w^2} effectively, we also introduce additional overhead into the code, which is extra time spent on nodal formation T_n and elemental formation T_e after

Table 21.5 Absolute and Relative Error on Unsaturated Case at Different TimeSteps for Problem Size 20,000

Saturated	$200\Delta t$	$300\Delta t$	$500\Delta t$	$600\Delta t$
Absolute error	0.0139	0.0652	0.1659	0.1843
Relative error(%)	0.019	0.091	0.23	0.26

Table 21.6 Half-bandwidth of Problem Size 2,000,000 Nodes with Different PARM Element Size versus That of Finest Grid

	Using PARM			
silt	4/3	4/3	4/3	1
sand	1	4/3	2	4
b_{W^2}	0.304×1012	0.252×1012	0.251×1012	0.251×1012
	Without PARM			
b_{W^2}	1.0×1012			

Table 21.7 PARM Overhead

Problem size	0.32	0.72	1.28	2.0	2.88
Overhead	6.03	7.87	11.02	15.02	20.62
Total execution time	155.2	360.0	615.1	1003.8	1445.7
Percentile	3.89%	2.19%	1.79%	1.49%	1.42%

Time in Seconds, and problem size in million nodes.

phase changes as well as additional global matrix formation T_m. Table 21.7 shows the overhead that is a summation of T_n, T_e, and T_m on different problem sizes versus the total execution with 1 processor for that problem size with only 10 timesteps. (It is not very likely that a phase will change within 10 timesteps. Therefore, we can assume that there is only one PARM overhead within this execution) Here, we only evaluated the performance for the grid size with silt = 4/3 and sand = 1 since other combination will produce smaller overhead because of the coarser grid.

We notice that when the problem size becomes larger and larger, the overhead introduced by PARM approach becomes more and more insignificant compared with the total execution time. The total overhead introduced by PARM is small enough to be neglected.

21.5 CONCLUSION AND FUTURE WORK

In this chapter, we presented an autonomic programming framework PARM that can dynamically self-configure the application execution environment to exploit the heterogeneity and the dynamism of the application execution states. We described our implementation approach PARM based on this programming paradigm and evaluated its performance on a hydrology application (VSAFT2D). VSAFT2D is a 2D finite element hydrodynamics application to model water flow and chemical transport through variably saturated porous media. Our preliminary results showed that by exploiting the application physics characteristics (e.g., sand saturated/unsaturated, silt saturated/unsaturated, etc.) and its current state (e.g., phase 2, phase 3, or phase 4), selecting the appropriate numerical scheme (e.g., Picard or Newton–Raphson etc.), up to 62% speedup can be achieved.

REFERENCES

1. P. Horn. Autonomic computing: IBM's perspective on the state of information technology. http://www.research.ibm.com/autonomic/, 2001.
2. J.O. Kephart and D.M. Chess. The vision of autonomic computing. *IEEE Comput.*. 36:41–50, 2003.
3. M. Agarwal, et al. AutoMate: Enabling Autonomic Applications on the Grid. *Proceedings of the Autonomic Computing Workshop, 5th Annual International Active Middleware Services Workshop (AMS2003)*, June 2003, pp. 48–57.
4. B. Khargharia, S. Hariri, et al. vGrid: a framework for building autonomic applications. *International Workshop on Challenges for Large Applications in Distributed Environments (CLADE 2003)*, June 2003, pp. 19–26.
5. Y. Zhang, J. Yang, S. Hariri, S. Chandra, M. Parashar. Autonomic proactive runtime partitioning strategies for SAMR applications. IPDPS Next Generation Software Program—NSFNGS—PI Workshop 2004.
6. J. Bilmes, K. Asanovic, C.-W. Chin, J. Demmel. Optimizing matrix multiply using PHiPAC: a portable, high-performance ACSI C coding methodology. In *Proceedings of the International Conference on Supercomputing*, Vienna, Austria, July 1997.
7. R.C. Whaley, A. Petitet, and J. Dongarra. Automated empirical optimizations of software and the ATLAS project. *Parallel Comput.*, 27(1–2):3–35, 2001.
8. Z. Chen, J. Dongarra, P. Luszczek, and K. Roche. Selfadapting software for numerical linear algebra and LAPACK for clusters. *Parallel Comput.*, 29(11–12):1723–1743, 2008.
9. J. Dongarra and V. Eijkhout. Self-adapting numerical software for next generation applications. Lapack Working Note 157, ICL-UT-02-07.
10. R. Whaley and J. Dongarra. Automatically tuned linear algebra software. Technical report UT CS-97-366, LAPACK Working Note No.131, University of Tennessee, 1997.
11. C.L. Lawson, R.J. Hanson, D.'Kincaid, and F.T. Krogh. Basic linear algebra subprograms for FORTRAN usage. *ACM Trans. Math. Software*, 5:308–323, 1979.
12. http://www.netlib.org/lapack/lug/index.html
13. A. Burrows, T. Young, P. Pinto, R. Eastman, and T.A. Thompson. *Ap. J.*, 539:865, 2000.
14. T.A. Thompson, A. Burrows, and P.A. Pinto. *Ap. J.*, 592:434, 2003.
15. G. Zumbusch. *Parallel Multilevel Methods: Adaptive Mesh Refinement and Loadbalancing*. Teubner, 2003.
16. J.H. Ferziger. *Numerical Methods for Engineering Application*. John Wiley & Sons, Inc., 1998.
17. B.A. Allan. The CCA core specification in a distributed memory SPMD framework, *Concurrency Comput. Pract. Exper.*, 14:1–23, 2002.
18. W. Press, S. Teukolsky, W. Vetterling, and B. Flannery. *Numerical Recipes in Fortran 77*. Cambridge University Press, 1992.
19. J.D. Istok. *Groundwater Modeling by the Finite Element Method (Water Resources Monograph)*. Amer Geophysical Union, 1989.
20. M. Parashar, R. Muralidhar, W. Lee, M. Wheeler, D. Arnold, and J. Dongarra. Enabling interactive oil reservoir simulations on the grid. *Concurrency Comput. Pract. Exper.*, 17(2):1–28, 2005.
21. http://math.nist.gov/MatrixMarket/
22. S. Balay, K. Buschelman, V. Eijkhout, W.D. Gropp, D. Kaushik, M.G. Knepley, L.C. McInnes, B.F. Smith, and H. Zhang. *PETSc Users Manual*, ANL-95/11—Revision 2.1.5, Argonne National Laboratory, 2004.
23. Y. Zhang, X.S. Li, and O. Marques. Towards an automatic and application-based eigensolver selection. *LACSI Symposium*, 2005.

24. X.S. Li and J.W. Demmel. *SuperLU_DIST*: A scalable distributed-memory sparse direct solver for unsymmetric linear systems. *ACM Trans. Math. Software*, 2003.
25. R. Srivastava, and T.-C.J. Yeh. A three-dimensional numerical model for water flow and transport of chemically reactive solute through porous media under variably saturated conditions. *Adv. Water Resour.*, 15:275–287, 1992.
26. E. Anderson, et al. *LAPACK User's Guide*, 3rd. edition. Society for Industrial and Applied Mathematics, Philadelphia, 1999.
27. R. Barret, et. al. *Templates for the Solution of Linear Systems: Building Blocks for Iterative Methods*, Society for Industrial and Applied Mathematics, Philadelphia, 1994.
28. http://www.osc.edu/hpc/hardware/index.shtml#beo.
29. G. Hornberger and P. Wiberg. *Numerical Methods in the Hydrological Sciences*, American Geophysical Union, 2005.
30. O.C. Zienkiewicz. *The Finite Element Method*, 3rd edition. McGraw-Hill UK, 1977.
31. P. Bochev, M. Gunzburger, and R. Lehoucq. On stabilized finite element methods for transient problems with varying time scales. *Proceedings of the European Congress on Computational Methods in Applied Sciences and Engineering* (ECCOMAS' 04), 2004.
32. S. Liu, M. Rodgers, Q. Wang, and L. Keer. A fast and effective method for transient thermoelastic displacement analyses. *J. Tribol.*, 123(3):479–485, 2001.
33. N. Touheed, P. Selwood, P.K. Jimack, M. Berzins. Parallel dynamic load-balancing for the solution of transient CFD problems using adaptive tetrahedral meshes. In D.R Emerson, A. Ecer, J. Periaux, N. Satofuka, and P. Fox, editors, *Parallel Computational Fluid Dynamics: Recent Developments and Advances Using Parallel Computers*. Elsevier Science, 1998, pp. 81–88.
34. C. Goodyer, R. Fairlie, M. Berzins, L. Scales. An in-depth investigation of the multigrid approach for steady and transient EHL problems. D. Dowson, editors, *Thinning Films and Tribological Interfaces*. Elsevier Science, 1999, pp. 95–102.
35. G.M. Amdahl. Validity of the single-processor approach to achieving large scale computing capabilities. *AFIPS Conference Proceedings*, Vol. 30, 1967, pp. 483–485.

Chapter 22

DistDLB: Improving Cosmology SAMR Simulations on Distributed Computing Systems Through Hierarchical Load Balancing*

Zhiling Lan, Valerie E. Taylor, and Yawei Li

22.1 INTRODUCTION

The structured adaptive mesh refinement (SAMR) algorithm has played a prominent role in cosmology simulations. In most cosmological simulations, only a relatively small volume of domain needs to be refined at a higher resolution. Therefore, SAMR, a temporally and spatially adaptive algorithm, has been widely adopted for cosmic modeling. It enables scientists to run previously intractable cosmological simulations on the present supercomputing systems [7]. The basic components in SAMR are uniform grids; therefore, existing accurate and well-tested grid-based methods are ready to be used for solving the hydrodynamics equations in cosmology SAMR simulations [6]. Over the past decades, cosmology SAMR simulations have been widely adopted to explore various astrophysics concepts and ideas. Cosmologists use

*Reprinted from "DistDLB: Improving Cosmology SAMR Simulations on Distributed Computing Systems through Hierarchical Load Balancing," Z. Lan, V. Taylor, and Y. Li, *Journal of Parallel and Distributed Coumpting*, 66(5):716–731. Copyright (2006), with permission from Elsevier.

Advanced Computational Infrastructures For Parallel and Distributed Adaptive Applications. Edited by Manish Parashar and Xiaolin Li

the comparison between simulations and telescopic observations of distant galaxies to verify and refine the theory of the origin of the universe and the formation of stars and galaxies.

A typical cosmology SAMR simulation requires a large amount of computing power. For instance, simulation of cosmic evolution takes more than 100 h on an IBM SP system with more than 1000 CPUs [27]. Distributed systems, composed of multiple supercomputers connected by various networks, provide an economical alternative to traditional parallel systems [14, 16, 17, 25, 26, 32, 37, 41, 42, 48]. By using distributed systems, researchers are no longer limited by the computing power of a single site and are able to execute cosmology simulations that require vast computing power, that is, beyond that available at any single site. An important issue of conducting distributed cosmology simulations is related to performance and efficiency. In particular, cosmology SAMR simulations are adaptive in that their computational load varies throughout the execution. Efficiently partitioning the cosmological workload and transferring excess workload from overloaded processors to underloaded processors during execution are critical techniques needed for the efficient execution of distributed cosmology simulations. The paper is focused on designing a load balancing scheme to improve the efficiency of cosmology simulations in distributed computing environments.

The unique characteristics of cosmology simulations and the heterogeneous sharing features of distributed computing environments, however, pose several research challenges to dynamic load balancing of such simulations:

- *Unique Features of Cosmology SAMR Simulations*: Several existing research on load balancing have been focused on graph-based partitioning [4, 9, 15, 19, 23, 33, 35, 36, 43, 46]. With graph partitioning, the computational workload and the interprocessor communication are represented as a weighted graph of vertices and edges. The objective of graph partitioning is to find a repartition of the graph so as to equalize the workload among processors and minimize the edge cut. Cosmology SAMR applications have very different data structures from graphs used in graph-based partitioning schemes. First, the basic building block used in cosmic modeling is "grid," which is a self-contained object with dozens of variables that need to be calculated at runtime. Besides, two other data structures are used to keep track of parent–child and sibling relations among grids. Second, both the computational workload per grid and the communication cost among grids are changing dynamically at runtime. Hence, the complicated and dynamic data structures used in cosmology SAMR simulations cannot be transformed into a graph that is represented as a static set of vertices and edges. In addition, cosmology SAMR applications have several unique adaptive characteristics, namely, high frequency of adaptations and different patterns of imbalances, that prevent the use of either scratch–remap or diffusion-based repartitioning techniques [22].
- *Heterogeneous and Fluctuating Performance of Computing Resources*: First, computing resources of a distributed system may be located at different sites. They may have different architectures, operating systems, processor speeds,

and compilers. All of these factors result in different performances across sites. Second, a typical distributed system includes different types of networks where network performance gap can be of different orders of magnitude. Therefore, the redistribution cost can be of more orders of magnitude than the actual partitioning when the excess workload is transferred across geographically distributed machines [13]. Furthermore, the shared networking resources are highly dynamic, which makes it difficult to make an accurate data transferring decision. To efficiently partition the application and then migrate the excess workload from overloaded processors to underloaded processors, the fluctuating performance of networks should be taken into consideration. Simply applying a load balancing scheme that is designed for homogeneous parallel systems to heterogeneous distributed systems can bring in a significant performance penalty [21].

In this paper, we present DistDLB, a dynamic load balancing scheme for cosmology SAMR simulations running on heterogeneous distributed computing systems. The primary goal of DistDLB is to reduce the redistribution cost as well as to maintain the quality of load balancing. More specifically, techniques are proposed to address the following issues: (1) the heterogeneity of networks, (2) the fluctuating performance of networks, (3) the heterogeneity of processors, and (4) the unique features of cosmology simulations. To address the heterogeneity of networks, DistDLB employs a hierarchical load balancing approach. One of the key issues is to decide when the workload should be redistributed across remotely connected machines to produce a performance gain. Heuristic methods are developed to evaluate the computational gain and the redistribution cost. The fluctuating performance of networks is addressed by adaptively choosing an appropriate action, for example, repartitioning across sites or limiting repartitioning within each site, based on the network traffic. To address the unique characteristics of cosmology applications, the load balancing technique presented in Ref. [22] is adopted. Experiments with the cosmology modeling code ENZO [11] on production distributed systems show that DistDLB can effectively reduce the execution times of cosmology simulations by 2.56–79.14% depending on the underlying network performance and the application parameters, as compared to the scheme that does not consider the heterogeneous and fluctuating performance of distributed systems.

The load balancing problem has been studied extensively over the past decades. A wealth of literatures is available to cover a wide range of issues related to load balancing [5, 9, 12, 23, 29, 33, 38, 43, 47]. To date, most load balancing techniques are focused on homogeneous parallel system, where the primary objective is to maintain a good quality of load balancing as well as to reduce the interprocessor communication during the computation. There are several well-known partitioning/repartitioning tools for scientific computing; examples of such tools include JOSTLE [44, 45], ParMETIS [30, 33], Zoltan [5, 13], and GridARM [8, 50]. The proposed DistDLB scheme complements existing works on load balancing in three aspects. First, it targets cosmology SAMR applications that currently lack the efficient load balancing techniques. Second, DistDLB emphasizes on the techniques that reduce the substantial redistribution cost incurred in distributed computing, which is rarely addressed in the literature. Finally, DistDLB addresses both the heterogeneous and fluctuating performance of distributed systems through the novel use of a hierarchical approach and a gain/cost evaluation model.

The rest of the paper is organized as follows. Section 22.2 presents an overview of cosmology SAMR simulations and the cosmology simulation code ENZO. Section 22.3 discusses the related work. Section 22.4 describes the detailed design of DistDLB. Section 22.5 presents the experimental results to evaluate DistDLB. Finally, Section 22.6 summarizes the paper and identifies our future work.

22.2 COSMOLOGY SAMR APPLICATIONS

Cosmology modeling simulates the evolution of the universe from the big bang to the present day through the formation of the stars, galaxies, and clusters of galaxies. SAMR has been widely adopted for such a modeling due to its adaptivity.

The community code, ENZO, is a successful parallel cosmology SAMR modeling tool designed for high resolution, multiphysics, and cosmological structure formation simulations [6, 11, 28]. To incorporate relevant dynamic, chemical, and thermodynamic process calculation, ENZO combines an Euler solver for the primordial gas, an N-body solver for the collisionless dark matter, a Poisson solver for the gravitational field, and a 12-species stiff reaction flow solver for the primordial gas chemistry [7]. The package is written in C++ with FORTRAN routines for computationally intensive sections and MPI functions for message passing among processors. Additional details about ENZO can be found in Refs [11, 22].

In this section, we present an overview of SAMR algorithm, unique characteristics of cosmology simulations that are related to dynamic load balancing, and a load balancing scheme for cosmology SAMR simulations on homogeneous parallel systems.

22.2.1 SAMR Algorithm

The structured adaptive mesh refinement (SAMR) algorithm was developed by Berger et al. [1, 3]. The central idea behind SAMR is deceptively simple [7]. It represents the grid hierarchy as a tree of grids[1] at any instant of time. The number of levels, the number of grids, and the locations of the grids change with each adaptation. Initially, a uniform mesh covers the entire computational domain, and in local regions that require higher resolution, finer subgrids are added. If a region still needs more resolution, a finer subgrid is added. This process repeats recursively with each adaptation resulting in a tree of grids, as shown in Figure 22.1. The top graph in this figure shows the overall structure after several adaptations. The remainder of the figure shows the grid

[1]We use "grid" to denote the basic entity used in the SAMR algorithm, and "Grid" to denote the computational grid.

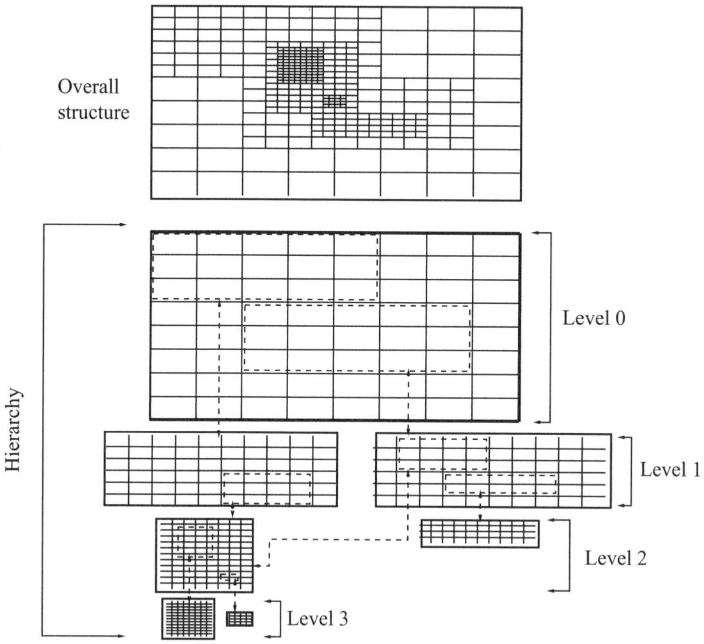

Figure 22.1 SAMR grid hierarchy.

hierarchy for the overall structure with the dotted regions corresponding to those that require further refinement [24]. In this grid hierarchy, there are four levels of grids going from level 0 to level 3. Throughout the execution of an SAMR application, the grid hierarchy changes with each adaptation.

Figure 22.2 presents the overall control algorithm used in SAMR [6]. As shown in the figure, the execution of cosmology simulations can be divided into multiple

```
InitializeHierarchy
While (Time<StopTime) {
    dt=ComputeTimeStep(TopGrid);
    Time+=dt;
    EvolveLevel(0,Time);
    CheckForOutput(Time);
}

EvolveLevel(level, ParentTime) {
    while (Time<ParentTime) {
            dt=ComputeTimeStep(all grids at level);
            Solver(dt);
            Time+=dt;
            SetBoundaryValues;
            EvolveLevel(level=1,Time);
            FluxCorrection;
            Projection;
            RebuildHierarchy(level+1);  //load balancing at level+1
    }
}
```

Figure 22.2 SAMR control algorithm.

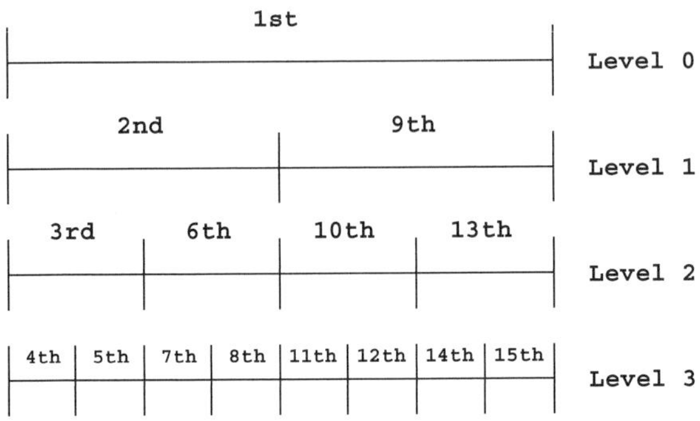

Figure 22.3 Integrated execution order (refinement factor = 2).

iterations at level 0. Each iteration starts with a time advance at level 0 by a timestep. For those regions that require higher resolutions, finer grids are constructed and then be time advanced with a smaller time-step. This process continues until all the grids at finer levels reach the same physical time as that at level 0. The subroutine *Rebuild-Hierarchy* is the adaptive part of SAMR, which completely rebuilds the grid hierarchy for the level specified in the argument and the finer levels [6]. Figure 22.3 illustrates the corresponding execution sequence for a simulation with four levels and a refinement factor of 2. The sequence number above the line shows the order in which the subgrids are evolved.

22.2.2 Data Structures and Adaptations

The basic component used in cosmology SAMR simulations is very different from that used in general scientific applications, such as those using finite element and difference methods (FD/FEM). In cosmology simulations, the basic entity for data movement is a self-contained unit called "grid." In other words, each subroutine in Figure 22.2 is applied to grids. Differing from meshes used in finite element and difference methods, *a grid is in fact an object*. It consists of several fields, including baryon field, particle data field, and gravity data field. Each field includes multiple variables that need to be calculated during execution. In addition, to keep track of parent–child and sibling relationships among grids, two other data structures are used: one is a linked list and the other is a tree. Furthermore, both the computational workload per grid and the communication cost among grids are changing dynamically at runtime, thus, it is not feasible to transform the complicated changing data structures used in cosmology SAMR applications into a graph that is represented as a static set of vertices and edges. From a more physical standpoint, in cosmology simulations, each level of the hierarchy has its own timestep, so that highly refined regions require many short steps, while coarser regions require fewer. For a FD/FEM, typically the entire domain is advanced with one timetstep.

Cosmology modeling has four unique adaptive characteristics relating to the repartitioning requirements: (1) coarse granularity, (2) high magnitude of imbalance,

(3) different patterns of imbalance, and (4) high frequency of adaptations [22]. Coarse granularity means that the basic component for cosmology simulations is large, usually ranging from 100 kB to 10 MB. The last three characteristics indicate that in a typical cosmological simulation, the nature of the grid hierarchy changes rapidly and the adaptation may occur in several local regions or through the entire computational domain. According to Ref. [34], existing repartitioning schemes can be classified as either *scratch–remap schemes* or *diffusion-based schemes*. In *scratch–remap* schemes, the workload is repartitioned from scratch and then remapped to the original partition. *Diffusion-based schemes* employ the neighboring information to redistribute the load between adjacent processors such that global balance is achieved by successive migration of workload between neighboring processors. The unique characteristics of cosmology simulations indicate that neither of them is effective for cosmology simulations. The fourth characteristic, the high frequency of adaptations, and the use of complex data structures result in *scratch–remap schemes* being intolerable because of the cost to completely modify the data structures without considering the previous load distribution. *Diffusion-based schemes* are local schemes that do not fully utilize some global information provided in cosmological simulations [22]. In Ref.[34], it was determined that *scratch–remap schemes* are advantageous for problems in which high magnitude of imbalance occurs in localized regions, while *diffusion-based schemes* generally provide better results for the problems in which imbalance occurs globally throughout the computational domain. The third characteristic, different patterns of imbalance, implies that an appropriate DLB scheme for SAMR should provide good balancing for both situations. Further, the first characteristic, coarse granularity, is a challenge for a DLB scheme because it limits the quality of load balancing.

22.2.3 ParaDLB: Load Balancing for Parallel Cosmology Simulations

Due to the complicated data structures and complexity of the algorithm itself used in SAMR, a simple load balancing strategy is at present used in cosmological simulations and we denote it as *original DLB*. In Ref. [22], it is shown that this simple load balancing strategy suffers from poor quality of load balancing; therefore, a dynamic load balancing scheme is proposed for cosmology SAMR simulations running on *homogeneous parallel systems* (denoted as *ParaDLB*). ParaDLB takes into consideration the unique characteristics of cosmology simulations and divides each load balancing step into one or more iterations of two phases: *moving grid phase* and *splitting grid phase*. The *moving grid phase* utilizes the global information to send grids directly from overloaded processors to underloaded processors. The use of direct communication to move the grids eliminates the variability in time to reach the equal balance and avoids chances of thrashing [39]. The *splitting grid phase* splits a grid into two smaller grids along the longest dimension, thereby addressing the first characteristic, coarse granularity. These two phases are interleaved and executed in parallel. Experiments show that ParaDLB can improve the performance of cosmology SAMR simulations on parallel systems by up to 57% as compared to *original DLB*.

```
Done=0; LastMax=LastMin=0;
while (MaxLoad>threashold * AvgLoad && Done ==0) {
    for (j=0;j<NumberOfGrids;j++) {                          //moving-grid phase
        for (i=0;i<NumberOfGrids;i++) {
            if (grid(i) resides on MaxProc && grid(i) >AvgLoad/threshold-MinLoad
                                          && grid (i) <AvgLoad*threshold-MinLoad) {
              move grid(i) from MaxProx to MinProc;
              update load information of MaxProc and MinProc;
              find new maxProc and MinProc;
              break;
            }
        }
        if (i==NumberOfGrids)
           break;
    }
    if (MaxLoad >threshold *AvgLoad) {                       //splitting-grid phase
        if (MaxProc==LastMax && MinProc == LastMin)
           Done=1;
        LastProc=MaxProc; LastMin=MinProc;
        find the largest grid MaxGrid on MaxProc;
        split MaxGrid into two and one of them redistribute to MinProc;
        update MaxProc, MinProc, MaxLoad, MinLoad, and AvgLoad;
    } else {
        Done=1;
    }
}
```

Figure 22.4 The pseudocode of ParaDLB for cosmology SAMR simulations on homogeneous parallel machines.

The detailed pseudocode of ParaDLB is shown in Figure 22.4. Here, *AvgLoad* denotes the required load for which all the processors would have an equal workload. *MaxProc* denotes the processor that has the maximal amount of workload *MaxLoad*, while *MinProc* denotes the processor that has the minimal amount of workload *minLoad*. In Ref. [20], a number of experiments with different input parameters are conducted to study the optimal value for the threshold. The sensitivity analysis shows the optimal value of *threshold* is around 1.25, which can result in the best performance in terms of execution time as well as the acceptable quality of load balancing.

ParaDLB is not a *scratch–remap scheme* because it takes into consideration the previous load distribution during the current repartitioning. It differs from *diffusion-based scheme* in two manners. First, ParaDLB addresses the issue of coarse granularity of SAMR applications. It splits large-sized grids located on overloaded processors if just the movement of grids is not enough to handle load imbalance. Second and more important, it employs the direct data movement between overloaded and underloaded processors instead of employing successive data migration of workload between neighboring processes as used in *diffusion-based schemes*.

22.3 DESIGN OF DISTDLB

To address the unique characteristics of cosmology SAMR applications and the heterogeneous shared features of distributed systems, we propose a dynamic load balancing scheme called DistDLB. A hierarchical approach, combined with runtime performance evaluation, is proposed to reduce the redistribution cost as well as maintain a satisfying quality of load balancing. The primary objective is to improve the performance, for example, reduce the overall execution time, of cosmology simulations. The following sections provide the details of DistDLB.

22.3.1 Two-Level Approach

Because a typical distributed system is composed of computers linked through interconnected networks, DistDLB divides a distributed system into "groups" [9, 10]. A "group" is defined as a set of *homogeneous* processors connected with *dedicated system area networks* (SAN). A group can be a shared-memory parallel computer, a distributed-memory parallel computer, or a cluster of Linux computers. Communication within a group is referred to as *local communication* and that between different groups as *remote communication*. Each group is assumed to be a space-shared parallel machine. This is reasonable as most high-performance centers use this policy for resource scheduling of their high-performance resources. All the processors involved in a distributed system will be divided into groups as determined by the configuration.

DistDLB explores a two-level approach when performing load balancing, that is, the load balancing process is divided into two phases: *global balancing phase* and *local balancing phase*. Global balancing phase is performed on grids at level 0 with the objective of appropriately partitioning workload among groups based on their relative capacity. Local balancing phase is performed on grids at finer levels with the objective of equally partitioning workload among processors within a group. The corresponding pseudocode of DistDLB is presented in Figure 22.5.

- *Global Balancing Phase*: At the beginning of each iterative step at level 0, DistDLB evaluates the load distribution among the groups based on the information collected from the previous iterative step. If imbalance is observed, the heuristic methods described in the following sections are invoked to calculate the computational gain from repartitioning the workload and the overhead of performing the load redistribution among groups. If the computational gain is larger than the redistribution overhead, this phase will be invoked and the top grids at level 0 will be repartitioned by considering the relative performance of each group.
- *Local Balancing Phase*: After each iterative step at level 0, finer grids imposed on a coarse grid (the parent grid) are constructed for those regions that require higher resolutions. Before each smaller iterative step at these finer levels, DistDLB entails a balancing process within each group, in which the workload of each group is evenly and equally distributed among its processors. An overloaded processor can only transfer its excess workload to an underloaded processor in the same group. In this manner, children grids as finer grids are always located at the same group as their parent grids; thus, no remote communication is needed between parent and children grids. This phase occurs with each iterative step at finer levels.

P : total number of processes; G : total number of groups; $root_i$: the root process in group i;
n_i : number of processes in group i; p_i : relative process performance in group i;
w_i : total amount of workload in group i for the previous iteration of level 0;
T^i : execution time of group i in the previous iteration of level 0;
$T^i_{rebuild}$: time for rebuilding data structures in the previous iteration of level 0;
$T^i_{evaluate}$: evaluation time for global balancing phase in the previous iteration of level 0;
if (level == 0) { //Global Balancing Phase
  if ($\max_{i \in G}(\frac{w_i}{n_i \times p_i}) > \min_{i \in G}(\frac{w_i}{n_i \times p_i})$){
    for (each group i) {
      $root_i$ calculates $T^i_{projected} = \frac{T^i}{w_i} \times \sum_{i \in G} w_i \times \frac{n_i \times p_i}{\sum_{j \in G}(n_j \times p_j)}$;
      $root_i$ calculates $\max_{i \in G}(T^i_{projected})$ and $\max_{i \in G}(T^i)$ via MPI_Allreduce;
      $root_i$ calculates Gain $= (\max_{i \in G}(T^i) - \max_{i \in G}(T^i_{projected}))$;
    }
    for (each group i) {
      $root_i$ exchanges two messages with $root_j$ $(j = i+1, P)$;
      $root_i$ calculates the communciation latency $\alpha^{i,j}$ and the communication rate $\beta^{i,j}$ $(j = i+1, P)$;
      $root_i$ calculates $T^i_{cost} = \max_j(\max(T^i_{rebuild}, T^j_{rebuild}) + \alpha^{i,j} \times N^{i,j} + \beta^{i,j} \times L^{i,j} + \max(T^i_{evaluate}, T^j_{evaluate}))$;
      $root_i$ calculates Cost $= \max_{i \in G}(T^i_{cost})$ via MPI_Allreduce;
    }
    if (Gain > Cost)
      repartition TopGrid among the groups and then equal repartition within each group;
  }
} else { //Local Balancing Phase
    load balancing using ParaDLB within each group;
}

Figure 22.5 The pseudocode of DistDLB for cosmology SAMR simulations on heterogeneous distributed systems.

The hierarchical approach exploited in DistDLB provides several benefits. First, it addresses the heterogeneity of networks and reduces the number of remote communications. Figure 22.6, corresponding to Figure 22.3, illustrates the executing points of *global balancing* and *local balancing* processes. As shown in the figure, there are much fewer *global balancing* processes during the runtime as compared to *local balancing* processes. Note that *global balancing phase* is more time consuming than *local balancing phase* due to the fact that *global balancing* involves in remote communication that is time consuming. Second, by separating the two phases, we can explore different load balancing schemes for each phase. For the *local balancing phase*, we can utilize the ParaDLB presented in Section 22.2.3 or another scheme. For the *global balancing phase*, the major challenge is how to effectively reduce the redistribution cost in a heterogeneous distributed environment. Section 22.4.2 presents heuristic methods to address this issue.

In a distributed computing environment, it may have more than two levels of networks: intercontinental WANs, WANs within a country, campus networks, and

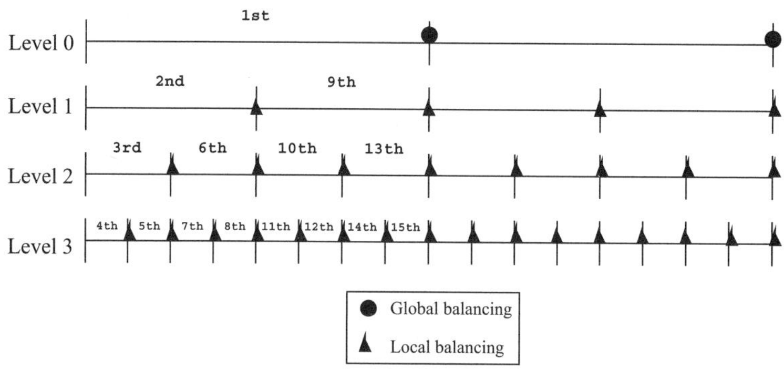

Figure 22.6 Integrated execution order showing points of load balancing.

various intraconnected networks within a cluster. DistDLB abstracts different levels of networks into two categories: (1) the dedicated tightly coupled system area networking level and (2) the interconnected networks connecting different machines. Compared to SAN, intermachine networks have much worse performance in terms of larger latency and lower bandwidth. DistDLB emphasizes on limiting the number of load balancing across intermachine networks so as to reduce the data redistribution cost. For different levels of intermachine networks, DistDLB distinguishes them by considering their performance through the evaluation model (as shown in Section "Quality of Load Balancing"). That is, if the underlying intermachine network is slower, global balancing phase will be skipped one or few times.

22.3.2 Global Balancing Phase

Global balancing phase is invoked periodically, that is, it is triggered during the iterative steps at the top level. Each global balancing phase consists of three steps: *imbalance detection*, *evaluation process*, and *global redistribution*.

Imbalance Detection DistDLB detects whether there is a global imbalance among groups by comparing the left and right side of the following equation:

$$W_i \Longleftrightarrow \sum_{j=1}^{G} W_j \times \frac{(n_i \times p_i)}{\sum_{j=1}^{G}(n_j \times p_j)}. \tag{22.1}$$

Here, G denotes the number of groups, n_i denotes the number of processors in the ith group, p_i denotes the relative performance of the processors in the ith group, and W_i is the amount of workload in the ith group. Thus, the left side represents the actual amount of workload of the ith group, and the right side represents the desired amount of workload of the ith group corresponding to its relative performance. If the actual workload is larger than the desired workload, then this group is overloaded; if the actual workload is smaller than the desired workload, then the group is underloaded; otherwise, the group is balanced.

At present, p_i is a static value that can be calculated before computation using a microbenchmark with computation similar to the application. We are at present working on adaptively changing this value at runtime when nondedicated processors are used.

Evaluation Process If global imbalance exists, DistDLB proceeds to estimate the computational gain and the redistribution cost of performing a global redistribution. This process is called *evaluation process*. The primary goal of DistDLB is to improve the performance of distributed applications; therefore, simple schemes are used in the evaluation step so as to minimize the DLB overhead. Based on the assumption that computation time is proportional to the amount of workload, DistDLB uses the following heuristic method to estimate the computational gain:

- First, DistDLB records several historical data from the previous iteration. The data include the execution time of the previous iteration and the amount of workload for each processor.
- According to the above information, DistDLB generates a prediction of the computational gain by the following equation:

$$\text{Gain} = \max_{1 \le i \le G}(T_t^i) - \max_{1 \le i \le G}\left[\frac{T_t^i}{W_i} \times \sum_{j=1}^{G} W_j \times \frac{n_i \times p_i}{\sum_{j=1}^{G}(n_j \times p_j)}\right] \quad (22.2)$$

  Here, T_t^i is the previous iterative time of group i with amount of workload W_i and used to predict the execution time for the current iteration without global balancing. The second part denotes the projected iterative time of group i if the total workload is redistributed corresponding to the relative performance of the group. The above equation represents the computational gain that can be achieved by global load balancing if we assign the appropriate amount of workload to each group corresponding to its relative performance. Note that the computational gain is calculated as the reduction of iterative time resulting from performing a global balancing.

The global balancing process will inevitably introduce some overheads, such as the computational overhead by rebuilding data structures of the application and the communication overhead by redistributing the workload among groups. Therefore, the redistribution cost is calculated based on the following heuristic method:

- Because the networks in distributed environments are shared resources and their performance are changing dynamically at runtime, DistDLB monitors the performance of networks by sending two messages (size of L_0 and L_1) between groups; the conventional communication model $T_{\text{comm}} = \alpha + \beta \times L$ [40] is used to calculate the current performance of the networks, which is represented by parameters α $(= (T_0 \times L_1 - T_1 \times L_0)/(L_1 - L_0))$ and β $(= (T_1 - T_0)/(L_1 - L_0))$.

- The time to rebuild data structures is recorded and used to predict the overhead of rebuilding process for the current iteration as T_1.
- This evaluation step introduces some overhead, so DistDLB records this overhead and denotes as T_2.
- Finally, DistDLB estimates the redistribution cost as

$$\text{Cost} = \max_{1 \le i,j \le G} [T_1 + (\alpha^{i,j} \times N_{\text{msg}}^{i,j} + \beta^{i,j} \times L_{\text{msg}}^{i,j}) + T_2], \tag{22.3}$$

where $T_1 = \max(T_1^i, T_1^j)$ and $T_2 = \max(T_2^i, T_2^j)$. In general, $T_2 \ll T_1$ because of the complicated data structures used in cosmology SAMR applications. Here, we assume that multiple redistribution processes occur in parallel; therefore, redistribution cost is calculated as the maximum of cost of all redistribution pairs. Here, $\alpha^{i,j}$ and $\beta^{i,j}$ are the estimated network latency and transfer rate between group i and j, $N_{\text{msg}}^{i,j}$ and $L_{\text{msg}}^{i,j}$ denote the number of messages and the total amount of the messages transferred between group i and j, respectively.

Global Redistribution Global redistribution is triggered if the computational gain is larger than the redistribution cost. When redistribution is triggered, DistDLB identifies the amount of workload that should be moved from overloaded groups to underloaded groups. Considering the unique adaptive characteristics of cosmology simulations (see Figure 22.3), DistDLB redistributes the grids on the top-level because the finer grids are reconstructed completely from the top level grids during the future timesteps (see Section 22.2.1). Suppose group i is overloaded whose grid at level 0 has a size of W_i^0, then the grid at the top level is decreased to a size of $[W_0^i \times (\sum_{j=1}^{G} W_j / \sum_{j=1}^{G}(n_j \times p_j))/(W_i/(n_i \times p_i))]$.

Figure 22.7 shows an example to illustrate the global redistribution process. Suppose the total workload is W, which needs to be repartitioned into two groups. Group A consists of n_{A} processors and each processor has performance p_{A}; group B consists of n_{B} processors and each processor has performance p_{B}. The top graph shows the overall grid hierarchy at time t, in which group A is overloaded because more refinements occur in its local region. DistDLB keeps track of this information and uses it as the load prediction for the next iteration at $t + \mathrm{d}t$. Since DistDLB notices that group A has more refinements in the previous iteration, it anticipates that in the next iteration, group A will be overloaded. Therefore, at the beginning of the iteration at $t + \mathrm{d}t$, DistDLB first reduces the size of the grid at level 0 for group A. After calculating the gain and the cost of a global redistribution by using the heuristic methods proposed above, DistDLB determines that performing a global load balancing is advantageous; thus, a global redistribution is invoked. Figure 22.7(b) shows the level 0 grids at time t, and Figure 22.7(c) represents the level 0 grids after global redistribution process at time $t + \mathrm{d}t$. The boundary between two groups is moved slightly to the overloaded group A (reducing the load of group A), and the shaded portion of grids at the top level is redistributed from the overloaded group A to the underloaded group B.

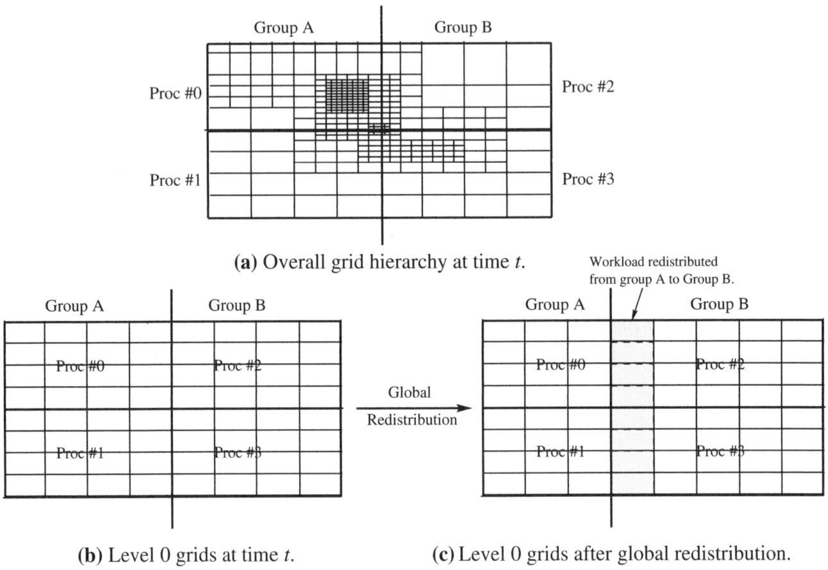

Figure 22.7 An example of global redistribution for cosmology simulations.

22.3.3 Local Balancing Phase

Between two consecutive global balancing steps, DistDLB focuses on local balancing within each group. During this phase, DistDLB concentrates on equal redistribution within a group because each group is a homogeneous system connected by a dedicated network. The major requirement is to consider the adaptive characteristics of cosmology simulations. At present, DistDLB utilizes ParaDLB (described in Section 22.2.3) during *local balancing phase*.

Recall that ParaDLB consists of two steps: *imbalance detection* and *local redistribution*. Local redistribution is performed through the integration of *moving grid step* and *splitting grid step*, and imbalance detection is based on whether $MaxLoad/AvgLoad > threshold$. It does not contain an explicit evaluation step due to the fact that the redistribution cost is generally small within a group. Therefore the implicit evaluation process of ParaDLB always chooses to perform a local redistribution.

22.4 EXPERIMENTS

In this section, we present the experimental results evaluating the performance of DistDLB against ParaDLB on production distributed systems. Both of them are designed for cosmology SAMR applications: while ParaDLB is for traditional parallel systems, DistDLB is for heterogeneous distributed systems. Hence, the difference in their performance demonstrates the benefit by considering the heterogeneous and dynamic features of resources on distributed systems. MPICH-G2 [18] is used for message passing across machines, and *Globus* [31] is used to launch the experiments. The data presented below are consistent across multiple runs.

22.4.1 Experiment Setup

We implemented the proposed techniques in the ENZO code. Further, to evaluate the performance of DistDLB, we manually instrumented the code with performance counters and timers. The instrumentation does not require any extra communication through networks and only one I/O operation is required at the end of simulation to generate the output of performance data. The performance data being collected include execution time, imbalance ratio, repartition cost, overhead introduced by DistDLB, among others. At runtime, each process collects its own performance data and prints out its profiling result at the end of execution.

Two production systems were used in the experiments. One is the Alliance Grid [37] and the other is the nationwide TeraGrid [42]. On the Alliance Grid, two different configurations, Alliance_1 and Alliance_2, were used. Our experiments on the TeraGrid were conducted on the clusters at two different sites across the United States. Table 22.1 describes the details of these systems. Here, ANL denotes the Argonne National Laboratory, NCSA denotes the National Center for Supercomputing Application, SDSC denotes the San Diego Supercomputer Center, and SARA is the Dutch Computing Center in the Netherlands.

Two real data sets provided by ENZO developers were used in the experiments: 3D_Data and 2D_Data. As the names suggest, they represent three-dimensional and two-dimensional cosmology simulations, respectively. We chose these data sets as they provide cosmology simulations that are interested to cosmologists. In addition, these two data sets are quite different in the number of adaptations at level 0. Table 22.2 illustrates the major differences between these data sets.

The main goal of high-performance computing is performance, for example, to reduce the execution time. Therefore, we use it as our primary performance metric.

Table 22.1 Configurations of Distributed Systems

System	Machines	Interconnection
TeraGrid	1.5 GHz Intel Itanium2 Cluster at SDSC 1.5 Ghz Intel Itanium2 Cluster at NCSA	TeraGrid backbone
Alliance_1	250 MHz R10000 SGI Origin2000 at ANL 250 MHz R10000 SGI Origin2000 at NCSA	ATM OC-3
Alliance_2	500 MHz R14000 SGI Origin3800 at SARA 250 MHz R10000 SGI Origin2000 at NCSA	Wide area networks

Table 22.2 Profiles of Data Sets

Data set	Initial problem size	Adaptations at level 0	Memory (MB)	Message size (MB)
3D_Data	50 × 50 × 50	57	50	8
2D_Data	500 × 500	2511	80	10

We also evaluate the quality of load balancing that is defined as

$$\text{imbalance\_ratio} = \frac{\max_{1\le i\le G}[W_i/(n_i \times p_i)]}{\sum_{1\le i\le G}(W_i)/\sum_{1\le i\le G}(n_i \times p_i)}, \tag{22.4}$$

where W_i is the amount of workload of group i. The denominator represents the weighted average amount of workload and the nominator represents the maximal weighted workload for a single processor. This metric is an extension of *imbalance_ratio* used in Ref. [22] for homogeneous parallel systems, in which it is defined as $MaxLoad/AvgLoad$. Note that *imbalance_ratio* is always greater than or equal to 1.0. The closer this metric is to 1.0, the better quality the load balancing achieves.

22.4.2 Performance Data

Execution Times Figure 22.8 presents the execution times with varying number of processors by evaluating DistDLB against ParaDLB on the TeraGrid. Tables 22.3 and 22.4 present the corresponding raw data. Since both ParaDLB and DistDLB are designed for cosmology SAMR applications, the results here indicate that DistDLB can effectively reduce the execution times by considering the heterogeneous and fluctuating performance of distributed systems. We also notice that the average improvement achieved by DistDLB over ParaDLB depends on data sets. For instance, the average improvement for 3D_Data is larger than that for 2D_Data. A major reason is that the repartition cost (including the time for rebuilding data structures and transferring data among processors) is higher for 3D_Data than for

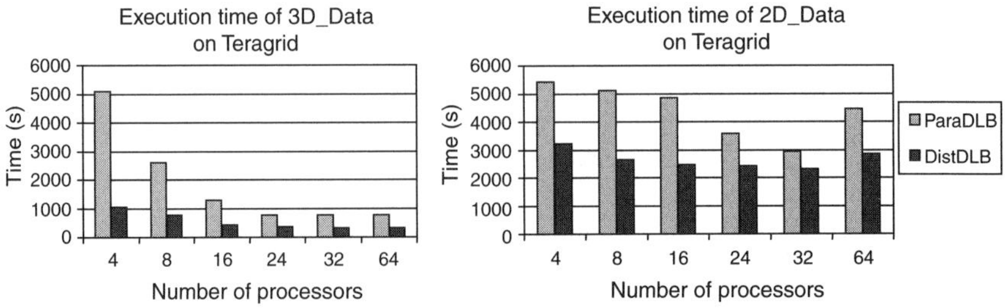

Figure 22.8 Comparison of execution times on the TeraGrid.

Table 22.3 Raw Data of Execution Times of 3D_Data on the TeraGrid

	4 CPUs	8 CPUs	16 CPUs	24 CPUs	32 CPUs	64 CPUs
ParaDLB	5094.78	2592.24	1300.24	769.60	774.78	780.00
DistDLB	1062.73	778.49	423.10	369.27	313.77	314.00
Improvement	79.14%	69.97%	67.46%	52.02%	59.50%	59.78%

Table 22.4 Raw Data of Execution Times of 2D_Data on the TeraGrid

	4 CPUs	8 CPUs	16 CPUs	24 CPUs	32 CPUs	64 CPUs
ParaDLB	5426.76	5116.67	4861.95	3573.17	2954.92	4458.07
DistDLB	3225.90	2652.16	2453.47	2422.27	2299.70	2856.56
Improvement	40.56%	48.17%	49.54%	32.21%	22.17%	35.92%

2D_Data; therefore, the techniques proposed in DistDLB can more effectively reduce the repartitioning and redistribution cost for 3D_Data.

As seen in Table 22.1, the Alliance Grid were composed of SGI Origin machines. However, working with the MPICH-G2 developers, we found out that the IRIX TCP/IP implementation has a bug that prevents us from executing large data sets. Thus, we were only able to run a smaller version of 3D_Data on the Alliance Grid. We present our experimental results on the Alliance Grid as it gives us an evaluation of DistDLB on different architectures.

The configuration of Alliance_1 consists of processors with the same performance; therefore, the difference in performance between DistDLB and ParaDLB reflects the advantages of taking into consideration the heterogeneity and dynamic feature of the networks. The processors used in Alliance_2 have different performance, so the difference between DistDLB and ParaDLB for this configuration also reflects the advantage of considering the heterogeneity of processors. To calculate the relative performance of processors on Alliance_2, we use the NAS Parallel Benchmarks (NPB) [2]. Figure 22.9 shows the relative performance of two machines of Alliance_2.

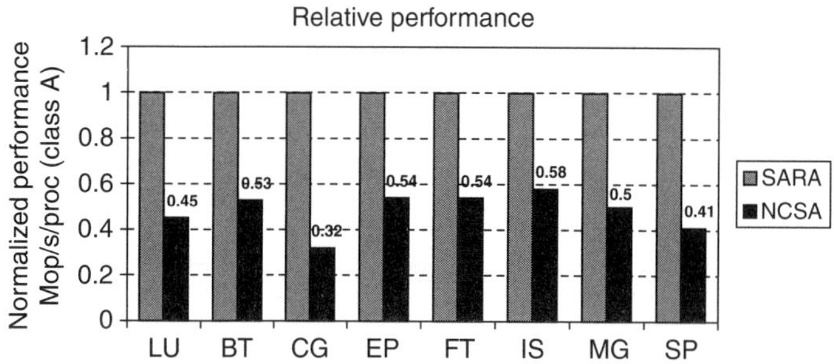

Figure 22.9 Relative performance between two machines of Alliance_2.

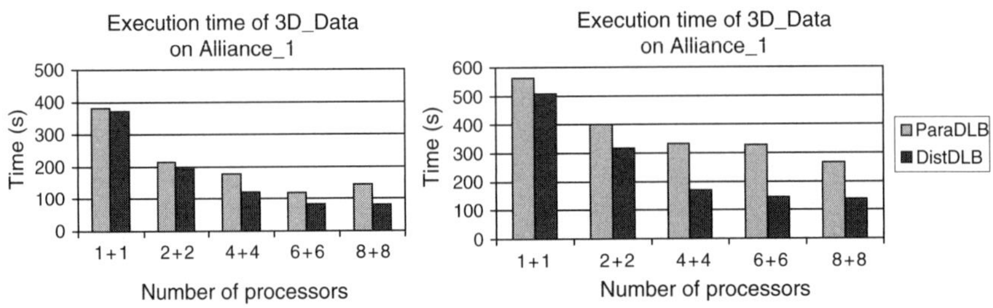

Figure 22.10 Comparison of execution times on Alliance_1 and Alliance_2.

Here, we use the option of class A with eight processors. By using arithmetic average, we conclude that the relative performance of the two machines at SARA and NCSA are 1.0 and 0.48, respectively, which are used in DistDLB.

Figure 22.10 compares the total execution times with varying configurations for 3D_Data on Alliance_1 and Alliance_2. Tables 22.5 and 22.6 present the corresponding raw data. Again, the results indicate that DistDLB outperforms ParaDLB on the Alliance Grid with different configurations. In addition, the results also show that the average improvement achieved by DistDLB over ParaDLB is influenced by the underlying interconnections. Alliance_1 has a specially designed interconnection with better performance (i.e., ATM OC-3) than that used in Alliance_2 (i.e., wide area networks). As mentioned, DistDLB is aimed to reduce remote communication when the interconnection has poor performance. Thus, for Alliance_2 with low performance interconnection, there are more opportunities for performance improvement by using DistDLB.

Quality of Load Balancing As mentioned earlier, the primary goal of DistDLB is to reduce the execution time. It will be interesting to see how much sacri-

Table 22.5 Raw Data of 3D_Data Execution Times on Alliance_1

	2 CPUs	4 CPUs	8 CPUs	12 CPUs	16 CPUs
ParaDLB	382.25	215.93	178.1	119.56	145.99
DistDLB	372.46	194.37	121.66	83.84	81.39
Improvement	2.56%	9.98%	31.69%	29.87%	44.25%

Table 22.6 Raw Data of 3D_Data Execution Times on Alliance_2

	2 CPUs	4 CPUs	8 CPUs	12 CPUs	16 CPUs
ParaDLB	563.19	400.99	333.77	328.70	267.94
DistDLB	507.08	316.98	170.57	144.46	138.56
Improvement	9.96%	20.95%	48.90%	56.05%	48.29%

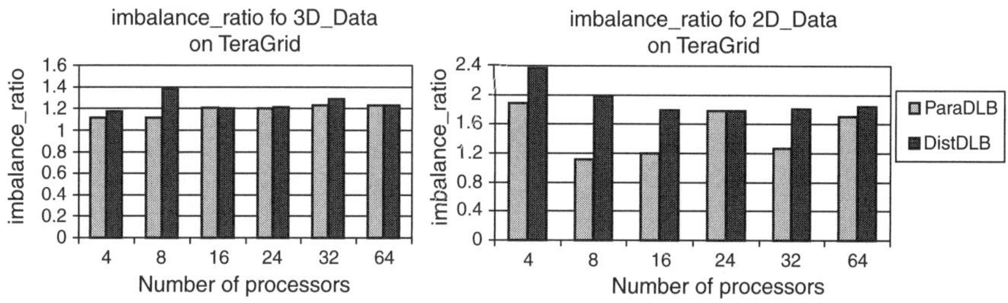

Figure 22.11 Comparison of load balancing quality on the TeraGrid.

fice DistDLB gives in terms of the quality of load balancing so as to achieve this goal. Figures 22.11 and 22.12 summarize the quality of load balancing by using DistDLB and ParaDLB on these systems. Here, the y-axis represents the value for *imbalance_ratio*. The closer the *imbalance_ratio* is to 1.0, the better quality the load balancing achieves. The figures show that when homogeneous processors are used (i.e., Alliance_1 and TeraGrid), the load balancing quality obtained by ParaDLB is better than DistDLB. In other words, DistDLB can reduce remote communication at the expense of lower quality of load balancing. We also notice that for most cases, the values of *imbalance_ratio* are less than 2.0, which is still acceptable. On the other hand, when heterogeneous processors are used (i.e., Alliance_2), DistDLB can achieve better results for the load balancing quality. This is due to the fact that DistDLB takes into consideration the heterogeneity of processors when partitioning and repartitioning workload among processors.

DistDLB Overhead Now we will evaluate the overhead introduced by DistDLB. First, we measure the percentage of overhead introduced by DistDLB, that is, the ratio between the DistDLB overhead and the execution time. The left part of Figure 22.13 presents the corresponding results for 3D_Data and 2D_Data with varying number of processors. The overhead brought by DistDLB is higher for 2D_data compared to 3D_Data: it is ranging between 0.8% and 3% for 3D_Data and between 11.6% and 16.4% for 2D_Data. DistDLB invokes global balancing process during each iteration at level 0. Recall that for 2D_Data, there are much more number of

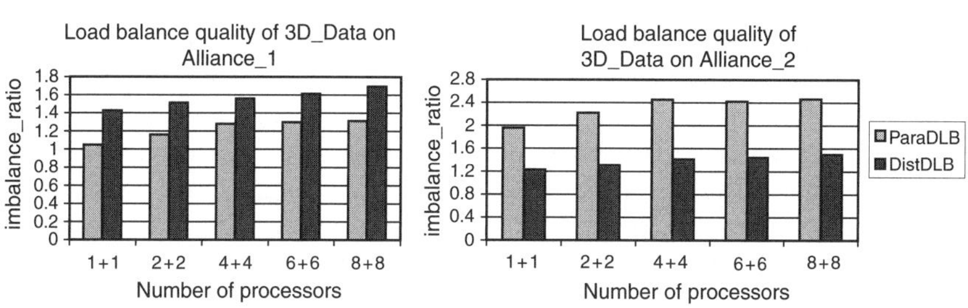

Figure 22.12 Comparison of load balancing quality on Alliance_1 and Alliance_2.

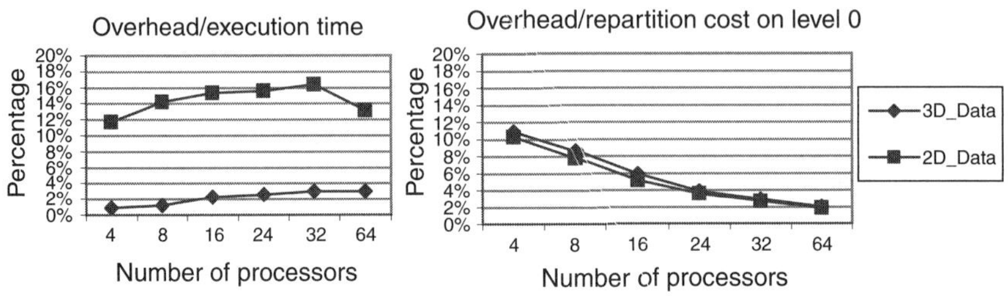

Figure 22.13 DistDLB overhead.

adaptations on level 0 (see Table 22.2), therefore, the overhead brought by DistDLB is higher for 2D_Data as compared to 3D_Data. Although the overhead brought by DistDLB might be nontrivial in some cases, both Figures 22.8 and 22.10 indicate that DistDLB can effectively reduce the overall execution times as compared to the scheme that does not consider the heterogeneous shared features of distributed systems. The main reason is that DistDLB can significantly reduce the repartition cost, which is illustrated in the right part of Figure 22.13.

In the right part of Figure 22.13, we study the ratio between the DistDLB overhead and the saved repartition cost at level 0. The saved repartition cost includes the time to rebuild data structures and transfer data among processors. Recall that DistDLB makes runtime decision on whether to perform global balancing or not. The results show that the ratio is getting decreased with increasing number of processors. For instance, the curves shown in the figure are decreasing from about 10% ($P = 4$) to about 1.9% ($P = 64$) for both data sets. When the number of processors increases, the saved repartition cost is increased dramatically while the overhead brought by DistDLB is increased in a much slower pace. In other words, DistDLB can perform better when a large number of processors is used. Because the overhead caused by DistDLB is always much smaller than the repartition cost on level 0, in case that DistDLB determines not to invoke a global balancing process, the performance gain obtained by omitting global balancing is generally much larger than the cost introduced by the DistDLB decision making.

22.5 CONCLUSION AND FUTURE WORK

In the paper, we presented a dynamic load balancer DistDLB to improve the performance and efficiency of cosmology SAMR simulations running on distributed systems. It focuses on reducing the redistribution cost through a hierarchical load balancing approach and a runtime decision-making mechanism. Heuristic methods have been proposed to adaptively adjust load balancing strategies based on the observation of the current system and application state. Experiments with real cosmology data sets on production systems indicate that DistDLB can effectively improve the performance of distributed cosmology simulations by 2.56%–79.14% as compared to the scheme that does not consider the heterogeneous and dynamic features of distributed systems. The major contributions of this work are as follows: (1) A hierarchical approach is proposed to address the heterogeneous feature of distributed systems, (2) A performance-based decision-making mechanism is designed to address the fluctuating performance of the underlying computing resources at runtime, (3) The proposed techniques have been tested with real-world cosmology applications on production systems, (4) The experiments show that with an appropriate load balancing scheme, large-scale cosmology simulations can make an efficient utilization of distributed computing systems, such as the TeraGrid.

At present, we are working on generalizing the proposed load balancing techniques to other applications. We believe that the proposed techniques can be easily incorporated into other partitioning tools such as those listed in Section 22.3: the hierarchical load balancing approach to address the heterogeneity of networks, and the performance-based runtime decision making to deal with the fluctuating performance of distributed systems. Note that the performance-based gain/cost model presented in Section 22.4 does not include any application-specific information, so they should be applicable to a range of applications. At present, a two-level approach is used in DistDLB to address the heterogeneity of distributed systems. It is interesting to investigate a multilevel approach and evaluate it against the proposed two-level approach. Finally, we are also working on incorporating the existing system monitoring tools such as NWS [49] in DistDLB.

ACKNOWLEDGMENTS

The authors would like to thank Greg Bryan at Columbia University and Michael Norman at University of California at San Diego for numerous comments and suggestions that contributed to this work. We would like to acknowledge NCSA and SDSC for the use of the TeraGrid clusters. We would also like to acknowledge NCSA, ANL, and the Dutch Computing Center SARA for the use of the SGI Origin machines.

REFERENCES

1. S. Baden, N. Chrisochoides, M. Norman, and D. Gannon. Structured adaptive mesh refinement (SAMR) grid methods. *IMA Volumes in Mathematics and Its Applications*. Springer-Verlag, New York, 1999, p. 117.
2. Nas parallel benchmarks. http://www.nas.nasa.gov/Software/NPB/.
3. M. Berger and P. Colella. Local adaptive mesh refinement for shock hydrodynamics. *J. Comput. Phys.*, 82(1):64–84, 1989.
4. R. Biswas and L. Oliker. Experiments with repartitioning and load balancing adaptive meshes. Technical report, NASA Ames Research Center, 1998.
5. E. Boman, K. Devine, B. Hendrickson, W. Mitchell, M. John, and C. Vaughan. Zoltan: a dynamic load-balancing library for parallel applications. http://www.snl.gov/zoltan.
6. G. Bryan. Fluid in the Universe: adaptive mesh refinement in cosmology. *Comput. Sci. Engi.*, 1(2):46–53, 1999.
7. G. Bryan, T. Abel, and M. Norman. Achieving extreme resolution in numerical cosmology using adaptive mesh refinement: resolving primordial star formation. In *Proceedings of the 2001 ACM/IEEE Conference on Supercomputing*, Denver, CO, 2001.

8. S. Chandra and M. Parashar. Armada: an adaptive application-sensitive partitioning framework for SAMR applications. In *Proceedings of the 14th IASTED International Conference on Parallel and Distributed Computing and Systems*, Cambridge, MA, 2002.
9. J. Chen and V. Taylor. ParaPART: parallel mesh partitioning tool for distributed systems. *Concurrency Pract. Exper.*, 12:111–123, 2000.
10. J. Chen and V. Taylor. PART: mesh partitioning for efficient use of distributed systems. *IEEE Trans. Parallel Distrib. Sys.*, 12:111–123, 2000.
11. ENZO: cosmological simulation code. http://cosmos.ucsd.edu/enzo/.
12. G. Cybenko. Dynamic load balancing for distributed memory multiprocessors. *IEEE Trans. Parallel Distrib. Syst.*, 7:279–301, 1989.
13. K. D. Devine, E. G. Boman, R. T. Heaphy, B.A. Hendrickson. J.D. Teresco, J. Faik, J.E. Flaherty, and L.G. Gervasio. New challenges in dynamic load balancing. *Appl. Numer. Math.*, 52(2–3):133–152, 2005.
14. The ASCI distributed resource management (DRM) environment. http://www.llnl.gov/asci/pse/hpcs/drm/.
15. C. Farhat. A simple and efficient automatic FEM domain decomposer. *Comput. Struct.*, 28(5):579–602, 1988.
16. The network for earthquake engineering simulation grid (NEESgrid). http://www.neesgrid.org/index.php.
17. I. Foster and C. Kesselman. *The Grid: Blueprint for a New Computing Infrastructure*. Morgan Kaufmann Publishers, San Francisco, CA, 1999.
18. N. Karonis, B. Toonen, and I. Foster. MPICH-G2: A grid-enabled implementation of the message passing interface. *J. Parallel Distrib. Comput.*, 63(5):551–563, 2003.
19. B. Kernighan and S. Lin. An efficient heuristic procedure for partitioning graphs. *Bell Syst. Tech. J.*, 49:291–307, 1970.
20. Z. Lan, V. Taylor, and G. Bryan. Dynamic load balancing for adaptive mesh refinement applications: improvements and sensitivity analysis. In *Proceedings of the IASTED Parallel and Distributed Computing Systems*, Anaheim, CA, 2001.
21. Z. Lan, V. Taylor, and G. Bryan. Dynamic load balancing of SAMR applications on distributed systems. In *Proceedings of the 2001 ACM/IEEE Conference on Supercomputing*, Denver, CO, 2001.
22. Z. Lan, V. Taylor, and G. Bryan. A novel dynamic load balancing scheme for parallel systems. *J. Parallel Distrib. Comput.*, 62(12):1763—1781, 2002.
23. B. Maerten, D. Roose, A. Basermann, J. Fingberg, and G. Lonsdale. Drama: a library for parallel dynamic load balancing of finite element applications. In *Proceedings of the 9th SIAM Conference on Parallel Processing for Scientific Computing*, San Antonio, TX, 1999.
24. H. Neeman. Autonomous hierarchical adaptive mesh refinement for multiscale simulations. PhD thesis. University of Illinois at Urbana-Champaign, 1996.
25. Collaborative Advanced Internet Research Network. http://www.isi.edu/CAIRN/.
26. The Grid Physics Network(GriPhyN). http://www.griphyn.org/index.php.
27. HPC wire breaking news. http://www.tgc.com/breaking/1593.html.
28. M. Norman and G. Bryan. Cosmological adaptive mesh refinement. In S. Miyama and K. Tomisaka, editors, *Numerical Astrophysics*, Tokyo, March 1988, p. 10–13.
29. L. Oliker and R. Biswas. PLUM: parallel load balancing for adaptive refined meshes. *J. Parallel Distrib. Comput.*, 47(2):109–124, 1997.
30. ParMETIS. http://www-users.cs.umn.edu/ karypis/metis/parmetis/index.html.
31. Globus project. http://www.globus.org.
32. The European DataGrid project. http://eu-datagrid.web.cern.ch/eu-datagrid/.
33. K. Schloegel, G. Karypis, and V. Kumar. Multilevel diffusion schemes for repartitioning of adaptive meshes. *J. Parallel Distrib. Comput.*, 47(2):109–124, 1997.
34. K. Schloegel, G. Karypis, and V. Kumar. A performance study of diffusive Vs. remapped load-balancing schemes. *Proceedings of the ISCA 11th International Conference on Parallel and Distributed Computing Systems*, 1998, pp. 59–66.
35. H. Simon. Harp: a dynamic spectral partitioner. *J. Parallel Distrib. Comput.*, 50:83–96, 1998.

36. S. Kumar, S. Das, and R. Biswas. Graph partitioning for parallel applications in heterogeneous grid environments. In *Proceedings of the International Parallel and Distributed Processing Symposium (IPDS'02)*, 2002.
37. L. Smarr. Toward the 21st century. *Communi. ACM*, 40(11):28–32, 1997.
38. A. Sohn and H. Simon. Jove: a dynamic load balancing framework for adaptive computations on an SP-2 distributed multiprocessor. NJIT CIS Technical Report, New Jersey, 1994.
39. F. Stangenberg. Recognizing and avoiding thrashing in dynamic load balancing. Technical Report. EPCC-SS94-04, September 1994.
40. A.S. Tanenbaum. *Computer Networks*. Prentice-Hall, 1996.
41. V. Taylor(PI), I. Foster, J. Mambretti, P. Dinda, X. Sun, and A. Choudhary. DOT: distributed optical testbed to facilitate the development of techniques for efficient execution of distributed applications. NSF EIA-0224377, 2002–2004.
42. The NSF TeraGrid. http://www.teragrid.org.
43. C. Walshaw, M. Cross, M. G. Everett, and S. Johnson. JOSTLE: partitioning of unstructured meshes for massively parallel machines. *Parallel Computational Fluid Dynamics: New Algorithms and Applications*, 1995.
44. C. Walshaw and M. Cross. Mesh partitioning: a multilevel balancing and refinement algorithm. *SIAM J. Sci. Comput.*, 22(1):63–80, 2000.
45. C. Walshaw and M. Cross. Multilevel mesh partitioning for heterogeneous communication networks. *Future Gener. Comput. Syst.*, 17(5):601–623, 2001.
46. C. Walshaw, M. Cross, and M. Everett. Parallel dynamic graph partitioning for adaptive unstructured meshes. *J. Parallel Distrib. Comput.*, 47(2):102–108, 1997.
47. M. Willebeek-LeMair and A. Reeves. Strategies for dynamic load balancing on highly parallel computers. *IEEE Trans. Parallel Distrib. Syst.*, 4(9):979–993, 1993.
48. W. Johnson, D. Gannon, and B. Nitzberg. Grids as production computing environments: the engineering aspect of NASA's information power grid. *Proceedings of the 8th IEEE Symposium on High-Performance Distributed Computing (HPDC'99)*, 1999.
49. R. Wolski, N. Spring, and J. Hayes. The network weather service: a distributed resource performance forecasting system. *J. Future Gener. Comput. Syst.*, 15:757–768, 1999.
50. Y. Zhang, S. Chandra, S. Hariri, and M. Parashar. Autonomic proactive runtime partitioning strategies for SAMR applications. *Proceedings of the NSF Next Generation Systems Program Workshop, IEEE/ACM 18th IPDPS*, Santa Fe, NM, 2004.

Index

Advanced Computational Infrastructures For Parallel and Distributed Adaptive Applications. Edited by Manish Parashar and Xiaolin Li